ENGLAND
THE CRICKET FACTS

ENGLAND
THE CRICKET FACTS

DEAN HAYES

Michael O'Mara Books Limited

First published in Great Britain in 2006 by
Michael O'Mara Books Limited
9 Lion Yard
Tremadoc Road
London SW4 7NQ

A CIP catalogue record for this book is available from the British Library

ISBN (10-digit): 1-84317-215-1
ISBN (13-digit): 978-1-84317-215-4

1 3 5 7 9 10 8 6 4 2

www.mombooks.com

Designed and typeset by E-Type

Printed and bound in England by Clays Ltd, St Ives plc

Author's note

Every effort has been made by the author and editor to ensure the accuracy of each fact and statistic in this book (which have been checked up to 10 September 2006). In the event of any errors, however, I offer apologies in advance.

CONTENTS

FOREWORD

When I was capped for the first time in July 1951, I was the 358th player to represent England. It is therefore remarkable to discover that, following the end of the Second World War, a total of 324 men have since played for their country.

Selection was difficult in my day. Even though we had people like Len Hutton and Denis Compton to build around, it still proved to be a very challenging task for selectors – indeed, it still is!

These days, if you are fortunate enough to be called up, in most cases it means you will probably get a reasonable run in the side, as long as you fulfil your potential and put in some good performances. This is in contrast to many England players chosen in the early days of Test match cricket, who, in comparison, would often make only a handful of appearances.

My own career in Test matches lasted from 1951 to 1969, which was a long span, though the selectors kept giving me a couple of three-year rests! However, I was also very lucky. In 1966, when England played host to the touring West Indian team, after we lost the first Test by an innings I was fortunate enough to be recalled for the next Test on my thirty-ninth birthday. The selectors kept faith in me, and I played in the next twenty-four games and only lost my place on my forty-second birthday.

This book, filled with facts, stats and the history of Test cricket, will make fascinating reading for the followers of our great game.

Tom Graveney, August 2006

INTRODUCTION

England: The Cricket Facts is a unique work of reference about the English national cricket team, providing an in-depth history of all aspects of the summer sport. It features full details of every England cricketer since 1877, including date of birth, teams played for, number of Tests played and Test match debut, along with a full Test-playing record; complete results of every England Test match, including top individual performances; profiles of England's top fifty players; performances in the World Cup and One-Day Internationals; a statistical section devoted to England's record holders; and a history of the England team through the years. Also interspersed throughout the text is a selection of fascinating facts and trivia.

In March 1877, when the eleven men representing England took to the field against Australia at Melbourne, little could they have realized that they were initiating one of the great sporting institutions – the Ashes. There have, of course, been other Test series that have been more adventurous and entertaining, but none receive the same attention and generate the same feeling as those matches played between England and Australia.

As a young boy, I travelled the short distance from my home in Bolton to witness the 'Old Trafford Bowling Massacre' in 1964, when four centuries were scored – Simpson 311, Barrington 256, Dexter 174 and Lawry 106. That's how it all started for me. I've loved every Ashes series since, and, like the rest of the nation, celebrated in style when England regained the famous urn in September 2005.

But of course England don't just play Australia, and over the years matches against both the old enemy and the other Test-playing nations have thrown up many memorable moments, such as Jessop's match at The Oval in 1902, the Bodyline series of 1932–3, Hutton's marathon at The Oval in 1938, Jim Laker's record-breaking performance at Old Trafford in 1956, the West Indies tour of 1963, Geoff Boycott's hundredth hundred at Headingley in 1977, Ian Botham's match at Headingley in 1981, Graham Gooch's innings against India at Lord's in 1990, and, of course, England's tremendous Ashes performance in 2005. All these and more will be highlighted throughout the pages of this book.

As a former cricket professional, though still playing regularly and captaining my local side, I remain a proud supporter of the England cricket team. I hope all England cricket fans will consider the book an indispensable work of reference, my personal contribution to more than 125 years of Test-match cricket.

Dean Hayes, August 2006

1 A HISTORY OF ENGLAND TESTS – SUMMARIES AND RESULTS

THE EARLY YEARS: 1877–1900

Test matches in the nineteenth century were organized somewhat differently from international cricket matches today, as the teams were not fully representative. Two Englishmen tried to promote separate tours to Australia for 1876–7: James Lillywhite wanted a team of pure professionals, while G. F. Grace was prepared to take amateurs. However, Grace's planned tour fell through and it was Lillywhite's team that ultimately went to Australia to play in what became recognized as the first two 'Test' matches. However, it was not the strongest side, as it didn't include the leading amateur of the day in W. G. Grace.

In March 1877, when the first 'Test' match was played at Melbourne, the view of English cricket followers was that Australia could not hope to beat England at full strength on level terms. Yet Australia would be the ultimate victors, winning the match by 45 runs. Right from this first encounter no quarter was asked and none given. Indeed, Charles Bannerman, whose hard-hitting innings of 165 set Australia on the road to victory, had his knuckles so badly bruised by the rising deliveries of Yorkshire's George Ulyett that he was eventually forced to retire.

The English tourists won the second meeting two weeks later, but the Australians, against whom England played their first thirty Test matches, certainly confirmed their new status as international cricketers at Melbourne, in 1879, by beating another touring English side by 10 wickets.

The following year, it was the turn of the Australians to test their mettle on foreign soil, meeting England at The Oval in September in the first Test match played in England – the only one of that Australian tour. W. G. Grace's 152 in the first innings was bettered by Billy Murdoch's 153 not out, but not before Australia had followed on. England were left with only 57 to win, but they lost 5 wickets in the process.

Two years later, another single-Test series was played in England, also at The Oval. Needing only 85 to win in a low-scoring match, England were bowled out for 77, thanks to the demon bowling of Fred Spofforth (14–90). The feat was duly immortalized in a mock obituary published in the *Sporting Times* of 2 September 1882, which read: 'In Affectionate Remembrance of

English Cricket, which died at the Oval on 29th August, 1882. Deeply lamented by a large circle of Sorrowing Friends and Acquaintances, R.I.P. N.B. – The body will be cremated, and the Ashes taken to Australia.'

A few months later, an England team led by the Hon. Ivo Bligh went to Australia and renewed England's pride by winning two of a rubber of three matches. The achievement was noted for posterity when Bligh was presented with a small urn containing the ashes of a set of bails that had been burned. After this first 'Ashes' victory, England went on to retain the Ashes for the next nine years and enjoy a period of ascendancy over their Australian rivals: from 1886 to 1890, eleven Test matches were played and England, losing only once to Australia at Lord's, won the other ten. This period coincided with the peak of the Surrey pace bowler George Lohmann and the emergence of the slow left-arm bowlers Johnny Briggs and Bobby Peel.

The early days of England–South Africa meetings were not at all significant as trials of strength between the two nations. The first Test match between the two countries took place at Port Elizabeth in March 1889, when England, led by C. Aubrey Smith, who many years later would be knighted as a world-famous Hollywood film actor, won by 8 wickets. In the second Test at Cape Town, Johnny Briggs had the astonishing figures of 7–17 and 8–11. Briggs hit the stumps fourteen times and got one man out lbw – an achievement unlikely to be equalled for individual devastation in Test cricket.

The recovery of Australian cricket came in 1891–2, when England sent a strong side led by W. G. Grace, but lost the first two Tests out of a series of three. However, England came back to win the next three series in 1893, 1894–5 and 1896, when they owed much to their batting strength: Arthur Shrewsbury, F. S. Jackson, William Gunn, W. G. Grace, Andrew Stoddart and Kumar Ranjitsinhji in particular were outstanding. But the power that tipped the scales in this period was the fast bowling of Tom Richardson – his tally of 88 wickets in only fourteen Tests has kept his name among those with the highest striking rates of wickets taken per Test match to this day, and it was not until his power began to wane that Australia won another series.

Lord Hawke's team that played three Tests in South Africa in 1896 included Charles Fry and Sammy Woods, but its most successful player was George Lohmann, who took 7–38 and 8–7 in the first Test at Port Elizabeth – so redeeming himself for his 'pair' as an opening batsman. In the next match at Johannesburg, he took the last 9 wickets for 28 runs in South Africa's first innings, and in all three Tests he took 35 wickets. In April 1899, the last game before the start of the Boer War in South Africa, England dismissed the home side for just 35 thanks to some fine bowling from Albert Trott (4–19) and Schofield Haigh (6–11). When war broke out a few weeks later, it could not be said that South African cricket had advanced very far at Test level. But a visit from Joe Darling's Australians on their way home from England in 1902 did much to raise standards, and the next England team to tour South Africa in 1906 would be in for a rude awakening.

TEST MATCH RESULTS: 1877–1900

1. Australia v England
First Test at Melbourne – 15, 16, 17, 19 March 1877
AUSTRALIA 245 (Bannerman 165 ret. hurt) and 104 (Shaw 5–38)
ENGLAND 196 (Jupp 63, Midwinter 5–78) and 108 (Kendall 7–55)
Australia won by 45 runs

2. Australia v England
Second Test at Melbourne – 31 March, 2, 3, 4 April 1877
AUSTRALIA 122 (Hill 4–27) and 259 (Gregory 43, Thomson 41)
ENGLAND 261 (Ulyett 52, Greenwood 49, Hill 49, Emmett 48, Kendall 4–82) and 122–6 (Ulyett 63)
England won by 4 wickets

3. Australia v England
Only Test at Melbourne – 2, 3, 4 January 1879
ENGLAND 113 (Absolom 52, Spofforth 6–48) and 160 (Spofforth 7–62)
AUSTRALIA 256 (Bannerman 73, Emmett 7–68) and 19–0
Australia won by 10 wickets

4. England v Australia
Only Test at The Oval – 6, 7, 8 September 1880
ENGLAND 420 (W. G. Grace 152, Lucas 55, Lord Harris 52, Steel 42) and 57–5
AUSTRALIA 149 (Morley 5–56) and 327 (Murdoch 153*, McDonnell 43)
England won by 5 wickets

5. Australia v England
First Test at Melbourne – 31 December 1881, 2, 3, 4 January 1882
ENGLAND 294 (Ulyett 87, Bates 58, Selby 55) and 308 (Selby 70, Scotton 50*, Bates 47, Shaw 40, Cooper 6–120)
AUSTRALIA 320 (Horan 124) and 127–3
Match drawn

6. Australia v England
Second Test at Sydney – 17, 18, 20, 21 February 1882
ENGLAND 133 (Palmer 7–68) and 232 (Ulyett 67, Barlow 62, Palmer 4–97, Garrett 4–62)
AUSTRALIA 197 (Massie 49, Blackham 40, Bates 4–52) and 169–5 (Murdoch 49)
Australia won by 5 wickets

7. Australia v England
Third Test at Sydney – 3, 4, 6, 7 March 1882
ENGLAND 188 (Shrewsbury 82, Palmer 5–46) and 134 (Shrewsbury 47, Garrett 6–78, Palmer 4–44)
AUSTRALIA 262 (McDonnell 147, Bannerman 70, Peate 5–43) and 64–4
Australia won by 6 wickets

8. Australia v England
Fourth Test at Melbourne – 10, 11, 13, 14 March 1882
ENGLAND 309 (Ulyett 149, Garrett 5–80) and 234–2 (Ulyett 64, Barlow 56, Bates 52*, Selby 48*)
AUSTRALIA 300 (Murdoch 85, McDonnell 52, Midwinter 4–81)
Match drawn

9. England v Australia
Only Test at The Oval – 28, 29 August 1882
AUSTRALIA 63 (Barlow 5–19, Peate 4–31) and 122 (Massie 55, Peate 4–40)
ENGLAND 101 (Spofforth 7–46) and 77 (Spofforth 7–44)
Australia won by 7 runs

10. Australia v England
First Test at Melbourne – 30 December 1882, 1, 2 January 1883
AUSTRALIA 291 (Bonnor 85, Murdoch 48, McDonnell 43) and 58–1
ENGLAND 177 (Palmer 7–65) and 169 (Giffen 4–38)
Australia won by 9 wickets

 DID YOU KNOW...?

In 1887, England were bowled out for 45 by Australia in the first Test at Sydney, but fought back thanks to the bowling efforts of Billy Barnes and George Lohmann to win by 13 runs.

11. Australia v England
Second Test at Melbourne – 19, 20, 22 January 1883
ENGLAND 294 (Read 75, Bates 55, Leslie 54, Palmer 5–103, Giffen 4–89)
AUSTRALIA 114 (Massie 43, Bates 7–28) and 153 (Bates 7–74)
England won by an innings and 27 runs

12. Australia v England
Third Test at Sydney – 26, 27, 29, 30 January 1883
ENGLAND 247 (Read 66, Tylecote 66, Spofforth 4–73) and 123 (Spofforth 7–44)
AUSTRALIA 218 (Bannerman 94, Giffen 41, Morley 4–47) and 83 (Barlow 7–40)
England won by 69 runs

13. Australia v England
Only Test at Sydney – 17, 19, 20, 21 February 1883
ENGLAND 263 (Steel 135*, Studd 48) and 197 (Bates 48*)
AUSTRALIA 262 (Bonnor 87, Blackham 57) and 199–6 (Bannerman 63, Blackham 58*)
Australia won by 4 wickets

14. England v Australia
First Test at Old Trafford – 10 (no play), 11, 12 July 1884
ENGLAND 95 (Shrewsbury 43, Boyle 6–42, Spofforth 4–42) and 180–9 (Palmer 4–47)
AUSTRALIA 182 (Midwinter 37, McDonnell 36)
Match drawn

15. England v Australia
Second Test at Lord's – 21, 22, 23 July 1884
AUSTRALIA 229 (Scott 75, Giffen 63, Peate 6–85) and 145 (Ulyett 7–36)
ENGLAND 379 (Steel 148, Palmer 6–111)
England won by an innings and 5 runs

16. England v Australia
Third Test at The Oval – 11, 12, 13 August 1884
AUSTRALIA 551 (Murdoch 211, McDonnell 103, Scott 102, Lyttelton 4–19)
ENGLAND 346 (Read 117, Scotton 90, Palmer 4–90) and 85–2
Match drawn

17. Australia v England
First Test at Adelaide – 12, 13, 15, 16 December 1884
AUSTRALIA 243 (McDonnell 124, Blackham 66, Bates 5–31) and 191 (McDonnell 83, Giffen 47, Peel 5–51)
ENGLAND 369 (W. Barnes 134, Scotton 82, Ulyett 68, Palmer 5–81) and 67–2
England won by 8 wickets

18. Australia v England
Second Test at Melbourne – 1, 2, 3, 5 January 1885
ENGLAND 401 (Briggs 121, Shrewsbury 72, W. Barnes 58, Jones 4–47) and 7–0
AUSTRALIA 279 (Jarvis 82, Horan 63, Trumble 59) and 126 (Bruce 45, W. Barnes 6–31)
England won by 10 wickets

19. Australia v England
Third Test at Sydney – 20, 21, 23, 24 February 1885
AUSTRALIA 181 (Garrett 51*, Flowers 5–46, Attewell 4–53) and 165 (Bates 5–24)
ENGLAND 133 (Horan 6–40, Spofforth 4–54) and 207 (Flowers 56, Read 56, Spofforth 6–90)
Australia won by 6 runs

20. Australia v England
Fourth Test at Sydney – 14, 16, 17 March 1885
ENGLAND 269 (Bates 64, W. Barnes 50, Read 47, Shrewsbury 40, Giffen 7–117) and 77 (Spofforth 5–30, Palmer 4–32)
AUSTRALIA 309 (Bonnor 128, Bannerman 51, Jones 40, W. Barnes 4–61) and 38–2
Australia won by 8 wickets

21. Australia v England
Fifth Test at Melbourne – 21, 23, 24, 25 March 1885
AUSTRALIA 163 (Spofforth 50, Ulyett 4–52) and 125
ENGLAND 386 (Shrewsbury 105*, W. Barnes 74, Bates 61, Briggs 43, Trumble 3–29)
England won by an innings and 98 runs

22. England v Australia
First Test at Old Trafford – 5, 6, 7 July 1886
AUSTRALIA 205 (Jones 87, Jarvis 45, Ulyett 4–46) and 123 (Scott 47, Barlow 7–44)
ENGLAND 223 (Read 51, Spofforth 4–82) and 107–6
England won by 4 wickets

23. England v Australia
Second Test at Lord's – 19, 20, 21 July 1886
ENGLAND 353 (Shrewsbury 164, W. Barnes 58, Spofforth 4–73)
AUSTRALIA 121 (Briggs 5–29) and 126 (Palmer 48, Briggs 6–45)
England won by an innings and 106 runs

24. England v Australia
Third Test at The Oval – 12, 13, 14 August 1886
ENGLAND 434 (W. G. Grace 170, Read 94, Briggs 53, Shrewsbury 44, Spofforth 4–65)

AUSTRALIA 68 (Lohmann 7–36) and 149 (Giffen 47, Lohmann 5–68)
England won by an innings and 217 runs

25. Australia v England
First Test at Sydney – 28, 29, 31 January 1887
ENGLAND 45 (Turner 6–15, Ferris 4–27) and 184 (Ferris 5–76)
AUSTRALIA 119 and 97 (W. Barnes 6–28, Lohmann 3–20)
England won by 13 runs

26. Australia v England
Second Test at Sydney – 25, 26, 28 February, 1 March 1887
ENGLAND 151 (Turner 5–41, Ferris 5–71) and 154 (Barlow 42*, Turner 4–52, Ferris 4–69)
AUSTRALIA 84 (Lohmann 8–35) and 150 (Bates 4–26)
England won by 71 runs

27. Australia v England
Only Test at Sydney – 10, 11 (no play), 13 (no play), 14, 15 February 1888
ENGLAND 113 (Shrewsbury 44, Turner 5–44, Ferris 4–60) and 137 (Turner 7–43)
AUSTRALIA 42 (Lohmann 5–17, Peel 5–18) and 82 (Lohmann 4–35, Peel 4–40)
England won by 126 runs

28. England v Australia
First Test at Lord's – 16, 17 July 1888
AUSTRALIA 116 (Peel 4–36) and 60 (Peel 4–14, Lohmann 4–33)
ENGLAND 53 (Turner 5–27) and 62 (Ferris 5–26, Turner 5–36)
Australia won by 61 runs

29. England v Australia
Second Test at The Oval – 13, 14 August 1888
AUSTRALIA 80 (Briggs 5–25) and 100 (W. Barnes 5–32, Peel 4–49)
ENGLAND 317 (Abel 70, W. Barnes 62, Lohmann 62*, Turner 6–112)
England won by an innings and 137 runs

30. England v Australia
Third Test at Old Trafford – 30, 31 August 1888
ENGLAND 172 (Turner 5–86)
AUSTRALIA 81 (Peel 7–31) and 70 (Peel 4–37)
England won by an innings and 21 runs

 DID YOU KNOW...?

Johnny Briggs took 8–11 (all clean-bowled) in a Test innings in 1889. He was one of the very few players to achieve a hat-trick and score a century in Tests.

31. South Africa v England
First Test at Port Elizabeth – 12, 13 March 1889
SOUTH AFRICA 84 (Smith 5–19, Briggs 4–39) and 129 (Fothergill 4–19)
ENGLAND 148 (Abel 46, Rose-Innes 5–43) and 67–2
England won by 8 wickets

32. South Africa v England
Second Test at Cape Town – 25, 26 March 1889
ENGLAND 292 (Abel 120, Wood 59, Ashley 7–95)
SOUTH AFRICA 47 (Briggs 7–17) and 43 (Briggs 8–11)
England won by an innings and 202 runs

33. England v Australia
First Test at Lord's – 21, 22, 23 July 1890
AUSTRALIA 132 (Lyons 55, Attewell 4–42) and 176 (Barrett 67*)
ENGLAND 173 (Ulyett 74, Lyons 5–30) and 137–3 (W. G. Grace 75*)
England won by 7 wickets

34. England v Australia
Second Test at The Oval – 11, 12 August 1890
AUSTRALIA 92 (Martin 6–50) and 102 (Martin 6–52)
ENGLAND 100 (Ferris 4–25) and 95–8 (Ferris 5–49)
England won by 2 wickets

England v Australia
Third Test at Old Trafford
Match cancelled without a ball being bowled: rain

35. Australia v England
First Test at Melbourne – 1, 2, 4, 5, 6 January 1892
AUSTRALIA 240 (Bruce 57, Bannerman 45, Sharpe 6–84) and 236 (Lyons 51, Bannerman 41, Bruce 40)
ENGLAND 264 (W. G. Grace 50, Bean 50, Briggs 41, McLeod 5–53) and 158 (Turner 5–51)
Australia won by 54 runs

36. Australia v England
Second Test at Sydney – 29, 30 January, 1, 2, 3 February 1892
AUSTRALIA 144 (Lyons 41, Lohmann 8–58) and 391 (Lyons 134, Bannerman 91, Bruce 72, Giffen 49, Briggs 4–69)
ENGLAND 307 (Abel 132*, Giffen 4–88) and 156 (Stoddart 69, Giffen 6–72, Turner 4–46)
Australia won by 72 runs

37. South Africa v England
Only Test at Cape Town – 19, 21, 22 March 1892
SOUTH AFRICA 97 (Ferris 6–54) and 83 (Ferris 7–37)
ENGLAND 369 (Wood 134*, Chatterton 48)
England won by an innings and 189 runs

38. Australia v England
Third Test at Adelaide – 24, 25, 26, 28 March 1892
ENGLAND 499 (Stoddart 134, Peel 83, W. G. Grace 58)
AUSTRALIA 100 (Briggs 6–49) and 169 (Briggs 6–87)
England won by an innings and 230 runs

39. England v Australia
First Test at Lord's – 17, 18, 19 July 1893
ENGLAND 334 (Shrewsbury 106, Jackson 91, Turner 6–67) and 234–8 dec. (Shrewsbury 81, W. Gunn 77, Giffen 5–43)
AUSTRALIA 269 (Graham 107, Gregory 57, Lockwood 6–101)
Match drawn

40. England v Australia
Second Test at The Oval – 14, 15, 16 August 1893
ENGLAND 483 (Jackson 103, Stoddart 83, W. G. Grace 68, Shrewsbury 66, Ward 55, Read 52, Giffen 7–128)
AUSTRALIA 91 (Briggs 5–34, Lockwood 4–37) and 349 (Trott 92, Bannerman 55, Giffen 53, Graham 42, Briggs 5–114, Lockwood 4–96)
England won by an innings and 43 runs

41. England v Australia
Third Test at Old Trafford – 24, 25, 26 August 1893
AUSTRALIA 204 (Bruce 68, Richardson 5–49, Briggs 4–81) and 236 (Bannerman 60, Richardson 5–107)
ENGLAND 243 (W. Gunn 102*, W. G. Grace 40, Giffen 4–113) and 118–4 (W. G. Grace 45, Stoddart 42)
Match drawn

42. Australia v England
First Test at Sydney – 14, 15, 17, 18, 19, 20 December 1894
AUSTRALIA 586 (Gregory 201, Giffen 161, Iredale 81, Richardson 5–181) and 166 (Darling 53, Peel 6–67)
ENGLAND 325 (Ward 75, Briggs 57, Brockwell 49, Giffen 4–75) and 437 (Ward 117, Brown 53, Ford 48, Briggs 42, Giffen 4–164)
England won by 10 runs

DID YOU KNOW...?

The first England Test captain to put the opposition in to bat was Andrew Stoddart, against Australia in 1895. England were dismissed for 65 and 72, and lost by an innings and 147 runs.

43. Australia v England
Second Test at Melbourne – 29, 31 December 1894, 1, 2, 3 January 1895
ENGLAND 75 (Turner 5–32) and 475 (Stoddart 173, Peel 53, Ward 41, Giffen 6–155)
AUSTRALIA 123 (Richardson 5–57) and 333 (Trott 95, Iredale 68, Bruce 54, Giffen 43, Peel 4–77)
England won by 94 runs

44. Australia v England
Third Test at Adelaide – 11, 12, 14, 15 January 1895
AUSTRALIA 238 (Giffen 58, Trott 48, Callaway 41, Richardson 5–75) and 411 (Iredale 140, Bruce 80, Trott 72*, Peel 4–96)
ENGLAND 124 (Callaway 5–37, Giffen 5–76) and 143 (Trott 8–43)
Australia won by 382 runs

45. Australia v England
Fourth Test at Sydney – 1, 2 (no play), 4 February 1895
AUSTRALIA 284 (Graham 105, Trott 85*, Briggs 4–65)
ENGLAND 65 and 72 (Giffen 5–26, Turner 4–33)
Australia won by an innings and 147 runs

46. Australia v England
Fifth Test at Melbourne – 1, 2, 4, 5, 6 March 1895
AUSTRALIA 414 (Darling 74, Gregory 70, Giffen 57, Lyons 55, Trott 42, Peel 4–14) and 267 (Giffen 51, Darling 50, Trott 42, Richardson 6–104)
ENGLAND 385 (MacLaren 120, Peel 73, Stoddart 68, Trott 4–71) and 298–4 (Brown 140, Ward 93)
England won by 6 wickets

47. South Africa v England
First Test at Port Elizabeth – 13, 14 February 1896
ENGLAND 185 (Fry 43, Middleton 5–64) and 226 (Woods 53, Middleton 4–66)
SOUTH AFRICA 93 (Lohmann 7–38) and 30 (Lohmann 8–7)
England won by 288 runs

48. South Africa v England
Second Test at Johannesburg – 2, 3, 4 March 1896
ENGLAND 482 (Hayward 122, Bromley-Davenport 84, Wright 71, Hill 65, Fry 64, Rowe 5–115, Sinclair 4–118)
SOUTH AFRICA 151 (Sinclair 40, Lohmann 9–28) and 134 (Halliwell 41, Heseltine 5–38)
England won by an innings and 197 runs

49. South Africa v England
Third Test at Cape Town – 21, 23 March 1896
SOUTH AFRICA 115 (Lohmann 7–42) and 117 (Hill 4–8)
ENGLAND 265 (Hill 124)
England won by an innings and 33 runs

50. England v Australia
First Test at Lord's – 22, 23, 24 June 1896
AUSTRALIA 53 (Richardson 6–39) and 347 (Trott 143, Gregory 103, Richardson 5–134, J. T. Hearne 5–76)
ENGLAND 292 (Abel 94, W. G. Grace 66, Jackson 44) and 111–4
England won by 6 wickets

 DID YOU KNOW...?

J. T. Hearne took the first Test hat-trick in England in 1899, dismissing three notable Australian batsman – Hill, Gregory and Noble – for nought apiece.

51. England v Australia
Second Test at Old Trafford – 16, 17, 18 July 1896
AUSTRALIA 412 (Iredale 108, Giffen 80, Trott 53, Richardson 7–168) and 125–7 (Richardson 6–76)
ENGLAND 231 (Lilley 65*, Ranjitsinhji 62) and 305 (Ranjitsinhji 154*, Stoddart 41)
Australia won by 3 wickets

52. England v Australia
Third Test at The Oval – 10, 11, 12 August 1896
ENGLAND 145 (Jackson 45, Trumble 6–59) and 84 (Trumble 6–30)
AUSTRALIA 119 (Darling 47, J. T. Hearne 6–41) and 44 (Peel 6–23, J. T. Hearne 4–19)
England won by 66 runs

53. Australia v England
First Test at Sydney – 13, 14, 15, 16, 17 December 1897
ENGLAND 551 (Ranjitsinhji 175, MacLaren 109, Hayward 72, Hirst 62, Storer 43) and 96–1 (MacLaren 50*)
AUSTRALIA 237 (Trumble 70, McLeod 50*, Gregory 46, J. T. Hearne 5–42) and 408 (Darling 101, Hill 96, Kelly 46*, J. T. Hearne 4–99)
England won by 9 wickets

54. Australia v England
Second Test at Melbourne – 1, 3, 4, 5 January 1898
AUSTRALIA 520 (McLeod 112, Iredale 89, Trott 79, Gregory 71, Hill 58)
ENGLAND 315 (Ranjitsinhji 71, Storer 51, Briggs 46*, Druce 44, Trumble 4–54) and 150 (Noble 6–49, Trumble 4–53)
Australia won by an innings and 55 runs

55. Australia v England
Third Test at Adelaide – 14, 15, 17, 18, 19 January 1898
AUSTRALIA 573 (Darling 178, Iredale 84, Hill 81, Gregory 52, Richardson 4–164)
ENGLAND 278 (Hirst 85, Hayward 70, Howell 4–70) and 282 (MacLaren 124, Ranjitsinhji 77, McLeod 5–65, Noble 5–84)
Australia won by an innings and 13 runs

56. Australia v England
Fourth Test at Melbourne – 29, 31 January, 1, 2 February 1898
AUSTRALIA 323 (Hill 188, Trumble 46, J. T. Hearne 6–98) and 115–2 (McLeod 64*)
ENGLAND 174 (Jones 4–56) and 263 (Ranjitsinhji 55, MacLaren 45)
Australia won by 8 wickets

57. Australia v England
Fifth Test at Sydney – 26, 28 February, 1, 2 March 1898
ENGLAND 335 (MacLaren 65, Druce 64, Wainwright 49, Hayward 47, Storer 44, Hirst 44, Jones 6–82) and 178 (Hayward 43, Trumble 4–37)
AUSTRALIA 239 (McLeod 64, Richardson 8–94) and 276–4 (Darling 160, Worrall 62)
Australia won by 6 wickets

58. South Africa v England
First Test at Johannesburg – 14, 15, 16 February 1899
ENGLAND 145 and 237 (Warner 132*, Middleton 5–51)
SOUTH AFRICA 251 (Sinclair 86, Trott 4–61) and 99 (Trott 5–49)
England won by 32 runs

59. South Africa v England
Second Test at Cape Town – 1, 3, 4 April 1899
ENGLAND 92 (Sinclair 6–26, Middleton 4–18) and 330 (J. Tyldesley 112, Mitchell 41)
SOUTH AFRICA 177 (Sinclair 106, Trott 4–69) and 35 (Haigh 6–11, Trott 4–19)
England won by 210 runs

60. England v Australia
First Test at Trent Bridge – 1, 2, 3 June 1899
AUSTRALIA 252 (Hill 52, Gregory 48, Darling 47, Noble 41, Rhodes 4–58, J. T. Hearne 4–71) and 230–8 dec. (Hill 80, Noble 45)
ENGLAND 193 (Fry 50, Ranjitsinhji 42, E. Jones 5–88) and 155–7 (Ranjitsinhji 93*)
Match drawn

61. England v Australia
Second Test at Lord's – 15, 16, 17 June 1899
ENGLAND 206 (Jackson 73, Jessop 51, E. Jones 7–88) and 240 (MacLaren 88*, Hayward 77)
AUSTRALIA 421 (Hill 135, Trumper 135*, Noble 54) and 28–0
Australia won by 10 wickets

62. England v Australia
Third Test at Headingley – 29, 30 June, 1 July (no play)
1899
AUSTRALIA 172 (Worrall 76, Young 4–30) and 224
(Trumble 56, Laver 45, J. T. Hearne 4–50)
ENGLAND 220 (Lilley 55, Hayward 40*, Trumble 5–60) and
19–0
Match drawn

63. England v Australia
Fourth Test at Old Trafford – 17, 18, 19 July 1899
ENGLAND 372 (Hayward 130, Lilley 58, Jackson 44, Young
43) and 94–3 (Ranjitsinhji 49*)

AUSTRALIA 196 (Noble 60*, Trumble 44, Bradley 5–67,
Young 4–79) and 346–7 dec. (Noble 89, Trumper 63,
Worrall 53)
Match drawn

64. England v Australia
Fifth Test at The Oval – 14, 15, 16 August 1899
ENGLAND 576 (Hayward 137, Jackson 118, Fry 60,
Ranjitsinhji 54, MacLaren 49, E. Jones 4–164)
AUSTRALIA 352 (Gregory 117, Darling 71, Worrall 55,
Lockwood 7–71) and 254–5 dec. (McLeod 77, Worrall
75, Noble 69*)
Match drawn

CRICKET IN THE EARLY TWENTIETH CENTURY: 1901–1914

The England tour of Australia in 1901–2, led by Archie MacLaren, was the fifteenth and last under private management. A number of England's leading players were not available, but the inclusion of Sydney Barnes, plucked out of league cricket and plunged straight into the turmoil of an Australian tour, was a surprise. As in the previous series in Australia in 1897–8, England won the first Test but the home side won the next four. MacLaren scored a century in the first Test at Sydney, making him the first batsman to score four Test centuries. A record 25 wickets fell on the first day of the second Test at Melbourne on a rain-affected pitch. In reply to Australia's first-innings score of 112, England were dismissed for 61 in just sixty-eight minutes. Barnes, who had taken 19 wickets in the first two Tests, twisted his knee after just seven overs of the third Test, and his loss was critical to the balance of the match and the series.

Having dominated the first series of the twentieth century on home turf, the Australians travelled to England a few months later and recorded a 2–1 series victory, which meant that Australia had won four successive rubbers. The series began with the first-ever Test to be staged at Edgbaston, where, after England had amassed a substantial total, heavy rain led to a dismal innings of 36 from Australia – their lowest on record. Wilfred Rhodes took 7–17, but the rain that had treated the tourists so unkindly would eventually return to save them and lead to a draw. The second Test at Lord's was abandoned because of heavy rain and the third, the only Test ever played at Bramall Lane, saw Australia win by 143 runs. At Old Trafford, Australia's Victor Trumper became the first player to score a century before lunch on the first day of a Test. Australia, who were 37 ahead on first innings, were struggling at 10–3 in their second innings when Joe Darling was dropped on the square-leg boundary by Test debutant Fred Tate, and the score advanced to 64 before another wicket fell. Wickets then tumbled quickly, with the result that England needed 124 to win. Four runs were required as last man Tate joined Rhodes. It was the perfect chance for him to redeem himself, but he was bowled by a quicker ball and never played Test cricket again, although his son Maurice would go on to become an outstanding Test bowler. Known as 'Jessop's Match', the final Test of the series saw England hopelessly placed at 48–5 with 263 needed for victory. Gilbert Jessop arrived to complete an astonishing century in seventy-five minutes – then the fastest on record in Test cricket. With his departure, much responsibility fell on George Hirst. When Rhodes joined his fellow Yorkshireman for England's last wicket, 15 runs were needed for victory. The runs were not obtained in singles as legend has it, but the last-wicket partnership did see England to victory.

The first Test of England's tour to Australia in 1903–4 saw 'Tip' Foster make 287 on his debut, which set a string of records. It remained the record highest Test score until 1929–30, when Andy Sandham scored 325, and it is still the most scored by a player in his first Test, the highest for England in Australia, and the record for any Test in Sydney. Foster was also the first batsman to share in three century partnerships in the same Test innings and his tenth-wicket stand of 130 with Wilfred Rhodes is still the record for Ashes Tests. England also won the second Test at Melbourne, with Rhodes taking 15 wickets, a new England record at the time – this despite having eight catches dropped from his bowling. In between Australia's victories in the third and fifth Tests, England won the fourth, with Bernard Bosanquet taking 6–51 in Australia's second innings.

The 1905 Ashes series became known as 'Jackson's Year' with F. S. (Stanley) Jackson leading England to victory over a strong Australian side. The England captain won the toss in each of the five Tests, and headed both the batting averages with 70.28 and the bowling averages with 15.46. Bosanquet, who played in only seven Tests, helped England to victory in the first at Trent Bridge with figures of 8–107, while Archie MacLaren scored a record fifth Test century – the first at the Nottingham ground. The next two Tests at Lord's and Headingley were drawn, though Jackson scored the first Test century at Leeds, and in the fourth Test he led his team to another win to take the Ashes with a successive hundred at Old Trafford.

In the first Test of England's 1905–6 tour, South Africa recorded their first-ever Test victory at Johannesburg. It proved to be a thrilling affair as the home side won by just one wicket. Needing 284 to win after being bowled out for 91 in the first innings, South Africa made the runs largely through an unbroken last-wicket stand of 48 between the left-handed Dave Nourse and his captain P. W. Sherwell. In this series the South African selectors took the unique step of picking the same side for all five Tests and their confidence was confirmed when Sherwell's side won all but the fourth Test against an under-strength England team led by Plum Warner.

After their success on home turf, South Africa were accorded full Test status when they visited England the following year. In the second of the three Tests, the others being drawn, England were bowled out for 76 after rain, Aubrey Faulkner taking 6–17. South Africa led on the first innings and needed only 129 to win in the second, but after more rain, Kent's Colin Blythe had the last word, taking 7–40 to help England to a 53-run victory.

In the 1907–8 Ashes series, England were unsettled by captaincy problems as the appointed captain, Arthur Jones of Nottinghamshire, missed the first three Tests after falling ill. In his absence Frederick Fane took over the leadership, becoming the first Essex player to captain England. Due to Jones's illness, another Nottinghamshire batsman, George Gunn, made an unexpected debut in the first Test at Sydney. Although not an official member of the touring party, Gunn made the most of his opportunity, topscoring with 119 and 74, though it was not enough to save England from defeat. The second Test marked the debut of Jack Hobbs, who hit 83 as England made 382. Australia's second innings saw five of their batsmen score half-centuries, leaving England 282 to win. Though Fane made a decent half-century, it was the last pair (Barnes and Fielder) who put on 39 to see England home. After defeat in the third Test, England's hopes of retaining the Ashes were washed away with a rain-affected wicket on day two of the fourth Test at Melbourne, when they were bowled out for 105. Though they hit back well to pin down Australia at 77–5, Warwick Armstrong made an unbeaten 133 to help Australia set England 495 to win. The tourists were dismissed for 186 to give Australia the Ashes, and the home side completed the series with another victory in the final Test at Sydney.

Though England won the first Test of the 1909 Ashes series by 10 wickets, it was a spell of rain before the Edgbaston match that would ultimately dictate its course. Australia found the swerve of Hirst and the spin of Blythe too much, and were bowled out for 74. England then made 121 before England's two left-arm bowlers again had their way to restrict the Aussies to 151 in the second innings, and the hosts were left needing 105 for victory. Hobbs and Fry, who both went first ball to Charles Macartney in the first innings, remained unbeaten as England romped home. The turning point in the series came in the second Test when Australia won comfortably by 9 wickets. England made six changes for the third Test at Headingley, and though the wicket gave both sets of bowlers a chance, it was Australia who triumphed by 126 runs. One up, Australia concentrated on avoiding defeat in the two remaining Tests, which they managed with two draws. In the final Test, at The Oval, Australia's Warren Bardsley became the first batsman ever to make two centuries in a Test.

H. D. G. Leveson-Gower's England team to tour South Africa in 1910–11 was much stronger in its early batting than some of its predecessors, boasting an order that read Hobbs, Rhodes, Denton, Fane and Woolley. But its bowling was much less menacing for South African batting, which by now had grown in confidence. South Africa had in Faulkner a world-class all-rounder, and in the first Test, which the home side won by 19 runs, he made 78 and 123 as well as taking 8 wickets. South Africa clinched the series in the fourth Test at Cape Town, Hobbs's 187 in the last Test coming too late to affect the outcome.

When England's appointed captain for the 1911–12 tour to Australia, Plum Warner, fell ill, it was Johnny Douglas, who three years previously had won an Olympic Games gold medal as a middleweight boxer, who took over the captaincy. The series, which England won 4–1 to regain the Ashes, is best remembered for the expert bowling of Frank Foster and Sydney Barnes, but England had a poor start in the first Test at Sydney, which Australia won by 146 runs. A famous opening spell by Barnes in the second Test at Melbourne – at one point he had figures of 11–7–6–5 – saw England get a grip on the match, which they refused to relinquish. At Adelaide, Hobbs made 187, the highest of his centuries against Australia, as England won by 7 wickets. For the fourth Test at Melbourne, Douglas put Australia in to bat, and by late afternoon the Foster–Barnes combination had already done its work, with the home side dismissed for 191. England's openers Hobbs and Rhodes scored 178 and 179 respectively – their partnership of 323 remaining England's best for any wicket in Australia. Douglas rammed home his decision to field first by taking half the wickets in the second innings, the final one ensuring that the Ashes would be coming back home to England. The final Test saw England triumph by 70 runs, in a match that saw Frank Woolley's unbeaten 133 become the first century by an England left-hander in Australia.

In 1912, the experiment of running a triangular tournament between England, Australia and South Africa proved a failure, partly because of a disastrously wet summer. South Africa lost more easily to England than they did to Australia, however, in particular falling foul of Sydney Barnes, who took 34 wickets over the three matches. In the meetings with Australia, rain ruined the first two matches, both of which were drawn, and so the overall result of the tournament hinged on the third Test between the two countries in August at The Oval – the ninth match of the tournament. To ensure a result, the encounter was declared a 'timeless Test' – the first to be staged in England – but as it turned out only four days were needed to produce a result. England set up their victory with a 134-run lead on the first innings. Australia were bowled out for 111 with Barnes and Woolley taking 5 wickets apiece as the last 8 wickets fell for just 21 runs. Fry, who trod on his stumps without dislodging a bail, made 79 in England's second innings, but, with Gerry Hazlitt taking England's last 5 wickets for 1 run, England were bowled out for 175, leaving Australia 310 to win. In an inglorious second innings, Australia were dismissed for 65 with Woolley taking 5–20 and Lancashire's Harry Dean with figures of 4–19.

If ever one man dominated a Test series, then it was Sydney Barnes on England's tour of South Africa in the last tournament before the First World War. He did not play in the final Test at Port Elizabeth, but in the first four he captured 49 wickets. South Africa had a high-class opening batsman in Herbie Taylor, but in an England side in which Hobbs, Rhodes, Woolley and Philip Mead all made runs, Barnes did the business with the ball. In the second Test at Johannesburg, he took 17 wickets, a feat not exceeded until Jim Laker's historic 19-wicket haul in 1956. England returned home as 4–0 series champions.

TEST MATCH RESULTS: 1901–14

65. Australia v England
First Test at Sydney – 13, 14, 16 December 1901
ENGLAND 464 (MacLaren 116, Lilley 84, Hayward 69,
    Braund 58, McLeod 4–84)
AUSTRALIA 168 (Gregory 48, Hill 46, S. Barnes 5–65) and
    172 (Gregory 43, Braund 5–61, Blythe 4–30)
England won by an innings and 124 runs

66. Australia v England
Second Test at Melbourne – 1, 2, 3, 4 January 1902
AUSTRALIA 112 (S. Barnes 6–42, Blythe 4–64) and 353
    (Duff 104, Hill 99, Armstrong 45*, S. Barnes 7–121)
ENGLAND 61 (Noble 7–17) and 175 (J. Tyldesley 66, Noble
    6–60, Trumble 4–49)
Australia won by 229 runs

67. Australia v England
Third Test at Adelaide – 17, 18, 20, 21, 22, 23 January 1902
ENGLAND 388 (Braund 103*, Hayward 90, Quaife 68,
    MacLaren 67) and 247 (Hayward 47, MacLaren 44,
    Quaife 44, Trumble 6–74)
AUSTRALIA 321 (Hill 98, Trumper 65, Gregory 55, Duff 43, J.
    Gunn 5–76) and 315–6 (Hill 97, Darling 69, Trumble 62*)
Australia won by 4 wickets

68. Australia v England
Fourth Test at Sydney – 14, 15, 17, 18 February 1902
ENGLAND 317 (MacLaren 92, J. Tyldesley 79, Hayward 41,
    Lilley 40, J. Saunders 4–119) and 99 (J. Saunders 5–43,
    Noble 5–54)
AUSTRALIA 299 (Noble 56, Armstrong 55, Hopkins 43,
    Jessop 4–68, Braund 4–118) and 121–3 (Duff 51*)
Australia won by 7 wickets

69. Australia v England
Fifth Test at Melbourne – 28 February, 1, 3, 4 March 1902
AUSTRALIA 144 (Hayward 4–22, J. Gunn 4–38) and 255
    (Hill 87, Gregory 41, Braund 5–95)
ENGLAND 189 (Lilley 41, Trumble 5–62) and 178
    (MacLaren 49, Noble 6–98)
Australia won by 32 runs

70. England v Australia
First Test at Edgbaston – 29, 30, 31 May 1902
ENGLAND 376–9 dec. (J. Tyldesley 138, Jackson 53,
    Lockwood 52*, Hirst 48)
AUSTRALIA 36 (Rhodes 7–17) and 46–2
Match drawn

71. England v Australia
Second Test at Lord's – 12, 13 (no play), 14 (no play) June
    1902
ENGLAND 102–2 (Jackson 55*, MacLaren 47*)
AUSTRALIA did not bat
Match drawn

72. England v Australia
Third Test at Bramall Lane, Sheffield – 3, 4, 5 July 1902
AUSTRALIA 194 (Noble 47, S. Barnes 6–49) and 289 (Hill
    119, Trumper 62, Hopkins 40*, Rhodes 5–63)
ENGLAND 145 (Saunders 5–50, Noble 5–51) and 195
    (MacLaren 63, Jessop 55, Noble 6–52, Trumble 4–49)
Australia won by 143 runs

73. England v Australia
Fourth Test at Old Trafford – 24, 25, 26 July 1902
AUSTRALIA 299 (Trumper 104, Hill 65, Lockwood 6–48,
    Rhodes 4–104) and 86 (Lockwood 5–28)
ENGLAND 262 (Jackson 128, Braund 65, Trumble 4–75)
    and 120 (Trumble 6–53, Saunders 4–52)
Australia won by 3 runs

74. England v Australia
Fifth Test at The Oval – 11, 12, 13 August 1902
AUSTRALIA 324 (Trumble 64*, Noble 52, Trumper 42,
    Hopkins 40, Hirst 5–77) and 121 (Lockwood 5–45)
ENGLAND 183 (Hirst 43, Trumble 8–65) and 263–9 (Jessop
    104, Hirst 58, Jackson 49, Trumble 4–108, Saunders
    4–105)
England won by 1 wicket

 DID YOU KNOW…?

England's innings of 61 against Australia in 1902
lasted only 94 balls, the fewest they have faced in
any Test innings.

75. Australia v England
First Test at Sydney – 11, 12, 14, 15, 16, 17 December 1903
AUSTRALIA 285 (Noble 133, Armstrong 48, Arnold 4–76)
    and 485 (Trumper 185*, Duff 84, Hill 51, Gregory 43,
    Rhodes 5–94)
ENGLAND 577 (Foster 287, Braund 102, J. Tyldesley 53,
    Rhodes 40*) and 194–5 (Hayward 91, Hirst 60*)
England won by 5 wickets

76. Australia v England
Second Test at Melbourne – 1, 2, 4, 5 January 1904
ENGLAND 315 (J. Tyldesley 97, Warner 68, Hayward 58,
    Foster 49 ret. hurt, Howell 4–43, Trumble 4–107) and
    103 (J. Tyldesley 62, Trumble 5–34)
AUSTRALIA 122 (Trumper 74, Rhodes 7–56) and 111
    (Rhodes 8–68)
England won by 185 runs

77. Australia v England
Third Test at Adelaide – 15, 16, 18, 19, 20 January 1904
AUSTRALIA 388 (Trumper 113, Hill 88, Duff 79, Noble 59)
    and 351 (Gregory 112, Noble 65, Trumper 59,
    Bosanquet 4–73)
ENGLAND 245 (Hirst 58, Warner 48) and 278 (Warner 79,
    Hayward 67, Hirst 44, Hopkins 4–81)
Australia won by 216 runs

78. Australia v England
Fourth Test at Sydney – 26, 27, 29 (no play) February, 1, 2,
    3 March 1904
ENGLAND 249 (Knight 70*, Noble 7–100) and 210
    (Hayward 52)
AUSTRALIA 131 (Duff 47, Arnold 4–28, Rhodes 4–33) and
    171 (Noble 53*, Bosanquet 6–51)
England won by 157 runs

79. Australia v England
Fifth Test at Melbourne – 5, 7, 8 March 1904
AUSTRALIA 247 (Trumper 88, Braund 8–81) and 133 (Hirst 5–48)
ENGLAND 61 (Cotter 6–40, Noble 4–19) and 101 (Trumble 7–28)
Australia won by 218 runs

80. England v Australia
First Test at Trent Bridge – 29, 30, 31 May 1905
ENGLAND 196 (J. Tyldesley 56, Laver 7–64) and 426–5 dec. (MacLaren 140, Jackson 82*, J. Tyldesley 61, Hayward 47)
AUSTRALIA 221 (Hill 54, Noble 50, Cotter 45, Jackson 5–52) and 188 (Gregory 51, Darling 40, Bosanquet 8–107)
England won by 213 runs

81. England v Australia
Second Test at Lord's – 15, 16, 17 (no play) June 1905
ENGLAND 282 (Fry 73, MacLaren 56, J. Tyldesley 43) and 151–5 (MacLaren 79)
AUSTRALIA 181 (Darling 41, Jackson 4–50)
Match drawn

82. England v Australia
Third Test at Headingley – 3, 4, 5 July 1905
ENGLAND 301 (Jackson 144*) and 295–5 dec. (J. Tyldesley 100, Hayward 60, Hirst 40*, Armstrong 5–122)
AUSTRALIA 195 (Armstrong 66, Duff 48, Warren 5–57) and 224–7 (Noble 62)
Match drawn

83. England v Australia
Fourth Test at Old Trafford – 24, 25, 26 July 1905
ENGLAND 446 (Jackson 113, Hayward 82, Spooner 52, McLeod 5–125)
AUSTRALIA 197 (Darling 73, Brearley 4–72) and 169 (Duff 60, Brearley 4–54)
England won by an innings and 80 runs

84. England v Australia
Fifth Test at The Oval – 14, 15, 16 August 1905
ENGLAND 430 (Fry 144, Jackson 76, Hayward 59, Arnold 40, Cotter 7–148) and 261–6 dec. (J. Tyldesley 112*, Spooner 79)
AUSTRALIA 363 (Duff 146, Darling 57, Kelly 42, Brearley 5–110) and 124–4
Match drawn

85. South Africa v England
First Test at Johannesburg – 2, 3, 4 January 1906
ENGLAND 184 (Crawford 44) and 190 (Warner 51, Crawford 43, Faulkner 4–26)
SOUTH AFRICA 91 (Lees 5–34) and 287–9 (Nourse 93*, White 81)
South Africa won by 1 wicket

86. South Africa v England
Second Test at Johannesburg – 6, 7, 8 March 1906
ENGLAND 148 (Sinclair 3–35) and 160 (Fane 65, Schwarz 4–30)
SOUTH AFRICA 277 (Sinclair 66, Haigh 4–64) and 34–1
South Africa won by 9 wickets

87. South Africa v England
Third Test at Johannesburg – 10, 12, 13, 14 March 1906
SOUTH AFRICA 385 (Hathorn 102, Nourse 61, White 46, Lees 6–78) and 349–5 dec. (White 147, Tancred 73, Nourse 55, Sinclair 48)
ENGLAND 295 (Fane 143, Snooke 4–57, Schwarz 4–67) and 196 (Denton 61, Snooke 8–70)
South Africa won by 243 runs

88. South Africa v England
Fourth Test at Cape Town – 24, 26, 27 March 1906
SOUTH AFRICA 218 (Snooke 44, White 41, Blythe 6–68) and 138 (White 73, Blythe 5–50, Lees 4–27)
ENGLAND 198 (Sinclair 4–41, Faulkner 4–49) and 160–6 (Fane 66*)
England won by 4 wickets

89. South Africa v England
Fifth Test at Cape Town – 30, 31 March, 2 April 1906
ENGLAND 187 (Crawford 74, Sinclair 4–45) and 130 (Nourse 4–25)
SOUTH AFRICA 333 (Vogler 62*, Snooke 60, Faulkner 45)
South Africa won by an innings and 16 runs

90. England v South Africa
First Test at Lord's – 1, 2, 3 July 1907
ENGLAND 428 (Braund 104, Jessop 93, J. Tyldesley 52, Lilley 48, Vogler 7–128)
SOUTH AFRICA 140 (Nourse 62, Faulkner 44, Arnold 5–37) and 185–3 (Sherwell 115)
Match drawn

91. England v South Africa
Second Test at Headingley – 29, 30, 31 July 1907
ENGLAND 76 (Faulkner 6–17, Sinclair 3–23) and 162 (Fry 54, White 4–47)
SOUTH AFRICA 110 (Blythe 8–59) and 75 (Blythe 7–40)
England won by 53 runs

92. England v South Africa
Third Test at The Oval – 19, 20, 21 August 1907
ENGLAND 295 (Fry 129, Foster 51, Lilley 42) and 138 (Vogler 4–49)
SOUTH AFRICA 178 (Snooke 63, Blythe 5–61) and 159–5 (Faulkner 42)
Match drawn

93. Australia v England
First Test at Sydney – 13, 14, 16, 17, 18 (no play), 19 December 1907
ENGLAND 273 (G. Gunn 119, Hutchings 42, Cotter 6–101) and 300 (G. Gunn 74, Hardstaff Snr 63, Saunders 4–68)
AUSTRALIA 300 (Hill 87, Trumper 43, Fielder 6–82) and 275–8 (Carter 61, Armstrong 44, McAlister 41)
Australia won by 2 wickets

94. Australia v England
Second Test at Melbourne – 1, 2, 3, 4, 6, 7 January 1908
AUSTRALIA 266 (Noble 61, Trumper 49, Crawford 5–79)
and 397 (Armstrong 77, Noble 64, Trumper 63,
Macartney 54, Carter 53, S. Barnes 5–72)
ENGLAND 382 (Hutchings 126, Hobbs 83, Braund 49,
Cotter 5–142) and 282–9 (Fane 50)
England won by 1 wicket

95. Australia v England
Third Test at Adelaide – 10, 11, 13, 14, 15, 16 January 1908
AUSTRALIA 285 (Macartney 75, Hartigan 48, Ransford 44,
Fielder 4–80) and 506 (Hill 160, Hartigan 116, Noble 65)
ENGLAND 363 (G. Gunn 65, Crawford 62, Hardstaff Snr 61,
Fane 48) and 183 (Hardstaff Snr 72, Braund 47,
O'Connor 5–40, J. Saunders 5–65)
Australia won by 245 runs

96. Australia v England
Fourth Test at Melbourne – 7, 8, 10, 11 February 1908
AUSTRALIA 214 (Ransford 51, Noble 48, Crawford 5–48,
Fielder 4–54) and 385 (Armstrong 133*, Carter 66,
Ransford 54, Fielder 4–91)
ENGLAND 105 (Hobbs 57, J. Saunders 5–28) and 186 (G.
Gunn 43, J. Saunders 4–76)
Australia won by 308 runs

97. Australia v England
Fifth Test at Sydney – 21, 22, 24, 25, 26, 27 February 1908
AUSTRALIA 137 (Gregory 44, S. Barnes 7–60) and 422
(Trumper 166, Gregory 56, Hill 44, Crawford 5–141,
Rhodes 4–102)
ENGLAND 281 (G. Gunn 122*, Hobbs 72) and 229 (Rhodes
69, Fane 46, J. Saunders 5–82)
Australia won by 49 runs

98. England v Australia
First Test at Edgbaston – 27, 28, 29 May 1909
AUSTRALIA 74 (Blythe 6–44, Hirst 4–28) and 151 (Gregory
43, Ransford 43, Blythe 5–58, Hirst 5–58)
ENGLAND 121 (Armstrong 5–27) and 105–0 (Hobbs 62*)
England won by 10 wickets

99. England v Australia
Second Test at Lord's – 14, 15, 16 June 1909
ENGLAND 269 (King 60, Lilley 47, J. Tyldesley 46, Cotter
4–80) and 121 (Armstrong 6–35)
AUSTRALIA 350 (Ransford 143*, Bardsley 46, Relf 5–85)
and 41–1
Australia won by 9 wickets

100. England v Australia
Third Test at Headingley – 1, 2, 3 July 1909
AUSTRALIA 188 (Gregory 46, Ransford 45, Rhodes 4–38)
and 207 (Armstrong 45, S. Barnes 6–63)
ENGLAND 182 (Sharp 61, J. Tyldesley 55, Macartney 7–58)
and 87 (Cotter 5–38, Macartney 4–27)
Australia won by 126 runs

101. England v Australia
Fourth Test at Old Trafford – 26, 27, 28 July 1909
AUSTRALIA 147 (S. Barnes 5–56, Blythe 5–63) and 279–9
dec. (Ransford 54*, Macartney 51, Trumper 48, Rhodes
5–83)
ENGLAND 119 (Laver 8–31) and 108–3 (Spooner 58)
Match drawn

102. England v Australia
Fifth Test at The Oval – 9, 10, 11 August 1909
AUSTRALIA 325 (Bardsley 136, Trumper 73, Macartney 50,
Carr 5–146) and 339–5 dec. (Bardsley 130, Gregory 74,
Noble 55)
ENGLAND 352 (Sharp 105, Rhodes 66, Fry 62, Hutchings
59, Cotter 6–95) and 104–3 (Rhodes 54)
Match drawn

 DID YOU KNOW...?

George Gunn, who was in Australia for his health in
1907–8, was called up for the first Test, and scored
119 and 74 on his England debut.

103. South Africa v England
First Test at Johannesburg – 1, 3, 4, 5 January 1910
SOUTH AFRICA 208 (Faulkner 78, Nourse 53, Simpson-
Hayward 6–43) and 345 (Faulkner 123, Snooke 47,
Buckenham 4–110)
ENGLAND 310 (Hobbs 89, Rhodes 66, Vogler 5–87,
Faulkner 5–120) and 224 (Thompson 63, Vogler 7–94)
South Africa won by 19 runs

104. South Africa v England
Second Test at Durban – 21, 22, 24, 25, 26 January 1910
SOUTH AFRICA 199 (Campbell 48, Faulkner 47, Simpson-
Hayward 4–42) and 347 (White 118, Nourse 69, Snooke
53)
ENGLAND 199 (Hobbs 53, Rhodes 44, Vogler 5–83) and
252 (Hobbs 70, Thompson 46*, Bird 42, Faulkner 6–87)
South Africa won by 95 runs

105. South Africa v England
Third Test at Johannesburg – 26, 28 February, 1, 2, 3 March
1910
SOUTH AFRICA 305 (Faulkner 76, White 72, Vogler 65,
Buckenham 5–115) and 237 (Snooke 52, Faulkner 44,
Simpson-Hayward 5–69)
ENGLAND 322 (Denton 104, Woolley 58*, Faulkner 4–89,
Vogler 4–98) and 221–7 (Hobbs 93*, Bird 45, Vogler
4–109)
England won by 3 wickets

106. South Africa v England
Fourth Test at Cape Town – 7, 8, 9 March 1910
ENGLAND 203 (Woolley 69, Bird 57) and 178 (Woolley 64,
Vogler 5–72)
SOUTH AFRICA 207 (Commaille 42, Thompson 4–50) and
175–6 (Faulkner 49*)
South Africa won by 4 wickets

107. South Africa v England
Fifth Test at Cape Town – 11, 12, 14 March 1910
ENGLAND 417 (Hobbs 187, Rhodes 77, Thompson 51,
Norton 4–47) and 16–1
SOUTH AFRICA 103 (Zulch 43*, Blythe 7–46) and 327
(Faulkner 99, Snooke 47, Schwarz 44)
England won by 9 wickets

108. Australia v England
First Test at Sydney – 15, 16, 18, 19, 20, 21 December 1911
AUSTRALIA 447 (Trumper 113, Minnett 90, Armstrong 60,
  Hill 46) and 308 (Kelleway 70, Hill 65, F. Foster 5–92,
  Douglas 4–50)
ENGLAND 318 (J. W. Hearne 76, Hobbs 63, F. Foster 56,
  Rhodes 41, Hordern 5–85) and 291 (G. Gunn 62, J. W.
  Hearne 43, Hordern 7–90)
Australia won by 146 runs

109. Australia v England
Second Test at Melbourne – 30 December 1911, 1, 2, 3
  January 1912
AUSTRALIA 184 (Hordern 49*, Ransford 43, S. Barnes 5–44)
  and 299 (Armstrong 90, Cotter 41, F. Foster 6–91)
ENGLAND 265 (J. W. Hearne 114, Rhodes 61, Hordern 4–66,
  Cotter 4–73) and 219–2 (Hobbs 126*, G. Gunn 43)
England won by 8 wickets

110. Australia v England
Third Test at Adelaide – 12, 13, 15, 16, 17 January 1912
AUSTRALIA 133 (F. Foster 5–36) and 476 (Hill 98, Carter
  72, Bardsley 63, Matthews 53, S. Barnes 5–105)
ENGLAND 501 (Hobbs 187, F. Foster 71, Rhodes 59, Mead
  46, Cotter 4–125) and 112–3 (Rhodes 57*, G. Gunn 45)
England won by 7 wickets

111. Australia v England
Fourth Test at Melbourne – 9, 10, 12, 13 February 1912
AUSTRALIA 191 (Minnett 56, S. Barnes 5–74, F. Foster
  4–77) and 173 (Douglas 5–46)
ENGLAND 589 (Rhodes 179, Hobbs 178, G. Gunn 75,
  Woolley 56, F. Foster 50)
England won by an innings and 225 runs

112. Australia v England
Fifth Test at Sydney – 23, 24, 26 (no play), 27, 28, 29
  February, 1 March 1912
ENGLAND 324 (Woolley 133*, G. Gunn 52, Hordern 5–95)
  and 214 (G. Gunn 61, Hobbs 45, Hordern 5–66)
AUSTRALIA 176 and 292 (Minnett 61, Trumper 50, Gregory
  40, F. Foster 4–43, S. Barnes 4–106)
England won by 70 runs

113. England v South Africa
First Test at Lord's – 10, 11, 12 June 1912
SOUTH AFRICA 58 (F. Foster 5–16, S. Barnes 5–25) and 217
  (Llewellyn 75, S. Barnes 6–85)
ENGLAND 337 (Spooner 119, Woolley 73, Pegler 7–65)
England won by an innings and 62 runs

114. England v Australia
First Test at Lord's – 24, 25, 26 June 1912
ENGLAND 310–7 dec. (Hobbs 107, Rhodes 59, Fry 42)
AUSTRALIA 282–7 (Macartney 99, Kelleway 61)
Match drawn

115. England v South Africa
Second Test at Headingley – 8, 9, 10 July 1912
ENGLAND 242 (Woolley 57, J. W. Hearne 45, Nourse 4–52)
  and 238 (Spooner 82, Hobbs 55, Faulkner 4–50)
SOUTH AFRICA 147 (S. Barnes 6–52) and 159 (S. Barnes
  4–63)
England won by 174 runs

116. England v Australia
Second Test at Old Trafford – 29, 30, 31 (no play) July 1912

ENGLAND 203 (Rhodes 92, Whitty 4–43, Hazlitt 4–77)
AUSTRALIA 14–0
Match drawn

117. England v South Africa
Third Test at The Oval – 12, 13 August 1912
SOUTH AFRICA 95 (S. Barnes 5–28, Woolley 5–41) and 93
  (Nourse 42, S. Barnes 8–29)
ENGLAND 176 (Hobbs 68, Faulkner 7–84) and 14–0
England won by 10 wickets

118. England v Australia
Third Test at The Oval – 19, 20, 21, 22 August 1912
ENGLAND 245 (Hobbs 66, Woolley 62, Rhodes 49, Minnett
  4–34, Witty 4–69) and 175 (Fry 79, Hazlitt 7–25)
AUSTRALIA 111 (Kelleway 43, Woolley 5–29, S. Barnes
  5–30) and 65 (Woolley 5–20, Dean 4–19)
England won by 244 runs

119. South Africa v England
First Test at Durban – 13, 15, 16, 17 December 1913
SOUTH AFRICA 182 (Taylor 109, S. Barnes 5–57) and 111
  (Nourse 46, S. Barnes 5–48)
ENGLAND 450 (Douglas 119, Hobbs 82, Bird 61, Tennyson 52)
England won by an innings and 157 runs

120. South Africa v England
Second Test at Johannesburg – 26, 27, 29, 30 December
  1913
SOUTH AFRICA 160 (Hartigan 51, S. Barnes 8–56) and 231
  (Nourse 56, P. Hands 40, Taylor 40, S. Barnes 9–103)
ENGLAND 403 (Rhodes 152, Mead 102, A. Relf 63,
  Blanckenberg 5–83)
England won by an innings and 12 runs

121. South Africa v England
Third Test at Johannesburg – 1, 2, 3, 5 January 1914
ENGLAND 238 (Hobbs 92, Taylor 3–15) and 308 (Mead 86,
  Douglas 77, Hobbs 41, Newberry 4–72)
SOUTH AFRICA 151 (J. W. Hearne 5–49) and 304 (Zulch 82,
  Taylor 70, Blanckenberg 59, S. Barnes 5–102)
England won by 91 runs

122. South Africa v England
Fourth Test at Durban – 14, 16, 17, 18 February 1914
SOUTH AFRICA 170 (P. Hands 51, S. Barnes 7–56) and 305–9
  dec. (Taylor 93, Carter 45, Nourse 45, S. Barnes 7–88)
ENGLAND 163 (Hobbs 64, Carter 6–50) and 154–5 (Hobbs
  97)
Match drawn

123. South Africa v England
Fifth Test at Port Elizabeth – 27, 28 February, 2, 3 March
  1914
SOUTH AFRICA 193 (P. Hands 83, Taylor 42, Douglas 4–14)
  and 228 (Taylor 87, Zulch 60, P. Hands 49, Booth 4–49)
ENGLAND 411 (Mead 117, Lundie 4–101) and 11–0
England won by 10 wickets

 DID YOU KNOW...?

Wilfred Rhodes took fifteen wickets in one Test in
1904 – despite having eight catches dropped off his
bowling.

TEST CRICKET BETWEEN THE WARS: 1920–39

In the 1920–1 series, Australia subjected England to a 5–0 defeat for the only time in a five-match Ashes series, winning by 377 runs, an innings and 91 runs, 119 runs, 8 wickets and 9 wickets respectively. The only Test in which England got the merest glimpse of a win was in the third match at Adelaide. This was the highest-scoring of all Ashes Test series with a total of 1,753 runs. Six centuries were scored, four by Australians and two by Englishmen – Jack Russell and Jack Hobbs. For Australia, Arthur Mailey finished with an Australian record of 36 wickets in the series.

Australia then extended their run of victories by winning the first three Tests in England in 1921 and the margins were again nearer to routs – 10 wickets, 8 wickets and 219 runs. Few England batsmen could cope with the lifting ball as propelled by Jack Gregory, while the pace and accuracy of Ted McDonald proved the perfect foil. At Old Trafford, with the rubber and the Ashes safe, new captain the Hon. Lionel Tennyson famously declared too late after what had become the first day of a two-day match following rain. Australian skipper Warwick Armstrong, who bowled the last over before the twenty-five minute dispute, then bowled the first afterwards, which added more confusion to the incident. At The Oval, Armstrong read a newspaper in the outfield, in a novel way of protesting at Tests limited to three days.

Though ill-health kept Jack Hobbs out of the England team to tour South Africa in 1922–3, the side captained by Frank Mann was a strong one. South Africa's leading player, Herbie Taylor, made 176 in the first Test, enabling the home side to win by 168 runs. England won the second in a thrilling match in Cape Town but by only one wicket. George Macaulay, making his Test debut, joined Alec Kennedy for the last wicket when England needed 5 runs to win – his first scoring stroke in Test cricket ended up being the match-winner. Phil Mead and Frank Woolley scored centuries in the next two Tests, both of which were drawn, which left all depending on the final Test in Durban. A hundred in each innings by England opener Jack Russell was the deciding factor as England went on to win by 109 runs.

Arthur Gilligan was the England captain when the Springboks came to England in 1924 and he played a major part in the sensational events of the first Test at Edgbaston. Put in by Taylor, England made 438 before bowling the South Africans out for just 30 – Gilligan taking 6–7 and Maurice Tate 4–12. They made 390 following on, but had suffered a severe blow from which they never recovered. At Lord's, England made a mammoth 531–2 declared with Jack Hobbs (211) and Herbert Sutcliffe making 268 for the first wicket, before Frank Woolley (134 not out) and Patsy Hendren (50 not out) added to the agony.

Since the start of Test cricket, the number of balls per over had varied from four to five and then six in England. In the 1924–5 Ashes series, Australia's authorities switched to eight-ball overs. Beaten by 193 runs in the first Test and by 81 in the second, England lost by only 11 runs at Adelaide and would almost certainly have won but for an injury to Sussex's Maurice Tate. England went on to win the fourth Test by an innings and 29 runs – it was the first victory over Australia in twelve years, Australia having won eleven of the previous thirteen Tests. England suffered a heavy defeat in the final Test, a game which rightly emphasized the solidity of the Australian batting, but the decisive factor was the introduction of a new bowler, thirty-three-year-old New Zealand-born Clarrie Grimmett.

After the heavy run-scoring and seven-day Tests of England's previous tour to Australia, the 1926 Ashes series got under way with rain – and plenty of it, resulting in just fifty minutes of play on the first day and none thereafter at Trent Bridge. The first four Tests were all drawn but were remarkable for the aggressive batting of Charlie Macartney, who made hundreds in the three middle Tests, and the consistency of England's opening pair Hobbs and Sutcliffe. This meant that in the final 'timeless' Test at The Oval, there was all to play for. England dropped their captain Arthur Carr for Percy Chapman – they also restored Harold Larwood and the forty-eight-year-old Wilfred Rhodes. Despite winning the toss, they frittered away the advantage by being bowled out for 280 on the first day, so that Australia led on the first innings by 22 runs.

The story of how Hobbs and Sutcliffe defied the Australian spinners on a 'sticky dog' has become legendary. The bowlers best suited to the conditions were Arthur Richardson, off-spin round the wicket, and Macartney, left-arm over, and they spun and kicked viciously from an impeccable length. But somehow Hobbs and Sutcliffe survived. Hobbs made 100 out of 172, by which time the match was virtually won; Sutcliffe went on to make 161 as England set their opponents a target of 415 for victory. Rhodes spun the ball off the worn area and amidst noisy jubilation the Australian innings fell apart – England had regained the Ashes.

When captain R. T. Stanyforth took a reasonably strong England team to South Africa in 1927–8, Herbie Taylor's long tenure as skipper had come to an end, though he was still to play in several more Test series. The new captain, H. G. Deane, did well to bring South Africa from being two down after two Tests to halve the series. Centuries by Ernest Tyldesley and Herbert Sutcliffe and 12 wickets by George Geary won England the first Test, and then Sutcliffe, Percy Holmes and Tyldesley won them the second after South Africa had held a first-innings lead of 117. After a drawn third Test, South Africa came back boldly as the pace bowling of Alf Hall and George Bissett took 17 wickets to defeat England, and then in the final Test, Bob Catterall made 119 and Bissett took 7–29 in the second innings as South Africa won by 8 wickets.

Since 1900, teams from the West Indies had toured England and English teams had visited the Caribbean for many years before West Indies were considered strong enough to be given Test status, in 1928. For many years, West Indian batting had been dependent on George Challenor, a great player when West Indies had gone to England in 1923. But by the time the first Test was played at Lord's he was forty years old, and no longer enjoying the successes of his youth. The Tests were played over three days and England won all three by an innings. Ernest Tyldesley (122) made the first hundred in the series at Lord's, Tich Freeman took five wickets in each innings at Old Trafford and Jack Hobbs scored 159 at The Oval.

In December 1928, the Exhibition Ground in Brisbane staged its first-ever Test. The match was also notable for marking the debut of the greatest batsman of all time, Don Bradman. However, the series would be most memorable for the monolithic batting of England's Wally Hammond. After a moderate first Test, he made 251 in the second, 200 in the third, and 119 not out and 177 in the fourth. A disappointing final match left him 95 runs short of a thousand for the series. England's strong all-round side began a successful series with an overwhelming victory, made so by the wise decision taken not to enforce a follow-on in a 'timeless' Test. When England batted a second time, they declared their innings closed at 342–8 – the first declaration of an innings in a Test in Australia. Having been set 742 for victory, Australia had two players unavailable to bat and were bowled out for 66, giving England victory by the huge margin of 675 runs. England had gone into the first Test with three bowlers plus Hammond, but didn't take the risk again with George Geary playing in the remaining four Tests. After making 636 in the second Test and winning by 8 wickets, England won the third and fourth Tests by narrow margins. Australia won the final Test by consistent batting after England had set the pace with 519.

When South Africa visited England in 1929, they led England on the first innings on four occasions, but each time they were unable to press home their advantage and England won at Headingley and Old Trafford. R. E. S. Wyatt and Frank Woolley made hundreds at Manchester, where Tich Freeman's leg spin took 12 wickets. At The Oval, Herbert Sutcliffe made two hundreds and with Wally Hammond (101 not out) prevented South Africa from winning after they led by 234 runs on the first innings – Tests were still of three days' duration then. It had long been realized that the disparity between South Africa's performances at home, where they had won ten Tests, and in England, where they had not won any, was largely connected with the matting pitches.

When England played their very first Test against New Zealand, they also had another team playing a series in the West Indies, so they were by no means at full strength. England won the first match at Christchurch by 8 wickets; they could only draw the remaining three.

The first series in England may have been disappointing to West Indies, but their first series at home in 1930 showed how difficult they would be to beat in the Caribbean. Tests were played over five days, but England, though they had the better of the match, could not force a win in the first Test, a second-innings 176 by the great George Headley holding them up. England won the second Test after the home side had led on first innings, while at Georgetown the West Indian team gained their first win over England. The final Test at Kingston, though a draw, was remarkable in several ways. As the series was level it was decided to play it to a finish, but rain prevented play on the eighth and ninth days and it was given up. England began by making 849, with Andy Sandham's 325 then the highest Test score. They led by no fewer than 563 runs, but did not enforce the follow-on and eventually declared, setting West Indies a target of 836 to win. The score had reached 408–5 when the match was abandoned. George Headley having contributed 227 runs to the total.

The 1930 Ashes series will be remembered for England's first sight of Don Bradman. Eight and 131; 254 and 1; 334; 14; and 232 – those were his scores in the five Tests, totalling 974 runs at an average of 139. Forty-seven-year-old Hobbs began the series well, but Hammond could not reproduce his Australian form and only Sutcliffe, who missed the second Test through injury, batted up to his reputation. England won the first Test by 93 runs, but they had the best of the conditions, and at one point it even looked as if Australia would get the 429 runs they needed for victory. In the second Test at Lord's, England made enough runs batting first to have ensured a draw in most circumstances, but they reckoned without the speed and certainty of Bradman's run-getting, and Australia replied to England's first-innings 425 with 729–6, with Bradman making 254. During the Headingley Test, in which a cloudburst saved England, Bradman made 334, of which 309 runs came on the first day. The Old Trafford Test was spoiled by rain and so it all came down to the final match at The Oval. England scored 405 thanks in the main to a sixth-wicket partnership of 170 between Sutcliffe (160) and new captain Bob Wyatt. In any normal series this total would have ensured a fight, but Australia now demonstrated their batting superiority beyond all doubt in producing a total of 695, and England lost by an innings.

The first match on grass in South Africa was played in Cape Town during England's tour of 1930–1. England had lost the first Test in Johannesburg by 28 runs and only narrowly avoided an innings defeat at Newlands, Cape Town, where three South African batsmen made hundreds in their total of 513–8. Three more draws followed with South Africa having slightly the better of them, so that their victory in the series, by the first-Test win, was well deserved.

When New Zealand Tom Lowry took his country's first Test-playing side to England in 1931, it was intended the only Test should be at Lord's, but in a wet summer the New Zealanders did so well that two other Tests were arranged at Old Trafford and The Oval. After a draw at Lord's, rain almost completely washed out the Old Trafford Test, while at The Oval, Herbert Sutcliffe, Kumar Duleepsinhji and Wally Hammond made centuries. After some rain, New Zealand were beaten by an innings.

In the summer of 1932, India embarked on their first tour of England, and in June played in the first Test match between the two countries, which was the only Test of the series. In the event, the home side won without too much trouble, although Holmes, Sutcliffe and Woolley were all back in the pavilion for 19 runs. Douglas Jardine and Les Ames led a recovery, but India were unable to consolidate their advantage and found the task of scoring 346 to win in the second innings too much.

Faith in fast bowling as the only form of attack likely to subdue Don Bradman was triumphantly vindicated in the 1932–3 Ashes series, but the manner it which it was deployed was bitterly resented throughout Australia. Fast leg theory, as conceived by Jardine, or 'Bodyline', as it was dubbed by the Australians, took on a different connotation when projected by bowlers of the pace and accuracy of Harold Larwood and Bill Voce, and the batsmen found themselves under continual physical attack. Nevertheless, Jardine persisted with his policy throughout an explosive series, which at one point seemed likely to be abandoned as forthright and bitter cables were exchanged between the respective governing bodies.

Australia went into the first Test without Bradman, but were saved on the opening day by a superb innings from Stan McCabe, whose 187 not out was the greatest innings played against Bodyline. Nevertheless, hundreds from Sutcliffe, Hammond and the Nawab of Pataudi gave England a huge lead before the Australians crumpled against Larwood. In the second Test on a slow wicket, Bodyline was less successful and the batting of Bradman and the bowling of O'Reilly got Australia home in a low-scoring match. The series erupted at Adelaide, where Woodfull, hit sickeningly over the heart by Larwood, who then reverted to his leg-side attack, told 'Plum' Warner, the MCC manager, that only one of the sides was playing cricket. Oldfield suffered a cracked skull as he mishooked at Larwood. Mounted police lined up in readiness as the crowd's fury reached fever pitch. The Australian Board sent a cable of protest to Lord's; the MCC responded that they had full confidence in their team management. Though the genius of Bill O'Reilly (27 wickets in the series) ensured that England did not have matters all their own way in the remaining matches, they still won them all, with Harold Larwood breaking all records for a fast bowler by taking 33 wickets.

The two Tests in New Zealand at the end of the 'Bodyline' tour produced two scores of over 500 by England, but no result. Rain affected both matches, which were notable mainly for two enormous innings by Wally Hammond – 227 in Christchurch and 336 not out in Auckland, out of a total of 548–7 declared. This innings lasted five and a quarter hours, a historic piece of hitting including 10 sixes and 33 fours, and, by exceeding Bradman's 334 made at Headingley, it became the highest Test innings to date.

The West Indies' share in the previous colourful series in the Caribbean had roused hopes that they would show great improvement when they went to England in 1933. Of the three Tests, only the second was not one-sided. England won the other two by an innings, Walter Robins taking 6–32 with his leg spin at Lord's and Charles Marriott 11 wickets at The Oval. At Old Trafford, West Indies led by 1 run on the first innings in a draw famous for the Bodyline bowling of Leary Constantine and Manny Martindale to England captain Jardine. He met it with characteristic courage and skill, and scored 127.

England sent a comparatively strong team for the first Test series in India in 1933–4 and proved too good all round. At Bombay Kent's Bryan Valentine (136) helped England to 438 and, despite 118 by Lala Amarnath in India's second innings, England won by 9 wickets. India followed on at Calcutta, only to save the match, but England clinched the series in the last Test, winning by 202 runs.

With feelings still running high after the 'Bodyline' series, Woodfull's Australians journeyed to England for the 1934 Ashes series. But the England side were without Jardine, Larwood and Voce, and injuries to other key players crucially weakened the team. A wicket that took spin helped Australia to a thrilling victory in the first Test at Trent Bridge with only ten minutes to spare. Luck went England's way in the second Test at Lord's, where centuries from Ames and Leyland helped England make 440. They then caught Australia on a rain-affected wicket and Verity took 14 wickets in a single day and 15 in the match as England won by an innings and 38 runs. At Old Trafford came the famous O'Reilly over after the ball was changed and England slumped from 68 without loss to 72–3. But Hendren (132) and Leyland (153) then led a recovery and England totalled 627. The wicket was over-prepared and the match was drawn, as was the fourth meeting at Headingley, where Bradman made 304 putting on a record 388 with Bill Ponsford (181). At The Oval, where Australia won the toss, Bradman (244) and Ponsford (266) broke their own record with a partnership of 451 on the first day, and England were overwhelmed, beaten by 562 runs.

It was clear by now that England had to be at their best to win in the Caribbean, and, in 1934–5, their only success was at Bridgetown in a unique first Test of only 309 runs. The pitch began wet and rain intervened later so that both sides manoeuvred to get the other in when the pitch was at its worst. England declared their first innings at 81–7, 21 runs behind the West Indies. Then the home side declared their second innings at 51–6, leaving England to score 73 runs on what appeared to be an impossible pitch. But Bob Wyatt reversed his batting order and, though England were at one time 48–6, Wyatt himself and Wally Hammond were there to steer England home by four wickets.

When South Africa visited these shores in 1935, it was the last time that Tests were of three days' duration. Of the five Tests played, four were drawn, with England being a shade superior. However, at Lord's, South Africa won their first-ever victory in England by 157 runs. They were not to know then that it would decide the series – their first-innings total of 228 containing a magnificent innings of 90 out of 126 in 105 minutes by Jock Cameron, who, sadly, was to die a few weeks after the end of the tour. England needed 309 to win, but were easily dismissed by the Greek leg-spin bowler Xenophon Balaskas, who added 4 wickets to the 5 he got in the first innings.

India's chances of winning their first Test on their tour of England in 1936 were upset when their leading all-rounder Amarnath was sent home for disciplinary reasons before the Lord's Test. England won two of the matches handsomely, but India had their moment of glory in the drawn Test at Old Trafford, when Vijay Merchant (114) and Mushtaq Ali (112) put on 203 for the first wicket. For England, Wally Hammond made 167 in a total of 571–8 declared.

England surprised everyone on their tour of Australia in 1936–7 by winning the first two Tests, the first at Brisbane after they'd been 20–3. That they made 358 was due to a fine innings of 126 by Leyland, and, though Jack Fingleton made a hundred for the Australians, Voce and Allen bowled England to a substantial first-innings lead. Set 381 to win, the home side found their task eventually made impossible by rain. The second Test brought a double century by Hammond before an overnight thunderstorm at the end of the second day compounded England's advantage. The Ashes seemed as good as won on the first afternoon of the third Test with Australia 130–6 on a good wicket. Soon, the rain came, and Australia declared at 200–9 and bowled England out for 76. Bradman then held himself and Fingleton back until the wicket had recovered and the two batsmen put on 346 together. Not even another Leyland hundred could save England. An innings of 212 from Bradman and fine bowling from Bill O'Reilly and Chuck Fleetwood-Smith helped Australia level the series at Adelaide, while Bradman (169) and the two spin bowlers dominated the final Test and Australia came from behind to retain the Ashes.

England's three-match Test series against New Zealand in 1937 introduced Len Hutton to Test cricket in the first Test and Denis Compton in the third. Hutton was out for 0 and 1 in the first, a match that was drawn with England comfortably on top. The Yorkshire batsman made 100 in the second Test at Old Trafford, which England won by 130 runs. The third Test was also drawn, with Joe Hardstaff hitting his second century of the series and Compton making 65 before being run out by a deflection off the bowler.

The 1938 Ashes series in England was reduced to four matches with the Manchester rain striking again – the third Test at Old Trafford being abandoned without a ball being bowled. It was ironic that a dusty pitch at Headingley should decide the fate of the Ashes in a drawn series. At Trent Bridge, for the first time in Tests, four batsmen scored centuries in the same innings in England's 658–6 declared – Barnett 126, Hutton 100, Paynter 216 not out and Compton 102. Yet the innings of the match was made by Australia's Stan McCabe, who made 232 out of a total of 411 – including 127 out of the last 148 runs in eighty minutes. Australia still followed on, but Bradman hit his thirteenth hundred against England, setting a new record in Ashes Tests. At Lord's, it was England's turn to scent defeat, despite a great knock of 240 from Hammond in their first innings, but they closed their ranks and a draw was the outcome. After Manchester came the dusty wicket at Headingley, a great hundred by Bradman in appalling light, and magnificent bowling by O'Reilly, who took 10–122 in Australia's 5-wicket win. At The Oval England proceeded to draw the series with Len Hutton making a record 364 and Joe Hardstaff 169 not out – Hammond declaring at 903–7. This crushing weight of runs, plus injuries to Bradman and Fingleton, made the rest of the match a formality.

It was clear by now that if England were to have any success when touring South Africa, they must field as strong a side as possible. The one that Walter Hammond took in the last pre-war season lacked a few of England's best players, but even so, numerous runs were scored and England took the series by winning the third Test in Durban, where Eddie Paynter made 243 and Hammond 120. Seven wickets by giant fast bowler Ken Farnes helped to complete the job. But it was the last Test, one of the four draws on that tour, that has gone down in history as the breaker of many records. Scheduled to be played to a finish, it was given up after ten days' play, when the England team had to leave Durban to catch their ship home. They were then 42 runs short of victory with 5 wickets still in hand, a remarkable state of affairs because they needed 696 runs to win when they started their last innings late on the sixth day. South Africa opened by making 530. England were then bowled out for 316 before the home side made 481 in their second innings. Thereafter the pitch was restored by rain, which also took away the eighth day's play, but England batted steadily on. Paul Gibb, who opened the innings, made 120, Bill Edrich 219 and Hammond 140, but further rain interrupted play and eventually the match was abandoned. It was the last 'timeless' Test.

However convincing their cricket was at home, West Indies were still immature in the Test sense when they visited England in the summer of 1939. England, with such gifted young players as Len Hutton and Denis Compton, were on a rising tide of strength and they won the first of three Tests at Lord's – the other two being drawn. Hutton made 196 and Compton 120, sharing in a stand of 248 in 140 minutes. For West Indies, George Headley made a century in each innings, but he had little support, and West Indies did not reach 300 in either innings.

TEST MATCH RESULTS: 1920–39

124. Australia v England
First Test at Sydney – 17, 18, 20, 21, 22 December 1920
AUSTRALIA 267 (Collins 70) and 581 (Armstrong 158, Collins 104, Kelleway 78, Macartney 69, Bardsley 57, Taylor 51)
ENGLAND 190 (Woolley 52, Hobbs 49) and 281 (Hobbs 59, J. W. Hearne 57, Hendren 56, Rhodes 45)
Australia won by 377 runs

125. Australia v England
Second Test at Melbourne – 31 December 1920, 1, 3, 4 January 1921
AUSTRALIA 499 (Pellew 116, Gregory 100, Taylor 68, Collins 64, Bardsley 51)
ENGLAND 251 (Hobbs 122, Hendren 67, Gregory 7–69) and 157 (Woolley 50, Armstrong 4–26)
Australia won by an innings and 91 runs

126. Australia v England
Third Test at Adelaide – 14, 15, 17, 18, 19, 20 January 1921
AUSTRALIA 354 (Collins 162, Oldfield 50, Ryder 44, Parkin 5–60) and 582 (Kelleway 147, Armstrong 121, Pellew 104, Gregory 78*, Howell 4–115)
ENGLAND 447 (Russell 135*, Woolley 79, Douglas 60, Makepeace 60, Mailey 5–160) and 370 (Hobbs 123, Russell 59, Hendren 51, Fender 42, Mailey 5–142)
Australia won by 119 runs

127. Australia v England
Fourth Test at Melbourne – 11, 12, 14, 15, 16 February 1921
ENGLAND 284 (Makepeace 117, Douglas 50, Mailey 4–115) and 315 (Rhodes 73, Douglas 60, Fender 59, Makepeace 54, Mailey 9–121)
AUSTRALIA 389 (Armstrong 123*, Gregory 77, Collins 59, Bardsley 56, Fender 5–122) and 211–2 (Gregory 76*, Ryder 52*)
Australia won by 8 wickets

128. Australia v England
Fifth Test at Sydney – 25, 26, 28 February, 1 March 1921
ENGLAND 204 (Woolley 53, Hobbs 40, Kelleway 4–27) and 280 (Douglas 68, Fender 40, Mailey 5–119)
AUSTRALIA 392 (Macartney 170, Gregory 93, Fender 5–90) and 93–1 (Bardsley 50*)
Australia won by 9 wickets

129. England v Australia
First Test at Trent Bridge – 28, 30 May 1921
ENGLAND 112 (Gregory 6–58) and 147 (McDonald 5–32)
AUSTRALIA 232 (Bardsley 66) and 30–0
Australia won by 10 wickets

130. England v Australia
Second Test at Lord's – 11, 13, 14 June 1921
ENGLAND 187 (Woolley 95, Mailey 4–55, McDonald 4–58) and 283 (Woolley 93, Tennyson 74*, Dipper 40, Gregory 4–76, McDonald 4–89)
AUSTRALIA 342 (Bardsley 88, Gregory 52, Carter 46, Pellew 43, Durston 4–102) and 131–2 (Bardsley 63*, Andrews 49)
Australia won by 8 wickets

131. England v Australia
Third Test at Headingley – 2, 4, 5 July 1921
AUSTRALIA 407 (Macartney 115, Armstrong 77, Pellew 52, Taylor 50, Parkin 4–106) and 273–7 dec. (Andrews 92, Carter 47)
ENGLAND 259 (Douglas 75, Tennyson 63, Brown 57, McDonald 4–105) and 202 (Brown 46)
Australia won by 219 runs

132. England v Australia
Fourth Test at Old Trafford – 23 (no play), 25, 26 July 1921
ENGLAND 362–4 dec. (Russell 101, E. Tyldesley 78*, Mead 47, Fender 44*, Woolley 41) and 44–1
AUSTRALIA 175 (Collins 40, Parkin 5–38)
Match drawn

DID YOU KNOW...?

England set a Test record by scoring 503 runs in a day against South Africa in 1924.

133. England v Australia
Fifth Test at The Oval – 13, 15, 16 August 1921
ENGLAND 403–8 dec. (Mead 182*, Tennyson 51, McDonald 5–143) and 244–2 (Russell 102*, Brown 84, Hitch 51*)
AUSTRALIA 389 (Andrews 94, Taylor 75, Macartney 61)
Match drawn

134. South Africa v England
First Test at Johannesburg – 23, 26, 27, 28 December 1922
SOUTH AFRICA 148 (Kennedy 4–37, Jupp 4–59) and 420 (Taylor 176, Brann 50, Kennedy 4–132)
ENGLAND 182 (Kennedy 41*, Blanckenberg 6–76) and 218 (Mead 49, Nupen 5–53)
South Africa won by 168 runs

135. South Africa v England
Second Test at Cape Town – 1, 2, 3, 4 January 1923
SOUTH AFRICA 113 (Fender 4–29) and 242 (Catterall 76, Taylor 68, Macaulay 5–64, Kennedy 4–58)
ENGLAND 183 (Carr 42, Blanckenberg 5–61, Hall 4–49) and 173–9 (Mann 45, Hall 7–63)
England won by 1 wicket

136. South Africa v England
Third Test at Durban – 18, 19, 20, 22 January 1923
ENGLAND 428 (Mead 181, Mann 84, Fender 60, Hall 4–105) and 11–1
SOUTH AFRICA 368 (Taylor 91, Francois 72, Catterall 52, Nourse 52, Kennedy 5–88)
Match drawn

137. South Africa v England
Fourth Test at Johannesburg – 9, 10, 12, 13 February 1923
ENGLAND 244 (Carr 63, Fender 44, Hall 6–82) and 376–6 dec. (Woolley 115*, Russell 96, Mann 59, Sandham 58)
SOUTH AFRICA 295 (Ward 64, Nourse 51, Tapscott 50*) and 247–4 (Taylor 101, Nourse 63)
Match drawn

138. South Africa v England
Fifth Test at Durban – 16, 17, 19, 20, 21, 22 February 1923
ENGLAND 281 (Russell 140, Mead 66) and 241 (Russell 111, Sandham 40)
SOUTH AFRICA 179 (Nourse 44, Francois 43) and 234 (Taylor 102, Kennedy 5–76)
England won by 109 runs

139. England v South Africa
First Test at Edgbaston – 14, 16, 17 June 1924
ENGLAND 438 (Hobbs 76, Hendren 74, Sutcliffe 64, Woolley 64, Kilner 59, Parker 6–152)
SOUTH AFRICA 30 (Gilligan 6–7, Tate 4–12) and 390 (Catterall 120, Blanckenberg 56, Susskind 51, Gilligan 5–83, Tate 4–103)
England won by an innings and 18 runs

140. England v South Africa
Second Test at Lord's – 28, 30 June, 1 July 1924
SOUTH AFRICA 273 (Catterall 120, Susskind 64) and 240 (Susskind 53, Catterall 45)
ENGLAND 531–2 dec. (Hobbs 211, Woolley 134*, Sutcliffe 122, Hendren 50*)
England won by an innings and 18 runs

141. England v South Africa
Third Test at Headingley – 12, 14, 15 July 1924
ENGLAND 396 (Hendren 132, Sutcliffe 83, Pegler 4–116) and 60–1
SOUTH AFRICA 132 (Taylor 59*, Tate 6–42) and 323 (Catterall 56, Taylor 56, Deane 47*)
England won by 9 wickets

142. England v South Africa
Fourth Test at Old Trafford – 26, 28, 29 July 1924
SOUTH AFRICA 116–4 (Ward 50, Tate 3–34)
Match drawn

143. England v South Africa
Fifth Test at The Oval – 16, 18, 19 August 1924
SOUTH AFRICA 342 (Catterall 95, Susskind 65, Blanckenberg 46*)
ENGLAND 421–8 (Hendren 142, Woolley 51, Tate 50, Sandham 46)
Match drawn

144. Australia v England
First Test at Sydney – 19, 20, 22, 23, 24, 26, 27 December 1924
AUSTRALIA 450 (Collins 114, Ponsford 110, Taylor 43, Richardson 42, Tate 6–130) and 452 (Taylor 108, Richardson 98, Collins 60, Mailey 46*, Tate 5–98)
ENGLAND 298 (Hobbs 115, Hendren 74*, Sutcliffe 59, Gregory 5–111, Mailey 4–129) and 411 (Woolley 123, Sutcliffe 115, Hobbs 57, Freeman 50*, Chapman 44)
Australia won by 193 runs

145. Australia v England
Second Test at Melbourne – 1, 2, 3, 5, 6, 7, 8 January 1925
AUSTRALIA 600 (Richardson 138, Ponsford 128, Hartkopf 80, Taylor 72, Gregory 44) and 250 (Taylor 90, Tate 6–99, Hearne 4–84)
ENGLAND 479 (Sutcliffe 176, Hobbs 154) and 290 (Sutcliffe 127, Woolley 50, Mailey 5–92, Gregory 4–87)
Australia won by 81 runs

146. Australia v England
Third Test at Adelaide – 16, 17, 19, 20, 21, 22, 23 January 1925
AUSTRALIA 489 (Ryder 201*, Andrews 72, Richardson 69, Oldfield 47, Kilner 4–127) and 250 (Ryder 88, Ponsford 43, Kilner 4–51, Woolley 4–77)
ENGLAND 365 (Hobbs 119, Hendren 92) and 363 (Whysall 75, Sutcliffe 59, Chapman 58)
Australia won by 11 runs

147. Australia v England
Fourth Test at Melbourne – 13, 14, 16, 17, 18 February 1925
ENGLAND 548 (Sutcliffe 143, Whysall 76, Kilner 74, Hobbs 66, Hendren 65, J. W. Hearne 44, Woolley 40, Mailey 4–186)
AUSTRALIA 269 (Taylor 86) and 250 (Taylor 68, Gregory 45, Kelleway 42, Tate 5–75)
England won by an innings and 29 runs

148. Australia v England
Fifth Test at Sydney – 27, 28 February, 2, 3, 4 March 1925
AUSTRALIA 295 (Ponsford 80, Kippax 42, Tate 4–92, Kilner 4–97) and 325 (Andrews 80, Kelleway 73, Oldfield 65*, Tate 5–115)
ENGLAND 167 (Woolley 47, Grimmett 5–45) and 146 (Grimmett 6–37)
Australia won by 307 runs

149. England v Australia
First Test at Trent Bridge – 12, 14 (no play), 15 (no play) June 1926
ENGLAND 32–0
AUSTRALIA did not bat
Match drawn

150. England v Australia
Second Test at Lord's – 26, 28, 29 June 1926
AUSTRALIA 383 (Bardsley 193, Kilner 4–70) and 194–5 (Macartney 133*)
ENGLAND 475–3 dec. (Hendren 127*, Hobbs 119, Woolley 87, Sutcliffe 82, Chapman 50*)
Match drawn

151. England v Australia
Third Test at Headingley – 10, 12, 13 July 1926
AUSTRALIA 494 (Macartney 151, Woodfull 141, Richardson 100, Ryder 42, Tate 4–99)
ENGLAND 294 (Macaulay 76, Hobbs 49, Grimmett 5–88) and 254–3 (Sutcliffe 94, Hobbs 88, Chapman 42*)
Match drawn

152. England v Australia
Fourth Test at Old Trafford – 24, 26, 27 July 1926
AUSTRALIA 335 (Woodfull 117, Macartney 109, Root 4–84)
ENGLAND 305–5 (G. E. Tyldesley 81, Hobbs 74, Woolley 58)
Match drawn

153. England v Australia
Fifth Test at The Oval – 14, 16, 17, 18 August 1926
ENGLAND 280 (Sutcliffe 76, Chapman 49, Mailey 6–138) and 436 (Sutcliffe 161, Hobbs 100)
AUSTRALIA 302 (Gregory 73, Collins 61) and 125 (Rhodes 4–44)
England won by 289 runs

154. South Africa v England
First Test at Johannesburg – 24, 26, 27 December 1927
SOUTH AFRICA 196 (Catterall 86, Geary 7–70) and 170 (Vincent 53, Coen 41*, Hammond 5–36, Geary 5–60)
ENGLAND 313 (G. E. Tyldesley 122, Sutcliffe 102, Hammond 51, Promnitz 5–58) and 57–0
England won by 10 wickets

155. South Africa v England
Second Test at Cape Town – 31 December 1927, 2, 3, 4 January 1928
ENGLAND 133 (Bissett 5–37, Vincent 4–22) and 428 (Sutcliffe 99, Wyatt 91, Holmes 88, G. E. Tyldesley 87)
SOUTH AFRICA 250 (Taylor 68, Deane 41, Freeman 4–58) and 224 (Taylor 71, Commaille 47)
England won by 87 runs

 DID YOU KNOW...?

Wally Hammond's 905 runs in 1928–9 are still the record for an England batsman in a Test series.

156. South Africa v England
Third Test at Durban – 21, 23, 24, 25 January 1928
SOUTH AFRICA 246 (Deane 77, Nupen 51, Wyatt 3–4) and 464–8 dec. (Nicolson 78, Catterall 76, Deane 73, Nupen 69, Taylor 50)
ENGLAND 430 (Hammond 90, G. E. Tyldesley 78, Holmes 70, Stevens 69, Astill 40, Vincent 6–131, Nupen 4–94) and 132–2 (G. E. Tyldesley 62*, Holmes 56)
Match drawn

157. South Africa v England
Fourth Test at Johannesburg – 28, 30, 31 January, 1 February 1928
ENGLAND 265 (Wyatt 58, G. E. Tyldesley 42, Hall 6–100, Bissett 4–43) and 215 (Holmes 63, Bissett 4–70)
SOUTH AFRICA 328 (Taylor 101, Cameron 64) and 156–6 (Morkel 45)
South Africa won by 4 wickets

158. South Africa v England
Fifth Test at Durban – 4, 6, 7, 8 February 1928
ENGLAND 282 (G. E. Tyldesley 100, Hammond 66, Sutcliffe 51, Nupen 5–83) and 118 (Bissett 7–29)
SOUTH AFRICA 332–7 dec. (Catterall 119, Cameron 53) and 69–2
South Africa won by 8 wickets

159. England v West Indies
First Test at Lord's – 23, 25, 26 June 1928
ENGLAND 401 (G. E. Tyldesley 122, Chapman 50, Sutcliffe 48, Constantine 4–82)
WEST INDIES 177 (Martin 44, Jupp 4–37) and 166 (Small 52, Browne 44, Freeman 4–37)
England won by an innings and 58 runs

160. England v West Indies
Second Test at Old Trafford – 21, 23, 24 July 1928
WEST INDIES 206 (Roach 50, Freeman 5–54) and 115 (Freeman 5–39)
ENGLAND 351 (Jardine 83, Hammond 63, Sutcliffe 54, Hobbs 53)
England won by an innings and 30 runs

161. England v West Indies
Third Test at The Oval – 11, 13, 14 August 1928
WEST INDIES 238 (Roach 53, Challenor 46, Tate 4–59) and 129 (Martin 41, Freeman 4–47)
ENGLAND 438 (Hobbs 159, G. E. Tyldesley 73, Sutcliffe 63, Tate 54, Griffiths 6–103, Francis 4–112)
England won by an innings and 71 runs

162. Australia v England
First Test at Brisbane – 30 November, 1, 3, 4, 5 December 1928
ENGLAND 521 (Hendren 169, Larwood 70, Chapman 50, Hobbs 49, Hammond 44) and 342–8 dec. (Mead 73, Jardine 65*, Hendren 45, Grimmett 6–131)
AUSTRALIA 122 (Larwood 6–32) and 66 (White 4–7)
England won by 675 runs

163. Australia v England
Second Test at Sydney – 14, 15, 17, 18, 19, 20 December 1928
AUSTRALIA 253 (Woodfull 68, Oldfield 41*, Geary 5–35) and 397 (Hendry 112, Woodfull 111, Ryder 79, Nothling 44, Tate 4–99)
ENGLAND 636 (Hammond 251, Hendren 74, Geary 66, Larwood 43, Hobbs 40, Blackie 4–148) and 16–2
England won by 8 wickets

DID YOU KNOW...?

England beat Australia by 675 runs at the Exhibition Ground in Brisbane in 1928. It was the first Test match at the ground and England's winning margin was the biggest, by runs alone, in Test cricket.

164. Australia v England
Third Test at Melbourne – 29, 31 December 1928, 1, 2, 3, 4, 5 January 1929
AUSTRALIA 397 (Ryder 112, Kippax 100, Bradman 79, a'Beckett 41) and 351 (Bradman 112, Woodfull 107, Kippax 41, White 5–107)
ENGLAND 417 (Hammond 200, Jardine 62, Sutcliffe 58, Blackie 6–94) and 332–7 (Sutcliffe 135, Hobbs 49, Hendren 45)
England won by 3 wickets

165. Australia v England
Fourth Test at Adelaide – 1, 2, 4, 5, 6, 7, 8 February 1929
ENGLAND 334 (Hammond 119*, Hobbs 74, Sutcliffe 64, Grimmett 5–102) and 383 (Hammond 177, Jardine 98, Tate 47, Oxenham 4–67)
AUSTRALIA 369 (Jackson 164, Ryder 63, Bradman 40, White 5–130, Tate 4–77) and 336 (Ryder 87, Bradman 58, Kippax 51, White 8–126)
England won by 12 runs

166. Australia v England
Fifth Test at Melbourne – 8, 9, 11, 12, 13, 14, 15, 16 March 1929
ENGLAND 519 (Hobbs 142, Leyland 137, Hendren 95) and 257 (Hobbs 65, Tate 54, Leyland 53*, Wall 5–66)
AUSTRALIA 491 (Bradman 123, Woodfull 102, Fairfax 65, Geary 5–105) and 287–5 (Ryder 57*, Oldfield 48)
Australia won by 5 wickets

167. England v South Africa
First Test at Edgbaston – 15, 17, 18 June 1929
ENGLAND 245 (Hendren 70, Tate 40, Ochse 4–79) and 308–4 dec. (Hammond 138*, Sutcliffe 114)
SOUTH AFRICA 250 (Mitchell 88, Catterall 67, Larwood 5–57) and 171–1 (Catterall 98, Mitchell 61*)
Match drawn

168. England v South Africa
Second Test at Lord's – 29 June, 1, 2 July 1929
ENGLAND 302 (Sutcliffe 100, Leyland 73, Hendren 43, Bell 6–99, Morkel 4–93) and 312–8 dec. (Leyland 102, Tate 100*, Ochse 4–99)
SOUTH AFRICA 322 (Morkel 88, Christy 70, Owen-Smith 52*) and 90–5 (Christy 41, Robbins 3–32)
Match drawn

169. England v South Africa
Third Test at Headingley – 13, 15, 16 July 1929
SOUTH AFRICA 236 (Catterall 74, Vincent 60, Freeman 7–115) and 275 (Owen-Smith 129)
ENGLAND 328 (Woolley 83, Hammond 65, Leyland 45, Quinn 6–92) and 186–5 (Woolley 95*, Bowley 46)
England won by 5 wickets

170. England v South Africa
Fourth Test at Old Trafford – 27, 29, 30 July 1929
ENGLAND 427–7 dec. (Woolley 154, Wyatt 113, Leyland 55)

SOUTH AFRICA 130 (Morkel 63, Freeman 7–71) and 265 (Cameron 83, Taylor 70, Freeman 5–100)
England won by an innings and 32 runs

171. England v South Africa
Fifth Test at The Oval – 17, 19, 20 August 1929
ENGLAND 258 (Sutcliffe 104, Woolley 46, Vincent 5–105) and 264–1 (Sutcliffe 109*, Hammond 101*)
SOUTH AFRICA 492–8 dec. (Taylor 121, Deane 93, Morkel 81, Cameron 62)
Match drawn

172. New Zealand v England
First Test at Christchurch – 10, 11, 13 January 1930
NEW ZEALAND 112 (Blunt 45*, Allom 5–38, Nichols 4–28) and 131 (Lowry 40, Allom 3–17)
ENGLAND 181 (Duleepsinhji 49, Blunt 3–17) and 66–2
England won by 8 wickets

173. West Indies v England
First Test at Bridgetown, Barbados – 11, 13, 14, 15, 16 January 1930
WEST INDIES 369 (Roach 122, de Caires 80, Sealy 58, Stevens 5–105) and 384 (Headley 176, Roach 77, de Caires 70, Stevens 5–90)
ENGLAND 467 (Sandham 152, Hendren 80, Haig 47, Calthorpe 40) and 167–3 (Sandham 51, Ames 44*)
Match drawn

174. New Zealand v England
Second Test at Wellington – 24, 25, 27 January 1930
NEW ZEALAND 440 (Dempster 136, Mills 117, Page 67, Woolley 7–76) and 164–4 dec. (Dempster 80*)
ENGLAND 320 (Nichols 78*, Dawson 44, Duleepsinhji 40, Badcock 4–80) and 107–4 (Duleepsinhji 56*)
Match drawn

175. West Indies v England
Second Test at Port-of-Spain, Trinidad – 1, 3, 4, 5, 6 February 1930
ENGLAND 208 (Hendren 77, Ames 42, Griffith 5–63) and 425–8 dec. (Hendren 205*, Ames 105, Constantine 4–165)
WEST INDIES 254 (Hunte 58, Constantine 52, Astill 4–58, Voce 4–79) and 212 (de Caires 45, Voce 7–70)
England won by 167 runs

176. New Zealand v England
Third Test at Auckland – 14 (no play), 15 (no play), 17 February 1930
ENGLAND 330–4 dec. (Duleepsinhji 117, Bowley 109, Woolley 59)
NEW ZEALAND 96–1 (Dempster 62*)
Match drawn

177. New Zealand v England
Fourth Test at Auckland – 21, 22, 24 February 1930
ENGLAND 540 (Legge 196, Nichols 75, Duleepsinhji 63, Dawson 55, Bowley 42) and 22–3
NEW ZEALAND 387 (Lowry 80, Weir 63, Allom 4–42)
Match drawn

 DID YOU KNOW...?

On 13 January 1930, England played two Test matches on the same day – against New Zealand at Christchurch and against West Indies at Bridgetown – the only instance in Test history.

178. West Indies v England

Third Test at Georgetown, British Guiana – 21, 22, 24, 25, 26 February 1930
WEST INDIES 471 (Roach 209, Headley 114, Hunte 53) and 290 (Headley 112, Browne 70*, Astill 4–70)
ENGLAND 145 (Hendren 56, Constantine 4–35, Francis 4–40) and 327 (Hendren 123, Calthorpe 49, G. Gunn 45, Constantine 5–87)
West Indies won by 289 runs

179. West Indies v England

Fourth Test at Kingston, Jamaica – 3, 4, 5, 7, 8, 9, 10, 11 (no play), 12 April 1930
ENGLAND 849 (Sandham 325, Ames 149, G. Gunn 85, Hendren 61, Wyatt 58, Scott 5–266) and 272 (Hendren 55, Sandham 50, G. Gunn 47, Scott 4–108)
WEST INDIES 286 (Nunes 66, Passailaigue 44) and 408–5 (Headley 223, Nunes 92)
Match drawn

180. England v Australia

First Test at Trent Bridge – 13, 14, 16, 17 June 1930
ENGLAND 270 (Hobbs 78, Chapman 52, Robins 50*, Grimmett 5–107) and 302 (Hobbs 74, Hendren 72, Sutcliffe 58 ret. hurt, Grimmett 5–94)
AUSTRALIA 144 (Kippax 64*, Robins 4–51) and 335 (Bradman 131, McCabe 49)
England won by 93 runs

181. England v Australia

Second Test at Lord's – 27, 28, 30 June, 1 July 1930
ENGLAND 425 (Duleepsinhji 173, Tate 54, Hendren 48, Woolley 41, Fairfax 4–101) and 375 (Chapman 121, Allen 57, Duleepsinhji 48, Grimmett 6–167)
AUSTRALIA 729–6 dec. (Bradman 254, Woodfull 155, Kippax 83, Ponsford 81, McCabe 44) and 72–3
Australia won by 7 wickets

182. England v Australia

Third Test at Headingley – 11, 12, 14, 15 July 1930
AUSTRALIA 566 (Bradman 334, Kippax 77, Woodfull 50, Tate 5–124)
ENGLAND 391 (Hammond 113, Chapman 45, Leyland 44, Grimmett 5–135) and 95–3
Match drawn

183. England v Australia

Fourth Test at Old Trafford – 25, 26, 28, 29 (no play) July 1930
AUSTRALIA 345 (Ponsford 83, Woodfull 54, Kippax 51, Grimmett 50, Fairfax 49)
ENGLAND 251–8 (Sutcliffe 74, Duleepsinhji 54, McCabe 4–41)
Match drawn

184. England v Australia

Fifth Test at The Oval – 16, 18, 19, 20, 21 (no play), 22 August 1930
ENGLAND 405 (Sutcliffe 161, Wyatt 64, Duleepsinhji 50, Hobbs 47, Grimmett 4–135) and 251 (Hammond 60, Sutcliffe 54, Hornibrook 7–92)
AUSTRALIA 695 (Bradman 232, Ponsford 110, Jackson 73, Woodfull 54, McCabe 54, Fairfax 53*, Peebles 6–204)
Australia won by an innings and 39 runs

185. South Africa v England

First Test at Johannesburg – 24, 26, 27 December 1930
SOUTH AFRICA 126 (McMillan 45*, Peebles 4–43, Voce 4–45) and 306 (Mitchell 72, Catterall 54, Cameron 51, Viljoen 44, Voce 4–59, Hammond 4–63)
ENGLAND 193 (Hammond 49, Nupen 5–63) and 211 (Hammond 63, Turnbull 61, Nupen 6–87)
South Africa won by 28 runs

 DID YOU KNOW...?

In 1930, England were bowled out for 849 on the third day v West Indies at Kingston. Sandham (325) made a new highest individual Test score, and Les Ames (149) scored the first Test century by a wicketkeeper.

186. South Africa v England

Second Test at Cape Town – 1, 2, 3, 5 January 1931
SOUTH AFRICA 513–8 dec. (Siedle 141, Mitchell 123, Taylor 117, Catterall 56)
ENGLAND 350 (Hendren 93, Hammond 57, Leyland 52, Wyatt 40) and 252 (Hendren 86, Hammond 65, Catterall 3–15)
Match drawn

187. South Africa v England

Third Test at Durban – 16, 17 (no play), 19, 20 January 1931
SOUTH AFRICA 177 (Cameron 41, Voce 5–58) and 145–8 (Taylor 64*, White 3–33)
ENGLAND 223–1 dec. (Hammond 136*, Wyatt 54)
Match drawn

188. South Africa v England

Fourth Test at Johannesburg – 13, 14, 16, 17 February 1931
ENGLAND 442 (Leyland 91, Hammond 75, Hendren 64, Hall 4–105) and 169–9 dec. (Leyland 46, Hendren 45, Nupen 6–46)
SOUTH AFRICA 295 (Taylor 72, Mitchell 68, Siedle 62, Peebles 6–63) and 280–7 (Mitchell 74, Cameron 69*, Voce 4–87)
Match drawn

189. South Africa v England

Fifth Test at Durban – 21, 23, 24, 25 February 1931
SOUTH AFRICA 252 (Mitchell 73, Siedle 57, Peebles 4–67) and 219–7 dec. (Cameron 41*)
ENGLAND 230 (Tate 50, Vincent 6–51) and 72–4
Match drawn

190. England v New Zealand

First Test at Lord's – 27, 29, 30 June 1931
NEW ZEALAND 224 (Dempster 53, Peebles 5–77) and 469–9 dec. (Dempster 120, Page 104, Blunt 96, Weir 40, Peebles 4–150)
ENGLAND 454 (Ames 137, Allen 122, Woolley 80, Merritt 4–104) and 146–5 (Hammond 46)
Match drawn

191. England v New Zealand
Second Test at The Oval – 29, 30, 31 July 1931
ENGLAND 416–4 dec. (Sutcliffe 117, Duleepsinhji 109, Hammond 100*, Ames 41, Bakewell 40)
NEW ZEALAND 193 (Lowry 62, Allen 5–14) and 197 (Vivian 51, Blunt 43, Peebles 4–63)
England won by an innings and 26 runs

192. England v New Zealand
Third Test at Old Trafford – 15 (no play), 17 (no play), 18 August 1931
ENGLAND 224–3 (Sutcliffe 109*, Duleepsinhji 63)
NEW ZEALAND did not bat
Match drawn

193. England v India
Only Test at Lord's – 25, 27, 28 June 1932
ENGLAND 259 (Jardine 79, Ames 65, Nissar 5–93) and 275–8 dec. (Jardine 85*, Paynter 54, Jahangir Khan 4–60)
INDIA 189 (Nayudu 40, Bowes 4–49) and 187 (Amar Singh 51, Hammond 3–9)
England won by 158 runs

194. Australia v England
First Test at Sydney – 2, 3, 5, 6, 7 December 1932
AUSTRALIA 360 (McCabe 187*, Richardson 49, Larwood 5–96, Voce 4–110) and 164 (Fingleton 40, Larwood 5–28)
ENGLAND 524 (Sutcliffe 194, Hammond 112, Nawab of Pataudi Snr 102) and 1–0
England won by 10 wickets

195. Australia v England
Second Test at Melbourne – 30, 31 December 1932, 2, 3 January 1933
AUSTRALIA 228 (Fingleton 83) and 191 (Bradman 103*)
ENGLAND 169 (Sutcliffe 52, O'Reilly 5–63, Wall 4–52) and 139 (O'Reilly 5–66, Ironmonger 4–26)
Australia won by 111 runs

196. Australia v England
Third Test at Adelaide – 13, 14, 16, 17, 18, 19 January 1933
ENGLAND 341 (Leyland 83, Wyatt 78, Paynter 77, Verity 45, Wall 5–72) and 412 (Hammond 85, Ames 69, Jardine 56, Wyatt 49, Leyland 42, Verity 40, O'Reilly 4–79)
AUSTRALIA 222 (Ponsford 85, Allen 4–71) and 193 (Woodfull 73*, Bradman 66, Allen 4–50, Larwood 4–71)
England won by 338 runs

197. Australia v England
Fourth Test at Brisbane – 10, 11, 13, 14, 15, 16 February 1933
AUSTRALIA 340 (Richardson 83, Bradman 76, Woodfull 67, Larwood 4–101) and 175
ENGLAND 356 (Sutcliffe 86, Paynter 83, Jardine 46, O'Reilly 4–120) and 162–4 (Leyland 86)
England won by 6 wickets

198. Australia v England
Fifth Test at Sydney – 23, 24, 25, 27, 28 February 1933
AUSTRALIA 435 (Darling 85, McCabe 73, O'Brien 61, Oldfield 52, Bradman 48, Lee 42, Larwood 4–98) and 182 (Bradman 71, Woodfull 67, Verity 5–33)
ENGLAND 454 (Hammond 101, Larwood 98, Sutcliffe 56, Wyatt 51, Allen 48, Leyland 42, Lee 4–111) and 168–2 (Hammond 75*, Wyatt 61*)
England won by 8 wickets

199. New Zealand v England
First Test at Christchurch – 24, 25, 27 March 1933
ENGLAND 560–8 dec. (Hammond 227, Ames 103, Brown 74, Voce 66, Jardine 45)
NEW ZEALAND 223 (Weir 66, Kerr 59, Voce 3–27) and 35–0
Match drawn

200. New Zealand v England
Second Test at Auckland – 31 March, 1, 3 April 1933
NEW ZEALAND 158 (Dempster 83*, Bowes 6–34) and 16–0
ENGLAND 548–7 dec. (Hammond 336*, Wyatt 60)
Match drawn

201. England v West Indies
First Test at Lord's – 24, 26, 27 June 1933
ENGLAND 296 (Ames 83*, Walters 51, Martindale 4–85)
WEST INDIES 97 (Robins 6–32) and 172 (Headley 50, Verity 4–45, Macaulay 4–57)
England won by an innings and 27 runs

202. England v West Indies
Second Test at Old Trafford – 22, 24, 25 July 1933
WEST INDIES 375 (Headley 169*, Barrow 105, Clark 4–99) and 225 (Constantine 64, Roach 64, Langridge 7–56)
ENGLAND 374 (Jardine 127, Robins 55, Ames 47, Walters 46, Martindale 5–73)
Match drawn

203. England v West Indies
Third Test at The Oval – 12, 14, 15 August 1933
ENGLAND 312 (Bakewell 107, Barnett 52, Nichols 49, Martindale 5–93)
WEST INDIES 100 (Marriott 5–37, Clark 3–16) and 195 (Roach 56, Marriott 6–59)
England won by an innings and 17 runs

204. India v England
First Test at Bombay – 15, 16, 17, 18 December 1933
INDIA 219 and 258 (Amarnath 118, Nayudu 67, Nichols 5–55)
ENGLAND 438 (Valentine 136, Walters 78, Jardine 60, Nissar 5–90) and 40–1
England won by 9 wickets

205. India v England
Second Test at Calcutta – 5, 6, 7, 8 January 1934
ENGLAND 403 (Langridge 70, Jardine 61, Verity 55*, Mitchell 47, Townsend 40, Valentine 40, Amar Singh 4–106) and 7–2
INDIA 247 (Dilawar Hussain 59, Merchant 54, Verity 4–64) and 237 (Dilawar Hussain 57, Jaoomal 43, Verity 4–76)
Match drawn

206. India v England
Third Test at Madras – 10, 11, 12, 13 February 1934
ENGLAND 335 (Bakewell 85, Jardine 65, Walters 59, Verity 42, Amar Singh 7–86) and 261–7 dec. (Walters 102, Langridge 46, Nazir Ali 4–83)
INDIA 145 (Verity 7–49) and 249 (Yuvraj of Patiala 60, Amar Singh 48, Langridge 5–63, Verity 4–104)
England won by 202 runs

207. England v Australia
First Test at Trent Bridge – 8, 9, 11, 12 June 1934
AUSTRALIA 374 (Chipperfield 99, McCabe 65, Ponsford 53,
Farnes 5–102) and 273–8 dec. (McCabe 88, Brown 73,
Farnes 5–77)
ENGLAND 268 (Hendren 79, Sutcliffe 62, Geary 53,
Grimmett 5–81) and 141 (Walters 46, O'Reilly 7–54)
Australia won by 238 runs

208. England v Australia
Second Test at Lord's – 22, 23, 25 June 1934
ENGLAND 440 (Ames 120, Leyland 109, Walters 82, Wall
4–108)
AUSTRALIA 284 (Brown 105, Verity 7–61) and 118
(Woodfull 43, Verity 8–43)
England won by an innings and 38 runs

209. England v Australia
Third Test at Old Trafford – 6, 7, 9, 10 July 1934
ENGLAND 627–9 dec. (Leyland 153, Hendren 132, Ames
72, Sutcliffe 63, Allen 61, Verity 60*, Walters 52,
O'Reilly 7–189) and 123–0 dec. (Sutcliffe 69*, Walters
50*)
AUSTRALIA 491 (McCabe 137, Woodfull 73, Brown 72,
Verity 4–78) and 66–1
Match drawn

210. England v Australia
Fourth Test at Headingley – 20, 21, 23, 24 July 1934
ENGLAND 200 (Walters 44, Grimmett 4–57) and 229–6
(Leyland 49*, Walters 45, Wyatt 44, Hendren 42)
AUSTRALIA 584 (Bradman 304, Ponsford 181, Bowes
6–142)
Match drawn

211. England v Australia
Fifth Test at The Oval – 18, 20, 21, 22 August 1934
AUSTRALIA 701 (Ponsford 266, Bradman 244, Woodfull 49,
Oldfield 42*, Bowes 4–164, Allen 4–170) and 327
(Bradman 77, McCabe 70, Ebeling 41, Bowes 5–55,
Clark 5–98)
ENGLAND 321 (Leyland 110, Walters 64) and 145
(Hammond 43, Grimmett 5–64)
Australia won by 562 runs

212. West Indies v England
First Test at Bridgetown, Barbados – 8, 9, 10 January
1935
WEST INDIES 102 (Headley 44, Farnes 4–40) and 51–6 dec.
(Smith 5–16)
ENGLAND 81–7 dec. (Hammond 43, Hylton 3–8) and 75–6
(Martindale 5–22)
England won by 4 wickets

213. West Indies v England
Second Test at Port-of-Spain, Trinidad – 24, 25, 26, 28
January 1935
WEST INDIES 302 (Sealy 92, Constantine 90, Smith 4–100)
and 280–6 dec. (Headley 93)
ENGLAND 258 (Holmes 85*, Iddon 73, Hendren 41) and
107 (Constantine 3–11)
West Indies won by 217 runs

214. West Indies v England
Third Test at Georgetown, British Guiana – 14, 15, 16, 18
February 1935

ENGLAND 226 (Paine 49, Hammond 47, Hylton 4–27) and
160–6 dec. (Wyatt 71)
WEST INDIES 184 (Headley 53, Wishart 52, Hollies 7–50)
and 104–5
Match drawn

215. West Indies v England
Fourth Test at Kingston, Jamaica – 14, 15, 16, 18 March
1935
WEST INDIES 535–7 dec. (Headley 270*, Sealy 91, Grant
77, Paine 5–168)
ENGLAND 271 (Ames 126, Iddon 54, Hendren 40) and 103
(Martindale 4–28)
West Indies won by an innings and 161 runs

216. England v South Africa
First Test at Trent Bridge – 15, 17, 18 June 1935
ENGLAND 384–7 dec. (Wyatt 149, Leyland 69, Sutcliffe
61)
SOUTH AFRICA 220 (Siedle 59, Cameron 52, Nichols 6–35)
and 17–1
Match drawn

217. England v South Africa
Second Test at Lord's – 29 June, 1, 2 July 1935
SOUTH AFRICA 228 (Cameron 90) and 278–7 dec.
(Mitchell 164*, Langton 44, Rowan 44)
ENGLAND 198 (Wyatt 53, Balaskas 5–49) and 151
(Langton 4–31, Balaskas 4–54)
South Africa won by 157 runs

218. England v South Africa
Third Test at Headingley – 13, 15, 16 July 1935
ENGLAND 216 (Hammond 63, Mitchell 58, Vincent 4–45,
Langton 4–59) and 294–7 dec. (Hammond 87*,
Mitchell 72, Smith 57, Wyatt 44, Vincent 4–104)
SOUTH AFRICA 171 (Rowan 62) and 194–5 (Mitchell 58,
Cameron 49)
Match drawn

219. England v South Africa
Fourth Test at Old Trafford – 27, 29, 30 July 1935
ENGLAND 357 (Robins 108, Bakewell 63, Leyland 53, Crisp
5–99) and 231–6 dec. (Hammond 63*, Bakewell 54,
Barber 44, Vincent 4–78)
SOUTH AFRICA 318 (Viljoen 124, Cameron 53, Dalton 47,
Bowes 5–100) and 169–2 (Nourse 53*, Rowan 49,
Mitchell 48*)
Match drawn

220. England v South Africa
Fifth Test at The Oval – 17, 19, 20 August 1935
SOUTH AFRICA 476 (Mitchell 128, Dalton 117, Langton
73*, Viljoen 60, Read 4–136) and 287–6 (Dalton 57*,
Viljoen 45, Cameron 42)
ENGLAND 534–6 dec. (Leyland 161, Ames 148*, Hammond
65)
Match drawn

221. England v India
First Test at Lord's – 27, 29, 30 June 1936
INDIA 147 (Allen 5–35) and 93 (Allen 5–43, Verity 4–17)
ENGLAND 134 (Leyland 60, Amar Singh 6–35) and 108–1
(Gimblett 67*)
England won by 9 wickets

222. England v India

Second Test at Old Trafford – 25, 27, 28 July 1936
INDIA 203 (Wazir Ali 42, Ramaswami 40, Verity 4–41) and
390–5 (Merchant 114, Mushtaq Ali 112, Ramaswami
60, Amar Singh 48*)
ENGLAND 571–8 dec. (Hammond 167, Hardstaff Jnr 94,
Worthington 87, Robins 76, Verity 66*)
Match drawn

DID YOU KNOW...?

In 1935, Les Ames scored 123 before lunch for
England v South Africa at The Oval, the highest
score made before lunch in a Test match.

223. England v India

Third Test at The Oval – 15, 17, 18 August 1936
ENGLAND 471–8 dec. (Hammond 217, Worthington 128,
Barnett 43, Nissar 5–120) and 64–1
INDIA 222 (Merchant 52, Mushtaq Ali 52, Sims 5–73) and
312 (Nayudu 81, Dilawar Hussain 54, Merchant 48,
Amar Singh 44, Allen 7–80)
England won by 9 wickets

224. Australia v England

First Test at Brisbane – 4, 5, 7, 8, 9 December 1936
ENGLAND 358 (Leyland 126, Barnett 69, Hardstaff Jnr 43,
O'Reilly 5–102) and 256 (Allen 68, Ward 6–102)
AUSTRALIA 234 (Fingleton 100, McCabe 51, Voce 6–41)
and 58 (Allen 5–36, Voce 4–16)
England won by 322 runs

225. Australia v England

Second Test at Sydney – 18, 19, 21, 22 December 1936
ENGLAND 426–6 dec. (Hammond 231*, Barnett 57,
Leyland 42)
AUSTRALIA 80 (Voce 4–10) and 324 (McCabe 93, Bradman
82, Fingleton 73)
England won by an innings and 22 runs

226. Australia v England

Third Test at Melbourne – 1, 2, 4, 5, 6, 7 January 1937
AUSTRALIA 200–9 dec. (McCabe 63) and 564 (Bradman
270, Fingleton 136, Rigg 47)
ENGLAND 76–9 dec. (Sievens 5–21) and 323 (Leyland
111*, Robins 61, Hammond 51, Fleetwood-Smith
5–124)
Australia won by 365 runs

227. Australia v England

Fourth Test at Adelaide – 29, 30 January, 1, 2, 3, 4 February
1937
AUSTRALIA 288 (McCabe 88, Chipperfield 57*, Brown 42)
and 433 (Bradman 212, McCabe 55, Gregory 50,
Hammond 5–57)
ENGLAND 330 (Barnett 129, Ames 52, Leyland 45, O'Reilly
4–51, Fleetwood-Smith 4–129) and 243 (Wyatt 50,
Hardstaff Jnr 43, Fleetwood-Smith 6–110)
Australia won by 148 runs

228. Australia v England

Fifth Test at Melbourne – 26, 27 February, 1, 2, 3 March
1937
AUSTRALIA 604 (Bradman 169, Badcock 118, McCabe 112,
Gregory 80, Farnes 6–96)
ENGLAND 239 (Hardstaff Jnr 83, Worthington 44,
O'Reilly 5–51, Nash 4–70) and 165 (Hammond 56,
Barnett 41)
Australia won by an innings and 200 runs

229. England v New Zealand

First Test at Lord's – 26, 28, 29 June 1937
ENGLAND 424 (Hammond 140, Hardstaff Jnr 114, Paynter
74, Roberts 4–101, Cowie 4–118) and 226–4 dec.
(Barnett 83*, Hardstaff Jnr 64)
NEW ZEALAND 295 (Roberts 66*, Moloney 64, Wallace 52)
and 175–8 (Wallace 56)
Match drawn

230. England v New Zealand

Second Test at Old Trafford – 24, 26, 27 July 1937
ENGLAND 358–9 dec. (Hutton 100, Barnett 62, Hardstaff
Jnr 58, Cowie 4–73) and 187 (Brown 57, Cowie 6–67)
NEW ZEALAND 281 (Hadlee 93, Vivian 58, Wellard 4–81)
and 134 (Vivian 50, Goddard 6–29)
England won by 130 runs

231. England v New Zealand

Third Test at The Oval – 14, 16, 17 August 1937
NEW ZEALAND 249 (Donnelly 58, Page 53, Roberts 50,
Robins 4–40) and 187 (Vivian 57)
ENGLAND 254–7 dec. (Hardstaff Jnr 103, Compton 65)
and 31–1
Match drawn

232. England v Australia

First Test at Trent Bridge – 10, 11, 13, 14 June 1938
ENGLAND 658–8 dec. (Paynter 216*, Barnett 126,
Compton 102, Hutton 100, Ames 46, Fleetwood-Smith
4–153)
AUSTRALIA 411 (McCabe 232, Bradman 51, Brown 48,
Farnes 4–106, Wright 4–153) and 427–6 dec. (Bradman
144*, Brown 133, Fingleton 40)
Match drawn

233. England v Australia

Second Test at Lord's – 24, 25, 27, 28 June 1938
ENGLAND 494 (Hammond 240, Paynter 99, Ames 83,
O'Reilly 4–93, McCormick 4–101) and 242–8 dec.
(Compton 76*, Paynter 43)
AUSTRALIA 422 (Brown 206*, Hassett 56, O'Reilly 42) and
204–6 (Bradman 102*, Hassett 42)
Match drawn

England v Australia
Third Test at Old Trafford – July 1938
Match abandoned without a ball being bowled: rain

234. England v Australia

Fourth Test at Headingley – 22, 23, 25 July 1938
ENGLAND 223 (Hammond 76, O'Reilly 5–66) and 123
(O'Reilly 5–56, Fleetwood-Smith 4–34)
AUSTRALIA 242 (Bradman 103, Barnett 57, Farnes 4–77)
and 107–5
Australia won by 5 wickets

DID YOU KNOW...?

On 3 March 1939, the 'Timeless' Test began between South Africa and England at Durban. It continued until 14 March, when the tourists' boat was due to sail for London.

235. England v Australia
Fifth Test at The Oval – 20, 22, 23, 24 August 1938
ENGLAND 903–7 dec. (Hutton 364, Leyland 187, Hardstaff Jnr 169*, Hammond 59, Wood 53)
AUSTRALIA 201 (Brown 69, Hassett 42, Barnes 41, Bowes 5–49) and 123 (Barnett 46, Farnes 4–63)
England won by an innings and 579 runs

236. South Africa v England
First Test at Johannesburg – 24, 26, 27, 28 December 1938
ENGLAND 422 (Paynter 117, Valentine 97, Gibb 93, Ames 42, Gordon 5–103) and 291–4 dec. (Gibb 106, Paynter 100, Hammond 58)
SOUTH AFRICA 390 (Dalton 102, Mitchell 73, Nourse 73, Langton 64*, Viljoen 50, Verity 4–61) and 108–1 (Mitchell 48*)
Match drawn

237. South Africa v England
Second Test at Cape Town – 31 December 1938, 2, 3, 4 January 1939
ENGLAND 559–9 dec. (Hammond 181, Ames 115, Valentine 112, Gibb 58, Gordon 5–157)
SOUTH AFRICA 286 (Nourse 120, Mitchell 42, Verity 5–70) and 201–2 (Rowan 89*, van der Bijl 87)
Match drawn

238. South Africa v England
Third Test at Durban – 20, 21, 23 January 1939
ENGLAND 469–4 dec. (Paynter 243, Hammond 120)
SOUTH AFRICA 103 (Farnes 4–29) and 353 (Mitchell 109, Rowan 67, Viljoen 61)
England won by an innings and 13 runs

239. South Africa v England
Fourth Test at Johannesburg – 18, 20, 21, 22 February 1939
ENGLAND 215 (Hutton 92, Paynter 40, Langton 5–58) and 203–4 (Hammond 61*, Gibb 45)

SOUTH AFRICA 349–8 dec. (Rowan 85, Melville 67, Mitchell 63)
Match drawn

240. South Africa v England
Fifth Test at Durban – 3, 4, 6, 7, 8, 9, 10, 11, 13, 14 March 1939
SOUTH AFRICA 530 (van der Bijl 125, Nourse 103, Melville 78, Grieveson 75, Dalton 57, Perks 5–100) and 481 (Melville 103, van der Bijl 97, Mitchell 89, Viljoen 74, Farnes 4–74)
ENGLAND 316 (Ames 84, Paynter 62, Dalton 4–59) and 654–5 (Edrich 219, Hammond 140, Gibb 120, Paynter 75, Hutton 55)
Match drawn (by agreement)

241. England v West Indies
First Test at Lord's – 24, 26, 27 June 1939
WEST INDIES 277 (Headley 106, Stollmeyer 59, Copson 5–85) and 225 (Headley 107, Copson 4–67)
ENGLAND 404–5 dec. (Hutton 196, Compton 120) and 100–2
England won by 8 wickets

242. England v West Indies
Second Test at Old Trafford – 22, 24, 25 July 1939
ENGLAND 164–7 dec. (Hardstaff Jnr 76) and 128–6 dec. (Constantine 4–42)
WEST INDIES 133 (Headley 51, Grant 47, Bowes 6–33) and 43–4
Match drawn

243. England v West Indies
Third Test at The Oval – 19, 21, 22 August 1939
ENGLAND 352 (Hardstaff Jnr 94, Oldfield 80, Hutton 73, Hammond 43, Constantine 5–75) and 366–3 dec. (Hutton 165*, Hammond 138)
WEST INDIES 498 (Weekes 137, V. H. Stollmeyer 96, Constantine 79, Headley 65, J. B. Stollmeyer 59, Perks 5–156)
Match drawn

DID YOU KNOW...?

England's 654–5 in the 'Timeless' Test in Durban in 1939 is the highest fourth-innings total in first-class cricket.

POST-WAR CRICKET: 1946–59

After the Second World War, the only match to finish in England's first Test series against India came at Lord's when the home side won by 10 wickets. But India only just escaped defeat at Old Trafford, while the Oval Test was ruined by the weather. The series was notable for the introduction to Test cricket of Alec Bedser, who took 11 wickets in each of the first two games. He claimed 7–49 and 4–96 at Lord's, where Joe Hardstaff hit a magnificent 205 not out.

The last pre-war Ashes Test had ended in England's biggest-ever victory, but the first post-war meeting between the two countries brought a record victory for Australia. Yet England might have come much closer to recovering the

Ashes but for Bradman. After a rather uncertain beginning at Brisbane he had made 28 when he appeared to give a perfect catch to Jack Ikin in the gully, only to be given not out. He went on to make 187 in that match and 234 in the next, both of which Australia won by an innings. For the rest of the series, Bradman's scores were kept within reasonable limits with Compton, Hutton and Washbrook finding their form. England drew the next two Tests with Compton making a hundred in each innings in the fourth Test. England were on top in the final Test until Hutton, who had made 122, had to retire with tonsilitis and Australia went on to win by 5 wickets.

Only one Test, at Christchurch, was played by Wally Hammond's team in New Zealand. It was Hammond's last appearance for England and he made 79 in a drawn game that was badly affected by the weather. In fact, for the first time in history, an extra day was added when rain prevented play on the third day.

When Alan Melville brought South Africa to England in 1947, their cricket was suffering from much the same post-war ailments as English cricket. The Springboks' batsmen, Melville, Dudley Nourse and Bruce Mitchell, made a lot of runs and they could take satisfaction from their contribution to a spectacular series that was a great advertisement for the game of cricket. But their shortage of penetrative bowling coincided with a glorious English summer and the series is remembered for the superb batting of Compton and Edrich. Compton made 753 runs in the series at 94.12 and scored four hundreds. Edrich played in only four Tests, making 552 runs at 110.40. South Africa led by 325 runs on the first innings of the opening Test, but could manage only a draw after making England follow on. Following three successive Test wins for England, Mitchell made a hundred in each innings of the last Test as South Africa finished on 423–7, only 28 runs adrift of an unconsidered victory.

The England team that visited the West Indies in 1947–8 was even more below strength than its predecessors. In those days, England depended heavily on players such as Hutton, Compton, Edrich and Bedser, but none of those went on this tour, though Hutton joined it later. England succeeded in drawing the first two Tests with wicketkeeper Billy Griffith playing in his first Test as an opening batsman and making his maiden first-class hundred. Generally, though, England's cricket was unexceptional and West Indies comfortably won the remaining two Tests.

When Australia visited these shores in 1948, Ray Lindwall and Keith Miller were reaching their peak, ably backed up by Bill Johnston, and, with Arthur Morris emerging as a left-hander in the great Australian tradition, and with Bradman, Barnes and Lindsay Hassett as effective as ever, the side lacked only a top-class spinner. Australia had four big victory margins and it was only at Old Trafford that they were unable to force a win. England were somewhat unlucky at Trent Bridge to bat first on a wicket enlivened by rain and the visitors led on the first innings by 344 with Bradman and Hassett making hundreds. Compton fell on his wicket after making 184 and with his dismissal went any chance England had of saving the game. At Lord's England were facing defeat towards the end of the second day and never recovered. At Old Trafford, England made

363 after being 19–5. Compton, struck on the head by a Lindwall bouncer, returned to make 145 not out. Bedser and Dick Pollard bowled Australia out for 221, but England lost a great chance of victory when rain completely washed out the fourth day. The Headingley Test saw England throw away the chance of victory. Centuries from Washbrook and Edrich helped England to a total of 496 and Australia replied with 458. Following England's declaration, Australia needed 404 to win in 344 minutes, but a number of dropped catches allowed Australia to win by 7 wickets. In the final Test at The Oval, England were bowled out for just 52, and, though Eric Hollies dismissed Bradman just four runs adrift of having a Test average of a 100, Australia won by an innings and 149 runs.

If the previous series against South Africa did much to restore cricket in England after the war, the visit of George Mann's England side to South Africa in 1948–9 did the same there. England won two narrow victories in the first and last Tests to clinch the series. The first, by 2 wickets, came in one of the most exciting finishes in Test cricket history. England needed 128 to win on an unpredictable pitch and only scraped home when Cliff Gladwin and Alec Bedser ran a desperate leg bye off the last ball of the match. The second Test in Johannesburg was notable for an opening stand of 359 between Washbrook and Hutton that lasted throughout the first day. The last Test was also unusual, for England won after a declaration by South African skipper Dudley Nourse, made, as it were, in desperation on the last day as his side were one down in the series. He set England a target of 172 to win in an hour and a half – a target they reached with seven wickets down and just a minute to spare.

The New Zealand team to tour England in 1949 was a strong side, especially rich in batting, and, in a glorious summer of hard pitches, they scored plenty of runs. But the Test matches were still of three days' duration and all were drawn – remembered still today as monuments of stalemate and frustration.

Though the West Indies had easily won the 1947–8 series, they had not really given any idea of how, for the first time, they would dominate a series in England. The 1950 series saw England win the first Test at Old Trafford, but from the second Test at Lord's, which West Indies won by 326 runs to record their first win in England, there was only one team in it. Compton was unfit for most of that summer, but when he was fit he played in the last Test, being needlessly run out for 44. In that match, Len Hutton played undefeated for 202 out of a total of 344. For West Indies, a number of their batsmen played sparkling innings – Clyde Walcott made 168 not out at Lord's, Frank Worrell hit a memorable 261 and Everton Weekes 129 at Trent Bridge, while Worrell's 138 accompanied Alan Rae's second hundred of the series at The Oval. Alf Valentine's slow left-arm took 33 wickets and Sonny Ramadhin, with his well-disguised leg-breaks, 26 – West Indies had arrived.

After twenty years of trying to counter Australia's batting genius Don Bradman, by 1950–1 England were now taking on an Australian team without him. After dismissing Australia for 228, England were caught on a rain-affected wicket and declared at 68–7. Australia in turn declared at 32–7. Needing 193 to win, England slumped to 30–6, and even a great last-day innings of 62 by

Hutton could not save them. England showed again with a smaller margin of defeat at Melbourne that there wasn't a great deal between the sides, but in the third Test at Sydney, injuries to Bailey and Wright saw Australia win by an innings. A fine 206 by Arthur Morris was matched by 156 not out by Hutton at Adelaide, possibly his greatest innings, but the remaining England batsmen all failed and they lost a match they really should have saved. Consolation came in the final Test at Melbourne, when England, thanks largely to Reg Simpson (156 not out) and Hutton, won their first Test against Australia since the war.

In New Zealand, Trevor Bailey made 134 not out in another high-scoring draw between the two countries, but England won the other Test by six wickets after being made to work hard on a deteriorating pitch.

Though Dudley Nourse's South African side of 1951 was much younger than previous sides to have played England and was well beaten, it contained much promise for the future. Indeed, the young team began by winning the first Test at Trent Bridge, where Nourse made 208 despite a broken thumb. Though Reg Simpson and Denis Compton both made hundreds for England, Athol Rowan and 'Tufty' Mann ran through the England second innings. At Lord's, the rain helped Lancashire's Roy Tattersall to take 12 wickets for 101 runs and England won by 10 wickets. Twelve wickets by Alec Bedser in wet conditions at Old Trafford brought England a 9-wicket victory there. Peter May scored a hundred in his first Test at Headingley, but Eric Rowan made 236 and the game was drawn. At The Oval, England won inside three days, but only after some moments of doubt as to whether the last-innings target of 163 was within their range.

On England's tour of India in 1951–2, the first three Tests were drawn. At New Delhi, England had a hard fight after being dismissed for 203 and the hosts ran up 418–6 with Merchant (154) and Hazare (164 not out) adding 211 for the third wicket before a determined 138 not out from Allan Watkins saved England. Hazare hit another hundred at Bombay, as did Pankaj Roy, but Tom Graveney replied for England with a brilliant 175. As with the next Test in Calcutta, there wasn't much chance of a finish. England won the fourth Test at Kanpur but India then made history by recording their first victory over England at Madras, winning by an innings and 8 runs thanks to Vinoo Mankad, who had match figures of 12–108, and centuries from Roy and Polly Umrigar.

However, when India arrived in England the following summer, they were totally outclassed. Only rain saved them from overwhelming defeat in all four games. The first Test at Headingley was noted for the worst start to an innings in Test history. Facing arrears of 41, India lost their first four wickets of their second innings without a run being scored – England went on to win by 7 wickets. A magnificent all-round performance by Mankad at Lord's, where he made 72 and 184 and bowled 73 overs for 5–196, couldn't prevent England from winning by 8 wickets. Fred Trueman demoralized India at Old Trafford, taking 8–31 in their first-innings total of 58. They fared little better when they followed on and were bowled out for 82 and so were dismissed twice in a day.

In 1953 after almost twenty years of domination by Australia, England regained the Ashes. Four draws and a victory at The Oval to England was history repeating itself. But there the comparisons ended, for the four drawn games were packed with drama. At Trent Bridge, great bowling in the match by Alec Bedser (14–99) left England needing 229 to win, but rain spoilt the match with the home side on 42–1. The Lord's Test was remarkable for the great match-saving stand between Willie Watson (109) and Trevor Bailey (71) after England had begun the final day facing almost certain defeat. Rain ruined the Old Trafford Test, but England got a horrible fright on the last day of the fourth Test at Headingley, where Australia, needing 177 to win in 115 minutes, set off at a gallop. Bailey put the brakes on by bowling wide of the leg stump off a long run, but his tactics were not widely approved. In the deciding Test at The Oval, Australia had no answers to Jim Laker and Tony Lock, but without a doubt the bowler of the series was Alec Bedser, who took a record 39 wickets.

When Len Hutton went to the West Indies early in 1954, he had with him a team that could at last be considered representative of the best of English cricket. However, the English batsmen failed to conquer the West Indian bowling, especially that of Sonny Ramadhin, in the first two Tests. In the third, however, England batted first for the first time and Hutton made 169 – West Indies followed on and were beaten. A match of huge scores in Port-of-Spain was drawn after Walcott, Weekes and Worrell had all made centuries and May and Compton had replied for England. But in Kingston, England won a remarkable victory in the last Test to square the series. Trevor Bailey took 7–34 as West Indies were bowled out for 139 and Len Hutton made 205 out of an England score of 414. West Indies were then bowled out a second time, allowing England to win by 9 wickets.

In 1954 Pakistan achieved the unexpected and the unprecedented on their first tour of England by winning one Test and so drawing the series. However, the series began in depressing manner for the tourists with rain preventing any play until mid-afternoon on the fourth day of the first Test. Further frustration followed at Trent Bridge, this time in the form of the batting of Compton (278) and Simpson (101) and England won by an innings and 129 runs. Rain proved to be Pakistan's saviour at Old Trafford when they were 25–4 in their second innings, having made only 90 in their first in reply to England's 359–8 declared. Then came the thrilling last Test at The Oval, where Pakistan won by 24 runs. Needing 168 to win, England were comfortably placed at 109–2 but collapsed completely and were out for 143.

England, with the Ashes safely in their grasp, took with them to Australia two secret weapons in the form of speed twins Frank 'Typhoon' Tyson and Brian Statham. In a series in which the Australian batting proved vulnerable, they took 46 wickets between them, ensuring that England held on to the Ashes with a 3–1 margin. After a wretched start at Brisbane, where Len Hutton misread the pitch and put the hosts in to bat – Australia totalled 601–8 – England were beaten by an innings and 154 runs. In the second Test at Sydney, England themselves were put in and after lagging behind on the first innings by 74 runs were struggling in their second innings at 55–3, when May and Cowdrey put on 116. Needing 223 to win, Australia were bowled out for 184 with Frank Tyson, who had been knocked unconscious by a Lindwall bouncer when batting, taking 6–85. At Melbourne, early life in the wicket put England in trouble, but Cowdrey and Bailey pulled the game round before Tyson and Statham did the rest. The pace bowlers were also responsible for England winning the fourth Test. The first three days of the final Test were lost through rain, but there was time for a superb century from Tom Graveney and for some inept Australian batting that left England pressing for victory.

When Len Hutton's team went to New Zealand after retaining the Ashes, they found the Kiwis' standards had declined. The first Test was interrupted by rain and the third and fourth days of what, unusually, was a five-day match were lost through rain. However, the English bowlers finished off the earlier work of Tyson and Statham and England won by 8 wickets. The second Test, which England won by an innings with a score of only 246 and a first-innings lead of only 46, was remarkable for New Zealand's melancholy achievement of the lowest score in Test history. On a pitch of varying bounce that took some spin, Statham with 3–9 and Tyson with 2–10 made the early inroads before Appleyard with 4–7 and Wardle, 1–0, bowled the home side out for just 26 in 27 overs.

The visit of South Africa in 1955 produced what many people still believe to be the finest post-war Test series. In what was a fine summer, England won the first two Tests and South Africa the next two and all depended on the final Test at The Oval. The result of the first Test was deceptive, England winning by an innings. Frank Tyson, fresh from his triumphs 'Down Under', took 6–28 in South Africa's second innings. At Lord's, however, England were bowled out on a fast track for 133 on the first day and McLean's dazzling innings helped give South Africa a 171-run lead. But May, captaining England in his first series, made a spectacular 112 and Brian Statham (7–39) bowled South Africa out. At Old Trafford, Compton made 158 for England in the first innings and May 117 in the second, but in between South Africa scored 521–8 declared, with McGlew, Waite and Winslow all making hundreds. The Springboks went on to win a historic match by three wickets with a few minutes to spare. They won more easily at Headingley, where Tayfield and Goddard shared the wickets in the last innings. And so to The Oval, where Laker and Lock spun England to victory, though it is widely acknowledged that if a very close lbw decision had not been given in Peter May's favour when he was on four – he went on to make 89 – the series might have had another ending.

With Hutton retired, Compton crippled and Statham, Trueman and Tyson all injured, England had to rebuild their side for the opening Test of the 1956 Ashes series at Trent Bridge. Even so, England were the better side, but their hopes were dashed by constant interruptions by rain. At Lord's, Trueman and Statham returned, but Keith Miller, with match figures of 10–152, helped Australia to win by 185 runs. The selectors recalled Lancashire's Cyril Washbrook for the Headingley Test. Joining May when England were 17–3, he helped to add 187 for the fourth wicket and the partnership proved decisive. The wicket then began to help the spinners Laker and Lock and England won by an innings and 42 runs. The fourth Test at Old Trafford will always be known simply as 'Laker's Match'. The Surrey off-spinner Jim Laker was handed the ball at the Stretford End and promptly took 9–37 in Australia's first innings, while in the second he took all 10 wickets for the amazing match analysis of 68–27–90–19. Yet the greatest bowling feat of all time was not without controversy. Pitch preparation was never easy in this wet summer and patches were apparent during England's first innings. In the final Test, Denis Compton became the third inspired comeback selection for England in the series, making 94 despite the recent loss of his right kneecap. The match, though, was spoilt by rain and May left the tourists two hours in which to make 228 to level the series. It was time enough for further humiliations – Australia 27–5 – with Laker taking his tally of wickets for the series to a record 46 at 9.60 apiece.

Another fine series in South Africa in 1956–7 saw England begin with dourly earned victories at Durban and Cape Town, the latter pressed home by Johnny Wardle taking 7–36 on a pitch taking some spin. England were not far off winning the third Test and the rubber, but after South Africa won an exciting victory at Johannesburg in the fourth Test by 17 runs it meant there was all to play for in the final Test at Port Elizabeth. South Africa won a vital toss and Endean's first-innings 70 out of 164 on a pitch of impossibly low bounce was a winning score in the conditions and allowed the home side to halve the series.

When West Indies toured England in 1957, the English batsmen had still never really worked out how to play Ramadhin and it was the wearing down of him by captain Peter May and Colin Cowdrey that in the first Test at Edgbaston turned the series England's way. In the first innings of this match, England were bowled out for 186 with Ramadhin taking 7–49. West Indies replied with 474, but then Peter May, with 285 not out, accompanied by Colin Cowdrey, who made 154, put on 411 in a record-breaking stand and England were eventually able to declare. The game was drawn but Ramadhin had taken 2–179 off 98 overs and he was never the same force again. England went on to win three Tests by an innings with Cowdrey making 152 at Lord's and Peter Richardson 107 and Tom Graveney 164 at The Oval, where West Indies were bowled out for 89 and 86 by Lock and Laker.

The summer of 1958 was extremely wet and this gave England an extra advantage for the home series against New Zealand. England, with Peter May playing some magnificent innings, were far too good. They began by bowling the Kiwis out for 94 at Edgbaston and in a calamitous match at Lord's, which was over by 3.30 p.m. on the third day, dismissed New Zealand for 47 and 74 with Lock (5–17) and Laker (4–13) in the first innings. The two spin bowlers, along with Trueman, Loader and Bailey, were almost as devastating in the second. New Zealand's torment at the hands of Laker and Lock continued at Headingley, where they were bowled out for 67 and again lost by an innings. The Kiwis lost by an innings again at Old Trafford, where May made another hundred, but the almost incessant rain came to their aid in the last Test.

The 1958–9 Ashes series in Australia was the first series to be televised and, though the occasion may have been momentous, the cricket most certainly was not. With Norman O'Neill in fine form, Australia ran out easy winners at Brisbane, while, following centuries from Neil Harvey and Peter May, the match was evenly poised as England batted a second time. They then collapsed to the erratic Ian Meckiff (6–38) and Australia went on to win, as in Brisbane, by 8 wickets. In the third Test at Sydney, Australia led by 138 on the first innings and the rubber seemed decided as England slid to 64–3. Then May (92) and Cowdrey (100 not out) put on 182 and the match was saved. At Adelaide, with Laker injured, England lost by 10 wickets, allowing Australia to claim back the Ashes. In the final Test, England lost by 9 wickets and Ray Lindwall, playing in his last Test against England, became Australia's leading Test wicket-taker by passing Clarrie Grimmett's record of 216 wickets.

Stopping off at New Zealand, England won the first Test at Christchurch by an innings with Ted Dexter scoring 141 and Tony Lock taking 11 wickets. But rain interrupted the second Test when Peter May (124 not out) had taken England into a big lead.

For the first time ever, in 1959 England won all five Tests in a series, India's contribution to this feat being a somewhat dubious distinction. Three of England's victories came with an innings to spare and the other two were won with plenty in hand. Brian Statham and Fred Trueman consistently upset the Indian batting and the bowlers encountered Peter May, Geoff Pullar, Ken Barrington and Colin Cowdrey full of runs. Only the fourth Test of the series provided any interest and it was the only one that went into the fifth day. Geoff Pullar and Mike Smith scored centuries for England and, when India batted a second time wanting 548 to win, A. A. Baig, an Oxford University freshman recruited during the tour, made 112 and Umrigar 118 before they went down by 171 runs.

TEST MATCH RESULTS: 1946–59

244. England v India
First Test at Lord's – 22, 24, 25 June 1946
INDIA 200 (Modi 57*, Abdul Hafeez 43, Bedser 7–49) and 275 (Mankad 63, Amarnath 50, Bedser 4–96)
ENGLAND 428 (Hardstaff Jnr 205*, Gibb 60, Amarnath 5–118) and 48–0
England won by 10 wickets

245. England v India
Second Test at Old Trafford – 20, 22, 23 July 1946
ENGLAND 294 (Hammond 69, Hutton 67, Washbrook 52, Compton 51, Amarnath 5–96, Mankad 5–101) and 153–5 dec. (Compton 71*)
INDIA 170 (Merchant 78, Mushtaq Ali 46, Pollard 5–24, Bedser 4–41) and 152–9 (Hazare 44, Bedser 7–52)
Match drawn

246. England v India
Third Test at The Oval – 17, 19, 20 August 1946
INDIA 331 (Merchant 128, Mushtaq Ali 59, Mankad 42, Edrich 4–68)
ENGLAND 95–3
Match drawn

247. Australia v England
First Test at Brisbane – 29, 30 November, 2, 3, 4 December 1946
AUSTRALIA 645 (Bradman 187, Hassett 128, McCool 95, Miller 79, Johnson 47, Wright 5–167)
ENGLAND 141 (Miller 7–60) and 172 (Toshack 6–82)
Australia won by an innings and 332 runs

248. Australia v England
Second Test at Sydney – 13, 14, 16, 17, 18, 19 December 1946
ENGLAND 255 (Edrich 71, Ikin 60, Johnson 6–42) and 371 (Edrich 119, Compton 54, Washbrook 41, McCool 5–109)
AUSTRALIA 659–8 dec. (Bradman 234, Barnes 234, Miller 40)
Australia won by an innings and 33 runs

249. Australia v England
Third Test at Melbourne – 1, 2, 3, 4, 6, 7 January 1947
AUSTRALIA 365 (McCool 104*, Bradman 79, Barnes 45) and 536 (Morris 155, Lindwall 100, Tallon 92, Bradman 49, McCool 43)
ENGLAND 351 (Edrich 89, Washbrook 62, Yardley 61, Ikin 48, Dooland 4–69) and 310–7 (Washbrook 112, Yardley 53*, Hutton 40)
Match drawn

250. Australia v England
Fourth Test at Adelaide – 31 January, 1, 3, 4, 5, 6 February 1947
ENGLAND 460 (Compton 147, Hutton 94, Hardstaff Jnr 67, Washbrook 65, Lindwall 4–52) and 340–8 dec. (Compton 103*, Hutton 76, Edrich 46, Toshack 4–76)
AUSTRALIA 487 (Miller 141*, Morris 122, Hassett 78, Johnson 52) and 215–1 (Morris 124*, Bradman 56*)
Match drawn

251. Australia v England
Fifth Test at Sydney – 28 February, 1 (no play), 3, 4, 5 March 1947
ENGLAND 280 (Hutton 122 ret. hurt, Edrich 60, Lindwall 7–63) and 186 (Compton 76, McCool 5–44)
AUSTRALIA 253 (Barnes 71, Morris 57, Wright 7–105) and 214–5 (Bradman 63, Hassett 47)
Australia won by 5 wickets

252. New Zealand v England
Only Test at Christchurch – 21, 22, 24 (no play), 25 March 1947
NEW ZEALAND 345–9 dec. (Hadlee 116, Sutcliffe 58, Cowie 45, Bedser 4–95)
ENGLAND 265–7 dec. (Hammond 79, Ikin 45, Edrich 42, Cowie 6–83)
Match drawn

DID YOU KNOW...?

The first Test in which an extra day was added because of rain was between New Zealand and England in March 1947.

253. England v South Africa
First Test at Trent Bridge – 7, 9, 10, 11 June 1947
SOUTH AFRICA 533 (Melville 189, Nourse 149, Harris 60, Dawson 48, Hollies 5–123) and 166–1 (Melville 104*, Viljoen 51*)
ENGLAND 208 (Compton 65, Edrich 57, Tuckett 5–68) and 551 (Compton 163, Yardley 99, Evans 74, Washbrook 59, Edrich 50, Smith 4–143)
Match drawn

254. England v South Africa
Second Test at Lord's – 21, 23, 24, 25 June 1947
ENGLAND 554–8 dec. (Compton 208, Edrich 189, Washbrook 65, Tuckett 5–115) and 26–0
SOUTH AFRICA 327 (Melville 117, Nourse 61, Mitchell 46, Wright 5–95) and 252 (Mitchell 80, Nourse 58, Wright 5–80)
England won by 10 wickets

255. England v South Africa
Third Test at Old Trafford – 5, 7, 8, 9 July 1947
SOUTH AFRICA 339 (Viljoen 93, Mitchell 80, Dyer 62, Edrich 4–95) and 267 (Nourse 115, Melville 59, Edrich 4–77)
ENGLAND 478 (Edrich 191, Compton 115, Yardley 41, Tuckett 4–148) and 130–3 (Washbrook 40)
England won by 7 wickets

256. England v South Africa
Fourth Test at Headingley – 26, 28, 29 July 1947
SOUTH AFRICA 175 (Mitchell 53, Nourse 51, Butler 4–34) and 184 (Nourse 57, Cranston 4–12)
ENGLAND 317–7 dec. (Hutton 100, Washbrook 75, Edrich 43, Mann 4–68) and 47–0
England won by 10 wickets

257. England v South Africa
Fifth Test at The Oval – 16, 18, 19, 20 August 1947
ENGLAND 427 (Hutton 83, Yardley 59, Compton 53, Gladwin 51*, Mann 4–93) and 325–6 dec. (Compton 113, Howorth 45*, Washbrook 43)
SOUTH AFRICA 302 (Mitchell 120, Dawson 55) and 423–7 (Mitchell 189*, Nourse 97, Tuckett 40*)
Match drawn

258. West Indies v England
First Test at Bridgetown, Barbados – 21, 22, 23, 24, 26 January 1948
WEST INDIES 296 (Gomez 86, J. B. Stollmeyer 78, Laker 7–103) and 351–9 dec. (Christiani 99, Williams 72, Ferguson 56*, Howorth 6–124)
ENGLAND 253 (Hardstaff Jnr 98, Robertson 80, Jones 4–54) and 86–4 (Robertson 51*)
Match drawn

259. West Indies v England
Second Test at Port-of-Spain, Trinidad – 11, 12, 13, 14, 16 February 1948
ENGLAND 362 (Griffith 140, Laker 55, Ferguson 5–137) and 275 (Robertson 133, Ferguson 6–92)
WEST INDIES 497 (Ganteaume 112, Carew 107, Worrell 97, Gomez 62) and 72–3
Match drawn

260. West Indies v England
Third Test at Georgetown, British Guiana – 3, 4, 5, 6 March 1948
WEST INDIES 297–8 dec. (Worrell 131*, Cranston 4–78) and 78–3
ENGLAND 111 (Goddard 5–31) and 263 (Hardstaff Jnr 63, Ferguson 5–116)
West Indies won by 7 wickets

261. West Indies v England
Fourth Test at Kingston, Jamaica – 27, 29, 30, 31 March, 1 April 1948
ENGLAND 227 (Robertson 64, Hutton 56, Johnson 5–41) and 336 (Place 107, Hardstaff Jnr 64, Hutton 60, Johnson 5–55)
WEST INDIES 490 (Weekes 141, Ferguson 75, Rickards 67, Walcott 45) and 76–0 (Goddard 46*)
West Indies won by 10 wickets

262. England v Australia
First Test at Trent Bridge – 10, 11, 12, 14, 15 June 1948
ENGLAND 165 (Laker 63, Johnston 5–36) and 441 (Compton 184, Hutton 74, Evans 50, Hardstaff Jnr 43, Miller 4–125, Johnston 4–147)
AUSTRALIA 509 (Bradman 138, Hassett 137, Barnes 62, Lindwall 42, Laker 4–138) and 98–2 (Barnes 64*)
Australia won by 8 wickets

263. England v Australia
Second Test at Lord's – 24, 25, 26, 28, 29 June 1948
AUSTRALIA 350 (Morris 105, Tallon 53, Hassett 47, Bedser 4–100) and 460–7 dec. (Barnes 141, Bradman 89, Miller 74, Morris 62)
ENGLAND 215 (Compton 53, Yardley 44, Lindwall 5–70) and 186 (Toshack 5–40)
Australia won by 409 runs

264. England v Australia
Third Test at Old Trafford – 8, 9, 10, 12 (no play), 13 July 1948
ENGLAND 363 (Compton 145*, Lindwall 4–99) and 174–3 dec. (Washbrook 85*, Edrich 53)
AUSTRALIA 221 (Morris 51, Bedser 4–81) and 92–1 (Morris 54*)
Match drawn

265. England v Australia
Fourth Test at Headingley – 22, 23, 24, 26, 27 July 1948
ENGLAND 496 (Washbrook 143, Edrich 111, Hutton 81, Bedser 79) and 365–8 dec. (Compton 66, Washbrook 65, Hutton 57, Edrich 54, Evans 47*, Johnston 4–95)
AUSTRALIA 458 (Harvey 112, Loxton 93, Lindwall 77, Miller 58) and 404–3 (Morris 182, Bradman 173*)
Australia won by 7 wickets

266. England v Australia
Fifth Test at The Oval – 14, 16, 17, 18 August 1948
ENGLAND 52 (Lindwall 6–20) and 188 (Hutton 64, Johnston 4–40)
AUSTRALIA 389 (Morris 196, Barnes 61, Hollies 5–131)
Australia won by an innings and 149 runs

267. South Africa v England
First Test at Durban – 16, 17, 18, 20 December 1948
SOUTH AFRICA 161 (Bedser 4–39) and 219 (Wade 63, Begbie 48, Wright 4–72)
ENGLAND 253 (Hutton 83, Compton 72, Mann 6–59, A. M. B. Rowan 4–108) and 128–8 (McCarthy 6–43)
England won by 2 wickets

268. South Africa v England
Second Test at Johannesburg – 27, 28, 29, 30 December 1948
ENGLAND 608 (Washbrook 195, Hutton 158, Compton 114, Crapp 56)
SOUTH AFRICA 315 (Mitchell 86, Wade 85) and 270–2 (E. A. B. Rowan 156*, Nourse 56*, Mitchell 40)
Match drawn

269. South Africa v England
Third Test at Cape Town – 1, 3, 4, 5 January 1949
ENGLAND 308 (Washbrook 74, Mann 44, Hutton 41, A. M. B. Rowan 5–80) and 276–3 dec. (Hutton 87, Watkins 64*, Crapp 54, Compton 51*)
SOUTH AFRICA 356 (Mitchell 120, Nourse 112, Wynne 50, Compton 5–70) and 142–4 (Wynne 46, Jenkins 4–48)
Match drawn

270. South Africa v England
Fourth Test at Johannesburg – 12, 14, 15, 16 February 1949
ENGLAND 379 (Watkins 111, Washbrook 97, Crapp 51, McCarthy 5–114) and 253 (Hutton 123, A. M. B. Rowan 4–69)
SOUTH AFRICA 257–9 dec. (Nourse 129*, Wade 54) and 194–4 (E. A. B. Rowan 86*, Viljoen 63)
Match drawn

271. South Africa v England
Fifth Test at Port Elizabeth – 5, 7, 8, 9 March 1949
SOUTH AFRICA 379 (Wade 125, Mitchell 99, Nourse 73, Bedser 4–61) and 187–3 dec. (Mitchell 56)
ENGLAND 395 (Mann 136*, Compton 49, Hutton 46, A. M. B. Rowan 5–167) and 174–7 (Compton 42, Washbrook 40, Mann 4–65)
England won by 3 wickets

272. England v New Zealand
First Test at Headingley – 11, 13, 14 June 1949
ENGLAND 372 (Compton 114, Hutton 101, Burtt 5–97, Cowie 5–127) and 267–4 dec. (Washbrook 103*, Edrich 70, Mann 49*)
NEW ZEALAND 341 (Smith 96, Donnelly 64, Mooney 46, Bailey 6–118) and 195–2 (Sutcliffe 82, Smith 54*, Scott 43)
Match drawn

273. England v New Zealand
Second Test at Lord's – 25, 27, 28 June 1949
ENGLAND 313–9 dec. (Compton 116, Bailey 93, Burtt 4–102) and 306–5 (Robertson 121, Hutton 66, Watkins 49*)
NEW ZEALAND 484 (Donnelly 206, Sutcliffe 57, Hadlee 43, Scott 42, Hollies 5–133)
Match drawn

274. England v New Zealand
Third Test at Old Trafford – 23, 25, 26 July 1949
NEW ZEALAND 293 (Donnelly 75, Reid 50, Bailey 6–84) and 348–7 (Sutcliffe 101, Donnelly 80)
ENGLAND 440–9 dec. (Simpson 103, Edrich 78, Hutton 73, Bailey 72*, Burtt 6–162)
Match drawn

275. England v New Zealand
Fourth Test at The Oval – 13, 15, 16 August 1949
NEW ZEALAND 345 (Sutcliffe 88, Scott 60, Wallace 55, Bedser 4–74) and 308 (Reid 93, Wallace 58, Sutcliffe 54, Laker 4–78)
ENGLAND 482 (Hutton 206, Edrich 100, Simpson 68, Cresswell 6–168, Cowie 4–123)
Match drawn

276. England v West Indies
First Test at Old Trafford – 8, 9, 10, 12 June 1950
ENGLAND 312 (Evans 104, Bailey 82*, Valentine 8–104) and 288 (Edrich 71, Hutton 45, Laker 40)
WEST INDIES 215 (Weekes 52, J. B. Stollmeyer 43, Berry 5–63) and 183 (J. B. Stollmeyer 78, Hollies 5–63, Berry 4–53)
England won by 202 runs

277. England v West Indies
Second Test at Lord's – 24, 26, 27, 28, 29 June 1950
WEST INDIES 326 (Rae 106, Weekes 63, Worrell 52, Jenkins 5–116) and 425–6 dec. (Walcott 168*, Gomez 70, Weekes 63, Worrell 45, Jenkins 4–174)
ENGLAND 151 (Ramadhin 5–66, Valentine 4–48) and 274 (Washbrook 114, Parkhouse 48, Ramadhin 6–86)
West Indies won by 326 runs

278. England v West Indies

Third Test at Trent Bridge – 20, 21, 22, 24, 25 July 1950
ENGLAND 223 (Shackleton 42, Yardley 41) and 436
(Washbrook 102, Simpson 94, Parkhouse 69, Dewes 67,
Evans 63, Ramadhin 5–135)
WEST INDIES 558 (Worrell 261, Weekes 129, Rae 68,
J. B. Stollmeyer 46, Bedser 5–127) and 103–0
(J. B. Stollmeyer 52*, Rae 46*)
West Indies won by 10 wickets

279. England v West Indies

Fourth Test at The Oval – 12, 14, 15, 16 August 1950
WEST INDIES 503 (Worrell 138, Rae 109, Gomez 74,
Goddard 58*, Wright 5–141)
ENGLAND 344 (Hutton 202*, Compton 44, Goddard 4–25,
Valentine 4–121) and 103 (Valentine 6–39)
West Indies won by an innings and 56 runs

280. Australia v England

First Test at Brisbane – 1, 2 (no play), 4, 5 December 1950
AUSTRALIA 228 (Harvey 74, Lindwall 41, Bedser 4–45) and
32–7 dec. (Bailey 4–22)
ENGLAND 68–7 dec. (Johnston 5–35) and 122 (Hutton
62*, Iverson 4–43)
Australia won by 70 runs

281. Australia v England

Second Test at Melbourne – 22, 23, 26, 27 December 1950
AUSTRALIA 194 (Hassett 52, Harvey 42, Bedser 4–37,
Bailey 4–40) and 181 (Archer 46, Brown 4–26)
ENGLAND 197 (Brown 62, Evans 49, Iverson 4–37) and
150 (Hutton 40, Johnston 4–26)
Australia won by 28 runs

282. Australia v England

Third Test at Sydney – 5, 6, 8, 9 January 1951
ENGLAND 290 (Brown 79, Hutton 62, Simpson 49, Miller
4–37) and 123 (Iverson 6–27)
AUSTRALIA 426 (Miller 145*, Johnson 77, Hassett 70,
Archer 48, Bedser 4–107, Brown 4–153)
Australia won by an innings and 13 runs

283. Australia v England

Fourth Test at Adelaide – 2, 3, 5, 6, 7, 8 February 1951
AUSTRALIA 371 (Morris 206, Miller 44, Hassett 43, Harvey
43, Wright 4–99) and 403–8 dec. (Burke 101*, Miller
99, Harvey 68)
ENGLAND 272 (Hutton 156*) and 228 (Simpson 61, Hutton
45, Sheppard 41, Johnston 4–73)
Australia won by 274 runs

284. Australia v England

Fifth Test at Melbourne – 23, 24 (no play), 26, 27, 28
February 1951
AUSTRALIA 217 (Hassett 92, Morris 50, Bedser 5–46,
Brown 5–49) and 197 (Hole 63, Harvey 52, Hassett 48,
Bedser 5–59)
ENGLAND 320 (Simpson 156*, Hutton 79, Miller 4–76) and
95–2 (Hutton 60*)
England won by 8 wickets

285. New Zealand v England

First Test at Christchurch – 17, 19, 20, 21 March 1951
NEW ZEALAND 417–8 dec. (Sutcliffe 116, Wallace 66, Reid
50, Hadlee 50, Burtt 42) and 46–3
ENGLAND 550 (Bailey 134*, Simpson 81, Compton 79,
Brown 62, Washbrook 58, Wright 45, Moir 6–155)
Match drawn

286. New Zealand v England

Second Test at Wellington – 24, 26, 27, 28 March 1951
NEW ZEALAND 125 (Wright 5–48) and 189 (Scott 60,
Tattersall 6–44)
ENGLAND 227 (Hutton 57, Brown 47, Cresswell 3–18) and
91–4
England won by 6 wickets

287. England v South Africa

First Test at Trent Bridge – 7, 8, 9, 11, 12 June 1951
SOUTH AFRICA 483–9 dec. (Nourse 208, Waite 76,
Fullerton 54) and 121 (Bedser 6–37)
ENGLAND 419–9 dec. (Simpson 137, Compton 112, Hutton
63, Watson 57, McCarthy 4–104, Chubb 4–146) and
114 (A. M. B. Rowan 5–68, Mann 4–24)
South Africa won by 71 runs

288. England v South Africa

Second Test at Lord's – 21, 22, 23 June 1951
ENGLAND 311 (Compton 79, Watson 79, Ikin 51, Chubb
5–77, McCarthy 4–76) and 16–0
SOUTH AFRICA 115 (Tattersall 7–52) and 211 (Fullerton
60, Cheetham 54, Tattersall 5–49)
England won by 10 wickets

289. England v South Africa

Third Test at Old Trafford – 5, 6, 7, 9, 10 July 1951
SOUTH AFRICA 158 (van Rynveld 40, Bedser 7–58) and
191 (E. A. B. Rowan 57, Cheetham 46, Bedser 5–54)
ENGLAND 211 (Brown 42, Chubb 6–51) and 142–1
(Hutton 98*)
England won by 9 wickets

290. England v South Africa

Fourth Test at Headingley – 26, 27, 28, 30, 31 July 1951
SOUTH AFRICA 538 (E. A. B. Rowan 236, Mansell 90, van
Rynveld 83, McLean 67) and 87–0 (E. A. B. Rowan
60*)
ENGLAND 505 (May 138, Hutton 100, Bailey 95, Lowson
58, A. M. B. Rowan 5–174)
Match drawn

291. England v South Africa

Fifth Test at The Oval – 16, 17, 18 August 1951
SOUTH AFRICA 202 (E. A. B. Rowan 55, A. M. B. Rowan 41,
Laker 4–64) and 154 (E. A. B. Rowan 45, Laker 6–55)
ENGLAND 194 (Compton 73, Melle 4–9) and 164–6
(Brown 40)
England won by 4 wickets

292. India v England

First Test at Delhi – 2, 3, 4, 6, 7 November 1951
ENGLAND 203 (Robertson 50, Watkins 40, Shinde 6–91)
and 368–6 (Watkins 137*, Carr 76, Lowson 68, Mankad
4–58)
INDIA 418–6 dec. (Hazare 164*, Merchant 154)
Match drawn

293. India v England

Second Test at Bombay – 14, 15, 16, 18, 19 December
1951
INDIA 485–9 dec. (Hazare 155, Roy 140, Gopinath 50*,
Statham 4–96) and 208 (Gopinath 42, Mankad 41,
Watkins 3–20)
ENGLAND 456 (Graveney 175, Watkins 80, Spooner 46,
Robertson 44, Mankad 4–91) and 55–2
Match drawn

294. India v England
Third Test at Calcutta – 30, 31 December 1951, 1, 3, 4 January 1952
ENGLAND 342 (Spooner 71, Watkins 68, Poole 55, Mankad 4–89) and 252–5 dec. (Spooner 92, Poole 69*)
INDIA 344 (Phadkar 115, Mankad 59, Manjrekar 48, Roy 42, Ridgway 4–83, Tattersall 4–104) and 103–0 (Mankad 71*)
Match drawn

295. India v England
Fourth Test at Kanpur – 12, 13, 14 January 1952
INDIA 121 (Tattersall 6–48, Hilton 4–32) and 157 (Adhikari 60, Hilton 5–61)
ENGLAND 203 (Watkins 66, Ghulam Ahmed 5–70, Mankad 4–54) and 76–2 (Graveney 48*)
England won by 8 wickets

296. India v England
Fifth Test at Madras – 6, 8, 9, 10 February 1952
ENGLAND 266 (Robertson 77, Spooner 66, Carr 40, Mankad 8–55) and 183 (Robertson 56, Watkins 48, Mankad 4–53, Ghulam Ahmed 4–77)
INDIA 457–9 dec. (Umrigar 130*, Roy 111, Phadkar 61)
India won by an innings and 8 runs

297. England v India
First Test at Headingley – 5, 6, 7, 9 June 1952
INDIA 293 (Manjrekar 133, Hazare 89, Laker 4–39) and 165 (Phadkar 64, Hazare 56, Trueman 4–27, Jenkins 4–50)
ENGLAND 334 (Graveney 71, Evans 66, Watkins 48, Ghulam Ahmed 5–100) and 128–3 (Simpson 51)
England won by 7 wickets

298. England v India
Second Test at Lord's – 19, 20, 21, 23, 24 June 1952
INDIA 235 (Mankad 72, Hazare 69*, Trueman 4–72) and 378 (Mankad 184, Hazare 49, Ramchand 42, Laker 4–102, Trueman 4–110)
ENGLAND 537 (Hutton 150, Evans 104, May 74, Graveney 73, Simpson 53, Mankad 5–196) and 79–2
England won by 8 wickets

299. England v India
Third Test at Old Trafford – 17, 18, 19 July 1952
ENGLAND 347 (Hutton 104, Evans 71, May 69)
INDIA 58 (Trueman 8–31) and 82 (Bedser 5–27, Lock 4–36)
England won by an innings and 207 runs

300. England v India
Fourth Test at The Oval – 14, 15, 16 (no play), 18, 19 August 1952
ENGLAND 326–6 dec. (Sheppard 119, Hutton 86, Ikin 53)
INDIA 98 (Bedser 5–41, Trueman 5–48)
Match drawn

301. England v Australia
First Test at Trent Bridge – 11, 12, 13, 15 (no play), 16 June 1953
AUSTRALIA 249 (Hassett 115, Morris 67, Miller 55, Bedser 7–55) and 123 (Morris 60, Bedser 7–44)
ENGLAND 144 (Hutton 43, Lindwall 5–57) and 120–1 (Hutton 60*)
Match drawn

302. England v Australia
Second Test at Lord's – 25, 26, 27, 29, 30 June 1953
AUSTRALIA 346 (Hassett 104, Davidson 76, Harvey 59, Bedser 5–105, Wardle 4–77) and 368 (Miller 109, Morris 89, Lindwall 50, Hole 47, Brown 4–82)
ENGLAND 372 (Hutton 145, Graveney 78, Compton 57, Lindwall 5–66) and 282–7 (Watson 109, Bailey 71)
Match drawn

303. England v Australia
Third Test at Old Trafford – 9, 10, 11, 13 (no play), 14 July 1953
AUSTRALIA 318 (Harvey 122, Hole 66, de Courcy 41, Bedser 5–115) and 35–8 (Wardle 4–7)
ENGLAND 276 (Hutton 66, Compton 45, Evans 44*)
Match drawn

304. England v Australia
Fourth Test at Headingley – 23, 24, 25, 27, 28 July 1953
ENGLAND 167 (Graveney 55, Lindwall 5–54) and 275 (Edrich 64, Compton 61, Laker 48, Miller 4–63)
AUSTRALIA 266 (Harvey 71, Hole 53, Bedser 6–95) and 147–4
Match drawn

305. England v Australia
Fifth Test at The Oval – 15, 17, 18, 19 August 1953
AUSTRALIA 275 (Lindwall 62, Hassett 53, Trueman 4–86) and 162 (Archer 49, Lock 5–45, Laker 4–75)
ENGLAND 306 (Hutton 82, Bailey 64, Lindwall 4–70) and 132–2 (Edrich 55*)
England won by 8 wickets

306. West Indies v England
First Test at Kingston, Jamaica – 15, 16, 18, 19, 20, 21 January 1954
WEST INDIES 417 (Holt 94, Walcott 65, J. B. Stollmeyer 60, Weekes 55, McWatt 54, Gomez 47*, Statham 4–90) and 209–6 dec. (Weekes 90*)
ENGLAND 170 (Ramadhin 4–65) and 316 (Watson 116, May 69, Hutton 56, Kentish 5–49)
West Indies won by 140 runs

307. West Indies v England
Second Test at Bridgetown, Barbados – 6, 8, 9, 10, 11, 12 February 1954
WEST INDIES 383 (Walcott 220, Atkinson 53, Laker 4–81) and 292–2 dec. (Holt 166, Worrell 76*)
ENGLAND 181 (Hutton 72, Ramadhin 4–50) and 313 (Compton 93, Hutton 77, Graveney 64*, May 62)
West Indies won by 181 runs

308. West Indies v England
Third Test at Georgetown, British Guiana – 24, 25, 26, 27 February, 1, 2 March 1954
ENGLAND 435 (Hutton 169, Compton 64, Bailey 49, Ramadhin 6–113) and 75–1
WEST INDIES 251 (Weekes 94, McWatt 54, Holt 48*, Statham 4–64) and 256 (Holt 64, J. B. Stollmeyer 44)
England won by 9 wickets

309. West Indies v England
Fourth Test at Port-of-Spain, Trinidad – 17, 18, 19, 20, 22, 23 March 1954
WEST INDIES 681–8 dec. (Weekes 206, Worrell 167, Walcott 124, Atkinson 74, J. B. Stollmeyer 41, Holt 40) and 212–4 dec. (Worrell 56, Atkinson 53*, Walcott 51*, Ferguson 44)
ENGLAND 537 (May 135, Compton 133, Graveney 92, Bailey 46, Hutton 44) and 98–3
Match drawn

310. West Indies v England
Fifth Test at Kingston, Jamaica – 30, 31 March, 1, 2, 3 April 1954
WEST INDIES 139 (Walcott 50, Bailey 7–34) and 346 (Walcott 116, J. B. Stollmeyer 64, Atkinson 40, Laker 4–71)
ENGLAND 414 (Hutton 205, Wardle 66, Sobers 4–75) and 72–1 (May 40*)
England won by 9 wickets

311. England v Pakistan
First Test at Lord's – 10 (no play), 11 (no play), 12 (no play), 14, 15 June 1954
PAKISTAN 87 (Statham 4–18, Wardle 4–33) and 121–3 (Waqar Hasan 53)
ENGLAND 117–9 dec. (Simpson 40, Khan Mohammad 5–61, Fazal Mahmood 4–54)
Match drawn

312. England v Pakistan
Second Test at Trent Bridge – 1, 2, 3, 5 July 1954
PAKISTAN 157 (Appleyard 5–51) and 272 (Maqsood Ahmed 69, Hanif Mohammad 51)
ENGLAND 558–6 dec. (Compton 278, Simpson 101, Graveney 84)
England won by an innings and 129 runs

313. England v Pakistan
Third Test at Old Trafford – 22, 23 (no play), 24, 26 (no play), 27 July 1954
ENGLAND 359–8 dec. (Compton 93, Graveney 65, Wardle 54, Bailey 42, Fazal Mahmood 4–107)
PAKISTAN 90 (Wardle 4–19) and 25–4 (Bedser 3–9)
Match drawn

314. England v Pakistan
Fourth Test at The Oval – 12, 13, 14, 16, 17 August 1954
PAKISTAN 133 (Tyson 4–35) and 164 (Wazir Mohammad 42*, Wardle 7–56)
ENGLAND 130 (Compton 53, Fazal Mahmood 6–53, Mahmood Hussain 4–58) and 143 (May 53, Fazal Mahmood 6–46)
Pakistan won by 24 runs

315. Australia v England
First Test at Brisbane – 26, 27, 29, 30 November, 1 December 1954
AUSTRALIA 601–8 dec. (Harvey 162, Morris 153, Lindwall 64*, Hole 57, Miller 49)
ENGLAND 190 (Bailey 88, Cowdrey 40) and 257 (Edrich 88, May 44)
Australia won by an innings and 154 runs

316. Australia v England
Second Test at Sydney – 17, 18, 20, 21, 22 December 1954
ENGLAND 154 and 296 (May 104, Cowdrey 54)
AUSTRALIA 228 (Archer 49, Burke 44, Tyson 4–45, Bailey 4–59) and 184 (Harvey 92*, Tyson 6–85)
England won by 38 runs

317. Australia v England
Third Test at Melbourne – 31 December 1954, 1, 3, 4, 5 January 1955
ENGLAND 191 (Cowdrey 102, Archer 4–33) and 279 (May 91, Hutton 42, Johnston 5–85)
AUSTRALIA 231 (Maddocks 47, Statham 5–60) and 111 (Tyson 7–27)
England won by 128 runs

318. Australia v England
Fourth Test at Adelaide – 28, 29, 31 January, 1, 2 February 1955
AUSTRALIA 323 (Maddocks 69, McDonald 48, Miller 44, Johnson 41) and 111
ENGLAND 341 (Hutton 80, Cowdrey 79, Compton 44, Benaud 4–120) and 97–5
England won by 5 wickets

319. Australia v England
Fifth Test at Sydney – 25 (no play), 26 (no play), 28 (no play) February, 1, 2, 3 March 1955
ENGLAND 371–7 dec. (Graveney 111, Compton 84, May 79, Bailey 72)
AUSTRALIA 221 (McDonald 72, Wardle 5–79) and 118–6
Match drawn

320. New Zealand v England
First Test at Dunedin – 11, 12, 14 (no play), 15 (no play), 16 March 1955
NEW ZEALAND 125 (Sutcliffe 74, Statham 4–24) and 132 (Tyson 4–16)
ENGLAND 209–8 dec. (Cowdrey 42, Graveney 41, Reid 4–36) and 49–2
England won by 8 wickets

321. New Zealand v England
Second Test at Auckland – 25, 26, 28 March 1955
NEW ZEALAND 200 (Reid 73, Sutcliffe 49, Statham 4–28) and 26 (Appleyard 4–7)
ENGLAND 246 (Hutton 53, May 48, Moir 5–62)
England won by an innings and 20 runs

322. England v South Africa
First Test at Trent Bridge – 9, 10, 11, 13 June 1955
ENGLAND 334 (Kenyon 87, May 83, Bailey 49, Graveney 42)
SOUTH AFRICA 181 (McGlew 68, Cheetham 54, Wardle 4–24) and 148 (McGlew 51, Tyson 6–28)
England won by an innings and 5 runs

323. England v South Africa
Second Test at Lord's – 23, 24, 25, 27 June 1955
ENGLAND 133 (Heine 5–60, Goddard 4–59) and 353 (May 112, Compton 69, Graveney 60, Tayfield 5–80)
SOUTH AFRICA 304 (McLean 142, Keith 57, Endean 48, Wardle 4–65) and 111 (Statham 7–39)
England won by 71 runs

324. England v South Africa
Third Test at Old Trafford – 7, 8, 9, 11, 12 July 1955
ENGLAND 284 (Compton 158, Bailey 44) and 381 (May 117, Cowdrey 50, Heine 5–86)
SOUTH AFRICA 521–8 dec. (Waite 113, Winslow 108, McGlew 104*, Goddard 62) and 145–7 (McLean 50, McGlew 48)
South Africa won by 3 wickets

325. England v South Africa
Fourth Test at Headingley – 21, 22, 23, 24, 25, 26 July 1955
SOUTH AFRICA 171 (Endean 41, McLean 41, Loader 4–52)
and 500 (McGlew 133, Endean 116*, Goddard 74,
Keith 73, Wardle 4–100)
ENGLAND 191 (Compton 61, May 47, Heine 4–70, Tayfield
4–70) and 256 (May 97, Insole 47, Goddard 5–69,
Tayfield 5–94)
South Africa won by 224 runs

326. England v South Africa
Fifth Test at The Oval – 13, 15, 16, 17 August 1955
ENGLAND 151 (Goddard 5–31) and 204 (May 89*,
Graveney 42, Tayfield 5–60)
SOUTH AFRICA 112 (Lock 4–39) and 151 (Waite 60, Laker
5–56, Lock 4–62)
England won by 92 runs

327. England v Australia
First Test at Trent Bridge – 7, 8 (no play), 9, 11, 12 June 1956
ENGLAND 217–8 dec. (Richardson 81, May 73, Miller
4–69) and 188–3 dec. (Cowdrey 81, Richardson 73)
AUSTRALIA 148 (Harvey 64, Laker 4–58) and 120–3 (Burke
58*)
Match drawn

328. England v Australia
Second Test at Lord's – 21, 22, 23, 25, 26 June 1956
AUSTRALIA 285 (McDonald 78, Burke 65) and 257 (Benaud
97, Trueman 5–90, Bailey 4–64)
ENGLAND 171 (May 63, Miller 5–72) and 186 (May 53,
Miller 5–80, Archer 4–71)
Australia won by 185 runs

329. England v Australia
Third Test at Headingley – 12, 13, 14 (no play), 16, 17 July
1956
ENGLAND 325 (May 101, Washbrook 98, Evans 40)
AUSTRALIA 143 (Burke 41, Miller 41, Laker 5–58, Lock
4–41) and 140 (Harvey 69, Laker 6–55)
England won by an innings and 42 runs

330. England v Australia
Fourth Test at Old Trafford – 26, 27, 28, 30, 31 July 1956
ENGLAND 459 (Sheppard 113, Richardson 104, Cowdrey
80, Evans 47, May 43, Johnson 4–151)
AUSTRALIA 84 (Laker 9–37) and 205 (McDonald 89, Laker
10–53)
England won by an innings and 170 runs

331. England v Australia
Fifth Test at The Oval – 23, 24, 25, 27 (no play), 28 August
1956
ENGLAND 247 (Compton 94, May 83*, Archer 5–53, Miller
4–91) and 182–3 dec. (Sheppard 62)
AUSTRALIA 202 (Miller 61, Laker 4–80) and 27–5
Match drawn

332. South Africa v England
First Test at Johannesburg – 24, 26, 27, 28, 29 December
1956
ENGLAND 268 (Richardson 117, Cowdrey 59, Adcock
4–36) and 150
SOUTH AFRICA 215 (Goddard 49, Keith 42) and 72 (Bailey
5–20)
England won by 131 runs

333. South Africa v England
Second Test at Cape Town – 1, 2, 3, 4, 5 January 1957
ENGLAND 369 (Cowdrey 101, Evans 62, Compton 58,
Richardson 45, Tayfield 5–130) and 220–6 dec.
(Compton 64, Cowdrey 61, Richardson 44)
SOUTH AFRICA 205 (Waite 49, McLean 42, Wardle 5–53)
and 72 (Wardle 7–36)
England won by 312 runs

334. South Africa v England
Third Test at Durban – 25, 26, 28, 29, 30 January 1957
ENGLAND 218 (Bailey 80, Richardson 68, Adcock 4–39)
and 254 (Insole 110*, Tayfield 8–69)
SOUTH AFRICA 283 (McLean 100, Goddard 69, Wardle
5–61) and 142–6 (Funston 44)
Match drawn

335. South Africa v England
Fourth Test at Johannesburg – 15, 16, 18, 19, 20 February
1957
SOUTH AFRICA 340 (McLean 93, Goddard 67, Waite 61)
and 142 (Goddard 49)
ENGLAND 251 (May 61, Insole 47, Compton 42, Tayfield
4–79) and 214 (Insole 68, Cowdrey 55, Tayfield
9–113)
South Africa won by 17 runs

336. South Africa v England
Fifth Test at Port Elizabeth – 1, 2, 4, 5 March 1957
SOUTH AFRICA 164 (Endean 70) and 134 (Tyson 6–40)
ENGLAND 110 (Bailey 41, Adcock 4–20, Heine 4–22) and
130 (Tayfield 6–78)
South Africa won by 58 runs

337. England v West Indies
First Test at Edgbaston – 30, 31 May, 1, 3, 4 June 1957
ENGLAND 186 (Richardson 47, Ramadhin 7–49) and
583–4 dec. (May 285*, Cowdrey 154, Close 42)
WEST INDIES 474 (Smith 161, Walcott 90, Worrell 81,
Sobers 53, Kanhai 42, Laker 4–119) and 72–7
Match drawn

338. England v West Indies
Second Test at Lord's – 20, 21, 22 June 1957
WEST INDIES 127 (Bailey 7–44) and 261 (Weekes 90,
Sobers 66, Bailey 4–54)
ENGLAND 424 (Cowdrey 152, Evans 82, Richardson 76,
Gilchrist 4–115)
England won by an innings and 36 runs

339. England v West Indies
Third Test at Trent Bridge – 4, 5, 6, 8, 9 July 1957
ENGLAND 619–6 dec. (Graveney 258, Richardson 126, May
104, Cowdrey 55) and 64–1
WEST INDIES 372 (Worrell 191*, Sobers 47, Kanhai 42,
Trueman 5–63) and 367 (Smith 168, Goddard 61,
Atkinson 46, Statham 5–118, Trueman 4–80)
Match drawn

340. England v West Indies
Fourth Test at Headingley – 25, 26, 27 July 1957
WEST INDIES 142 (Kanhai 47, Loader 6–36) and 132
ENGLAND 279 (May 69, Cowdrey 68, Sheppard 68,
Worrell 7–70)
England won by an innings and 5 runs

341. England v West Indies
Fifth Test at The Oval – 22, 23, 24 August 1957
ENGLAND 412 (Graveney 164, Richardson 107, Evans 40, Sheppard 40, Ramadhin 4–107)
WEST INDIES 89 (Lock 5–28) and 86 (Sobers 42, Lock 6–20)
England won by an innings and 237 runs

342. England v New Zealand
First Test at Edgbaston – 5, 6, 7, 9 June 1958
ENGLAND 221 (May 84, Cowdrey 81, MacGibbon 5–64, Alabaster 4–46) and 215–6 dec. (Richardson 100, Cowdrey 70)
NEW ZEALAND 94 (Trueman 5–31) and 137
England won by 205 runs

343. England v New Zealand
Second Test at Lord's – 19, 20, 21 June 1958
ENGLAND 269 (Cowdrey 65, M. J. K. Smith 47, Hayes 4–36, MacGibbon 4–86)
NEW ZEALAND 47 (Lock 5–17, Laker 4–13) and 74 (Lock 4–12)
England won by an innings and 148 runs

344. England v New Zealand
Third Test at Headingley – 3 (no play), 4 (no play), 5, 7, 8 July 1958
NEW ZEALAND 67 (Laker 5–17, Lock 4–14) and 129 (Lock 7–51)
ENGLAND 267–2 dec. (May 113*, Milton 104*)
England won by an innings and 71 runs

345. England v New Zealand
Fourth Test at Old Trafford – 24, 25, 26, 28, 29 July 1958
NEW ZEALAND 267 (MacGibbon 66, Sparling 50, Petrie 45 ret. hurt, Statham 4–71) and 85 (Lock 7–35)
ENGLAND 365–9 dec. (May 101, Richardson 74, Watson 66, Dexter 52)
England won by an innings and 13 runs

346. England v New Zealand
Fifth Test at The Oval – 21, 22, 23 (no play), 25 (no play), 26 August 1958
NEW ZEALAND 161 (Moir 41*, Lock 2–19) and 91–3
ENGLAND 219–9 dec. (Trueman 39*, MacGibbon 4–65)
Match drawn

347. Australia v England
First Test at Brisbane – 5, 6, 8, 9, 10 December 1958
ENGLAND 134 and 198 (Bailey 68, Benaud 4–66)
AUSTRALIA 186 (McDonald 42, Loader 4–56) and 147–2 (O'Neill 71*)
Australia won by 8 wickets

348. Australia v England
Second Test at Melbourne – 31 December 1958, 1, 2, 3, 5 January 1959
ENGLAND 259 (May 113, Bailey 48, Cowdrey 44, Davidson 6–64) and 87 (Meckiff 6–38)
AUSTRALIA 308 (Harvey 167, McDonald 47, Statham 7–57) and 42–2
Australia won by 8 wickets

349. Australia v England
Third Test at Sydney – 9, 10, 12, 13, 14, 15 January 1959
ENGLAND 219 (May 42, Swetman 41, Benaud 5–83) and 287–7 dec. (Cowdrey 100*, May 92, Benaud 4–94)

AUSTRALIA 357 (O'Neill 77, Davidson 71, Mackay 57, Favell 54, Laker 5–107, Lock 4–130) and 54–2
Match drawn

350. Australia v England
Fourth Test at Adelaide – 30, 31 January, 2, 3, 4, 5 February 1959
AUSTRALIA 476 (McDonald 170, Burke 66, O'Neill 56, Benaud 46, Davidson 43, Harvey 41, Trueman 4–90) and 36–0
ENGLAND 240 (Cowdrey 84, Graveney 41, Benaud 5–91) and 270 (May 59, Graveney 53*, Richardson 43, Watson 40, Benaud 4–82)
Australia won by 10 wickets

351. Australia v England
Fifth Test at Melbourne – 13, 14, 16, 17, 18 February 1959
ENGLAND 205 (Richardson 68, Mortimore 44*, Benaud 4–43) and 214 (Graveney 54, Cowdrey 46)
AUSTRALIA 351 (McDonald 133, Grout 74, Benaud 64, Trueman 4–92, Laker 4–93) and 69–1 (McDonald 51*)
Australia won by 9 wickets

352. New Zealand v England
First Test at Christchurch – 27, 28, February, 2 March 1959
ENGLAND 374 (Dexter 141, May 71, Graveney 42)
NEW ZEALAND 142 (Reid 40, Lock 5–31) and 133 (Guy 56, Lock 6–53)
England won by an innings and 99 runs

353. New Zealand v England
Second Test at Auckland – 14, 16, 17 (no play), 18 March 1959
NEW ZEALAND 181 (Sutcliffe 61)
ENGLAND 311–7 (May 124*, Richardson 67, Graveney 46)
Match drawn

354. England v India
First Test at Trent Bridge – 4, 5, 6, 8 June 1959
ENGLAND 422 (May 106, Evans 73, Horton 58, Barrington 56, Gupte 4–102)
INDIA 206 (Roy 54, Trueman 4–45) and 157 (Roy 49, Manjrekar 44, Statham 5–31)
England won by an innings and 59 runs

355. England v India
Second Test at Lord's – 18, 19, 20 June 1959
INDIA 168 (Contractor 81, Ghorpade 41, Greenhough 5–35) and 165 (Manjrekar 61, Kripal Singh 41)
ENGLAND 226 (Barrington 80, Desai 5–89) and 108–2 (Cowdrey 63*)
England won by 8 wickets

356. England v India
Third Test at Headingley – 2, 3, 4 July 1959
INDIA 161 (Rhodes 4–50) and 149 (Borde 41, Close 4–35)
ENGLAND 483–8 dec. (Cowdrey 160, Barrington 80, Parkhouse 78, Pullar 75, Gupte 4–111)
England won by an innings and 173 runs

357. England v India
Fourth Test at Old Trafford – 23, 24, 25, 27, 28 July 1959
ENGLAND 490 (Pullar 131, M. J. K. Smith 100, Barrington
87, Cowdrey 67, Surendranath 5–115) and 265–8
dec. (Parkhouse 49, Illingworth 47*, Barrington 46,
Dexter 45, Gupte 4–76)
INDIA 208 (Borde 75) and 376 (Umrigar 118, Baig 112,
Contractor 56)
England won by 171 runs

358. England v India
Fifth Test at The Oval – 20, 21, 22, 24 August 1959
INDIA 140 (Trueman 4–24) and 194 (Nadkarni 76)
ENGLAND 361 (M. J. K. Smith 98, Subba Row 94,
Swetman 65, Illingworth 50, Surendranath 5–75)
England won by an innings and 27 runs

TEST MATCHES IN THE SIXTIES: 1960–9

The 1959–60 series in the Caribbean was decided by a dramatic second Test in Trinidad. Ken Barrington (121) and Mike Smith (108) made hundreds in England's first innings of 382 and on the third day the West Indian batting broke down against the pace of Trueman and Statham. The match had been tensely fought with much hostile fast bowling by both sides. The crowd, for the varying reasons that cause a West Indian crowd to riot, stopped the match with a storm of bottle-throwing and an invasion of the playing area. The last three days of the match were peaceful, however, and England went on to win by 256 runs. They held their lead without much difficulty in the three remaining matches.

The South African tour of England in 1960 was one of the most disappointing ever undertaken by the Springboks. The summer was damp and miserable and it gave the tourists no chance to settle in. The tour was further marred by the inclusion of Geoff Griffin, who was frequently no-balled for throwing and did not bowl in the second-half of the tour. England won the first three Tests and, though the Springboks led by 264 runs in the fifth Test at The Oval, a second-innings opening stand of 290 between Geoff Pullar (175) and Colin Cowdrey (155) prevented them from coming anywhere near victory.

The 1961 Ashes series came just a few months after the famous rubber between Australia and the West Indies, featuring the first-ever tied Test at the Gabba. Under the captaincy of Richie Benaud, Australian cricket was on a high: the Ashes won back in 1958–9 and now, on English soil, the success continued with a 2–1 victory. Ashes cricket returned to Edgbaston for the first time in more than fifty years. Led by 321 on the first innings, England saved the game through Ted Dexter (180) and Ramon Subba Row (112) but they lost the Lord's Test by five wickets through a faulty appreciation of the wicket. England played two spinners, whereas Australia after losing Benaud to injury, opted to replace him with an extra pace bowler. Bill Lawry, in only his second Test, caught the eye with 130 and, though Trueman and Statham reduced Australia to 19–4 in chasing just 69 for victory, Burge saw his side home. Two extraordinary breakthroughs by Trueman on an unpredictable Headingley wicket settled the third Test. After being 183–2, the Yorkshire paceman took 5–16 in 6 overs as the tourists tumbled to 208–9. In their second innings, Trueman proceeded to take 5 wickets without conceding a run and 6–4 in 45 balls all told. Australia's last 8 wickets fell in fifty minutes and England made the necessary runs that evening. In the fourth Test at Old Trafford, fine bowling by Statham (5–33) reduced Australia to 190 all out. With the wicket playing a little easier, England made 367 and Australia were 334–9, just 157 ahead, when Alan Davidson suddenly hit Allen for 20 in one over as 98 were added for the final wicket. England needed 256 to win at a run a minute and, though Ted Dexter hit 76 in eighty-four minutes, Australia won by 54 runs with just over a quarter of an hour to spare. Australia did much to confirm their superiority at The Oval by scoring 494 in the best batting of the series, but England held on for a draw.

England's first Test victory against Pakistan at Lahore by 5 wickets, with a little over half a hour to spare, proved decisive as Pakistan collapsed from 315–3 to 387–9. A fine innings of 139 from Ken Barrington kept England in striking distance. Before the second and third Tests were played in Dacca and Karachi, England went to India and played five Tests there.

India won a Test series against England for the first time, their success being well deserved. At Bombay, England scored 500–8 with Barrington making an unbeaten 151, but India saved the game comfortably. England were made to follow on against India for the first time at Kanpur but, with Pullar (119), Barrington (172) and Ted Dexter (126 not out) showing a return to form, they made 497–5 without inviting the hosts to bat again. After rain had washed out the last two days at New Delhi, the two teams met at Calcutta, where India won by 187 runs prior to the final Test at Madras, which again the home side won, this time by 128 runs to take the series by two Tests.

Back in Pakistan, Hanif Mohammad scored a century in each innings of a dull draw at Dacca, while Ted Dexter's double century and Peter Parfitt's 111 gave Pakistan no hope of squaring the series.

Hopes that the Pakistanis would do well in England in 1962 were not fulfilled and only the weather saved them from defeat in all five Tests. Bowling was the tourists' main weakness and only once did they dismiss England for fewer than 400. Both Parfitt and Graveney enjoyed averages of over 100. The Pakistani side was a young, inexperienced touring side and it found the English conditions vastly different from those at home. Pakistan had only recently been changing from matting wickets to lifeless turf that allowed little movement off the pitch. Consequently, they were at a complete loss against the bowling of Trueman and Statham and suffered four defeats in the five-match series.

In touring Australia for the Ashes series of 1962–3, England ruined their chances by dropping too many catches and, by drawing the series, the Australians retained the Ashes. At Brisbane, after Australia had scored 404, fine defensive innings by Barrington and Parfitt enabled England to score 389. England could make little headway when Australia batted a second time and were left to make 378 for victory. Though Dexter made 99, England ended the game by staving off defeat. In the second Test at Melbourne, England gained a narrow lead on the first innings, thanks to a fine stand of 175 by Cowdrey (113) and Dexter (93). Brian Booth hit his second century of the series to set England a sizeable target for victory. The final day saw Sheppard, who had failed to score in the first innings and dropped two catches, steer England to a 7-wicket victory. At Sydney, England were bowled out for 279 and after Fred Titmus took 4–5 in the space of 58 balls, Australia's lead was only 40 runs. However, Alan Davidson destroyed England in their second innings and Australia won by 8 wickets. At Adelaide, more dropped catches helped Australia to 393 but England held on for a draw, thanks to another fine innings of 132 not out by Ken Barrington. With all to play for in the final Test, neither side was prepared to take chances and for the first time in a five-match Ashes series in Australia, the rubber had ended with an even scoreline.

England then visited New Zealand and won all three Tests. In the first, at Auckland, Ken Barrington (126), Peter Parfitt (131) and Barry Knight (125) all made hundreds as England went on to win by an innings and 215 runs. The second Test, at Wellington, was also won by an innings with Colin Cowdrey making an unbeaten 128, while a century by New Zealand's John Reid kept the margin to 7 wickets in the third Test at Christchurch.

Though West Indies' strength as a Test-playing nation had been growing, no one expected the scintillating victory that was won. Worrell won the toss on a deteriorating Old Trafford pitch and West Indies, making England follow on, spun them out a second time and won by 10 wickets. At Lord's, after an even first innings, England were denied victory thanks to Basil Butcher's 133, the rain, an injury to Colin Cowdrey and the fast-bowling marathon of Wes Hall and Charlie Griffith, which led to one of the most pulsating finishes in Test cricket. In the end, Colin Cowdrey, with broken arm, had to return to partner the last man for the last two balls when England were only 6 runs short of victory. England levelled the series by winning the third Test at Edgbaston, where Fred Trueman took 7–44 as West Indies were bowled out for 91 in their second innings. West Indies then won the last two Tests at Headingley and The Oval with an exhibition that warmed the heart of a public already stimulated by the excitement of the Lord's finish.

Though five draws in a five-Test series was not a novel experience for India, who had achieved it twice before against Pakistan, it was for England when they toured the subcontinent in 1963–4. Not that it affected attendances, because the grounds were packed to capacity for the run-glut encouraged by the easy pitches. England suffered heavily from injury and sickness and both Cowdrey and Parfitt were flown out to strengthen the side. Cowdrey's arrival brought England their first century in the series when he scored 107 in the third Test at Calcutta, though Kunderam and Manjrekar had opened India's century account in the first Test at madras. The Kent batsman also made 151 at New Delhi but Hanumant Singh and Nawab of Pataudi, who made 203 not out, gave India a century advantage of six to two as Jaisimha had scored 129 at Calcutta. With Barry Knight (127) and Parfitt (121) to the fore, England made 59–8 at Kanpur and Fred Titmus took 6–73 to make India follow on, but an unbeaten 122 from Nadkarni ensured the stalemate would not be broken.

England fancied their chances of regaining the Ashes in 1964 but unfortunately rain affected the series with four matches being drawn. Australia's victory at Headingley in the third Test was sufficient to win the series. Half the playing time was lost in the first Test at Trent Bridge, although England still had a chance of victory when rain returned on the final day. The first two days of the Lord's Test were also lost to rain, and though Australia recovered from 88–6 to 176 all out, John Edrich's 120 gave England a lead of 70. Australia were batting more solidly in reply when the game was washed out. At Headingley, England had made 268 and Australia were 187–7 when Dexter took the new ball. Peter Burge then proceeded to make 160 in an innings that won the series, and Australia led by 121 runs. England fared little better in their second innings and Australia won by 7 wickets. At Old Trafford, with Bobby Simpson making 311, Australia declared at 656–8. Dexter (174) and Barrington (256) eclipsed the great stand of Lawry and Simpson and lifted England to within 45 of the mammoth total, but the inevitable draw meant that the Ashes stayed with Australia. At The Oval, England batted first in unfavourable conditions and were led on first innings by 197. But Geoff Boycott (113) and Colin Cowdrey (93 not out) had more than restored the balance when rain washed out the final day.

South Africa were the better side when England toured there in 1964–5 but the tourists won the first Test at Durban, where the pitch deteriorated after hundreds by Barrington (148) and Jim Parks (108) and the England spinners Titmus and Allen bowled the Springboks out twice.

In the second Test, at Johannesburg, England were in sight of what would have been a dashing and worthy win at the start of the last day, for Bob Barber (97) and Ted Dexter (172) had played superbly at the start. But one of the many fine innings by Colin Bland, who made an unbeaten 144, thwarted them. Thereafter, increasingly hampered by injuries, England hung on to their lead against strengthening opposition.

Throughout his country's lean years, New Zealand's John Reid was often fighting a lone battle supported by players of considerably less ability and experience than himself. When he took the 1965 side to England for the first half-season tour, the weakness in batting and spin remained, and wet weather and bad pitches did not help. England, captained by Mike Smith, made big scores, and after wins at Edgbaston and Lord's this culminated in the 546–4 declared at Headingley. John Edrich made 310 not out and Ken Barrington 163 as the Surrey pair put on 369 for the second wicket in a game England won by an innings and 187 runs.

In the second half of the summer of 1965, England played South Africa in what was the last series between the two countries before politics intruded. It produced three thrilling matches: two draws with close finishes and one easy win for the Springboks. In the first Test at Lord's England's eighth-wicket pair were defending grimly when the end came. In the second, South Africa were always in control after Graeme Pollock had played an incredible innings of 125 in damp English conditions. The last Test at The Oval was drawn in an atmosphere of frustration. Chasing 399 to win, England were 308–4 and needed another 91 in an hour and a quarter when a thunderstorm finished the match.

The weather had prevented a tremendous climax just as politicians and agitators were to prevent the playing of some almost certainly tremendous cricket in the series of 1968–9 and 1970 that never took place.

England's visit to Australia in 1965–6 saw them take the lead in the series in the third Test, at Sydney, but their hopes of regaining the Ashes were snuffed out by Simpson and Lawry in the following match. At Brisbane rain interruptions left the home side, after they had declared at 443–6, just eleven hours to bowl England out twice, and this they failed to do. The second Test, at Melbourne, was also drawn, with Edrich and Cowdrey both making centuries. England's best match was at Sydney, where Boycott and Bob Barber, who made 185, put on 234 for the first wicket and Edrich made 103. On a wicket known to favour spin, Australia lost by an innings. At Adelaide, England were bowled out for 241 before Simpson (225) and Lawry (119) emulated the opening stand of Boycott and Barber at Sydney and actually put Australia in front. Despite a fighting 102 from Barrington, England were a beaten side. Even though the Surrey batsman made 115 and England totalled 485, the attack was simply not good enough to force a result.

Although the run of defeats ended in the series in New Zealand, the Kiwis were within a fraction of defeat in the first two Tests and their failings, as well as one cause of them, were painfully obvious. The low bounce of pitches prepared on rugby grounds discouraged stroke-play and this, plus New Zealand's many years of struggle against England, produced a negative approach to the game. Such negativity robbed New Zealand of the elusive first victory when they had England in difficulties in the final Test at Auckland. With a first-innings lead of 74, they took over six hours to make 129 in their second and then they bowled defensively in the last innings.

When West Indies toured England in 1966, their team, under the leadership of Garry Sobers, showed signs of decline and inevitably had a difficult job matching the feats of 1963. That it triumphed was due to Sobers himself, who scored 722 runs and took 20 wickets to beat an England side captained by Mike Smith at the start, Colin Cowdrey in the middle and Brian Close at the end. Sobers was fortunate in winning the toss at Old Trafford but, on a pitch that took spin increasingly, West Indies won by an innings and 40 runs. At Lord's West Indies were within sight of defeat on the fourth day but an unbeaten sixth-wicket stand of 274 between cousins Sobers and David Holford saved them. The West Indies won the next two Tests and the series was settled when England, against relatively light-hearted opposition, won by an innings and 34 runs at The Oval, with Tom Graveney making 165.

Upset by terrible weather and injuries, India gave a dismal display in the first half of a shared tour with Pakistan. Geoff Boycott's unbeaten 246 in the first Test at Headingley helped England to a 6-wicket win, but India, following on, did distinguish themselves in their second innings by making 510 when Pataudi's 148 proved to be their only Test century. Brian Close's men found less resistance in the other two Tests, winning by an innings and 124 runs at Lord's, where Graveney made 151, and by 132 runs at Edgbaston.

Solid batting from Hanif Mohammad (187 not out) and Asif Iqbal helped Pakistan to open the series at Lord's with a draw. Barrington scored 148 in England's first innings and rain interfered with the second Test, at Trent Bridge, where England won by 10 wickets after Barrington had made a seven-hour unbeaten 109. The conditions were tailor-made for Derek Underwood when India batted a second time and he took 5–52 as they were dismissed for 114. At The Oval, Barrington hit his third century in three games as Pakistan batted again 224 in arrears. At 65–8 they looked doomed to an innings defeat. Then Asif came to the wicket and with Intikhab Alam increased the Test record for the ninth wicket to 190. Unprecedented scenes greeted his century as hundreds of Pakistanis raced onto the field and hoisted him shoulder high until the police intervened. He continued the entertainment until he was stumped by Alan Knott for 146. Fittingly, Ken Barrington hit the winning runs as England won by 8 wickets with a day to spare.

Though there had been signs of cracks in the West Indies team in 1966, few expected England to beat them in their own backyard in 1967–8, but under the captaincy of Colin Cowdrey, who batted superbly himself, England did it by wining the fourth Test. The tourists came close to winning the first Test, at Port-of-Spain, and also the second, at Kingston, where John Snow, who didn't play in the first Test, took 7–49 in West Indies' first innings. The game here was interrupted by a riot. When England did win, it was through a remarkable declaration by Sobers, who set England to make 215 in 165 minutes. Cowdrey followed up his first innings 148 with 71, Boycott acted as the anchorman with 80 not out and, with three minutes to spare, England won by 7 wickets. They were perilously near losing the last Test in Georgetown, but a four-hour stand between Cowdrey and Alan Knott held West Indies up and England's last pair earned the vital draw.

In 1968, the youngest-ever Australian side to visit England used the conditions better than the home side. At Old Trafford, Australia had made 357 when England, on 86–0, collapsed to 165 all out, with only the last pair saving the follow-on. Australia's lead was over 400 when England began their fourth innings with over nine hours remaining. Although Basil D'Oliveira averted a debacle, Australia still won by 159 runs. At Lord's, Cowdrey declared England's first innings at 351–7 before Snow, Brown and Knight ripped through the Australian batting to bowl them out for 78. Beginning the last day needing 273 to avoid an innings defeat, they were saved by the rain. England dominated the third Test at Edgbaston but were frustrated by the weather and, in the fourth Test at Headingley, dropped catches and further periods of rain allowed Australia to draw and so retain the Ashes. Few more dramatic denouements have occurred on a cricket field than the final scenes at The Oval in the last Test. After England had made 494, with Edrich 164 and D'Oliveira 158 the major run-getters, Australia were dismissed for 324. England then went for quick runs and Australia were a beaten side when a storm flooded the playing area. With the crowd willingly helping, the deluge was mopped up just in time and, with Underwood taking 7–50, England achieved victory with just six minutes to spare.

Internal political riots ruined the 1968–9 series in Pakistan and finally caused the abandonment of the third Test. The unrest was apparent from the first Test at Lahore, in which Cowdrey scored 100, while D'Oliveira's unbeaten 114 was the outstanding innings of a dull second Test at Dacca. At Karachi, Colin Milburn enlivened the proceedings with a quick-fire 139, Graveney scored 105 and Alan Knott was within four runs of a maiden Test century, when rioting stopped play.

A much-weakened and less experienced West Indies side were beaten in a short half-season series in 1969. This time, England, captained by Ray Illingworth, won the toss and the match at Old Trafford, where Boycott's 128 went a long way in helping them total 413 in the first innings. An even second Test at Lord's was drawn, where Yorkshire players Illingworth (113) and Hampshire (107) both made centuries. England clinched the rubber with an exciting win by 30 runs in the third Test at Headingley. They batted slowly in a low-scoring match but the pitch eased on the last two days and at one time West Indies, needing 303 to win, were 219–3 with Sobers to come. But when a brilliant innings of 91 from Basil Butcher ended, Sobers played on for 0 and the effort died away.

There was a heartening improvement in New Zealand's performance on their tour of England in the second half of 1969. They were unlucky to play the first Test on a bad pitch at Lord's, where John Edrich made the first of two hundreds and Derek Underwood had match figures of 11–70, including a match-winning 7–32 in New Zealand's second innings. After the second Test, at Trent Bridge, was drawn, New Zealand were left to play the last Test at The Oval amid showers, and, with Underwood producing match figures of 12–101, England won by 8 wickets.

TEST MATCH RESULTS: 1960–9

359. West Indies v England
First Test at Bridgetown, Barbados – 6, 7, 8, 9, 11, 12 January 1960
ENGLAND 482 (Dexter 136*, Barrington 128, Pullar 65, Swetman 45) and 71–0 (Pullar 46*)
WEST INDIES 563–8 dec. (Sobers 226, Worrell 197*, Hunte 42, Kanhai 40, Trueman 4–93)
Match drawn

360. West Indies v England
Second Test at Port-of-Spain, Trinidad – 28, 29, 30 January, 1, 2, 3 February 1960
ENGLAND 382 (Barrington 121, M. J. K. Smith 108, Dexter 77) and 230–9 dec. (Barrington 49, Illingworth 41*)
WEST INDIES 112 (Trueman 5–35) and 244 (Kanhai 110, Hunte 47)
England won by 256 runs

361. West Indies v England
Third Test at Kingston, Jamaica – 17, 18, 19, 20, 22, 23 February 1960
ENGLAND 277 (Cowdrey 114, Hall 7–69) and 305 (Cowdrey 97, Pullar 66, May 45, Watson 4–62)

WEST INDIES 353 (Sobers 147, McMorris 73, Nurse 70) and 175–6 (Kanhai 57, Hunte 40, Trueman 4–54)
Match drawn

362. West Indies v England
Fourth Test at Georgetown, Guyana – 9, 10, 11, 12, 14, 15 March 1960
ENGLAND 295 (Cowdrey 65, Allen 55, Hall 6–90) and 334–8 (Dexter 110, Subba Row 100, Pullar 47, Worrell 4–49)
WEST INDIES 402–8 dec. (Sobers 145, Kanhai 55)
Match drawn

363. West Indies v England
Fifth Test at Port-of-Spain, Trinidad – 25, 26, 28, 29, 30, 31 March 1960
ENGLAND 393 (Cowdrey 119, Dexter 76, Barrington 69, Parks 43, Ramadhin 4–73) and 350–7 dec. (Parks 101*, M. J. K. Smith 96, Pullar 54, Dexter 47)
WEST INDIES 338–8 dec. (Sobers 92, Hunte 72*, Walcott 53) and 209–5 (Worrell 61, Sobers 49*)
Match drawn

364. England v South Africa

First Test at Edgbaston – 9, 10, 11, 13, 14 June 1960
ENGLAND 292 (Subba Row 56, M. J. K. Smith 54, Dexter
52, Adcock 5–62) and 203 (Tayfield 4–62)
SOUTH AFRICA 186 (Waite 58, O'Linn 42, Trueman 4–58)
and 209 (McLean 68, Waite 56*)
England won by 100 runs

365. England v South Africa

Second Test at Lord's – 23, 24, 25, 27 June 1960
ENGLAND 362–8 dec. (M. J. K. Smith 99, Subba Row 90,
Dexter 56, Walker 52, Griffin 4–87)
SOUTH AFRICA 152 (Statham 6–63, Moss 4–35) and 137
(Statham 5–34)
England won by an innings and 73 runs

366. England v South Africa

Third Test at Trent Bridge – 7, 8, 9, 11 July 1960
ENGLAND 287 (Barrington 80, Cowdrey 67, Goddard 5–80)
and 49–2
SOUTH AFRICA 88 (Trueman 5–27) and 247 (O'Linn 98,
Waite 60, McGlew 45, Trueman 4–77)
England won by 8 wickets

367. England v South Africa

Fourth Test at Old Trafford – 21, 22, 23, 25, 26 July 1960
ENGLAND 260 (Barrington 76, Adcock 4–66) and 153–7 dec.
SOUTH AFRICA 229 (McLean 109, Allen 4–58) and 46–0
Match drawn

368. England v South Africa

Fifth Test at The Oval – 18, 19, 20, 22, 23 August 1960
ENGLAND 155 (Pullar 59, Adcock 6–65, Pothecary 4–58)
and 479–9 dec. (Pullar 175, Cowdrey 155)
SOUTH AFRICA 419 (Goddard 99, Waite 77, O'Linn 55,
Tayfield 46*, Carlstein 42) and 97–4
Match drawn

369. England v Australia

First Test at Edgbaston – 8, 9, 10, 12, 13 June 1961
ENGLAND 195 (Subba Row 59, Mackay 4–57) and 401–4
(Dexter 180, Subba Row 112, Barrington 48*)
AUSTRALIA 516–9 dec. (Harvey 114, O'Neill 82, Simpson
76, Mackay 64, Lawry 57)
Match drawn

370. England v Australia

Second Test at Lord's – 22, 23, 24, 26 June 1961
ENGLAND 206 (Subba Row 48, Davidson 5–42) and 202
(Barrington 66, Pullar 42, McKenzie 5–37)
AUSTRALIA 340 (Lawry 130, Mackay 54, Burge 46,
Trueman 4–118) and 71–5
Australia won by 5 wickets

371. England v Australia

Third Test at Headingley – 6, 7, 8 July 1961
AUSTRALIA 237 (Harvey 73, McDonald 54, Trueman 5–58)
and 120 (Harvey 53, Trueman 6–30)
ENGLAND 299 (Cowdrey 93, Pullar 53, Davidson 5–63)
and 62–2
England won by 8 wickets

372. England v Australia

Fourth Test at Old Trafford – 27, 28, 29, 31 July, 1 August
1961
AUSTRALIA 190 (Lawry 74, Booth 46, Statham 5–53) and
432 (Lawry 102, Davidson 77*, O'Neill 67, Simpson 51,
Allen 4–58)

ENGLAND 367 (May 95, Barrington 78, Pullar 63, Allen 42,
Simpson 4–23) and 201 (Dexter 76, Subba Row 49,
Benaud 6–70)
Australia won by 54 runs

373. England v Australia

Fifth Test at The Oval – 17, 18, 19, 21, 22 August 1961
ENGLAND 256 (May 71, Barrington 53, Davidson 4–83)
and 370–8 (Subba Row 137, Barrington 83, Allen 42*,
Murray 40, Mackay 5–121)
AUSTRALIA 494 (Burge 181, O'Neill 117, Booth 71,
Simpson 40, Allen 4–133)
Match drawn

374. Pakistan v England

First Test at Lahore – 21, 22, 24, 25, 26 October 1961
PAKISTAN 387–9 dec. (Javed Burki 138, Mushtaq
Mohammad 76, Saeed Ahmed 74) and 200
ENGLAND 380 (Barrington 139, M. J. K. Smith 99, Allen 40,
Mohammad Munaf 4–42) and 209–5 (Dexter 66*,
Richardson 48)
England won by 5 wickets

375. India v England

First Test at Bombay – 11, 12, 14, 15, 16 November 1961
ENGLAND 500–8 dec. (Barrington 151*, Dexter 85, Pullar
83, Richardson 71, Ranjane 4–76) and 184–5 dec.
(Barrington 52*, Richardson 43)
INDIA 390 (Durani 71, Borde 69, Manjrekar 68, Jaisimha
56, Lock 4–74) and 180–5 (Manjrekar 84, Jaisimha 51)
Match drawn

376. India v England

Second Test at Kanpur – 1, 2, 3, 5, 6 December 1961
INDIA 467–8 dec. (Umrigar 147*, Manjrekar 96, Jaisimha
70)
ENGLAND 244 (Barber 69*, Lock 49, Pullar 46, Gupte
5–90) and 497–5 (Barrington 172, Dexter 126*, Pullar
119, Richardson 48)
Match drawn

377. India v England

Third Test at Delhi – 13, 14, 16, 17 (no play), 18 December
1961
INDIA 466 (Manjrekar 189*, Jaisimha 127, Allen 4–87)
ENGLAND 256–3 (Barrington 113*, Pullar 89, Dexter 45*)
Match drawn

378. India v England

Fourth Test at Calcutta – 30, 31 December 1961, 1, 3, 4
January 1962
INDIA 380 (Borde 68, Nawab of Pataudi Jnr 64, Mehra 62,
Durani 43, Allen 5–67) and 252 (Borde 61, Allen 4–95,
Lock 4–111)
ENGLAND 212 (Richardson 62, Dexter 57, Durani 5–47,
Borde 4–65) and 233 (Dexter 62, Parfitt 46, Richardson
42)
India won by 187 runs

379. India v England

Fifth Test at Madras – 10, 11, 13, 14, 15 January 1962
INDIA 428 (Nawab of Pataudi Jnr 103, Contractor 86,
Engineer 65, Nadkarni 63) and 190 (Manjrekar 85, Lock
6–65)
ENGLAND 281 (M. J. K. Smith 73, Durani 6–105) and 209
(Barrington 48, Durani 4–72)
India won by 128 runs

380. Pakistan v England
Second Test at Dacca – 19, 20, 21, 23, 24 January 1962
PAKISTAN 393–7 dec. (Javed Burki 140, Hanif Mohammad 111, Saeed Ahmed 69, Lock 4–155) and 216 (Hanif Mohammad 104, Alimuddin 50, Allen 5–30, Lock 4–70)
ENGLAND 439 (Pullar 165, Barber 86, Barrington 84, D'Souza 4–94) and 38–0
Match drawn

381. Pakistan v England
Third Test at Karachi – 2, 3, 4, 6, 7 February 1962
PAKISTAN 253 (Alimuddin 109, Hanif Mohammad 67, Knight 4–66) and 404–8 (Hanif Mohammad 89, Imtiaz Ahmed 86, Alimuddin 53, Mushtaq Mohammad 41, Nasim-ul-Ghani 41)
ENGLAND 507 (Dexter 205, Parfitt 111, Pullar 60, M. J. K. Smith 56, D'Souza 5–112)
Match drawn

382. England v Pakistan
First Test at Edgbaston – 31 May, 1, 2, 4 June 1962
ENGLAND 544–5 dec. (Cowdrey 159, Parfitt 101*, Graveney 97, Allen 79*, Dexter 72)
PAKISTAN 246 (Mushtaq Mohammad 63, Hanif Mohammad 47, Statham 4–54) and 274 (Saeed Ahmed 65, Imtiaz Ahmed 46)
England won by an innings and 24 runs

383. England v Pakistan
Second Test at Lord's – 21, 22, 23 June 1962
PAKISTAN 100 (Trueman 6–31) and 355 (Javed Burki 101, Nasim-ul-Ghani 101, Coldwell 6–85)
ENGLAND 370 (Graveney 153, Dexter 65, Cowdrey 41, Mohammad Farooq 4–70) and 86–1
England won by 9 wickets

384. England v Pakistan
Third Test at Headingley – 5, 6, 7 July 1962
ENGLAND 428 (Parfitt 119, Stewart 86, Allen 62, Munir Malik 5–128)
PAKISTAN 131 (Alimuddin 50, Dexter 4–10) and 180 (Alimuddin 60, Saeed Ahmed 54)
England won by an innings and 117 runs

385. England v Pakistan
Fourth Test at Trent Bridge – 26, 27, 28, 30, 31 July 1962
ENGLAND 428–5 dec. (Graveney 114, Parfitt 101*, Dexter 85, Sheppard 83)
PAKISTAN 219 (Mushtaq Mohammad 55, Saeed Ahmed 43, Nasim-ul-Ghani 41, Knight 4–38, Trueman 4–71) and 216–6 (Mushtaq Mohammad 100*, Saeed Ahmed 64)
Match drawn

386. England v Pakistan
Fifth Test at The Oval – 16, 17, 18, 20 August 1962
ENGLAND 480–5 dec. (Cowdrey 182, Dexter 172, Sheppard 57, Barrington 50*) and 27–0
PAKISTAN 183 (Imtiaz Ahmed 49, Hanif Mohammad 46, Mushtaq Mohammad 43, Larter 5–57) and 323 (Imtiaz Ahmed 98, Mushtaq Mohammad 72, Mathias 48, Javed Burki 42, Larter 4–88)
England won by 10 wickets

387. Australia v England
First Test at Brisbane – 30 November, 1, 3, 4, 5 December 1962

AUSTRALIA 404 (Booth 112, Mackay 86*, Benaud 51, Simpson 50) and 362–4 dec. (Lawry 98, Simpson 71, Harvey 57, O'Neill 56, Burge 47*)
ENGLAND 389 (Parfitt 80, Barrington 78, Dexter 70, Benaud 6–115) and 278–6 (Dexter 99, Pullar 56, Sheppard 53)
Match drawn

388. Australia v England
Second Test at Melbourne – 29, 31 December 1962, 1, 2, 3 January 1963
AUSTRALIA 316 (Lawry 52, Mackay 49, Davidson 40, Titmus 4–43) and 248 (Booth 103, Lawry 57, Trueman 5–62)
ENGLAND 331 (Cowdrey 113, Dexter 93, Graveney 41, Davidson 6–75) and 237–3 (Sheppard 113, Cowdrey 58*, Dexter 52)
England won by 7 wickets

389. Australia v England
Third Test at Sydney – 11, 12, 14, 15 January 1963
ENGLAND 279 (Cowdrey 85, Pullar 53, Simpson 5–57, Davidson 4–54) and 104 (Davidson 5–25)
AUSTRALIA 319 (Simpson 91, Shepherd 71*, Harvey 64, Titmus 7–79) and 67–2
Australia won by 8 wickets

390. Australia v England
Fourth Test at Adelaide – 25, 26, 28, 29, 30 January 1963
AUSTRALIA 393 (Harvey 154, O'Neill 100, Davidson 46) and 293 (Booth 77, Simpson 71, Benaud 48, Trueman 4–60)
ENGLAND 331 (Barrington 63, Dexter 61, Titmus 59*, McKenzie 5–89) and 223–4 (Barrington 132*)
Match drawn

391. Australia v England
Fifth Test at Sydney – 15, 16, 18, 19, 20 February 1963
ENGLAND 321 (Barrington 101, Dexter 47) and 268–8 dec. (Barrington 94, Sheppard 68, Cowdrey 53)
AUSTRALIA 349 (Burge 103, O'Neill 73, Benaud 57, Titmus 5–103) and 152–4 (Burge 52*, Lawry 45*)
Match drawn

392. New Zealand v England
First Test at Auckland – 23, 25, 26, 27 February 1963
ENGLAND 562–7 dec. (Parfitt 131*, Barrington 126, Knight 125, Cowdrey 86, Cameron 4–118)
NEW ZEALAND 258 (Yuile 64, Motz 60, Reid 59) and 89 (Larter 4–26, Illingworth 4–34)
England won by an innings and 215 runs

393. New Zealand v England
Second Test at Wellington – 1, 2, 4 March 1963
NEW ZEALAND 194 (Blair 64*, Trueman 4–46) and 187 (Playle 65, Titmus 4–50)
ENGLAND 428–8 dec. (Cowdrey 128*, Barrington 76, A. C. Smith 69*, Illingworth 46)
England won by an innings and 47 runs

394. New Zealand v England
Third Test at Christchurch – 15, 16, 18, 19 March 1963
NEW ZEALAND 266 (Reid 74, Sinclair 44, Dowling 40, Trueman 7–75) and 159 (Reid 100, Titmus 4–46)
ENGLAND 253 (Barrington 47, Dexter 46, Cowdrey 43, Sheppard 42) and 173–3 (Barrington 45)
England won by 7 wickets

395. England v West Indies
First Test at Old Trafford – 6, 7, 8, 10 June 1963
WEST INDIES 501–6 dec. (Hunte 182, Kanhai 90, Worrell
74*, Sobers 64) and 1–0
ENGLAND 205 (Dexter 73, Gibbs 5–59) and 296 (Stewart
87, Gibbs 6–98)
West Indies won by 10 wickets

396. England v West Indies
Second Test at Lord's – 20, 21, 22, 24, 25 June 1963
WEST INDIES 301 (Kanhai 73, Solomon 56, Hunte 44,
Sobers 42, Trueman 6–100) and 229 (Butcher 133,
Trueman 5–52, Shackleton 4–72)
ENGLAND 297 (Barrington 80, Dexter 70, Titmus 52*, Griffith
5–91) and 228–9 (Close 70, Barrington 60, Hall 4–93)
Match drawn

397. England v West Indies
Third Test at Edgbaston – 4, 5, 6, 8, 9 July 1963
ENGLAND 216 (Close 55, Sobers 5–60) and 278–9 dec.
(Sharpe 85*, Dexter 57, Lock 56, Gibbs 4–49)
WEST INDIES 186 (Carew 40, Trueman 5–75, Dexter 4–38)
and 91 (Trueman 7–44)
England won by 217 runs

398. England v West Indies
Fourth Test at Headingley – 25, 26, 27, 29 July 1963
WEST INDIES 397 (Sobers 102, Kanhai 92, Solomon 62,
Trueman 4–117) and 229 (Butcher 78, Sobers 52,
Kanhai 44, Titmus 4–44)
ENGLAND 174 (Lock 53, Griffith 6–36) and 231 (Parks 57,
Close 56, Bolus 43, Gibbs 4–76)
West Indies won by 221 runs

399. England v West Indies
Fifth Test at The Oval – 22, 23, 24, 26 August 1963
ENGLAND 275 (Sharpe 63, Close 46, Griffith 6–71) and
223 (Sharpe 83, Hall 4–39)
WEST INDIES 246 (Hunte 80, Butcher 53) and 255–2
(Hunte 108*, Kanhai 77)
West Indies won by 8 wickets

400. India v England
First Test at Madras – 10, 11, 12, 14, 15 January 1964
INDIA 457–7 dec. (Kunderan 192, Manjrekar 108, Sardesai
65, Jaisimha 51, Titmus 5–116) and 152–9 dec. (Titmus
4–46)
ENGLAND 317 (Bolus 88, Barrington 80, Wilson 42, Borde
5–88) and 241–5 (Mortimore 73*, M. J. K. Smith 57)
Match drawn

401. India v England
Second Test at Bombay – 21, 22, 23, 25, 26 January 1964
INDIA 300 (Durani 90, Borde 84) and 249–8 dec. (Sardesai
66, Jaisimha 66, Manjrekar 43*)
ENGLAND 233 (Titmus 84*, M. J. K. Smith 46, Chandrasekhar
4–67) and 206–3 (Bolus 57, Binks 55, Parks 40*)
Match drawn

402. India v England
Third Test at Calcutta – 29, 30 January, 1, 2, 3 February
1964
INDIA 241 (Sardesai 54, Nadkarni 43*, Price 5–73) and
300–7 dec. (Jaisimha 129)
ENGLAND 267 (Cowdrey 107, Desai 4–62) and 145–2
(M. J. K. Smith 75*)
Match drawn

403. India v England
Fourth Test at Delhi – 8, 9, 11, 12, 13 February 1964
INDIA 344 (Hanumant Singh 105, Jaisimha 47, Sardesai 44,
Kunderan 40) and 463–4 (Nawab of Pataudi Jnr 203*,
Kunderan 100, Borde 67*, Jaisimha 50)
ENGLAND 451 (Cowdrey 151, Parfitt 67, Bolus 58, Edrich
41)
Match drawn

404. India v England
Fifth Test at Kanpur – 15, 16, 18, 19, 20 February 1964
ENGLAND 559–8 dec. (Knight 127, Parfitt 121, Bolus 67,
Parks 51*)
INDIA 266 (Sardesai 79, Nadkarni 52*, Titmus 6–73) and
347–3 (Nadkarni 122*, Sardesai 87, Durani 61*,
Kunderan 55)
Match drawn

405. England v Australia
First Test at Trent Bridge – 4, 5, 6 (no play), 8, 9 June 1964
ENGLAND 216–8 dec. (Boycott 48) and 193–9 dec. (Dexter
68, McKenzie 5–53)
AUSTRALIA 168 (Simpson 50) and 40–2
Match drawn

406. England v Australia
Second Test at Lord's – 18 (no play), 19 (no play), 20, 22,
23 June 1964
AUSTRALIA 176 (Veivers 54, Trueman 5–48) and 168–4
(Burge 59)
ENGLAND 246 (Edrich 120, Corling 4–60)
Match drawn

407. England v Australia
Third Test at Headingley – 2, 3, 4, 6 July 1964
ENGLAND 268 (Parks 68, Dexter 66, Hawke 5–75,
McKenzie 4–74) and 229 (Barrington 85)
AUSTRALIA 389 (Burge 160, Lawry 78, Titmus 4–69) and
111–3 (Redpath 58*)
Australia won by 7 wickets

408. England v Australia
Fourth Test at Old Trafford – 23, 24, 25, 27, 28 July 1964
AUSTRALIA 656–8 dec. (Simpson 311, Lawry 106, Booth
98, O'Neill 47) and 4–0
ENGLAND 611 (Barrington 256, Dexter 174, Parks 60,
Boycott 58, McKenzie 7–153)
Match drawn

409. England v Australia
Fifth Test at The Oval – 13, 14, 15, 17, 18 (no play) August
1964
ENGLAND 182 (Barrington 47, Hawke 6–47) and 381–4
(Boycott 113, Cowdrey 93*, Titmus 56, Barrington 54*)
AUSTRALIA 379 (Lawry 94, Booth 74, Veivers 67*, Redpath
45, Trueman 4–87)
Match drawn

410. South Africa v England
First Test at Durban – 4, 5, 7, 8 December 1964
ENGLAND 485–5 dec. (Barrington 148*, Parks 108*,
Barber 74, Boycott 73)
SOUTH AFRICA 155 (Allen 5–41) and 226 (Bland 68, Pithey
43, Titmus 5–66)
England won by an innings and 104 runs

411. South Africa v England
Second Test at Johannesburg – 23, 24, 26, 28, 29 December 1964
ENGLAND 531 (Dexter 172, Barrington 121, Barber 97, Parfitt 52, P. Pollock 5–129)
SOUTH AFRICA 317 (Pithey 85, Barlow 71, Goddard 40, Titmus 4–73) and 336–6 (Bland 144*, G. Pollock 55, Goddard 50, Allen 4–87)
Match drawn

412. South Africa v England
Third Test at Cape Town – 1, 2, 4, 5, 6 January 1965
SOUTH AFRICA 501–7 dec. (Pithey 154, Barlow 138, Bland 78, Goddard 40) and 346 (Barlow 78, G. Pollock 73, Bland 64, Lindsay 50, Barrington 3–4)
ENGLAND 442 (M. J. K. Smith 121, Dexter 61, Parks 59, Barber 58, Barrington 49, Parfitt 44, Bromfeld 5–88) and 15–0
Match drawn

413. South Africa v England
Fourth Test at Johannesburg – 22, 23, 25, 26, 27 January 1965
SOUTH AFRICA 390–6 dec. (Barlow 96, Pithey 95, Waite 64, Goddard 60, Bland 55) and 307–3 dec. (Goddard 112, G. Pollock 65*, Barlow 42)
ENGLAND 384 (Parfitt 122*, Barrington 93, Barber 61, M. J. K. Smith 42, McKinnon 4–128) and 153–6 (Boycott 76*)
Match drawn

414. South Africa v England
Fifth Test at Port Elizabeth – 12, 13, 15, 16, 17 February 1965
SOUTH AFRICA 502 (G. Pollock 137, Barlow 69, van der Merwe 66, Goddard 61, Bland 48) and 178–4 dec. (G. Pollock 77*, Barlow 47)
ENGLAND 435 (Boycott 117, Barrington 72, Dexter 40) and 29–1
Match drawn

415. England v New Zealand
First Test at Edgbaston – 27, 28, 29, 31 May, 1 June 1965
ENGLAND 435 (Barrington 137, Cowdrey 85, Dexter 57, Motz 5–108) and 96–1 (Barber 51, Boycott 44*)
NEW ZEALAND 116 (Titmus 4–18) and 413 (Pollard 81*, Sutcliffe 53, Congdon 47, Reid 44, Morgan 43, Dick 42, Dowling 41, Barber 4–132)
England won by 9 wickets

416. England v New Zealand
Second Test at Lord's – 17, 18, 19, 21, 22 June 1965
NEW ZEALAND 175 (Pollard 55, Taylor 51, Rumsey 4–25) and 347 (Sinclair 72, Dowling 66, Pollard 55)
ENGLAND 307 (Cowdrey 119, Dexter 62, M. J. K. Smith 44, Collinge 4–85) and 218–3 (Dexter 80*, Boycott 76)
England won by 7 wickets

417. England v New Zealand
Third Test at Headingley – 8, 9, 10, 12, 13 July 1965
ENGLAND 546–4 dec. (Edrich 310*, Barrington 163)
NEW ZEALAND 193 (Reid 54, Yuile 46, Illingworth 4–42, Larter 4–66) and 166 (Pollard 53, Dowling 41, Titmus 5–19)
England won by an innings and 187 runs

418. England v South Africa
First Test at Lord's – 22, 23, 24, 26, 27 July 1965
SOUTH AFRICA 280 (G. Pollock 56, Lindsay 40) and 248 (Bland 70, Barlow 52)
ENGLAND 338 (Barrington 91, Titmus 59, Barber 56) and 145–7 (Dumbrill 4–30)
Match drawn

419. England v South Africa
Second Test at Trent Bridge – 5, 6, 7, 9 August 1965
SOUTH AFRICA 269 (G. Pollock 125, Cartwright 6–94) and 289 (Barlow 76, Bacher 67, G. Pollock 59, Larter 5–68)
ENGLAND 240 (Cowdrey 105, Barber 41, P. Pollock 5–53) and 224 (Parfitt 86, Parks 44*, P. Pollock 5–34)
South Africa won by 94 runs

420. England v South Africa
Third Test at The Oval – 26, 27, 28, 30, 31 August 1965
SOUTH AFRICA 208 (Lance 69, Statham 5–40, Higgs 4–47) and 392 (Bland 127, Bacher 70, Lance 53, Higgs 4–96)
ENGLAND 202 (Cowdrey 58, Parks 42, Barber 40, P. Pollock 5–43) and 308–4 (Cowdrey 78*, Barrington 73, Russell 70, Parfitt 46)
Match drawn

421. Australia v England
First Test at Brisbane – 10, 11 (no play), 13, 14, 15 December 1965
AUSTRALIA 443–6 dec. (Lawry 166, Walters 155, Veivers 56*)
ENGLAND 280 (Titmus 60, Barrington 53, Parks 52, Boycott 45, Philpott 5–90) and 186–3 (Boycott 63*)
Match drawn

422. Australia v England
Second Test at Melbourne – 30, 31 December 1965, 1, 3, 4 January 1966
AUSTRALIA 358 (Cowper 99, Lawry 88, Simpson 59, Knight 4–84) and 426 (Burge 120, Walters 115, Lawry 78, Simpson 67)
ENGLAND 558 (Edrich 109, Cowdrey 104, Parks 71, Barrington 63, Titmus 56*, Boycott 51, Barber 48, M. J. K. Smith 41, McKenzie 5–134) and 5–0
Match drawn

423. Australia v England
Third Test at Sydney – 7, 8, 10, 11 January 1966
ENGLAND 488 (Barber 185, Edrich 103, Boycott 84, Allen 50*, Hawke 7–105)
AUSTRALIA 221 (Cowper 60, Thomas 51, Brown 5–63) and 174 (Titmus 4–40, Allen 4–47)
England won by an innings and 93 runs

424. Australia v England
Fourth Test at Adelaide – 28, 29, 31 January, 1 February 1966
ENGLAND 241 (Barrington 60, Parks 49, McKenzie 6–48) and 266 (Barrington 102, Titmus 53, Hawke 5–54)
AUSTRALIA 516 (Simpson 225, Lawry 119, Thomas 52, Stackpole 43, Jones 6–118)
Australia won by an innings and 9 runs

425. Australia v England
Fifth Test at Melbourne – 11, 12, 14, 15 (no play), 16 February 1966
ENGLAND 485–9 dec. (Barrington 115, Parks 89, Edrich 85, Cowdrey 79, Titmus 42*, Walters 4–53) and 69–3
AUSTRALIA 543–8 dec. (Cowper 307, Lawry 108, Walters 60)
Match drawn

426. New Zealand v England
First Test at Christchurch – 25, 26, 28 February, 1 March 1966
ENGLAND 342 (Allen 88, M. J. K. Smith 54, Parfitt 54, Brown 44) and 201–5 dec. (M. J. K. Smith 87, Parfitt 46*)
NEW ZEALAND 347 (Congdon 104, Motz 58, Petrie 55, Jones 4–71) and 48–8 (Higgs 4–5)
Match drawn

427. New Zealand v England
Second Test at Dunedin – 4, 5, 7, 8 March 1966
NEW ZEALAND 192 (Motz 57) and 147–9 (Allen 4–46)
ENGLAND 254–8 dec. (Cowdrey 89*, Murray 50)
Match drawn

428. New Zealand v England
Third Test at Auckland – 11, 12, 14, 15 March 1966
NEW ZEALAND 296 (Sinclair 114, Congdon 64, Allen 5–123) and 129
ENGLAND 222 (Cowdrey 59, Russell 56, Pollard 3–3) and 159–4 (Parks 45*)
Match drawn

429. England v West Indies
First Test at Old Trafford – 2, 3, 4 June 1966
WEST INDIES 484 (Sobers 161, Hunte 135, Nurse 49, Butcher 44, Titmus 5–83)
ENGLAND 167 (Parks 43, Gibbs 5–37) and 277 (Milburn 94, Cowdrey 69, Gibbs 5–69)
West Indies won by an innings and 40 runs

430. England v West Indies
Second Test at Lord's – 16, 17, 18, 20, 21 June 1966
WEST INDIES 269 (Nurse 64, Butcher 49, Sobers 46, Higgs 6–91) and 369–5 dec. (Sobers 163*, Holford 105*, Kanhai 40)
ENGLAND 355 (Graveney 96, Parks 91, Boycott 60, Hall 4–106) and 197–4 (Milburn 126*)
Match drawn

431. England v West Indies
Third Test at Trent Bridge – 30 June, 1, 2, 4, 5 July 1966
WEST INDIES 235 (Nurse 93, Lashley 49, Higgs 4–71, Snow 4–82) and 482–5 dec. (Butcher 209*, Sobers 94, Kanhai 63, Nurse 53)
ENGLAND 325 (Graveney 109, Cowdrey 96, D'Oliveira 76, Sobers 4–90, Hall 4–105) and 253 (Boycott 71, D'Oliveira 54)
West Indies won by 139 runs

432. England v West Indies
Fourth Test at Headingley – 4, 5, 6, 8 August 1966
WEST INDIES 500–9 dec. (Sobers 174, Nurse 137, Hunte 48, Kanhai 45, Higgs 4–94)
ENGLAND 240 (D'Oliveira 88, Higgs 49, Sobers 5–41) and 205 (Barber 55, Milburn 42, Gibbs 6–39)
West Indies won by an innings and 55 runs

433. England v West Indies
Fifth Test at The Oval – 18, 19, 20, 22 August 1966
WEST INDIES 268 (Kanhai 104, Sobers 81) and 225 (Nurse 70, Butcher 60)
ENGLAND 527 (Graveney 165, Murray 112, Higgs 63, Snow 59*)
England won by an innings and 34 runs

434. England v India
First Test at Headingley – 8, 9, 10, 12, 13 June 1967
ENGLAND 550–4 dec. (Boycott 246*, D'Oliveira 109, Barrington 93, Graveney 59) and 126–4 (Barrington 46)
INDIA 164 (Nawab of Pataudi Jnr 64, Engineer 42) and 510 (Nawab of Pataudi Jnr 148, Wadekar 91, Engineer 87, Hanumant Singh 73, Illingworth 4–100)
England won by 6 wickets

435. England v India
Second Test at Lord's – 22, 23, 24, 26 June 1967
INDIA 152 (Wadekar 57) and 110 (Kunderan 47, Illingworth 6–29)
ENGLAND 386 (Graveney 151, Barrington 97, Chandrasekhar 5–127)
England won by an innings and 124 runs

436. England v India
Third Test at Edgbaston – 13, 14, 15 July 1967
ENGLAND 298 (Murray 77, Barrington 75, Milburn 40) and 203 (Close 47, Amiss 45, Prasanna 4–60)
INDIA 92 and 277 (Wadekar 70, Nawab of Pataudi Jnr 47, Close 4–68, Illingworth 4–92)
England won by 132 runs

437. England v Pakistan
First Test at Lord's – 27, 28, 29, 31 July, 1 August 1967
ENGLAND 369 (Barrington 148, Graveney 81, D'Oliveira 59, Russell 43) and 241–9 dec. (D'Oliveira 81*)
PAKISTAN 354 (Hanif Mohammad 187*, Asif Iqbal 76) and 88–3
Match drawn

438. England v Pakistan
Second Test at Trent Bridge – 10, 11, 12, 14 (no play), 15 August 1967
PAKISTAN 140 (Saeed Ahmed 44, Higgs 4–35) and 114 (Saeed Ahmed 68, Underwood 5–52)
ENGLAND 252–8 dec. (Barrington 109*, Close 41) and 3–0
England won by 10 wickets

439. England v Pakistan
Third Test at The Oval – 24, 25, 26, 28 August 1967
PAKISTAN 216 (Mushtaq Mohammad 66, Arnold 5–58) and 255 (Asif Iqbal 146, Intikhab Alam 51, Higgs 5–58)
ENGLAND 440 (Barrington 142, Graveney 77, Titmus 65, Arnold 59, Mushtaq Mohammad 4–80) and 34–2
England won by 8 wickets

440. West Indies v England
First Test at Port-of-Spain, Trinidad – 19, 20, 22, 23, 24 January 1968
ENGLAND 568 (Barrington 143, Graveney 118, Cowdrey 72, Boycott 68, Parks 42, Griffith 5–69)
WEST INDIES 363 (Lloyd 118, Kanhai 85, Nurse 41) and 243–8 (Butcher 52, Camacho 43, Nurse 42)
Match drawn

441. West Indies v England
Second Test at Kingston, Jamaica – 8, 9, 10, 12, 13, 14 February 1968
ENGLAND 376 (Cowdrey 101, Edrich 96, Barrington 63, Hall 4–63) and 68–8
WEST INDIES 143 (Snow 7–49) and 391–9 dec. (Sobers 113*, Nurse 73)
Match drawn

DID YOU KNOW...?

In the 1968 Ashes series, Colin Cowdrey scored his 7,000th Test run, set a world record for most Test catches, and became the first player to play in a hundred Tests.

442. West Indies v England
Third Test at Bridgetown, Barbados – 29 February, 1, 2, 4, 5 March 1968
WEST INDIES 349 (Butcher 86, Sobers 68, Camacho 57, Snow 5–86) and 284–6 (Lloyd 113*, Butcher 60)
ENGLAND 449 (Edrich 146, Boycott 90, Graveney 55, D'Oliveira 51)
Match drawn

443. West Indies v England
Fourth Test at Port-of-Spain, Trinidad – 14, 15, 16, 18, 19 March 1968
WEST INDIES 526–7 dec. (Kanhai 153, Nurse 136, Camacho 87, Sobers 48, Lloyd 43) and 92–2 dec. (Carew 40*)
ENGLAND 404 (Cowdrey 148, Knott 69*, Boycott 62, Barrington 48, Butcher 5–34) and 215–3 (Boycott 80*, Cowdrey 71)
England won by 7 wickets

444. West Indies v England
Fifth Test at Georgetown, Guyana – 28, 29, 30 March, 1, 2, 3 April 1968
WEST INDIES 414 (Sobers 152, Kanhai 150, Snow 4–82) and 264 (Sobers 95*, Nurse 49, Snow 6–60)
ENGLAND 371 (Boycott 116, Lock 89, Cowdrey 59) and 206–9 (Cowdrey 82, Knott 73*, Gibbs 6–60)
Match drawn

445. England v Australia
First Test at Old Trafford – 6, 7, 8, 10, 11 June 1968
AUSTRALIA 357 (Sheahan 88, Lawry 81, Walters 81, I. Chappell 73, Snow 4–97) and 220 (Walters 86, Jarman 41, Pocock 6–79)
ENGLAND 165 (Edrich 49, Cowper 4–48) and 253 (D'Oliveira 87*, Barber 46)
Australia won by 159 runs

446. England v Australia
Second Test at Lord's – 20, 21, 22, 24, 25 June 1968
ENGLAND 351–7 dec. (Milburn 83, Barrington 75, Boycott 49, Cowdrey 45)
AUSTRALIA 78 (Brown 5–42) and 127–4 (Redpath 53)
Match drawn

447. England v Australia
Third Test at Edgbaston – 11 (no play), 12, 13, 15, 16 July 1968
ENGLAND 409 (Cowdrey 104, Graveney 96, Edrich 88, Freeman 4–78) and 142–3 dec. (Edrich 64)
AUSTRALIA 222 (I. Chappell 71, Cowper 57, Walters 46) and 68–1
Match drawn

448. England v Australia
Fourth Test at Headingley – 25, 26, 27, 29, 30 July 1968
AUSTRALIA 315 (Redpath 92, I. Chappell 65, Walters 42, Underwood 4–41) and 312 (I. Chappell 81, Walters 56, Redpath 48, Illingworth 6–87)
ENGLAND 302 (Prideaux 64, Edrich 62, Barrington 49, Underwood 45*, Connolly 5–72) and 230–4 (Edrich 65, Barrington 46*, Graveney 41)
Match drawn

449. England v Australia
Fifth Test at The Oval – 22, 23, 24, 26, 27 August 1968
ENGLAND 494 (Edrich 164, D'Oliveira 158, Graveney 63) and 181 (Connolly 4–65)
AUSTRALIA 324 (Lawry 135, Redpath 67, Mallett 43*) and 125 (Inverarity 56, Underwood 7–50)
England won by 226 runs

450. Pakistan v England
First Test at Lahore – 21, 22, 23, 24 February 1969
ENGLAND 306 (Cowdrey 100, Edrich 54, Knott 52, Saeed Ahmed 4–64, Intikhab Alam 4–117) and 225–9 dec. (Fletcher 83, Brown 44*)
PAKISTAN 209 (Asif Iqbal 70, Cottam 4–50) and 203–5 (Majid Khan 68)
Match drawn

451. Pakistan v England
Second Test at Dacca – 28 February, 1, 2, 3 March 1969
PAKISTAN 246 (Mushtaq Mohammad 52, Asif Iqbal 44, Snow 4–70) and 195–6 dec. (Majid Khan 49*, Underwood 5–94)
ENGLAND 274 (D'Oliveira 114*, Graveney 46, Pervez Sajjad 4–75) and 33–0
Match drawn

452. Pakistan v England
Third Test at Karachi – 6, 7, 8 March 1969
ENGLAND 502–7 (Milburn 139, Graveney 105, Knott 96*)
Match abandoned as a draw

453. England v West Indies
First Test at Old Trafford – 12, 13, 14, 16, 17 June 1969
ENGLAND 413 (Boycott 128, Graveney 75, Edrich 58, D'Oliveira 57, Shepherd 5–104) and 12–0
WEST INDIES 147 (Brown 4–39, Snow 4–54) and 275 (Fredericks 64, Butcher 48, Sobers 48, Carew 44)
England won by 10 wickets

454. England v West Indies
Second Test at Lord's – 26, 27, 28, 30 June, 1 July 1969
WEST INDIES 380 (Davis 103, Camacho 67, Fredericks 63, Snow 5–114) and 295–9 dec. (Lloyd 70, Fredericks 60, Sobers 50*, Camacho 45)
ENGLAND 344 (Illingworth 113, Hampshire 107, Knott 53) and 295–7 (Boycott 106, Sharpe 86)
Match drawn

455. England v West Indies
Third Test at Headingley – 10, 11, 12, 14, 15 July 1969
ENGLAND 223 (Edrich 79, D'Oliveira 48, Knott 44, Holder 4–48) and 240 (Sobers 5–42)
WEST INDIES 161 (Knight 4–63) and 272 (Butcher 91, Camacho 71, Underwood 4–55)
England won by 30 runs

456. England v New Zealand
First Test at Lord's – 24, 25, 26, 28 July 1969
ENGLAND 190 (Illingworth 53) and 340 (Edrich 115, Knight 49, Boycott 47, Sharpe 46)
NEW ZEALAND 169 (Congdon 41, Dowling 41, Illingworth 4–37, Underwood 4–38) and 131 (Turner 43*, Underwood 7–32)
England won by 230 runs

457. England v New Zealand
Second Test at Trent Bridge – 7, 8, 9, 11, 12 August 1969
NEW ZEALAND 294 (Hastings 83, Congdon 66, Ward 4–61) and 66–1 (Murray 40*)
ENGLAND 451–8 dec. (Edrich 155, Sharpe 111, D'Oliveira 45, Hadlee 4–88)
Match drawn

458. England v New Zealand
Third Test at The Oval – 21, 22, 23, 25, 26 August 1969
NEW ZEALAND 150 (Turner 53, Underwood 6–41) and 229 (Hastings 61, Underwood 6–60)
ENGLAND 242 (Edrich 68, Sharpe 48, Boycott 46, Taylor 4–47) and 138–2 (Denness 55*, Sharpe 45*)
England won by 8 wickets

ENGLAND CRICKET, SEVENTIES STYLE: 1970–9

England's visit to Australia in 1970–1 was the longest Test series in cricket history and went to a seventh Test (although the third Test was abandoned without a ball being bowled). The series definitely belonged to England, who won the fourth and seventh Tests to recapture the Ashes. Keith Stackpole's 207 at Brisbane supported by Doug Walters' 112 ensured a sizeable Australian score of 433, but England got a first-innings lead of 31 before having Australia in trouble in their second innings. Then Bill Lawry led a dour recovery and the match ended as a draw. The second Test at Perth saw England surrender a good position after Brian Luckhurst had made 131 in their total of 397. Australia were 107–5 when Greg Chappell went in and, with Redpath making 171 and Chappell, on his debut, 102, it was England who had to steer clear of defeat. After the third was abandoned and replaced by another, six having been originally arranged, England won a great victory in the fourth at Sydney. Gaining a first-innings lead of 96, they consolidated through an unbeaten 142 from Geoff Boycott before John Snow's 7–40 blasted Australia out for 116. At Melbourne, D'Oliveira (117) and Luckhurst (109) helped England to draw the game. The sixth Test at Adelaide saw Geoff Boycott make 119 not out in England's second innings after Ray Illingworth with good precedent had decided to enforce the follow-on. A great final conflict at Sydney was overshadowed by long-threatened confrontation between Illingworth and the umpires. Terry Jenner was hit by a Snow bouncer; Snow, as had happened several times previously in the series, was warned for intimidation; the crowd demonstrated; a spectator manhandled Snow; and Illingworth led his team off the field. England, 80 behind on the first innings, held together to make 302 and set Australia a target of 223 to win, which proved beyond the home side, despite an injury to Snow, who took 31 wickets in the series.

After winning in Australia, Ray Illingworth's side arrived in New Zealand. They won the first Test, in Christchurch, after bowling New Zealand out for 65 on a damp pitch on the first day, with Derek Underwood taking 6–12. In the second Test, on a splendid pitch at Auckland, they came as near to winning as they have done in the long history of the series. Graham Dowling declared just a few runs behind England's first-innings total of 321, and, after England lost four second-innings wickets cheaply and had Cowdrey and D'Oliveira injured, Knott followed up his first-innings hundred with a dogged 96 to delay New Zealand's first win for yet another series.

In 1971, Pakistan kept England in the field for more than two days of the first Test at Edgbaston as they amassed 608–7 declared with a young Zaheer Abbas making 274. Asif Iqbal and Mushtaq Mohammad also made hundreds and it needed fighting innings from D'Oliveira (78) and Knott (116) to give England first-innings respectability. England followed on 255 behind but, even with Luckhurst making 108, rain on the final day deprived Pakistan of a certain victory. Rain for most of the second Test meant that all depended on Headingley, where England won an exciting victory by 25 runs. Boycott followed his second Test 121 not out with 112 but Pakistan still needed only 231 for victory, with more than a day to play. The younger Mohammad, Sadiq, scored 91 but it wasn't enough to save his side.

The first Test of the 1971 series against India was ruined by rain, with India 38 runs short of a target of 183 with two wickets in hand. Rain saved the tourists at Old Trafford when they were 65–3, needing 420 to win. Illingworth and Luckhurst made hundreds and Lancashire's Peter Lever, on his home ground, made 88 not out batting at No. 9. But at The Oval, India needed only 173 for victory, which they accomplished with 6 wickets down. After England had led by 71 on first innings, they crumbled in the face of Chandrasekhar, whose bounce and turn proved mesmeric. He finished with 6–38 to win both the match and the series.

England retained the Ashes in 1972 but only after a terrific fight against Ian Chappell's Australian side. England won the first Test by 89 runs in a low-scoring match in which the Australians never recovered after being bowled out by Arnold and Snow for 142 in their first innings. The series was squared at Lord's in a remarkable match dominated by the swing bowling of Bob Massie, who took 8 wickets in each innings to finish with match figures of 16–137. Greg Chappell made 131 and the tourists won by 8 wickets. Poor fielding in the third Test at Trent Bridge let England down but, after Massie and Lillee had bowled England out for 189 and Ross Edwards had made 170 not out, the England batsman competently saved the match. The fate of the Ashes was determined in controversial circumstances in the fourth Test at Headingley. Derek Underwood, who had been out of favour, was recalled to bowl on a turning pitch and he returned match figures of 10–82 as England won by 9 wickets on the third day. Dennis Lillee's pace brought the series level at The Oval, taking 10 wickets in the match to complete 31 for the series, and, with both Chappells getting hundreds, Australia won a great victory by 6 wickets.

It wasn't until towards the end of the 1972–3 tour of India that England got to grips with the spin of Bedi and Chandrasekhar. Nevertheless, England won the first Test, in Delhi, by six wickets, a remarkable start for captain Tony Lewis, playing his first Test. Although Chandrasekhar had 8–79 in the first innings, Greig, 68 not out and 70 not out, saw England home. The Indian spinners held sway in Calcutta and Madras, earning the home side wins by 28 runs and 4 wickets respectively. But Tony Lewis steadied the ship in the fourth match, at Kanpur, which ensured his side would not lose. The bat was always in command at Bombay and England could not square the series. Engineer and Viswanath made hundreds for India while Fletcher and Greig hit their first three-figure scores for England.

Following these five keenly contested Tests, England journeyed on to Pakistan, where in the first Test, at Lahore, Dennis Amiss became the fourth player on the tour to make his maiden Test century and though Asif Iqbal and Sadiq Mohammad both made hundreds to give the home side a lead on first innings, England came away with a draw. In the second Test, Amiss led the way with a fine innings of 158 as England amassed 487. Pakistan replied with 569–9 declared with Mushtaq 157 and Intikhab Alam 138. They looked to be on their way to victory after England slumped to 77–5 but Greig and Knott added 112 to stave off defeat. The last Test provided, if nothing else, a remarkable statistic – in that three batsmen were dismissed for 99. One of those batsman was Dennis Amiss, who was seeking his third hundred in successive Tests.

The New Zealand side visiting England in 1973 twice had chances to record their first win in England. In the first Test, at Trent Bridge, England struggled to make 250 but then the pace trio of Arnold, Greig and Snow bowled the Kiwis out for 97. After Greig had followed that with 139 to add to Amiss's 138, England looked set for a massive win as they set the visitors 479 for victory. Bev Congden (176) and Vic Pollard (116) masterminded such a recovery, however, that they fell only 38 runs short of their target. New Zealand should have won the second Test at Lord's after Congden (175) and Pollard (105 not out) had given them a first-innings lead of 302. But a dropped catch behind the wicket and a fine innings of 178 by Keith Fletcher saved the day for England. In the third Test, Boycott made an excellent 115 and, with Arnold taking 5–27, New Zealand were beaten by an innings and 1 run.

West Indies put an end to their losing streak against England by winning the first Test of this 1973 miniseries at The Oval. After Clive Lloyd had made 132, England suffered from a virtuoso performance from Keith Boyce. Coming in at No. 9, the Essex all-rounder slammed 72 and then took 5–70 and 6–77, and, though Frank Hayes on debut made 106, West Indies won by 158 runs. A draw in the second Test, at Edgbaston, had its controversial moments. Umpire Arthur Fagg threatened to withdraw after he had been intimidated by West Indian fielders after turning down an appeal for a catch behind the wicket against Boycott. He later received an apology. There was more drama at Lord's in the final Test when the ground was evacuated because of a 'bomb scare' – the players took their sanctuary in the middle of the pitch. The match itself saw Kanhai (157), Sobers (150 not out) and Julien (121) all hit hundreds as England capitulated to Boyce and Holder and lost by an innings and 226 runs.

Touring the Caribbean in 1973–4, England lost the first Test and were largely outplayed in the series but then surprisingly squared the rubber in the final game. At Trinidad, West Indies won by 7 wickets after bowling England out for 131, and, with Kallicharran making 158, earned a huge first-innings lead. Dennis Amiss's second-innings 174 was in vain. The Warwickshire opener did perform a rescue miracle in Kingston when he batted for nine and a half hours for 262 not out to save the game. At Bridgetown, it was Fletcher's turn to mastermind the escape, although Greig (148) and Knott (87) pulled the first innings together. Lawrence Rowe then made 302, the highest score by a West Indian, and, in England's second innings, Keith Fletcher, with an unbeaten 129, held firm after England's first four wickets had fallen cheaply. Rain ruined the fourth Test, at Georgetown, after both Amiss and Greig had made centuries. In the final Test, at Trinidad, England found superb performances from Boycott (99 and 112) and Greig (8–86 and 5–70) and West Indies fell 26 runs short of their target of 226. England had climaxed a series of near-defeats by escaping with a drawn rubber.

England took full advantage of the damp, cold conditions of 1974 when India visited England for the first half of the summer. At Old Trafford in the first Test, rain fell on the first four days, but, with Fletcher making 123 not out, England were able to declare at 328–9. India lost early wickets but a fine century from Sunil Gavaskar supported by Abid Ali helped them recover to 246. Edrich, on his return to the Test side, made another hundred and India were bowled out on the last day to lose by 113 runs. At Lord's, the margin was even wider as England won by a massive innings and 285 runs. England amassed 629 with Amiss 188, Denness 118, Greig 106 and Edrich 96. Forced to follow on, India then crumbled to just 42 all out, the lowest score in Test history at Lord's, with Old taking 5–21 and Arnold 4–19. India again conceded defeat by an innings in the third Test and David Lloyd, in only his second Test, made 214 not out and he put on 207 with his skipper Mike Denness, reaching his second century of a one-sided series.

The second half of the summer saw Pakistan bring perhaps their strongest-ever side to England and return home undefeated as all three Tests ended in draws. Rain robbed England of victory at Headingley when they finished on 238–6 in chasing 282 for victory – this in the face of some penetrating seam bowling from Sarfraz Nawaz. The second Test, at Lord's, was steeped in controversy and the weather conditions, which stopped a certain England win, probably prevented a loud outcry from Pakistan. The complaint was of an inadequate covering of the wicket and each time the rain fell it was the tourists who suffered. The first downpour reduced their innings from 71–0 to 130 all out with Underwood taking 5–20. Pakistan's second innings was similarly affected when Underwood took 8–51. Needing just 87 to win, England had reached 27 without loss when rain finally won the day. The final Test, at The Oval, produced a high-scoring draw, with Zaheer Abbas making 240 and England's Amiss (183) and Fletcher (122) both making hundreds. Nevertheless, it was a frustrating end to a contest between two evenly matched sides.

With a revitalized Dennis Lillee and a new bowling sensation in Jeff Thomson, Australia crushed England in the Ashes series of 1974–5. At

Brisbane, Tony Greig dodged the bouncers to make a splendid 110 but Thomson broke the England batsmen's resistance in the second innings to give Australia victory by 166 runs. Centuries by Edwards and Walters in the second Test at Perth gave the home side a huge lead on first innings before Jeff Thomson reigned supreme in the second innings despite gallant resistance from Titmus and won by 9 wickets. After an exciting low-scoring draw at Melbourne – Australia were 8 runs short of victory with 2 wickets remaining – the home side regained the Ashes by winning the fourth Test by 171 runs. England squandered a splendid chance to win the fifth Test after having Australia 84–5, and, though Knott made a flamboyant century, Australia went on to win by 163 runs. All this made the sixth Test the more remarkable as Peter Lever took 6–38 and Denness, in the face of mounting criticism, made 188 and Fletcher 146. Greg Chappell made another hundred in his side's second innings, but England won by an innings and 4 runs.

A comprehensive victory by England in the first Test against New Zealand at Auckland was marred by a fearful accident to Ewan Chatfield, the New Zealand No. 11. Chatfield's heart actually stopped beating for several seconds after he was struck on the temple by a lifting delivery from Lever. Only swift action by England physiotherapist Bernard Thomas saved Chatfield. For England, Fletcher and Denness continued in good vein, making 181 and 216 respectively, and Greig had match figures of 10–149 as the visitors won by an innings and 83 runs. Amiss, after his personal disaster in Australia, made an impressive 164 not out in a rain-ruined second Test.

The four-match 1975 Ashes series was arranged to fill a gap in the Test match calendar. When the series began after the first World Cup had finished in July, it was quite clear that England were still suffering from their defeat Down Under the previous winter. Replying to Australia's 359 in the first Test, at Edgbaston, England had just begun their innings when a thunderstorm drenched the ground. On resumption they capitulated to Dennis Lillee and Max Walker for 101 and went on to lose by an innings and 85 runs. Denness resigned the captaincy to be replaced by Tony Greig for the second Test at Lord's, and though he didn't get off to a winning start, he scored 96 and 41. Edrich made 175 while David Steele on his Test debut made 50 and 45. Following this drawn match, the Headingley Test was perfectly balanced when it had to be abandoned in unique and controversial circumstances. On the final day Australia required a further 225 runs with 7 wickets in hand. Yet no play was possible because, overnight, vandals dug holes in and spread oil on the wicket. With the Ashes now out of reach, England fought a stern rearguard action at The Oval to earn yet another draw. This Test saw Bob Woolmer occupy the crease for 499 minutes in scoring 149, the slowest century made by an Englishman against Australia. Grey-haired, bespectacled Steele enjoyed a popular triumph, averaging 60 in his first series.

After managing to draw the first two Tests of the 1976 series at home to West Indies, England were finally outplayed by the tourists. In the first Test, at Trent Bridge, Steele made a patient hundred and two elder statesmen, Close and Edrich, played out the draw. England might even have won at Lord's after forty-three-year-old Close made a gallant 60 and Snow and Underwood had earned a first innings lead. With West Indies needing 323 for victory, Roy Fredericks made 138 as the visitors finished on 241–6. The rout began in the third Test at Old Trafford, even though West Indies had been reduced at one stage to 26–4. There followed a fine century from Greenidge but, even so, they were all out for 211. In reply, England collapsed to 71 all out in the face of some hostile bowling from Andy Roberts, Michael Holding and Wayne Daniel. They improved in their second innings but their margin of defeat was a stunning 425 runs. Greenidge made his third successive century at Headingley but England battled back into the game with both Greig and Knott making 116. Willis then took 5–42 to give his side a fighting chance, but, though Greig was again defiant, West Indies won by 55 runs. In the final Test, at The Oval, Viv Richards was at his most punishing, scoring 291, but Dennis Amiss made a marvellous comeback with 203. Then England's batting collapsed, and Greenidge and Fredericks set up a declaration by hitting 182 off 32 overs. Holding, who had claimed 8–92 in the first innings, later sustained his assault with 6–57 to become the first West Indian bowler to take 14 wickets in a Test.

After the hardships of the last three years or so, England came back strongly in the 1976–7 tour of India to win their first series here in five rubbers since the war. The first Test, at New Delhi, was won by an innings and 25 runs after Amiss had weathered an ominous start to score a magnificent 179. John Lever, who made 53 in this his first Test, then took 7–46 as India were bowled out for 122. He continued to swing the ball prodigiously in the second innings as India reached 234, with only Gavaskar (71) surviving for any length of time. England's victory at Calcutta was almost as overwhelming as they won by 10 wickets. Bob Willis took 5–27 as India collapsed to 155 all out before a punishing century by Greig saw England to 321.The lead of 166 was adequate as India were bowled out for 181 in their second innings. England won the series at Madras with their third win in a row, this time by 200 runs. On a deteriorating pitch, Brearley and Greig made the only half-centuries of the match, while Lever's 5–59 in the first innings and Underwood's 4–28 in the second brought about the victory. India came back to win by 140 runs in the fourth Test, at Bangalore, while the fifth, in Bombay, saw England left to make 214 in four hours. Both sides had some nervous moments before stumps were drawn with England 152–7.

With the hundredth anniversary of the first-ever Test match approaching, the authorities in Melbourne set about planning an appropriate celebration, and in March 1977, Australia met England. Though not for the Ashes, the match was as fluctuating and thrilling as any in the long saga of England–Australia encounters. Australia were bowled out for 138 but this was put into perspective when England crashed to Lillee and Walker for just 95.The match then settled down and, with Rodney Marsh recording the first Test century by a regular wicketkeeper for Australia, England were set the unlikely target of 463 with plenty of time. By the end of the fourth day they were a promising 191–2 with Nottinghamshire's Derek Randall 87 not out. On a memorable last day, England forged nearer and nearer to their 'impossible' requirement as Randall made 174 in his first Test against Australia. While he was in, there was always the chance of an England win but when he left, there was a slender hope. Lillee took the final wicket, that of Underwood, and the jubilant scenes at the end was for the glory of the game as much for Australia's success.

The 1977 Ashes series in England was staged in the shadow of the most dramatic shake-up in cricket history. Kerry Packer's World Series Cricket was set to split the game wide open, involving most of the world's top players. Tony Greig's close involvement cost him the England captaincy and he was replaced by Mike Brearley. The first Test, at Lord's, known as the Jubilee Test in honour of the Queen's twenty-five years on the throne, was curtailed by rain with honours even. England then won by 9 wickets at Old Trafford with Bob Woolmer scoring his third century in consecutive home Tests against Australia. Greg Chappell made 112 when Australia batted a second time but the cause was lost and England needed just 79 runs for victory. Another victory came at Trent Bridge when Geoff Boycott returned after three-and-a-half years' self-imposed exile and made 107. The sensation of Australia's first innings was England debutant Ian Botham's 5–74, but Australia's second knock of 309 left England 189 to get, and, with Brearley and Boycott both making eighties, England won by 7 wickets.

England demolished Australia in the fourth Test at Headingley to recover the Ashes and to provide a dramatic background to Boycott's hundredth century in first-class cricket. Long and loud was the admiration from the Yorkshire crowd when he straight-drove Chappell to bring up his century. He was last man out for 191 as England totalled 436. With Botham taking 5–21 and Hendrick 4–41, Australia were bowled out for 103 and following on were dismissed for 248 to lose by an innings and 85 runs. At The Oval, Mick Malone took 5–63 off 47 overs in his first Test and followed with 46 in a ninth-wicket stand of 100 with Walker, but rain was the victor.

Three Tests were played by England in Pakistan in 1977–8 and three more draws were added to the Asian country's long list of uncompleted matches. The first Test at Lahore was remarkable for Mudassar Nazar's 557-minute century – the slowest ever in any Test, which was drawn as play ended prematurely due to a second crowd disturbance. England had some anxious moments before the second Test at Hyderabad was drawn, with Brearley and Boycott batting throughout the last day and England not losing a wicket. The Karachi Test was overshadowed by events off the field. It was thought that Pakistan might call up some of their Packer players and, if this was the case, then some of the England team would refuse to take to the field against them. As it was, both teams did their best to put spectators to sleep in another drawn match.

Crossing from Pakistan to New Zealand, England met their destiny in the first Test at Wellington, where the Kiwis, after 47 attempts, won their first Test against them. On a worsening pitch and against some short, aggressive bowling by both sides, the innings totals were progressively smaller. Chris Old took 6–54 as New Zealand were bowled out for 228, and then, despite Boycott's 77, England fell 13 runs short of the Kiwis' total. Bob Willis had 5–32 as New Zealand made 123, leaving England to make 137 for victory. With Richard Hadlee (6–26) virtually unplayable, England collapsed to 64 all out. England gained revenge at Christchurch, where Ian Botham scored his first Test century and took 5–73 in New Zealand's first-innings total of 235. Following England's declaration at 96–4, Bob Willis, with 4–14, made early inroads into the Kiwis' batting as they were bowled out for 105. With all to play for at Auckland, New Zealand made 315 before England crawled to 429 with Clive Radley's 158 being just minute quicker than Peter Richardson's 488-minute slowest Test century for England. Geoff Howarth then made another century and the match petered out into a draw.

The 1978 series against Pakistan was the first to be sponsored by Cornhill Insurance and the first in which Ian Botham really established himself as a Test all-rounder. In the first Test, at Edgbaston, Chris Old took 7–50, including 4 in 5 balls, as Pakistan were bowled out for 164. With Radley and Botham both hitting hundreds, England declared at 452–8, going on to win by an innings. At Lord's, Botham hit another century in England's total of 364 before Willis (5–47) and Phil Edmonds (4–6) dismissed the tourists for 105. Following on, they were bowled out a second time with Botham taking 8–34 – the best analysis at Lord's – as England won by an innings and 120 runs. Sadly, rain ruined the final Test at Headingley.

England's other opponents in that summer of 1978 were New Zealand, who, batting first in the opening Test at The Oval, were dismissed for 234. England took a lead of 45 on first innings thanks to David Gower making 111, his maiden Test century. Phil Edmonds took 4–20 off 37 overs as New Zealand set England a target of just 138. Rain washed out the entire fourth day but Gooch blasted an unbeaten 91 as the home side won by 7 wickets. At Trent Bridge, Boycott made 131 in England's total of 429 before Botham took 6–34 as New Zealand were skittled out for 120. Following on, they did a little better with 190 but still lost by an innings and 119 runs. New Zealand had a lead of 50 on first innings in the final Test, at Lord's, but, with Botham taking 5–39, they were dismissed for just 67 in their second innings, leaving England to make 118 for victory, which they did for the loss of 3 wickets.

For the 1978–9 Ashes series, both England and Australia were without players who had joined Kerry Packer's World Cricket Series. In the first Test at Brisbane, despite Graham Yallop (102) and Kim Hughes (129) batting with great determination in Australia's second innings and adding 170 for the fourth wicket, England were left to make just 170 for victory, a target they reached with 7 wickets remaining. At Perth, Gower made 102 and Boycott hit 77 from 337 balls, as England went on to win by 66 runs. In the third Test, at Melbourne, Graeme Wood made 100 in Australia's total of 258 – it proved a winning total as England were bowled out for 143 and then 179 after Australia had made 167 in their second innings. Rodney Hogg took his total of wickets in the three Tests to 27, a total that included 5 wickets in each of the five completed innings. At Sydney, Derek Randall made the slowest century in Ashes Tests – 353 balls – but Australia, chasing 205 to win, were bowled out for just 111 as England retained the Ashes. In the fifth Test, at Adelaide, Australia's Rick Darling required heart massage when a ball from Willis struck him under the heart. Though he recovered to resume his innings the following day, England won by 205 runs. The tourists also won the final Test at Sydney by 9 wickets. Rodney Hogg's aggregate of wickets for the series was 41 – an Australian Ashes record.

With India the visitors in 1979, England amassed 633–5 declared, their highest post-war total. Gower, with 200 not out, led the way, while Boycott made 155. Remarkably, Kapil Dev took all the wickets to finish with 5–146. Despite Gavaskar and Viswanath hitting half-centuries in each innings, England won by an innings and 83 runs. Rain helped India save the second Test at Lord's after they'd been bowled out for 96. England declared at 419–9 and, when Botham dismissed Gavaskar in India's second knock, it was his hundredth Test wicket, taken in a record time of two years and nine days. Vengsarkar and Viswanath turned the tide for India, both making hundreds and adding 210 for the third wicket in a drawn game. At Headingley, Botham hit 99 before lunch on the fourth day after most of the previous three days had been lost to rain, while the fourth and final Test at The Oval provided one of the best finishes in Test cricket. England batted and made 305, India replying with 202. Boycott made 125 when England went in again, allowing them to declare at 334–8. India needed 438 with over eight hours in which to get them. They made an impressive start, putting on 213 for the first wicket. When the last hour began, India had still lost only one wicket in over a day's play – 328–1. They needed 110 from the last 25 overs but, following Gavaskar's dismissal for a magnificent 221, they lost a little momentum and wickets fell – at 429–8 at the close, they were just nine runs short of a great victory. Botham completed 1,000 Test runs during the match and became the quickest to a Test double of 1,000 runs and 100 wickets, achieved in only twenty-one matches.

TEST MATCH RESULTS: 1970–9

459. Australia v England
First Test at Brisbane – 27, 28, 29 November, 1, 2 December 1970
AUSTRALIA 433 (Stackpole 207, Walters 112, I. Chappell 59, Snow 6–114) and 214 (Lawry 84, Shuttleworth 5–47)
ENGLAND 464 (Edrich 79, Luckhurst 74, Knott 73, D'Oliveira 57) and 39–1
Match drawn

460. Australia v England
Second Test at Perth – 11, 12, 13, 15, 16 December 1970
ENGLAND 397 (Luckhurst 131, Boycott 70, Edrich 47, Cowdrey 40, McKenzie 4–66) and 287–6 dec. (Edrich 115*, Boycott 50)
AUSTRALIA 440 (Redpath 171, G. Chappell 108, I. Chappell 50, Marsh 44, Snow 4–143) and 100–3
Match drawn

Australia v England
Third Test at Melbourne – December 1970–January 1971
Match abandoned without a ball being bowled: rain

461. Australia v England
Fourth Test at Sydney – 9, 10, 11, 13, 14 January 1971
ENGLAND 332 (Boycott 77, Edrich 55, Mallett 4–40, Gleeson 4–83) and 319–5 dec. (Boycott 142*, D'Oliveira 56, Illingworth 53)
AUSTRALIA 236 (Redpath 64, Walters 55, Underwood 4–66) and 116 (Lawry 60*, Snow 7–40)
England won by 299 runs

462. Australia v England
Fifth Test at Melbourne – 21, 22, 23, 25, 26 January 1971
AUSTRALIA 493–9 dec. (I. Chappell 111, Marsh 92*,
   Redpath 72, Lawry 56, Walters 55) and 169–4 dec.
   (Lawry 42)
ENGLAND 392 (D'Oliveira 117, Luckhurst 109, Illingworth
   41) and 161–0 (Boycott 76*, Edrich 74*)
Match drawn

DID YOU KNOW...?

Pace bowler John Price missed out on a possible
Test hat-trick at Lord's in June 1971 when
Pakistan's last man fell ill.

463. Australia v England
Sixth Test at Adelaide – 29, 30 January, 1, 2, 3 February
1971
ENGLAND 470 (Edrich 130, Fletcher 80, Boycott 58,
   Hampshire 55, D'Oliveira 47, Lillee 5–84) and 233–4
   dec. (Boycott 119*, Illingworth 48*, Edrich 40)
AUSTRALIA 235 (Stackpole 87, P. Lever 4–49) and 328–3
   (Stackpole 136, I. Chappell 104)
Match drawn

464. Australia v England
Seventh Test at Sydney – 12, 13, 14, 16, 17 February 1971
ENGLAND 184 (Illingworth 42) and 302 (Luckhurst 59,
   Edrich 57, D'Oliveira 47)
AUSTRALIA 264 (G. Chappell 65, Redpath 59, Walters 42)
   and 160 (Stackpole 67)
England won by 62 runs

465. New Zealand v England
First Test at Christchurch – 25, 26, 27 February, 1 March
1971
NEW ZEALAND 65 (Underwood 6–12, Shuttleworth 3–14)
   and 254 (Turner 76, Congdon 55, Underwood 6–85)
ENGLAND 231 (D'Oliveira 100, Hampshire 40, Howarth
   4–46) and 89–2 (Hampshire 51*)
England won by 8 wickets

466. New Zealand v England
Second Test at Auckland – 5, 6, 7, 8 March 1971
ENGLAND 321 (Knott 101, P. Lever 64, D'Oliveira 58,
   Cowdrey 54, Cunis 6–76) and 237 (Knott 96, Cowdrey
   45, Collinge 4–41)
NEW ZEALAND 313–7 dec. (Burgess 104, Turner 65,
   Dowling 53, Shrimpton 46, Underwood 5–108) and
   40–0
Match drawn

467. England v Pakistan
First Test at Edgbaston – 3, 4, 5, 7, 8 June 1971
PAKISTAN 608–7 dec. (Zaheer Abbas 274, Asif Iqbal 104*,
   Mushtaq Mohammad 100)
ENGLAND 353 (Knott 116, D'Oliveira 73, P. Lever 47, Asif
   Masood 5–111) and 229–5 (Luckhurst 108*, Asif
   Masood 4–49)
Match drawn

468. England v Pakistan
Second Test at Lord's – 17, 18, 19, 21, 22 June 1971
ENGLAND 241–2 dec. (Boycott 121*, Luckhurst 46) and
   117–0 (Hutton 58*, Luckhurst 53*)
PAKISTAN 148 (Zaheer Abbas 40)
Match drawn

469. England v Pakistan
Third Test at Headingley – 8, 9, 10, 12, 13 July 1971
ENGLAND 316 (Boycott 112, D'Oliveira 74) and 264
   (D'Oliveira 72, Amiss 56, Illingworth 45, Saleem Altaf
   4–11)
PAKISTAN 350 (Zaheer Abbas 72, Wasim Bari 63, Mushtaq
   Mohammad 57) and 205 (Sadiq Mohammad 91,
   P. Lever 3–10)
England won by 25 runs

470. England v India
First Test at Lord's – 22, 23, 24, 26, 27 July 1971
ENGLAND 304 (Snow 73, Knott 67, Bedi 4–70) and 191
   (Edrich 62, Venkataraghavan 4–52)
INDIA 313 (Wadekar 85, Viswanath 68, Solkar 67, Gifford
   4–84) and 145–8 (Gavaskar 53, Gifford 4–43)
Match drawn

471. England v India
Second Test at Old Trafford – 5, 6, 7, 9, 10 August 1971
ENGLAND 386 (Illingworth 107, P. Lever 88*, Luckhurst 78,
   Knott 41, Abid Ali 4–64) and 245–3 dec. (Luckhurst
   101, Edrich 59)
INDIA 212 (Gavaskar 57, Solkar 50, P. Lever 5–70) and 65–3
Match drawn

472. England v India
Third Test at The Oval – 19, 20, 21, 23, 24 August 1971
ENGLAND 355 (Knott 90, Jameson 82, Hutton 81, Edrich
   41) and 101 (Chandrasekhar 6–38)
INDIA 284 (Engineer 59, Sardesai 54, Wadekar 48, Solkar
   44, Illingworth 5–70) and 174–6 (Wadekar 45, Sardesai
   40)
India won by 4 wickets

473. England v Australia
First Test at Old Trafford – 8, 9, 10, 12, 13 June 1972
ENGLAND 249 (Greig 57, Edrich 49) and 234 (Greig 62,
   Boycott 47, Lillee 6–66)
AUSTRALIA 142 (Stackpole 53, Snow 4–41, Arnold 4–62) and
   252 (Marsh 91, Stackpole 67, Greig 4–53, Snow 4–87)
England won by 89 runs

474. England v Australia
Second Test at Lord's – 22, 23, 24, 26 June 1972
ENGLAND 272 (Greig 54, Knott 43, Massie 8–84) and 116
   (Massie 8–53)
AUSTRALIA 308 (G. Chappell 131, I. Chappell 56, Marsh
   50, Snow 5–57) and 81–2 (Stackpole 57*)
Australia won by 8 wickets

475. England v Australia
Third Test at Trent Bridge – 13, 14, 15, 17, 18 July 1972
AUSTRALIA 315 (Stackpole 114, Colley 54, Marsh 41, Snow
   5–92) and 324–4 dec. (Edwards 170*, G. Chappell 72,
   I. Chappell 50)
ENGLAND 189 (Lillee 4–35, Massie 4–43) and 290–4
   (Luckhurst 96, D'Oliveira 50*, Parfitt 46)
Match drawn

476. England v Australia
Fourth Test at Headingley – 27, 28, 29 July 1972
AUSTRALIA 146 (Stackpole 52, Underwood 4–37) and 136
(Sheahan 41*, Underwood 6–45)
ENGLAND 263 (Illingworth 57, Snow 48, Edrich 45, Mallett
5–114) and 21–1
England won by 9 wickets

477. England v Australia
Fifth Test at The Oval – 10, 11, 12, 14, 15, 16 August
1972
ENGLAND 284 (Knott 92, Parfitt 51, Hampshire 42, Lillee
5–58) and 356 (Wood 90, Knott 63, D'Oliveira 43, Lillee
5–123)
AUSTRALIA 399 (I. Chappell 118, G. Chappell 113, Edwards
79, Underwood 4–90) and 242–5 (Stackpole 79,
Sheahan 44*, Marsh 43*)
Australia won by 5 wickets

478. India v England
First Test at Delhi – 20, 21, 22, 23, 25 December 1972
INDIA 173 (Abid Ali 58, Arnold 6–45) and 233 (Solkar 75,
Engineer 63, Underwood 4–56)
ENGLAND 200 (Greig 68*, Amiss 46, Chandrasekhar 8–79)
and 208–4 (Lewis 70*, Wood 45, Greig 40*)
England won by 6 wickets

479. India v England
Second Test at Calcutta – 30, 31 December 1972, 1, 3, 4
January 1973
INDIA 210 (Engineer 75, Wadekar 44) and 155 (Durani 53,
Greig 5–24, Old 4–43)
ENGLAND 174 (Chandrasekhar 5–65) and 163 (Greig 67,
Bedi 5–63, Chandrasekhar 4–42)
India won by 28 runs

480. India v England
Third Test at Madras – 12, 13, 14, 16, 17 January 1973
ENGLAND 242 (Fletcher 97*, Chandrasekhar 6–90) and
159 (Denness 76, Prasanna 4–16, Bedi 4–38)
INDIA 316 (Ali Khan 73, Wadekar 44, Pocock 4–114) and
86–6 (Pocock 4–28)
India won by 4 wickets

481. India v England
Fourth Test at Kanpur – 25, 27, 28, 29, 30 January 1973
INDIA 357 (Wadekar 90, Gavaskar 69, Ali Khan 54, Abid Ali
41, Old 4–69) and 186–6 (Viswanath 75*)
ENGLAND 397 (Lewis 125, Birkenshaw 64, Fletcher 58,
Arnold 45, Knott 40, Chandrasekhar 4–86)
Match drawn

482. India v England
Fifth Test at Bombay – 6, 7, 8, 10, 11 February 1973
INDIA 448 (Engineer 121, Viswanath 113, Wadekar 87,
Durani 73) and 244–5 dec. (Gavaskar 67, Engineer 66,
Viswanath 48)
ENGLAND 480 (Greig 148, Fletcher 113, Knott 56,
Chandrasekhar 5–135) and 67–2
Match drawn

483. Pakistan v England
First Test at Lahore – 2, 3, 4, 6, 7 March 1973
ENGLAND 355 (Amiss 112, Fletcher 55, Denness 50, Greig
41) and 306–7 dec. (Lewis 74, Greig 72, Denness 68,
Intikhab Alam 4–80)

PAKISTAN 422 (Sadiq Mohammad 119, Asif Iqbal 102,
Mushtaq Mohammad 66, Greig 4–86) and 124–3 (Talat
Ali 57, Majid Khan 43)
Match drawn

484. Pakistan v England
Second Test at Sind – 16, 17, 18, 20, 21 March 1973
ENGLAND 487 (Amiss 158, Fletcher 78, Knott 71, Mushtaq
Mohammad 4–93, Intikhab Alam 4–137) and 218–6
(Greig 64, Knott 63*)
PAKISTAN 569–9 dec. (Mushtaq Mohammad 157, Intikhab
Alam 138, Asif Iqbal 68, Wasim Bari 48, Pocock 5–169)
Match drawn

485. Pakistan v England
Third Test at Karachi – 24, 25, 27, 28, 29 March 1973
PAKISTAN 445–6 dec. (Majid Khan 99, Mushtaq
Mohammad 99, Sadiq Mohammad 89, Intikhab Alam
61) and 199 (Wasim Bari 41, Gifford 5–55, Birkenshaw
5–57)
ENGLAND 386 (Amiss 99, Lewis 88, Fletcher 54, Greig 48,
Denness 47, Intikhab Alam 4–105) and 30–1
Match drawn

486. England v New Zealand
First Test at Trent Bridge – 7, 8, 9, 11, 12 June 1973
ENGLAND 250 (Boycott 51, Knott 49, Amiss 42, D. Hadlee
4–42, Taylor 4–53) and 325–8 dec. (Greig 139, Amiss
138*)
NEW ZEALAND 97 (Greig 4–33) and 440 (Congdon 176,
Pollard 116, Wadsworth 46, Arnold 5–131)
England won by 38 runs

487. England v New Zealand
Second Test at Lord's – 21, 22, 23, 25, 26 June 1973
ENGLAND 253 (Greig 63, Boycott 61, Roope 56) and
463–9 (Fletcher 178, Boycott 92, Amiss 53, Roope 51,
Howarth 4–144)
NEW ZEALAND 551–9 dec. (Congdon 175, Pollard 105*,
Burgess 105, Hastings 86, Old 5–113)
Match drawn

488. England v New Zealand
Third Test at Headingley – 5, 6, 7, 9, 10 July 1973
NEW ZEALAND 276 (Burgess 87, Pollard 62, Old 4–71) and
142 (Turner 81, Arnold 5–27)
ENGLAND 419 (Boycott 115, Fletcher 81, Illingworth 65,
Collinge 5–74)
England won by an innings and 1 run

489. England v West Indies
First Test at The Oval – 26, 27, 28, 30, 31 July 1973
WEST INDIES 415 (Lloyd 132, Kallicharran 80, Boyce 72,
Arnold 5–113) and 255 (Kallicharran 80, Sobers 51,
Headley 42)
ENGLAND 257 (Boycott 97, Boyce 5–70) and 255 (Hayes
106*, Illingworth 40, Boyce 6–77)
West Indies won by 158 runs

490. England v West Indies
Second Test at Edgbaston – 9, 10, 11, 13, 14 August 1973
WEST INDIES 327 (Fredericks 150, Julien 54) and 302
(Lloyd 94, Sobers 74, Kanhai 54, Arnold 4–43)
ENGLAND 305 (Boycott 56*, Amiss 56, Fletcher 52) and
182–2 (Amiss 86*, Fletcher 44*, Luckhurst 42)
Match drawn

491. England v West Indies
Third Test at Lord's – 23, 24, 25, 27 August 1973
WEST INDIES 652–8 dec. (Kanhai 157, Sobers 150*, Julien 121, Lloyd 63, Fredericks 51, Willis 4–118)
ENGLAND 233 (Fletcher 68, Greig 44, Boyce 4–50, Holder 4–56) and 193 (Fletcher 86*, Boyce 4–49)
West Indies won by an innings and 226 runs

492. West Indies v England
First Test at Port-of-Spain, Trinidad – 2, 3, 5, 6, 7 February 1974
ENGLAND 131 (Boyce 4–42) and 392 (Amiss 174, Boycott 93, Denness 44, Gibbs 6–108)
WEST INDIES 392 (Kallicharran 158, Julien 86*, Pocock 5–110) and 132–3 (Fredericks 65*)
West Indies won by 7 wickets

493. West Indies v England
Second Test at Kingston, Jamaica – 16, 17, 19, 20, 21 February 1974
ENGLAND 353 (Boycott 68, Denness 67, Greig 45) and 432–9 (Amiss 262*)
WEST INDIES 583–9 dec. (Rowe 120, Fredericks 94, Kallicharran 93, Julien 66, Sobers 57, Lloyd 49)
Match drawn

494. West Indies v England
Third Test at Bridgetown, Barbados – 6, 7, 9, 10, 11 March 1974
ENGLAND 395 (Greig 148, Knott 87, Julien 5–57) and 277–7 (Fletcher 129*, Knott 67)
WEST INDIES 596–8 dec. (Rowe 302, Kallicharran 119, Murray 53*, Greig 6–164)
Match drawn

495. West Indies v England
Fourth Test at Georgetown, Guyana – 22, 23, 24, 26 (no play), 27 March 1974
ENGLAND 448 (Greig 121, Amiss 118, Knott 61, Denness 42, Fletcher 41)
WEST INDIES 198–4 (Fredericks 98, Kanhai 44)
Match drawn

496. West Indies v England
Fifth Test at Port-of-Spain, Trinidad – 30, 31 March, 2, 3, 4, 5 April 1974
ENGLAND 267 (Boycott 99, Amiss 44) and 263 (Boycott 112, Fletcher 45, Knott 44)
WEST INDIES 305 (Rowe 123, Fredericks 67, Lloyd 52, Greig 8–86) and 199 (Greig 5–70)
England won by 26 runs

497. England v India
First Test at Old Trafford – 6, 7, 8, 10, 11 June 1974
ENGLAND 328–9 dec. (Fletcher 123*, Amiss 56, Greig 53) and 213–3 dec. (Edrich 100*, Amiss 47, Denness 45*)
INDIA 246 (Gavaskar 101, Abid Ali 71, Viswanath 40, Willis 4–64) and 182 (Gavaskar 58, Viswanath 50, Old 4–20)
England won by 113 runs

498. England v India
Second Test at Lord's – 20, 21, 22, 24 June 1974
ENGLAND 629 (Amiss 188, Denness 118, Greig 106, Edrich 96, Lloyd 46, Bedi 6–226)
INDIA 302 (Engineer 86, Viswanath 52, Gavaskar 49, Solkar 43, Old 4–67) and 42 (Old 5–21, Arnold 4–19)
England won by an innings and 285 runs

499. England v India
Third Test at Edgbaston – 4 (no play), 5, 6, 8 July 1974
INDIA 165 (Engineer 64*, Hendrick 4–28) and 216 (Naik 77, Mankad 43)
ENGLAND 459–2 dec. (Lloyd 214*, Denness 100, Amiss 79, Fletcher 51*)
England won by an innings and 78 runs

500. England v Pakistan
First Test at Headingley – 25, 26, 27, 29, 30 July 1974
PAKISTAN 285 (Majid Khan 75, Sarfraz Nawaz 53, Zaheer Abbas 48) and 179 (Mushtaq Mohammad 43)
ENGLAND 183 (Lloyd 48) and 238–6 (Edrich 70, Fletcher 67*, Denness 44, Sarfraz Nawaz 4–56)
Match drawn

501. England v Pakistan
Second Test at Lord's – 8, 9, 10, 12, 13 August 1974
PAKISTAN 130 (Majid Khan 48, Sadiq Mohammad 40, Underwood 5–20) and 226 (Mushtaq Mohammad 76, Wasim Raja 53, Sadiq Mohammad 43, Underwood 8–51)
ENGLAND 270 (Knott 83, Old 41, Edrich 40) and 27–0
Match drawn

502. England v Pakistan
Third Test at The Oval – 22, 23, 24, 26, 27 August 1974
PAKISTAN 600–7 dec. (Zaheer Abbas 240, Majid Khan 98, Mushtaq Mohammad 76) and 94–4
ENGLAND 545 (Amiss 183, Fletcher 122, Old 65, Underwood 43, Intikhab Alam 5–116)
Match drawn

503. Australia v England
First Test at Brisbane – 29, 30 November, 1, 3, 4 December 1974
AUSTRALIA 309 (I. Chappell 90, G. Chappell 58, Walker 41*, Willis 4–56) and 288–5 dec. (G. Chappell 71, Walters 62*, Edwards 53, Marsh 46*)
ENGLAND 265 (Greig 110, Edrich 48, Walker 4–73) and 166 (Thomson 6–46)
Australia won by 166 runs

504. Australia v England
Second Test at Perth – 13, 14, 15, 17 December 1974
ENGLAND 208 (Knott 51, Lloyd 49) and 293 (Titmus 61, Old 43, Cowdrey 41, Thomson 5–93)
AUSTRALIA 481 (Edwards 115, Walters 103, G. Chappell 62, Redpath 41, Marsh 41) and 23–1
Australia won by 9 wickets

505. Australia v England
Third Test at Melbourne – 26, 27, 28, 30, 31 December 1974
ENGLAND 242 (Knott 52, Edrich 49, Thomson 4–72) and 244 (Amiss 90, Greig 60, Lloyd 44, Mallett 4–60, Thomson 4–71)
AUSTRALIA 241 (Redpath 55, Marsh 44, Willis 5–61) and 238–8 (G. Chappell 61, Marsh 40, Greig 4–56)
Match drawn

506. Australia v England
Fourth Test at Sydney – 4, 5, 6, 8, 9 January 1975
AUSTRALIA 405 (G. Chappell 84, McCosker 80, I. Chappell 53, Arnold 5–86, Greig 4–104) and 289–4 dec. (G. Chappell 144, Redpath 105)
ENGLAND 295 (Knott 82, Edrich 50, Thomson 4–74) and 228 (Greig 54, Mallett 4–21)
Australia won by 171 runs

507. Australia v England
Fifth Test at Adelaide – 25 (no play), 26, 27, 29, 30 January 1975
AUSTRALIA 304 (Jenner 74, Walters 55, Walker 41, Underwood 7–113) and 272–5 dec. (Walters 71*, Marsh 55, Redpath 52, I. Chappell 41, Underwood 4–102)
ENGLAND 172 (Denness 51, Fletcher 40, Lillee 4–49) and 241 (Knott 106*, Fletcher 63, Lillee 4–69)
Australia won by 163 runs

508. Australia v England
Sixth Test at Melbourne – 8, 9, 10, 12, 13 February 1975
AUSTRALIA 152 (I. Chappell 65, P. Lever 6–38) and 373 (G. Chappell 102, Redpath 83, McCosker 76, I. Chappell 50, Greig 4–88)
ENGLAND 529 (Denness 188, Fletcher 146, Greig 89, Edrich 70, Walker 8–143)
England won by an innings and 4 runs

509. New Zealand v England
First Test at Auckland – 20, 21, 22, 23, 25 February 1975
ENGLAND 593–6 dec. (Fletcher 216, Denness 181, Edrich 64, Greig 51)
NEW ZEALAND 326 (Parker 121, Morrison 58, Wadsworth 58, Greig 5–98) and 184 (Morrison 58, Howarth 51*, Greig 5–51)
England won by an innings and 83 runs

510. New Zealand v England
Second Test at Christchurch – 28 February (no play), 1 (no play), 2, 3, 4, 5 March 1975
NEW ZEALAND 342 (Turner 98, Wadsworth 58, Parker 41)
ENGLAND 272–2 (Amiss 164*, Denness 59*)
Match drawn

 DID YOU KNOW...?

Dennis Amiss, Derek Underwood and Geoff Arnold all made a pair in the fifth Test of the 1974–5 Ashes series at Adelaide.

511. England v Australia
First Test at Edgbaston – 10, 11, 12, 14 July 1975
AUSTRALIA 359 (Marsh 61, McCosker 59, Edwards 56, I. Chappell 52, Thomson 49)
ENGLAND 101 (Lillee 5–15, Walker 5–48) and 173 (Fletcher 51, Thomson 5–38)
Australia won by an innings and 85 runs

512. England v Australia
Second Test at Lord's – 31 July, 1, 2, 4, 5 August 1975
ENGLAND 315 (Greig 96, Knott 69, Steele 50, Lillee 4–84) and 436–7 dec. (Edrich 175, Wood 52, Steele 45, Greig 41)
AUSTRALIA 268 (Edwards 99, Lillee 73*, Snow 4–66)
Match drawn

513. England v Australia
Third Test at Headingley – 14, 15, 16, 18, 19 (no play) August 1975
ENGLAND 288 (Steele 73, Edrich 62, Greig 51, Gilmour 6–85) and 291 (Steele 92, Greig 49)
AUSTRALIA 135 (Edmonds 5–28) and 220–3 (McCosker 95*, I. Chappell 62)
Match drawn

514. England v Australia
Fourth Test at The Oval – 28, 29, 30 August, 1, 2, 3 September 1975
AUSTRALIA 532–9 dec. (I. Chappell 192, McCosker 127, Walters 65, Edwards 44) and 40–2
ENGLAND 191 (Thomson 4–50, Walker 4–63) and 538 (Woolmer 149, Edrich 96, Roope 77, Steele 66, Knott 64, Walters 4–34, Lillee 4–91)
Match drawn

515. England v West Indies
First Test at Trent Bridge – 3, 4, 5, 7, 8 June 1976
WEST INDIES 494 (Richards 232, Kallicharran 97, Fredericks 42, Underwood 4–82) and 176–5 dec. (Richards 63, Snow 4–53)
ENGLAND 332 (Steele 106, Woolmer 82, Daniel 4–53) and 156–2 (Edrich 76*)
Match drawn

516. England v West Indies
Second Test at Lord's – 17, 18, 19, 21, 22 June 1976
ENGLAND 250 (Close 60, Brearley 40, Roberts 5–60) and 254 (Steele 64, Close 46, Roberts 5–63)
WEST INDIES 182 (Greenidge 84, Lloyd 50, Underwood 5–39, Snow 4–68) and 241–6 (Fredericks 138)
Match drawn

517. England v West Indies
Third Test at Old Trafford – 8, 9, 10, 12, 13 July 1976
WEST INDIES 211 (Greenidge 134, Selvey 4–41) and 411–5 dec. (Richards 135, Greenidge 101, Fredericks 50, Lloyd 43)
ENGLAND 71 (Holding 5–17) and 126 (Roberts 6–37)
West Indies won by 425 runs

518. England v West Indies
Fourth Test at Headingley – 22, 23, 24, 26, 27 July 1976
WEST INDIES 450 (Greenidge 115, Fredericks 109, Richards 66, Rowe 50, Snow 4–77) and 196 (King 58, Willis 5–42)
ENGLAND 387 (Greig 116, Knott 116) and 204 (Greig 76*, Willey 45)
West Indies won by 55 runs

519. England v West Indies
Fifth Test at The Oval – 12, 13, 14, 16, 17 August 1976
WEST INDIES 687–7 dec. (Richards 291, Lloyd 84, Fredericks 71, Rowe 70, King 63) and 182–0 dec. (Fredericks 86*, Greenidge 85*)
ENGLAND 435 (Amiss 203, Knott 50, Steele 44, Holding 8–92) and 203 (Knott 57, Steele 42, Holding 6–57)
West Indies won by 231 runs

520. India v England
First Test at Delhi – 17, 18, 19, 21, 22 December 1976
ENGLAND 381 (Amiss 179, Knott 75, J. Lever 53, Bedi 4–92)
INDIA 122 (J. Lever 7–46) and 234 (Gavaskar 71, Underwood 4–78)
England won by an innings and 25 runs

521. India v England
Second Test at Calcutta – 1, 2, 3, 5, 6 January 1977
INDIA 155 (Willis 5–27) and 181 (Patel 56)
ENGLAND 321 (Greig 103, Tolchard 67, Old 52, Bedi
5–110, Prasanna 4–93) and 16–0
England won by 10 wickets

522. India v England
Third Test at Madras – 14, 15, 16, 18, 19 January 1977
ENGLAND 262 (Brearley 59, Greig 54, Knott 45, Bedi 4–72)
and 185–9 dec. (Amiss 46, Greig 41, Chandrasekhar
5–50, Prasanna 4–55)
INDIA 164 (J. Lever 5–59) and 83 (Underwood 4–28, Willis
3–18)
England won by 200 runs

523. India v England
Fourth Test at Bangalore – 28, 29, 30 January, 1, 2 February
1977
INDIA 253 (Amarnath 63, Kirmani 52, Willis 6–53) and 259–9
dec. (Viswanath 79*, Gavaskar 50, Underwood 4–76)
ENGLAND 195 (Amiss 82, Chandrasekhar 6–76) and 177
(Knott 81*, Bedi 6–71)
India won by 140 runs

524. India v England
Fifth Test at Bombay – 11, 12, 14, 15, 16 February 1977
INDIA 338 (Gavaskar 108, Patel 83, Amarnath 40,
Underwood 4–89) and 192 (Amarnath 63, Gavaskar 42,
Underwood 5–84)
ENGLAND 317 (Brearley 91, Greig 76, Amiss 50, Prasanna
4–73, Bedi 4–109) and 152–7 (Fletcher 58*, Ghavri 5–33)
Match drawn

525. Australia v England
Centenary Test at Melbourne – 12, 13, 14, 16, 17 March 1977
AUSTRALIA 138 (G. Chappell 40) and 419–9 dec. (Marsh
110*, Davis 68, Walters 66, Hookes 56, Old 4–104)
ENGLAND 95 (Lillee 6–26, Walker 4–54) and 417 (Randall
174, Amiss 64, Brearley 43, Knott 42, Greig 41, Lillee
5–139)
Australia won by 45 runs

526. England v Australia
First Test at Lord's – 16, 17, 18, 20, 21 June 1977
ENGLAND 216 (Woolmer 79, Randall 53, Thomson 4–41)
and 305 (Woolmer 120, Greig 91, Brearley 49, Thomson
4–86)
AUSTRALIA 296 (Serjeant 81, G. Chappell 66, Walters 53,
Willis 7–78) and 114–6 (Hookes 50)
Match drawn

527. England v Australia
Second Test at Old Trafford – 7, 8, 9, 11, 12 July 1977
AUSTRALIA 297 (Walters 88, G. Chappell 44) and 218
(G. Chappell 112, Underwood 6–66)
ENGLAND 437 (Woolmer 137, Randall 79, Greig 76) and
82–1 (Brearley 44)
England won by 9 wickets

528. England v Australia
Third Test at Trent Bridge – 28, 29, 30 July, 1, 2 August 1977
AUSTRALIA 243 (McCosker 51, O'Keeffe 48*, Botham
5–74) and 309 (McCosker 107, Hookes 42, Willis 5–88)
ENGLAND 364 (Knott 135, Boycott 107, Pascoe 4–80) and
189–3 (Brearley 81, Boycott 80*)
England won by 7 wickets

529. England v Australia
Fourth Test at Headingley – 11, 12, 13, 15 August 1977
ENGLAND 436 (Boycott 191, Knott 57, Greig 43, Pascoe
4–91, Thomson 4–113)
AUSTRALIA 103 (Botham 5–21, Hendrick 4–41) and 248
(Marsh 63, Hendrick 4–54)
England won by an innings and 85 runs

530. England v Australia
Fifth Test at The Oval – 25 (no play), 26, 27, 29, 30 August
1977
ENGLAND 214 (Malone 5–63, Thomson 4–87) and 57–2
AUSTRALIA 385 (Hookes 85, Walker 78*, Marsh 57,
Malone 46, Willis 5–102)
Match drawn

531. Pakistan v England
First Test at Lahore – 14, 15, 16, 18, 19 December 1977
PAKISTAN 407–9 dec. (Haroon Rashid 122, Mudassar
Nazar 114, Javed Miandad 71) and 106–3 (Haroon
Rashid 45*)
ENGLAND 288 (Miller 98*, Boycott 63, Sarfraz Nawaz
4–68)
Match drawn

532. Pakistan v England
Second Test at Sind – 2, 3, 4, 6, 7 January 1978
PAKISTAN 275 (Haroon Rashid 108, Javed Miandad 88*) and
259–4 dec. (Mudassar Nazar 66, Javed Miandad 61*)
ENGLAND 191 (Boycott 79, Abdul Qadir 6–44) and 186–1
(Boycott 100*, Brearley 74)
Match drawn

533. Pakistan v England
Third Test at Karachi – 18, 19, 20, 22, 23 January 1978
ENGLAND 266 (Roope 56, Abdul Qadir 4–81) and 222–5
(Boycott 56, Randall 55)
PAKISTAN 281 (Mudassar Nazar 76, Wasim Raja 47,
Mohsin Khan 44, Edmonds 7–66)
Match drawn

534. New Zealand v England
First Test at Wellington – 10, 11, 12, 14, 15 February 1978
NEW ZEALAND 228 (Wright 55, Congdon 44, Old 6–54)
and 123 (Willis 5–32)
ENGLAND 215 (Boycott 77, Hadlee 4–74) and 64 (Hadlee
6–26)
New Zealand won by 72 runs

535. New Zealand v England
Second Test at Christchurch – 24, 25, 26, 28 February, 1
March 1978
ENGLAND 418 (Botham 103, Miller 89, Edmonds 50,
Roope 50, Taylor 45, Hadlee 4–147) and 96–4 dec.
NEW ZEALAND 235 (Anderson 62, Parker 53*, Botham
5–73, Edmonds 4–38) and 105 (Willis 4–14)
England won by 174 runs

536. New Zealand v England
Third Test at Auckland – 4, 5, 6, 8, 9, 10 March 1978
NEW ZEALAND 315 (Howarth 122, Edwards 55, Burgess
50, Botham 5–109) and 382–8 (Howarth 102, Anderson
55, Edwards 54, Parker 47*)
ENGLAND 429 (Radley 158, Roope 68, Boycott 54, Botham
53, Collinge 4–98)
Match drawn

537. England v Pakistan

First Test at Edgbaston – 1, 2, 3, 5 June 1978
PAKISTAN 164 (Old 7–50) and 231 (Sadiq Mohammad 79, Edmonds 4–44)
ENGLAND 452–8 dec. (Radley 106, Botham 100, Gower 58, Miller 48, Sikander Bakht 4–132)
England won by an innings and 57 runs

538. England v Pakistan

Second Test at Lord's – 15, 16, 17, 19 June 1978
ENGLAND 364 (Botham 108, Roope 69, Gower 56, Gooch 54)
PAKISTAN 105 (Willis 5–47, Edmonds 4–6) and 139 (Mohsin Khan 46, Talat Ali 40, Botham 8–34)
England won by an innings and 120 runs

539. England v Pakistan

Third Test at Headingley – 29, 30 June, 1, 3, 4 July 1978
PAKISTAN 201 (Sadiq Mohammad 97, Mohsin Khan 41, Old 4–41, Botham 4–59)
ENGLAND 119–7 (Sarfraz Nawaz 5–39)
Match drawn

540. England v New Zealand

First Test at The Oval – 27, 28, 29, 31 July, 1 August 1978
NEW ZEALAND 234 (Howarth 94, Wright 62, Willis 5–42) and 182 (Edmonds 4–20)
ENGLAND 279 (Gower 111, Radley 49) and 138–3 (Gooch 91*)
England won by 7 wickets

541. England v New Zealand

Second Test at Trent Bridge – 10, 11, 12, 14 August 1978
ENGLAND 429 (Boycott 131, Radley 59, Gooch 55, Brearley 50, Gower 46, Hadlee 4–94)
NEW ZEALAND 120 (Botham 6–34) and 190 (Edgar 60, Edmonds 4–44)
England won by an innings and 119 runs

542. England v New Zealand

Third Test at Lord's – 24, 25, 26, 28 August 1978
NEW ZEALAND 339 (Howarth 123, Burgess 68, Botham 6–101) and 67 (Botham 5–39, Willis 4–16)
ENGLAND 289 (Radley 77, Gower 71, Hadlee 5–84) and 118–3 (Gower 46, Gooch 42*)
England won by 7 wickets

543. Australia v England

First Test at Brisbane – 1, 2, 3, 5, 6 December 1978
AUSTRALIA 116 (Willis 4–44) and 339 (Hughes 129, Yallop 102)
ENGLAND 286 (Randall 75, Botham 49, Gower 44, Hogg 6–74, Hurst 4–93) and 170–3 (Randall 74*, Gower 48*)
England won by 7 wickets

544. Australia v England

Second Test at Perth – 15, 16, 17, 19, 20 December 1978
ENGLAND 309 (Gower 102, Boycott 77, Miller 40, Hogg 5–65) and 208 (Randall 45, Gooch 43, Hogg 5–57)
AUSTRALIA 190 (Toohey 81*, Willis 5–44) and 161 (Wood 64, Cosier 47, J. Lever 4–28)
England won by 166 runs

545. Australia v England

Third Test at Melbourne – 29, 30 December 1978, 1, 2, 3 January 1979
AUSTRALIA 258 (Wood 100, Yallop 41) and 167 (Hughes 48)
ENGLAND 143 (Hogg 5–30) and 179 (Gower 49, Gooch 40, Hogg 5–36)
Australia won by 103 runs

546. Australia v England

Fourth Test at Sydney – 6, 7, 8, 10, 11 January 1979
ENGLAND 152 (Botham 59, Hurst 5–28) and 346 (Randall 150, Brearley 53, Higgs 5–148, Hogg 4–67)
AUSTRALIA 294 (Darling 91, Border 60*, Hughes 48, Yallop 44) and 111 (Border 45*, Emburey 4–46)
England won by 93 runs

547. Australia v England

Fifth Test at Adelaide – 27, 28, 29, 31 January, 1 February 1979
ENGLAND 169 (Botham 74, Hogg 4–26) and 360 (Taylor 97, Miller 64, Boycott 49, Emburey 42, Hurst 4–97)
AUSTRALIA 164 (Botham 4–42) and 160 (Hughes 46)
England won by 205 runs

548. Australia v England

Sixth Test at Sydney – 10, 11, 12, 14 February 1979
AUSTRALIA 198 (Yallop 121, Botham 4–57) and 143 (Yardley 61*, Miller 5–44, Emburey 4–52)
ENGLAND 308 (Gooch 74, Gower 65, Brearley 46, Higgs 4–69) and 35–1
England won by 9 wickets

549. England v India

First Test at Edgbaston – 12, 13, 14, 16 July 1979
ENGLAND 633–5 dec. (Gower 200*, Boycott 155, Gooch 83, Miller 63*, Kapil Dev 5–146)
INDIA 297 (Viswanath 78, Gavaskar 61) and 253 (Gavaskar 68, Chauhan 56, Viswanath 51, Botham 5–70, Hendrick 4–45)
England won by an innings and 83 runs

550. England v India

Second Test at Lord's – 2, 3, 4, 6, 7 August 1979
INDIA 96 (Gavaskar 42, Botham 5–35) and 318–4 (Viswanath 113, Vengsarkar 103, Gavaskar 59)
ENGLAND 419–9 dec. (Gower 82, Taylor 64, Miller 62, Randall 57)
Match drawn

551. England v India

Third Test at Headingley – 16, 17 (no play), 18 (no play), 20, 21 August 1979
ENGLAND 270 (Botham 137)
INDIA 223–6 (Gavaskar 78, Vengsarkar 65*)
Match drawn

552. England v India

Fourth Test at The Oval – 30, 31 August, 1, 3, 4 September 1979
ENGLAND 305 (Gooch 79, Willey 52) and 334–8 dec. (Boycott 125, Bairstow 59)
INDIA 202 (Viswanath 62, Y. Singh 43*, Botham 4–65) and 429–8 (Gavaskar 221, Chauhan 80, Vengsarkar 52)
Match drawn

THE DAWN OF A NEW ERA: 1980–9

With peace made between the Packer organization and established cricket, England went to Australia to play a three-match series against the home country. In the course of the first Test at Perth, Dennis Lillee strode out to bat with an aluminium bat and was ordered to change it for a more traditional appliance. Needing 354 to win, they were bowled out for 215 with Boycott finishing unbeaten on 99 – the first English batsman to carry his bat through a completed innings without reaching a century. He was also the first player to finish 99 not out in a Test. The pitch for the second Test at Sydney was the subject of much controversy. Soaked by rain for days beforehand, it was underprepared and, on a shortened first day, England ended it at 90–7 before being bowled out for 123. Australia reached only 145 before David Gower scored 98 not out, but he ran out of partners as England set the home side only 216 to make for victory. The wicket was now improving and Australia won by 6 wickets. In the final Test at Melbourne, Gooch was run out for 99, attempting a single for his first Test century, and Australia made 477, a lead of 171 on first innings. Despite an unbeaten 119 from Botham, Australia needed a mere 103 to win, and did so by 8 wickets.

The Test match played at the Wankhede Stadium in Bombay to celebrate India's Golden Jubilee was a triumph for Ian Botham and, to a lesser extent, Bob Taylor. In India's first innings total of 242, Botham took 6–58 and Taylor held seven catches. England looked in trouble at 58–5 but Botham (114) and Taylor (43) added 171 in a total of 296. Botham then skittled India out even more dramatically second time round, taking 7–48 as the Indians were all out for 149. Gooch and Boycott made 98 without loss as England won by 10 wickets. Botham became the first player to score a century and take 10 wickets in a Test match.

Ian Botham was the new England captain when West Indies toured in 1980 and he top-scored with 57 in England's first-innings total of 263 at Trent Bridge. West Indies scored 308 in reply and though Boycott batted obstinately in England's second innings, the tourists were left to make just 208 for victory. They were made to fight hard on the last day and, at 180–7, the game could have gone either way, but the match had been one of missed catches and one more on the last day proved crucial as West Indies won by 2 wickets. At Lord's, Graham Gooch made a brilliant 123 in a total of 269 before Viv Richards made 145 and Desmond Haynes 184 as they added 223 for the second wicket. West Indies made 518 but rain cut short England's knock, which ended at 133–2. Rain severely affected the third Test, at Old Trafford, while the fourth, at The Oval, also drawn, saw England make 370 and West Indies 265 before England looked in trouble at 92–9 in their second innings. Willis joined Peter Willey and the Northamptonshire all-rounder made 100 not out in a total of 209–9 declared. England needed to win at Headingley to tie the series but, with rain washing out the first and fourth days, they had little chance.

After the huge success of the 1977 Centenary Test in Melbourne, another was held at Lord's in 1980, this time marking the centenary of the first Test match played in England. Sadly, with rain interruptions, the match failed to live up to the drama of the match three years earlier. Greg Chappell declared Australia's first innings at 385–5 with both Hughes and Wood making hundreds, while England were bowled out for 205. Chappell declared a second time at 189–4, setting England 370 to win at just over a run a minute. The chase was soon given up but Boycott enjoyed himself, batting out time for 128 not out and passing 7,000 Test runs along the way.

In 1980–1, England toured the Caribbean, having lost 1–0 to the West Indies in the summer. The first Test, at Port-of-Spain, began late because rain had left wet patches on the pitch, both covers and pitch having been sabotaged by locals protesting at the omission of Deryck Murray. West Indies made 426–9 declared and bowled England out for 178, forcing them to follow on. England were bowled out a second time and West Indies won by an innings and 79 runs. The second Test, at Georgetown, was cancelled, the first ever to be called off for political reasons, days before its scheduled start. Robin Jackman had arrived in Guyana as a replacement for the injured Willis and was immediately served with a deportation order. Jackman, married to a South African, had played in South Africa for the previous eleven winters and was unacceptable to the Guyana authorities. The third Test, at Bridgetown, was marred by the sudden death through a heart attack of Ken Barrington, the assistant manager and coach of the England team. With Clive Lloyd making a hundred, West Indies made 265 before England were rapidly shot out for 122. After Richards had made 182 not out, Lloyd declared at 379–7, leaving England needing 523 to win. Gooch showed his colleagues how fast bowling should be played with a fine innings of 116, but West Indies won by 298 runs. In the fourth Test, in Antigua, Peter Willey made 102 not out in a total of 271. Richards, on his home island, made 114 as West Indies declared at 468–9 but England easily saved the game with Boycott unbeaten on 104 in a total of 234–3. Gooch again batted brilliantly in the fifth Test, at Kingston, making 153, but, once he was out at 249–5, they tumbled to 285 all out. West Indies totalled 442 before Gower, with 154 not out, aided by Willey and Downton, helped England draw the game.

One of the most memorable series in Ashes history occurred during the summer of 1981. The opening day of the first Test, at Trent Bridge, saw England, bowled out for 185, reduce Australia to 33–4. Rain interrupted play the following day but, nevertheless, Australia were all out for 179 on the Saturday. England were then dismissed for 125 and, though Australia had a few alarms in reaching 132–6, they went 1–0 up in the series. The second Test, at Lord's, always looked a draw and after the game Ian Botham resigned the captaincy and Mike Brearley was appointed to resume the duties for the remainder of the series. The third Test, at Headingley, was one of the most exciting of modern times and featured the biggest reversal of fortune in living memory. Australia won the toss and made 401–9 declared, using up almost all of the first two rain-interrupted days. England were shot out for 174 and were forced to follow on. England's situation was so bleak that, on the morning of the fourth day, with them 6–1 – still 221 runs in arrears – the bookmakers offered odds of 500–1 against an England win. Lillee and Marsh both placed bets in the unlikely event of their opponents turning things around. England slid to 41–4 before Boycott and Willey took the score to 105–5. Boycott and then Taylor fell in quick succession to leave England 135–7, still 92 runs short of avoiding an innings defeat. Dilley joined Botham and the pair added 117 in 18 overs. When Dilley was out for 56, Botham went on to blast 149 not out. England made 356, leaving Australia needing 130 to win. After Bob Willis had been switched to the Kirkstall Lane End, he dismissed Chappell, Hughes and Yallop within the space of a few minutes just before lunch. After lunch, the rout continued as Old bowled Border and Dilley held a Marsh hook on the boundary. Willis then beat Lawson for pace and after Lillee and Bright had taken 35 off four overs, Lillee popped a ball from Willis to Gatting, who dived forward to take the catch. A Willis yorker then accounted for Bright. He had taken a career best 8–43 and England had won the most remarkable game of cricket by 18 runs. At Edgbaston, England were dismissed for 189 before Australia made 258, a lead of 69. England were in trouble at 167–8 but a stand of 50 between Emburey and Old meant England totalled 219. Set 151 to win, Australia soon lost Wood, and on Sunday, 142 were needed with 9 wickets left. At 105–5, Brearley called on Botham. The last 5 wickets fell for just 7 runs, all to Botham, and Australia were all out for 121. The Old Trafford Test was a match of contrasts – high and low innings, fast and slow scoring. England made 231 and Australia 130, with Willis picking up his hundredth wicket in Ashes cricket. In England's second innings, Botham passed 100 in 86 balls and when he was out, he had scored 118 from the 149 runs he added with Chris Tavare. The Kent batsman scored the slowest 50 in an English first-class match (75 overs, 306 minutes). England reached 404 and Australia needed 506 to win. Yallop and Border both made hundreds but Australia were all out for 402. The final Test, at The Oval, could not live up to the previous three and, after Brearley mistakenly put Australia into bat, the game ended in a draw.

During the first Test of England's tour of India in 1981–2, the tourists were unhappy at several umpiring decisions. On a pitch of variable bounce, India made 179 and England, after being 95–1, were bowled out for 166. India then struggled to 157–8 before Kapil Dev took the score to 227. With Madan Lal and Kapil Dev taking 5 wickets apiece, England lost by 138 runs. At Bangalore, England made 400 on a benign pitch but, as it took two days, the game was destined to be a draw from the start. Gavaskar made 172 as India replied with 428 and England made 174–3 in the time left. The third Test followed the same pattern as the previous one as Geoff Boycott, with 105, overtook Garry Sobers as the leading run-getter in Test history, while Chris Tavare made 149. The match at Calcutta was watched by an estimated 425,000 – a world record for any match. It was here that England had their best chance to level the series, giving themselves just over a day to bowl out India for 306. However, the last day started late because of bad light and, with Gavaskar unbeaten on 83, India finished on 170–3. In the fifth Test, at Madras, India declared at 481–4 with

Viswanath making 222 and Yashpal Sharma 140. Gooch made 127 as England avoided the follow-on with a total of 328 and India were 160–3 when stumps were drawn. The sixth Test, at Kanpur, was a victim of mist and rain but Botham hit 142 in England's total of 378–9 declared. India avoided the follow-on and on the last day, Kapil Dev scored an entertaining 116, passing his century off 83 balls, one of the quickest in Test history.

Elevated to full Test status, Sri Lanka played their first Test match against England in Colombo in February 1982. Warnapura won the toss and batted on a damp pitch and was himself one of the first four batsmen out, with just 34 runs on the board. Madugalle and Ranatunga then hit half-centuries, allowing Sri Lanka to make 218. England's first-innings lead was only five and, with Roy Dias making 77, a shock win looked on the cards. Then John Emburey produced a spell of 5–5 and the home side lost their last 7 wickets while adding only 8 runs. Emburey's final figures were 6–33 as Sri Lanka were dismissed for 175. Needing 171 to win, England won by 7 wickets with Chris Tavare making 85.

For the visit of India in 1982, Bob Willis was England's new captain and he elected to bat in the first Test, at Lord's, where Derek Randall top-scored with 126 in a total of 433. India made a desperate start and with Botham taking 5–46 were all out for 128. They looked to be going the same way when following on, but a masterly innings of 157 by Vengsarkar and a quickfire knock of 89 by Kapil Dev allowed India to reach 369. Needing 65, England lost 3 wickets while 18 were scored in 8 overs on the fourth night, but then reached the target without further loss on the last morning. In the second Test, at Old Trafford, Botham hit 128 in England's total of 425 and with Miler (98) helped in a stand of 169. With rain interruptions throughout, India had made 379–8 before the last day was washed out completely. England batted first again at The Oval and provided some brilliant attacking batting, with Botham leading the way with 208 and Lamb 107 in a total of 594. The Indian batsmen made a spirited reply and, in making 410 with Kapil Dev hitting 97 in 93 balls, avoided the follow-on. Willis later declared and set India 376 to win in an impossible time to the disgruntlement of the spectators.

Pakistan followed India to England for the second half of the summer of 1982. David Gower, who top-scored with 74 in England's moderate first innings total of 272, led a charmed life and even played on without disturbing a bail. Imran Khan took 7–52, a reward for his pace and control. Pakistan ended 21 runs behind on first innings with Ian Greig claiming 4–53 on his Test debut. England's second innings depended heavily on Derek Randall, who made 105, until Taylor and Willis added 79 for the last wicket to enable England to total 291. Needing 313 to win, Pakistan started badly and were 0–2 and, though Imran hit a defiant 65, they lost by 113 runs. In the second Test, at Lord's, Mohsin Khan made a brilliant 200, after a rain stoppage had forced him to wait for four hours on 199. Pakistan declared at 428–8 before Abdul Qadir took 4–38 as England were dismissed for 227. Worse was to come as Mudasser Nazar took 6–32 and England had to follow on. When they were all out for 276,

Pakistan were left with 18 overs to make the 77 runs for victory and scored them without loss with almost 5 overs to spare. The final Test, the decider at Headingley, was fought evenly throughout and after Pakistan had made 275, England replied with 256. Willis then dismissed both Pakistani openers for ducks before Miandad and Imran brought a touch of respectability to the score. Even so, England needed only 219 to win and, after Fowler and Tavare put on 106 for the first wicket, they looked to be in no trouble. Fowler, on his debut, went on to make 86 but when he was out, England lost 6 wickets for 31 runs before Marks and Taylor saw them home.

England, without South African 'rebels' Gooch, Boycott, Emburey, Knott and Underwood, headed to Australia to contest the 1982–3 Ashes series. The series began at Perth on a batsman's wicket on which England, put in, made 411. When England had reached 400 there was a pitch invasion by drunken English supporters, which developed into a skirmish, and Terry Alderman, who tried to do some personal policing, dislocated a shoulder and stretched a nerve. Australia passed England's total and declared at 424–9. With England struggling at 80–4 there was the possibility of a result but Randall's 115 helped England recover and the match ended in a draw. At Brisbane, Geoff Lawson's 6–47 wrecked the tourists' first innings and they were bowled out for 219. Kepler Wessels, making his debut for Australia, then scored 162 and the home side had a lead of 122 on first innings. England totalled 309 in their second knock. With Wessels dropped before he had scored, Dyson retired hurt and, with three men out for 93, there was just a hint of a collapse, but Hughes and Hookes saw Australia home by 7 wickets. Willis won the toss in the third Test, at Adelaide, and sent Australia in to bat. The plan backfired as Australia totalled 438 with Greg Chappell making his ninth hundred against England. Only Lamb, Gower and Botham batted well for England their last seven wickets fell for 35 runs; England, 216 all out, followed on. This time Gower made 114 but the lower order was again disappointing and Australia made the 83 needed for the loss of two wickets.

The Boxing Day Test in Melbourne provided one of cricket's great finishes. Put in again, England made 284. Australia passed it only by three before England recovered from 129–5 in their second to reach 294, leaving Australia 292 to win. The home side were struggling at 71–3 when Hughes and Hookes added exactly 100, putting Australia on top. Six wickets then fell for 47 runs, leaving Border and Thomson to make 74 for the last wicket. Half of these were made by the close of play and 18,000 entered the ground free on the last morning to see if they could make the other 37. They almost did. When three runs short of the target, Thomson nicked Botham to Tavare at second slip. He could only knock the ball up over his head but Miller at first slip came round the back of him to hold the ball just above the ground. One of the worst umpiring decisions of the series came in the final Test, at Sydney, when John Dyson, clearly run out by almost a yard, was allowed to stay, and he went on to make 79. Border made 89 and Australia totalled 314. England replied with 237, while Kim Hughes hit a hundred as Australia set England a virtually impossible 452 to win. Eddie Hemmings, who had been sent in as night-watchman, made 95 and the match ended with England 315–7.

During the New Zealand visit to England in 1983, the Kiwis recorded their first-ever victory on English soil. In the first Test, at The Oval, England made 209 with Richard Hadlee taking 6–53 prior to top-scoring with 84 as Willis and Botham helped bowl out New Zealand for 196. England began their second innings with a 223 opening stand and ground their way to 446–6 declared with Tavare, Fowler and Lamb all hitting hundreds. New Zealand were then bowled out for 270, giving England victory by 189 runs. New Zealand put England in at Headingley and bowled them out for 225 with Lance Cairns taking 7–74. New Zealand were 168–1 but minutes later found themselves 169–4 before eventually recovering to make 377. Gower made an unbeaten 112 in England's second innings but the Kiwis were left with just 101 to win. Bob Willis took 5–35 but the tourists won by 5 wickets. New Zealand came down to earth with a bump at Lord's. Howarth won the toss and put England in to bat, Gower making 108 in a total of 326. Nick Cook was the most impressive of England's three debutants (Foster and Chris Smith were the others) and he took 5–35 as New Zealand were bowled out for 191. England were then dismissed for 211 but the visitors never looked like making 347 and lost by 127 runs. In the fourth and final Test, at Trent Bridge, Botham (103) and Randall (83) shared a brilliant stand of 186 – 164 glorious runs coming in 32 overs after tea. England totalled 420. Cook bowled brilliantly again to take 5–63 and New Zealand were out for 207. Lamb then made a splendid 137 not out, almost half of England's second innings total of 297. New Zealand needed 511 in nearly two days but, despite useful knocks from Hadlee, Edgar and Coney, they lost by 165 runs.

Five months after their last meeting, New Zealand were playing England at home but after winning the toss in the first Test at Wellington and electing to bat, they were bowled out for 219. At 115–5, the England innings was follow-ing a similar pattern until Randall (164) and Botham (138) got together to add 232 in a total of 463. The pitch had eased somewhat and Martin Crowe made 100 and Jeremy Coney an unbeaten 174 as the Kiwis totalled 537 to save the game. England were 69 without loss when stumps were drawn. Play in the second Test, at Christchurch, lasted only twelve hours on a controversial wicket. New Zealand made 307 with Richard Hadlee out one short of his century, on a suspect pitch. The wicket, full of cracks, was now also spongy and England were bowled out for 82. Following on, they fared little better and were dismissed for 93. England had to win the last Test in Auckland to avoid a series defeat by New Zealand for the first time. Three players dominated New Zealand's first innings, John Wright (130), Jeff Crowe (128) and wicketkeeper Ian Smith (113 not out), as they declared at 496–9. After interruptions for rain, the match was already virtually drawn, though Randall made another hundred in England's total of 439. There was just time for five overs of New Zealand's second innings before the celebrations began – the Kiwis winning their first series victory over England, six months after their first win in England.

The three Tests in Pakistan in 1983–4 were threatened by student disruptions and went ahead under heavy security precautions. In the first Test, at Karachi, no English batsman, with the possible exception of David Gower, mastered Qadir. Needing only 65 to record their first home win against England, the Pakistanis batted nervously but at 66–7, they had just scraped home. Botham, Dilley and Willis all returned home through injury and illness and played no further part in the tour. The second Test was a batting feast and after Pakistan had declared at 449–8, England replied with 546–8 declared, with Gower making a splendid 152. Not surprisingly the match was drawn, as was the third Test, at Lahore, although this match was far more exciting. England, batting first, made 241 thanks to a stand of 120 between Fowler and Marks after Pakistan had reduced them to 83–5. Pakistan were also in trouble but an astonishing innings of 90 by Sarfraz Nawaz gave them a lead of 102 runs on first innings. Gower then played another captain's innings and his unbeaten 173 enabled him to declare at 344–9 to set Pakistan 243 to win in a generous 59 overs. Norman Cowans, with 5–42, bowled beautifully but at the close of play the home side were 217–6, having batted out the last half an hour.

England captain David Gower decided to bat first on what proved a lively Edgbaston wicket in the first Test of the 1985 series against West Indies. Fowler and Randall departed early while Andy Lloyd was struck on the head by a Marshall bouncer and spent the next eight days in hospital. All out for 191, England struggled to contain the West Indian batsmen and Larry Gomes (143) and Richards (117) shared a third-wicket stand of 206 before Baptiste and Holding flogged a tired attack for a ninth-wicket stand of 150 – West Indies were 606 all out. In their second innings, England's batsmen showed determination in delaying the inevitable but soon after lunch on the fourth day, West Indies had won by an innings and 180 runs. At Lord's, Fowler (106) and Broad (55) had 100 on the board without loss but nobody else did much and England were all out for 286. Botham then bowled with plenty of venom to take 8–103 as West Indies were bowled out for 245. With Lamb making 110 and that man Botham a swashbuckling 81, England declared at 300–9, setting West Indies 342 to win. A magnificent innings by Greenidge (214 not out) supported by Gomes (92 not out) saw West Indies run out comfortable 9-wicket winners. The third Test, at Headingley, was another overwhelming victory for the West Indies who won by 8 wickets after Allan Lamb had made a second successive hundred in England's 270. A century by Gomes helped the tourists to a 32 run lead on first innings before Malcolm Marshall took 7–53 as England slumped to 159 all out. At Old Trafford, England had West Indies at 70–4 but Greenidge's second double century of the series and Dujon, with 101, added 197 as they went on to make 500. Lamb made his third century in successive matches but, at 280 all out, England were forced to follow on. With the pitch now taking spin, Harper took 6–57 as West Indies won by an innings and 64 runs. The final Test, at The Oval, saw Botham take his 300th Test wicket as West Indies were bowled out for 190. England fell 28 runs short before Desmond Haynes, the only West Indian batsman to fail in the series so far, made 125 in a second-innings total of 346. Needing 375 to win, the home side could only score 202 and West Indies had achieved what they called a 5–0 'blackwash'.

When Sri Lanka visited England for their first ever Test match in this country, Wettimuny played the longest innings in a Test match at Lord's – 642 minutes. He made 190 and skipper Mendis contributed 111 runs as Sri Lanka declared at 491–7. When England saved the follow-on with five men out, the game was destined for a draw – Lamb went on to make 107 in a total of 370. Sri Lanka batted on, offering England no consolation, Silva making 102 not out and Mendis smashing 94 from 97 balls.

Tragedy accompanied England's tour to India in 1984–5, when the Prime Minister Mrs Gandhi was assassinated. The rioting and unrest that followed and the period of mourning led to the tourists retreating to Sri Lanka for a while. In the first Test, at Bombay, England were dismissed for 195 before Shastri and Kirmani hit hundreds to enable India to declare at 465–8. Sivaramakrishnan took his second 6-wicket haul of the match and India won by 8 wickets. At Delhi India were bowled out for 307 before Tim Robinson, playing in only his second Test, made an eight-hour 160 to give England a lead of 111 runs on first innings. India played rashly in their second innings with many batsmen getting themselves out, and England found themselves with two hours to make the 125 for victory, which they did for the loss of 2 wickets. The third Test, at Calcutta, was a disappointing draw before records fell in the fourth test at Madras. After India were bowled out for 272, Fowler (201) and Gatting (207) both hit double centuries – the first occasion that two England batsmen had passed 200 in the same Test match. England declared at 652–7 and then Foster again bowled beautifully to finish with match figures of 11–163 as India made 412 and England won by 9 wickets. For the first time in a series in India, a visiting side had come from a match down to lead in the series. The final Test, at Kanpur, saw Vengsarkar and Azharuddin make hundreds as India declared at 553–8, but Fowler and Robinson put on 156 for the wicket as England, in no hurry, made their total of 417 stretch over into the last day. After India declared at 97–1, England made no attempt to make 234 to win in 46 overs.

The England side for the first Test of the 1985 Ashes series contained players now eligible after the lifting of the three-year ban for touring South Africa with a rebel XI. At Headingley, Australia, after passing 200 with only two men out, collapsed to 331. Tim Robinson then made a splendid 175 and, supported by Gatting, Botham and Downton, England made 533. Australia's second innings closed on 324, leaving England three hours to make 123 for victory, a target they achieved but not without losing 5 wickets. In the second Test, at Lord's, England made 290 before Allan Border, with 196, helped Australia to a first-innings lead of 135. In their second innings, England lost 6 wickets in reaching 100 but recovered to be all out for 261. Australia needed 127 to win but made hard work of it, losing 6 wickets in the process. At Trent Bridge, England at one stage were 358 for 2 but were bowled out for 456 –

Gower was the top scorer with 166. For Australia, Wood made 172 and Ritchie 146 in a total of 569 but the pitch was too good and the game drawn. Rain was the victor at Old Trafford, although England were pressing for a result until the last day. Australia made 257 and England passed this total with only three men out, going on to declare at 482–9 with Gatting (160) making his first century in this country. Border then went on to make an unbeaten 146 as Australia ended on 340–5. For the fifth Test, at Edgbaston, Richard Ellison was recalled to the England team and he took 6–77 as Australia were bowled out for 335. England raced past the tourists' total and declared at 595–5 with Gower making 215 not out, Robinson 148 and Gatting 100 not out. Ellison then took 4–1 in the evening to reduce Australia to 35–5. They were eventually all out for 142 to give England victory by an innings and 118 runs. Australia needed to win the final Test at The Oval and so retain the Ashes. But this looked impossible after Gooch (196) and Gower (157) added 351 for the second wicket. However, England were all out for 464 and Australia, after being dismissed for 241, followed on. For the first time in England all seats were sold in advance for a fourth day but Australia were soon out for 129 and England had won the series 3–1.

In 1985–6, England were defeated convincingly in all five Tests on their tour to the West Indies. In the opening Test at Kingston, Patterson made the most of the uneven pitch to help the West Indies to a 10-wicket win, the game being over inside three days. The second Test just crept into the final day before West Indies won by 7 wickets. Richie Richardson hit his second hundred in successive Tests in the third game at Bridgetown and Patterson picked up another 6 wickets as West Indies went 3–0 up in the series. There was no relief for England at Port-of-Spain as Viv Richards made his 6,000th Test run in another 10-wicket win for the home side. In the final Test, Viv Richards treated his home crowd at St John's with a brilliant 100 in 81 minutes. England made a more determined effort but they were still 164 runs behind on first innings and lost the match by 240 runs.

Following this trouncing, England entertained India for the first half of the summer of 1986 but in the opening Test, at Lord's, Dilip Vengsarkar hit his traditional hundred (it was his third century on the ground – a record for an overseas player). Kapil Dev then destroyed the England batting and India won by 5 wickets. In the second Test, at Headingley, Vengsarkar hit another hundred before the English batsmen were bemused by some plain bowling from Binny that resulted with India's victory by 279 runs. In the third Test, both teams made 390 in their first innings, but then India, chasing 236 to win, were content to let the game run to a draw on the last day.

England's visitors for the second half of the summer were New Zealand, and their habit of losing Test series continued. At Lord's, the game is in the history books as the 'Keepers' Test', as England used four wicketkeepers (Athey, Taylor, Parks and French) in a single innings – the game was drawn. At Trent Bridge, Richard Hadlee on his home ground, helped New Zealand to an 8-wicket win by taking 10 wickets, while John Bracewell made a brave hundred.

At The Oval, New Zealand were bowled out for 287 before Gower and Gatting scored hundreds in a total of 388–5 declared. The New Zealanders were quite content to see the rain, which more or less washed away the fourth and fifth days, give them victory in the series.

After their succession of defeats, England went to Australia in 1986–7 regarded by the press as underdogs. However, they completely outgunned Australia in the opening Test at Brisbane. Botham, with 138, helped England to 456 and then Dilley bowled the home side out cheaply. The follow-on was enforced and England won by 7 wickets. In the second Test, at Perth, Broad, Gower and Richards all made hundreds while Border held Australia together and any hope of a definite result disappeared when England scored too slowly second time. The third Test, in Adelaide, resulted in more high scoring and another draw. Australia reached 514–5 with David Boon top-scoring with 103 and then Broad and Gatting made hundreds for England. At Melbourne, Gladstone Small took 5–48 as Australia were bowled out for 141 before Chris Broad hit his third hundred in successive Tests to give England a commanding lead. Australia then collapsed against the spin of Edmonds and Emburey and England won by an innings and 14 runs and retained the Ashes. For the final Test, off-spinner Peter Taylor was a controversial selection but he took 6–78 to remove England for 275, this after Dean Jones had made a superb 184 not out for Australia. At lunch on the final day, the game was evenly poised, but Peter Sleep's leg breaks saw Australia home by 55 runs, with an over in hand.

Weather ruined the first Test of the 1987 Pakistan tour of England when, following Tim Robinson's patient 166 in a total of 447, showers allowed the tourists to make only 140–5 in reply. Lord's was worse, with the second, fourth and fifth days blank. In fact, there was just time for one innings with Bill Athey making 123 in England's total of 368. At Headingley, Gatting rather surprisingly opted to bat and England, who at one time were 31–5, were 136 all out. Pakistan batted down the order and made 353, with Salim Malik falling one run short of a hundred. Inspired bowling by Imran Khan (7–40) meant an innings defeat for England. The Edgbaston Test had an exciting finish. Pakistan made 439 and England 521, a lead of 82 runs, before Pakistan were whittled out for 205 in their second innings, leaving England 124 to win. There were 18 overs to get them in and, after just 4, England were 32 without loss. However, wickets then began to tumble and two run-outs in the final over ended the chase with England on 109–7. Pakistan batted first on a perfect Oval wicket and, with Miandad making 260, Imran Khan 118 and Salim Malik 102, totalled 708. Ian Botham took 3–217 – the record number of runs conceded by an England bowler in one innings. England were bowled out for 232 and followed on, but, with Gatting making 150 not out, the match was saved, though Pakistan recorded their first series victory in England.

England's tour of Pakistan in 1987–8 was one of the most acrimonious ever with unseemly rows between England captain Gatting and the umpires. The trouble began in the first Test, at Lahore, when Broad was reluctant to leave after being given out. However, Abdul Qadir took 9–56 to dismiss England for 175 and then Mudassar Nazar made 120 in Pakistan's reply of 392. England were bowled out for 130 in their second innings to suffer defeat by an innings and 87 runs. Trouble really flared in the second Test after England had made 292 with Broad scoring 116. Pakistan were struggling at 106–5 when Gatting called his deep square-leg in closer. Umpire Shakoor Rana halted Hemmings in his delivery stride on the grounds that the fielder had not completed his positional change. There followed an altercation in which Gatting claims he was called a cheat and the umpire that he was abused. Rana refused to umpire the following day unless Gatting apologized and Gatting would do so only if Rana would apologize also (which he wouldn't) and so the third day was lost. Play resumed on the fourth day but the game dragged out into a draw. The umpiring 'errors' continued in the final Test and there were more examples of dissent over decisions as the game ended in a draw.

England visited Australia to play a Bicentennial Test in January 1988 and made 425 in their first innings with Chris Broad top-scoring with 139. Annoyed at his dismissal he knocked his off stump out of the ground and was fined £500. Australia were dismissed for 214 and the follow-on enforced but a very disappointing match ended with Boon (184 not out) batting out time at 328–2.

In New Zealand, Chris Broad made another hundred at Christchurch as England totalled 319 and were in a strong position when Dilley (6–38) helped remove the hosts for 168. England made only 152 in their second innings but bad weather prevented a finish with New Zealand on 130–4. The second Test at Auckland was hampered by poor weather and slow batting, both of which contributed to the game being drawn. An easy wicket at Wellington and a cyclone that washed out the last two days meant a boring end to a rather tedious series.

When West Indies toured England in 1988, the first Test, at Trent Bridge, was often interrupted by the weather. England made 245 and West Indies responded by declaring their innings closed at 448 for 9. Graham Gooch made an excellent 146 and David Gower an unbeaten 88 in England's second innings 301 for 3 in a drawn match. After ten defeats by West Indies, this was a welcome result. England made an excellent start to the second Test, having West Indies at 54–5, but Logie and Dujon led a recovery to 209. England subsided to 165 all out before Greenidge, with 103, and Logie, with 95 not out, helped the tourists reach 397, setting England 442 to win. Lamb made 113 but England were all out for 307. At Old Trafford, where thirty-seven-year-old John Childs made his Test debut, England were bowled out for 135 before a good combined effort with the bat allowed West Indies to declare at 384–7. England were then shot out for 93, the last 7 wickets falling while only 20 runs were added. Malcolm Marshall took 7–22, his best-ever Test return. In the fourth Test at Headingley, England were captained by Chris Cowdrey but after being put in, they were bowled out for 201. West Indies gained a lead of 74 before England were bowled out cheaply a second time, their total of 138 meaning that West Indies needed only 66 – a target they achieved without losing a wicket. At The Oval, England had their fourth captain, Graham Gooch, in five matches. Bowled out for 205, England, thanks to Neil Foster's figures of 5–64, gained a lead of 22 on first innings. Gooch did his best to consolidate, being last out for 84 in England's second-innings total of 202. West Indies were thus set 225 to win and, with Greenidge and Haynes in outstanding form, they triumphed by 8 wickets.

The Test against Sri Lanka in the summer of 1988 saw the visitors bowled out for 194, but, with Jack Russell on his debut making 94 and Kim Barnett on his, 66, along with useful contributions from Gooch and Lamb, England made 429. Sri Lanka did better in their second innings with 331, leaving England to make 97 to win. They lost 3 wickets in achieving their target, but the match ended a record sequence for England of eighteen matches without a victory.

Though an evenly fought Ashes series was expected in 1989, England captain David Gower won the toss in the first Test at Headingley and asked Australia to bat. The Australian batsmen seized the initiative, which they kept for the entire series. Mark Taylor, in his first Ashes Test, made 136 and Steve Waugh 177 not out as the tourists declared at 601–7. Allan Lamb played a magnificent innings of 125 for England as they replied with 430. England had avoided the follow-on but after Australia declared at 230–3, England crashed to 191 all out in their second innings. At Lord's, England were dismissed for 286 and, with Australia at one stage 276–6, the match was well poised. However, Steve Waugh hit an unbeaten 152 and he took Australia to 528. Gower (106) and Robin Smith (96) fought back well for England but a total of 359 left Australia needing only 118 – a total achieved for the loss of 4 wickets. At Edgbaston, Dean Jones was Australia's batting hero with 157 in a total of 424 but, though England made 242 to avoid the follow-on, Australia were 158–2 as the game ended in a draw. The fourth Test, at Old Trafford, saw England batting first after winning the toss, and, with Smith holding the innings together as Lawson took 7–62, they managed to total 260. Good contributions from Australia's first five batsmen saw them reach 447 and England collapsed to 59–6 before a seventh-wicket stand of 142 between Jack Russell (128 not out) and John Emburey (64) gave England some respectability in a score of 264. Australia needed only 78 to win and won by 9 wickets. This win gave Australia a winning 3–0 lead in the series with two matches still to come. Records were broken at Trent Bridge when Australian openers Geoff Marsh and Mark Taylor batted throughout the first day and their side were 301–0 at stumps. Taylor went on to make 219 and Marsh 138 as Australia declared at 602–6. England, with a much-changed side, made 255, with Robin Smith scoring another century, but they were bundled out for 167 when following on and lost by an innings and 180 runs. For the final Test, at The Oval, England brought the number of players selected for the series to 29, one fewer than the record 30 of 1921. Australia batted and made 468 with Dean Jones leading the way with 122. England, with 285, avoided the follow-on before Border declared at 219–4. England had one or two anxious moments before gaining the draw at 143–5.

TEST MATCH RESULTS: 1979–89

553. Australia v England
First Test at Perth − 14, 15, 16, 18, 19 December 1979
AUSTRALIA 244 (Hughes 99, Marsh 42, Botham 6−78) and
337 (Border 115, Wiener 58, Botham 5−98)
ENGLAND 228 (Brearley 64, Lillee 4−73) and 215 (Boycott
99*, Dymock 6−34)
Australia won by 138 runs

554. Australia v England
Second Test at Sydney − 4, 5, 6, 8 January 1980
ENGLAND 123 (Lillee 4−40, Dymock 4−42) and 237
(Gower 98*, Underwood 43)
AUSTRALIA 145 (I. Chappell 42, Botham 4−29) and 219−4
(G. Chappell 98*, Hughes 47, McCosker 41)
Australia won by 6 wickets

555. Australia v England
Third Test at Melbourne − 1, 2, 3, 5, 6 February 1980
ENGLAND 306 (Gooch 99, Brearley 60*, Boycott 44, Lillee
6−60) and 273 (Botham 119*, Gooch 51, Lillee 5−78,
Pascoe 4−80)
AUSTRALIA 477 (G. Chappell 114, I. Chappell 75, Laird 74,
Border 63, J. Lever 4−111) and 103−2 (G. Chappell 40*)
Australia won by 8 wickets

556. India v England
Only Test at Bombay − 15, 17, 18, 19 February 1980
INDIA 242 (Gavaskar 49, Kirmani 40*, Botham 6−58) and
149 (Kapil Dev 45*, Botham 7−48)
ENGLAND 296 (Botham 114, Taylor 43, Ghavri 5−52) and
98−0 (Gooch 49*, Boycott 43*)
England won by 10 wickets

557. England v West Indies
First Test at Trent Bridge − 5, 6, 7, 9, 10 June 1980
ENGLAND 263 (Botham 57, Woolmer 46, Roberts 5−72)
and 252 (Boycott 75, Garner 4−30)
WEST INDIES 308 (Murray 64, Richards 64, Greenidge 53,
Willis 4−82) and 209−8 (Haynes 62, Willis 5−65)
West Indies won by 2 wickets

558. England v West Indies
Second Test at Lord's − 19, 20, 21, 23, 24 June 1980
ENGLAND 269 (Gooch 123, Tavare 42, Holding 6−67,
Garner 4−36) and 133−2 (Boycott 49*, Gooch 47)
WEST INDIES 518 (Haynes 184, Richards 145, Lloyd 56)
Match drawn

559. England v West Indies
Third Test at Old Trafford − 10, 11, 12 (no play), 14, 15 July
1980
ENGLAND 150 (Rose 70) and 391−7 (Boycott 86, Willey
62*, Gatting 56)
WEST INDIES 260 (Lloyd 101, Richards 65)
Match drawn

560. England v West Indies
Fourth Test at The Oval − 24, 25, 26 (no play), 28, 29 July
1980
ENGLAND 370 (Gooch 83, Boycott 53, Rose 50, Gatting 48)
and 209−9 dec. (Willey 100*, Rose 41, Holding 4−79)
WEST INDIES 265 (Bacchus 61, Garner 46, Marshall 45,
Dilley 4−57)
Match drawn

561. England v West Indies
Fifth Test at Headingley − 7 (no play), 8, 9, 11 (no play), 12
August 1980
ENGLAND 143 (Bairstow 40) and 227−6 dec. (Gooch 55,
Boycott 47, Rose 43*)
WEST INDIES 245 (Haynes 42, Dilley 4−79)
Match drawn

562. England v Australia
Centenary Test at Lord's − 28, 29, 30 August, 1, 2
September 1980
AUSTRALIA 385−5 dec. (Hughes 117, Wood 112, Border
56*, G. Chappell 47) and 189−4 dec. (Hughes 84,
G. Chappell 59)
ENGLAND 205 (Boycott 62, Gower 45, Pascoe 5−59, Lillee
4−43) and 244−3 (Boycott 128*, Gatting 51*)
Match drawn

563. West Indies v England
First Test at Port-of-Spain, Trinidad − 13, 14, 16, 17, 18
February 1981
WEST INDIES 426−9 dec. (Haynes 96, Greenidge 84, Lloyd
64, Roberts 50*, Murray 46, Emburey 5−124)
ENGLAND 178 (Gower 48, Gooch 41, Croft 5−40) and 169
(Boycott 70)
West Indies won by an innings and 79 runs

West Indies v England
Second Test at Georgetown, Guyana − February–March
1981
Match cancelled without a ball being bowled

564. West Indies v England
Third Test at Bridgetown, Barbados − 13, 14, 15, 17, 18
March 1981
WEST INDIES 265 (Lloyd 100, Gomes 58, Botham 4−77)
and 379−7 dec. (Richards 182*, Lloyd 66)
ENGLAND 122 (Croft 4−39) and 224 (Gooch 116, Gower 54)
West Indies won by 298 runs

565. West Indies v England
Fourth Test at St John's, Antigua − 27, 28, 29, 31 March, 1
April 1981
ENGLAND 271 (Willey 102*, Croft 6−74) and 234−3
(Boycott 104*, Gooch 83)
WEST INDIES 468−9 dec. (Richards 114, Mattis 71,
Greenidge 63, Lloyd 58, Holding 58*, Botham 4−127)
Match drawn

566. West Indies v England
Fifth Test at Kingston, Jamaica − 10, 11, 12, 14, 15 April
1981
ENGLAND 285 (Gooch 153, Boycott 40, Holding 5−56) and
302−6 dec. (Gower 154*, Willey 67)
WEST INDIES 442 (Lloyd 95, Gomes 90*, Haynes 84,
Greenidge 62, Dilley 4−116)
Match drawn

567. England v Australia
First Test at Trent Bridge − 18, 19, 20, 21 June 1981
ENGLAND 185 (Gatting 52, Alderman 4−68) and 125
(Lillee 5−46, Alderman 5−62)
AUSTRALIA 179 (Border 63) and 132−6 (Dilley 4−24)
Australia won by 4 wickets

568. England v Australia
Second Test at Lord's – 2, 3, 4, 6, 7 July 1981
ENGLAND 311 (Willey 82, Gatting 59, Gooch 44, Lawson
7–81) and 265–8 dec. (Gower 89, Boycott 60)
AUSTRALIA 345 (Border 64, Marsh 47, Wood 44, Hughes
42, Lillee 40*) and 90–4 (Wood 62*)
Match drawn

569. England v Australia
Third Test at Headingley – 16, 17, 18, 20, 21 July 1981
AUSTRALIA 401–9 dec. (Dyson 102, Hughes 89, Yallop 58,
Botham 6–95) and 111 (Willis 8–43)
ENGLAND 174 (Botham 50, Lillee 4–49) and 356 (Botham
149*, Dilley 56, Boycott 46, Alderman 6–135)
England won by 18 runs

570. England v Australia
Fourth Test at Edgbaston – 30, 31 July, 1, 2 August 1981
ENGLAND 189 (Brearley 48, Alderman 5–42) and 219
(Bright 5–68)
AUSTRALIA 258 (Hughes 47, Kent 46, Emburey 4–43) and
121 (Border 40, Botham 5–11)
England won by 29 runs

571. England v Australia
Fifth Test at Old Trafford – 13, 14, 15, 16, 17 August 1981
ENGLAND 231 (Tavare 69, Allott 52*, Lillee 4–55,
Alderman 4–88) and 404 (Botham 118, Tavare 78,
Knott 59, Emburey 57, Alderman 5–109)
AUSTRALIA 130 (Kent 52, Willis 4–63) and 402 (Border
123*, Yallop 114, Marsh 47, Hughes 43)
England won by 103 runs

572. England v Australia
Sixth Test at The Oval – 27, 28, 29, 31 August, 1 September
1981
AUSTRALIA 352 (Border 106*, Wood 66, Kent 54, Botham
6–125, Willis 4–91) and 344–9 dec. (Wellham 103,
Border 84, Marsh 52, Hendrick 4–82, Botham 4–128)
ENGLAND 314 (Boycott 137, Gatting 53, Lillee 7–89) and
261–7 (Knott 70*, Gatting 56, Brearley 51, Lillee 4–70)
Match drawn

573. India v England
First Test at Bombay – 27, 28, 29 November, 1 December
1981
INDIA 179 (Gavaskar 55, Dilley 4–47, Botham 4–72) and
227 (Kapil Dev 46, Botham 5–61)
ENGLAND 166 (Boycott 60, Tavare 56, Doshi 5–39) and
102 (Madan Lal 5–23, Kapil Dev 5–70)
India won by 138 runs

574. India v England
Second Test at Bangalore – 9, 10, 12, 13, 14 December 1981
ENGLAND 400 (Gower 82, Gooch 58, Botham 55, Dilley 52,
Shastri 4–83) and 174–3 dec. (Boycott 50, Gooch 40)
INDIA 428 (Gavaskar 172, Srikkanth 65, Kapil Dev 59,
Vengsarkar 43, J. Lever 5–100)
Match drawn

575. India v England
Third Test at Delhi – 23, 24, 26, 27, 28 December 1981
ENGLAND 476–9 dec. (Tavare 149, Boycott 105, Gooch 71,
Botham 66, Fletcher 51, Madan Lal 5–85) and 68–0 dec.
INDIA 487 (Viswanath 107, Shastri 93, Kirmani 67,
Gavaskar 46, Madan Lal 44)
Match drawn

DID YOU KNOW...?

England's game against India in Calcutta in 1982
was watched by 394,000 spectators – a record for
any cricket match.

576. India v England
Fourth Test at Calcutta – 1, 2, 3, 5, 6 January 1982
ENGLAND 248 (Fletcher 69, Botham 58, Gooch 47, Kapil
Dev 6–91) and 265–5 dec. (Gower 74, Gooch 63,
Fletcher 60*)
INDIA 208 (Vengsarkar 70, Gavaskar 42) and 170–3
(Gavaskar 83*)
Match drawn

577. India v England
Fifth Test at Madras – 13, 14, 15, 17, 18 January 1982
INDIA 481–4 dec. (Viswanath 222, Yashpal Sharma 140,
Vengsarkar 71 ret. hurt) and 160–3 dec. (Roy 60*)
ENGLAND 328 (Gooch 127, Gower 64, Botham 52, Doshi
4–69)
Match drawn

578. India v England
Sixth Test at Kanpur – 30, 31 January, 1, 3, 4 February 1982
ENGLAND 378–9 dec. (Botham 142, Gower 85, Gooch 58,
Doshi 4–81)
INDIA 377–7 dec. (Kapil Dev 116, Viswanath 74, Yashpal
Sharma 55*, Gavaskar 52, Vengsarkar 46)
Match drawn

579. Sri Lanka v England
Only Test at Colombo – 17, 18, 20, 21 February 1982
SRI LANKA 218 (Madugalle 65, Ranatunga 54, Underwood
5–28) and 175 (Dias 77, Emburey 6–33)
ENGLAND 223 (Gower 89, Fletcher 45, de Mel 4–70) and
171–3 (Tavare 85, Gower 42*)
England won by 7 wickets

580. England v India
First Test at Lord's – 10, 11, 12, 14, 15 June 1982
ENGLAND 433 (Randall 126, Botham 67, Edmonds 64,
Allott 41*, Kapil Dev 5–125) and 67–3
INDIA 128 (Gavaskar 48, Kapil Dev 41, Botham 5–46) and
369 (Vengsarkar 157, Kapil Dev 89, Willis 6–101)
England won by 7 wickets

581. England v India
Second Test at Old Trafford – 24, 25, 26, 27, 28 June 1982
ENGLAND 425 (Botham 128, Miller 98, G. Cook 66, Tavare
57, Doshi 6–102)
INDIA 379–8 (Patil 129*, Kapil Dev 65, Kirmani 58,
Viswanath 54)
Match drawn

582. England v India
Third Test at The Oval – 8, 9, 10, 12, 13 July 1982
ENGLAND 594 (Botham 208, Lamb 107, Randall 95,
G. Cook 50, Gower 47, Doshi 4–175) and 191–3 dec.
(Tavare 75*, Lamb 45, Gower 45)
INDIA 410 (Kapil Dev 97, Shastri 66, Patil 62, Viswanath
56, Kirmani 43) and 111–3 (Viswanath 75*)
Match drawn

583. England v Pakistan
First Test at Edgbaston – 29, 30, 31 July, 1 August 1982
ENGLAND 272 (Gower 74, Tavare 54, Miller 47, Imran
  Khan 7–52) and 291 (Randall 105, Taylor 54, Tahir
  Naqqash 5–40)
PAKISTAN 251 (Mansoor Akhtar 58, Zaheer Abbas 40,
  I. Greig 4–53) and 199 (Imran Khan 65, Botham 4–70)
England won by 113 runs

584. England v Pakistan
Second Test at Lord's – 12, 13, 14, 15, 16 August 1982
PAKISTAN 428–8 dec. (Mohsin Khan 200, Zaheer Abbas 75,
  Mansoor Akhtar 57, Jackman 4–110) and 77–0
ENGLAND 227 (Abdul Qadir 4–39) and 276 (Tavare 82,
  Botham 69, Mudassar Nazar 6–32)
Pakistan won by 10 wickets

585. England v Pakistan
Third Test at Headingley – 26, 27, 28, 30, 31 August
  1982
PAKISTAN 275 (Imran Khan 67*, Mudassar Nazar 65,
  Javed Miandad 54, Botham 4–70) and 199 (Javed
  Miandad 52, Imran Khan 46, Botham 5–74)
ENGLAND 256 (Gower 74, Botham 57, Imran Khan 5–49)
  and 219–7 (Fowler 86, Mudassar Nazar 4–55)
England won by 3 wickets

586. Australia v England
First Test at Perth – 12, 13, 14, 16, 17 November 1982
ENGLAND 411 (Tavare 89, Randall 78, Gower 72, Lamb 46,
  Yardley 5–107) and 358 (Randall 115, Lamb 56, Pringle
  47*, Lawson 5–108)
AUSTRALIA 424–9 dec. (G. Chappell 117, Hughes 62,
  Hookes 56, Dyson 52, Lawson 50, Miller 4–70) and
  73–2
Match drawn

587. Australia v England
Second Test at Brisbane – 26, 27, 28, 30 November, 1
  December 1982
ENGLAND 219 (Lamb 72, Botham 40, Lawson 6–47) and
  309 (Fowler 83, Miller 60, Thomson 5–73, Lawson
  5–87)
AUSTRALIA 341 (Wessels 162, G. Chappell 53, Yardley 53,
  Willis 5–66) and 190–3 (Hookes 66*, Wessels 46)
Australia won by 7 wickets

588. Australia v England
Third Test at Adelaide – 10, 11, 12, 14, 15 December
  1982
AUSTRALIA 438 (G. Chappell 115, Hughes 88, Dyson 44,
  Wessels 44, Botham 4–112) and 83–2
ENGLAND 216 (Lamb 82, Gower 60, Lawson 4–56) and
  304 (Gower 114, Botham 58, Lawson 5–66)
Australia won by 8 wickets

589. Australia v England
Fourth Test at Melbourne – 26, 27, 28, 29, 30 December
  1982
ENGLAND 284 (Tavare 89, Lamb 83, Hogg 4–69, Yardley
  4–89) and 294 (Fowler 65, Botham 46, Pringle 42,
  Lawson 4–66)
AUSTRALIA 287 (Hughes 66, Hookes 53, Marsh 53, Wessels
  47) and 288 (Hookes 68, Border 62*, Hughes 48,
  Cowans 6–77)
England won by 3 runs

590. Australia v England
Fifth Test at Sydney – 2, 3, 4, 6, 7 January 1983
AUSTRALIA 314 (Border 89, Dyson 79, Botham 4–75) and
  382 (Hughes 137, Border 83, Wessels 53, Marsh 41)
ENGLAND 237 (Gower 70, Randall 70, Thomson 5–50) and
  314–7 (Hemmings 95, Randall 44, Yardley 4–139)
Match drawn

591. England v New Zealand
First Test at The Oval – 14, 15, 16, 17, 18 July 1983
ENGLAND 209 (Randall 75*, Tavare 45, Hadlee 6–53) and
  446–6 dec. (Tavare 109, Fowler 105, Lamb 102*,
  Edmonds 43*)
NEW ZEALAND 196 (Hadlee 84, Coney 44, Willis 4–43,
  Botham 4–62) and 270 (Wright 88, Howarth 67)
England won by 189 runs

 DID YOU KNOW...?

Against Pakistan in 1982, Robin Jackman, David
Gower and Allan Lamb were all out for 0 after
eating duck the night before.

592. England v New Zealand
Second Test at Headingley – 28, 29, 30 July, 1 August
  1983
ENGLAND 225 (Tavare 69, Lamb 58, Cairns 7–74) and 252
  (Gower 112*, Chatfield 5–95)
NEW ZEALAND 377 (Wright 93, Edgar 84, Hadlee 75, Willis
  4–57) and 103–5 (Willis 5–35)
New Zealand won by 5 wickets

593. England v New Zealand
Third Test at Lord's – 11, 12, 13, 15 August 1983
ENGLAND 326 (Gower 108, Gatting 81, Tavare 51, Hadlee
  5–93) and 211 (Botham 61, C. Smith 43)
NEW ZEALAND 191 (Edgar 70, M. Crowe 46, N. Cook
  5–35, Botham 4–50) and 219 (Coney 68)
England won by 127 runs

594. England v New Zealand
Fourth Test at Trent Bridge – 25, 26, 27, 28, 29 August 1983
ENGLAND 420 (Botham 103, Randall 83, Gower 72,
  Bracewell 4–108) and 297 (Lamb 137*, Hadlee 4–85)
NEW ZEALAND 207 (Edgar 62, N. Cook 5–63) and 345
  (Hadlee 92*, Edgar 76, Coney 68, N. Cook 4–87)
England won by 165 runs

595. New Zealand v England
First Test at Wellington – 20, 21, 22, 23, 24 January 1984
NEW ZEALAND 219 (J. Crowe 52, Botham 5–59) and 537
  (Coney 174*, M. Crowe 100, Cairns 64)
ENGLAND 463 (Randall 164, Botham 138, Cairns 7–143)
  and 69–0
Match drawn

596. New Zealand v England
Second Test at Christchurch – 3, 4, 5 February 1984
NEW ZEALAND 307 (Hadlee 99, J. Crowe 47, Coney 41,
  Willis 4–51)
ENGLAND 82 (Chatfield 3–10, Hadlee 3–16) and 93
  (Hadlee 5–28)
New Zealand won by an innings and 132 runs

597. New Zealand v England
Third Test at Auckland – 10, 11, 12, 14, 15 February 1984
NEW ZEALAND 496–9 dec. (Wright 130, J. Crowe 128,
Smith 113*) and 16–0
ENGLAND 439 (Randall 104, C. Smith 91, Botham 70,
Lamb 49)
Match drawn

598. Pakistan v England
First Test at Karachi – 2, 3, 4, 6 March 1984
ENGLAND 182 (Gower 58, Abdul Qadir 5–74, Sarfraz
Nawaz 4–42) and 159 (Gower 57)
PAKISTAN 277 (Salim Malik 74, Mohsin Khan 54, Abdul
Qadir 40, N. Cook 6–65) and 66–7 (N. Cook 5–18)
Pakistan won by 3 wickets

599. Pakistan v England
Second Test at Faisalabad – 12, 13, 14, 16, 17 March 1984
PAKISTAN 449–8 dec. (Salim Malik 116, Wasim Raja 112,
Zaheer Abbas 68, Abdul Qadir 50) and 137–4 (Salim
Malik 76)
ENGLAND 546–8 dec. (Gower 152, Marks 83, Gatting 75,
C. Smith 66, Randall 65, Fowler 57)
Match drawn

600. Pakistan v England
Third Test at Lahore – 19, 20, 21, 23, 24 March 1984
ENGLAND 241 (Marks 74, Fowler 58, Abdul Qadir 5–84)
and 344–9 dec. (Gower 173*, Marks 55, Gatting 53,
Abdul Qadir 5–110)
PAKISTAN 343 (Sarfraz Nawaz 90, Zaheer Abbas 82*,
Qasim Umar 73, Foster 5–67) and 217–6 (Mohsin Khan
104, Shoaib Mohammad 80, Cowans 5–42)
Match drawn

601. England v West Indies
First Test at Edgbaston – 14, 15, 16, 18 June 1984
ENGLAND 191 (Botham 64, Garner 4–53) and 235
(Downton 56, Pringle 46*, Garner 5–55)
WEST INDIES 606 (Gomes 143, Richards 117, Baptiste 87*,
Lloyd 71, Holding 69, Pringle 5–108)
West Indies won by an innings and 180 runs

602. England v West Indies
Second Test at Lord's – 28, 29, 30 June, 2, 3 July 1984
ENGLAND 286 (Fowler 106, Broad 55, Marshall 6–85) and
300–9 dec. (Lamb 110, Botham 81)
WEST INDIES 245 (Richards 72, Baptiste 44, Botham
8–103) and 344–1 (Greenidge 214*, Gomes 92*)
West Indies won by 9 wickets

603. England v West Indies
Third Test at Headingley – 12, 13, 14, 16 July 1984
ENGLAND 270 (Lamb 100, Botham 45, Holding 4–70) and
159 (Fowler 50, Gower 43, Marshall 7–53)
WEST INDIES 302 (Gomes 104*, Holding 59, Lloyd 48,
Allott 6–61) and 131–2 (Greenidge 49, Haynes 43)
West Indies won by 8 wickets

604. England v West Indies
Fourth Test at Old Trafford – 26, 27, 28, 30, 31 July 1984
WEST INDIES 500 (Greenidge 223, Dujon 101, Davis 77,
Pocock 4–121)
ENGLAND 280 (Lamb 100*, Broad 42, Garner 4–51) and
156 (Gower 57*, Harper 6–57)
West Indies won by an innings and 64 runs

605. England v West Indies
Fifth Test at The Oval – 9, 10, 11, 13, 14 August 1984
WEST INDIES 190 (Lloyd 60*, Botham 5–72) and 346
(Haynes 125, Dujon 49)
ENGLAND 162 (Marshall 5–35) and 202 (Botham 54,
Tavare 49, Holding 5–43, Garner 4–51)
West Indies won by 172 runs

606. England v Sri Lanka
Only Test at Lord's – 23, 24, 25, 27, 28 August 1984
SRI LANKA 491–7 dec. (Wettimuny 190, Mendis 111,
Ranatunga 84) and 294–7 dec. (Silva 102*, Mendis 94,
Botham 6–90)
ENGLAND 370 (Lamb 107, Broad 86, Gower 55, Ellison 41,
John 4–98, de Mel 4–110)
Match drawn

607. India v England
First Test at Bombay – 28, 29 November, 1, 2, 3 December
1984
ENGLAND 195 (Edmonds 48, Sivaramakrishnan 6–64) and
317 (Gatting 136, Downton 62, Fowler 55,
Sivaramakrishnan 6–117)
INDIA 465–8 dec. (Shastri 142, Kirmani 102, Amarnath 49,
Kapil Dev 42) and 51–2
India won by 8 wickets

608. India v England
Second Test at Delhi – 12, 13, 15, 16, 17 December 1984
INDIA 307 (Kapil Dev 60, Amarnath 42, Ellison 4–66) and
235 (Gavaskar 65, Amarnath 64, Patil 41, Edmonds
4–60, Pocock 4–93)
ENGLAND 418 (Robinson 160, Downton 74, Lamb 52,
Sivaramakrishnan 6–99) and 127–2
England won by 8 wickets

609. India v England
Third Test at Calcutta – 31 December 1984, 1, 3, 4, 5
January 1985
INDIA 437–7 dec. (Shastri 111, Azharuddin 110,
Vengsarkar 48, Amarnath 42) and 29–1
ENGLAND 276 (Lamb 67, Fowler 49, Gatting 48, Sharma
4–38, Yadav 4–86)
Match drawn

610. India v England
Fourth Test at Madras – 13, 14, 15, 17, 18 January 1985
INDIA 272 (Amarnath 78, Kapil Dev 53, Azharuddin 48,
Foster 6–104) and 412 (Azharuddin 105, Amarnath 95,
Kirmani 75, Kapil Dev 49, Foster 5–59)
ENGLAND 652–7 dec. (Gatting 207, Fowler 201, Robinson
74, Lamb 62) and 35–1
England won by 9 wickets

611. India v England
Fifth Test at Kanpur – 31 January, 1, 3, 4, 5 February
1985
INDIA 553–8 dec. (Vengsarkar 137, Azharuddin 122,
Srikkanth 84, Shastri 59, Kapil Dev 42) and 97–1 dec.
(Azharuddin 54*, Srikkanth 41*)
ENGLAND 417 (Robinson 96, Gower 78, Fowler 69,
Gatting 62, Edmonds 49, Kapil Dev 4–81) and 91–0
(Gatting 41*)
Match drawn

612. England v Australia
First Test at Headingley – 13, 14, 15, 17, 18 June 1985
AUSTRALIA 331 (Hilditch 119, Ritchie 46) and 324 (Phillips 91, Hilditch 80, Wessels 64, Emburey 5–82, Botham 4–107)
ENGLAND 533 (Robinson 175, Botham 60, Downton 54, Gatting 53, McDermott 4–134) and 123–5
England won by 5 wickets

613. England v Australia
Second Test at Lord's – 27, 28, 29 June, 1, 2 July 1985
ENGLAND 290 (Gower 86, Lamb 47, McDermott 6–70) and 261 (Botham 85, Gatting 75*, Holland 5–68)
AUSTRALIA 425 (Border 196, Ritchie 94, O'Donnell 48, Botham 5–109) and 127–6 (Border 41*)
Australia won by 4 wickets

614. England v Australia
Third Test at Trent Bridge – 11, 12, 13, 15, 16 July 1985
ENGLAND 456 (Gower 166, Gatting 74, Gooch 70, Lawson 5–103) and 196–2 (Robinson 77*, Gooch 48)
AUSTRALIA 539 (Wood 172, Ritchie 146, Hilditch 47, O'Donnell 46)
Match drawn

615. England v Australia
Fourth Test at Old Trafford – 1, 2, 3, 5, 6 August 1985
AUSTRALIA 257 (Boon 61, Hilditch 49, O'Donnell 45, Edmonds 4–40, Botham 4–79) and 340–5 (Border 146*, Wessels 50, Hilditch 40, Emburey 4–99)
ENGLAND 482–9 dec. (Gatting 160, Gooch 74, Lamb 67, Gower 47, McDermott 8–141)
Match drawn

616. England v Australia
Fifth Test at Edgbaston – 15, 16, 17, 19, 20 August 1985
AUSTRALIA 335 (Wessels 83, Lawson 53, Border 45, Ellison 6–77) and 142 (Phillips 59, Ellison 4–27)
ENGLAND 595–5 dec. (Gower 215, Robinson 148, Gatting 100*, Lamb 46)
England won by an innings and 118 runs

617. England v Australia
Sixth Test at The Oval – 29, 30, 31 August, 2 September 1985
ENGLAND 464 (Gooch 196, Gower 157, Lawson 4–101, McDermott 4–108)
AUSTRALIA 241 (Ritchie 64*) and 129 (Border 58, Ellison 5–46)
England won by an innings and 94 runs

618. West Indies v England
First Test at Kingston, Jamaica – 21, 22, 23 February 1986
ENGLAND 159 (Gooch 51, Lamb 49, Patterson 4–30) and 152 (Willey 71)
WEST INDIES 307 (Greenidge 58, Gomes 56, Dujon 54, Ellison 5–78) and 5–0
West Indies won by 10 wickets

619. West Indies v England
Second Test at Port-of-Spain, Trinidad – 7, 8, 9, 11, 12 March 1986
ENGLAND 176 (Gower 66, Lamb 62, Marshall 4–38) and 315 (Gower 47, Gooch 43, Lamb 40, Walsh 4–74, Marshall 4–94)

WEST INDIES 399 (Richardson 102, Haynes 67, Marshall 62*, Emburey 5–78) and 95–3 (Greenidge 45)
West Indies won by 7 wickets

620. West Indies v England
Third Test at Bridgetown, Barbados – 21, 22, 23, 25 March 1986
WEST INDIES 418 (Richardson 160, Haynes 84, Richards 51, Thomas 4–70)
ENGLAND 189 (Gower 66, Gooch 53, Marshall 4–42) and 199 (Robinson 43, Garner 4–69)
West Indies won by an innings and 30 runs

621. West Indies v England
Fourth Test at Port-of-Spain, Trinidad – 3, 4, 5 April 1986
ENGLAND 200 (D. M. Smith 47, Garner 4–43) and 150
WEST INDIES 312 (Richards 87, Gomes 48, Greenidge 42, Botham 5–71) and 39–0
West Indies won by 10 wickets

622. West Indies v England
Fifth Test at St John's, Antigua – 11, 12, 13, 15, 16 April 1986
WEST INDIES 474 (Haynes 131, Marshall 76, Holding 73, Harper 60) and 246–2 dec. (Richards 110*, Haynes 70)
ENGLAND 310 (Gower 90, Slack 52, Gooch 51, Garner 4–67) and 170 (Gooch 51)
West Indies won by 240 runs

623. England v India
First Test at Lord's – 5, 6, 7, 9, 10 June 1986
ENGLAND 294 (Gooch 114, Pringle 63, Sharma 5–64) and 180 (Gatting 40, Kapil Dev 4–52)
INDIA 341 (Vengsarkar 126*, Amarnath 69, Dilley 4–146) and 136–5
India won by 5 wickets

624. England v India
Second Test at Headingley – 19, 20, 21, 23 June 1986
INDIA 272 (Vengsarkar 61) and 237 (Vengsarkar 102*, J. Lever 4–64, Pringle 4–73)
ENGLAND 102 (Binny 5–40) and 128 (Maninder Singh 4–26)
India won by 279 runs

625. England v India
Third Test at Edgbaston – 3, 4, 5, 7, 8 July 1986
ENGLAND 390 (Gatting 183*, Gower 49, Pringle 44, Sharma 4–130) and 235 (Gooch 40, Sharma 6–58)
INDIA 390 (Amarnath 79, Azharuddin 64, More 48, Binny 40) and 174–5 (Gavaskar 54, Edmonds 4–31)
Match drawn

626. England v New Zealand
First Test at Lord's – 24, 25, 26, 28, 29 July 1986
ENGLAND 307 (Moxon 74, Gower 62, Athey 44, Willey 44, Hadlee 6–80) and 295–6 dec. (Gooch 183, Willey 42)
NEW ZEALAND 342 (M. Crowe 106, Edgar 83, Coney 51, Dilley 4–82, Edmonds 4–97) and 41–2
Match drawn

627. England v New Zealand
Second Test at Trent Bridge – 7, 8, 9, 11, 12 August 1986
ENGLAND 256 (Gower 71, Athey 55, Hadlee 6–80) and 230 (Emburey 75, Hadlee 4–60)
NEW ZEALAND 413 (Bracewell 110, Hadlee 68, Wright 58, Gray 50) and 7–2 (M. Crowe 48*)
New Zealand won by 8 wickets

628. England v New Zealand
Third Test at The Oval – 21, 22, 23, 25, 26 August 1986
NEW ZEALAND 287 (Wright 119, Dilley 4–92) and 7–0
ENGLAND 388–5 dec. (Gower 131, Gatting 121, Botham
59*)
Match drawn

629. Australia v England
First Test at Brisbane – 14, 15, 16, 18, 19 November
1986
ENGLAND 456 (Botham 138, Athey 76, Gatting 61, Gower
51, Lamb 40, DeFreitas 40) and 77–3
AUSTRALIA 248 (Marsh 56, Matthews 56*, Ritchie 41,
Dilley 5–68) and 282 (Marsh 110, Emburey 5–80)
England won by 7 wickets

630. Australia v England
Second Test at Perth – 28, 29, 30 November, 2, 3 December
1986
ENGLAND 592–8 dec. (Broad 162, Gower 136, Richards
133, Athey 96, Reid 4–115) and 199–8 dec. (Gatting
70, Gower 48, S. Waugh 5–69)
AUSTRALIA 401 (Border 125, S. Waugh 71, Matthews 45,
Dilley 4–79) and 197–4 (Jones 69, Marsh 49)
Match drawn

631. Australia v England
Third Test at Adelaide – 12, 13, 14, 15, 16 December
1986
AUSTRALIA 514–5 dec. (Boon 103, Jones 93, S. Waugh
79*, Matthews 73*, Border 70, Marsh 43) and 201–3
dec. (Border 100*, Ritchie 46*, Marsh 41)
ENGLAND 455 (Broad 116, Gatting 100, Athey 55,
Emburey 49, Reid 4–64, Sleep 4–132) and 39–2
Match drawn

632. Australia v England
Fourth Test at Melbourne – 26, 27, 28 December 1986
AUSTRALIA 141 (Jones 59, Botham 5–41, Small 5–48) and
194 (Marsh 60, S. Waugh 49)
ENGLAND 349 (Broad 112, Lamb 43, Gatting 40, Reid
4–78, McDermott 4–83)
England won by an innings and 14 runs

633. Australia v England
Fifth Test at Sydney – 10, 11, 12, 14, 15 January 1987
AUSTRALIA 343 (Jones 184*, Small 5–75) and 251
(S. Waugh 73, Border 49, Taylor 42, Emburey 7–78)
ENGLAND 275 (Gower 72, Emburey 69, Richards 46, Taylor
6–78) and 264 (Gatting 96, Sleep 5–72)
Australia won by 55 runs

634. England v Pakistan
First Test at Old Trafford – 4, 5, 6, 8, 9 June 1987
ENGLAND 447 (Robinson 166, French 59, Botham 48,
Gatting 44, Wasim Akram 4–111, Mohsin Kamal
4–127)
PAKISTAN 140–5 (Mansoor Akhtar 75)
Match drawn

635. England v Pakistan
Second Test at Lord's – 18, 19 (no play), 20, 22 (no play),
23 June 1987
ENGLAND 368 (Athey 123, Broad 55, Gatting 43, French
42)
Match drawn

636. England v Pakistan
Third Test at Headingley – 2, 3, 4, 6 July 1987
ENGLAND 136 (Capel 53) and 199 (Gower 55, Imran Khan
7–40)
PAKISTAN 353 (Salim Malik 99, Ijaz Ahmed 50, Wasim
Akram 43, Foster 8–107)
Pakistan won by an innings and 18 runs

637. England v Pakistan
Fourth Test at Edgbaston – 23, 24, 25, 27, 28 July 1987
PAKISTAN 439 (Mudassar Nasar 124, Saleem Yousuf 91*,
Javed Miandad 75, Dilley 5–92) and 205 (Shoaib
Mohammad 50, Foster 4–59)
ENGLAND 521 (Gatting 124, Robinson 80, Gower 61,
Emburey 58, Imran Khan 6–129) and 109–7
Match drawn

638. England v Pakistan
Fifth Test at The Oval – 6, 7, 8, 10, 11 August 1987
PAKISTAN 708 (Javed Miandad 260, Imran Khan 118, Salim
Malik 102, Mudassar Nasar 73, Ijaz Ahmed 69, Saleem
Yousuf 42, Dilley 6–154)
ENGLAND 232 (Gatting 61, Emburey 53, Abdul Qadir 7–96)
and 315–4 (Gatting 150*, Botham 51*, Broad 42)
Match drawn

639. Pakistan v England
First Test at Lahore – 25, 26, 27, 28 November 1987
ENGLAND 175 (Broad 41, Abdul Qadir 9–56) and 130
(Abdul Qadir 4–45)
PAKISTAN 392 (Mudassar Nasar 120, Javed Miandad 65,
Ijaz Ahmed 44, Wasim Akram 40)
Pakistan won by an innings and 87 runs

640. Pakistan v England
Second Test at Faisalabad – 7, 8, 9, 11, 12 December 1987
ENGLAND 292 (Broad 116, Gatting 79, Iqbal Qasim 5–83,
Abdul Qadir 4–105) and 137–6 dec. (Gooch 65)
PAKISTAN 191 (Salim Malik 60, Foster 4–42) and 51–1
Match drawn

641. Pakistan v England
Third Test at Karachi – 16, 17, 18, 20, 21 December 1987
ENGLAND 294 (Capel 98, Emburey 70, Abdul Qadir 5–88)
and 258–9 (Gooch 93, Emburey 74*, Abdul Qadir
5–98)
PAKISTAN 353 (Aamer Malik 98*, Abdul Qadir 61, Salim
Malik 55, Ramiz Raja 50, DeFreitas 5–86)
Match drawn

642. Australia v England
Bicentenary Test at Sydney – 29, 30, 31 January, 1, 2
February 1988
ENGLAND 425 (Broad 139, French 47, Robinson 43, Moxon
40, Taylor 4–84)
AUSTRALIA 214 (Jones 56, Sleep 41) and 328–2 (Boon
184*, Marsh 56, Border 48*)
Match drawn

643. New Zealand v England
First Test at Christchurch – 12, 13, 14, 16, 17 February 1988
ENGLAND 319 (Broad 114, Robinson 70, Emburey 42,
Morrison 5–69, Chatfield 4–87) and 152 (Chatfield
4–36, Snedden 4–45)
NEW ZEALAND 168 (Dilley 6–38) and 130–4 (Jones 54*)
Match drawn

644. New Zealand v England
Second Test at Auckland – 25, 26, 27, 28, 29 February 1988
NEW ZEALAND 301 (Wright 103, Dilley 5–60) and 350–7
dec. (Greatbatch 107*, Franklin 62, Wright 49)
ENGLAND 323 (Moxon 99, Robinson 54, Emburey 45,
Gatting 42, Chatfield 4–37)
Match drawn

645. New Zealand v England
Third Test at Wellington – 3, 4, 5, 6 (no play), 7 March 1988
NEW ZEALAND 512–6 dec. (M. Crowe 143, Rutherford
107*, Greatbatch 68, Bracewell 54, Vance 47)
ENGLAND 183–2 (Moxon 81*, Broad 61)
Match drawn

646. England v West Indies
First Test at Trent Bridge – 2, 3, 4, 6, 7 June 1988
ENGLAND 245 (Gooch 73, Broad 54, Marshall 6–69,
Ambrose 4–53) and 301–3 (Gooch 146, Gower 88*)
WEST INDIES 448–9 dec. (Hooper 84, Richards 80,
Marshall 72, Haynes 60, Ambrose 43)
Match drawn

647. England v West Indies
Second Test at Lord's – 16, 17, 18, 20, 21 June 1988
WEST INDIES 209 (Logie 81, Dujon 53, Dilley 5–55, Small
4–64) and 397 (Greenidge 103, Logie 95*, Richards 72,
Dujon 52, Dilley 4–73, Jarvis 4–107)
ENGLAND 165 (Gower 46, Gooch 44, Marshall 6–32) and
307 (Lamb 113, Marshall 4–60)
West Indies won by 134 runs

648. England v West Indies
Third Test at Old Trafford – 30 June, 1, 2, 4, 5 July 1988
ENGLAND 135 (Walsh 4–46) and 93 (Marshall 7–22)
WEST INDIES 384–7 dec. (Harper 74, Dujon 67, Richards
47, Greenidge 45, Marshall 43*, Dilley 4–99)
West Indies won by an innings and 156 runs

649. England v West Indies
Fourth Test at Headingley – 21, 22, 23, 25, 26 July 1988
ENGLAND 201 (Lamb 64 ret. hurt, Ambrose 4–58) and 138
(Gooch 50)
WEST INDIES 275 (Harper 56, Haynes 54, Logie 44, Pringle
5–95) and 67–0 (Dujon 40*)
West Indies won by 10 wickets

650. England v West Indies
Fifth Test at The Oval – 4, 5, 6, 8 August 1988
ENGLAND 205 (R. Smith 57, Bailey 43) and 202 (Gooch 84,
Benjamin 4–52)
WEST INDIES 183 (Dujon 64, Logie 47, Foster 5–64) and
226–2 (Haynes 77*, Greenidge 77)
West Indies won by 8 wickets

651. England v Sri Lanka
Only Test at Lord's – 25, 26, 27, 29, 30 August 1988

SRI LANKA 194 (Ratnayeke 59*, Kuruppu 46) and 331
(Ranatunga 78, Samarasekera 57, Mendis 56, Newport
4–87)
ENGLAND 429 (Russell 94, Gooch 75, Barnett 66, Lamb 63,
Labrooy 4–119) and 100–3
England won by 7 wickets

652. England v Australia
First Test at Headingley – 8, 9, 10, 12, 13 June 1989
AUSTRALIA 601–7 dec. (S. Waugh 177*, Taylor 136, Jones
79, Hughes 71, Border 66) and 230–3 dec. (Border 60*,
Taylor 60, Boon 43, Jones 40*)
ENGLAND 430 (Lamb 125, Barnett 80, R. Smith 66,
Alderman 5–107) and 191 (Gooch 68, Alderman 5–44)
Australia won by 210 runs

653. England v Australia
Second Test at Lord's – 22, 23, 24, 26, 27 June 1989
ENGLAND 286 (Russell 64*, Gooch 60, Gower 57, Hughes
4–71) and 359 (Gower 106, R. Smith 96, Alderman
6–128)
AUSTRALIA 528 (S. Waugh 152*, Boon 94, Lawson 74,
Taylor 62, Emburey 4–88) and 119–4 (Boon 58*)
Australia won by 6 wickets

654. England v Australia
Third Test at Edgbaston – 6, 7, 8, 10, 11 July 1989
AUSTRALIA 424 (Jones 157, Taylor 43, S. Waugh 43, Marsh 42,
Hohns 40, Fraser 4–63) and 158–2 (Taylor 51, Marsh 42)
ENGLAND 242 (Botham 46, Russell 42, Curtis 41)
Match drawn

655. England v Australia
Fourth Test at Old Trafford – 27, 28, 29, 31 July, 1 August
1989
ENGLAND 260 (R. Smith 143, Lawson 6–72) and 264
(Russell 128*, Emburey 64, Alderman 5–66)
AUSTRALIA 447 (S. Waugh 92, Taylor 85, Border 80, Jones
69, Marsh 47) and 81–1
Australia won by 9 wickets

656. England v Australia
Fifth Test at Trent Bridge – 10, 11, 12, 14 August 1989
AUSTRALIA 602–6 dec. (Taylor 219, Marsh 138, Boon 73,
Border 65*)
ENGLAND 255 (R. Smith 101, Alderman 5–69) and 167
(Atherton 47)
Australia won by an innings and 180 runs

657. England v Australia
Sixth Test at The Oval – 24, 25, 26, 28, 29 August 1989
AUSTRALIA 468 (Jones 122, Border 76, Taylor 71, Boon 46,
Healy 44, Pringle 4–70) and 219–4 dec. (Border 51*,
Jones 50, Taylor 48)
ENGLAND 285 (Gower 79, Small 59, Alderman 5–66) and
143–5 (R. Smith 77*)
Match drawn

TEST-MATCH CRICKET IN THE 1990s

The West Indies, who had lost only one home Test match during the 1980s and had beaten England in 14 of their last 15 games, lost the first Test at Kingston by 9 wickets. Accurate bowling by Fraser (5–28) helped dismiss West Indies for 164 while Allan Lamb (132) scored his first hundred for England overseas in a total of 364. Small and Malcolm claimed four wickets apiece as the home side totalled 240, leaving England just 41 to get, which they did for the loss of Gooch. The second Test, in Georgetown, was declared a washout but at Port-of-Spain, Devon Malcolm was in devastating form as West Indies were bowled out for 199. England then dawdled, fatally as it turned out, in making 288 before Malcolm (6–77) bowled out West Indies for 239 in their second innings. Needing 151 to win, England were 73–2 at lunch on the last day and looking on the verge of another outstanding victory. It then rained for three hours. On resumption, West Indies' bowlers managed just 17 overs in two hours of bizarre play – England 120–5 – when Gooch called Russell and Capel in from the gloom. The West Indies levelled the series when they won the fourth Test at Bridgetown by 161 runs with about half an hour of playable daylight left on the final day. Clyde Best (164) made his maiden Test hundred and the home side made 446. With Gooch injured, Lamb captained England and his faultless hundred was the first by an England captain on his first appearance in that role since Archie MacLaren in 1897, when he deputized for Andrew Stoddart. England were 88 runs behind on first innings and with Haynes making 109, West Indies declared their second innings at 267–8. Curtley Ambrose then produced a match-winning spell of 8–45 to bowl England out for 191. In the final Test, West Indies overwhelmed their tired and battered opponents by an innings and 32 runs. A depleted England side struggled against the short-pitched bowling and were all out for 260. Greenidge (149) then crowned his hundredth Test with his eighteenth Test hundred and with Haynes (167) shared in a new West Indies record of 298 for the first wicket. West Indies were eventually all out for 446. England's second innings was a melancholy procession of batsmen as they were bowled out for 154 to leave West Indies the winners by an innings and 32 runs.

The first Test of New Zealand's tour of 1990 was ruined by the weather, though there were fine performances by Phil DeFreitas (5–53), as New Zealand were bowled out for 208, and an innings of 151 by Mike Atherton as England declared at 345–9. Sadly, with New Zealand 36–2 in their second innings, the game petered out into a draw. As at Trent Bridge, the second Test at Lord's was hampered by the weather and this prevented any other result than a draw. This was Sir Richard Hadlee's last appearance at the home of cricket and, though he did little with the ball, he made 86 and Trevor Franklin 101 in New Zealand's total of 462–9 declared – this after England had made 334. England were then 272–4 with Allan Lamb unbeaten on 84. The third Test, at Edgbaston, saw Hadlee produce a final memorable bowling performance, though England won the Test by 114 runs. Skipper Graham Gooch (154) and Mike Atherton (82) added 170 for the first wicket and, with useful contributions lower down the order, England totalled 435. Eddie Hemmings took 6–58 as New Zealand succumbed to 249 and, though Hadlee claimed 5–53 in a disappointing England second-innings total of 158, it was Devon Malcolm's 5-wicket haul that helped England to victory.

The first Test against India, at Lord's, in the second half of the summer of

1990, produced one of the most vividly entertaining of all the Tests held at the most famous of all grounds. The match contained the monumental innings of 333 by Graham Gooch – the sixth highest in Test history – and dominating hundreds by Lamb and Smith in a total of 653–4 declared. Centuries by Shastri and Azharuddin and a burst of audacious hitting by Kapil Dev saw India save the follow-on by one run despite some superb bowling by Fraser. A second thunderous century by Gooch saw England declare at 272–4 prior to a decisive performance by the bowlers that saw the home side win by 247 runs. In the second Test, at Old Trafford, Gooch (116) and Atherton (131) put on 225 for the first wicket and with Robin Smith making an unbeaten 121, England totalled 519. Azharuddin hit a chanceless 179 for India but they still fell 87 runs behind on first innings. Lamb then battled hard and made 109, enabling Gooch to declare and set India 408 to win. After Sidhu was out first ball, India collapsed to 109–4 but in came seventeen-year-old Sachin Tendulkar to stroke 119 not out and save the tourists. India won the toss at The Oval and, batting first, made 606–9 declared with Shastri (187) and Kapil Dev (110) making hundreds. They made all the running after getting England out for 340 and inviting the home side to follow on. A fine opening stand between Gooch and Atherton of 176 set England on their way to saving the match before David Gower hit an unbeaten 157 – an innings played under intense public scrutiny and with his career under threat – enabling England to clinch the series.

For the Ashes series of 1990–1, England, as they say, were lucky to get nil. In the opening Test at Brisbane, acting captain Allan Lamb called incorrectly and with conditions perfect for swing bowling, England were all out for 194. Even though there was bright blue sky on the second day, Fraser and Small made good use of the movement off the seam and the home side were dismissed for 152. With Bruce Reid (6–47) almost unplayable, England were bowled out for 114 and, needing 157 for victory, Taylor and Marsh knocked off the runs with disdainful ease. Until tea on the fourth day of the second Test, at Melbourne, England were on level terms with Australia, but, with superb pace bowling by Reid, along with Marsh and Boon batting heroically all through what was supposed to be an intensely difficult last day, Australia all but assured themselves of the Ashes for three more years.

Though the third Test at Sydney was drawn, England at least restored some honour. Australia, batting first, made 518 before Gooch declared England's innings closed at 469–8. With the ball now turning sharply, Tufnell and Hemmings bowled the home side out for 205, leaving England to make 254 to win. They were 113–4 in a game watched by 106,304, who provided the record receipts for a Test in Australia. No one felt robbed of their money in the fourth test at Adelaide, where, with Australia on top for much of the game, England were set a mammoth 472 to win. Gooch (117) and Atherton (87) played so well that there were visions of the tourists getting somewhere near the improbable target. But after the second new ball had been taken, the scoring rate dropped and England ended on 335–5. Australia's tougher, more resilient and thoughtful cricket had its reward with a 9-wicket win in the final

Test at Perth. Craig McDermott took 8–97 as England went from 191–2 to 244 all out. Australia made 307 before persistent and accurate fast bowling proved too much for England in their second innings, and, needing only 120 to win, Marsh and Boon saw Australia home.

Despite several interruptions by rain, the first Test against the West Indies in 1991 saw an intriguing and hard-fought contest end in England's favour by 115 runs. In a game full of suspense, the home side held a 25-run lead on first innings before Graham Gooch turned the match on its head with an outstanding innings of 154 not out – it scaled new heights of responsibility, discipline and determination in an England total of 252. Gooch's score was the highest by an England player at Headingley and he became the fourth player to score a hundred on each of the six Test-playing grounds. West Indies were then bowled out for 162 in an innings that saw several batsmen get out to excessive stroke-making. The Lord's Test was destroyed by the weather, though Robin Smith, with an innings of 148 not out, saved England from following on after the home side had been 110–5 in the wake of West Indies' first-innings total of 419. The West Indies squared the series at Trent Bridge with their superior firepower – Ambrose, Walsh and Marshall all making telling contributions as the tourists won by 9 wickets. At Edgbaston, Richie Richardson made 104 in a low-scoring game that saw West Indies win by 7 wickets, although Chris Lewis took 6–111 in their first innings. England won the fifth Test, at The Oval, to share the rubber 2–2 with the deciding moment being an astonishing piece of cricket in which 7 West Indian wickets fell for 18 runs in 10 overs either side of lunch on the third day. When England won the match almost two days later, Robin Smith had made 109 in England's first-innings total of 419, while Phil Tufnell (6–25) ran through the West Indies batting and they were all out for 176. Following on, the Middlesex spinner didn't find it as easy and, with Richardson (121) making another hundred, England were left to make 145 to win, which they did through their refusal to be overwhelmed by superior forces.

In an entertaining one-off Test against Sri Lanka, Alec Stewart made his maiden Test hundred and Phil DeFreitas claimed his best Test figures of 7–70 as England led by 58 runs on first innings. Gooch then hit 174 as England batted a second time and kept the game alive by declaring and dangling the carrot of a target of 423 to win – gettable in both time and conditions – but England's all-round experience eventually told and they won by 137 runs.

New Zealand won the toss in the first Test, at Christchurch, and put England in to bat. Alec Stewart made 148 and both Smith and Lamb got into the nineties in a total of 580–9 declared. In the Kiwis' first innings, Dilip Patel was run out for 99 and, as the home side followed on, John Wright was also dismissed 1 run short of his century, being stumped off Tufnell, who took 7–47 (match figures of 11–147) as England won by an innings and 4 runs. England then became the first side to win a Test series in New Zealand for thirteen years after their emphatic 168-run triumph in Auckland. The victory underlined the gulf in application and talent, highlighted by the performances of Gooch (114) and Lewis (5–31) in New Zealand's first-innings total of 142.

England drew the third Test but they have never completed a victorious over-seas Test series in such a sombre mood as in Wellington. Once Allan Lamb had notched his fourteenth Test century on the final afternoon, the match was destined to fizzle out into a draw. Sadly, the match is remembered for the career-threatening injury to David Lawrence, who fractured a kneecap as he collapsed in agony after delivering the ball.

After rain and bad light had accounted for the first two days of the Edgbaston Test against Pakistan, Javed Miandad (153) and Salim Malik (165) added 322 – a record for any wicket between the two countries – while for England Alec Stewart and Robin Smith both hit hundreds on a relaid strip that was a bowlers' graveyard. The second Test produced one of the most tense and exciting endings at Lord's since England drew with West Indies in 1963. After Pakistan had gained a 38-run advantage on first innings, England, with Alec Stewart carrying his bat for 69 not out, set Pakistan 138 to win. At 95–8, England seemed likely to register their first win against Pakistan since 1978 but in the end it was the tourists' pace bowlers, Wasim Akram and Waqar Younis, who came together to painstakingly guide their side home by 2 wickets. In the final Test, a blameless pitch, showing no signs of wear or tear, allowed Aamir Sohail to make 205 in Pakistan's first-innings total of 505–9 declared and, with England saving the follow-on, the game ended as a draw – although if Pakistan had held their catches it could have been a different story.

England torpedoed their chances of winning the first Test against India in Calcutta in 1992–3 when, on a wicket favouring the spinners, they opted to play with four seamers. It was also soon apparent that Azharuddin had rediscovered his form and he hit 182 in an Indian first-innings total of 371. India's three spinners, Kumble, Raju and Chauhan, took three wickets apiece as England were dismissed for 163. The England batsmen decided on a completely different strategy in the second innings and attacked whenever possible, but, on a pitch that was now spinning appreciably, they were bowled out for 286, leaving India needing 79 to win, which they did with ease. At Madras, India won the toss and, with Tendulkar (165) and Sidhu (106) scoring hundreds, they were able to declare at 560–6. England, who'd lost Gooch on the morning of the match to food poisoning, found that only Stewart, Hick and Fairbrother could survive for long and they were all out for 286. Following on, Chris Lewis struck a magnificent 117 but the home side won by an innings and 22 runs. India's superiority on their own turning pitches was confirmed beyond all doubt in the final Test, at Bombay, as they completed their first-ever whitewash over England. Graeme Hick hit a superb 178 as England made 347 but Vinod Kambli in only his third Test hit 224 as India totalled 591. Anil Kumble then took four wickets as England were beaten by an innings and 15 runs.

In the one-off Test against Sri Lanka in Colombo in March 1993, England began brightly with Robin Smith opening the innings, making 128 in a total of 380. Sri Lanka responded with flair and purpose and, with all the top order contributing, made 469. After conceding a lead of 89, England hit out rashly as if the surface was breaking up and were dismissed for just 228. Needing 140 to win, Sri Lanka had learnt from their recent panic against Australia and won by 5 wickets to record their first Test defeat of England.

In 1993, Australia retained the Ashes in convincing style – the first Test at Old Trafford producing a match of rare quality. The measure of Australia's eventual superiority was better reflected by the 179-run margin of their win rather than England's bold effort to save the game, which lasted until the fifth over of the mandatory final 15. Australia made 289 with Mark Taylor making 124 and Peter Such taking 6–67. England started well before Gatting was bowled by Warne's first ball in Ashes cricket – a ball that pitched wide of leg stump by a foot and turned viciously out of the rough to clip the off stump. He then proceeded to wreck the rest of the innings and Australia led by 79 on first innings. The weather then improved and Australia declared their second innings closed at 432–5. Needing 512 to win, Gooch hit a faultless 133, but the leg-spin of Warne and the bustling hostility of Hughes was too much. At Lord's Australia made a mammoth 632–4 declared, with Taylor (111) and Slater (152) posting a century opening stand before Boon (164) and Mark Waugh (99) took the honours on day two. Atherton battled hard to save the game but England were bowled out for 205 and followed on. Atherton was run out for 99 after slipping while going for a third run and Australia won by an innings and 62 runs.

At Trent Bridge, England made 321 while Australia's innings was a mirror image, though they did lead by 52 runs. In England's second innings, Graham Thorpe became the fourteenth England player to score a hundred on Test debut and only the third against Australia in England. Gooch declared the innings closed at 422–6, setting Australia 371 to win. At 115–6, the tourists looked in trouble but then Steve Waugh and Brendan Julien came together and thereafter the penetration of the attack was unsustainable. In the fourth Test, Australia's total of 653–4 declared set a new record for an innings of a Test at Headingley. The undefeated fifth-wicket partnership of 432 between Border and Steve Waugh was the highest stand for any Australian wicket in a Test match at the Yorkshire ground. England, 453 adrift of Australia's total, were made to follow on but, despite some gritty performances, Australia won by an innings and 148 runs. At Edgbaston, England were dismissed for 276 before making early inroads into the Australian batting to leave them 80–4. However, Mark Waugh (137) and Ian Healy (80) helped them to a total of 408. England made 305, leaving Australia just 120 to win, a target they achieved for the loss of two wickets. In the final Test, at The Oval, England made a useful total of 380 before Atherton's astute handling of his bowlers restricted the visitors to 303. During England's second innings, Gooch became his country's all-time leading run-scorer as Australia needed 391 to win. They fell 161 runs short to give England their first win in eighteen Tests against the old enemy.

Facing West Indies in the first Test at Kingston during the early part of 1994, England were beaten by 8 wickets as Keith Arthurton hit 126 and Jimmy Adams an unbeaten 95 in a total of 407 made in reply to England's 234. Graeme Hick fell four runs short of his century in the second innings as the tourists made 267, leaving West Indies just 95 to win. If ever England were going to stall the West Indian juggernaut it was in the second Test at Georgetown, but they were trounced by an innings and 44 runs. Mike Atherton made 144 in England's first-innings total of 322 but this was over-shadowed by Brian Lara's 167, and, with Jimmy Adams making 137, the hosts scored 556. England needed to bat for five sessions to save the game but this they failed to do. In the third Test, at Port-of-Spain, England were marvellously combative but on the fourth day they were swept away by Curtley Ambrose. West Indies made 252 before England replied with 328. Andy Caddick took 6–65 as the home side struggled to 269, leaving England to make 193 to win. Ambrose then devastated the England batsmen, taking 6–24 as they were shot out for just 46 – surpassing by one run their lowest-ever Test score, made in Sydney in 1887. England then stunned the locals in Bridgetown by beating the West Indies by 208 runs. The match highlighted the maturity of Alec Stewart as a batsman of international stature as he made 118 in England's total of 355. Angus Fraser was magnificently dogged in West Indies' reply, taking 8–75 as England led by 51 runs on first innings. Stewart's second century was even more impressive than his first and England declared at 394–7 with a lead of 445. It seemed as if West Indies were keen on making history themselves as Richardson blazed away at the new ball, but Caddick took 5–63 and the game was over by teatime on the final day. In the fifth Test, at Antigua, Brian Lara broke the world record for the highest Test score with a masterful innings of 375 in a total of 593–5 declared. The game then seemed to lose its sense of purpose and, with England needing 394 to save the follow-on, Atherton (135) and Smith (175) made hundreds as the tourists equalled the home side's score. The game then petered out into a draw but at least England had finished the series with their heads held high.

Against New Zealand at Trent Bridge in 1994, England bowled out the visitors for 251 before Atherton (101) and Gooch (210) added 263 for the second wicket and England declared at 567–8. Phil DeFreitas, who had hit an unbeaten 51 in that total, then took 5–71 to enable England to win by an innings and 90 runs. New Zealand were unrecognizable in the second Test at Lord's and, with Martin Crowe scoring a fine 142, they made 476. Dion Nash, who'd hit a composed half-century batting at No. 9, then took 6–76 as England stumbled to 281. Bryan Young then fell 6 runs short of a second-innings hundred for New Zealand, who set England 407 to win. Nash was again in fine form, taking 5–93, but Alec Stewart hit 119 and, with Rhodes and Taylor anxiously playing out the last twenty-three minutes in an enveloping gloom, England somehow avoided defeat. At Old Trafford, Mike Atherton hit 111 on his home ground in England's total of 382 before the Kiwis were dismissed for 151. Following on, New Zealand's Martin Crowe made another hundred before the Manchester weather saved the tourists from a heavy defeat.

England's other visitors that summer were South Africa, returning to the Test scene 29 years after playing at Lord's. The South Africans, accruing runs at a little over 2 an over, scored 357 with Kepler Wessels top-scoring with 105. England then gave way to Donald and De Villiers and were all out for 180 before the tourists declared at 278–8. Needing 456 to win, England had five sessions in which to make them, but were shot out for just 99. A drawn Test at Headingley is almost as rare as an England victory at Lord's. England's reshuffled batting order saw them make 477–9 before declaring, with Mike Atherton again out for 99. An innings of 104 by Peter Kirsten held the South African innings together as they finished 30 runs adrift of the England total. Graeme Hick hit a quickfire 110 as England set the Springboks 298 to win in a possible 70 overs – a target that was always academic. The third Test, at The Oval, simply surpassed all expectations. England had to win but history and statistics were against them. South Africa won the toss and elected to bat first, making 332. England's reply left them 28 runs behind but then Devon Malcolm produced the definitive fast-bowling performance. The South African batting disintegrated in the wake of an awesome performance as Malcolm took 9–57 from 16.3 overs to take the sixth best analysis ever recorded in Test cricket. England, set 204 to win, accelerated away and lost just 2 wickets in levelling the series.

A crucial difference throughout the 1994–5 Ashes series was the fielding – Australia's was routinely excellent while England's ground fielding was predictably laborious. The series was launched at Brisbane with two Australian centuries and the rehabilitation of Craig McDermott, but will for ever be remembered for the devastating performance of Shane Warne. Slater (176) and Mark Waugh (140) made their highest Test centuries as Australia totalled 426. McDermott then took 6–53 in England's poor total of 167. Australia declared at 248–8, leaving England an unlikely 508 to win. England's top order put up a brave fight before Shane Warne took 8–71 to lead his side to an 184-run victory. At Melbourne, Australia made 279 and England were going well at 119–1 but folded to be all out for 212. Australia built on their lead and declared at 320–7. In their second innings England's batsmen capitulated again to McDermott and Warne, with the latter performing the hat-trick as England were dismissed for just 92. Mike Atherton's team turned the form book upside down at Sydney. After making 309, they had Australia at 57–6 and in danger of having to follow on, but they rallied and finished 193 runs short. Atherton then declared with Hick on 98 not out and Australia were set 449 to win. Taylor and Slater cruised to 139–0 to set up an intriguing final day. Lunching on 206–0, Australia were on the brink of history, but rain after lunch meant one and a half hours were lost and, though Fraser removed the middle order, the light was bad and Atherton could only employ Tufnell and Hick. The game was drawn, England had salvaged some pride but Australia had retained the Ashes. The fourth Test at Adelaide saw Mike Gatting make 117 in England's total of 353 but Australia, with Greg Blewitt making his maiden Test hundred, led by 66 runs on first innings. In England's second innings, Phil DeFreitas blasted 88 in a total of 328. Needing 262 to win, Australia collapsed to 83–8 and eventually lost by 106 runs. The fifth Test offered England the chance to level the series but they lost by 329 runs. Slater made his third hundred of the series as the home side reached 402 and, after England had lost early wickets, Graham Thorpe made 123 in a total of 295. Declaring at 345–8, the Australian bowlers exploited the new ball and Craig McDermott took 6–38 as England were bowled out for just 123.

The West Indies' visit to England in 1995, saw them win the first Test, at Headingley, by 9 wickets, this after England had been bowled out for 199 in their first innings. The tourists led by 83 runs on first innings but another poor batting display meant that West Indies needed just 126 to win. This they achieved for the loss of just one wicket. At Lord's England won by 72 runs with Robin Smith top-scoring in each innings. West Indies needed 296 to win but with Dominic Cork producing figures of 7–43, England levelled the series. After being bowled out for 147 in the third Test, at Edgbaston, England were 153 behind when they went out to bat for a second time. With Walsh and Bishop in outstanding form, they were dismissed for just 89 to leave the West Indies the winners by an innings and 64 runs. The fourth Test, at Old Trafford, was the hundredth to be sponsored by Cornhill. West Indies won the toss and elected to bat but were bowled out for 216. England made 437 before Dominic Cork performed the hat-trick in West Indies' second innings total of 314 – a total helped by Brian Lara's 145. In their simple quest for 94 runs for victory, England almost derailed themselves but eventually won by 6 wickets. Centuries by Atherton (113) and Hick (118 not out) helped England to a total of 440 in the Trent Bridge Test and, though Lara (152) made yet another hundred, England led by 23 runs on first innings. A fine last-wicket partnership of 80 between Mike Watkinson (82 not out) and Angus Fraser helped England set the West Indies a victory target of 293. The game ended in a draw and England went into the sixth and final Test at The Oval, level at 2–2. England won the toss and batted first, making 454. With Brian Lara (179) and Carl Hooper (127) both hitting hundreds, West Indies took their total to 692–8 before declaring. In their second innings, England skipper Atherton took a pounding from the West Indies pacemen and though he deserved a century he fell five runs short as the game and the series ended in a draw.

On England's first visit to South Africa since their return to the fold, Graeme Hick made 141 in the first Test, at Pretoria, but the game was ruined by the weather. At Johannesburg, Peter Kirsten made 110 in South Africa's first-innings total of 332 before the tourists were bowled out for just 200. Brian McMillan hit 100 not out as South Africa declared at 346–9, leaving England 479 to win. It was here that skipper Mike Atherton made his highest Test score of 185 not out in a personal battle with Allan Donald as England finished on 351–5. The third Test, at Durban, was hampered by the rain and fizzled out into a draw. The fourth Test, at Fort Elizabeth, had the makings of a memorable one until England's totally negative tactics in the final four sessions ensured a most unsatisfactory conclusion. Set 328 to win, England, with a side full of stroke-makers, denied themselves an outside chance of victory and finished on 189–3. South Africa then duly overwhelmed England inside three days in the fifth and final Test to take the series 1–0.

India's visit to England in the first half of 1996 saw them lose the first Test, at Edgbaston, by 8 wickets. Bowled out for 214, England, thanks in the main to a fine hundred by Nasser Hussain, had a lead of 99 on first innings. Some effective bowling from Chris Lewis saw India bowled out for 219 in their second innings before England lost a couple of wickets in making the 121 they needed for victory. At Lord's, England had slumped to 107–5 before a superb innings of 124 by wicketkeeper Jack Russell took them to 344. Ganguly then hit 131 and Dravid fell five runs short of a century as India replied with 429, the game later ending in a draw. In the third Test, at Trent Bridge, both Ganguly (136) and Tendulkar (177) made hundreds in India's first-innings total of 521. England responded by passing the tourists' score with Atherton (160) and Hussain (107) – before he retired hurt – the major run-makers in a total of 564. Mark Ealham, on his debut, bowled well in India's second innings to take 4–21 but the game ended in a draw.

Pakistan were the visitors for the second half of the summer and they won the first Test at Lord's by 164 runs, this after Inzamam-ul-Haq had made 148 in a first-innings score of 340. England were 55 runs behind on first innings and, with Pakistan declaring at 352–5, the home side faced a target of 408 for victory. Mushtaq Ahmed bamboozled the majority of England batsmen to take 5–57. At Headingley, Ijaz Ahmed's innings of 141 and Moin Khan's 105 lower down the order helped Pakistan make 448. Alec Stewart (170) and Nick Knight (113) helped England pass this total but it was a good batting surface and the game ended in a draw. At The Oval, England were bowled out for 326 before Saeed Anwar made a faultless 176 and Salim Malik an unbeaten 100 in Pakistan's 521–8 declared. Mushtaq Ahmed then took 6–78 as the tourists went on to win the game by 9 wickets and so take the three-match series 2–0.

England's first Test match in Zimbabwe at Bulawayo not only ended in a draw, but finished with the scores level. Andy Flower (112) top-scored in Zimbabwe's first-innings total of 376, while both Hussain (113) and Crawley (112) hit hundreds as England gained a lead of 30 runs on the first innings. With the wicket beginning to take spin, Tufnell got amongst the wickets, leaving England needing 205 to win. Despite a brilliant 96 from Nick Knight and a fighting 73 from Alec Stewart, England finished on 204–6. The game at Harare also finished in a draw, with no play on the final day and Alec Stewart hitting a hundred in England's second innings.

It was then on to New Zealand and the first Test at Auckland, which produced plenty of runs in yet another drawn game. Stephen Fleming made 129 in the Kiwis' first-innings total of 390, but, with Alec Stewart (173) and his Surrey teammate Graham Thorpe (119) both making centuries, England led by 131 runs on first innings. New Zealand were in trouble at 142–9, just 11 runs ahead, when Nathan Astle (102 not out) and last man Danny Morrison put on an unbeaten 106 to save the game for the home side. At Wellington, Caddick and Gough ran through the Kiwis as they were bowled out for 124, and, with Thorpe (108) hitting his second century of the series, England were 259 runs in front as New Zealand batted a second time. Despite a better showing, England went on to win the game by an innings and 68 runs. Mike Atherton's decision to put New Zealand in to bat after winning the toss at Christchurch looked to have backfired, especially after England were bowled out for 228, some 118 runs behind New Zealand's first-innings total of 346. However, a disappointing second-innings total of 186 from the home side left England needing 305 for victory. Skipper Atherton saw England home by 4 wickets following a fine innings of 118.

When Australia visited England for the 1997 Ashes series, they had recon-firmed their status as the world's best Test-playing team following defeats of West Indies and South Africa. However, within a couple of hours of the start of the first day of the opening Test at Edgbaston, Australia, having won the toss and elected to bat, found themselves at 54–8. Shane Warne hit a belligerent 47 but the tourists were all out for 118. After England lost two early wickets, Hussain and Thorpe put on 288 runs for the third wicket, with the Essex player going on to make 207 before England declared at 478–9. Australia started well in their second innings and were 327–1 with both Taylor and Blewett making centuries. Gough then got England back on track and the home side won by 9 wickets with a day to spare. The opening day at Lord's was abandoned without a ball being bowled before Glenn McGrath destroyed England with figures of 8–38 as they were all out for just 77. With Australia looking for quick runs, Waugh declared at 213–7. Atherton and Butcher opened with a first-wicket partnership of 162 and England finished on 266–4. Dean Headley, making his debut at Old Trafford, became the first third-generation cricketer, following father Ron and grandfather George, both of whom appeared for the West Indies. Australia had a lead of 73 runs on the first innings, and with Steve Waugh making his second century of the match, Australia declared at 395–8, setting England 469 to win. Warne took early wickets and McGrath claimed 4 of the 5 to fall on the last day in a 268-run win for Australia.

At Headingley, Jason Gillespie ran through the England batting, taking 7–37 before Matthew Elliott (199) and Ricky Ponting (127) allowed the tourists to declare at 501–9. Needing 329 to make Australia bat again, they started badly and were 89–4 before Hussain (105) and Crawley (72) took the score to 222. But even so, Australia won by an innings and 51 runs. The fifth Test, at Trent Bridge, saw Adam and Ben Hollioake become the fifth set of brothers to play together for England but the first time this century that two brothers had made their debuts in the same Test. Australia made 427 before bowling England out for 313 and then set about extending their 114-run lead. England were left needing 451 but, with only Thorpe batting to potential, Australia won by 264 runs. At The Oval, McGrath took 7–76 to restrict England to 180 before Tufnell got the ball to turn prodigiously to take 7–66 off 34.3 overs – even so, the tourists had a useful lead. Then, for the third time in the match, a bowler took 7 wickets – Mike Kasprowicz with 7–36. Australia needed only 124 to win but Caddick ran in and bowled everything in the right area to take 5–42, and, with Tufnell taking 4–27 – finishing with a match return of 11–93 – England won by 19 runs.

The first Test against the West Indies at Sabina Park was abandoned on the first morning with England 17–3 – during the course of the 61 balls that were bowled, the England physio had to run on the field six times to treat batsmen who had suffered blows to the body. Safety was the paramount concern and there was no other option than to call the game off – the only Test match ever abandoned because of dangerous conditions. This meant there would be back-to-back Tests at Port-of-Spain. England lost the first by 3 wickets when it never looked likely that the West Indies would make the 282 needed for victory. But then England won the third Test as Fraser and Caddick took 5 wickets apiece as the home side were bowled out for 159. Curtley Ambrose also took 5 wickets and England were 14 runs behind on first innings. Bowlers were again on top when West Indies batted a second time and England were left to make 225 for victory. Alec Stewart, who'd top-scored in England's first innings, saw his side home by 3 wickets with a disciplined knock of 83. The toss was all-important at Georgetown and West Indies made 352 with Chanderpaul (118) and Lara (93) the major contributors. England were bowled out for 170 before Ian Bishop struck an unbeaten 44 to help West Indies set the tourists a target of 380 for victory. Not surprisingly, Ambrose demolished the top order and West Indies won by 242 runs. In the final Test at Barbados, Mark Ramprakash finally scored his maiden Test hundred and, with Graham Thorpe also making a century, England made 403. West Indies could muster only 262 in reply and with England's batsmen putting bat to ball, Atherton was able to declare and set West Indies 375 to win in ninety minutes and a day. With the pitch beginning to turn, England were in with a good chance of squaring the series but seasonal rains arrived to thwart the tourists.

Having resigned the captaincy, Mike Atherton registered his twelfth Test century in the opening match of the 1998 series against South Africa but the game ended as a draw. At Lord's, South Africa lost their first four wickets for 46 runs but fielding lapses allowed Cronje (81) and Rhodes (117) to make a spirited recovery in a fifth-wicket stand of 184. England were then bowled out for just 110 as the batsmen were unable to withstand the bowling of Donald and Pollock. Following on, they were bowled out for 264 with Hussain making 105 but the tourists needed only eight balls to make the 15 runs required for victory. In the third Test, at Old Trafford, England saved a game that they seemed destined to lose. With Gary Kirsten making 210 and Jacques Kallis 132, South Africa declared and their first innings closed at 552–5. With the exceptions of Atherton, Stewart and Ramprakash, England's spineless display of batting in the first innings saw them bowled out for 183. Following on, Atherton (89) and Stewart (164) put on 226 for the third wicket but it was down to Glamorgan's Robert Croft (37 not out) and Angus Fraser, who repelled Allan Donald for the final, tense hour of the match as England ended on 369–9.

The Trent Bridge Test is best remembered for the elevated passage of play between Atherton and Donald on the fourth evening. South Africa had the better of the early exchanges and led by 38 on the first innings. England, led by Fraser (5–62), bowled South Africa out for 208, leaving the home side needing 247 in a day and a half to win the match and level the series. Following the departure of Mark Butcher, Hussain joined Atherton at the crease midway through the final session on the Sunday evening. In a forty-minute spell of fierce, short-pitched fast bowling, the Lancashire opener stood firm and in making an unbeaten 98 helped England to an 8-wicket win. The Headingley Test was the decider and on a bowler-friendly surface, the match was compelling. England, despite Mark Butcher's 116, were bowled out for 230 but fine bowling by Angus Fraser restricted South Africa to a lead of 22 on first innings. A wonderful innings of 94 by Nasser Hussain enabled England to set South Africa 219 to win. By the end of the fourth day, the visitors were 185–8, 34 short of victory, but, instead of claiming the extra half-hour when England's bowlers were tired, they took the decision to come off. England wrapped the game up and with it the series early on the last day.

In the one-off Test against Sri Lanka at The Oval, England were completely outplayed as Muttiah Muralitharan took 16–220 – the best bowling ever recorded there in a Test. It certainly didn't look as though the visitors would win when, after Sri Lanka had won the toss and put England in to bat, Hick (107) and Crawley (156 not out) made hundreds in a total of 445. In reply, Sri Lanka, led by Jayasuriya (213) and Aravinda de Silva (152), made 591, a lead of 146 on first innings. Then, with Muralitharan taking 9–65, England were dismissed for 181 and Sri Lanka went on to win by 10 wickets.

In the first Test of the 1998–9 Ashes series at Brisbane, England escaped with a draw, thanks mainly to a thunderstorm, which flooded the ground. Australia had made 485 and England 375, thanks to a fine hundred from Butcher, before Taylor declared his side's second innings closed at 237–3. With England needing 348 to win in a probable 98 overs, wickets fell at regular inter-vals until rain ended play with England on 179–6. England paid the price of being dismissed in the first two sessions of the second Test at Perth. Their total of 112 was the lowest total at the WACA. Australia then made 240 before bowling England out for 191. Needing 64 for victory, the Aussies achieved this for the loss of 3 wickets. At Adelaide, Justin Langer made 179 not out in Australia's total of 391. England were 187–3 before their last 7 wickets fell for just 40 runs. Slater made another hundred, enabling Australia to declare at 278–5. There were moments when England could fantasize about a draw but they were bowled out for 237 and Australia had retained the Ashes. The fourth Test, at Melbourne, had it all. England, with Alec Stewart making his first hundred in 23 Tests against Australia, were bowled out for 270. The home side, thanks to Steve Waugh (122 not out) had a lead of 70 runs on first innings and though Hick, Hussain and Stewart all scored fifties in England's second innings, Australia were left with just 175 to win. At 103–2, they looked clear favourites but Headley (6–60) and Gough polished off the tail and England won by 12 runs. The final Test, at Sydney, swung from one side to the other. Darren Gough performed the first hat-trick in an Ashes Test this century, but, even so, Australia totalled 322. England struggled against Stuart MacGill and were dismissed for 220. The third day belonged to Mark Slater, who made 123, twice as many as all his teammates made together, setting England 287 to win. Hussain couldn't find anyone to stay with him and Australia won by 98 runs.

England won the first Test of the 1999 home series against New Zealand by 7 wickets, this after being 100 behind on first innings. New Zealand were bowled out for 226 and England 126 before Andy Caddick produced figures of 5–32 to dismiss the Kiwis a second time for just 107. After losing Alec Stewart, home debutant Alex Tudor came in as nightwatchman, going on to make 99 not out in England's winning score of 211–3 – the highest score by an England nightwatchman and the first such score ever made in a Test outside Perth. The Kiwis levelled the series in the second Test at Lord's. Chris Cairns took 6–77 as England were bowled out for 186 and Horne made 100 as New Zealand replied with 358. The home side were then dismissed for 229, leaving New Zealand just 58 to win – a total they reached for the loss of one wicket but spent a dreary hour and a half in getting them. The weather certainly spared England's blushes in the third Test at Old Trafford. England conceded a first-innings deficit of over 100 for the fourth time running against New Zealand, having been bowled out for 199, and then watched McMillan and Astle both make hundreds in a total of 496–9 declared. In reply, England were 181–2 but thanks to the weather they would be playing for the series in the final Test at The Oval. In a low-scoring match, Chris Cairns played his part in the Kiwis' victory by 83 runs, making 80 in their second-innings total of 162 and taking 5–31 as England were bowled out for 153 in their first knock.

After their defeat by New Zealand, England arrived in South Africa for Duncan Fletcher's first series in charge. The first Test in Johannesburg saw England in murky light reduced to 2–4 in the fourth over with Butcher, Hussain, Stewart and Atherton all back in the pavilion. England were eventually all out for 122 with Donald taking 6–53 and Pollock 4–16. Cullinan made 108 as South Africa declared at 403–9 but the home side's two pace bowlers again got amongst the English batsmen, enabling South Africa to win by an innings and 21 runs. The game at Port Elizabeth, in which Lance Klusener made 174 in South Africa's first-innings total of 450, was drawn, with Atherton (108) and Hussain (82) helping England to 373 before the hosts set England a victory target of 302. Hussain was unbeaten on 70 as England finished on 153–6. England had the better of the early exchanges at Durban when in-form batsman Nasser Hussain made 146 not out in a total of 366–9 declared. Andrew Caddick then produced figures of 7–46 as the Springboks were skittled out for 156, but after following on they made 572–7 thanks to a fine innings of 275 by Gary Kirsten, supported by wicketkeeper Mark Boucher's 108. South Africa wrapped up the series in Cape Town 2–0, winning by an innings and 37 runs, and both teams flew to Pretoria for the final match of a now dead rubber. It was to be the Test in which match-fixing was finally proved to the world, although the players did not know it then. Rain halted proceedings with South Africa 155–6 on the first day, and it didn't stop raining for another three days, leaving the last day for both teams to play out for the seemingly inevitable draw. Hansie Cronje then offered Hussain a game: if both sides would forfeit an innings, he would set England around 280 to win in 80 overs. As it transpired the offer was 249 in 76 overs. At 102–4, the game was evenly poised, but

Cronje brought on the debutant and part-time bowler Pieter Strydom and England's innings gained momentum. Stewart's 73 and Vaughan's 69 took their side to a position where only victory or defeat was contemplated by the England skipper and they scraped home by 2 wickets with Gough and Silverwood at the crease.

TEST MATCH RESULTS: 1990–2000

658. West Indies v England
First Test at Kingston, Jamaica – 24, 25, 26, 28 February, 1 March 1990
WEST INDIES 164 (Fraser 5–28) and 240 (Best 64, Small 4–58, Malcolm 4–77)
ENGLAND 364 (Lamb 132, R. Smith 57, Larkins 46, Walsh 5–68) and 41–1
England won by 9 wickets

West Indies v England
Second Test at Georgetown, Guyana – March 1990
Match abandoned without a ball being bowled: rain

659. West Indies v England
Third Test at Port-of-Spain, Trinidad – 23, 24, 25, 27, 28 March 1990
WEST INDIES 199 (Logie 98, Malcolm 4–60) and 239 (Haynes 45, Greenidge 42, Malcolm 6–77)
ENGLAND 288 (Gooch 84, Larkins 54, Capel 40, Ambrose 4–59) and 120–5
Match drawn

660. West Indies v England
Fourth Test at Bridgetown, Barbados – 5, 6, 7, 8, 10 April 1990
WEST INDIES 446 (Best 164, Richards 70, Richardson 45, Greenidge 41, Small 4–109) and 267 (Haynes 109, Logie 48, Small 4–74)
ENGLAND 358 (Lamb 119, R. Smith 62, Stewart 45, Bishop 4–70) and 191 (Russell 55, R. Smith 40*, Ambrose 8–45)
West Indies won by 164 runs

661. West Indies v England
Fifth Test at St John's, Antigua – 12, 14, 15, 16 April 1990
ENGLAND 260 (Bailey 42, Bishop 5–84) and 154 (Ambrose 4–22)
WEST INDIES 446 (Haynes 167, Greenidge 149, Malcolm 4–126)
West Indies won by an innings and 32 runs

662. England v New Zealand
First Test at Trent Bridge – 7, 8, 9, 11, 12 June 1990
NEW ZEALAND 208 (M. Crowe 59, DeFreitas 5–53) and 36–2
ENGLAND 345–9 dec. (Atherton 151, R. Smith 55, Hadlee 4–89)
Match drawn

663. England v New Zealand
Second Test at Lord's – 21, 22, 23, 25, 26 June 1990
ENGLAND 334 (Gooch 85, R. Smith 64, Stewart 54, Morrison 4–64) and 272–4 dec. (Lamb 84*, Atherton 54, Stewart 42)
NEW ZEALAND 462–9 dec. (Franklin 101, Wright 98, Hadlee 86, Jones 49, Greatbatch 47, Malcolm 5–94)
Match drawn

664. England v New Zealand
Third Test at Edgbaston – 5, 6, 7, 9, 10 July 1990
ENGLAND 435 (Gooch 154, Atherton 82, Small 44*, Russell 43) and 158 (Atherton 70, Hadlee 5–53, Bracewell 4–38)
NEW ZEALAND 249 (Franklin 66, Greatbatch 45, Hemmings 6–58) and 230 (Wright 46, Jones 40, Malcolm 5–46)
England won by 114 runs

665. England v India
First Test at Lord's – 26, 27, 28, 30, 31 July 1990
ENGLAND 653–4 dec. (Gooch 333, Lamb 139, R. Smith 100*, Gower 40) and 272–4 dec. (Gooch 123, Atherton 72)
INDIA 454 (Azharuddin 121, Shastri 100, Kapil Dev 77*, Vengsarkar 52, Fraser 5–104) and 224
England won by 247 runs

666. England v India
Second Test at Old Trafford – 9, 10, 11, 13, 14 August 1990
ENGLAND 519 (Atherton 131, R. Smith 121*, Gooch 116, Hirwani 4–174) and 320–4 dec. (Lamb 109, Atherton 74, R. Smith 61*)
INDIA 432 (Azharuddin 179, Manjrekar 93, Tendulkar 68, Fraser 5–124) and 343–6 (Tendulkar 119*, Prabhakar 67*, Manjrekar 50)
Match drawn

667. England v India
Third Test at The Oval – 23, 24, 25, 27, 28 August 1990
INDIA 606–9 dec. (Shastri 187, Kapil Dev 110, Azharuddin 78, More 61*)
ENGLAND 340 (Gooch 85, R. Smith 57, Hemmings 51, Prabhakar 4–74) and 477–4 dec. (Gower 157*, Gooch 88, Atherton 86, Lamb 52)
Match drawn

668. Australia v England
First Test at Brisbane – 23, 24, 25 November 1990
ENGLAND 194 (Gower 61, Reid 4–53) and 114 (Alderman 6–47)
AUSTRALIA 152 and 157–0 (Marsh 72*, Taylor 67*)
Australia won by 10 wickets

669. Australia v England

Second Test at Melbourne – 26, 27, 28, 29, 30 December 1990
ENGLAND 352 (Gower 100, Stewart 79, Larkins 64, Reid 6–97) and 150 (Gooch 58, Larkins 54, Reid 7–51)
AUSTRALIA 306 (Border 62, Taylor 61, Jones 44, Fraser 6–82) and 197–2 (Boon 94*, Marsh 79*)
Australia won by 8 wickets

670. Australia v England

Third Test at Sydney – 4, 5, 6, 7, 8 January 1991
AUSTRALIA 518 (Matthews 128, Boon 97, Border 78, Jones 60, S. Waugh 48, Malcolm 4–128) and 205 (Healy 69, Tufnell 5–61)
ENGLAND 469–8 dec. (Gower 123, Atherton 105, Stewart 91, Gooch 59) and 113–4 (Gooch 54)
Match drawn

671. Australia v England

Fourth Test at Adelaide – 25, 26, 27, 28, 29 January 1991
AUSTRALIA 386 (M. Waugh 138, Matthews 65, Boon 49, McDermott 42*, DeFreitas 4–56) and 314–6 dec. (Boon 121, Border 83*)
ENGLAND 229 (Gooch 87, R. Smith 53, DeFreitas 45, McDermott 5–97, Reid 4–53) and 335–5 (Gooch 117, Atherton 87, Lamb 53)
Match drawn

672. Australia v England

Fifth Test at Perth – 1, 2, 3, 5 February 1991
ENGLAND 244 (Lamb 91, R. Smith 58, McDermott 8–97) and 182 (R. Smith 43, Newport 40*, Hughes 4–37)
AUSTRALIA 307 (Boon 64, Matthews 60*, Healy 42) and 120–1 (Marsh 63*)
Australia won by 9 wickets

673. England v West Indies

First Test at Headingley – 6, 7, 8, 9, 10 June 1991
ENGLAND 198 (R. Smith 54) and 252 (Gooch 154*, Ambrose 6–52)
WEST INDIES 173 (Richards 73, DeFreitas 4–34) and 162 (Richardson 68, DeFreitas 4–59)
England won by 115 runs

674. England v West Indies

Second Test at Lord's – 20, 21, 22, 23 (no play), 24 June 1991
WEST INDIES 419 (Hooper 111, Richards 63, Haynes 60, Richardson 57, Pringle 5–100) and 12–2
ENGLAND 354 (R. Smith 148*, Russell 46, Ambrose 4–87)
Match drawn

675. England v West Indies

Third Test at Trent Bridge – 4, 5, 6, 8, 9 July 1991
ENGLAND 300 (Gooch 68, R. Smith 64*, Hick 43, Ambrose 5–74) and 211 (DeFreitas 55*, Walsh 4–64)
WEST INDIES 397 (Richards 80, Logie 78, Marshall 67) and 115–1 (Haynes 57*, Richardson 52*)
West Indies won by 9 wickets

676. England v West Indies

Fourth Test at Edgbaston – 25, 26, 27, 28 July 1991
ENGLAND 188 (Gooch 45, Marshall 4–33) and 255 (Lewis 65, Pringle 45, Gooch 40, Patterson 5–81)
WEST INDIES 292 (Richardson 104, Lewis 6–111) and 157–3 (Richards 73*, Hooper 55*)
West Indies won by 7 wickets

677. England v West Indies

Fifth Test at The Oval – 8, 9, 10, 11, 12 August 1991
ENGLAND 419 (R. Smith 109, Gooch 60, Lewis 47*, H. Morris 44) and 146–5
WEST INDIES 176 (Haynes 75*, Tufnell 6–25) and 385 (Richardson 121, Richards 60, Hooper 54, Haynes 43, Lawrence 5–106)
England won by 5 wickets

678. England v Sri Lanka

Only Test at Lord's – 22, 23, 24, 26, 27 August 1991
ENGLAND 282 (Stewart 113*, H. Morris 42, Ratnayake 5–69) and 364–3 dec. (Gooch 174, Smith 63*, Stewart 43)
SRI LANKA 224 (Hathurusingha 66, Ratnayake 52, de Silva 42, DeFreitas 7–70) and 285 (Jayasuriya 66, Tufnell 5–94)
England won by 137 runs

679. New Zealand v England

First Test at Christchurch – 18, 19, 20, 21, 22 January 1992
ENGLAND 580–9 dec. (Stewart 148, R. Smith 96, Lamb 93, Lewis 70, Reeve 59)
NEW ZEALAND 312 (Patel 99, Cairns 61, Tufnell 4–100) and 264 (Wright 99, M. Crowe 48, Hartland 45, Tufnell 7–47)
England won by an innings and 4 runs

680. New Zealand v England

Second Test at Auckland – 30, 31 January, 1, 2, 3 February 1992
ENGLAND 203 (Pringle 41, Cairns 6–52) and 321 (Gooch 114, Lamb 60)
NEW ZEALAND 142 (M. Crowe 45, Lewis 5–31) and 214 (M. Crowe 56, DeFreitas 4–62)
England won by 168 runs

681. New Zealand v England

Third Test at Wellington – 6, 7, 8, 9, 10 February 1992
ENGLAND 305 (Stewart 107, Hick 43, Patel 4–87) and 359–7 dec. (Lamb 142, R. Smith 76, Stewart 63)
NEW ZEALAND 432–9 dec. (Jones 143, Wright 116, Hick 4–126) and 43–3
Match drawn

682. England v Pakistan

First Test at Edgbaston – 4 (no play), 5, 6, 7, 8 June 1992
PAKISTAN 446–4 dec. (Salim Malik 165, Javed Miandad 153*, Ramiz Raja 47, DeFreitas 4–121)
ENGLAND 459–7 dec. (Stewart 190, R. Smith 127, Hick 51)
Match drawn

683. England v Pakistan

Second Test at Lord's – 18, 19, 20, 21 June 1992
ENGLAND 255 (Stewart 74, Gooch 69, Waqar Younis 5–91) and 175 (Stewart 69*, Wasim Akram 4–66)
PAKISTAN 293 (Aamer Sohail 73, Asif Mujtaba 59, Salim Malik 55, Malcolm 4–70) and 141–8 (Wasim Akram 45*)
Pakistan won by 2 wickets

684. England v Pakistan

Third Test at Old Trafford – 2, 3 (no play), 4, 6, 7 July 1992
PAKISTAN 505 (Aamer Sohail 205, Javed Miandad 88, Asif Mujtaba 57, Ramiz Raja 54) and 239–5 dec. (Ramiz Raja 88, Javed Miandad 45*, Asif Mujtaba 40)
ENGLAND 390 (Gooch 78, Gower 73, Lewis 55, Salisbury 50, Wasim Akram 5–128, Aaqib Javed 4–100)
Match drawn

685. England v Pakistan
Fourth Test at Headingley – 23, 24, 25, 26 July 1992
PAKISTAN 197 (Salim Malik 82*) and 221 (Salim Malik
84*, Ramiz Raja 63, Mallender 5–50)
ENGLAND 320 (Gooch 135, Atherton 76, R. Smith 42,
Waqar Younis 5–117) and 99–4
England won by 6 wickets

686. England v Pakistan
Fifth Test at The Oval – 6, 7, 8, 9 August 1992
ENGLAND 207 (Atherton 60, Wasim Akram 6–67) and 174
(R. Smith 84*, Waqar Younis 5–52)
PAKISTAN 380 (Javed Miandad 59, Shoaib Mohammad 55,
Asif Mujtaba 50, Rashid Latif 50, Aamer Sohail 49,
Salim Malik 40, Malcolm 5–94) and 5–0
Pakistan won by 10 wickets

687. India v England
First Test at Calcutta – 29, 30, 31 January, 1, 2 February 1993
INDIA 371 (Azharuddin 182, Tendulkar 50, Prabhakar 46)
and 82–2
ENGLAND 163 and 286 (Gatting 81, Stewart 49)
India won by 8 wickets

688. India v England
Second Test at Madras – 11, 12, 13, 14, 15 February 1993
INDIA 560–6 dec. (Tendulkar 165, Sidhu 106, Amre 78,
Kapil Dev 66*, Kambli 59)
ENGLAND 286 (Fairbrother 83, Stewart 74, Hick 64, Raju
4–103) and 252 (Lewis 117, R. Smith 56, Kumble 6–64)
India won by an innings and 22 runs

689. India v England
Third Test at Bombay – 19, 20, 21, 22, 23 February 1993
ENGLAND 347 (Hick 178, Lewis 49) and 229 (R. Smith 62,
Gatting 61, Hick 47, Kumble 4–70)
INDIA 591 (Kambli 224, Sidhu 79, Tendulkar 78, Amre 57,
Prabhakar 44, Tufnell 4–142)
India won by an innings and 15 runs

690. Sri Lanka v England
Only Test at Colombo – 13, 14, 15, 17, 18 March 1993
ENGLAND 380 (R. Smith 128, Hick 68, Stewart 63,
Warnaweera 4–90, Muralitharan 4–118) and 228
(Emburey 59, Lewis 45, Warnaweera 4–98)
SRI LANKA 469 (Tillakaratne 93*, de Silva 80, Mahanama
64, Ranatunga 64, Hathurusingha 59, Gurusinha 43,
Lewis 4–66) and 142–5
Sri Lanka won by 5 wickets

691. England v Australia
First Test at Old Trafford – 3, 4, 5, 6, 7 June 1993
AUSTRALIA 289 (Taylor 124, Slater 58, Such 6–67) and
432–5 dec. (Healy 102*, Boon 93, S. Waugh 78*, M.
Waugh 64)
ENGLAND 210 (Gooch 65, Warne 4–51, Hughes 4–59) and
332 (Gooch 133, Lewis 43, Warne 4–86, Hughes 4–92)
Australia won by 179 runs

692. England v Australia
Second Test at Lord's – 17, 18, 19, 20, 21 June 1993
AUSTRALIA 632–4 dec. (Boon 164*, Slater 152, Taylor 111,
M. Waugh 99, Border 77)
ENGLAND 205 (Atherton 80, Hughes 4–52, Warne 4–57)
and 365 (Atherton 99, Hick 64, Stewart 62, Gatting 59,
May 4–81, Warne 4–102)
Australia won by an innings and 62 runs

693. England v Australia
Third Test at Trent Bridge – 1, 2, 3, 5, 6 July 1993
ENGLAND 321 (R. Smith 86, Hussain 71, Hughes 5–92) and
422–6 dec. (Gooch 120, Thorpe 114*, R. Smith 50,
Hussain 47*)
AUSTRALIA 373 (Boon 101, M. Waugh 70, Slater 40,
McCague 4–121) and 202–6 (Julian 56*, S. Waugh
47*)
Match drawn

694. England v Australia
Fourth Test at Headingley – 22, 23, 24, 25, 26 July 1993
AUSTRALIA 653–4 dec. (Border 200*, S. Waugh 157*, Boon
107, Slater 67, M. Waugh 52)
ENGLAND 200 (Gooch 59, Atherton 55, Reiffel 5–65) and
305 (Stewart 78, Atherton 63, May 4–65)
Australia won by an innings and 148 runs

 DID YOU KNOW...?

Mike Atherton's 553 runs in 1993 were the record
for an Ashes series by a batsman who didn't score
a century.

695. England v Australia
Fifth Test at Edgbaston – 5, 6, 7, 8, 9 August 1993
ENGLAND 276 (Atherton 72, Emburey 55*, Stewart 45,
Reiffel 6–71) and 251 (Thorpe 60, Gooch 48, Warne
5–82, May 5–89)
AUSTRALIA 408 (M. Waugh 137, Healy 80, S. Waugh 59)
and 120–2 (M. Waugh 62*)
Australia won by 8 wickets

696. England v Australia
Sixth Test at The Oval – 19, 20, 21, 22, 23 August 1993
ENGLAND 380 (Hick 80, Stewart 76, Gooch 56, Atherton
50) and 313 (Gooch 79, Ramprakash 64, Atherton 42)
AUSTRALIA 303 (Healy 83*, Taylor 70, Border 48, Fraser
5–87) and 229 (M. Waugh 49, Reiffel 42, Watkin
4–65)
England won by 161 runs

697. West Indies v England
First Test at Kingston, Jamaica – 19, 20, 21, 23, 24 February
1994
ENGLAND 234 (Stewart 70, Atherton 55, K. Benjamin
6–66) and 267 (Hick 96)
WEST INDIES 407 (Arthurton 126, Adams 95*, Lara 83)
and 95–2 (Haynes 43*)
West Indies won by 8 wickets

698. West Indies v England
Second Test at Georgetown, Guyana – 17, 18, 19, 20, 22
March 1994
ENGLAND 322 (Atherton 144, R. Smith 84, Ambrose
4–58) and 190 (Stewart 79, K Benjamin 4–34,
Ambrose 4–37)
WEST INDIES 556 (Lara 167, Adams 137, Haynes 63,
Chanderpaul 62, W. Benjamin 44, Salisbury 4–163)
West Indies won by an innings and 44 runs

699. West Indies v England

Third Test at Port-of-Spain, Trinidad – 25, 26, 27, 29, 30 March 1994
WEST INDIES 252 (Richardson 63, Lara 43, Fraser 4–49, Lewis 4–61) and 269 (Chanderpaul 50, Adams 43, Arthurton 42, Caddick 6–65)
ENGLAND 328 (Thorpe 86, Atherton 48, Hick 40, Ambrose 5–60) and 46 (Ambrose 6–24)
West Indies won by 147 runs

700. West Indies v England

Fourth Test at Bridgetown, Barbados – 8, 9, 10, 12, 13 April 1994
ENGLAND 355 (Stewart 118, Atherton 85, Ambrose 4–86) and 394–7 dec. (Stewart 143, Thorpe 84, Hick 59, Walsh 5–94)
WEST INDIES 304 (Chanderpaul 77, Ambrose 44, K. Benjamin 43*, Fraser 8–75) and 237 (Lara 64, Arthurton 52, Caddick 5–63)
England won by 208 runs

701. West Indies v England

Fifth Test at St John's, Antigua – 16, 17, 18, 20, 21 April 1994
WEST INDIES 593–5 dec. (Lara 375, Chanderpaul 75*, Adams 59, Arthurton 47) and 43–0
ENGLAND 593 (R. Smith 175, Atherton 135, Lewis 75*, Russell 62, K. Benjamin 4–110)
Match drawn

702. England v New Zealand

First Test at Trent Bridge – 2, 3, 4, 5, 6 June 1994
NEW ZEALAND 251 (Fleming 54, DeFreitas 4–94) and 226 (Young 53, Parore 42, DeFreitas 5–71)
ENGLAND 567–8 dec. (Gooch 210, Atherton 101, R. Smith 78, DeFreitas 51*, Rhodes 49)
England won by an innings and 90 runs

703. England v New Zealand

Second Test at Lord's – 16, 17, 18, 19, 20 June 1994
NEW ZEALAND 476 (M. Crowe 142, Thomson 69, Nash 56, Fleming 41, Parore 40) and 211–5 dec. (Young 94)
ENGLAND 281 (Hick 58, White 51, Stewart 45, Nash 6–76) and 254–8 (Stewart 119, Nash 5–93)
Match drawn

704. England v New Zealand

Third Test at Old Trafford – 30 June, 1, 2, 4, 5 July 1994
ENGLAND 382 (Atherton 111, DeFreitas 69, Gough 65, White 42, Owens 4–99, Nash 4–107)
NEW ZEALAND 151 (M. Crowe 70, Gough 4–47) and 308–7 (M. Crowe 115, Parore 71)
Match drawn

705. England v South Africa

First Test at Lord's – 21, 22, 23, 24 July 1994
SOUTH AFRICA 357 (Wessels 105, G. Kirsten 72, Matthews 41, Gough 4–76) and 278–8 dec. (G. Kirsten 44, P. Kirsten 42, Gough 4–46)
ENGLAND 180 (Donald 5–74) and 99
South Africa won by 356 runs

706. England v South Africa

Second Test at Headingley – 4, 5, 6, 7, 8 August 1994
ENGLAND 477–9 dec. (Atherton 99, Stewart 89, Thorpe 72, Rhodes 65*) and 267–5 dec. (Hick 110, Thorpe 73)

SOUTH AFRICA 447 (P. Kirsten 104, McMillan 78, Matthews 62*, Richardson 48, Rhodes 46, DeFreitas 4–89) and 116–3 (G. Kirsten 65)
Match drawn

707. England v South Africa

Third Test at The Oval – 18, 19, 20, 21 August 1994
SOUTH AFRICA 332 (McMillan 93, Richardson 58, Wessels 45, Benjamin 4–42, DeFreitas 4–93) and 175 (Cullinan 94, Malcolm 9–57)
ENGLAND 304 (Thorpe 79, Stewart 62, Gough 42*, de Villiers 4–62) and 205–2 (Hick 81*, Atherton 63)
England won by 8 wickets

708. Australia v England

First Test at Brisbane – 25, 26, 27, 28, 29 November 1994
AUSTRALIA 426 (Slater 176, M. Waugh 140, Taylor 59, Gough 4–107) and 248–8 dec. (Taylor 58, Healy 45*, Slater 45, Tufnell 4–79)
ENGLAND 167 (Atherton 54, McDermott 6–53) and 323 (Hick 80, Thorpe 67, Gooch 56, Warne 8–71)
Australia won by 184 runs

709. Australia v England

Second Test at Melbourne – 24, 26, 27, 28, 29 December 1994
AUSTRALIA 279 (S. Waugh 94*, M. Waugh 71, Gough 4–60) and 320–7 dec. (Boon 131, Slater 44)
ENGLAND 212 (Thorpe 51, Atherton 44, Warne 6–64) and 92 (McDermott 5–42)
Australia won by 295 runs

710. Australia v England

Third Test at Sydney – 1, 2, 3, 4, 5 January 1995
ENGLAND 309 (Atherton 88, Crawley 72, Gough 51, McDermott 5–101) and 255–2 dec. (Hick 98*, Atherton 67, Thorpe 47*)
AUSTRALIA 116 (Taylor 49, Gough 6–49) and 344–7 (Taylor 113, Slater 103, Fraser 5–73)
Match drawn

711. Australia v England

Fourth Test at Adelaide – 26, 27, 28, 29, 30 January 1995
ENGLAND 353 (Gatting 117, Atherton 80) and 328 (DeFreitas 88, Thorpe 83, Crawley 71, M. Waugh 5–40)
AUSTRALIA 419 (Blewett 102*, Taylor 90, Healy 74, Slater 67) and 156 (Healy 51*, Lewis 4–24, Malcolm 4–39)
England won by 106 runs

712. Australia v England

Fifth Test at Perth – 3, 4, 5, 6, 7 February 1995
AUSTRALIA 402 (Slater 124, S. Waugh 99*, M. Waugh 88) and 345–8 dec. (Blewett 115, S. Waugh 80, Taylor 52, Slater 45)
ENGLAND 295 (Thorpe 123, Ramprakash 72) and 123 (Ramprakash 42, McDermott 6–38)
Australia won by 329 runs

713. England v West Indies

First Test at Headingley – 8, 9, 10, 11 June 1995
ENGLAND 199 (Atherton 81, Bishop 5–32, Benjamin 4–60) and 208 (Thorpe 61, Walsh 4–60)
WEST INDIES 282 (Campbell 69, Adams 58, Lara 53, Arthurton 42) and 129–1 (Hooper 73*, Lara 48*)
West Indies won by 9 wickets

714. England v West Indies
Second Test at Lord's — 22, 23, 24, 25, 26 June 1995
ENGLAND 283 (R. Smith 61, Thorpe 52) and 336 (R. Smith 90, Hick 67, Thorpe 42, Ambrose 4–70)
WEST INDIES 324 (Arthurton 75, Adams 54, Richardson 49, Hooper 40, Fraser 5–66) and 223 (Campbell 93, Lara 54, Cork 7–43)
England won by 72 runs

715. England v West Indies
Third Test at Edgbaston — 6, 7, 8 July 1995
ENGLAND 147 (R. Smith 46) and 89 (R. Smith 41, Walsh 5–45, Bishop 4–29)
WEST INDIES 300 (Campbell 79, Richardson 69, Hooper 40, Cork 4–69)
West Indies won by an innings and 64 runs

716. England v West Indies
Fourth Test at Old Trafford — 27, 28, 29, 30 July 1995
WEST INDIES 216 (Lara 87, Fraser 4–45, Cork 4–86) and 314 (Lara 145, Campbell 44, Cork 4–111)
ENGLAND 437 (Thorpe 94, Cork 56*, Atherton 47, R. Smith 44, Walsh 4–92) and 94–4
England won by 6 wickets

DID YOU KNOW...?

Dominic Cork's 7–43 against the West Indies in 1995 were the best figures by a bowler making his England debut. Jack Ferris took 7–37 in 1892, but had previously played for Australia.

717. England v West Indies
Fifth Test at Trent Bridge — 10, 11, 12, 13, 14 August 1995
ENGLAND 440 (Hick 118*, Atherton 113, Knight 57, Benjamin 5–105) and 269–9 dec. (Watkinson 82*, Thorpe 76, Atherton 43, Benjamin 5–69)
WEST INDIES 417 (Lara 152, Williams 62, Campbell 47, Richardson 40, Illingworth 4–96) and 42–2
Match drawn

718. England v West Indies
Sixth Test at The Oval — 24, 25, 26, 27, 28 August 1995
ENGLAND 454 (Hick 96, Russell 91, Thorpe 74, Crawley 50, Ambrose 5–96) and 223–4 (Atherton 95, Hick 51*)
WEST INDIES 692–8 dec. (Lara 179, Hooper 127, Richardson 93, Campbell 89, Chanderpaul 80)
Match drawn

719. South Africa v England
First Test at Pretoria — 16, 17, 18 (no play), 19 (no play), 20 (no play) November 1995
ENGLAND 381–9 dec. (Hick 141, Atherton 78, Russell 50*, R. Smith 43)
Match drawn

720. South Africa v England
Second Test at Johannesburg — 30 November, 1, 2, 3, 4 December 1995
SOUTH AFRICA 332 (G. Kirsten 110, Cullinan 69, Cork 5–84, Malcolm 4–62) and 346–9 dec. (McMillan 100*, Cullinan 61, Rhodes 57, Cronje 48, Cork 4–78)
ENGLAND 200 (R. Smith 52, Stewart 45) and 351–5 (Atherton 185*, R. Smith 44)
Match drawn

721. South Africa v England
Third Test at Durban — 14, 15, 16, 17 (no play), 18 (no play) December 1995
SOUTH AFRICA 225 (Hudson 45, Martin 4–60)
ENGLAND 152–5 (Stewart 41)
Match drawn

722. South Africa v England
Fourth Test at Port Elizabeth — 26, 27, 28, 29, 30 December 1995
SOUTH AFRICA 428 (Cullinan 91, Richardson 84, G. Kirsten 51, McMillan 49, Rhodes 49, Cork 4–113) and 162–9 dec. (G. Kirsten 69)
ENGLAND 263 (Atherton 72, Hick 62) and 189–3 (Stewart 81)
Match drawn

723. South Africa v England
Fifth Test at Cape Town — 2, 3, 4 January 1996
ENGLAND 153 (Smith 66, Donald 5–46) and 157 (Thorpe 59, Pollock 5–32)
SOUTH AFRICA 244 (Cullinan 62, Richardson 54*) and 70–0 (G. Kirsten 41*)
South Africa won by 10 wickets

724. England v India
First Test at Edgbaston — 6, 7, 8, 9 June 1996
INDIA 214 (Srinath 52, Cork 4–61) and 219 (Tendulkar 122, Lewis 5–72)
ENGLAND 313 (Hussain 128, Prasad 4–71, Srinath 4–103) and 121–2 (Atherton 53*)
England won by 8 wickets

725. England v India
Second Test at Lord's — 20, 21, 22, 23, 24 June 1996
ENGLAND 344 (Russell 124, Thorpe 89, Prasad 5–76) and 278–9 dec. (Stewart 66, Irani 41)
INDIA 429 (Ganguly 131, Dravid 95)
Match drawn

726. England v India
Third Test at Trent Bridge — 4, 5, 6, 8, 9 July 1996
INDIA 521 (Tendulkar 177, Ganguly 136, Dravid 84, Manjrekar 53) and 211 (Tendulkar 74, Ganguly 48, Mongia 45, Ealham 4–21)
ENGLAND 564 (Atherton 160, Hussain 107 ret. hurt, Ealham 51, Stewart 50, Thorpe 45)
Match drawn

727. England v Pakistan
First Test at Lord's — 25, 26, 27, 28, 29 July 1996
PAKISTAN 340 (Inzamam-ul-Haq 148, Saeed Anwar 74, Rashid Latif 45) and 352–5 dec. (Saeed Anwar 88, Ijaz Ahmed 76, Inzamam-ul-Haq 55)
ENGLAND 285 (Thorpe 77, Knight 51, Russell 41*, Ata-ur-Rehman 4–50, Waqar Younis 4–69) and 243 (Stewart 89, Atherton 64, Salisbury 40, Mushtaq Ahmed 5–57, Waqar Younis 4–85)
Pakistan won by 164 runs

728. England v Pakistan
Second Test at Headingley – 8, 9, 10, 11, 12 August 1996
PAKISTAN 448 (Ijaz Ahmed 141, Moin Khan 105, Salim
Malik 55, Asif Mujtaba 51, Cork 5–113) and 242–7 dec.
(Inzamam-ul-Haq 65, Ijaz Ahmed 52)
ENGLAND 501 (Stewart 170, Knight 113, Crawley 53,
Hussain 48)
Match drawn

729. England v Pakistan
Third Test at The Oval – 22, 23, 24, 25, 26 August 1996
ENGLAND 326 (Crawley 106, Thorpe 54, Stewart 44, Waqar
Younis 4–95) and 242 (Stewart 54, Hussain 51,
Atherton 43, Mushtaq Ahmed 6–78)
PAKISTAN 521–8 dec. (Saeed Anwar 176, Salim Malik
100*, Ijaz Ahmed 61, Aamer Sohail 46) and 48–1
Pakistan won by 9 wickets

730. Zimbabwe v England
First Test at Bulawayo – 18, 19, 20, 21, 22 December 1996
ZIMBABWE 376 (A. Flower 112, Campbell 84, G. Flower
43) and 234 (Whittall 56, Waller 50, Tufnell 4–61)
ENGLAND 406 (Hussain 113, Crawley 112, Knight 56,
Stewart 48, P. A. Strang 5–123) and 204–6 (Knight 96,
Stewart 73)
Match drawn (scores level)

731. Zimbabwe v England
Second Test at Harare – 26, 27, 28, 29, 30 (no play)
December 1996
ENGLAND 156 (Crawley 47*, Whittall 4–18, Streak 4–43)
and 195–3 (Stewart 101*, Thorpe 50*)
ZIMBABWE 215 (G. Flower 73, P. A. Strang 47*, Gough 4–40)
Match drawn

732. New Zealand v England
First Test at Auckland – 24, 25, 26, 27, 28 January 1997
NEW ZEALAND 390 (Fleming 129, Pocock 70, Cairns 67,
Young 44, Gough 4–91) and 248–9 dec. (Astle 102*)
ENGLAND 521 (Stewart 173, Thorpe 119, Atherton 83,
Cork 59)
Match drawn

733. New Zealand v England
Second Test at Wellington – 6, 7, 8, 9, 10 February 1997
NEW ZEALAND 124 (Patel 45, Gough 5–40, Caddick 4–45)
and 191 (Pocock 64, Young 56, Gough 4–52)
ENGLAND 383 (Thorpe 108, Hussain 64, Crawley 56,
Stewart 52, Doull 5–75)
England won by an innings and 68 runs

734. New Zealand v England
Third Test at Christchurch – 14, 15, 16, 17, 18 February 1997
NEW ZEALAND 346 (Fleming 62, Parore 59, Cairns 57,
Horne 42, Croft 5–95) and 186 (Cairns 52, Young 49)
ENGLAND 228 (Atherton 94*, Allott 4–74) and 307–6
(Atherton 118, Crawley 40*, Vettori 4–97)
England won by 4 wickets

735. England v Australia
First Test at Edgbaston – 5, 6, 7, 8 June 1997
AUSTRALIA 118 (Warne 47, Caddick 5–50) and 477 (Taylor
129, Blewett 125, Elliott 66)
ENGLAND 478–9 dec. (Hussain 207, Thorpe 138, Ealham
53*, Kasprowicz 4–113) and 119–1 (Atherton 57*,
Stewart 40*)
England won by 9 wickets

736. England v Australia
Second Test at Lord's – 19 (no play), 20, 21, 22, 23 June
1997
ENGLAND 77 (McGrath 8–38) and 266–4 dec. (Butcher 87,
Atherton 77)
AUSTRALIA 213–7 dec. (Elliott 112, Caddick 4–71)
Match drawn

737. England v Australia
Third Test at Old Trafford – 3, 4, 5, 6, 7 July 1997
AUSTRALIA 235 (S. Waugh 108, Headley 4–72) and 395–8
dec. (S. Waugh 116, M. Waugh 55, Warne 53, Healy 47,
Reiffel 45, Headley 4–104)
ENGLAND 162 (Butcher 51, Warne 6–48) and 200 (Crawley
83, McGrath 4–46)
Australia won by 268 runs

738. England v Australia
Fourth Test at Headingley – 24, 25, 26, 27, 28 July 1997
ENGLAND 172 (Atherton 41, Gillespie 7–37) and 268
(Hussain 105, Crawley 72, Reiffel 5–49)
AUSTRALIA 501–9 dec. (Elliott 199, Ponting 127, Reiffel
54*, Gough 5–149)
Australia won by an innings and 61 runs

739. England v Australia
Fifth Test at Trent Bridge – 7, 8, 9, 10 August 1997
AUSTRALIA 427 (Taylor 76, S. Waugh 75, Elliott 69,
M. Waugh 68, Blewett 50, Headley 4–87) and 336
(Healy 63, Blewett 60, Taylor 45, Ponting 45)
ENGLAND 313 (Stewart 87, Thorpe 53, McGrath 4–71,
Warne 4–86) and 186 (Thorpe 82*)
Australia won by 264 runs

740. England v Australia
Sixth Test at The Oval – 21, 22, 23 August 1997
ENGLAND 180 (McGrath 7–76) and 163 (Thorpe 62,
Ramprakash 48, Kasprowicz 7–36)
AUSTRALIA 220 (Blewett 47, Tufnell 7–66) and 104
(Caddick 5–42, Tufnell 4–27)
England won by 19 runs

741. West Indies v England
First Test at Kingston, Jamaica – 29 January 1998
ENGLAND 17–3
Match abandoned as a draw

742. West Indies v England
Second Test at Port-of-Spain, Trinidad – 5, 6, 7, 8, 9
February 1998
ENGLAND 214 (Hussain 61*, Stewart 50) and 258 (Stewart
73, Ambrose 5–52)
WEST INDIES 191 (Lara 55, Fraser 8–53) and 282–7
(Hooper 94*, D. Williams 65, S. Williams 62)
West Indies won by 3 wickets

743. West Indies v England
Third Test at Port-of-Spain, Trinidad – 13, 14, 15, 16, 17
February 1998
WEST INDIES 159 (Lara 42, Fraser 5–40, Caddick 5–67)
and 210 (Adams 53, Lara 47, Fraser 4–40, Headley
4–77)
ENGLAND 145 (Stewart 44, Ambrose 5–25) and 225–7
(Stewart 83, Atherton 49)
England won by 3 wickets

744. West Indies v England
Fourth Test at Georgetown, Guyana – 27, 28 February, 1, 2 March 1998
WEST INDIES 352 (Chanderpaul 118, Lara 93, Hooper 43) and 197 (Bishop 44*)
ENGLAND 170 (Ramprakash 64*) and 137 (Ambrose 4–38)
West Indies won by 242 runs

745. West Indies v England
Fifth Test at Bridgetown, Barbados – 12, 13, 14, 15, 16 March 1998
ENGLAND 403 (Ramprakash 154, Thorpe 103, Hooper 5–80) and 233–3 dec. (Atherton 64, Stewart 48, Hussain 46*)
WEST INDIES 262 (Lambert 55, Wallace 45, Chanderpaul 45) and 112–2 (Wallace 61)
Match drawn

746. West Indies v England
Sixth Test at St John's, Antigua – 20, 21, 22, 23, 24 March 1998
ENGLAND 127 (Hussain 37, Ramnarine 4–29, Ambrose 3–28) and 321 (Hussain 106, Thorpe 84*, Stewart 79, Walsh 4–80)
WEST INDIES 500–7 dec. (Hooper 108*, Lambert 104, Wallace 92, Lara 89, Caddick 3–111)
West Indies won by an innings and 52 runs

747. England v South Africa
First Test at Edgbaston – 4, 5, 6, 7, 8 June 1998
ENGLAND 462 (Atherton 103, Butcher 77, Ramprakash 49, Stewart 49, Donald 4–95) and 170–8 dec. (Atherton 43, Thorpe 43)
SOUTH AFRICA 343 (Rhodes 95, Cullinan 78, Kallis 61, Klusener 57, Cork 5–93, Fraser 4–103)
Match drawn

748. England v South Africa
Second Test at Lord's – 18, 19, 20, 21 June 1998
SOUTH AFRICA 360 (Rhodes 117, Cronje 81, Cork 6–119) and 15–0
ENGLAND 110 (Donald 5–32) and 264 (Hussain 105, Stewart 56, Atherton 44, Kallis 4–24)
South Africa won by 10 wickets

749. England v South Africa
Third Test at Old Trafford – 2, 3, 4, 5, 6 July 1998
SOUTH AFRICA 552–5 dec. (G. Kirsten 210, Kallis 132, Cullinan 75, Cronje 69*)
ENGLAND 183 (Atherton 41, Stewart 40, Adams 4–63) and 369–9 (Stewart 164, Atherton 89, Donald 6–88)
Match drawn

750. England v South Africa
Fourth Test at Trent Bridge – 23, 24, 25, 26, 27 July 1998
SOUTH AFRICA 374 (Cronje 126, Pollock 50, Elworthy 48, Kallis 47, Fraser 5–60, Gough 4–116) and 208 (Cronje 67, Cullinan 56, Fraser 5–62, Cork 4–60)
ENGLAND 336 (Butcher 75, Ramprakash 67*, Atherton 58, Donald 5–109) and 247–2 (Atherton 98*, Hussain 58, Stewart 45*)
England won by 8 wickets

751. England v South Africa
Fifth Test at Headingley – 6, 7, 8, 9, 10 August 1998
ENGLAND 230 (Butcher 116, Ntini 4–72) and 240 (Hussain 94, Pollock 5–53, Donald 5–71)

SOUTH AFRICA 252 (Cronje 57, Kallis 40, Fraser 5–42) and 195 (Rhodes 85, McMillan 54, Gough 6–42)
England won by 23 runs

752. England v Sri Lanka
Only Test at The Oval – 27, 28, 29, 30, 31 August 1998
ENGLAND 445 (Crawley 156*, Hick 107, Ramprakash 53, Muralitharan 7–155) and 181 (Ramprakash 42, Muralitharan 9–65)
SRI LANKA 591 (Jayasuriya 213, de Silva 152, Ranatunga 51, Perera 43*) and 37–0
Sri Lanka won by 10 wickets

753. Australia v England
First Test at Brisbane – 20, 21, 22, 23, 24 November 1998
AUSTRALIA 485 (Healy 134, S. Waugh 112, Fleming 71*, Mullally 5–105) and 237–3 dec. (Slater 113, Langer 74)
ENGLAND 375 (Butcher 116, Thorpe 77, Ramprakash 69*, Hussain 59, McGrath 6–85) and 179–6 (Hussain 47)
Match drawn

754. Australia v England
Second Test at Perth – 28, 29, 30 November 1998
ENGLAND 112 (Fleming 5–46) and 191 (Hick 68, Ramprakash 47*, Gillespie 5–88, Fleming 4–45)
AUSTRALIA 240 (Taylor 61, Tudor 4–89) and 64–3
Australia won by 7 wickets

755. Australia v England
Third Test at Adelaide – 11, 12, 13, 14, 15 December 1998
AUSTRALIA 391 (Langer 179*, Taylor 59, S. Waugh 59, Headley 4–97) and 278–5 dec. (Slater 103, Langer 52, M. Waugh 51*)
ENGLAND 227 (Hussain 89*, Ramprakash 61, MacGill 4–53) and 237 (Stewart 63*, Ramprakash 57, McGrath 4–50)
Australia won by 205 runs

756. Australia v England
Fourth Test at Melbourne – 26 (no play), 27, 28, 29 December 1998
ENGLAND 270 (Stewart 107, Ramprakash 63, MacGill 4–61) and 244 (Hick 60, Stewart 52, Hussain 50)
AUSTRALIA 340 (S. Waugh 122*, Gough 5–96) and 162 (M. Waugh 43, Headley 6–60)
England won by 12 runs

757. Australia v England
Fifth Test at Sydney – 2, 3, 4, 5 January 1999
AUSTRALIA 322 (M. Waugh 121, S. Waugh 96, Headley 4–62) and 184 (Slater 123, Such 5–81, Headley 4–40)
ENGLAND 220 (Crawley 44, Hussain 42, MacGill 5–57) and 188 (Hussain 53, Stewart 42, MacGill 7–50)
Australia won by 98 runs

758. England v New Zealand
First Test at Edgbaston – 1, 2, 3 July 1999
NEW ZEALAND 226 (Parore 73) and 107 (Caddick 5–32)
ENGLAND 126 and 211–3 (Tudor 99*, Hussain 44)
England won by 7 wickets

759. England v New Zealand
Second Test at Lord's – 22, 23, 24, 25 July 1999
ENGLAND 186 (Hussain 61, Stewart 50, Cairns 6–77) and 229 (Caddick 45)
NEW ZEALAND 358 (Horne 100, Vettori 54, Twose 52, Astle 43) and 60–1
New Zealand won by 9 wickets

760. England v New Zealand
Third Test at Old Trafford – 5, 6, 7, 8, 9 August 1999
ENGLAND 199 (Ramprakash 69*) and 181–2 (Stewart 83*, Atherton 48)
NEW ZEALAND 496–9 dec. (McMillan 107, Astle 101, Bell 83, Cairns 41, Such 4–114)
Match drawn

761. England v New Zealand
Fourth Test at The Oval – 19, 20, 21, 22 August 1999
NEW ZEALAND 236 (Fleming 66*, Vettori 51) and 162 (Cairns 80)
ENGLAND 153 (Hussain 40, Cairns 5–31) and 162 (Atherton 64, Thorpe 44, Nash 4–39)
New Zealand won by 83 runs

762. South Africa v England
First Test at Johannesburg – 25, 26, 27, 28 November 1999
ENGLAND 122 (Donald 6–53, Pollock 4–16) and 260 (Stewart 86, Caddick 48, Donald 5–74, Pollock 4–64)
SOUTH AFRICA 403–9 dec. (Cullinan 108, Gibbs 85, Klusener 72, Cronje 44, Gough 5–70)
South Africa won by an innings and 21 runs

763. South Africa v England
Second Test at Port Elizabeth – 9, 10, 11, 12, 13 December 1999
SOUTH AFRICA 450 (Klusener 174, Cullinan 58, Rhodes 50, Gibbs 48, Boucher 42, Tufnell 4–124) and 224–4 dec. (Kallis 85*, Rhodes 57*)
ENGLAND 373 (Atherton 108, Hussain 82, Flintoff 42, Hayward 4–75) and 153–6 (Hussain 70*)
Match drawn

764. South Africa v England
Third Test at Durban – 26, 27, 28, 29, 30 December 1999
ENGLAND 366–9 dec. (Hussain 146*, Stewart 95, Butcher 48)
SOUTH AFRICA 156 (Pollock 64, Caddick 7–46) and 572–7 (G. Kirsten 275, Boucher 108, Kallis 69, Klusener 45)
Match drawn

765. South Africa v England
Fourth Test at Cape Town – 2, 3, 4, 5 January 2000
ENGLAND 258 (Atherton 71, Vaughan 42, Butcher 40, Stewart 40, Donald 5–47) and 126
SOUTH AFRICA 421 (Cullinan 120, Kallis 105, G. Kirsten 80, Silverwood 5–91)
South Africa won by an innings and 37 runs

766. South Africa v England
Fifth Test at Centurion – 14, 15 (no play), 16 (no play), 17 (no play), 18 January 2000
SOUTH AFRICA 248–8 dec. (Klusener 61*, Cullinan 46)
Second innings forfeited
ENGLAND 0–0 dec. and 251–8 (Stewart 73, Vaughan 69)
England won by 2 wickets

INTERNATIONAL CRICKET IN THE NEW MILLENNIUM: 2000–6

Zimbabwe's Test debut in England in early 2000 saw them collapse to 83 all out in the first Test at Lord's with Ed Giddins taking 5–15. The hosts amassed 415 with both Hick and Stewart making hundreds in a fourth-wicket stand of 149. With Gough and Caddick picking up 4 wickets apiece, Zimbabwe were bowled out for a second time for 123, leaving England to reflect on their largest winning margin – an innings and 209 runs – for twenty-six years. In a rain-affected second Test, Mike Atherton made 136 in England's 374 and in doing so became the highest Test-run scorer at Trent Bridge. Zimbabwe declared at 285–4 with Murray Goodwin unbeaten on 148, and, with England bowled out cheaply for 147, Zimbabwe were left with little time to bat.

The West Indies arrived in England while the Zimbabwe series was in progress and went on to win the first Test, at Edgbaston, comfortably by an innings and 93 runs. The second Test, at Lord's, was the pivotal match of the summer. Alec Stewart, captaining England in the absence of Nasser Hussain, who had broken a thumb the week before, won the toss and put the West Indies in to bat. But by mid-afternoon on the second day, following the tourists' total of 267, England had conceded a first-innings lead of 133. In the next two hours amid a fervent atmosphere, Andrew Caddick took 5–16 and West Indies were all out for 54. It was their lowest innings total against England. With England needing 188 to win on an increasingly uneven pitch, Atherton and Vaughan both played important innings for the team before Dominic Cork saw the side home by 2 wickets. The next Test, at Old Trafford, marked one hundred Test appearances for both Atherton and Stewart. After Cork had reduced West Indies to 157 all out, Stewart celebrated his hundredth Test with a fine century in a total of 303 but then Lara made the game safe for the West Indies, who later declared at 438–7, leaving England little time to go for victory. At Headingley, the series swung decisively in England's favour. After West Indies were bowled out for 172, England gained a lead of 101 runs on first innings before Caddick's 5–14 reduced the tourists to 61 all out and England won by an innings and 39 runs. The Oval pitch was bowler-friendly but two fine knocks from Mike Atherton (83 and 108) helped England win by 158 runs.

England then travelled to Pakistan for a three-Test series, the first two of which were drawn and somewhat dull affairs – though Graham Thorpe made 118 in the first Test at Lahore and Ashley Giles took 5–75 at Faisalabad, where Mike Atherton hit a match-saving 65 not out. The two draws put pressure on the Pakistani side as the third Test at Karachi approached. In reply to Pakistan's 405, in which Inzamam-ul-Haq and Yousuf Youhana both hit hundreds, Atherton scored a nine-hour century to bring England within 17 runs of the home side's total. In their second innings, Pakistan collapsed under pressure and were all out for 158. It left England needing 176 from a minimum of 44 overs. Atherton and Trescothick got England off to a flier before the light began to fade. Batting in near darkness against Waqar Younis, Thorpe and Hussain saw England home and, in doing so, they became the first England team to win a Test in Pakistan for thirty-nine years.

Moving on to Sri Lanka, England were beaten by an innings and 28 runs at Galle after Atapattu hit a fine double hundred in the home side's total of 470–5 declared. Despite 122 by Trescothick, England were bowled out for 253 and following on were dismissed a second time for 189. Jayawardene hit 101 in the second Test at the Asgiriya Stadium in Kandy as Sri Lanka made 297, but Nasser Hussain at last found some form with a fighting innings of 109 as England led by 90 runs on first innings. Jayasuriya was given out off a bump ball and Sri Lanka were all out for 250, leaving England to get 161 to win. Vaas ran through the top order but England won by 3 wickets to level the series. In the third and deciding Test at Colombo, Sri Lanka were bowled out for 241 before Graham Thorpe hit an unbeaten 113 in England's reply of 249. England's bowlers, and in particular Ashley Giles (4–11), demolished the Sri Lankan batting and they were all out for 81. England won an incredible victory against all the odds, though they lost 6 wickets in scoring the 74 runs necessary.

England's victory over Pakistan in the opening Test of 2001 was completed in less than three days, despite the complete loss of the first day. All England's top order scored runs in a total of 391 before Gough (5–61) and Caddick (4–52) bowled out Pakistan for 203. Hussain enforced the follow-on and the same two bowlers, along with Dominic Cork, dismissed the tourists for 179, leaving England the winners by an innings and 9 runs. The Old Trafford Test produced a wonderful, epic struggle. Inzamam-ul-Haq made 114 in Pakistan's first-innings total of 403 while Thorpe and Vaughan hit hundreds in England's reply of 357. Inzamam was again outstanding as Pakistan batted a second time and his knock enabled the visitors to set England 370 to win. Trescothick and Atherton put on 146 for the first wicket but after that wickets began to tumble and, though the Somerset opener made 117, Pakistan won by 108 runs. Their victory was tarnished somewhat by television evidence that showed that four of England's dismissals had been taken when the bowler demonstrably over-stepped the line.

Australia totally dominated the 2001 Ashes in England, winning the series 4–1. In the first Test, at Edgbaston, England had lurched to 191–9 before a remarkable tenth-wicket stand of 103 between Stewart and Caddick took them to 294. However, Australia's total of 576 gave the visitors a first-innings lead of 282 and they went on to win by an innings and 118 runs. At Lord's the home side were bowled out for 187 before the tourists lost their last wicket at 401. In England's second innings only Mark Butcher showed any form as Australia won by 8 wickets. At Trent Bridge, England were dismissed for 185 and though Australia were at one time 102–7, they still managed to pass England's total by 5 runs. Warne then took 6 wickets and Australia, needing 158 to win, triumphed by 7 wickets. The Headingley Test saw centuries by Ponting and Martyn help Australia to a first-innings total of 447. All England's batsmen made useful scores but the tourists still had a lead on first innings of 138. Acting captain Adam Gilchrist, who had replaced injured skipper Steve Waugh, declared at 176–4, setting England 315 to win. In scoring an undefeated 173, Mark Butcher played magnificently to lead his side home by 6 wickets. At The Oval, Steve Waugh was back to his best, making an unbeaten 157 alongside his brother Mark (120) and Justin Langer (102) as Australia declared at 641–4. Warne then took 7–165 but not before Ramprakash had made a splendid 133 in a total of 432. Nine runs short of avoiding the follow-on, England were then bowled out for 184.

In wake of the tragedies in the USA on 11 September 2001, fears over travel and security threatened England's tour of India. A below-strength England team will not remember the opening Test in Chandigarh with any fondness. England were bowled out for 238, but, with Dasgupta making a century and Tendulkar (88) and Dravid (86) both batting well, India had a lead of 231 on first innings. Anil Kumble then took 6–81 as England made 235 and India won by 10 wickets. Despite outplaying India for much of the second Test at Ahmedabad, the end result was a draw. Trescothick (99) and Craig White (121) helped England score 407 before Ashley Giles took 5–67 in India's reply of 291. England batted until they were all out for 257 but, in hindsight, Hussain might well have declared earlier. Needing 374 for victory, they closed on 198–3. In the third Test at Bangalore, Hussain gave his team the luxury of batting first after winning the toss. Most of the top order made runs in a total of 336 before Hoggard and Flintoff took 4 wickets apiece as India fell 98 runs short of the tourists' total. England were 33 without loss when the Test was abandoned due to rain, but coming back from oblivion after the first Test and dominating both the second and third was a terrific achievement.

It's not often that a double centurion ends up on the losing side but the first

Test against New Zealand in Christchurch was no ordinary Test. England, with Hussain making 106, totalled 228 before Matthew Hoggard, with 7–63, skittled out the Kiwis in their first innings for 147. In England's second innings, Graham Thorpe (200 not out) and Andrew Flintoff (137) added 281 for the sixth wicket – the fourth highest in Test history and the highest stand for England in New Zealand – enabling Hussain to declare at 468–6. With New Zealand needing a mammoth 550 to win, Nathan Astle hit an astonishing 222 from 168 balls; his second 100 took 39 balls as he reached 200 from 153 deliveries – the fastest double century in Test history – yet New Zealand still lost by 98 runs. The second Test at Wellington was overshadowed by the news of the tragic death of Ben Hollioake in a car accident. As a result, there was an air of futility as the match meandered to a draw. The final Test at Auckland saw the home side recover from being 19–4 on the first day to win by 78 runs on the last. On the fourth afternoon, there was the bizarre sight of Test cricket being played under floodlights while darkness descended over Auckland. New Zealand had made 202 and, with Tuffey taking 6–54, bowled England out for 160. In the second innings, Fleming then declared at 269–9, but, with the exception of Hussain, the England batsmen never came to terms with the Kiwis' bowling as the hosts levelled the series.

England took a pounding from the Sri Lankans in the first Test of their 2002 tour at Lord's but then regrouped in their second innings to secure a draw. Both Atapattu and Jayawardene hit hundreds and added 206 for the third wicket as Sri Lanka made 555–8 declared. Though conditions were less favourable when England batted, few expected their long batting line-up to succumb to Sri Lanka's limited bowling resources but they were bowled out for 275. Following on, England's batsmen responded superbly and, with Vaughan (115) and Butcher (105) leading the way, declared at 529–5 and honours were even. At Edgbaston, England bowled the tourists out for 162 and then, with Trescothick and Thorpe hitting hundreds and Butcher falling 6 runs short, they totalled 545. Needing 383 to make England bat again, Sri Lanka were undone by the swing of Hoggard, who took 5–92 as England won by an innings and 111 runs. England continued to dominate the series and made 512 in the final Test at Old Trafford. Facing the follow-on after being bowled out for 253, Sri Lanka's Russel Arnold then made 109 but the visitors' total of 308 left England with only 50 to make, which they did without losing a wicket.

England carried on their winning ways in the opening Test of the series against India later that summer with Hussain leading the way at Lord's with 155 in the home side's total of 487. All England's bowlers got amongst the wickets as India were bowled out for 221. A hundred from Michael Vaughan and an unbeaten century from John Crawley saw England declare their second innings at 301–6 before India, with Agarkar making 109 not out, were finally dismissed for 397. At Trent Bridge, Sehwag made 109 as India were all out for 357, but England, with Michael Vaughan making a magnificent 197 and Craig White 94 not out, made 617, a lead of 220. Despite losing both openers early on, India easily avoided an innings defeat, with Dravid (115) Ganguly (99) and

Tendulkar (92) all making useful contributions in a drawn game. In the third Test, at Headingley, India squared the series with a crushing innings defeat over England. The same three batsmen all made hundreds as the tourists ran up a total of 628–8 declared. England were dismissed for 273 in their first innings and then, with Kumble taking 4–66, they were all out for 309 – Hussain scoring his twelfth Test century – to lose by an innings and 46 runs. The final Test, at The Oval, did not produce the thrilling climax all cricket fans had been hoping for. Vaughan's fine innings of 195 helped England to a first-innings total of 515, but, with Rahul Dravid in superb form, his 217 saw India get within 7 runs of England's total, and, with the home side on 114–0, rain descended on the last day, leaving both teams with their heads held high.

In the first Test of the 2002–3 Ashes series, Nasser Hussain won the toss but then threw away any advantage by choosing to field despite the sight of a dry, flat pitch and a cloudless sky. At the end of the first day, Australia were 364–2, going on to make 492, with Hayden (197) and Ponting (123) dominating the attack before Giles claimed his fourth wicket. With Trescothick, Butcher, Crawley and Hussain all scoring half-centuries, England replied with 325. Matthew Hayden smashed another hundred and after extending their lead to 463, the Australians declared. With the cracks now widening, England collapsed to McGrath and Warne and were 79 all out. At Adelaide, Michael Vaughan, who had hit a magnificent 177, was dismissed off the last ball of the day and from that moment, the Australians took charge. From 295–3, England slumped to 342 all out. With useful contributions all down the order, Australia declared at 552–9, going on to win by an innings and 51 runs. In the third Test, at Perth, England were bowled out for 185 before Australia built an invincible lead. England, 271 behind, had slumped to 34–4 and, though Stewart and Hussain hit half-centuries, there was never much likelihood of Australia needing to bat a second time.

The fourth Test, at Melbourne, saw Australia scramble home for their least convincing victory of the series. Michael Vaughan scored his sixth century of 2002 and beat Dennis Amiss's record for the number of runs in a calendar year by an English batsman. Australia had declared their innings closed at 551–6 but with England bowled out for 270 they had no option but to follow on. The centrepiece of England's second innings was Vaughan's 145 but Australia needed just 107 for victory. Harmison and Caddick bowled with plenty of fire to remove the top five batsmen, but the hosts won by 5 wickets. Encouragingly, in the last Test, England eked out a total of 362, with Mark Butcher leading the way with 124. For Australia, Steve Waugh reached his twenty-ninth Test hundred to draw level with Sir Donald Bradman, but, even with Gilchrist hitting a characteristically buccaneering century, Australia had a lead of only one run. England made 452–9 declared, with Vaughan making 183. A target of 451 was just the sort of run chase the Australians fancied but, with Caddick taking 7–94, England triumphed by 225 runs.

England thumped an inexperienced Zimbabwe side in the first Test of their 2003 tour at Lord's inside three days, as they palpably failed to adjust to the conditions with bat and ball. Butcher made 137 in England's total of 472 before Lancashire's James Anderson became the youngest-ever player to take 5 wickets on debut, finishing with 5–73 as the tourists were bowled out for 147. Following on, Zimbabwe were ruthlessly exposed and Butcher, who had a magical match, had the final say to record figures of 4–60 as England won by an innings and 92 runs. Durham's Riverside became the first new Test ground in England for 101 years when it hosted the second Test against Zimbabwe. After England had amassed 416, Zimbabwe were found wanting in good batting conditions and were all out for a paltry 94, with Richard Johnson on debut taking 6–33. Again following on, Harmison and Anderson picked up 4 wickets apiece as England triumphed by an innings and 69 runs.

The first Test against South Africa, at Edgbaston, was a tale of two captains, Graeme Smith hitting the highest score ever achieved by a South African in Test cricket and Nasser Hussain at the end of the game announcing his departure as England's captain. Smith (277) and Gibbs (179) opened with a first-wicket partnership of 338 as the Springboks totalled 594–5 declared. England just avoided the follow-on thanks to another superb hundred from Vaughan and, though Smith hit 85 from just 70 balls to set England 321 to win, there was little time for the home side to be embarrassed in their second innings. At Lord's, Makhaya Ntini took 5–75 as England were dismissed for 173, and then Graeme Smith (259) hit another double century as he and Gary Kirsten (108) helped the tourists to 682–6 declared. England had never faced such a massive deficit (509) in their history. Butcher and Hussain hinted at a famous rearguard action and Andrew Flintoff entertained the crowd with some audacious hitting in an innings of 142, but despite their efforts South Africa won by an innings and 92 runs. In the third Test, at Trent Bridge, Butcher and Hussain both hit hundreds in an England first-innings total of 445, before James Anderson took another 5 wickets as the hosts gained a lead of 83 on first innings. Shaun Pollock, with 6–39, ripped through the England batting as they were all out for 118 to leave the Springboks needing 202 to win. Then, Sussex's James Kirtley took 6–34 – South Africa were all out for 131 and England had won by 70 runs to level the series. England made a flying start at Headingley to leave South Africa 21–4, but Kirsten dug in to reach a superb century and take his side to a respectable 342 all out. England started well but at 164–1, Butcher and Trescothick accepted the light and conceded the initiative. England were eventually all out for 307. In South Africa's second innings, Andrew Hall blasted an unbeaten 99 off 87 balls to swing the match out of England's reach before Kallis (6–54) helped bowl his side to a 191-run win. In the final Test, at The Oval, Michael Vaughan's side came back from the dead to level the series. Herschel Gibbs had flayed the England attack in helping the Springboks to a first-innings total of 484 but then Trescothick (219) and Thorpe (124) launched England's comeback prior to Flintoff hitting a ferocious 95. Vaughan declared at 604–9 before Bicknell and Harmison picked up 4 wickets each to bowl out South Africa for 229. Trescothick and Butcher saw the hosts home by 9 wickets, and England's amazing comeback was complete.

The first day of England's first Test against Bangladesh in Dhaka was a near washout but, with Harmison taking 5–35, the hosts were bowled out for 203. Trescothick made 113 but England's 295 was the lowest first-innings total by a touring team in Bangladesh. Hoggard and Harmison then took 4 wickets apiece and England were left to make 164 for victory, which they did for the loss of 3 wickets. At Chittagong four England batsmen made half-centuries in a total of 326 before Richard Johnson became the first England bowler to take five wickets in his first two Tests since Nick Cook in 1983. Leading by 174 on first innings, England declared their second innings closed at 293–5, going on to win the game by 329 runs.

In the first Test against Sri Lanka at Galle, England's bowlers restricted the home side to 331 before Butcher came in to keep the England side afloat. Muralitharan had taken 7–46 in the England total of 235 all out – the best in Tests at this ground. Ashley Giles then took his second 4-wicket haul of the match as the hosts set England 323 to win. When Paul Collingwood was dismissed in the last over before tea, England were 170–7 with Sri Lanka still having 35 overs at their disposal. Giles was smothering the spinners with a big forward stride, but as gloom descended the umpires finally offered the light with England on 210–9. At Kandy, Sri Lanka's last-day failure to secure victory against England was almost a carbon copy of that at Galle. Sri Lanka had a lead of 88 on first innings and, following Dilshan's hundred in the second innings, declared at 279–7, leaving England needing 368 for victory. Michael Vaughan scored his first century as England captain and – though when he went to a brilliant one-handed catch by Dilshan, England were 7 wickets down with 17 overs – Batty and Read played out time. A weary England ran out of fight in the third Test, at Colombo, for, after being bowled out for 265, they allowed Sri Lanka to make their highest total against England of 628–8 declared with both Samaraweera and Jayawardene making hundreds. The tourists were then bowled out for 148, giving Sri Lanka their first win over England in a series of more than one Test. The victory, by an innings and 215 runs, was England's third-heaviest defeat.

England started their tour of the Caribbean at Sabina Park, Kingston. Devon Smith made a first-day hundred as the West Indies totalled 311 and, though Best and Edwards were bowling in speeds in excess of 90 mph, the tourists gained a lead of 28 on first innings. Then three days of bruisingly competitive Test cricket were erased in 123 breathtaking and bizarre minutes. West Indies were bowled out for their lowest Test total of 47 with Steve Harmison producing his best Test figures of 7–12. England won by 10 wickets. After the second Test at Port-of-Spain, England found themselves for the first time ever, 2–0 up in a Test series in the Caribbean. Harmison carried on where he'd left off, taking 6–61 as the home side were all out for 208. With Thorpe leading the way, England's middle order helped make 319 before Simon Jones (5–57) destroyed the home side's second innings, for a 7-wicket victory. At Bridgetown, England not only claimed their third successive victory but secured their first series in the Caribbean since 1967–8. Flintoff took 5–58 as West Indies were bowled out for 224 and, though England managed only a 2-run lead on first innings, thanks to an unbeaten 119 by Thorpe, their pace bowlers – including Hoggard taking a hat-trick – demolished the West Indies batsmen the second time round for just 94, and England won by 8 wickets. At St John's, with West Indies 3–0 down and facing a whitewash, Brian Lara made a world record 400 not out as West Indies declared at 751–5. With 552 needed to avoid the follow-on, only Flintoff with an unbeaten 102 put up any fight and they were all out for 285. Following on, Vaughan led a second-innings rearguard, scoring 140 as England finished on 422–5.

New Zealand's visit to England in 2004 saw Andrew Strauss become the fourth player to make a century on his Test debut at Lord's. After New Zealand had scored 386 in their first innings. Strauss's heroics saw England lead by 55 runs on first innings. Mark Richardson, a former No. 11 made 101 in the Kiwis' second innings and, with McCullum making 96, England were left needing 282 to win. Strauss was run out on 83, but Hussain hit an unbeaten 103 and England won by 7 wickets. At Headingley, New Zealand skipper Stephen Fleming made 97 in his side's total of 409 but Trescothick (132) and Geraint Jones (100), along with Flintoff's swashbuckling 94, helped the home side to a lead of 117 on first innings. New Zealand's depleted side were then bowled out for 161, England going on to win by 9 wickets. Despite having lost the series, New Zealand produced a sturdy first-innings performance in the final Test at Trent Bridge, making 384 before bowling England out for 319. A better performance by England's bowlers in the Kiwis' second innings left the home side needing 284 for victory. Despite the loss of early wickets, Graham Thorpe became the tenth Englishman to make 6,000 Test runs when making his unbeaten 104 in England's 4-wicket win.

In the second half of the summer England played host to the West Indies. At Lord's in the first Test, Robert Key's 221 was the third-highest maiden Test century by an England batsman, and, with Strauss (137) and Vaughan (101) also making hundreds, England totalled 568. There was no way back for the West Indies, though they utilized the conditions well enough for Chanderpaul to make 128 not out and save the follow-on. In England's second innings, Michael Vaughan became the second England captain to score hundreds in both innings of the same match after Graham Gooch, and he declared, setting the tourists 478 to win. Giles then took 5–81, including the wicket of Lara, beaten in flight and by sharp turn, as England won by 210 runs. At Edgbaston, England, with centuries from Trescothick and Flintoff, put the game out of West Indies' reach with a first-innings total of 566. Sarwan completed his first hundred against England in West Indies' score of 326 and then Trescothick hit back-to-back centuries as England set the tourists a target of 479. Ashley Giles then took 5–57 as England won by 256 runs and in doing so became the first England spinner since Tony Lock in 1958 to take 9 wickets or more in consecutive Tests. In winning the third Test at Old Trafford, England had to overcome not only a West Indian side showing more heart, but also the Manchester weather. After West Indies had made 395, Thorpe gave an exemplary display of how to build an innings in making 114 in England's 330 before the tourists were bowled out for 165 second time round. Left with 231 to make for victory, Key and Flintoff shared the match-clinching partnership of 120 as dark clouds hovered, and, the threat of rain hung in the air, England won by 7 wickets. In the final Test, at The Oval, England were 321–7 early on the second morning and they were falling short of an adequate total, but Giles and Hoggard added 87 and then Harmison and Anderson hit 60 to leave West Indies facing another massive climb for safety. Harmison then roughed up the West Indies, batsmen to take 6–46 in their first-innings total of 152. Following on, Gayle made 105 but England went on to win by 10 wickets. It was England's first home season to include two clean sweeps and this, their seventh successive win, equalled their best runs of 1885–8 and 1928–9.

Visiting South Africa, England beat the Springboks by 7 wickets in the first Test at Port Elizabeth. Dippenaar hit 110 in South Africa's first-innings total of 337 while Strauss became the seventh player to score centuries in his first Test both at home and away. Facing a deficit of 88 runs on first innings, South Africa were bowled out for 229, leaving England just 142 to win. The second Test saw England bowled out for 139 and, with Jacques Kallis (162) in imperious form, the home side led by 193 runs on first innings. England then turned the tables and with Trescothick (132) and Strauss (136) putting 273 for the first wicket and Graham Thorpe hitting an unbeaten 118, they were able to declare at 570–7 and set the Springboks 378 to win in a little over a day. England chipped and chivvied away, session by session, but they met staunch resistance as South Africa finished on 290–8.

At Cape Town, after South Africa had rattled up a first-innings total of 441, Michael Vaughan's thirteen-match unbeaten run was undermined by a death-wish batting display as England were bowled out for 163. Smith refused to enforce the follow-on and South Africa succeeded not only in extending their lead to 500 but in stretching England's resistance to breaking point. Facing 167 overs to bat out for the draw, the tourists found Pollock's nagging accuracy and Boje's increasingly influential turn an irresistible combination and they lost by 196 runs. The fourth Test, at Johannesburg, was the most compelling of the series. Strauss made another hundred as England declared at 411–8 but, with Gibbs making 161, South Africa gained an 8-run lead on first innings. Trescothick then hit a brilliant second-innings century, enabling Vaughan to declare for a second time and set the hosts 325 to win. Along came Matthew Hoggard, who kept on and on at the batsmen to take 7–61 (match figures of 12–205) and England won by 77 runs. Following South Africa's modest first-innings total of 247 at Centurion in the fifth Test, England, despite Andre Nel's 6–81, made 359, a lead of 112. With both de Villiers and Kallis making hundreds in South Africa's second innings, the home side declared at 296–6, leaving England 185 to win. In a game that had been bedevilled by daily storms, Ntini's relentless aggression in taking 3–12 in 11 overs reduced England to 73–4 at stumps.

In summer 2005, Bangladesh's first visit to England saw them bowled out for 108 before the home side amassed a score of 528–3 declared with

Trescothick and Vaughan making centuries. Bangladesh fared little better in their second innings and England won by an innings and 261 runs. The second meeting, at Chester-le-Street, saw England wrap up victory inside the first session of the third day once again. Having bowled out Bangladesh for 104, England scored 447–3 with Trescothick making another hundred and Ian Bell his maiden Test century. Bangladesh improved in their second innings but they eventually fell to Hoggard's swing as England won by an innings and 27 runs.

The biggest Test series in England for twenty years got under way at Lord's with the home side making a good start, bowling Australia out for 190 with Steve Harmison taking 5–43, including polishing off the tail with 4–7 in 14 deliveries. Glenn McGrath became the fourth bowler in Tests to take 500 wickets when he dismissed Trescothick and immediately set about adding to his tally. England were 21–5 but then debutant Kevin Pietersen and wicketkeeper Jones rescued England before they fell 35 runs short of Australia's total. The tourists were well on top by the end of the second day, when they remarkably led by 314. Eventually all out for 384, England required 420 to win. With Warne paired with paceman McGrath, England crumbled and, with the latter mopping up the tail with a devastating spell of 4–3 in 23 balls, Australia won by 239 runs.

The drama at Edgbaston began before the start with the news that Glenn McGrath had injured his right ankle in practice and would not play. Following their capitulation in the first Test, England's batsmen had decided to be positive and their total of 407 was their highest on the opening day of a Test since the Second World War. England took a 99-run lead on first innings but before the second day was over, Strauss was bowled by a fizzing leg-break by Shane Warne. Aiming for a large lead, England collapsed to 31–4 before Flintoff came to the rescue and his last-wicket stand of 51 off 49 balls with Simon Jones was England's most valuable last-wicket partnership since Hirst and Rhodes in 1902. Needing 282 to win, Australia had cruised to 47–0 before Flintoff removed Langer. Wickets fell at regular intervals before Warne trod on his wicket, leaving the last pair of Brett Lee and Mike Kasprowicz to make 62 runs for victory. With Lee playing a brave innings, English hearts were in their mouths as just 3 runs were needed for victory, when Kasprowicz gloved a ball from Harmison down the leg-side, where Geraint Jones took a tumbling catch. The 2-run margin is the narrowest yet in an Ashes Test – has there ever been a more exciting match?

At Old Trafford, England for once had the chance to go one up in an Ashes series, with everything still to play for. England ended the first day at 341–5, thanks to a captain's innings from Michael Vaughan, but they were bowled out for 444. England had Australia at 201–7 but then rain took too much time out of the third day for England's liking and in only one hour of play, the tourists added 54 runs without losing a wicket. However, the following morning, with Simon Jones (6–53) leading the way, England got amongst the wickets, but Warne's fighting knock of 90 ensured Australia avoided the follow-on. Following a brisk start from Trescothick and Strauss (106), Vaughan was able to declare, setting the tourists 423 to win. Though wickets fell around him, Ricky Ponting played a captain's innings under pressurized circumstances but, as ninth man out for 156, he was forced to watch from a nervous dressing-room balcony as Australia's last pair of Lee and McGrath batted out the last 24 balls of the game. Vaughan won the toss in the fourth Test at Trent Bridge and opted to bat. Trescothick and Strauss notched up an opening stand of 105 but wickets fell steadily before Flintoff (102) and Geraint Jones (85) added 177 for the sixth wicket and England ended with a total of 477. Hoggard reduced Australia's first innings to tatters with 3 wickets in his opening spell and, with Simon Jones taking 5–44, they were bowled out for 218. Michael Vaughan enforced the follow-on but England were made to toil as all bar last man Tait reached double figures in a total of 387. With the pitch still playing well, England needed 129 to go 2–1 up in the series. The England batsmen made it hard for themselves and blind panic set in as the top order seemed to lose their heads. England were 57–4 before Flintoff joined Pietersen and they added 46 for the fifth wicket. After Flintoff's dismissal, Jones followed soon after and England were 116–7, still 13 runs short of victory. Yet salvation was at hand as Giles and Hoggard waited for the bad ball and saw England home by 3 wickets.

As the final Test at The Oval dawned, all that stood between Michael Vaughan's side and a nation's adulation were eleven Australian cricketers desperate to avoid losing the Ashes after sixteen years of dominance. At the close of play on day one, England were 319–7, largely thanks to the partnership between Strauss and Flintoff, with the former making 129. However, they were all out for 373 and this looked a dangerously modest score after they had won the toss against a determined team forced to fight for their reputation. Australia had reached 112–0 when the openers, rather surprisingly, accepted the offer to walk off for bad light and supposedly impending rain. Both Langer and Hayden made centuries and Australia ended the third day on 277–2, still 96 runs behind England. The following morning, Flintoff, ably supported by Hoggard, unnerved the Australians. The tourists were no doubt thinking of a big lead but, after they had reached 323–3, their last 7 wickets fell for 44 runs in 15 overs and England had an improbable 6-run lead. In their second innings, England had struggled to 126–5 when Pietersen launched into the Australian attack. As he moved towards his maiden Test century, England were still some way from safety when Giles joined him at the crease but, by the time Pietersen perished to a McGrath delivery for a magnificent 158, the hosts were past 300 and guaranteed a draw – England had regained the Ashes.

The first post-Ashes Test against Pakistan in Multan was another roller-coaster of a match. The hosts were bowled out for 274 before stand-in skipper Marcus Trescothick hit a superb 193 in England's reply of 418. Salman Butt reached three figures for Pakistan in their second innings, leaving England 198 to win. But such a target against the likes of the leg-spinner Danish Kaneria never looked easy and the home side won by 22 runs. In the second Test, Pakistani skipper Inzamam-ul-Haq held his side's first innings together with a knock of 109 as they eventually totalled 462, but England, with Bell and Pietersen both scoring hundreds, fell just 16 runs adrift. A second century from Inzamam left England to bat out for a draw. At Lahore, England batted first and made 288 but, with Mohammad Yousuf reaching 223 and Kamran Akmal 154, Pakistan were able to declare at 636–8. England's batsmen, with the exception of Bell and Collingwood, then collapsed on the final afternoon – 8 wickets going down for 43 runs in a little over an hour to give Pakistan victory by an innings and 100 runs.

Andrew Flintoff took over the captaincy for the visit to India, and, in the opening Test at Nagpur, Paul Collingwood made 134 not out in England's first-innings total of 393. Thanks to some fine bowling by Hoggard (6–57), the tourists had a lead of 70 runs on first innings and, with debutant Alistair Cook making an unbeaten 104, Flintoff declared at 297–3. Wasim Jaffer also reached his hundred as India finished on 260–6, some 107 runs short of the victory target. At Chandigarh, England were humbled by Anil Kumble, who became the first Indian bowler to take 500 Test wickets. India led by 38 runs on first innings after Kumble had taken 5–76, and then, after bowling England out for just 181, went on to win the game by 9 wickets. Missing five Ashes winners, England produced a resourceful performance in the final Test at Mumbai. Strauss made 128 in England's first-innings score of 400 and Owais Shah 88 before James Anderson took 4–40 as India were dismissed for 279. England were then shot out for 191, leaving India needing 312 to win. Cue England's oldest player Shaun Udal, who ended with figures of 4–14 as India were bowled out for 100, leaving England the winners by 212 runs.

In May 2006, England played host to Sri Lanka for the first of three Tests. The first meeting at Lord's saw England drop a string of catches, which would ultimately cost them the match. England had opted to bat first, and with Kevin Pietersen producing an outstanding innings of 158, supported by fellow centurion Marcus Trescothick and also Cook, Collingwood and Strauss, captain Freddie Flintoff declared at 551–6. Six Sri Lankan wickets on the evening of the second day certainly vindicated his decision to declare earlier than most expected, and the visitors were eventually all out for 192. Faced with the inevitable follow-on, however, Sri Lanka fared much better, with Jayawardene making 119 and six other batsman reaching a half century as the tourists ended the match on 537–9. At Edgbaston, Sri Lanka were bowled out for just 141, with England's pacemen sharing the wickets. England too found it difficult to bat with the exception of Pietersen, who made 142 scoring at a rate of a run a ball against Muralitharan. Sri Lanka's opening batsman Vandort made a brave 105 in his side's second innings, but England were left with just 78 needed for victory. As the home side took a 1–0 lead in the three-match series, Murali finished with 10 wickets in a Test for the fifteenth time. In the final Test at Trent Bridge, England sprung a surprise by selecting Jon Lewis ahead of Sajid Mahmood. Lewis took three wickets in Sri Lanka's first innings total of 231, but was wicketless in the second. England struggled and their first innings ended two runs adrift of Sri Lanka's total. Useful knocks from several Sri Lankan batsmen set England a total of 325 for victory. England's openers Trescothick and Strauss made a good start, putting on 84 for the first wicket, but then Murali produced his fourth-best analysis in Test cricket, taking 8–70 as England were dismissed for 190 and Sri Lanka levelled the series.

After winning the toss in the first of four Tests against Pakistan, England's captain, Andrew Strauss, elected to bat. Though he and Trescothick didn't make the most of the conditions, Cook, Collingwood and Bell all made centuries. England declared at 528–9, but Mohammad Yousuf, with a superb innings of 202, helped Pakistan reach 445 in reply. Strauss scored 128 in the second innings to become the fourth England player to score a Test century in his first match as captain. His second declaration of the match left the visitors needing 380 to win, but with less than a day to bowl Pakistan out, the match petered out into a draw. At Old Trafford, Steve Harmison's explosive return to form saw him take 6–19 on a pitch that might have been made for him as Pakistan were bowled out for 119. After Alastair Cook made a composed century and Bell also reached three figures, Strauss again declared England's innings closed, with the home side on 467–9. In Pakistan's second innings, Harmison took 5–57 and was rightly named Man of the Match, but Monty Panesar was the man of the moment: bowling 27 consecutive overs, he took 5–72 as he exploited the cracks in the pitch and produced subtle variations of pace and length. England recorded victory by an innings and 120 runs.

After two fairly quiet Tests, Kevin Pietersen made his first real impact on the series at Headingley and by the end of the first day had made 104, before being forced to retire through cramp. All the main batsmen contributed, as England piled up an impressive 515. Mohammad Yousuf led Pakistan's reply and made 192 while Younis Khan hit 173 as the tourists ended the third day with a lead of 23 runs on first innings. Highlight of the day for England fans was the unusual dismissal of Inzamam-ul-Haq, who overbalanced and dislodged the bails with his stomach. Strauss then hit 116 as England were dismissed for 345, leaving Pakistan 323 to win to level the series. On the final day a draw looked on the cards, but England secured their first series triumph since the Ashes with a 167-run win, with Panesar and Sajid Mahmood the pick of the England bowlers.

On the opening day of the final Test Inzamam won the toss, and with Umar Gul and Mohammad Asif bowling extremely well, England were out for just 173. In reply, two Pakistan players were dismissed in the nineties, but Mohammad Yousuf went on to yet another century in a total of 504. Despite losing Trescothick early, England batted much more resolutely in the second innings, and were on 230–3 on the fourth day when the umpires conferred over the state of the ball, and the home side were awarded 5 runs for alleged ball-tampering by Pakistan. Bad light later stopped play with England 33 runs in arrears and 6 wickets intact. When play was able to resume, the umpires waited in the middle with the England batsmen ready on the balcony, but the Pakistan team failed to emerge. The umpires then left the field of play, later returning to the middle with the England batsmen but not Pakistan. Half an hour later, Pakistan took to the field amid booing but returned to their dressing room after the umpires stayed off the pitch. Play was then officially called off for the day and England awarded victory following the stand-off between the visitors and the umpires – an historic and shaming first for the sport.

TEST MATCH RESULTS: 2000–6

767. England v Zimbabwe
First Test at Lord's – 18, 19, 20, 21 May 2000
ZIMBABWE 83 (Giddins 5–15) and 123 (Caddick 4–38,
   Gough 4–57)
ENGLAND 415 (Stewart 124*, Hick 101, Atherton 55,
   Knight 44, Streak 6–87)
England won by an innings and 209 runs

768. England v Zimbabwe
Second Test at Trent Bridge – 1, 2 (no play), 3, 4, 5 June
   2000
ENGLAND 374 (Atherton 136, Schofield 57, Ramprakash
   56) and 147
ZIMBABWE 285–4 dec. (Goodwin 148*, Johnson 51,
   A. Flower 42) and 25–1
Match drawn

769. England v West Indies
First Test at Edgbaston – 15, 16, 17 June 2000
ENGLAND 179 (Walsh 5–36) and 125
WEST INDIES 397 (Adams 98, Chanderpaul 73, Campbell
   59, Lara 50, Rose 48, Gough 5–109)
West Indies won by an innings and 93 runs

770. England v West Indies
Second Test at Lord's – 29, 30 June, 1 July 2000
WEST INDIES 267 (Campbell 82, Hinds 59, Cork 4–39,
   Gough 4–72) and 54 (Caddick 5–16)
ENGLAND 134 (Ambrose 4–30, Walsh 4–43) and 191–8
   (Atherton 45, Vaughan 41, Walsh 6–74)
England won by 2 wickets

771. England v West Indies
Third Test at Old Trafford – 3, 4, 5, 6, 7 August 2000
WEST INDIES 157 (Cork 4–23) and 438–7 dec. (Lara 112,
   Campbell 55, Griffith 54, Adams 53, Jacobs 42*)
ENGLAND 303 (Stewart 105, Trescothick 66, Walsh 4–50,
   Ambrose 4–70) and 80–1
Match drawn

772. England v West Indies
Fourth Test at Headingley – 17, 18 August 2000
WEST INDIES 172 (Sarwan 59*, White 5–57) and 61
   (Caddick 5–14, Gough 4–30)
ENGLAND 272 (Vaughan 76, Hick 59, Thorpe 46, Ambrose
   4–42, Walsh 4–51)
England won by an innings and 39 runs

773. England v West Indies
Fifth Test at The Oval – 31 August, 1, 2, 3, 4 September 2000
ENGLAND 281 (Atherton 83, Trescothick 78, Thorpe 40)
   and 217 (Atherton 108, Walsh 4–73)
WEST INDIES 125 (White 5–32) and 215 (Lara 47, Caddick
   4–54)
England won by 158 runs

774. Pakistan v England
First Test at Lahore – 15, 16, 17, 18, 19 November 2000
ENGLAND 480–8 dec. (Thorpe 118, White 93, Atherton 73,
   Trescothick 71, Saqlain Mushtaq 8–164) and 77–4 dec.
PAKISTAN 401 (Yousuf Youhana 124, Inzamam-ul-Haq 63,
   Shahid Afridi 52, Salim Elahi 44, Saeed Anwar 40, White
   4–54, Giles 4–113)
Match drawn

775. Pakistan v England
Second Test at Faisalabad – 29, 30 November, 1, 2, 3
   December 2000
PAKISTAN 316 (Yousuf Youhana 77, Moin Khan 65, Saeed
   Anwar 53, Salim Elahi 41, Giles 5–75) and 269–3 dec.
   (Abdul Razzaq 100*, Salim Elahi 72, Inzamam-ul-Haq
   71)
ENGLAND 342 (Thorpe 79, White 41) and 125–5 (Atherton
   65*)
Match drawn

776. Pakistan v England
Third Test at Karachi – 7, 8, 9, 10, 11 December 2000
PAKISTAN 405 (Inzamam-ul-Haq 142, Yousuf Youhana 117,
   Giles 4–94) and 158
ENGLAND 388 (Atherton 125, Hussain 51, Waqar Younis
   4–88) and 176–4 (Thorpe 64*, Hick 40)
England won by 6 wickets

777. Sri Lanka v England
First Test at Galle – 22, 23, 24, 25, 26 February 2001
SRI LANKA 470–5 dec. (Atapattu 201*, de Silva 106,
   Jayawardene 61, Sangakkara 58)
ENGLAND 253 (Trescothick 122, Jayasuriya 4–50) and 189
   (Trescothick 57, Atherton 44, Jayasuriya 4–44,
   Muralitharan 4–66)
Sri Lanka won by an innings and 28 runs

778. Sri Lanka v England
Second Test at Kandy – 7, 8, 9, 10, 11 March 2001
SRI LANKA 297 (Jayawardene 101, Arnold 65, Caddick
   4–55, Gough 4–73) and 250 (Sangakkara 95,
   Dharmasena 54, Gough 4–50)
ENGLAND 387 (Hussain 109, Thorpe 59, Stewart 54,
   Muralitharan 4–127) and 161–7 (Thorpe 46, Vaas
   4–39)
England won by 3 wickets

779. Sri Lanka v England
Third Test at Colombo – 15, 16, 17 March 2001
SRI LANKA 241 (Jayawardene 71, Jayasuriya 45,
   Sangakkara 45, Croft 4–56) and 81 (Giles 4–11)
ENGLAND 249 (Thorpe 113*, Vaas 6–73) and 74–6
   (Jayasuriya 4–24)
England won by 4 wickets

780. England v Pakistan
First Test at Lord's – 17 (no play), 18, 19, 20 May 2001
ENGLAND 391 (Thorpe 80, Hussain 64, Stewart 44,
   Atherton 42, Azhar Mahmood 4–50)
PAKISTAN 203 (Younis Khan 58, Gough 5–61, Caddick
   4–52) and 179 (Abdul Razzaq 53, Caddick 4–54)
England won by an innings and 9 runs

781. England v Pakistan
Second Test at Old Trafford – 31 May, 1, 2, 3, 4 June 2001
PAKISTAN 403 (Inzamam-ul-Haq 114, Rashid Latif 71,
   Younis Khan 65) and 323 (Inzamam-ul-Haq 85, Yousuf
   Youhana 49)
ENGLAND 357 (Thorpe 138, Vaughan 120) and 261
   (Trescothick 117, Atherton 51, Saqlain Mushtaq 4–74)
Pakistan won by 108 runs

782. England v Australia
First Test at Edgbaston – 5, 6, 7, 8 July 2001
ENGLAND 294 (Stewart 65, Atherton 57, Caddick 49*,
Warne 5–71) and 164 (Trescothick 76, Butcher 41)
AUSTRALIA 576 (Gilchrist 152, S. Waugh 105, Martyn 105,
Slater 77, M. Waugh 49, Butcher 4–42)
Australia won by an innings and 118 runs

783. England v Australia
Second Test at Lord's – 19, 20, 21, 22 July 2001
ENGLAND 187 (McGrath 5–54) and 227 (Butcher 83,
Ramprakash 40, Gillespie 5–53)
AUSTRALIA 401 (M. Waugh 108, Gilchrist 90, Martyn 52,
S. Waugh 45, Caddick 5–101) and 14–2
Australia won by 8 wickets

784. England v Australia
Third Test at Trent Bridge – 2, 3, 4 August 2001
ENGLAND 185 (Trescothick 69, Stewart 46, McGrath 5–49)
and 162 (Atherton 51, Warne 6–33)
AUSTRALIA 190 (Gilchrist 54, Tudor 5–44) and 158–3
(M. Waugh 42*, Hayden 42)
Australia won by 7 wickets

785. England v Australia
Fourth Test at Headingley – 16, 17, 18, 19, 20 August
2001
AUSTRALIA 447 (Ponting 144, Martyn 118, M. Waugh 72,
Gough 5–103) and 176–4 dec. (Ponting 72)
ENGLAND 309 (Stewart 76*, Butcher 47, Hussain 46,
Ramprakash 40, McGrath 7–76) and 315–4 (Butcher
173*, Hussain 55)
England won by 6 wickets

786. England v Australia
Fifth Test at The Oval – 23, 24, 25, 26, 27 August 2001
AUSTRALIA 641–4 dec. (S. Waugh 157*, M. Waugh 120,
Langer 102 ret. hurt, Hayden 68, Martyn 64*, Ponting
62)
ENGLAND 432 (Ramprakash 133, Trescothick 55, Afzaal 54,
Hussain 52, Warne 7–165) and 184 (McGrath 5–43,
Warne 4–64)
Australia won by an innings and 25 runs

787. India v England
First Test at Chandigarh – 3, 4, 5, 6 December 2001
ENGLAND 238 (Hussain 85, Trescothick 66, Harbhajan
Singh 5–51) and 235 (Thorpe 62, Trescothick 46,
Kumble 6–81)
INDIA 469 (Dasgupta 100, Tendulkar 88, Dravid 86,
Ganguly 47, Dawson 4–134) and 5–0
India won by 10 wickets

788. India v England
Second Test at Ahmedabad – 11, 12, 13, 14, 15 December
2001
ENGLAND 407 (White 121, Trescothick 99, Butcher 51,
Foster 40, Kumble 7–115) and 257 (Butcher 92, Hussain
50, Harbhajan Singh 5–71)
INDIA 291 (Tendulkar 103, Laxman 75, Das 41, Giles 5–67)
and 198–3 (Dasgupta 60, Das 58)
Match drawn

789. India v England
Third Test at Bangalore – 19, 20, 21, 22, 23 (no play)
December 2001

ENGLAND 336 (Vaughan 64, Ramprakash 58, Foster 48,
Hussain 43, Srinath 4–73) and 33–1
INDIA 238 (Tendulkar 90, Sehwag 66, Flintoff 4–50,
Hoggard 4–80)
Match drawn

790. New Zealand v England
First Test at Christchurch – 13, 14, 15, 16 March 2002
ENGLAND 228 (Hussain 106) and 468–6 dec. (Thorpe
200*, Flintoff 137)
NEW ZEALAND 147 (Vettori 42, McMillan 40, Hoggard
7–63) and 451 (Astle 222, Richardson 76, Fleming 48,
Caddick 6–122)
England won by 98 runs

791. New Zealand v England
Second Test at Wellington – 21 (no play), 22, 23, 24, 25
March 2002
ENGLAND 280 (Hussain 66, Butcher 47, Butler 4–60) and
293–4 dec. (Trescothick 88, Flintoff 75, Butcher 60)
NEW ZEALAND 218 (Richardson 60, Vincent 57, McMillan
41, Caddick 6–63, Giles 4–103) and 158–4 (Vincent 71)
Match drawn

792. New Zealand v England
Third Test at Auckland – 30, 31 (no play) March, 1, 2, 3
April 2002
NEW ZEALAND 202 (Harris 71, Parore 45, McMillan 41,
Caddick 4–70) and 269–9 dec. (Astle 65, McMillan 50*,
Harris 43, Hoggard 4–68)
ENGLAND 160 (Thorpe 42, Tuffey 6–54) and 233 (Hussain
82)
New Zealand won by 78 runs

793. England v Sri Lanka
First Test at Lord's – 16, 17, 18, 19, 20 May 2002
SRI LANKA 555–8 dec. (Atapattu 185, Jayawardene 107,
de Silva 88, Arnold 50) and 42–1
ENGLAND 275 (Vaughan 64, Hussain 57) and 529–5 dec.
(Vaughan 115, Butcher 105, Trescothick 76, Hussain 68,
Thorpe 65, Crawley 41*)
Match drawn

794. England v Sri Lanka
Second Test at Edgbaston – 30, 31 May, 1, 2 June 2002
SRI LANKA 162 (Jayawardene 47) and 272 (Jayawardene
59, Atapattu 56, de Silva 47, Hoggard 5–92)
ENGLAND 545 (Trescothick 161, Thorpe 123, Butcher 94,
Vaughan 46, Muralitharan 5–143)
England won by an innings and 111 runs

795. England v Sri Lanka
Third Test at Old Trafford – 13, 14, 15, 16, 17 June 2002
ENGLAND 512 (Butcher 123, Stewart 123, Trescothick 81,
Giles 45) and 50–0
SRI LANKA 253 (Arnold 62, Sangakkara 40, Tudor 4–65)
and 308 (Arnold 109, de Silva 40, Giles 4–62)
England won by 10 wickets

796. England v India
First Test at Lord's – 25, 26, 27, 28, 29 July 2002
ENGLAND 487 (Hussain 155, Crawley 64, Flintoff 59, White
53) and 301–6 dec. (Crawley 100*, Vaughan 100)
INDIA 221 (Sehwag 84, Dravid 46, Laxman 43*) and 397
(Agarkar 109*, Laxman 74, Dravid 63, Jaffer 53,
Hoggard 4–87)
England won by 170 runs

797. England v India
Second Test at Trent Bridge — 8, 9, 10, 11, 12 August 2002
INDIA 357 (Sehwag 106, Ganguly 68, Harbhajan Singh 54, Hoggard 4–105) and 424–8 dec. (Dravid 115, Ganguly 99, Tendulkar 92)
ENGLAND 617 (Vaughan 197, White 94*, Stewart 87, Butcher 53)
Match drawn

798. England v India
Third Test at Headingley — 22, 23, 24, 25, 26 August 2002
INDIA 628–8 dec. (Tendulkar 193, Dravid 148, Ganguly 128, Bangar 68)
ENGLAND 273 (Stewart 78*, Vaughan 61) and 309 (Hussain 110, Stewart 47, Butcher 42, Kumble 4–66)
India won by an innings and 46 runs

799. England v India
Fourth Test at The Oval — 5, 6, 7, 8, 9 (no play) September 2002
ENGLAND 515 (Vaughan 195, Trescothick 57, Butcher 54, Cork 52, Harbhajan Singh 5–115) and 114–0 (Trescothick 58*, Vaughan 47*)
INDIA 508 (Dravid 217, Tendulkar 54, Ganguly 51, Laxman 40, Caddick 4–114)
Match drawn

800. Australia v England
First Test at Brisbane — 7, 8, 9, 10 November 2002
AUSTRALIA 492 (Hayden 197, Ponting 123, Warne 57, Giles 4–101) and 296–5 dec. (Hayden 103, Martyn 64, Gilchrist 60*)
ENGLAND 325 (Trescothick 72, Crawley 69*, Butcher 54, Hussain 51, McGrath 4–87) and 79 (Butcher 40, McGrath 4–36)
Australia won by 384 runs

801. Australia v England
Second Test at Adelaide — 21, 22, 23, 24 November 2002
ENGLAND 342 (Vaughan 177, Hussain 47, Gillespie 4–78, Warne 4–93) and 159 (Stewart 57, Vaughan 41, McGrath 4–41)
AUSTRALIA 552 (Ponting 154, Martyn 95, Gilchrist 54, Bichel 48, Langer 48, Hayden 46, White 4–106)
Australia won by an innings and 51 runs

802. Australia v England
Third Test at Perth — 29, 30 November, 1 December 2002
ENGLAND 185 (Key 47) and 223 (Stewart 66*, Hussain 61)
AUSTRALIA 456 (Martyn 71, Ponting 68, S. Waugh 53, Lehmann 42, Lee 41, White 5–127)
Australia won by an innings and 48 runs

803. Australia v England
Fourth Test at Melbourne — 26, 27, 28, 29, 30 December 2002
AUSTRALIA 551–6 dec. (Langer 250, Hayden 102, S. Waugh 77, Love 62*) and 107–5
ENGLAND 270 (White 85*, Gillespie 4–25) and 387 (Vaughan 145, Key 52, MacGill 5–152)
Australia won by 5 wickets

804. Australia v England
Fifth Test at Sydney — 2, 3, 4, 5, 6 January 2003
ENGLAND 362 (Butcher 124, Hussain 75, Stewart 71) and 452 (Vaughan 183, Hussain 72)
AUSTRALIA 363 (Gilchrist 133, S. Waugh 102, Hoggard 4–92) and 226 (Bichel 49, Lee 46, Caddick 7–94)
England won by 225 runs

805. England v Zimbabwe
First Test at Lord's — 22, 23, 24 May 2003
ENGLAND 472 (Butcher 137, McGrath 69, Trescothick 59, Giles 52)
ZIMBABWE 147 (Ebrahim 68, Anderson 5–73) and 233 (Vermeulen 61, Friend 43, Butcher 4–60)
England won by an innings and 92 runs

806. England v Zimbabwe
Second Test at Chester-le-Street — 5, 6, 7 June 2003
ENGLAND 416 (McGrath 81, Stewart 68, Giles 50, Butcher 47, Trescothick 43, Streak 4–64)
ZIMBABWE 94 (Johnson 6–33) and 253 (Friend 65*, Ebrahim 55, Anderson 4–55, Harmison 4–55)
England won by an innings and 69 runs

807. England v South Africa
First Test at Edgbaston — 24, 25 (no play), 26, 27, 28 July 2003
SOUTH AFRICA 594–5 dec. (Smith 277, Gibbs 179, G. Kirsten 44) and 134–4 dec. (Smith 85)
ENGLAND 408 (Vaughan 156, Giles 41, Flintoff 40, Ntini 4–114, Pretorius 4–115) and 110–1 (Trescothick 52*)
Match drawn

808. England v South Africa
Second Test at Lord's — 31 July, 1, 2, 3 August 2003
ENGLAND 173 (Ntini 5–75) and 417 (Flintoff 142, Butcher 70, Hussain 61, Ntini 5–145)
SOUTH AFRICA 682–6 dec. (Smith 259, G. Kirsten 108, Dippenaar 92, Boucher 68, Gibbs 49)
South Africa won by an innings and 92 runs

809. England v South Africa
Third Test at Trent Bridge — 14, 15, 16, 17, 18 August 2003
ENGLAND 445 (Hussain 116, Butcher 106, Stewart 72, Smith 64) and 118 (Pollock 6–39)
SOUTH AFRICA 362 (McKenzie 90, Pollock 62, Boucher 48, Anderson 5–102) and 131 (Boucher 52, Kirtley 6–34)
England won by 70 runs

810. England v South Africa
Fourth Test at Headingley — 21, 22, 23, 24, 25 August 2003
SOUTH AFRICA 342 (G. Kirsten 130, Zondeki 59, Rudolph 55) and 365 (Hall 99*, G. Kirsten 60, Kallis 41)
ENGLAND 307 (Butcher 77, Trescothick 59, Flintoff 55, Hussain 42) and 209 (Butcher 61, Flintoff 50, Kallis 6–54)
South Africa won by 191 runs

811. England v South Africa
Fifth Test at The Oval — 4, 5, 6, 7, 8 September 2003
SOUTH AFRICA 484 (Gibbs 183, G. Kirsten 90, Kallis 66, Pollock 66*) and 229 (Pollock 43, Harmison 4–33, Bicknell 4–84)
ENGLAND 604–9 dec. (Trescothick 219, Thorpe 124, Flintoff 95) and 110–1 (Trescothick 69*)
England won by 9 wickets

812. Bangladesh v England
First Test at Dhaka – 21, 22, 23, 24, 25 October 2003
BANGLADESH 203 (Khaled Mashud 51, Harmison 5–35) and
255 (Hannan Sarkar 59, Habibul Bashar 58, Mushfiqur
Rahman 46*, Harmison 4–44, Hoggard 4–48)
ENGLAND 295 (Trescothick 113, Thorpe 64, Vaughan 48)
and 164–3 (Vaughan 81*)
England won by 7 wickets

813. Bangladesh v England
Second Test at Chittagong – 29, 30, 31 October, 1
November 2003
ENGLAND 326 (Hussain 76, Trescothick 60, Clarke 55,
Vaughan 54, Mashrafe Mortaza 4–60) and 293–5 dec.
(Hussain 95, Thorpe 54, Butcher 42)
BANGLADESH 152 (Johnson 5–49) and 138 (Johnson 4–44)
England won by 329 runs

814. Sri Lanka v England
First Test at Galle – 2, 3, 4, 5, 6 December 2003
SRI LANKA 331 (Sangakkara 71, Jayasuriya 48,
Samaraweera 45, Giles 4–69) and 226 (Jayawardene
86*, Giles 4–63)
ENGLAND 235 (Butcher 51, Thorpe 43, Muralitharan 7–46)
and 210–9 (Butcher 54, Muralitharan 4–47)
Match drawn

815. Sri Lanka v England
Second Test at Kandy – 10, 11, 12, 13, 14 December 2003
SRI LANKA 382 (Dilshan 63, Fernando 51*, Jayawardene
45, Giles 5–116) and 279–7 dec. (Dilshan 100,
Jayawardene 52)
ENGLAND 294 (Thorpe 57, Vaughan 52, Muralitharan
4–60, Vaas 4–77) and 285–7 (Vaughan 105, Thorpe 41,
Muralitharan 4–64)
Match drawn

816. Sri Lanka v England
Third Test at Colombo – 18, 19, 20, 21 December 2003
ENGLAND 265 (Flintoff 77, Trescothick 70) and 148
(Muralitharan 4–63)
SRI LANKA 628 (Samaraweera 142, Jayawardene 134,
Jayasuriya 85, Dilshan 83, Chandana 76)
Sri Lanka won by an innings and 215 runs

817. West Indies v England
First Test at Kingston, Jamaica – 11, 12, 13, 14 March 2004
WEST INDIES 311 (Smith 108, Hinds 84) and 47 (Harmison
7–12)
ENGLAND 339 (Butcher 58, Hussain 58, Flintoff 46) and 20–0
England won by 10 wickets

818. West Indies v England
Second Test at Port-of-Spain, Trinidad – 19, 20, 21, 22, 23
March 2004
WEST INDIES 208 (Gayle 62, Jacobs 40, Harmison 6–61)
and 209 (Jacobs 70, Chanderpaul 42, Jones 5–57)
ENGLAND 319 (Thorpe 90, Butcher 61, Hussain 58, Collins
4–71) and 99–3 (Butcher 46*)
England won by 7 wickets

819. West Indies v England
Third Test at Bridgetown, Barbados – 1, 2, 3 April 2004
WEST INDIES 224 (Sarwan 63, Chanderpaul 50, Flintoff
5–58) and 94 (Hoggard 4–35)
ENGLAND 226 (Thorpe 119*, Edwards 4–70) and 93–2
(Trescothick 42)
England won by 8 wickets

820. West Indies v England
Fourth Test at St John's, Antigua – 10, 11, 12, 13, 14 April
2004
WEST INDIES 751–5 dec. (Lara 400*, Jacobs 107*, Sarwan
90, Gayle 69)
ENGLAND 285 (Flintoff 102, Butcher 52, Collins 4–76) and
422–5 (Vaughan 140, Trescothick 88, Butcher 61,
Hussain 56)
Match drawn

821. England v New Zealand
First Test at Lord's – 20, 21, 22, 23, 24 May 2004
NEW ZEALAND 386 (Richardson 93, Cairns 82, Oram 67,
Astle 64, Harmison 4–126) and 336 (Richardson 101,
McCullum 96, Astle 49, Harmison 4–76)
ENGLAND 441 (Strauss 112, Trescothick 86, Flintoff 63,
G. Jones 46) and 282–3 (Hussain 103*, Strauss 83,
Thorpe 51*)
England won by 7 wickets

822. England v New Zealand
Second Test at Headingley – 3, 4, 5, 6, 7 June 2004
NEW ZEALAND 409 (Fleming 97, Papps 86, McCullum 54,
Cairns 41, Harmison 4–74) and 161 (Richardson 40,
Hoggard 4–75)
ENGLAND 526 (Trescothick 132, Jones 100, Flintoff 94,
Strauss 62) and 45–1
England won by 9 wickets

823. England v New Zealand
Third Test at Trent Bridge – 10, 11, 12, 13 June 2004
NEW ZEALAND 384 (Fleming 117, Styris 108, Richardson
73) and 218 (Richardson 49, Fleming 45, Giles 4–46)
ENGLAND 319 (Trescothick 63, Vaughan 61, Flintoff 54,
Giles 45*, Thorpe 45, Cairns 5–79, Franklin 4–104) and
284–6 (Thorpe 104*, Butcher 59, Cairns 4–108)
England won by 4 wickets

824. England v West Indies
First Test at Lord's – 22, 23, 24, 25, 26 July 2004
ENGLAND 568 (Key 221, Strauss 137, Vaughan 103, Collins
4–113) and 325–5 dec. (Vaughan 101*, Flintoff 58,
Trescothick 45)
WEST INDIES 416 (Chanderpaul 128*, Gayle 66, Banks 45,
Smith 45, Bravo 44, Giles 4–129) and 267 (Chanderpaul
97*, Gayle 81, Lara 44, Giles 5–81)
England won by 210 runs

825. England v West Indies
Second Test at Edgbaston – 29, 30, 31 July, 1 August 2004
ENGLAND 566 (Flintoff 167, Trescothick 105, G. Jones 74,
Thorpe 61, Bravo 4–76) and 248 (Trescothick 107,
Thorpe 54, Gayle 5–34, Lawson 4–94)
WEST INDIES 336 (Sarwan 139, Lara 95, Chanderpaul 45,
Giles 4–65) and 222 (Gayle 82, Chanderpaul 43, Giles
5–57)
England won by 256 runs

826. England v West Indies
Third Test at Old Trafford – 12, 13 (no play), 14, 15, 16
August 2004
WEST INDIES 395 (Bravo 77, Chanderpaul 76, Baugh 68,
Joseph 45, Sarwan 40, Hoggard 4–83) and 165 (Sarwan
60, Gayle 82, Harmison 4–44)
ENGLAND 330 (Thorpe 114, Strauss 90, Bravo 6–55) and
231–3 (Key 93*, Flintoff 57*)
England won by 7 wickets

827. England v West Indies
Fourth Test at The Oval – 19, 20, 21 August 2004
ENGLAND 470 (Flintoff 72, Bell 70, Vaughan 66, Giles 52)
and 4–0
WEST INDIES 152 (Lara 79, Harmison 6–46) and 318
(Gayle 105, Bravo 54, Anderson 4–52)
England won by 10 wickets

828. South Africa v England
First Test at Port Elizabeth – 17, 18, 19, 20, 21 December
2004
SOUTH AFRICA 337 (Dippenaar 110, Rudolph 93) and 229
(Kallis 61, Smith 55, S. Jones 4–39)
ENGLAND 425 (Strauss 126, Butcher 79, Trescothick 47)
and 145–3 (Strauss 94*)
England won by 7 wickets

829. South Africa v England
Second Test at Durban – 26, 27, 28, 29, 30 December 2004
ENGLAND 139 (Pollock 4–32) and 570–7 dec. (Strauss 136,
Trescothick 132, Thorpe 118*, G. Jones 73, Flintoff 60)
SOUTH AFRICA 332 (Kallis 162, Pollock 43) and 290–8
(Rudolph 61, de Villiers 52*, van Jaarsveld 49)
Match drawn

830. South Africa v England
Third Test at Cape Town – 2, 3, 4, 5, 6 January 2005
SOUTH AFRICA 441 (Kallis 149, Boje 76, Smith 74, Flintoff
4–79) and 222–8 dec. (Kallis 66, Dippenaar 44)
ENGLAND 163 (Strauss 45, Langeveldt 5–46, Ntini 4–50)
and 304 (Key 41, Pollock 4–65, Boje 4–71)
South Africa won by 196 runs

831. South Africa v England
Fourth Test at Johannesburg – 13, 14, 15, 16, 17 January
2005
ENGLAND 411–8 dec. (Strauss 147, Key 83, Vaughan 82, Ntini
4–111) and 332–9 dec. (Trescothick 180, Vaughan 54)
SOUTH AFRICA 419 (Gibbs 161, Boucher 64, Boje 48,
Hoggard 5–144) and 247 (Gibbs 98, Smith 67*,
Hoggard 7–61)
England won by 77 runs

832. South Africa v England
Fifth Test at Centurion – 21 (no play), 22, 23, 24, 25
January 2005
SOUTH AFRICA 247 (de Villiers 92, Flintoff 4–44, S. Jones
4–47) and 296–6 dec. (Kallis 136*, de Villiers 109)
ENGLAND 359 (Thorpe 86, Flintoff 77, G. Jones 50, Strauss
44, Nel 6–81) and 73–4 (Ntini 3–12)
Match drawn

833. England v Bangladesh
First Test at Lord's – 26, 27, 28 May 2005
BANGLADESH 108 (Hoggard 4–42) and 159 (Khaled
Mashud 44)
ENGLAND 528–3 dec. (Trescothick 194, Vaughan 120,
Strauss 69, Bell 65*, Thorpe 42*)
England won by an innings and 261 runs

834. England v Bangladesh
Second Test at Chester-le-Street – 3, 4, 5 June 2005
BANGLADESH 104 (Harmison 5–38) and 316 (Aftab Ahmed
82*, Javed Omar 71, Habibul Bashar 63, Hoggard 5–73)
ENGLAND 447–3 dec. (Bell 162*, Trescothick 151, Thorpe
66*, Vaughan 44)
England won by an innings and 27 runs

835. England v Australia
First Test at Lord's – 21, 22, 23, 24 July 2005
AUSTRALIA 190 (Langer 40, Harmison 5–43) and 384
(Clarke 91, Katich 67, Martyn 65, Ponting 42)
ENGLAND 155 (Pietersen 57, McGrath 5–53) and 180
(Pietersen 64*, Trescothick 44, McGrath 4–29, Warne
4–64)
Australia won by 239 runs

836. England v Australia
Second Test at Edgbaston – 4, 5, 6, 7 August 2005
ENGLAND 407 (Trescothick 90, Pietersen 71, Flintoff 68,
Strauss 48, Warne 4–116) and 182 (Flintoff 73, Warne
6–46, Lee 4–82)
AUSTRALIA 308 (Langer 82, Ponting 61, Gilchrist 49*,
Clarke 40) and 279 (Lee 43*, Warne 42, Flintoff 4–79)
England won by 2 runs

837. England v Australia
Third Test at Old Trafford – 11, 12, 13, 14, 15 August
2005
ENGLAND 444 (Vaughan 166, Trescothick 63, Bell 59,
Flintoff 46, G. Jones 42, Warne 4–99, Lee 4–100) and
280–6 dec. (Strauss 106, Bell 65, Trescothick 41,
McGrath 5–115)
AUSTRALIA 302 (Warne 90, S. Jones 6–53) and 371–9
(Ponting 156, Flintoff 4–71)
Match drawn

838. England v Australia
Fourth Test at Trent Bridge – 25, 26, 27, 28 August 2005
ENGLAND 477 (Flintoff 102, G. Jones 85, Trescothick 65,
Vaughan 58, Pietersen 45, Warne 4–102) and 129–7
(Warne 4–31)
AUSTRALIA 218 (Lee 47, Katich 45, S. Jones 5–44) and 387
(Langer 61, Katich 59, Clarke 56, Ponting 48, Warne 45)
England won by 3 wickets

839. England v Australia
Fifth Test at The Oval – 8, 9, 10, 11, 12 September 2005
ENGLAND 373 (Strauss 129, Flintoff 72, Trescothick 43,
Warne 6–122) and 335 (Pietersen 158, Giles 59,
Vaughan 45, Warne 6–124)
AUSTRALIA 367 (Hayden 138, Langer 105, Flintoff 5–78,
Hoggard 4–97) and 4–0
Match drawn

840. Pakistan v England
First Test at Multan – 12, 13, 14, 15, 16 November 2005
PAKISTAN 274 (Salman Butt 74, Inzamam-ul-Haq 53,
Flintoff 4–68) and 341 (Salman Butt 122, Inzamam-ul-
Haq 72, Younis Khan 48, Flintoff 4–88)
ENGLAND 418 (Trescothick 193, Bell 71, Flintoff 45,
Shabbir Ahmed 4–54) and 175 (Danish Kaneria 4–62)
Pakistan won by 22 runs

841. Pakistan v England
Second Test at Faisalabad – 20, 21, 22, 23, 24 November
2005
PAKISTAN 462 (Inzamam-ul-Haq 109, Shahid Afridi 92,
Mohammad Yousuf 78, Kamran Akmal 41) and 268–9
dec. (Inzamam-ul-Haq 100*, Salman Butt 50)
ENGLAND 446 (Bell 115, Pietersen 100, G. Jones 55,
Trescothick 48, Shahid Afridi 4–95) and 164–6 (Flintoff
56, Pietersen 42)
Match drawn

842. Pakistan v England

Third Test at Lahore – 29, 30 November, 1, 2, 3 December 2005
ENGLAND 288 (Collingwood 96, Vaughan 58, Trescothick 50) and 248 (Bell 92, Collingwood 80, Shoaib Akhtar 5–71, Danish Kaneria 4–52)
PAKISTAN 636–8 dec. (Mohammad Yousuf 223, Kamran Akmal 154, Inzamam-ul-Haq 97, Naved-ul-Hasan 42*)
Pakistan won by an innings and 100 runs

843. India v England

First Test at Nagpur – 1, 2, 3, 4, 5 March 2006
ENGLAND 393 (Collingwood 134*, Cook 60, Flintoff 43, Sreesanth 4–95) and 297–3 dec. (Cook 104*, Pietersen 87, Strauss 46)
INDIA 323 (Kaif 91, Jaffer 81, Kumble 58, Dravid 40, Hoggard 6–57) and 260–6 (Jaffer 100, Dravid 71)
Match drawn

844. India v England

Second Test at Chandigarh – 9, 10, 11, 12, 13 March 2006
ENGLAND 300 (Flintoff 70, Pietersen 64, G. Jones 52, Kumble 5–76) and 181 (Bell 57, Flintoff 51, Patel 4–25, Kumble 4–70)
INDIA 338 (Dravid 95, Pathan 52, Flintoff 4–96) and 144–1 (Sehwag 76*, Dravid 42*)
India won by 9 wickets

845. India v England

Third Test at Mumbai – 18, 19, 20, 21, 22 March 2006
ENGLAND 400 (Strauss 128, Shah 88, Flintoff 50, Sreesanth 4–70) and 191 (Flintoff 50, Kumble 4–49)
INDIA 279 (Dhoni 64, Dravid 52, Anderson 4–40) and 100 (Udal 4–14)
England won by 212 runs

846. England v Sri Lanka

First Test at Lord's – 11, 12, 13, 14, 15 May 2006
ENGLAND 551–6 dec. (Pietersen 158, Trescothick 106, Cook 89, Collingwood 57, Strauss 48)
SRI LANKA 192 (Jayawardene 61, Hoggard 4–27) and 537–9 (Jayawardene 119, Dilshan 69, Sangakkara 65, Kulasekara 64, Maharoof 59, Tharanga 52, Vaas 50*)
Match drawn

847. England v Sri Lanka

Second Test at Edgbaston – 25, 26, 27, 28 May 2006
SRI LANKA 141 and 231 (Vandort 105, Dilshan 59, Plunkett 3–17)

ENGLAND 295 (Pietersen 142, Muralitharan 6–86) and 81–4 (Muralitharan 4–29)
England won by 6 wickets

848. England v Sri Lanka

Third Test at Trent Bridge – 2, 3, 4, 5 June 2006
SRI LANKA 231 and 322 (Sangakkara 66, Kapugedera 50, Tharanga 46, Jayawardene 45, Panesar 5–78)
ENGLAND 229 (Collingwood 48, Pietersen 41) and 190 (Strauss 55, Muralitharan 8–70)
Sri Lanka won by 134 runs

849. England v Pakistan

First Test at Lord's – 13, 14, 15, 16, 17 July 2006
ENGLAND 528–9 dec. (Collingwood 186, Cook 105, Bell 100*) and 296–8 dec. (Strauss 128, Pietersen 41)
PAKISTAN 445 (Mohammad Yousuf 202, Inzamam-ul-Haq 69, Kamran Akmal 50, Harmison 4–94) and 214–4 (Inzamam-ul-Haq 56*, Faisal Iqbal 48, Mohammad Yousuf 48)
Match drawn

850. England v Pakistan

Second Test at Old Trafford – 27, 28, 29 July 2006
PAKISTAN 119 (Younis Khan 44, Harmison 6–19) and 222 (Younis Khan 62, Harmison 5–57, Panesar 5–72)
ENGLAND 461–9 dec. (Cook 127, Bell 106*, Collingwood 48, Strauss 42)
England won by an innings and 120 runs

851. England v Pakistan

Third Test at Headingley – 4, 5, 6, 7, 8 August 2006
ENGLAND 515 (Pietersen 135, Bell 119, Umar Gul 5–123) and 345 (Strauss 116, Trescothick 58, Read 55)
PAKISTAN 538 (Mohammad Yousuf 192, Younis Khan 173) and 155 (Younis Khan 41, Mahmood 4–22)
England won by 167 runs

852. England v Pakistan

Fourth Test at The Oval – 17, 18, 19, 20 August 2006
ENGLAND 173 (Cook 40, Umar Gul 4–46, Mohammad Asif 4–56) and 298–4 (Pietersen 96, Cook 83, Strauss 54)
PAKISTAN 504 (Mohammad Yousuf 128, Mohammad Hafeez 95, Imran Farhat 91, Faisal Iqbal 58*, Harmison 4–125)
England awarded a win after opposition refused to play

2 ENGLAND'S TEST PLAYERS

Inns	number of Test innings
NOs	number of times Not Out
HSc	high score
Runs	number of batting runs
Average	average number of runs per innings
100s	number of Test hundreds
Runs	number of runs conceded off bowling
Wkts	number of wickets taken
Average	average number of runs per wicket
Best	best bowling figures

1.   ARMITAGE Thomas
Born   Sheffield, Yorkshire, 25 April 1848
Died   Chicago, Illinois, USA, 21 September 1922
Career Yorkshire, 1872–9
Tests 2
Debut v Australia, Melbourne, March 1877

Inns	NOs	HSc	Runs	Average	100s
3	0	21	33	11.00	–

Runs	Wkts	Average	Best
15	0	–	–

2.   CHARLWOOD Henry Rupert James
Born   Horsham, Sussex, 19 December 1846
Died   Scarborough, Yorkshire, 6 June 1888
Career Sussex, 1865–82
Tests 2
Debut v Australia, Melbourne, March 1877

Inns	NOs	HSc	Runs	Average	100s
4	0	36	63	15.75	–

Runs	Wkts	Average	Best
–	–	–	–

3.   EMMETT Thomas
Born   Halifax, Yorkshire, 3 September 1841
Died   Leicester, 30 June 1904
Career Yorkshire, 1866–88
Tests 7
Debut v Australia, Melbourne, March 1877

Inn	NOs	HSc	Runs	Average	100s
13	1	48	160	13.33	–

Runs	Wkts	Average	Best
284	9	31.55	7–68

4.   GREENWOOD Andrew
Born   Huddersfield, Yorkshire, 20 August 1847
Died   Huddersfield, Yorkshire, 12 February 1889
Career Yorkshire, 1869–80
Tests 2
Debut v Australia, Melbourne, March 1877

Inn	NOs	HSc	Runs	Average	100s
4	0	49	77	19.25	–

Runs	Wkts	Average	Best
–	–	–	–

5.   HILL Allen
Born   Kirkheaton, Yorkshire, 14 November 1843
Died   Leyland, Lancashire, 29 August 1910
Career Yorkshire, 1871–82
Tests 2
Debut v Australia, Melbourne, March 1877

Inn	NOs	HSc	Runs	Average	100s
4	2	49	101	50.50	–

Runs	Wkts	Average	Best
130	7	18.57	4–27

6.   JUPP Henry
Born   Dorking, Surrey, 19 November 1841
Died   Bermondsey, London, 8 April 1889
Career Surrey, 1862–81
Tests 2
Debut v Australia, Melbourne, March 1877

Inns	NOs	HSc	Runs	Average	100s
4	0	63	68	17.00	–

Runs	Wkts	Average	Best
–	–	–	–

7.   LILLYWHITE James Jnr
Born   Westhampnett, Sussex, 23 February 1842
Died   Westerton, Sussex, 25 October 1929
Career Sussex, 1862–83
Tests 2
Debut v Australia, Melbourne, March 1877

Inns	NOs	HSc	Runs	Average	100s
3	1	10	16	8.00	–

Runs	Wkts	Average	Best
126	8	15.75	4–70

8.   SELBY John
Born   Nottingham, 1 July 1849
Died   Nottingham, 11 March 1894
Career Nottinghamshire, 1870–87
Tests 6
Debut v Australia, Melbourne, March 1877

Inns	NOs	HSc	Runs	Average	100s
12	1	70	256	23.27	–

Runs	Wkts	Average	Best
–	–	–	–

9.   SHAW Alfred
Born   Burton Joyce, Nottinghamshire, 29 August 1842
Died   Gedling, Nottinghamshire, 16 January 1907
Career Nottinghamshire, 1864–97; Sussex, 1894–5
Tests 7
Debut v Australia, Melbourne, March 1877

Inns	NOs	HSc	Runs	Average	100s
12	1	40	111	10.09	–

Runs	Wkts	Average	Best
285	12	23.75	5–38

10.   SOUTHERTON James
Born   Petworth, Sussex, 16 November 1827
Died   Mitcham, Surrey, 16 June 1880
Career Surrey, 1854–79; Sussex, 1858–72; Hampshire, 1861–7
Tests 2
Debut v Australia, Melbourne, March 1877

Inns	NOs	HSc	Runs	Average	100s
3	1	6	7	3.50	

Runs	Wkts	Average	Best
107	7	15.28	4–46

DID YOU KNOW...?

James Southerton was forty-nine when he played for England against Australia at Melbourne during the 1876–7 tour – the oldest Test debutant.

11.   ULYETT George
Born   Pitsmoor, Sheffield, Yorkshire, 21 October 1851
Died   Pitsmoor, Sheffield, Yorkshire, 18 June 1898
Career Yorkshire, 1873–93
Tests 25
Debut v Australia, Melbourne, March 1877

Inns	NOs	HSc	Runs	Average	100s
39	0	149	949	24.33	1

Runs	Wkts	Average	Best
1020	50	20.40	7–36

12.   ABSOLOM Charles Alfred
Born   Blackheath, Kent, 7 June 1846
Died   Port-of-Spain, Trinidad, 30 July 1889
Career Cambridge University, 1866–9; Kent 1868–79
Tests 1
Debut v Australia, Melbourne, January 1879

Inns	NOs	HSc	Runs	Average	100s
2	0	52	58	29.00	–

Runs	Wkts	Average	Best
–	–	–	–

13.   HARRIS 4th Lord GCSI, GCIE, CB
Born   St Anne's, Trinidad, 3 February 1851
Died   Faversham, Kent, 24 March 1932
Career Kent, 1870–1911; Oxford University, 1871–4
Tests 4
Debut v Australia, Melbourne, January 1879

Inns	NOs	HSc	Runs	Average	100s
6	1	52	145	29.00	–

Runs	Wkts	Average	Best
29	0	–	–

14.   HONE Leland
Born   Dublin, Ireland, 30 January 1853
Died   Dublin, Ireland, 31 December 1896
Career MCC, 1878–80
Tests 1
Debut v Australia, Melbourne, January 1879

Inns	NOs	HSc	Runs	Average	100s
2	0	7	13	6.50	

Runs	Wkts	Average	Best
–	–	–	–

15.   HORNBY Albert Neilson
Born   Blackburn, Lancashire, 10 February 1847
Died   Nantwich, Cheshire, 17 December 1925
Career Lancashire, 1867–99
Tests 3
Debut v Australia, Melbourne, January 1879

Inns	NOs	HSc	Runs	Average	100s
6	0	9	21	3.50	–

Runs	Wkts	Average	Best
0	1	0.00	1–0

16.   LUCAS Alfred Perry
Born   Westminster, London, 20 February 1857
Died   Great Waltham, Essex, 12 October 1923
Career Surrey, 1874–82; Cambridge University, 1875–8; Middlesex, 1883–8; Essex, 1894–1907
Tests 5
Debut v Australia, Melbourne, January 1879

Inns	NOs	HSc	Runs	Average	100s
9	1	55	157	19.62	–

Runs	Wkts	Average	Best
54	0	–	–

17.   MacKINNON Francis Alexander
Born   Kensington, London, 9 April 1848
Died   Forres, Morayshire, Scotland, 27 February 1947
Career Cambridge University, 1870; Kent, 1875–85
Tests 1
Debut v Australia, Melbourne, January 1879

Inns	NOs	HSc	Runs	Average	100s
2	0	5	5	2.50	–

Runs	Wkts	Average	Best
–	–	–	–

18.   ROYLE Rev Vernon Peter Fanshawe Archer
Born   Brooklands, Cheshire, 29 January 1854
Died   Stanmore Park, Middlesex, 21 May 1929
Career Lancashire, 1873–91; Oxford University, 1875–6
Tests 1
Debut v Australia, Melbourne, January 1879

Inns	NOs	HSc	Runs	Average	100s
2	0	18	21	10.50	–

Runs	Wkts	Average	Best
6	0	–	–

19.   SCHULTZ Sandford Spence
Born   Birkenhead, Cheshire, 29 August 1857
Died   Kensington, London, 18 December 1937
Career Cambridge University, 1876–7; Lancashire, 1877–82
Tests 1
Debut v Australia, Melbourne, January 1879

Inns	NOs	HSc	Runs	Average	100s
2	1	20	20	20.00	–

Runs	Wkts	Average	Best
26	1	26.00	1–16

20.   WEBBE Alexander Josiah
Born   Bethnal Green, London, 16 January 1855
Died   Abinger Hammer, Surrey, 19 February 1941
Career Oxford University, 1875–8; Middlesex, 1875–1900
Tests 1
Debut v Australia, Melbourne, January 1879

Inns	NOs	HSc	Runs	Average	100s
2	0	4	4	2.00	

Runs	Wkts	Average	Best
–	–	–	–

21.   BARNES William
Born Sutton-in-Ashfield, Nottinghamshire, 27 May 1852
Died Mansfield Woodhouse, Nottinghamshire, 24 March
1899
Career Nottinghamshire, 1875–94
Tests 21
Debut v Australia, The Oval, September 1880

Inns	NOs	HSc	Runs	Average	100s
33	2	134	725	23.38	1

Runs	Wkts	Average	Best
793	51	15.54	6–28

22.   GRACE Edward Mills
Born Downend, Bristol, 28 November 1841
Died Thornbury, Gloucestershire, 20 May 1911
Career Gloucestershire, 1870–95
Tests 1
Debut v Australia, The Oval, September 1880

Inns	NOs	HSc	Runs	Average	100s
2	0	36	36	18.00	–

Runs	Wkts	Average	Best
–	–	–	–

23.   GRACE George Frederick
Born Downend, Bristol, 13 December 1850
Died Basingstoke, Hampshire, 22 September 1880
Career Gloucestershire, 1870–80
Tests 1
Debut v Australia, The Oval, September 1880

Inns	NOs	HSc	Runs	Average	100s
2	0	0	0	0.00	–

Runs	Wkts	Average	Best
–	–	–	–

24   GRACE William Gilbert
Born Downend, Bristol, 18 July 1848
Died Mottingham, Kent, 23 October 1915
Career Gloucestershire, 1870–99; London County, 1900–4
Tests 22
Debut v Australia, The Oval, September 1880

Inns	NOs	HSc	Runs	Average	100s
36	2	170	1098	32.29	2

Runs	Wkts	Average	Best
236	9	26.22	2–12

25.   LYTTELTON Rt Hon. Alfred KC
Born Westminster, London, 7 February 1857
Died Marylebone, London, 5 July 1913
Career Cambridge University, 1876–9; Middlesex 1877–87
Tests 4
Debut v Australia, The Oval, September 1880

Inns	NOs	HSc	Runs	Average	100s
7	1	31	94	15.66	–

Runs	Wkts	Average	Best
19	4	4.75	4–19

26.   MORLEY Frederick
Born Sutton-in-Ashfield, Nottinghamshire, 16 December
1850
Died Sutton-in-Ashfield, Nottinghamshire, 28 September
1884
Career Nottinghamshire, 1872–83
Tests 4
Debut v Australia, The Oval, September 1880

Inns	NOs	HSc	Runs	Average	100s
6	2	2*	6	1.50	–

Runs	Wkts	Average	Best
296	16	18.50	5–56

27.   PENN Frank
Born Lee, Lewisham, London, 7 March 1851
Died Patrixbourne, Kent, 26 December 1916
Career Kent, 1875–81
Tests 1
Debut v Australia, The Oval, September 1880

Inns	NOs	HSc	Runs	Average	100s
2	1	27*	50	50.00	–

Runs	Wkts	Average	Best
2	0	–	–

28.   STEEL Allan Gibson
Born West Derby, Liverpool, 24 September 1858
Died Hyde Park, London, 15 June 1914
Career Lancashire, 1877–93; Cambridge University,
1878–81
Tests 13
Debut v Australia, The Oval, September 1880

Inns	NOs	HSc	Runs	Average	100s
20	3	148	600	35.29	2

Runs	Wkts	Average	Best
605	29	20.86	3–27

29.   BARLOW Richard Gorton
Born Barrow Bridge, Bolton, Lancashire, 28 May 1851
Died Stanley Park, Blackpool, Lancashire, 31 July 1919
Career Lancashire, 1871–91
Tests 17
Debut v Australia, Melbourne, Dec 1881–Jan 1882

Inns	NOs	HSc	Runs	Average	100s
30	4	62	591	22.73	–

Runs	Wkts	Average	Best
767	34	22.55	7–40

30.   BATES Willie
Born Huddersfield, Yorkshire, 19 November 1855
Died Lepton, Yorkshire, 8 January 1900
Career Yorkshire, 1877–87
Tests 15
Debut v Australia, Melbourne, Dec 1881–Jan 1882

Inns	NOs	HSc	Runs	Average	100s
26	2	64	656	27.33	–

Runs	Wkts	Average	Best
821	50	16.42	7–28

31.   MIDWINTER William Evans
Born St Briavels, Gloucestershire, 19 June 1851
Died Kew, Melbourne, Australia, 3 December 1890
Career Victoria, 1874–5; Gloucestershire, 1877–82;
Australia, 1876–7 to 1886–7
Tests 4
Debut v Australia, Melbourne, Dec 1881–Jan 1882

Inns	NOs	HSc	Runs	Average	100s
7	0	36	95	13.57	–

Runs	Wkts	Average	Best
272	10	27.20	4–81

32.   PEATE Edmund
Born Holbeck, Leeds, Yorkshire, 2 March 1855
Died Newlay, Horsforth, Yorkshire, 11 March 1900
Career Yorkshire, 1879–87
Tests 9
Debut v Australia, Melbourne, Dec 1881–Jan 1882

Inns	NOs	HSc	Runs	Average	100s
14	8	13	70	11.66	–

Runs	Wkts	Average	Best
683	31	22.03	6–85

33.   PILLING Richard

Born   Old Warden, Bedfordshire, 5 July 1855
Died   Old Trafford, Manchester, 28 March 1891
Career Lancashire, 1877–89
Tests   8
Debut v Australia, Melbourne, Dec 1881–Jan 1882

Inns	NOs	HSc	Runs	Average	100s
13	1	23	91	7.58	–

Runs	Wkts	Average	Best
–	–	–	–

34.   SCOTTON William Henry

Born   Nottingham, 15 January 1856
Died   St John's Wood, London, 9 July 1893
Career Nottinghamshire, 1875–90
Tests   15
Debut v Australia, Melbourne, Dec 1881–Jan 1882

Inns	NOs	HSc	Runs	Average	100s
25	2	90	510	22.17	–

Runs	Wkts	Average	Best
20	0	–	–

35.   SHREWSBURY Arthur

Born   New Lenton, Nottinghamshire, 11 April 1856
Died   Gedling, Nottinghamshire, 19 May 1903
Career Nottinghamshire, 1875–1902
Tests   23
Debut v Australia, Melbourne, Dec 1881–Jan 1882

Inns	NOs	HSc	Runs	Average	100s
40	4	164	1277	35.47	3

Runs	Wkts	Average	Best
2	0	–	–

36.   READ John Maurice

Born   Thames Ditton, Surrey, 9 February 1859
Died   Winchester, Hampshire, 17 February 1929
Career Surrey, 1880–95
Tests   17
Debut v Australia, The Oval, August 1882

Inns	NOs	HSc	Runs	Average	100s
29	2	57	461	17.07	–

Runs	Wkts	Average	Best
–	–	–	–

37.   STUDD Charles Thomas

Born   Spratton, Northamptonshire, 2 December 1860
Died   Ibambi, Belgian Congo, 16 July 1931
Career Middlesex, 1879–84; Cambridge University, 1880–3
Tests   5
Debut v Australia, The Oval, August 1882

Inns	NOs	HSc	Runs	Average	100s
9	1	48	160	20.00	–

Runs	Wkts	Average	Best
98	3	32.66	2–35

38.   BLIGH Hon. Ivo Francis Walter

Born   Westminster, London, 13 March 1859
Died   Shorne, Kent, 10 April 1927
Career Kent, 1877–83; Cambridge University, 1878–81
Tests   4
Debut v Australia, Melbourne, Dec 1882–Jan 1883

Inns	NOs	HSc	Runs	Average	100s
7	1	19	62	10.33	–

Runs	Wkts	Average	Best
–	–	–	–

39.   LESLIE Charles Frederick Henry

Born   Westminster, London, 8 December 1861
Died   Westminster, London, 12 February 1921
Career Oxford University, 1881–3; Middlesex, 1881–6
Tests   4
Debut v Australia, Melbourne, Dec 1882–Jan 1883

Inns	NOs	HSc	Runs	Average	100s
7	0	54	106	15.14	–

Runs	Wkts	Average	Best
44	4	11.00	3–31

40.   READ Walter William

Born   Reigate, Surrey, 23 November 1855
Died   Addiscombe Park, Surrey, 6 January 1907
Career Surrey, 1873–97
Tests   18
Debut v Australia, Melbourne, Dec 1882–Jan 1883

Inns	NOs	HSc	Runs	Average	100s
27	1	117	720	27.69	1

Runs	Wkts	Average	Best
63	0	–	–

41.   STUDD George Brown

Born   Netheravon, Wiltshire, 20 October 1859
Died   Pasadena, California, USA, 13 February 1945
Career Cambridge University, 1879–82; Middlesex, 1879–86
Tests   4
Debut v Australia, Melbourne, Dec 1882–Jan 1883

Inns	NOs	HSc	Runs	Average	100s
7	0	9	31	4.42	–

Runs	Wkts	Average	Best
–	–	–	–

42.   TYLECOTE Edward Ferdinando Sutton

Born   Marston Moretaine, Bedfordshire, 23 June 1849
Died   New Hunstanton, Norfolk, 15 March 1938
Career Oxford University, 1869–72; Kent, 1875–83
Tests   6
Debut v Australia, Melbourne, Dec 1882–Jan 1883

Inns	NOs	HSc	Runs	Average	100s
9	1	66	152	19.00	–

Runs	Wkts	Average	Best
–	–	–	–

43.   VERNON George Frederick

Born   Marylebone, London, 20 June 1856
Died   Elmina, Gold Coast (now Ghana), 10 August 1902
Career Middlesex, 1878–95
Tests   1
Debut v Australia, Melbourne, Dec 1882–Jan 1883

Inns	NOs	HSc	Runs	Average	100s
2	1	11*	14	14.00	–

Runs	Wkts	Average	Best
–	–	–	–

44.   O'BRIEN Sir Timothy Carew (3rd Baronet)

Born   Dublin, Ireland, 5 November 1861
Died   Ramsey, Isle of Man, 9 December 1948
Career Middlesex, 1881–98; Oxford University, 1884–5; Ireland 1902–7
Tests   5
Debut v Australia, Old Trafford, July 1884

Inns	NOs	HSc	Runs	Average	100s
8	0	20	59	7.37	–

Runs	Wkts	Average	Best
–	–	–	–

45. CHRISTOPHERSON Stanley
Born Kidbrooke, Kent, 11 November 1861
Died St John's Wood, London, 6 April 1949
Career Kent, 1883–90
Tests 1
Debut v Australia, Lord's, July 1884

Inns	NOs	HSc	Runs	Average	100s
1	0	17	17	17.00	–

Runs	Wkts	Average	Best
69	1	69.00	1–52

46. ATTEWELL William
Born Keyworth, Nottinghamshire, 12 June 1861
Died Long Eaton, Derbyshire, 11 June 1927
Career Nottinghamshire, 1881–99
Tests 10
Debut v Australia, Adelaide, December 1884

Inns	NOs	HSc	Runs	Average	100s
15	6	43*	150	16.66	–

Runs	Wkts	Average	Best
626	28	22.35	4–42

47. BRIGGS John
Born Sutton-in-Ashfield, Nottinghamshire, 3 October
1862
Died Cheadle, Cheshire, 11 January 1902
Career Lancashire, 1879–1900
Tests 33
Debut v Australia, Adelaide, December 1884

Inns	NOs	HSc	Runs	Average	100s
50	5	121	815	18.11	1

Runs	Wkts	Average	Best
2095	118	17.75	8–11

48. FLOWERS Wilfred
Born Calverton, Nottinghamshire, 7 December 1856
Died Carlton, Nottinghamshire, 1 November 1926
Career Nottinghamshire, 1877–96
Tests 8
Debut v Australia, Adelaide, December 1884

Inns	NOs	HSc	Runs	Average	100s
14	0	56	254	18.14	–

Runs	Wkts	Average	Best
296	14	21.14	5–46

49. HUNTER Joseph
Born Scarborough, Yorkshire, 3 August 1855
Died Rotherham, Yorkshire, 4 January 1891
Career Yorkshire, 1878–88
Tests 5
Debut v Australia, Adelaide, December 1884

Inns	NOs	HSc	Runs	Average	100s
7	2	39*	93	18.60	–

Runs	Wkts	Average	Best
–	–	–	–

50. PEEL Robert
Born Churwell, Leeds, Yorkshire, 12 February 1857
Died Morley, Leeds, Yorkshire, 12 August 1941
Career Yorkshire, 1882–97
Tests 20
Debut v Australia, Adelaide, December 1884

Inns	NOs	HSc	Runs	Average	100s
33	4	83	427	14.72	–

Runs	Wkts	Average	Best
1715	101	16.98	7–31

51. LOHMANN George Alfred
Born Kensington, London, 2 June 1865
Died Cape Province, South Africa, 1 December 1901
Career Surrey, 1884–96; Western Province, 1894–5 to
1896–7
Tests 18
Debut v Australia, Old Trafford, July 1886

Inns	NOs	HSc	Runs	Average	100s
26	2	62*	213	8.87	–

Runs	Wkts	Average	Best
1205	112	10.75	9–28

DID YOU KNOW...?

George Lohmann set world-record bowling figures
in consecutive Tests against South Africa in 1897
with figures of 8–7 and 9–28.

52. GUNN William
Born St Anne's, Nottingham, 4 December 1858
Died Standard Hill, Nottingham, 29 January 1921
Career Nottinghamshire, 1880–1904
Tests 11
Debut v Australia, Sydney, January 1887

Inns	NOs	HSc	Runs	Average	100s
20	2	102*	392	21.77	1

Runs	Wkts	Average	Best
–	–	–	–

53. SHERWIN Mordecai
Born Kimberley, Nottinghamshire, 26 February 1851
Died Nottingham, 3 July 1910
Career Nottinghamshire, 1876–96
Tests 3
Debut v Australia, Sydney, January 1887

Inns	NOs	HSc	Runs	Average	100s
6	4	21*	30	15.00	–

Runs	Wkts	Average	Best
–	–	–	–

54. WOOD Reginald
Born Woodchurch, Cheshire, 7 March 1860
Died Sydney, NSW, Australia, 6 January 1915
Career Lancashire, 1880–4; Victoria, 1886–7
Tests 1
Debut v Australia, Sydney, Feb–March 1887

Inns	NOs	HSc	Runs	Average	100s
2	0	6	6	3.00	–

Runs	Wkts	Average	Best
–	–	–	–

55. NEWHAM William
Born Shrewsbury, Shropshire, 12 December 1860
Died Brighton, Sussex, 26 June 1944
Career Sussex, 1881–1905
Tests 1
Debut v Australia, Sydney, February 1888

Inns	NOs	HSc	Runs	Average	100s
2	0	17	26	13.00	–

Runs	Wkts	Average	Best
–	–	–	–

DID YOU KNOW...?

Andrew Stoddart was a natural all-rounder. He captained England at cricket and rugby, was a good boxer and scratch golfer, and played real tennis, hockey and billiards extremely well.

---

56. STODDART Andrew Ernest
Born Westoe, South Shields, 11 March 1863
Died St John's Wood, London, 4 April 1915
Career Middlesex, 1885–1900
Tests 16
Debut v Australia, Sydney, February 1888

Inns	NOs	HSc	Runs	Average	100s
30	2	173	996	35.57	2

Runs	Wkts	Average	Best
94	2	47.00	1–10

57. ABEL Robert
Born Rotherhithe, London, 30 November 1857
Died Stockwell, London, 10 December 1936
Career Surrey, 1881–1904
Tests 13
Debut v Australia, Lord's, July 1888

Inns	NOs	HSc	Runs	Average	100s
22	2	132*	744	37.20	2

Runs	Wkts	Average	Best
–	–	–	–

58. SHUTER John
Born Thornton Heath, Surrey, 9 February 1855
Died Blackheath, Kent, 5 July 1920
Career Kent, 1874; Surrey, 1877–1909
Tests 1
Debut v Australia, The Oval, August 1888

Inns	NOs	HSc	Runs	Average	100s
1	0	28	28	28.00	–

Runs	Wkts	Average	Best
–	–	–	–

59. SUGG Frank Howe
Born Ilkeston, Derbyshire, 11 January 1862
Died Waterloo, Liverpool, 29 May 1933
Career Yorkshire, 1883; Derbyshire, 1884–6; Lancashire, 1887–99
Tests 2
Debut v Australia, The Oval, August 1888

Inns	NOs	HSc	Runs	Average	100s
2	0	31	55	27.50	–

Runs	Wkts	Average	Best
–	–	–	–

60. WOOD Henry
Born Dartford, Kent, 14 December 1853
Died Waddon, Surrey, 30 April 1919
Career Kent, 1876–82; Surrey, 1884–1900
Tests 4
Debut v Australia, The Oval, August 1888

Inns	NOs	HSc	Runs	Average	100s
4	1	134*	204	68.00	1

Runs	Wkts	Average	Best
–	–	–	–

61. BOWDEN Montague Parker
Born Stockwell, London, 1 November 1865
Died Umtali, Mashonaland, 19 February 1892
Career Surrey, 1883–8; Transvaal, 1889–90
Tests 2
Debut v South Africa, Port Elizabeth, March 1889

Inns	NOs	HSc	Runs	Average	100s
2	0	25	25	12.50	–

Runs	Wkts	Average	Best
–	–	–	–

62. COVENTRY Hon. Charles John
Born Marylebone, London, 26 February 1867
Died Earl's Croome, Worcestershire, 2 June 1929
Career –
Tests 2
Debut v South Africa, Port Elizabeth, March 1889

Inns	NOs	HSc	Runs	Average	100s
2	1	12	13	13.00	–

Runs	Wkts	Average	Best
–	–	–	–

63. FOTHERGILL Arnold James
Born Newcastle-upon-Tyne, 26 August 1854
Died Sunderland, County Durham, 1 August 1932
Career Somerset, 1882–4
Tests 2
Debut v South Africa, Port Elizabeth, March 1889

Inns	NOs	HSc	Runs	Average	100s
2	0	32	33	16.50	–

Runs	Wkts	Average	Best
90	8	11.25	4–19

64. GRIEVE Basil Arthur Firebrace
Born Kilburn, Middlesex, 28 May 1864
Died Eastbourne, Sussex, 19 November 1917
Career –
Tests 2
Debut v South Africa, Port Elizabeth, March 1889

Inns	NOs	HSc	Runs	Average	100s
3	2	14*	40	40.00	–

Runs	Wkts	Average	Best
–	–	–	–

65. HEARNE Frank
Born Ealing, Middlesex, 23 November 1858
Died Cape Town, South Africa, 14 July 1949
Career Kent, 1879–89; Western Province, 1889–90 to 1903–4; South Africa, 1891–2 to 1895–6
Tests 2
Debut v South Africa, Port Elizabeth, March 1889

Inns	NOs	HSc	Runs	Average	100s
2	0	27	47	23.50	–

Runs	Wkts	Average	Best
–	–	–	–

DID YOU KNOW...?

Aubrey Smith, later a Hollywood actor, was the only player to captain England in his one and only Test, which was against South Africa in March 1889.

66.   SMITH Sir Charles Aubrey
Born   City of London, 21 July 1863
Died   Beverley Hills, USA, 20 December 1948
Career Cambridge University, 1882–5; Sussex, 1882–96;
         Transvaal, 1889–90
Tests 1
Debut v South Africa, Port Elizabeth, March 1889

Inns	NOs	HSc	Runs	Average	100s
1	0	3	3	3.00	–

Runs	Wkts	Average	Best
61	7	8.71	5–19

67.   McMASTER Joseph Emile Patrick
Born   Gilford, County Down, N. Ireland, 16 March 1861
Died   Bloomsbury, London, 7 June 1929
Career –
Tests 1
Debut v South Africa, Cape Town, March 1889

Inns	NOs	HSc	Runs	Average	100s
1	0	0	0	0.00	–

Runs	Wkts	Average	Best
–	–	–	–

68.   MacGREGOR Gregor
Born   Merchiston, Edinburgh, 31 August 1869
Died   Marylebone, London, 20 August 1919
Career Cambridge University, 1888–91; Middlesex,
         1892–1907; Scotland, 1905
Tests 8
Debut v Australia, Lord's, July 1890

Inns	NOs	HSc	Runs	Average	100s
11	3	31	96	12.00	–

Runs	Wkts	Average	Best
–	–	–	–

69.   CRANSTON James
Born   Birmingham, 9 January 1859
Died   Bristol, 10 December 1904
Career Gloucestershire, 1876–99
Tests 1
Debut v Australia, The Oval, August 1890

Inns	NOs	HSc	Runs	Average	100s
2	0	16	31	15.50	–

Runs	Wkts	Average	Best
–	–	–	–

70.   MARTIN Frederick
Born   Dartford, Kent, 12 October 1861
Died   Dartford, Kent, 13 December 1921
Career Kent, 1885–99
Tests 2
Debut v Australia, The Oval, August 1890

Inns	NOs	HSc	Runs	Average	100s
2	0	13	14	7.00	–

Runs	Wkts	Average	Best
141	14	10.07	6–50

71.   SHARPE John William
Born   Ruddington, Nottinghamshire, 9 December 1866
Died   Ruddington, Nottinghamshire, 19 June 1936
Career Surrey, 1889–93; Nottinghamshire, 1894
Tests 3
Debut v Australia, The Oval, August 1890

Inns	NOs	HSc	Runs	Average	100s
6	4	26	44	22.00	–

Runs	Wkts	Average	Best
305	11	27.72	6–84

72.   BEAN George
Born   Sutton-in-Ashfield, Nottinghamshire, 7 March 1864
Died   Mansfield, Nottinghamshire, 16 March 1923
Career Nottinghamshire, 1885; Sussex, 1886–98
Tests 3
Debut v Australia, Melbourne, January 1892

Inns	NOs	HSc	Runs	Average	100s
5	0	50	92	18.40	–

Runs	Wkts	Average	Best
–	–	–	–

73.   BARTON Victor Alexander
Born   Hound, Netley, Hampshire, 6 October 1867
Died   Southampton, Hampshire, 23 March 1906
Career Kent, 1889–90; Hampshire, 1895–1902
Tests 1
Debut v South Africa, Cape Town, March 1892

Inns	NOs	HSc	Runs	Average	100s
1	0	23	23	23.00	–

Runs	Wkts	Average	Best
–	–	–	–

74.   CHATTERTON William
Born   Thornsett, Derbyshire, 27 December 1861
Died   Hyde, Cheshire, 19 March 1913
Career Derbyshire, 1882–1902
Tests 1
Debut v South Africa, Cape Town, March 1892

Inns	NOs	HSc	Runs	Average	100s
1	0	48	48	48.00	–

Runs	Wkts	Average	Best
–	–	–	–

 DID YOU KNOW...?

Three brothers called Hearne played in the same Test – South Africa v England at Cape Town in March 1892. G. G. and A. Hearne played for England, and F. Hearne made his debut for South Africa, having previously played twice for England.

75.   FERRIS John James
Born   Sydney, NSW, Australia, 21 May 1867
Died   Durban, South Africa, 17 November 1900
Career NSW, 1886–7 to 1897–8; Gloucestershire, 1892–5;
         South Australia, 1895–6; Australia, 1886–7 to 1890
Tests 1
Debut v South Africa, Cape Town, March 1892

Inns	NOs	HSc	Runs	Average	100s
1	0	16	16	16.00	–

Runs	Wkts	Average	Best
91	13	7.00	7–37

76.   HEARNE Alec
Born   Ealing, Middlesex, 22 July 1863
Died   Beckenham, Kent, 16 May 1952
Career Kent, 1884–1906
Tests 1
Debut v South Africa, Cape Town, March 1892

Inns	NOs	HSc	Runs	Average	100s
1	0	9	9	9.00	–

Runs	Wkts	Average	Best
–	–	–	–

77. HEARNE George Gibbons

Born Ealing, Middlesex, 7 July 1856
Died Denmark Hill, London, 13 February 1932
Career Kent, 1875–95
Tests 1
Debut v South Africa, Cape Town, March 1892

Inns	NOs	HSc	Runs	Average	100s
1	0	0	0	0.00	–

Runs	Wkts	Average	Best
–	–	–	–

78. HEARNE John Thomas

Born Chalfont St Giles, Buckinghamshire, 3 May 1867
Died Chalfont St Giles, Buckinghamshire, 17 April 1944
Career Middlesex, 1888–1923
Tests 12
Debut v South Africa, Cape Town, March 1892

Inns	NOs	HSc	Runs	Average	100s
18	4	40	126	9.00	–

Runs	Wkts	Average	Best
1082	49	22.08	6–41

79. MURDOCH William Lloyd

Born Sandhurst, Victoria, Australia, 18 October 1854
Died Melbourne, Victoria, Australia, 18 February 1911
Career NSW, 1875–6 to 1893–4; Sussex, 1893–9; London
County, 1901–4; Australia, 1876–7 to 1890
Tests 1
Debut v South Africa, Cape Town, March 1892

Inns	NOs	HSc	Runs	Average	100s
1	0	12	12	12.00	–

Runs	Wkts	Average	Best
–	–	–	–

80. POUGHER Arthur Dick

Born Humberstone, Leicester, 19 April 1865
Died Aylestone Park, Leicester, 20 May 1926
Career Leicestershire, 1886–1901
Tests 1
Debut v South Africa, Cape Town, March 1892

Inns	NOs	HSc	Runs	Average	100s
1	0	17	17	17.00	–

Runs	Wkts	Average	Best
26	3	8.66	3–26

81. PHILIPSON Hylton

Born Tynemouth, Northumberland, 8 June 1866
Died Hyde Park, London, 4 December 1935
Career Oxford University, 1887–9; Middlesex, 1895–8
Tests 5
Debut v Australia, Adelaide, March 1892

Inns	NOs	HSc	Runs	Average	100s
8	1	30	63	9.00	–

Runs	Wkts	Average	Best
–	–	–	–

82. JACKSON Rt Hon Sir Francis Stanley PC GCIE

Born Chapel Allerton, Yorkshire, 21 November 1870
Died Knightsbridge, London, 9 March 1947
Career Cambridge University, 1890–3; Yorkshire, 1890–1907
Tests 20
Debut v Australia, Lord's, July 1893

Inns	NOs	HSc	Runs	Average	100s
33	4	144*	1415	48.79	5

Runs	Wkts	Average	Best
799	24	33.29	5–52

83. LOCKWOOD William Henry

Born Old Radford, Nottinghamshire, 25 March 1868
Died Old Radford, Nottinghamshire, 26 April 1932
Career Nottinghamshire, 1886–7; Surrey, 1889–1904
Tests 12
Debut v Australia, Lord's, July 1893

Inns	NOs	HSc	Runs	Average	100s
16	3	52*	231	17.76	–

Runs	Wkts	Average	Best
883	43	20.53	7–71

84. MOLD Arthur Webb

Born Middleton Cheney, Northamptonshire, 27 May 1863
Died Middleton Cheney, Northamptonshire, 29 April 1921
Career Lancashire, 1889–1901
Tests 3
Debut v Australia, Lord's, July 1893

Inns	NOs	HSc	Runs	Average	100s
3	1	0*	0	0.00	–

Runs	Wkts	Average	Best
234	7	33.42	3–44

85. WAINWRIGHT Edward

Born Sheffield, Yorkshire, 8 April 1865
Died Sheffield, Yorkshire, 28 October 1919
Career Yorkshire, 1888–1902
Tests 5
Debut v Australia, Lord's, July 1893

Inns	NOs	HSc	Runs	Average	100s
9	0	49	132	14.66	–

Runs	Wkts	Average	Best
73	0	–	–

86. WARD Albert

Born Leeds, Yorkshire, 21 November 1865
Died Bolton, Lancashire, 6 January 1939
Career Yorkshire, 1886; Lancashire, 1889–1904
Tests 7
Debut v Australia, The Oval, August 1893

Inns	NOs	HSc	Runs	Average	100s
13	0	117	487	37.46	1

Runs	Wkts	Average	Best
–	–	–	–

87. BROCKWELL William

Born Kingston-upon-Thames, Surrey, 21 January 1865
Died Richmond, Surrey, 30 June 1935
Career Surrey, 1886–1903; Kimberley, 1889–90; London
County, 1901–3
Tests 7
Debut v Australia, Old Trafford, August 1893

Inns	NOs	HSc	Runs	Average	100s
12	0	49	202	16.83	–

Runs	Wkts	Average	Best
309	5	61.80	3–33

88. RICHARDSON Thomas

Born Byfleet, Surrey, 11 August 1870
Died St Jean D'Arvey, Savoie, France, 2 July 1912
Career Surrey, 1892–1904; London County, 1904;
Somerset, 1905
Tests 14
Debut v Australia, Old Trafford, August 1893

Inns	NOs	HSc	Runs	Average	100s
24	8	25*	177	11.06	–

Runs	Wkts	Average	Best
2220	88	25.22	8–94

89.   BROWN John Thomas
Born   Great Driffield, Yorkshire, 20 August 1869
Died   Westminster, London, 4 November 1904
Career Yorkshire, 1889–1904
Tests 8
Debut v Australia, Sydney, December 1894

Inns	NOs	HSc	Runs	Average	100s
16	3	140	470	36.15	1

Runs	Wkts	Average	Best
22	0	–	–

90.   FORD Francis Gilbertson Justice
Born   Paddington, London, 14 December 1866
Died   Burwash, Sussex, 7 February 1940
Career Middlesex, 1886–99; Cambridge University, 1887–90
Tests 5
Debut v Australia, Sydney, December 1894

Inns	NOs	HSc	Runs	Average	100s
9	0	48	168	18.66	–

Runs	Wkts	Average	Best
129	1	129.00	1–47

91.   GAY Leslie Hewitt
Born   Brighton, Sussex, 24 March 1871
Died   Salcombe Regis, Devon, 1 November 1949
Career Cambridge University, 1891–3; Somerset, 1894; Hampshire, 1900
Tests 1
Debut v Australia, Sydney, December 1894

Inns	NOs	HSc	Runs	Average	100s
2	0	33	37	18.50	–

Runs	Wkts	Average	Best
–	–	–	–

92.   MacLAREN Archibald Campbell
Born   Whalley Range, Manchester, 1 December 1871
Died   Bracknell, Berkshire, 17 November 1944
Career Lancashire, 1890–1914
Tests 35
Debut v Australia, Sydney, December 1894

Inns	NOs	HSc	Runs	Average	100s
61	4	140	1931	33.87	5

Runs	Wkts	Average	Best
–	–	–	–

93.   BROMLEY-DAVENPORT Hugh Richard
Born   Chelford, Cheshire, 18 August 1870
Died   South Kensington, London, 23 May 1954
Career Cambridge University, 1892–3; Middlesex, 1896–8
Tests 4
Debut v South Africa, Port Elizabeth, February 1896

Inns	NOs	HSc	Runs	Average	100s
6	0	84	128	21.33	–

Runs	Wkts	Average	Best
98	4	24.50	2–46

94.   BUTT Henry Rigden
Born   Fulham, London, 27 December 1865
Died   Hastings, Sussex, 21 December 1928
Career Sussex, 1890–1912
Tests 3
Debut v South Africa, Port Elizabeth, February 1896

Inns	NOs	HSc	Runs	Average	100s
4	1	13	22	7.33	–

Runs	Wkts	Average	Best
–	–	–	–

95.   FRY Charles Burgess
Born   West Croydon, Surrey, 25 April 1872
Died   Hampstead, Middlesex, 7 September 1956
Career Oxford University, 1892–5; Sussex, 1894–1908; London County, 1900–2; Hampshire, 1909–21; Europeans, 1921–2
Tests 26
Debut v South Africa, Port Elizabeth, February 1896

Inns	NOs	HSc	Runs	Average	100s
41	3	144	1223	32.18	2

Runs	Wkts	Average	Best
3	0	–	–

96.   HAWKE 7th Lord (Hon. Martin Bladen)
Born   Gainsborough, Lincolnshire, 16 August 1860
Died   West End, Edinburgh, Scotland, 10 October 1938
Career Yorkshire, 1881–1911; Cambridge University, 1882–5
Tests 5
Debut v South Africa, Port Elizabeth, February 1896

Inns	NOs	HSc	Runs	Average	100s
8	1	30	55	7.85	–

Runs	Wkts	Average	Best
–	–	–	–

97.   HAYWARD Thomas Walter
Born   Cambridge, 29 March 1871
Died   Cambridge, 19 July 1939
Career Surrey, 1893–1914
Tests 35
Debut v South Africa, Port Elizabeth, February 1896

Inns	NOs	HSc	Runs	Average	100s
60	2	137	1999	34.46	3

Runs	Wkts	Average	Best
514	14	36.71	4–22

98.   HILL Arthur James Ledger
Born   Bassett, Hampshire, 26 July 1871
Died   Sparsholt, Hampshire, 6 September 1950
Career Cambridge University, 1890–3; Hampshire, 1895–1921
Tests 3
Debut v South Africa, Port Elizabeth, February 1896

Inns	NOs	HSc	Runs	Average	100s
4	0	124	251	62.75	1

Runs	Wkts	Average	Best
8	4	2.00	4–8

99.   MILLER Audley Montague
Born   Westbury-on-Trym, Gloucestershire, 19 October 1869
Died   Clifton, Bristol, 26 June 1959
Career MCC, 1896–1903
Tests 1
Debut v South Africa, Port Elizabeth, February 1896

Inns	NOs	HSc	Runs	Average	100s
2	2	20*	24	–	–

Runs	Wkts	Average	Best
–	–	–	–

100.   WOODS Samuel Moses James
Born   Ashfield, Sydney, NSW, Australia, 13 April 1867
Died   Taunton, Somerset, 30 April 1931
Career Cambridge University, 1888–91; Somerset, 1891–1910
Tests 3
Debut v South Africa, Port Elizabeth, February 1896

Inns	NOs	HSc	Runs	Average	100s
4	0	53	122	30.50	–

Runs	Wkts	Average	Best
129	5	25.80	3–28

101. WRIGHT Charles William
Born Harewood, Yorkshire, 27 May 1863
Died Melton Mowbray, Leicestershire, 10 January 1936
Career Cambridge University, 1882–5; Nottinghamshire, 1882–9
Tests 3
Debut v South Africa, Port Elizabeth, February 1896

Inns	NOs	HSc	Runs	Average	100s
4	0	71	125	31.25	–

Runs	Wkts	Average	Best
–	–	–	–

102. HESELTINE Christopher
Born Knightsbridge, London, 26 November 1869
Died Lymington, Hampshire, 13 June 1944
Career Hampshire, 1895–1904
Tests 2
Debut v South Africa, Johannesburg, March 1896

Inns	NOs	HSc	Runs	Average	100s
2	0	18	18	9.00	–

Runs	Wkts	Average	Best
84	5	16.80	5–38

103. TYLER Edwin James
Born Kidderminster, Worcestershire, 13 October 1864
Died Taunton, Somerset, 25 January 1917
Career Somerset, 1891–1907
Tests 1
Debut v South Africa, Cape Town, March 1896

Inns	NOs	HSc	Runs	Average	100s
1	0	0	0	0.00	–

Runs	Wkts	Average	Best
65	4	16.25	3–49

104. LILLEY Arthur Frederick Augustus
Born Holloway Head, Birmingham, 28 November 1866
Died Brislington, Bristol, 17 November 1929
Career Warwickshire, 1894–1911; London County, 1900–1
Tests 35
Debut v Australia, Lord's, June 1896

Inns	NOs	HSc	Runs	Average	100s
52	8	84	903	20.52	–

Runs	Wkts	Average	Best
23	1	23.00	1–23

105. RANJITSINHJI Kumar Shri
Born Sarodar, India, 10 September 1872
Died Jamnagar, India, 2 April 1933
Career Cambridge University, 1893–4; Sussex, 1895–1920; London County, 1901–4
Tests 15
Debut v Australia, Old Trafford, July 1896

Inns	NOs	HSc	Runs	Average	100s
26	4	175	989	44.95	2

Runs	Wkts	Average	Best
39	1	39.00	1–23

106. WYNYARD Edward George
Born Saharanpur, India, 1 April 1861
Died Beaconsfield, Buckinghamshire, 30 October 1936
Career Hampshire, 1878–1908
Tests 3
Debut v Australia, The Oval, August 1896

Inns	NOs	HSc	Runs	Average	100s
6	0	30	72	12.00	–

Runs	Wkts	Average	Best
17	0	–	–

107. DRUCE Norman Frank
Born Denmark Hill, London, 1 January 1875
Died Milford-on-Sea, Hampshire, 27 October 1954
Career Cambridge University 1894–7; Surrey 1895–7
Tests 5
Debut v Australia, Sydney, December 1897

Inns	NOs	HSc	Runs	Average	100s
9	0	64	252	28.00	–

Runs	Wkts	Average	Best
–	–	–	–

108. HIRST George Herbert
Born Kirkheaton, Yorkshire, 7 September 1871
Died Huddersfield, Yorkshire, 10 May 1954
Career Yorkshire, 1891–1929; Europeans, 1921–2
Tests 24
Debut v Australia, Sydney, December 1897

Inns	NOs	HSc	Runs	Average	100s
38	3	85	790	22.57	–

Runs	Wkts	Average	Best
1770	59	30.00	5–48

109. MASON John Richard
Born Blackheath, Kent, 26 March 1874
Died Cooden, Sussex, 15 October 1958
Career Kent, 1893–1914
Tests 5
Debut v Australia, Sydney, December 1897

Inns	NOs	HSc	Runs	Average	100s
10	0	32	129	12.90	–

Runs	Wkts	Average	Best
149	2	74.50	1–8

110. STORER William
Born Butterley, Derbyshire, 25 January 1867
Died Derby, 28 February 1912
Career Derbyshire, 1887–1900; London County, 1900
Tests 6
Debut v Australia, Sydney, December 1897

Inns	NOs	HSc	Runs	Average	100s
11	0	51	215	19.54	–

Runs	Wkts	Average	Best
108	2	54.00	1–24

111. BOARD John Henry
Born Clifton, Bristol, 23 February 1867
Died On board SS *Kenilworth Castle* en route from South Africa to England, 15 April 1924
Career Gloucestershire, 1891–1914; London County, 1900–4; Hawke's Bay, 1910–14
Tests 6
Debut v South Africa, Johannesburg, February 1899

Inns	NOs	HSc	Runs	Average	100s
12	2	29	108	10.80	–

Runs	Wkts	Average	Best
–	–	–	–

112. CUTTELL Willis Robert
Born Sheffield, Yorkshire, 13 September 1864
Died Nelson, Lancashire, 9 December 1929
Career Lancashire, 1896–1906
Tests 2
Debut v South Africa, Johannesburg, February 1899

Inns	NOs	HSc	Runs	Average	100s
4	0	21	65	16.25	–

Runs	Wkts	Average	Best
73	6	12.16	3–17

113. HAIGH Schofield
Born Huddersfield, Yorkshire, 19 March 1871
Died Huddersfield, Yorkshire, 27 February 1921
Career Yorkshire, 1895–1913
Tests 11
Debut v South Africa, Johannesburg, February 1899

Inns	NOs	HSc	Runs	Average	100s
18	3	25	113	7.53	–

Runs	Wkts	Average	Best
622	24	25.91	6–11

114. MILLIGAN Frank William
Born Aldershot, Hampshire, 19 March 1870
Died Ramathlabama, Bechuanaland, 31 March 1900
Career Yorkshire, 1894–8
Tests 2
Debut v South Africa, Johannesburg, February 1899

Inns	NOs	HSc	Runs	Average	100s
4	0	38	58	14.50	–

Runs	Wkts	Average	Best
29	0	–	–

115. MITCHELL Frank
Born Market Weighton, Yorkshire, 13 August 1872
Died Blackheath, Kent, 11 October 1935
Career Cambridge University, 1894–7; Yorkshire 1894–1904; London County, 1911; Transvaal, 1902–3 to 1903–4; South Africa, 1912
Tests 2
Debut v South Africa, Johannesburg, February 1899

Inns	NOs	HSc	Runs	Average	100s
4	0	41	88	22.00	–

Runs	Wkts	Average	Best
–	–	–	–

116. TROTT Albert Edwin
Born Melbourne, Australia, 6 February 1873
Died Harlesden, Middlesex, 30 July 1914
Career Victoria, 1892–3 to 1895–6; Middlesex, 1898–1910; London County, 1900–4; Hawke's Bay, 1901–2; Australia, 1894–5
Tests 2
Debut v South Africa, Johannesburg, February 1899

Inns	NOs	HSc	Runs	Average	100s
4	0	16	23	5.75	–

Runs	Wkts	Average	Best
198	17	11.64	5–49

117. TYLDESLEY John Thomas
Born Worsley, Lancashire, 22 November 1873
Died Monton, Manchester, 27 November 1930
Career Lancashire, 1895–1923
Tests 31
Debut v South Africa, Johannesburg, February 1899

Inns	NOs	HSc	Runs	Average	100s
55	1	138	1661	30.75	4

Runs	Wkts	Average	Best
–	–	–	–

118 WARNER Sir Pelham Francis
Born Port-of-Spain, Trinidad, 2 October 1873
Died West Lavington, Sussex, 30 January 1963
Career Oxford University, 1894–6; Middlesex, 1894–1920
Tests 15
Debut v South Africa, Johannesburg, February 1899

Inns	NOs	HSc	Runs	Average	100s
28	2	132*	622	23.92	1

Runs	Wkts	Average	Best
–	–	–	–

119. WILSON Rev. Clement Eustace Macro
Born Bolsterstone, Yorkshire, 15 May 1875
Died Calverhall, Shropshire, 8 February 1944
Career Cambridge University, 1895–8; Yorkshire, 1896–9
Tests 2
Debut v South Africa, Johannesburg, February 1899

Inns	NOs	HSc	Runs	Average	100s
4	1	18	42	14.00	–

Runs	Wkts	Average	Best
–	–	–	–

120. ARCHER Alfred German
Born Richmond, Surrey, 6 December 1871
Died Seaford, Sussex, 15 July 1935
Career Worcestershire, 1900–1
Tests 1
Debut v South Africa, Cape Town, April 1899

Inns	NOs	HSc	Runs	Average	100s
2	1	24*	31	31.00	–

Runs	Wkts	Average	Best
–	–	–	–

121. RHODES Wilfred
Born Kirkheaton, Yorkshire, 29 October 1877
Died Branksome Park, Dorset, 8 July 1973
Career Yorkshire, 1898–1930; Europeans, 1921–2; Patiala, 1926–7
Tests 58
Debut v Australia, Trent Bridge, June 1899

Inns	NOs	HSc	Runs	Average	100s
98	21	179	2325	30.19	2

Runs	Wkts	Average	Best
3425	127	26.96	8–68

 DID YOU KNOW…?

Wilfred Rhodes was fifty-two when he played for England against the West Indies at Kingston, Jamaica, during the 1929–30 tour – the oldest ever Test player.

122. JESSOP Gilbert Laird
Born Cheltenham, Gloucestershire, 19 May 1874
Died Fordington, Dorset, 11 May 1955
Career Gloucestershire, 1894–1914; Cambridge University, 1896–9; London County, 1900–3
Tests 18
Debut v Australia, Lord's, June 1899

Inns	NOs	HSc	Runs	Average	100s
26	0	104	569	21.88	1

Runs	Wkts	Average	Best
354	10	35.40	4–68

123. MEAD Walter
Born Clapton, London, 1 April 1868
Died Chipping Ongar, Essex, 18 March 1954
Career Essex, 1894–1913; London County, 1904
Tests 1
Debut v Australia, Lord's, June 1899

Inns	NOs	HSc	Runs	Average	100s
2	0	7	7	3.50	–

Runs	Wkts	Average	Best
91	1	91.00	1–91

124. TOWNSEND Charles Lucas
Born Clifton, Bristol, 7 November 1876
Died Elton, County Durham, 17 October 1958
Career Gloucestershire, 1893–1922; London County, 1900
Tests 2
Debut v Australia, Lord's, June 1899

Inns	NOs	HSc	Runs	Average	100s
3	0	38	51	17.00	–

Runs	Wkts	Average	Best
75	3	25.00	3–50

125. QUAIFE William George
Born Newhaven, Sussex, 17 March 1872
Died Edgbaston, Birmingham, 13 October 1951
Career Warwickshire, 1894–1928; London County, 1900–3;
Griqualand West, 1912–13
Tests 7
Debut v Australia, Headingley, June 1899

Inns	NOs	HSc	Runs	Average	100s
13	1	68	228	19.00	–

Runs	Wkts	Average	Best
6	0	–	–

126. YOUNG Harding Isaac
Born Leyton, Essex, 5 February 1876
Died Rochford, Essex, 12 December 1964
Career Essex, 1898–1912
Tests 2
Debut v Australia, Headingley, June 1899

Inns	NOs	HSc	Runs	Average	100s
2	0	43	43	21.50	–

Runs	Wkts	Average	Best
262	12	21.83	4–30

127. BRADLEY Walter Morris
Born Sydenham, London, 2 January 1875
Died Wandsworth Common, London, 19 June 1944
Career Kent, 1895–1903; London County, 1903
Tests 2
Debut v Australia, Old Trafford, July 1899

Inns	NOs	HSc	Runs	Average	100s
2	1	23*	23	23.00	–

Runs	Wkts	Average	Best
233	6	38.83	5–67

128. JONES Arthur Owen
Born Shelton, Nottinghamshire, 16 August 1872
Died Dunstable, Bedfordshire, 21 December 1914
Career Cambridge University, 1892–3; Nottinghamshire,
1892–1914; London County, 1901
Tests 12
Debut v Australia, The Oval, August 1899

Inns	NOs	HSc	Runs	Average	100s
21	0	34	291	13.85	–

Runs	Wkts	Average	Best
133	3	44.33	3–73

129. BARNES Sydney Francis
Born Smethwick, Staffordshire, 19 April 1873
Died Chadsmoor, Staffordshire, 26 December 1967
Career Warwickshire, 1894–6; Lancashire, 1899–1903
Tests 27
Debut v Australia, Sydney, December 1901

Inns	NOs	HSc	Runs	Average	100s
39	9	38*	242	8.06	0

Runs	Wkts	Average	Best
3106	189	16.43	9–103

130. BLYTHE Colin
Born Deptford, Kent, 30 May 1879
Died Passchendaele, Belgium, 8 November 1917
Career Kent, 1899–1914
Tests 19
Debut v Australia, Sydney, December 1901

Inns	NOs	HSc	Runs	Average	100s
31	12	27	183	9.63	–

Runs	Wkts	Average	Best
1863	100	18.63	8–59

131. BRAUND Leonard Charles
Born Clewer, Berkshire, 18 October 1875
Died Putney Common, London, 23 December 1955
Career Surrey, 1896–8; Somerset, 1899–1920; London
County, 1900–4
Tests 23
Debut v Australia, Sydney, December 1901

Inns	NOs	HSc	Runs	Average	100s
41	3	104	987	25.97	3

Runs	Wkts	Average	Best
1810	47	38.51	8–81

132. GUNN John Richmond
Born Hucknall Torkard, Nottinghamshire, 19 July 1876
Died Basford, Nottinghamshire, 21 August 1963
Career Nottinghamshire, 1896–1925; London County,
1904
Tests 6
Debut v Australia, Sydney, December 1901

Inns	NOs	HSc	Runs	Average	100s
10	2	24	85	10.62	–

Runs	Wkts	Average	Best
387	18	21.50	5–76

133. McGAHEY Charles Percy
Born Hackney, Middlesex, 12 February 1871
Died Whipps Cross, Essex, 10 January 1935
Career Essex, 1894–1921; London County, 1901–4
Tests 2
Debut v Australia, Sydney, February 1902

Inns	NOs	HSc	Runs	Average	100s
4	0	18	38	9.50	–

Runs	Wkts	Average	Best
–	–	–	–

134. PALAIRET Lionel Charles Hamilton
Born Grange-over-Sands, Lancashire, 27 May 1870
Died Exmouth, Devon, 27 March 1833
Career Oxford University, 1890–3; Somerset, 1891–1909
Tests 2
Debut v Australia, Old Trafford, July 1902

Inns	NOs	HSc	Runs	Average	100s
4	0	20	49	12.25	–

Runs	Wkts	Average	Best
–	–	–	–

DID YOU KNOW...?

Sydney Barnes took his series haul against South
Africa to 49 wickets, a world record, with 7–56 and
7–88 in the match at Durban in 1914.

135. TATE Frederick William
Born Brighton, Sussex, 24 July 1867
Died Burgess Hill, Sussex, 24 February 1943
Career Sussex, 1887–1905
Tests 1
Debut v Australia, Old Trafford, July 1902

Inns	NOs	HSc	Runs	Average	100s
2	1	5*	9	9.00	–

Runs	Wkts	Average	Best
51	2	25.50	2–7

136. ARNOLD Edward George
Born Exmouth, Devon, 7 November 1876
Died Worcester, 25 October 1942
Career Worcestershire, 1899–1913; London County, 1900
Tests 10
Debut v Australia, Sydney, December 1903

Inns	NOs	HSc	Runs	Average	100s
15	3	40	160	13.33	–

Runs	Wkts	Average	Best
788	31	25.41	5–37

DID YOU KNOW...?

Bernard Bosanquet, generally regarded as the inventor of the googly, was the father of the well-known ITV newsreader Reginald Bosanquet.

137. BOSANQUET Bernard James Tindal
Born Enfield, Middlesex, 13 October 1877
Died Ewhurst, Surrey, 12 October 1936
Career Oxford University, 1898–1900; Middlesex, 1898–1919
Tests 7
Debut v Australia, Sydney, December 1903

Inns	NOs	HSc	Runs	Average	100s
14	3	27	147	13.36	–

Runs	Wkts	Average	Best
604	25	24.16	8–107

138. FOSTER Reginald Erskine
Born Malvern, Worcestershire, 16 April 1878
Died Kensington, London, 13 May 1914
Career Oxford University, 1897–1900; Worcestershire, 1899–1912
Tests 8
Debut v Australia, Sydney, December 1903

Inns	NOs	HSc	Runs	Average	100s
14	1	287	602	46.30	1

Runs	Wkts	Average	Best
–	–	–	–

139. RELF Albert Edward
Born Burwash, Sussex, 26 June 1874
Died Crowthorne, Berkshire, 26 March 1937
Career Sussex, 1900–21; London County, 1904; Auckland, 1907–8 to 1909–10
Tests 13
Debut v Australia, Sydney, December 1903

Inns	NOs	HSc	Runs	Average	100s
21	3	63	416	23.11	–

Runs	Wkts	Average	Best
624	25	24.96	5–85

140. FIELDER Arthur
Born Tonbridge, Kent, 19 July 1877
Died Lambeth, London, 30 August 1949
Career Kent, 1900–14
Tests 6
Debut v Australia, Melbourne, January 1904

Inns	NOs	HSc	Runs	Average	100s
12	5	20	78	11.14	–

Runs	Wkts	Average	Best
711	26	27.34	6–82

141. KNIGHT Albert Ernest
Born Leicester, 8 October 1872
Died Edmonton, Middlesex, 25 April 1946
Career Leicestershire, 1895–1912; London County, 1903–4
Tests 3
Debut v Australia, Melbourne, January 1904

Inns	NOs	HSc	Runs	Average	100s
6	1	70*	81	16.20	–

Runs	Wkts	Average	Best
–	–	–	–

142. DENTON David
Born Wakefield, Yorkshire, 4 July 1874
Died Wakefield, Yorkshire, 16 February 1950
Career Yorkshire, 1894–1920
Tests 11
Debut v Australia, Headingley, July 1905

Inns	NOs	HSc	Runs	Average	100s
22	1	104	424	20.19	1

Runs	Wkts	Average	Best
–	–	–	–

143. WARREN Arnold
Born Codnor Park, Derbyshire, 2 April 1875
Died Codnor, Derbyshire, 3 September 1951
Career Derbyshire, 1897–1920
Tests 1
Debut v Australia, Headingley, July 1905

Inns	NOs	HSc	Runs	Average	100s
1	0	7	7	7.00	–

Runs	Wkts	Average	Best
113	6	18.83	5–57

DID YOU KNOW...?

During his innings of 287 in 1903, Reginald 'Tip' Foster became the first batsman to share three century partnerships in the same Test innings.

144. BREARLEY Walter
Born Bolton, Lancashire, 11 March 1876
Died Middlesex Hospital, London, 30 January 1937
Career Lancashire, 1902–11; London County, 1904
Tests 4
Debut v Australia, Old Trafford, July 1905

Inns	NOs	HSc	Runs	Average	100s
5	2	11*	21	7.00	–

Runs	Wkts	Average	Best
359	17	21.11	5–110

145. SPOONER Reginald Herbert
Born Litherland, Lancashire, 21 October 1880
Died Lincoln, 2 October 1961
Career Lancashire, 1899–1921
Tests 10
Debut v Australia, Old Trafford, July 1905

Inns	NOs	HSc	Runs	Average	100s
15	0	119	481	32.06	1

Runs	Wkts	Average	Best
–	–	–	–

146. CRAWFORD John Neville
Born Cane Hill, Surrey, 1 December 1886
Died Epsom, Surrey, 2 May 1963
Career Surrey, 1904–21; South Australia, 1909–10 to 1913–14; Otago, 1914–15; Wellington, 1917–18
Tests 12
Debut v South Africa, Johannesburg, January 1906

Inns	NOs	HSc	Runs	Average	100s
23	2	74	469	22.33	–

Runs	Wkts	Average	Best
1150	39	29.48	5–48

147. FANE Frederick Luther
Born Curragh Camp, Ireland, 27 April 1875
Died Brentwood, Essex, 27 November 1960
Career Essex, 1895–1922; Oxford University, 1896–8; London County, 1901
Tests 14
Debut v South Africa, Johannesburg, January 1906

Inns	NOs	HSc	Runs	Average	100s
27	1	143	682	26.23	1

Runs	Wkts	Average	Best
–	–	–	–

148. HAYES Ernest George
Born Peckham, London, 6 November 1876
Died West Dulwich, London, 2 December 1953
Career Surrey, 1896–1919; London County, 1903; Leicestershire, 1926
Tests 5
Debut v South Africa, Johannesburg, January 1906

Inns	NOs	HSc	Runs	Average	100s
9	1	35	86	10.75	–

Runs	Wkts	Average	Best
52	1	52.00	1–28

149. LEES Walter Scott
Born Sowerby Bridge, Yorkshire, 25 December 1875
Died West Hartlepool, County Durham, 10 September 1924
Career Surrey, 1896–1911; London County, 1903
Tests 5
Debut v South Africa, Johannesburg, January 1906

Inns	NOs	HSc	Runs	Average	100s
9	3	25*	66	11.00	–

Runs	Wkts	Average	Best
467	26	17.96	6–78

150. MOON Leonard James
Born Kensington, London, 9 February 1878
Died Salonika, Greece, 23 November 1916
Career Cambridge University, 1897–1900; Middlesex, 1899–1909
Tests 4
Debut v South Africa, Johannesburg, March 1906

Inns	NOs	HSc	Runs	Average	100s
8	0	36	182	22.75	–

Runs	Wkts	Average	Best
–	–	–	–

151. HARTLEY John Cabourn
Born Lincoln, 15 November 1874
Died Woodhall Spa, Lincolnshire, 8 March 1963
Career Oxford University, 1895–7; Sussex 1895–8
Tests 2
Debut v South Africa, Johannesburg, March 1906

Inns	NOs	HSc	Runs	Average	100s
4	0	9	15	3.75	–

Runs	Wkts	Average	Best
115	1	115.00	1–62

152. KNOX Neville Alexander
Born Clapham, London, 10 October 1884
Died Surbiton, Surrey, 3 March 1935
Career Surrey, 1904–10
Tests 2
Debut v South Africa, Headingley, July 1907

Inns	NOs	HSc	Runs	Average	100s
4	1	8*	24	8.00	–

Runs	Wkts	Average	Best
105	3	35.00	2–39

153. GUNN George
Born Hucknall Torkard, Nottinghamshire, 13 June 1879
Died Cuckfield, Sussex, 29 June 1958
Career Nottinghamshire, 1902–32
Tests 15
Debut v Australia, Sydney, December 1907

Inns	NOs	HSc	Runs	Average	100s
29	1	122*	1120	40.00	2

Runs	Wkts	Average	Best
8	0	–	–

154. HARDSTAFF Joseph Snr
Born Kirkby-in-Ashfield, Nottinghamshire, 9 November 1882
Died Nuncargate, Nottinghamshire, 2 April 1947
Career Nottinghamshire, 1902–24
Tests 5
Debut v Australia, Sydney, December 1907

Inns	NOs	HSc	Runs	Average	100s
10	0	72	311	31.10	–

Runs	Wkts	Average	Best
–	–	–	–

155. HUTCHINGS Kenneth Lotherington
Born Southborough, Kent, 7 December 1882
Died Ginchy, France, 3 September 1916
Career Kent, 1902–12
Tests 7
Debut v Australia, Sydney, December 1907

Inns	NOs	HSc	Runs	Average	100s
12	0	126	341	28.41	1

Runs	Wkts	Average	Best
81	1	81.00	1–5

156. YOUNG Richard Alfred
Born Dharwar, India, 16 September 1885
Died Hastings, Sussex, 1 July 1968
Career Cambridge University, 1905–8; Sussex, 1905–25
Tests 2
Debut v Australia, Sydney, December 1907

Inns	NOs	HSc	Runs	Average	100s
4	0	13	27	6.75	–

Runs	Wkts	Average	Best
–	–	–	–

157. HOBBS Sir John Berry

Born Barnwell, Cambridge, 16 December 1882
Died Hove, Sussex, 21 December 1863
Career Surrey, 1905–34
Tests 61
Debut v Australia, Melbourne, January 1908

Inns	NOs	HSc	Runs	Average	100s
102	7	211	5410	56.94	15

Runs	Wkts	Average	Best
165	1	165.00	1–19

158. HUMPHRIES Joseph

Born Stonebroom, Derbyshire, 19 May 1876
Died Chesterfield, Derbyshire, 7 May 1946
Career Derbyshire, 1899–1914
Tests 3
Debut v Australia, Melbourne, January 1908

Inns	NOs	HSc	Runs	Average	100s
6	1	16	44	8.80	–

Runs	Wkts	Average	Best
–	–	–	–

159. THOMPSON George Joseph

Born Cogenhoe, Northampton, 27 October 1877
Died Clifton, Bristol, 3 March 1943
Career Northamptonshire, 1905–22; Auckland, 1911–12
Tests 6
Debut v Australia, Edgbaston, May 1909

Inns	NOs	HSc	Runs	Average	100s
10	1	63	273	30.33	–

Runs	Wkts	Average	Best
638	23	27.73	4–50

160. KING John Herbert

Born Lutterworth, Leicestershire, 16 April 1871
Died Denbigh, Clwyd, 18 November 1946
Career Leicestershire, 1895–1925
Tests 1
Debut v Australia, Lord's, June 1909

Inns	NOs	HSc	Runs	Average	100s
2	0	60	64	32.00	–

Runs	Wkts	Average	Best
99	1	99.00	1–99

161. SHARP John

Born Hereford, 15 February 1878
Died Wavertree, Liverpool, 28 January 1938
Career Lancashire, 1899–1925
Tests 3
Debut v Australia, Headingley, July 1909

Inns	NOs	HSc	Runs	Average	100s
6	2	105	188	47.00	1

Runs	Wkts	Average	Best
111	3	37.00	3–67

162. CARR Douglas Ward

Born Cranbrook, Kent, 17 March 1872
Died Sidmouth, Devon, 23 March 1950
Career Kent, 1909–14
Tests 1
Debut v Australia, The Oval, August 1909

Inns	NOs	HSc	Runs	Average	100s
1	0	0	0	0.00	–

Runs	Wkts	Average	Best
282	7	40.28	5–146

163. WOOLLEY Frank Edward

Born Tonbridge, Kent, 27 May 1887
Died Halifax, Nova Scotia, Canada, 18 October 1978
Career Kent, 1906–38
Tests 64
Debut v Australia, The Oval, August 1909

Inns	NOs	HSc	Runs	Average	100s
98	7	154	3283	36.07	5

Runs	Wkts	Average	Best
2815	83	33.91	7–76

164. BIRD Morice Carlos

Born Liverpool, 25 March 1888
Died Broadstone, Dorset, 9 December 1933
Career Lancashire, 1907; Surrey, 1909–21
Tests 10
Debut v South Africa, Johannesburg, January 1910

Inns	NOs	HSc	Runs	Average	100s
16	1	61	280	18.66	–

Runs	Wkts	Average	Best
120	8	15.00	3–11

165. BUCKENHAM Claude Percival

Born Herne Hill, London, 16 January 1876
Died Dundee, Scotland, 23 February 1937
Career Essex, 1899–1914
Tests 4
Debut v South Africa, Johannesburg, January 1910

Inns	NOs	HSc	Runs	Average	100s
7	0	17	43	6.14	–

Runs	Wkts	Average	Best
593	21	28.23	5–115

166. LEVESON-GOWER Sir Henry Dudley Gresham

Born Titsey, Surrey, 8 May 1873
Died Kensington, London, 1 February 1954
Career Oxford University, 1893–6; Surrey, 1895–1920
Tests 3
Debut v South Africa, Johannesburg, January 1910

Inns	NOs	HSc	Runs	Average	100s
6	2	31	95	23.75	–

Runs	Wkts	Average	Best
–	–	–	–

167. SIMPSON-HAYWARD George Hayward Thomas

Born Kenilworth, Warwickshire, 7 June 1875
Died Icomb, Gloucestershire, 2 October 1936
Career Cambridge University, 1895–7; Worcestershire, 1899–1914
Tests 5
Debut v South Africa, Johannesburg, January 1910

Inns	NOs	HSc	Runs	Average	100s
8	1	29*	105	15.00	–

Runs	Wkts	Average	Best
420	23	18.26	6–43

168. STRUDWICK Herbert
Born Mitcham, Surrey, 28 January 1880
Died Shoreham, Sussex, 14 February 1970
Career Surrey, 1902–27
Tests 28
Debut v South Africa, Johannesburg, January 1910

Inns	NOs	HSc	Runs	Average	100s
42	13	24	230	7.93	–

Runs	Wkts	Average	Best
–	–	–	–

DID YOU KNOW...?

N. C. Tufnell, replacing Herbert Strudwick, achieved the first Test stumping as he dismissed S. J. Snooke for 53 in the match against South Africa at Durban in 1910.

169. TUFNELL Neville Charsley
Born Simla, Punjab, India, 13 June 1887
Died Whitechapel, London, 3 August 1951
Career Cambridge University, 1908–10; Surrey, 1922
Tests 1
Debut v South Africa, Cape Town, March 1910

Inns	NOs	HSc	Runs	Average	100s
1	0	14	14	14.00	–

Runs	Wkts	Average	Best
–	–	–	–

170. DOUGLAS John William Henry Tyler
Born Clapton, London, 3 September 1882
Died Laeso, Denmark, 19 December 1930
Career Essex, 1901–28; London County, 1903–4
Tests 23
Debut v Australia, Sydney, December 1911

Inns	NOs	HSc	Runs	Average	100s
35	2	119	962	29.15	1

Runs	Wkts	Average	Best
1486	45	33.02	5–46

171. FOSTER Frank Rowbotham
Born Birmingham, 31 January 1889
Died Northampton, 3 May 1958
Career Warwickshire, 1908–14
Tests 11
Debut v Australia, Sydney, December 1911

Inns	NOs	HSc	Runs	Average	100s
15	1	71	330	23.57	–

Runs	Wkts	Average	Best
926	45	20.57	6–91

172. HEARNE John William
Born Hillingdon, Middlesex, 11 February 1891
Died West Drayton, Middlesex, 14 September 1965
Career Middlesex, 1909–36
Tests 24
Debut v Australia, Sydney, December 1911

Inns	NOs	HSc	Runs	Average	100s
36	5	114	806	26.00	1

Runs	Wkts	Average	Best
1462	30	48.73	5–49

173. KINNEIR Septimus Paul
Born Corsham, Wiltshire, 13 May 1871
Died Birmingham, 16 October 1928
Career Warwickshire, 1898–1914
Tests 1
Debut v Australia, Sydney, December 1911

Inns	NOs	HSc	Runs	Average	100s
2	0	30	52	26.00	–

Runs	Wkts	Average	Best
–	–	–	–

174. MEAD Charles Philip
Born Battersea, London, 9 March 1887
Died Boscombe, Hampshire, 26 March 1958
Career Hampshire, 1905–36
Tests 17
Debut v Australia, Sydney, December 1911

Inns	NOs	HSc	Runs	Average	100s
26	2	182*	1185	49.37	4

Runs	Wkts	Average	Best
–	–	–	–

175. HITCH John William
Born Radcliffe, Lancashire, 7 May 1886
Died Rumney, Cardiff, 7 July 1965
Career Surrey, 1907–25
Tests 7
Debut v Australia, Melbourne, Dec 1911–Jan 1912

Inns	NOs	HSc	Runs	Average	100s
10	3	51*	103	14.71	–

Runs	Wkts	Average	Best
325	7	46.42	2–31

DID YOU KNOW...?

Johnny Douglas, captain of Essex and England, was drowned while attempting to save his father when the Finnish ship they were aboard, *Oberon*, sank after a collision with its sister ship *Arcturus* in dense fog in the Kattegat in December 1930.

176. SMITH Ernest James
Born Birmingham, 6 February 1886
Died Birmingham, 31 August 1979
Career Warwickshire, 1904–30
Tests 11
Debut v Australia, Melbourne, Dec 1911–Jan 1912

Inns	NOs	HSc	Runs	Average	100s
14	1	22	113	8.69	–

Runs	Wkts	Average	Best
–	–	–	–

177. VINE Joseph
Born Willingdon, Sussex, 15 May 1875
Died Hove, Sussex, 25 April 1946
Career Sussex, 1896–1922; London County, 1901–4
Tests 2
Debut v Australia, Melbourne, February 1912

Inns	NOs	HSc	Runs	Average	100s
3	2	36	46	46.00	–

Runs	Wkts	Average	Best
–	–	–	–

DID YOU KNOW...?

In 1912, England's Joe Vine came on as a substitute fielder and took a catch for Australia.

178. DEAN Harry
Born Burnley, Lancashire, 13 August 1884
Died Garstang, Lancashire, 12 March 1957
Career Lancashire, 1906–21
Tests 3
Debut v Australia, Lord's, June 1912

Inns	NOs	HSc	Runs	Average	100s
4	2	8	10	5.00	–

Runs	Wkts	Average	Best
153	11	13.90	4–19

179. BOOTH Major William
Born Pudsey, Yorkshire, 10 December 1886
Died La Cigny, France, 1 July 1916
Career Yorkshire, 1908–14
Tests 2
Debut v South Africa, Durban, December 1913

Inns	NOs	HSc	Runs	Average	100s
2	0	32	46	23.00	–

Runs	Wkts	Average	Best
130	7	18.57	4–49

180. TENNYSON 3rd Lord (Hon. Lionel Hallam)
Born Westminster, London, 7 November 1889
Died Bexhill-on-Sea, Sussex, 6 June 1951
Career Hampshire, 1913–35
Tests 9
Debut v South Africa, Durban, December 1913

Inns	NOs	HSc	Runs	Average	100s
12	1	74*	345	31.36	–

Runs	Wkts	Average	Best
1	0	–	–

181. HENDREN Elias Henry
Born Turnham Green, Middlesex, 5 February 1889
Died Tooting Bec, London, 4 October 1962
Career Middlesex, 1907–37
Tests 51
Debut v Australia, Sydney, December 1920

Inns	NOs	HSc	Runs	Average	100s
83	9	205*	3525	47.63	7

Runs	Wkts	Average	Best
31	1	31.00	1–27

182. PARKIN Cecil Harry
Born Eaglescliffe, County Durham, 18 February 1886
Died Cheetham Hill, Manchester, 15 June 1943
Career Yorkshire, 1906; Lancashire, 1914–26
Tests 10
Debut v Australia, Sydney, December 1920

Inns	NOs	HSc	Runs	Average	100s
16	3	36	160	12.30	–

Runs	Wkts	Average	Best
1128	32	35.25	5–38

183. RUSSELL Charles Albert George
Born Leyton, Essex, 7 October 1887
Died Whipps Cross, Essex, 23 March 1961
Career Essex, 1908–30
Tests 10
Debut v Australia, Sydney, December 1920

Inns	NOs	HSc	Runs	Average	100s
18	2	140	910	56.87	5

Runs	Wkts	Average	Best
–	–	–	–

184. WADDINGTON Abraham
Born Thornton, Yorkshire, 4 February 1893
Died Scarborough, Yorkshire, 28 October 1959
Career Yorkshire, 1919–27
Tests 2
Debut v Australia, Sydney, December 1920

Inns	NOs	HSc	Runs	Average	100s
4	0	7	16	4.00	–

Runs	Wkts	Average	Best
119	1	119.00	1–35

185. HOWELL Henry
Born Ladywood, Birmingham, 29 November 1890
Died Selly Oak, Birmingham, 9 July 1932
Career Warwickshire, 1913–28
Tests 5
Debut v Australia, Melbourne, Dec 1920–Jan 1921

Inns	NOs	HSc	Runs	Average	100s
8	6	5	15	7.50	–

Runs	Wkts	Average	Best
559	7	79.85	4–115

186. MAKEPEACE Joseph William Henry
Born Middlesbrough, Yorkshire, 22 August 1881
Died Bebington, Cheshire, 19 December 1952
Career Lancashire, 1906–30
Tests 4
Debut v Australia, Melbourne, Dec 1920–Jan 1921

Inns	NOs	HSc	Runs	Average	100s
8	0	117	279	34.87	1

Runs	Wkts	Average	Best
–	–	–	–

187. FENDER Percy George Herbert
Born Balham, London, 22 August 1892
Died Exeter, Devon, 15 June 1985
Career Sussex, 1910–13; Surrey, 1914–35
Tests 13
Debut v Australia, Adelaide, January 1921

Inns	NOs	HSc	Runs	Average	100s
21	1	60	380	19.00	–

Runs	Wkts	Average	Best
1185	29	40.86	5–90

188. DOLPHIN Arthur
Born Wilsden, Yorkshire, 24 December 1885
Died Bradford, Yorkshire, 23 October 1942
Career Yorkshire, 1905–27; Patiala, 1926–7
Tests 1
Debut v Australia, Melbourne, February 1921

Inns	NOs	HSc	Runs	Average	100s
2	0	1	1	0.50	–

Runs	Wkts	Average	Best
–	–	–	–

189. WILSON Evelyn Rockley
Born Bolsterstone, Yorkshire, 25 March 1879
Died Winchester, Hampshire, 21 July 1957
Career Cambridge University, 1899–1902; Yorkshire, 1899–1923
Tests 1
Debut v Australia, Sydney, Feb–March 1921

Inns	NOs	HSc	Runs	Average	100s
2	0	5	10	5.00	–

Runs	Wkts	Average	Best
36	3	12.00	2–28

190. HOLMES Percy
Born Huddersfield, Yorkshire, 25 November 1886
Died Huddersfield, Yorkshire, 3 September 1971
Career Yorkshire, 1913–33
Tests 7
Debut v Australia, Trent Bridge, May 1921

Inns	NOs	HSc	Runs	Average	100s
14	1	88	357	27.46	–

Runs	Wkts	Average	Best
–	–	–	–

191. JUPP Vallance William Crisp
Born Burgess Hill, Sussex, 27 March 1891
Died Spratton, Northamptonshire, 9 July 1960
Career Sussex, 1909–22; Northamptonshire, 1923–38
Tests 8
Debut v Australia, Trent Bridge, May 1921

Inns	NOs	HSc	Runs	Average	100s
13	1	38	208	17.33	–

Runs	Wkts	Average	Best
616	28	22.00	4–37

192. KNIGHT Donald John
Born Sutton, Surrey, 12 May 1894
Died Marylebone, London, 5 January 1960
Career Surrey, 1911–37; Oxford University, 1914 and 1919
Tests 2
Debut v Australia, Trent Bridge, May 1921

Inns	NOs	HSc	Runs	Average	100s
4	0	38	54	13.50	–

Runs	Wkts	Average	Best
–	–	–	–

193. RICHMOND Thomas Leonard
Born Radcliffe-on-Trent, Nottinghamshire, 23 June 1890
Died Saxondale, Nottinghamshire, 29 December 1957
Career Nottinghamshire, 1912–28
Tests 1
Debut v Australia, Trent Bridge, May 1921

Inns	NOs	HSc	Runs	Average	100s
2	0	4	6	3.00	–

Runs	Wkts	Average	Best
86	2	43.00	2–69

194. TYLDESLEY George Ernest
Born Worsley, Lancashire, 5 February 1889
Died Rhos-on-Sea, Clwyd, 5 May 1962
Career Lancashire, 1909–36
Tests 14
Debut v Australia, Trent Bridge, May 1921

Inns	NOs	HSc	Runs	Average	100s
20	2	122	990	55.00	3

Runs	Wkts	Average	Best
2	0	–	–

195. DIPPER Alfred Ernest
Born Apperley, Gloucestershire, 9 November 1885
Died Lambeth, London, 7 November 1945
Career Gloucestershire, 1908–32
Tests 1
Debut v Australia, Lord's, June 1921

Inns	NOs	HSc	Runs	Average	100s
2	0	40	51	25.50	–

Runs	Wkts	Average	Best
–	–	–	–

196. DURSTON Frederick John
Born Clophill, Bedfordshire, 11 July 1893
Died Southall, Middlesex, 8 April 1965
Career Middlesex, 1919–33
Tests 1
Debut v Australia, Lord's, June 1921

Inns	NOs	HSc	Runs	Average	100s
2	1	6*	8	8.00	–

Runs	Wkts	Average	Best
136	5	27.20	4–102

197. EVANS Alfred John
Born Newtown, Hampshire, 1 May 1889
Died Marylebone, London, 18 September 1960
Career Hampshire, 1908–20; Oxford University, 1909–12; Kent, 1921–8
Tests 1
Debut v Australia, Lord's, June 1921

Inns	NOs	HSc	Runs	Average	100s
2	0	14	18	9.00	–

Runs	Wkts	Average	Best
–	–	–	–

198. HAIG Nigel Esme MC
Born Kensington, London, 12 December 1887
Died Eastbourne, Sussex, 27 October 1966
Career Middlesex, 1912–34
Tests 5
Debut v Australia, Lord's, June 1921

Inns	NOs	HSc	Runs	Average	100s
9	0	47	126	14.00	–

Runs	Wkts	Average	Best
448	13	34.46	3–73

199. BROWN George
Born Cowley, Oxford, 6 October 1887
Died Winchester, Hampshire, 3 December 1964
Career Hampshire, 1908–33
Tests 7
Debut v Australia, Headingley, July 1921

Inns	NOs	HSc	Runs	Average	100s
12	2	84	299	29.90	–

Runs	Wkts	Average	Best
–	–	–	–

200. DUCAT Andrew
Born Brixton, London, 16 February 1886
Died Lord's, St John's Wood, London, 23 July 1942
Career Surrey, 1906–31
Tests 1
Debut v Australia, Headingley, July 1921

Inns	NOs	HSc	Runs	Average	100s
2	0	3	5	2.50	–

Runs	Wkts	Average	Best
–	–	–	–

201. HARDINGE Harold Thomas William
Born Greenwich, London, 25 February 1886
Died Cambridge, 8 May 1965
Career Kent, 1902–33
Tests 1
Debut v Australia, Headingley, July 1921

Inns	NOs	HSc	Runs	Average	100s
2	0	25	30	15.00	–

Runs	Wkts	Average	Best
–	–	–	–

202. WHITE John Cornish
Born Holford, Somerset, 19 February 1891
Died Combe Florey, Somerset, 2 May 1961
Career Somerset, 1909–37
Tests 15
Debut v Australia, Headingley, July 1921

Inn	NOs	HSc	Runs	Average	100s
22	9	29	239	18.38	–

Runs	Wkts	Average	Best
1581	49	32.26	8–126

203. HALLOWS Charles
Born Little Lever, Lancashire, 4 April 1895
Died Bolton, Lancashire, 10 November 1972
Career Lancashire, 1914–32
Tests 2
Debut v Australia, Old Trafford, July 1921

Inns	NOs	HSc	Runs	Average	100s
2	1	26	42	42.00	–

Runs	Wkts	Average	Best
–	–	–	–

204. PARKER Charles Warrington Leonard
Born Prestbury, Gloucestershire, 14 October 1882
Died Cranleigh, Surrey, 11 July 1959
Career Gloucestershire, 1903–35
Tests 1
Debut v Australia, Old Trafford, July 1921

Inns	NOs	HSc	Runs	Average	100s
1	1	3*	3	–	–

Runs	Wkts	Average	Best
32	2	16.00	2–32

DID YOU KNOW...?

When Andy Sandham scored 325 against the West Indies in 1930, he was using Freddie Calthorpe's bat and wearing Patsy Hendren's boots.

205. SANDHAM Andrew
Born Streatham, London, 6 July 1890
Died Westminster, London, 20 April 1982
Career Surrey, 1911–37
Tests 14
Debut v Australia, The Oval, August 1921

Inns	NOs	HSc	Runs	Average	100s
23	0	325	879	38.21	2

Runs	Wkts	Average	Best
–	–	–	–

206. CARR Arthur William
Born Mickleham, Surrey, 21 May 1893
Died West Witton, Yorkshire, 7 February 1963
Career Nottinghamshire, 1910–34
Tests 11
Debut v South Africa, Johannesburg, December 1922

Inns	NOs	HSc	Runs	Average	100s
13	1	63	237	19.75	–

Runs	Wkts	Average	Best
–	–	–	–

207. GILLIGAN Arthur Edward Robert
Born Denmark Hill, London, 23 December 1894
Died Pulborough, Sussex, 5 September 1976
Career Cambridge University, 1919–20; Surrey, 1919; Sussex, 1920–32
Tests 11
Debut v South Africa, Johannesburg, December 1922

Inns	NOs	HSc	Runs	Average	100s
16	3	39*	209	16.07	–

Runs	Wkts	Average	Best
1046	36	29.05	6–7

208. KENNEDY Alexander Stuart
Born Edinburgh, Scotland, 24 January 1891
Died Hythe, Southampton, 15 November 1959
Career Hampshire, 1907–36
Tests 5
Debut v South Africa, Johannesburg, December 1922

Inns	NOs	HSc	Runs	Average	100s
8	2	41*	93	15.50	–

Runs	Wkts	Average	Best
599	31	19.32	5–76

209. MANN Francis Thomas
Born Winchmore Hill, Middlesex, 3 March 1888
Died Milton Lilbourne, Wiltshire, 6 October 1964
Career Cambridge University, 1909–11; Middlesex, 1909–31
Tests 5
Debut v South Africa, Johannesburg, December 1922

Inns	NOs	HSc	Runs	Average	100s
9	1	84	281	35.12	–

Runs	Wkts	Average	Best
–	–	–	–

210. STEVENS Greville Thomas Scott
Born Hampstead, Middlesex, 7 January 1901
Died Islington, London, 19 September 1970
Career Middlesex, 1919–32; Oxford University, 1920–3
Tests 10
Debut v South Africa, Johannesburg, December 1922

Inns	NOs	HSc	Runs	Average	100s
17	0	69	263	15.47	–

Runs	Wkts	Average	Best
648	20	32.40	5–90

211. MACAULAY George Gibson
Born Thirsk, Yorkshire, 7 December 1897
Died Sullom Voe, Shetland Islands, 13 December 1940
Career Yorkshire, 1920–35
Tests 8
Debut v South Africa, Cape Town, January 1923

Inns	NOs	HSc	Runs	Average	100s
10	4	76	112	18.66	–

Runs	Wkts	Average	Best
662	24	27.58	5–64

212. STREET George Benjamin
Born Charlwood, Surrey, 6 December 1889
Died Portslade, Sussex, 24 April 1924
Career Sussex, 1909–23
Tests 1
Debut v South Africa, Durban, January 1923

Inns	NOs	HSc	Runs	Average	100s
2	1	7*	11	11.00	–

Runs	Wkts	Average	Best
–	–	–	–

213. CHAPMAN Arthur Percy Frank
Born Reading, Berkshire, 3 September 1900
Died Alton, Hampshire, 16 September 1961
Career Cambridge University, 1920–2; Kent, 1924–38
Tests 26
Debut v South Africa, Edgbaston, June 1924

Inns	NOs	HSc	Runs	Average	100s
36	4	121	925	28.90	1

Runs	Wkts	Average	Best
20	0	–	–

214. KILNER Roy
Born Wombwell, Yorkshire, 17 October 1890
Died Barnsley, Yorkshire, 5 April 1928
Career Yorkshire, 1911–27
Tests 9
Debut v South Africa, Edgbaston, June 1924

Inns	NOs	HSc	Runs	Average	100s
8	1	74	233	33.28	–

Runs	Wkts	Average	Best
734	24	30.58	4–51

215. SUTCLIFFE Herbert
Born Harrogate, Yorkshire, 24 November 1894
Died Crosshills, Yorkshire, 22 January 1978
Career Yorkshire, 1919–45
Tests 54
Debut v South Africa, Edgbaston, June 1924

Inns	NOs	HSc	Runs	Average	100s
84	9	194	4555	60.73	16

Runs	Wkts	Average	Best
–	–	–	–

DID YOU KNOW...?

When Maurice Tate took 38 wickets in the 1924–5
Ashes series, to break Arthur Mailey's Ashes record
of 36, his thirty-seventh victim was Mailey himself.

216. TATE Maurice William
Born Brighton, Sussex, 30 May 1895
Died Wadhurst, Sussex, 18 May 1956
Career Sussex, 1912–37
Tests 39
Debut v South Africa, Edgbaston, June 1924

Inns	NOs	HSc	Runs	Average	100s
52	5	100*	1198	25.48	1

Runs	Wkts	Average	Best
4055	155	26.16	6–42

217. WOOD George Edward Charles
Born Blackheath, Kent, 22 August 1893
Died Christchurch, Hampshire, 18 March 1971
Career Cambridge University, 1913–20; Kent, 1919–27
Tests 3
Debut v South Africa, Edgbaston, June 1924

Inns	NOs	HSc	Runs	Average	100s
2	0	6	7	3.50	–

Runs	Wkts	Average	Best
–	–	–	–

218. TYLDESLEY Richard Knowles
Born Westhoughton, Lancashire, 11 March 1897
Died Bolton, Lancashire, 17 September 1943
Career Lancashire, 1919–31
Tests 7
Debut v South Africa, Lord's, June–July 1924

Inns	NOs	HSc	Runs	Average	100s
7	1	29	47	7.83	–

Runs	Wkts	Average	Best
619	19	32.57	3–50

219. DUCKWORTH George
Born Warrington, Lancashire, 9 May 1901
Died Warrington, Lancashire, 5 January 1966
Career Lancashire, 1923–38
Tests 24
Debut v South Africa, Old Trafford, July 1924

Inns	NOs	HSc	Runs	Average	100s
28	12	39*	234	14.62	–

Runs	Wkts	Average	Best
–	–	–	–

220. GEARY George
Born Barwell, Leicestershire, 9 July 1893
Died Leicester, 6 March 1981
Career Leicestershire, 1912–38
Tests 14
Debut v South Africa, Old Trafford, July 1924

Inns	NOs	HSc	Runs	Average	100s
20	4	66	249	15.56	–

Runs	Wkts	Average	Best
1353	46	29.41	7–70

221. MacBRYAN John Crawford William
Born Box, Wiltshire, 22 July 1892
Died Cambridge, 14 July 1983
Career Somerset, 1911–31; Cambridge University, 1919–20
Tests 1
Debut v South Africa, Old Trafford, July 1924

Inns	NOs	HSc	Runs	Average	100s
–	–	–	–	–	–

Runs	Wkts	Average	Best
–	–	–	–

DID YOU KNOW...?

Jack MacBryan, who won an Olympic gold medal
for hockey, didn't bat or bowl in his only Test for
England in 1924, which was almost completely
washed out.

222. FREEMAN Alfred Percy
Born Lewisham, London, 17 May 1888
Died Bearsted, Kent, 28 January 1965
Career Kent, 1914–36
Tests 12
Debut v Australia, Sydney, December 1924

Inns	NOs	HSc	Runs	Average	100s
16	5	50*	154	14.00	–

Runs	Wkts	Average	Best
1707	66	25.86	7–71

223. WHYSALL William Wilfrid
Born Woodborough, Nottinghamshire, 31 October 1887
Died Nottingham, 11 November 1930
Career Nottinghamshire, 1910–30
Tests 4
Debut v Australia, Adelaide, January 1925

Inns	NOs	HSc	Runs	Average	100s
7	0	76	209	29.85	–

Runs	Wkts	Average	Best
9	0	–	–

DID YOU KNOW...?

William Whysall, who played for Nottinghamshire for twenty years from 1910 and also in four Tests for England, died from blood poisoning after a fall on a dance floor when only forty-three years old.

224. ROOT Charles Frederick
Born Somercotes, Derbyshire, 16 April 1890
Died Wolverhampton, Staffordshire, 20 January 1954
Career Derbyshire, 1910–20; Worcestershire, 1921–32
Tests 3
Debut v Australia, Trent Bridge, June 1926

Inns	NOs	HSc	Runs	Average	100s
–	–	–	–	–	–

Runs	Wkts	Average	Best
194	8	24.25	4–84

225. LARWOOD Harold
Born Nuncargate, Nottinghamshire, 14 November 1904
Died Sydney, NSW, Australia, 22 July 1995
Career Nottinghamshire, 1924–38; Europeans, 1936–7
Tests 21
Debut v Australia, Lord's, June 1926

Inns	NOs	HSc	Runs	Average	100s
28	3	98	485	19.40	–

Runs	Wkts	Average	Best
2212	78	28.35	6–32

226. ASTILL William Ewart
Born Ratby, Leicestershire, 1 March 1888
Died Stoneygate, Leicester, 10 February 1948
Career Leicestershire, 1906–39
Tests 9
Debut v South Africa, Johannesburg, December 1927

Inns	NOs	HSc	Runs	Average	100s
15	0	40	190	12.66	–

Runs	Wkts	Average	Best
856	25	34.24	4–58

DID YOU KNOW...?

Wally Hammond was the first batsman to score double centuries in successive Test innings and the only one to do it twice: 251 and 200 against Australia in 1928–9, and 227 and 336 not out against New Zealand in 1933.

227. HAMMOND Walter Reginald
Born Dover, Kent, 19 June 1903
Died Durban, South Africa, 1 July 1965
Career Gloucestershire, 1920–51; South African Air Force, 1942–3
Tests 85
Debut v South Africa. Johannesburg, December 1927

Inns	NOs	HSc	Runs	Average	100s
140	16	336*	7249	58.45	22

Runs	Wkts	Average	Best
3138	83	37.80	5–36

228. LEGGE Geoffrey Bevington
Born Bromley, Kent, 26 January 1903
Died Brampford Speke, Devon, 21 November 1940
Career Kent, 1924–31; Oxford University, 1925–6
Tests 5
Debut v South Africa, Johannesburg, December 1927

Inns	NOs	HSc	Runs	Average	100s
7	1	196	299	49.83	1

Runs	Wkts	Average	Best
34	0	–	–

229. PEEBLES Ian Alexander Ross
Born Aberdeen, Scotland, 20 January 1908
Died Speen, Buckinghamshire, 27 February 1980
Career Middlesex, 1928–48; Oxford University, 1930; Scotland, 1937
Tests 13
Debut v South Africa, Johannesburg, December 1927

Inns	NOs	HSc	Runs	Average	100s
17	8	26	98	10.88	–

Runs	Wkts	Average	Best
1391	45	30.91	6–63

230. STANYFORTH Lt-Col Ronald Thomas
Born Chelsea, London, 30 May 1892
Died Kirk Hammerton, Yorkshire, 20 February 1964
Career Oxford University, 1914; Yorkshire, 1928
Tests 4
Debut v South Africa, Johannesburg, December 1927

Inns	NOs	HSc	Runs	Average	100s
6	1	6*	13	2.60	–

Runs	Wkts	Average	Best
–	–	–	–

231. WYATT Robert Elliott Storey
Born Milford, Surrey, 2 May 1901
Died Truro, Cornwall, 20 April 1995
Career Warwickshire, 1923–39; Worcestershire, 1946–51
Tests 40
Debut v South Africa, Johannesburg, December 1927

Inns	NOs	HSc	Runs	Average	100s
64	6	149	1839	31.70	2

Runs	Wkts	Average	Best
642	18	35.66	3–4

232. STAPLES Samuel James

Born Newstead Colliery, Nottinghamshire, 18 September 1892
Died Nottingham, 4 June 1950
Career Nottinghamshire, 1920–34
Tests 3
Debut v South Africa, Durban, January 1928

Inns	NOs	HSc	Runs	Average	100s
5	0	39	65	13.00	–

Runs	Wkts	Average	Best
435	15	29.00	3–50

233. DAWSON Edward William

Born Paddington, London, 13 February 1904
Died Idmiston, Wiltshire, 4 June 1979
Career Leicestershire, 1922–34; Cambridge University, 1924–7
Tests 5
Debut v South Africa, Durban, February 1928

Inns	NOs	HSc	Runs	Average	100s
9	0	55	175	19.44	–

Runs	Wkts	Average	Best
–	–	–	–

234. ELLIOTT Harry

Born Scarcliffe, Derbyshire, 2 November 1891
Died Derby, 2 February 1976
Career Derbyshire, 1920–47
Tests 4
Debut v South Africa, Durban, February 1928

Inns	NOs	HSc	Runs	Average	100s
5	1	37*	61	15.25	–

Runs	Wkts	Average	Best
–	–	–	–

235. JARDINE Douglas Robert

Born Malabar Hill, Bombay, India, 23 October 1900
Died Montreux, Switzerland, 18 June 1958
Career Oxford University, 1920–3; Surrey, 1921–33
Tests 22
Debut v West Indies, Lord's, June 1928

Inns	NOs	HSc	Runs	Average	100s
33	6	127	1296	48.00	1

Runs	Wkts	Average	Best
10	0	–	–

236. SMITH Harry

Born Fishponds, Bristol, 21 May 1891
Died Downend, Bristol, 12 November 1937
Career Gloucestershire, 1912–35
Tests 1
Debut v West Indies, Lord's, June 1928

Inns	NOs	HSc	Runs	Average	100s
1	0	7	7	7.00	–

Runs	Wkts	Average	Best
–	–	–	–

237. LEYLAND Maurice

Born Harrogate, Yorkshire, 20 July 1900
Died Harrogate, Yorkshire, 1 January 1967
Career Yorkshire, 1920–47; Patiala, 1926–7
Tests 41
Debut v West Indies, The Oval, August 1928

Inns	NOs	HSc	Runs	Average	100s
65	5	187	2764	46.06	9

Runs	Wkts	Average	Best
585	6	97.50	3–91

238. DULEEPSINHJI Kumar Shri

Born Sarodar, India, 13 June 1905
Died Bombay, India, 5 December 1959
Career Sussex, 1924–32; Cambridge University, 1925–8; Hindus, 1928–9
Tests 12
Debut v South Africa, Edgbaston, June 1929

Inns	NOs	HSc	Runs	Average	100s
19	2	173	995	58.52	3

Runs	Wkts	Average	Best
7	0	–	–

239. KILLICK Rev Edgar Thomas

Born Fulham, London, 9 May 1907
Died Northampton, 18 May 1953
Career Middlesex, 1926–39; Cambridge University, 1927–30
Tests 2
Debut v South Africa, Edgbaston, June 1929

Inns	NOs	HSc	Runs	Average	100s
4	0	31	81	20.25	–

Runs	Wkts	Average	Best
–	–	–	–

240. O'CONNOR Jack

Born Cambridge, 6 November 1897
Died Buckhurst Hill, Essex, 22 February 1977
Career Essex, 1921–39
Tests 4
Debut v South Africa, Lord's, June–July 1929

Inns	NOs	HSc	Runs	Average	100s
7	0	51	153	21.85	–

Runs	Wkts	Average	Best
72	1	72.00	1–31

241. ROBINS Robert Walter Vivian

Born Stafford, 3 June 1906
Died Marylebone, London, 12 December 1968
Career Middlesex, 1925–51; Cambridge University, 1926–8
Tests 19
Debut v South Africa, Lord's, June–July 1929

Inns	NOs	HSc	Runs	Average	100s
27	4	108	612	26.60	1

Runs	Wkts	Average	Best
1758	64	27.46	6–32

242. BOWLEY Edward Henry

Born Leatherhead, Surrey, 6 June 1890
Died Winchester, Hampshire, 9 July 1974
Career Sussex, 1912–34; Auckland, 1926–7 to 1928–9
Tests 5
Debut v South Africa, Headingley, July 1929

Inns	NOs	HSc	Runs	Average	100s
7	0	109	252	36.00	1

Runs	Wkts	Average	Best
116	0	–	–

243. BARRATT Fred

Born Annesley, Nottinghamshire, 12 April 1894
Died Nottingham, 29 January 1947
Career Nottinghamshire, 1914–31
Tests 5
Debut v South Africa, Old Trafford, July 1929

Inns	NOs	HSc	Runs	Average	100s
4	1	17	28	9.33	–

Runs	Wkts	Average	Best
235	5	47.00	1–8

244. AMES Leslie Ethelbert George
Born Elham, Kent, 3 December 1905
Died Canterbury, Kent, 26 February 1990
Career Kent, 1926–51
Tests 47
Debut v South Africa, The Oval, August 1929

Inns	NOs	HSc	Runs	Average	100s
72	12	149	2434	40.56	8

Runs	Wkts	Average	Best
–	–	–	–

245. CLARK Edward Winchester
Born Elton, Huntingdonshire, 9 August 1902
Died King's Lynn, Norfolk, 28 April 1982
Career Northamptonshire, 1922–47
Tests 8
Debut v South Africa, The Oval, August 1929

Inns	NOs	HSc	Runs	Average	100s
9	5	10	36	9.00	–

Runs	Wkts	Average	Best
899	32	28.09	5–98

246. ALLOM Maurice James Carrick
Born Northwood, Middlesex, 23 March 1906
Died Shipbourne, Kent, 8 April 1995
Career Cambridge University, 1926–8; Surrey, 1927–37
Tests 5
Debut v New Zealand, Christchurch, January 1930

Inns	NOs	HSc	Runs	Average	100s
3	2	8*	14	14.00	–

Runs	Wkts	Average	Best
265	14	18.92	5–38

 DID YOU KNOW...?

The smallest England players were both known as 'Tich': leg-spinner Percy Freeman was 5 feet 2 inches, while wicketkeeper Walter Cornford was barely over 5 feet tall.

247. CORNFORD Walter Latter
Born Hurst Green, Sussex, 25 December 1900
Died Brighton, Sussex, 6 February 1964
Career Sussex, 1921–47
Tests 4
Debut v New Zealand, Christchurch, January 1930

Inns	NOs	HSc	Runs	Average	100s
4	0	18	36	9.00	–

Runs	Wkts	Average	Best
–	–	–	–

248. GILLIGAN Alfred Herbert Harold
Born Denmark Hill, London, 29 June 1896
Died Shamley Green, Surrey, 5 May 1978
Career Sussex, 1919–31
Tests 4
Debut v New Zealand, Christchurch, January 1930

Inns	NOs	HSc	Runs	Average	100s
4	0	32	71	17.75	–

Runs	Wkts	Average	Best
–	–	–	–

249. NICHOLS Morris Stanley
Born Stondon Massey, Essex, 6 October 1900
Died Newark, Nottinghamshire, 26 January 1961
Career Essex, 1924–39
Tests 14
Debut v New Zealand, Christchurch, January 1930

Inns	NOs	HSc	Runs	Average	100s
19	7	78*	355	29.58	–

Runs	Wkts	Average	Best
1152	41	28.09	6–35

250. TURNBULL Maurice Joseph Lawson
Born Cardiff, Glamorgan, 16 March 1906
Died Montchamp, France, 5 August 1944
Career Glamorgan, 1924–39; Cambridge University, 1926–9
Tests 9
Debut v New Zealand, Christchurch, January 1930

Inns	NOs	HSc	Runs	Average	100s
13	2	61	224	20.36	–

Runs	Wkts	Average	Best
–	–	–	–

251. WORTHINGTON Thomas Stanley
Born Bolsover, Derbyshire, 21 August 1905
Died King's Lynn, Norfolk, 31 August 1973
Career Derbyshire, 1924–47
Tests 9
Debut v New Zealand, Christchurch, January 1930

Inns	NOs	HSc	Runs	Average	100s
11	0	128	321	29.18	1

Runs	Wkts	Average	Best
316	8	39.50	2–19

252. CALTHORPE Hon. Frederick Somerset Gough
Born Kensington, London, 27 May 1892
Died Worplesdon, Surrey, 19 November 1935
Career Sussex, 1911–12; Cambridge University, 1912–14 and 1919; Warwickshire, 1919–30
Tests 4
Debut v West Indies, Bridgetown, January 1930

Inns	NOs	HSc	Runs	Average	100s
7	0	49	129	18.42	–

Runs	Wkts	Average	Best
91	1	91.00	1–38

253. VOCE William
Born Annesley Woodhouse, Nottinghamshire, 8 August 1909
Died Nottingham, 6 June 1984
Career Nottinghamshire, 1927–52
Tests 27
Debut v West Indies, Bridgetown, January 1930

Inns	NOs	HSc	Runs	Average	100s
38	15	66	308	13.39	–

Runs	Wkts	Average	Best
2733	98	27.88	7–70

254. TOWNSEND Leslie Fletcher
Born Long Eaton, Derbyshire, 8 June 1903
Died Richmond, New Zealand, 17 February 1993
Career Derbyshire, 1922–39; Auckland, 1934–5 to 1935–6
Tests 4
Debut v West Indies, Georgetown, February 1930

Inns	NOs	HSc	Runs	Average	100s
6	0	40	97	16.16	–

Runs	Wkts	Average	Best
205	6	34.16	2–22

255. ALLEN Sir George Oswald Browning
Born Sydney, NSW, Australia, 31 July 1902
Died St John's Wood, London, 29 November 1989
Career Middlesex, 1921–50; Cambridge University, 1922–3
Tests 25
Debut v Australia, Lord's, June–July 1930

Inns	NOs	HSc	Runs	Average	100s
33	2	122	750	24.19	1

Runs	Wkts	Average	Best
2379	81	29.37	7–80

256. GODDARD Thomas William John
Born Gloucester, 1 October 1900
Died Gloucester, 22 May 1966
Career Gloucestershire, 1922–52
Tests 8
Debut v Australia, Old Trafford, July 1930

Inns	NOs	HSc	Runs	Average	100s
5	3	8	13	6.50	–

Runs	Wkts	Average	Best
588	22	26.72	6–29

257. FARRIMOND William
Born Daisy Hill, Lancashire, 23 May 1903
Died Bolton, Lancashire, 15 November 1979
Career Lancashire, 1924–45
Tests 4
Debut v South Africa, Johannesburg, February 1931

Inns	NOs	HSc	Runs	Average	100s
7	0	35	116	16.57	–

Runs	Wkts	Average	Best
–	–	–	–

258. LEE Henry William
Born Marylebone, London, 26 October 1890
Died Westminster, London, 21 April 1981
Career Middlesex, 1911–34; Cooch Behar's XI, 1917–18
Tests 1
Debut v South Africa, Johannesburg, February 1931

Inns	NOs	HSc	Runs	Average	100s
2	0	18	19	9.50	–

Runs	Wkts	Average	Best
–	–	–	–

259. ARNOLD John
Born Cowley, Oxford, 30 November 1907
Died Southampton, Hampshire, 4 April 1984
Career Hampshire, 1929–50
Tests 1
Debut v New Zealand, Lord's, June 1931

Inns	NOs	HSc	Runs	Average	100s
2	0	34	34	17.00	–

Runs	Wkts	Average	Best
–	–	–	–

260. BAKEWELL Alfred Harry
Born Walsall, Staffordshire, 2 November 1908
Died Westbourne, Dorset, 23 January 1983
Career Northamptonshire, 1928–36
Tests 6
Debut v New Zealand, Lord's, June 1931

Inns	NOs	HSc	Runs	Average	100s
9	0	107	409	45.44	1

Runs	Wkts	Average	Best
8	0	–	–

261. BROWN Frederick Richard
Born Lima, Peru, 16 December 1910
Died Ramsbury, Wiltshire, 24 July 1991
Career Cambridge University, 1930–1; Surrey, 1931–48; Northamptonshire, 1949–53
Tests 22
Debut v New Zealand, The Oval, July 1931

Inns	NOs	HSc	Runs	Average	100s
30	1	79	734	25.31	–

Runs	Wkts	Average	Best
1398	45	31.06	5–49

262. VERITY Hedley
Born Leeds, Yorkshire, 18 May 1905
Died Caserta, Italy, 31 July 1943
Career Yorkshire, 1930–9
Tests 40
Debut v New Zealand, The Oval, July 1931

Inns	NOs	HSc	Runs	Average	100s
44	12	66*	669	20.90	–

Runs	Wkts	Average	Best
3510	144	24.37	8–43

263. PAYNTER Edward
Born Oswaldtwistle, Lancashire, 5 November 1901
Died Keighley, Yorkshire, 5 February 1979
Career Lancashire, 1926–45
Tests 20
Debut v New Zealand, Old Trafford, August 1931

Inns	NOs	HSc	Runs	Average	100s
31	5	243	1540	59.23	4

Runs	Wkts	Average	Best
–	–	–	–

264. BOWES William Eric
Born Elland, Yorkshire, 25 July 1908
Died Leeds, Yorkshire, 5 September 1987
Career Yorkshire, 1929–47
Tests 15
Debut v India, Lord's, June 1932

Inns	NOs	HSc	Runs	Average	100s
11	5	10*	28	4.66	–

Runs	Wkts	Average	Best
1519	68	22.33	6–33

265. PATAUDI Nawab of, Sr (Iftikhar Ali Khan)
Born Pataudi, India, 16 March 1910
Died New Delhi, India, 5 January 1952
Career Oxford University, 1928–31; Patiala, 1931–2; Western Indian States, 1943–4; Southern Punjab, 1945–6; India, 1946
Tests 3
Debut v Australia, Sydney, December 1932

Inns	NOs	HSc	Runs	Average	100s
5	0	102	144	28.80	1

Runs	Wkts	Average	Best
–	–	–	–

266. MITCHELL Thomas Bignall
Born Creswell, Derbyshire, 4 September 1902
Died Hickleton, Yorkshire, 27 January 1996
Career Derbyshire, 1928–39
Tests 5
Debut v Australia, Brisbane, February 1933

Inns	NOs	HSc	Runs	Average	100s
6	2	9	20	5.00	–

Runs	Wkts	Average	Best
498	8	62.25	2–49

267. WALTERS Cyril Frederick

Born Bedlinog, Glamorgan, 28 August 1905
Died Neath, Glamorgan, 23 December 1992
Career Glamorgan, 1923–8; Worcestershire, 1928–35; Wales, 1927–9
Tests 11
Debut v West Indies, Lord's, June 1933

Inns	NOs	HSc	Runs	Average	100s
18	3	102	784	52.26	1

Runs	Wkts	Average	Best
–	–	–	–

DID YOU KNOW...?

Cyril Walters captained England in only one Test, the first of the 1934 Ashes series, in which he over-bowled leg-spinner Tommy Mitchell, 'because he was a chosen member of the team'.

268. LANGRIDGE James

Born Chailey, Sussex, 10 July 1906
Died Brighton, Sussex, 10 September 1966
Career Sussex, 1924–53; Auckland, 1927–8
Tests 8
Debut v West Indies, Old Trafford, July 1933

Inns	NOs	HSc	Runs	Average	100s
9	0	70	242	26.88	–

Runs	Wkts	Average	Best
413	19	21.73	7–56

269. BARNETT Charles John

Born Cheltenham, Gloucestershire, 3 July 1910
Died Stroud, Gloucestershire, 28 May 1993
Career Gloucestershire, 1927–48
Tests 20
Debut v West Indies, The Oval, August 1933

Inns	NOs	HSc	Runs	Average	100s
35	4	129	1098	35.41	2

Runs	Wkts	Average	Best
93	0	–	–

270. MARRIOTT Charles Stowell

Born Heaton Moor, Lancashire, 14 September 1895
Died Dollis Hill, Middlesex, 13 October 1966
Career Lancashire, 1919–21; Cambridge University, 1920–1; Kent, 1924–37
Tests 1
Debut v West Indies, The Oval, August 1933

Inns	NOs	HSc	Runs	Average	100s
1	0	0	0	0.00	–

Runs	Wkts	Average	Best
96	11	8.72	6–59

271. MITCHELL Arthur

Born Baildon, Yorkshire, 13 September 1902
Died Bradford, Yorkshire, 25 December 1976
Career Yorkshire, 1922–45
Tests 6
Debut v India, Bombay, December 1933

Inns	NOs	HSc	Runs	Average	100s
10	0	72	298	29.80	–

Runs	Wkts	Average	Best
4	0	–	–

272. VALENTINE Bryan Herbert

Born Blackheath, Kent, 17 January 1908
Died Otford, Kent, 2 February 1983
Career Kent, 1927–48; Cambridge University, 1928–9
Tests 7
Debut v India, Bombay, December 1933

Inns	NOs	HSc	Runs	Average	100s
9	2	136	454	64.85	2

Runs	Wkts	Average	Best
–	–	–	–

273. LEVETT William Howard Vincent

Born Goudhurst, Kent, 25 January 1908
Died Hastings, Sussex, 1 December 1995
Career Kent, 1930–47
Tests 1
Debut v India, Calcutta, January 1934

Inns	NOs	HSc	Runs	Average	100s
2	1	5	7	7.00	–

Runs	Wkts	Average	Best
–	–	–	–

274. FARNES Kenneth

Born Leytonstone, Essex, 8 July 1911
Died Chipping Warden, Oxfordshire, 20 October 1941
Career Essex, 1930–9; Cambridge University, 1931–3
Tests 15
Debut v Australia, Trent Bridge, June 1934

Inns	NOs	HSc	Runs	Average	100s
17	5	20	58	4.83	–

Runs	Wkts	Average	Best
1719	60	28.65	6–96

275. HOPWOOD John Leonard

Born Newton Hyde, Cheshire, 30 October 1903
Died Denton, Lancashire, 15 June 1985
Career Lancashire, 1923–39
Tests 2
Debut v Australia, Old Trafford, July 1934

Inns	NOs	HSc	Runs	Average	100s
3	1	8	12	6.00	–

Runs	Wkts	Average	Best
155	0	–	–

276. KEETON William Walter

Born Shirebrook, Derbyshire, 30 April 1905
Died Forest Town, Nottinghamshire, 10 October 1980
Career Nottinghamshire, 1926–52
Tests 2
Debut v Australia, Headingley, July 1934

Inns	NOs	HSc	Runs	Average	100s
4	0	25	57	14.25	–

Runs	Wkts	Average	Best
–	–	–	–

277. HOLLIES William Eric

Born Old Hill, Staffordshire, 5 June 1912
Died Chinley, Derbyshire, 16 April 1981
Career Warwickshire, 1932–57
Tests 13
Debut v West Indies, Bridgetown, January 1935

Inns	NOs	HSc	Runs	Average	100s
15	8	18*	37	5.28	–

Runs	Wkts	Average	Best
1332	44	30.27	7–50

278. HOLMES Errol Reginald Thorold
Born Calcutta, India, 21 August 1905
Died Marylebone, London, 16 August 1960
Career Surrey, 1924–55; Oxford University, 1925–7
Tests 5
Debut v West Indies, Bridgetown, January 1935

Inns	NOs	HSc	Runs	Average	100s
9	2	85*	114	16.28	–

Runs	Wkts	Average	Best
76	2	38.00	1–10

279. IDDON John
Born Mawdesley, Lancashire, 8 January 1902
Died Madeley, Staffordshire, 17 April 1946
Career Lancashire, 1924–45
Tests 5
Debut v West Indies, Bridgetown, January 1935

Inns	NOs	HSc	Runs	Average	100s
7	1	73	170	28.33	–

Runs	Wkts	Average	Best
27	0	–	–

280. PAINE George Alfred Edward
Born Paddington, London, 11 June 1908
Died Solihull, Warwickshire, 30 March 1978
Career Middlesex, 1926; Warwickshire, 1929–47
Tests 4
Debut v West Indies, Bridgetown, January 1935

Inns	NOs	HSc	Runs	Average	100s
7	1	49	97	16.16	–

Runs	Wkts	Average	Best
467	17	27.47	5–168

281. SMITH Cedric Ivan James
Born Corsham, Wiltshire, 25 August 1906
Died Mellor, Lancashire, 9 February 1979
Career Middlesex, 1934–9
Tests 5
Debut v West Indies, Bridgetown, January 1935

Inns	NOs	HSc	Runs	Average	100s
10	0	27	102	10.20	–

Runs	Wkts	Average	Best
393	15	26.20	5–16

282. TOWNSEND David Charles Humphery
Born Norton-on-Tees, County Durham, 20 April 1912
Died Norton-on-Tees, County Durham, 27 January 1997
Career Oxford University, 1933–4
Tests 3
Debut v West Indies, Port-of-Spain, January 1935

Inns	NOs	HSc	Runs	Average	100s
6	0	36	77	12.83	–

Runs	Wkts	Average	Best
9	0	–	–

283. MITCHELL-INNES Norman Stewart
Born Calcutta, India, 7 September 1914
Career Somerset, 1931–49; Oxford University, 1934–7; Scotland, 1937
Tests 1
Debut v South Africa, Trent Bridge, June 1935

Inns	NOs	HSc	Runs	Average	100s
1	0	5	5	5.00	–

Runs	Wkts	Average	Best
–	–	–	–

284. BARBER Wilfred
Born Cleckheaton, Yorkshire, 18 April 1901
Died Bradford, Yorkshire, 10 September 1968
Career Yorkshire, 1926–47
Tests 2
Debut v South Africa, Headingley, July 1935

Inns	NOs	HSc	Runs	Average	100s
4	0	44	83	20.75	–

Runs	Wkts	Average	Best
0	1	0.00	1–0

285. HARDSTAFF Joseph Jnr
Born Nuncargate, Nottingham, 3 July 1911
Died Worksop, Nottinghamshire, 1 January 1990
Career Nottinghamshire, 1930–55; Europeans, 1944–5; Auckland, 1948–9 to 1949–50
Tests 23
Debut v South Africa, Headingley, July 1935

Inns	NOs	HSc	Runs	Average	100s
38	3	205*	1636	46.74	4

Runs	Wkts	Average	Best
–	–	–	–

286. SIMS James Morton
Born Leyton, Essex, 13 May 1903
Died Canterbury, Kent, 27 April 1973
Career Middlesex, 1929–52
Tests 4
Debut v South Africa, Headingley, July 1935

Inns	NOs	HSc	Runs	Average	100s
4	0	12	16	4.00	–

Runs	Wkts	Average	Best
480	11	43.63	5–73

287. SMITH Denis
Born Somercotes, Derbyshire, 24 January 1907
Died Derby, 12 September 1979
Career Derbyshire, 1927–52
Tests 2
Debut v South Africa, Headingley, July 1935

Inns	NOs	HSc	Runs	Average	100s
4	0	57	128	32.00	–

Runs	Wkts	Average	Best
–	–	–	–

288. CLAY John Charles
Born Bonvilston, Glamorgan, 18 March 1898
Died Cowbridge, Glamorgan, 11 August 1973
Career Glamorgan, 1921–49; Wales, 1923–6
Tests 1
Debut v South Africa, The Oval, August 1935

Inns	NOs	HSc	Runs	Average	100s
–	–	–	–	–	–

Runs	Wkts	Average	Best
75	0	–	–

289. READ Holcombe Douglas
Born Woodford Green, Essex, 28 January 1910
Died Truro, Cornwall, 5 January 2000
Career Surrey, 1933; Essex, 1933–5
Tests 1
Debut v South Africa, The Oval, August 1935

Inns	NOs	HSc	Runs	Average	100s
–	–	–	–	–	–

Runs	Wkts	Average	Best
200	6	33.33	4–136

290. GIMBLETT Harold

Born Bicknoller, Somerset, 19 October 1914
Died Verwood, Dorset, 30 March 1978
Career Somerset, 1935–54
Tests 3
Debut v India, Lord's, June 1936

Inns	NOs	HSc	Runs	Average	100s
5	1	67*	129	32.25	–

Runs	Wkts	Average	Best
–	–	–	–

291. FAGG Arthur Edward

Born Chartham, Kent, 18 June 1915
Died Tunbridge Wells, Kent, 13 September 1977
Career Kent, 1932–57
Tests 5
Debut v India, Old Trafford, July 1936

Inns	NOs	HSc	Runs	Average	100s
8	0	39	150	18.75	–

Runs	Wkts	Average	Best
–	–	–	–

292. FISHLOCK Laurence Barnard

Born Battersea, London, 2 January 1907
Died Sutton, Surrey, 26 June 1986
Career Surrey, 1931–52
Tests 4
Debut v India, Old Trafford, July 1936

Inns	NOs	HSc	Runs	Average	100s
5	1	19*	47	11.75	–

Runs	Wkts	Average	Best
–	–	–	–

293. GOVER Alfred Richard

Born Epsom, Surrey, 29 February 1908
Died South London, 7 October 2001
Career Surrey, 1928–47
Tests 4
Debut v India, Old Trafford, July 1936

Inns	NOs	HSc	Runs	Average	100s
1	1	2*	2	–	–

Runs	Wkts	Average	Best
359	8	44.87	3–85

294. HUTTON Sir Leonard

Born Fulneck, Pudsey, Yorkshire, 23 June 1916
Died Kingston-upon-Thames, Surrey, 6 September 1990
Career Yorkshire, 1934–55
Tests 79
Debut v New Zealand, Lord's, June 1937

Inns	NOs	HSc	Runs	Average	100s
138	15	364	6971	56.67	19

Runs	Wkts	Average	Best
232	3	77.33	1–2

295. PARKS James Horace

Born Haywards Heath, Sussex, 12 May 1903
Died Cuckfield, Sussex, 21 November 1980
Career Sussex, 1924–39; Canterbury, 1946–7
Tests 1
Debut v New Zealand, Lord's, June 1937

Inns	NOs	HSc	Runs	Average	100s
2	0	22	29	14.50	–

Runs	Wkts	Average	Best
36	3	12.00	2–26

296. WELLARD Arthur William

Born Southfleet, Kent, 8 April 1902
Died Eastbourne, Sussex, 31 December 1980
Career Somerset, 1927–50
Tests 2
Debut v New Zealand, Old Trafford, July 1937

Inns	NOs	HSc	Runs	Average	100s
4	0	38	47	11.75	–

Runs	Wkts	Average	Best
237	7	33.85	4–81

297. COMPTON Denis Charles Scott

Born Hendon, Middlesex, 23 May 1918
Died Windsor, Berkshire, 23 April 1997
Career Middlesex, 1936–58; Holkar, 1944–5; Europeans, 1944–5 to 1945–6
Tests 78
Debut v New Zealand, The Oval, August 1937

Inns	NOs	HSc	Runs	Average	100s
131	15	278	5807	50.06	17

Runs	Wkts	Average	Best
1410	25	56.40	5–70

298. MATTHEWS Austin David George

Born Penarth, Glamorgan, 3 May 1904
Died Penrhyn Bay, Clwyd, 29 July 1977
Career Northamptonshire, 1927–36; Glamorgan, 1937–47
Tests 1
Debut v New Zealand, The Oval, August 1937

Inns	NOs	HSc	Runs	Average	100s
1	1	2*	2	–	–

Runs	Wkts	Average	Best
65	2	32.50	1–13

299. WASHBROOK Cyril

Born Blackburn, Lancashire, 6 December 1914
Died Manchester, 27 April 1999
Career Lancashire, 1933–59
Tests 37
Debut v New Zealand, The Oval, August 1937

Inns	NOs	HSc	Runs	Average	100s
66	6	195	2569	42.81	6

Runs	Wkts	Average	Best
33	1	33.00	1–25

300. EDRICH William John

Born Lingwood, Norfolk, 26 March 1916
Died Chesham, Buckinghamshire, 24 April 1986
Career Middlesex, 1937–58
Tests 39
Debut v Australia, Trent Bridge, June 1938

Inns	NOs	HSc	Runs	Average	100s
63	2	219	2440	40.00	6

Runs	Wkts	Average	Best
1693	41	41.29	4–68

301. SINFIELD Reginald Albert

Born Stevenage, Hertfordshire, 24 December 1900
Died Ham Green, Bristol, 17 March 1988
Career Gloucestershire, 1924–39
Tests 1
Debut v Australia, Trent Bridge, June 1938

Inns	NOs	HSc	Runs	Average	100s
1	0	6	6	6.00	–

Runs	Wkts	Average	Best
123	2	61.50	1–51

302. WRIGHT Douglas Vivian Parson
Born Sidcup, Kent, 21 August 1914
Died Canterbury, Kent, 13 November 1998
Career Kent, 1932–57
Tests 34
Debut v Australia, Trent Bridge, June 1938

Inns	NOs	HSc	Runs	Average	100s
39	13	45	289	11.11	–

Runs	Wkts	Average	Best
4224	108	39.11	7–105

303. PRICE Wilfred Frederick Frank
Born Westminster, London, 25 April 1902
Died Hendon, Middlesex, 13 January 1969
Career Middlesex, 1926–47
Tests 1
Debut v Australia, Lord's, June 1938

Inns	NOs	HSc	Runs	Average	100s
2	0	6	6	3.00	–

Runs	Wkts	Average	Best
–	–	–	–

304. WOOD Arthur
Born Bradford, Yorkshire, 25 August 1898
Died Ilkley, Yorkshire, 1 April 1973
Career Yorkshire, 1927–46
Tests 4
Debut v Australia, The Oval, August 1938

Inns	NOs	HSc	Runs	Average	100s
5	1	53	80	20.00	–

Runs	Wkts	Average	Best
–	–	–	–

305. GIBB Paul Antony
Born Brandsby, Yorkshire, 11 July 1913
Died Guildford, Surrey, 7 December 1977
Career Scotland, 1934–8; Cambridge University, 1935–8; Yorkshire, 1935–46; Essex, 1951–6
Tests 8
Debut v South Africa, Johannesburg, December 1938

Inns	NOs	HSc	Runs	Average	100s
13	0	120	581	44.69	2

Runs	Wkts	Average	Best
–	–	–	–

306. WILKINSON Leonard Litton
Born Northwich, Cheshire, 5 November 1916
Died Barrow-in-Furness, Cumbria, 3 September 2002
Career Lancashire, 1937–47
Tests 3
Debut v South Africa, Johannesburg, December 1938

Inns	NOs	HSc	Runs	Average	100s
2	1	2	3	3.00	–

Runs	Wkts	Average	Best
271	7	38.71	2–12

307. YARDLEY Norman Walter Dransfield
Born Barnsley, Yorkshire, 19 March 1915
Died Sheffield, Yorkshire, 3 October 1989
Career Cambridge University, 1935–8; Yorkshire, 1936–55
Tests 20
Debut v South Africa, Johannesburg, December 1938

Inns	NOs	HSc	Runs	Average	100s
34	2	99	812	25.37	–

Runs	Wkts	Average	Best
707	21	33.66	3–67

308. PERKS Reginald Thomas David
Born Hereford, 4 October 1911
Died Worcester, 22 November 1977
Career Worcestershire, 1930–55
Tests 2
Debut v South Africa, Durban, March 1939

Inns	NOs	HSc	Runs	Average	100s
2	2	2*	3	–	–

Runs	Wkts	Average	Best
355	11	32.27	5–100

309. COPSON William Henry
Born Stonebroom, Derbyshire, 27 April 1908
Died Clay Cross, Derbyshire, 14 September 1971
Career Derbyshire, 1932–50
Tests 3
Debut v West Indies, Lord's, June 1939

Inns	NOs	HSc	Runs	Average	100s
1	0	6	6	6.00	–

Runs	Wkts	Average	Best
297	15	19.80	5–85

 DID YOU KNOW...?

In 1947, Godfrey Evans set a record by taking 97 minutes to score his first run in a match against Australia.

310. OLDFIELD Norman
Born Dukinfield, Cheshire, 5 May 1911
Died Blackpool, Lancashire, 19 April 1996
Career Lancashire, 1935–9; Northamptonshire, 1948–54
Tests 1
Debut v West Indies, The Oval, August 1939

Inns	NOs	HSc	Runs	Average	100s
2	0	80	99	49.50	–

Runs	Wkts	Average	Best
–	–	–	–

311. BEDSER Alec Victor
Born Reading, Berkshire, 4 July 1918
Career Surrey, 1939–60
Tests 51
Debut v India, Lord's, June 1946

Inns	NOs	HSc	Runs	Average	100s
71	15	79	714	12.75	–

Runs	Wkts	Average	Best
5876	236	24.89	7–44

312. IKIN John Thomas
Born Bignall End, Staffordshire, 7 March 1918
Died Bignall End, Staffordshire, 15 September 1984
Career Lancashire, 1939–57
Tests 18
Debut v India, Lord's, June 1946

Inns	NOs	HSc	Runs	Average	100s
31	2	60	606	20.89	–

Runs	Wkts	Average	Best
354	3	118.00	1–38

313.   SMAILES Thomas Francis
Born   Ripley, Yorkshire, 27 March 1910
Died   Harrogate, Yorkshire, 1 December 1970
Career Yorkshire, 1932–48
Tests 1
Debut v India, Lord's, June 1946

Inns	NOs	HSc	Runs	Average	100s
1	0	25	25	25.00	–

Runs	Wkts	Average	Best
62	3	20.66	3–44

314.   POLLARD Richard
Born   Westhoughton, Lancashire, 19 June 1912
Died   Westhoughton, Lancashire, 16 December 1985
Career Lancashire, 1933–50
Tests 4
Debut v India, Old Trafford, July 1946

Inns	NOs	HSc	Runs	Average	100s
3	2	10*	13	13.00	–

Runs	Wkts	Average	Best
378	15	25.20	5–24

315.   EVANS Thomas Godfrey
Born   Finchley, Middlesex, 18 August 1920
Died   Northampton, 3 May 1999
Career Kent, 1939–67
Tests 91
Debut v India, The Oval, August 1946

Inns	NOs	HSc	Runs	Average	100s
133	14	104	2439	20.49	2

Runs	Wkts	Average	Best
–	–	–	–

316.   SMITH Thomas Peter Bromley
Born   Ipswich, Suffolk, 30 October 1908
Died   Hyères, France, 4 August 1967
Career Essex, 1929–51
Tests 4
Debut v India, The Oval, August 1946

Inns	NOs	HSc	Runs	Average	100s
5	0	24	33	6.60	–

Runs	Wkts	Average	Best
319	3	106.33	2–172

317.   COOK Cecil
Born   Tetbury, Gloucestershire, 23 August 1921
Died   Tetbury, Gloucestershire, 5 September 1996
Career Gloucestershire, 1946–64
Tests 1
Debut v South Africa, Trent Bridge, June 1947

Inns	NOs	HSc	Runs	Average	100s
2	0	4	4	2.00	–

Runs	Wkts	Average	Best
127	0	–	–

318.   DOLLERY Horace Edgar
Born   Reading, Berkshire, 14 October 1914
Died   Edgbaston, Birmingham, 20 January 1987
Career Warwickshire, 1934–55; Wellington, 1950–1
Tests 4
Debut v South Africa, Trent Bridge, June 1947

Inns	NOs	HSc	Runs	Average	100s
7	0	37	72	10.28	–

Runs	Wkts	Average	Best
–	–	–	–

319.   MARTIN John William
Born   Catford, London, 16 February 1917
Died   Woolwich, London, 4 January 1987
Career Kent, 1939–53
Tests 2
Debut v South Africa, Trent Bridge, June 1947

Inns	NOs	HSc	Runs	Average	100s
2	0	26	26	13.00	–

Runs	Wkts	Average	Best
129	1	129.00	1–111

320.   POPE George Henry
Born   Tibshelf, Derbyshire, 27 January 1911
Died   Chesterfield, Derbyshire, 29 October 1993
Career Derbyshire, 1933–48
Tests 1
Debut v South Africa, Lord's, June 1947

Inns	NOs	HSc	Runs	Average	100s
1	1	8*	8	–	–

Runs	Wkts	Average	Best
85	1	85.00	1–49

321.   CRANSTON Kenneth
Born   Aigburth, Liverpool, 20 October 1917
Career Lancashire, 1947–8
Tests 8
Debut v South Africa, Old Trafford, July 1947

Inns	NOs	HSc	Runs	Average	100s
14	0	45	209	14.92	–

Runs	Wkts	Average	Best
461	18	25.61	4–12

 DID YOU KNOW...?

In 1933, Peter Smith arrived at The Oval to play against the West Indies only to find that the invitation was a hoax. He finally made his Test debut some thirteen years later.

322.   GLADWIN Clifford
Born   Doe Lea, Derbyshire, 3 April 1916
Died   Chesterfield, Derbyshire, 10 April 1988
Career Derbyshire, 1939–58
Tests 8
Debut v South Africa, Old Trafford, July 1947

Inns	NOs	HSc	Runs	Average	100s
11	5	51*	170	28.33	–

Runs	Wkts	Average	Best
571	15	38.06	3–21

323.   BUTLER Harold James
Born   Clifton, Nottingham, 12 March 1913
Died   Lenton, Nottinghamshire, 17 July 1991
Career Nottinghamshire, 1933–54
Tests 2
Debut v South Africa, Headingley, July 1947

Inns	NOs	HSc	Runs	Average	100s
2	1	15*	15	15.00	–

Runs	Wkts	Average	Best
215	12	17.91	4–34

324. YOUNG John Albert
Born Paddington, London, 14 October 1912
Died St John's Wood, London, 5 February 1993
Career Middlesex, 1933–56
Tests 8
Debut v South Africa, Headingley, July 1947

Inns	NOs	HSc	Runs	Average	100s
10	5	10*	28	5.60	–

Runs	Wkts	Average	Best
757	17	44.52	3–65

DID YOU KNOW...?

At Trent Bridge, in 1948, England slow left-armer Jack Young bowled 11 consecutive maidens against Australia, a Test record at the time, and conceded only 79 runs from 60 overs.

325. HOWORTH Richard
Born Bacup, Lancashire, 26 April 1909
Died Worcester, 2 April 1980
Career Worcestershire, 1933–51; Europeans, 1944–5
Tests 5
Debut v South Africa, The Oval, August 1947

Inns	NOs	HSc	Runs	Average	100s
10	2	45*	145	18.12	–

Runs	Wkts	Average	Best
635	19	33.42	6–124

326. ROBERTSON John David Benbow
Born Chiswick, Middlesex, 22 February 1917
Died Bury St Edmonds, Suffolk, 12 October 1996
Career Middlesex, 1937–59
Tests 11
Debut v South Africa, The Oval, August 1947

Inns	NOs	HSc	Runs	Average	100s
21	2	133	881	46.36	2

Runs	Wkts	Average	Best
58	2	29.00	2–17

327. BROOKES Dennis
Born Kippax, Yorkshire, 29 October 1915
Died Northampton, 9 March 2006
Career Northamptonshire, 1934–59
Tests 1
Debut v West Indies, Bridgetown, January 1948

Inns	NOs	HSc	Runs	Average	100s
2	0	10	17	8.50	–

Runs	Wkts	Average	Best
–	–	–	–

328. LAKER James Charles
Born Bradford, Yorkshire, 9 February 1922
Died Putney, London, 23 April 1986
Career Surrey, 1946–59; Essex, 1962–4; Auckland, 1951–2
Tests 46
Debut v West Indies, Bridgetown, January 1948

Inns	NOs	HSc	Runs	Average	100s
63	15	63	676	14.08	–

Runs	Wkts	Average	Best
4101	193	21.24	10–53

329. PLACE Winston
Born Rawtenstall, Lancashire, 7 December 1914
Died Burnley, Lancashire, 25 January 2002
Career Lancashire, 1937–55
Tests 3
Debut v West Indies, Bridgetown, January 1948

Inns	NOs	HSc	Runs	Average	100s
6	1	107	144	28.80	1

Runs	Wkts	Average	Best
–	–	–	–

330. SMITHSON Gerald Arthur
Born Spofforth, Yorkshire, 1 November 1926
Died Abingdon, Berkshire, 6 September 1970
Career Yorkshire, 1946–50; Leicestershire, 1951–6
Tests 2
Debut v West Indies, Bridgetown, January 1948

Inns	NOs	HSc	Runs	Average	100s
3	0	35	70	23.33	–

Runs	Wkts	Average	Best
–	–	–	–

331. TREMLETT Maurice Fletcher
Born Stockport, Cheshire, 5 July 1923
Died Southampton, Hampshire, 30 July 1984
Career Somerset, 1947–60; Central Districts, 1951–2
Tests 3
Debut v West Indies, Bridgetown, January 1948

Inns	NOs	HSc	Runs	Average	100s
5	2	18*	20	6.66	–

Runs	Wkts	Average	Best
226	4	56.50	2–98

332. GRIFFITH Stewart Cathie
Born Wandsworth, London, 16 June 1914
Died Felpham, Sussex, 7 April 1993
Career Cambridge University, 1934–6; Surrey, 1934; Sussex, 1937–54
Tests 3
Debut v West Indies, Port-of-Spain, February 1948

Inns	NOs	HSc	Runs	Average	100s
5	0	140	157	31.40	1

Runs	Wkts	Average	Best
–	–	–	–

333. WARDLE John Henry
Born Ardsley, Yorkshire, 8 January 1923
Died Doncaster, Yorkshire, 23 July 1985
Career Yorkshire, 1946–58
Tests 28
Debut v West Indies, Port-of-Spain, February 1948

Inns	NOs	HSc	Runs	Average	100s
41	8	66	653	19.78	–

Runs	Wkts	Average	Best
2080	102	20.39	7–36

334. COXON Alexander
Born Huddersfield, Yorkshire, 18 January 1916
Died Roker, Sunderland, 22 January 2006
Career Yorkshire, 1945–50
Tests 1
Debut v Australia, Lord's, June 1948

Inns	NOs	HSc	Runs	Average	100s
2	0	19	19	9.50	–

Runs	Wkts	Average	Best
172	3	57.33	2–90

335. CRAPP John Frederick
Born St Columb Major, Cornwall, 14 October 1912
Died Knowle, Bristol, 13 February 1981
Career Gloucestershire, 1936–56
Tests 7
Debut v Australia, Old Trafford, July 1948

Inn	NOs	HSc	Runs	Average	100s
13	2	56	319	29.00	–

Runs	Wkts	Average	Best
–	–	–	–

336. EMMETT George Malcolm
Born Agra, India, 2 December 1912
Died Knowle, Bristol, 18 December 1976
Career Gloucestershire, 1936–59
Tests 1
Debut v Australia, Old Trafford, July 1948

Inns	NOs	HSc	Runs	Average	100s
2	0	10	10	5.00	–

Runs	Wkts	Average	Best
–	–	–	–

337. DEWES John Gordon
Born North Latchford, Cheshire, 11 October 1926
Career Cambridge University, 1948–50; Middlesex, 1948–56
Tests 5
Debut v Australia, The Oval, August 1948

Inns	NOs	HSc	Runs	Average	100s
10	0	67	121	12.10	–

Runs	Wkts	Average	Best
–	–	–	–

338. WATKINS Albert John
Born Usk, Monmouthshire, 21 April 1922
Career Glamorgan, 1939–62
Tests 15
Debut v Australia, The Oval, August 1948

Inns	NOs	HSc	Runs	Average	100s
24	4	137*	810	40.50	2

Runs	Wkts	Average	Best
554	11	50.36	3–20

339. JENKINS Roland Oliver
Born Rainbow Hill, Worcester, 24 November 1918
Died Worcester, 22 July 1995
Career Worcestershire, 1938–58
Tests 9
Debut v South Africa, Durban, December 1948

Inns	NOs	HSc	Runs	Average	100s
12	1`	39	198	18.00	–

Runs	Wkts	Average	Best
1098	32	34.31	5–116

340. MANN Francis George
Born Byfleet, Surrey, 6 September 1917
Died Berkshire, 8 August 2001
Career Middlesex, 1937–54; Cambridge University, 1938–9
Tests 7
Debut v South Africa, Durban, December 1948

Inns	NOs	HSc	Runs	Average	100s
12	2	136*	376	37.60	1

Runs	Wkts	Average	Best
–	–	–	–

341. SIMPSON Reginald Thomas
Born Sherwood Rise, Nottingham, 27 February 1920
Career Sind, 1944–5 to 1945–6; Europeans, 1944–to 1945–6; Nottinghamshire, 1946–63
Tests 27
Debut v South Africa, Durban, December 1948

Inns	NOs	HSc	Runs	Average	100s
45	3	156*	1401	33.35	4

Runs	Wkts	Average	Best
22	2	11.00	2–4

342. BAILEY Trevor Edward
Born Westcliff-on-Sea, Essex, 3 December 1923
Career Essex, 1946–67; Cambridge University, 1947–8
Tests 61
Debut v New Zealand, Headingley, June 1949

Inns	NOs	HSc	Runs	Average	100s
91	14	134*	2290	29.74	1

Runs	Wkts	Average	Best
3856	132	29.21	7–34

343. WHARTON Alan
Born Heywood, Lancashire, 30 April 1923
Died Colne, Lancashire, 26 August 1993
Career Lancashire, 1946–60; Leicestershire, 1961–3
Tests 1
Debut v New Zealand, Headingley, June 1949

Inns	NOs	HSc	Runs	Average	100s
2	0	13	20	10.00	–

Runs	Wkts	Average	Best
–	–	–	–

344. CLOSE Dennis Brian
Born Leeds, Yorkshire, 24 February 1931
Career Yorkshire, 1949–70; Somerset, 1971–7
Tests 22
Debut v New Zealand, Old Trafford, July 1949

Inns	NOs	HSc	Runs	Average	100s
37	2	70	887	25.34	–

Runs	Wkts	Average	Best
532	18	29.55	4–35

345. JACKSON Herbert Leslie
Born Whitwell, Derbyshire, 5 April 1921
Career Derbyshire, 1947–63
Tests 2
Debut v New Zealand, Old Trafford, July 1949

Inns	NOs	HSc	Runs	Average	100s
2	1	8	15	15.00	–

Runs	Wkts	Average	Best
155	7	22.14	2–26

 DID YOU KNOW...?

England captain George Mann made Test match history against New Zealand in 1949 by declaring on the first day.

346. BERRY Robert
Born West Gorton, Manchester, 29 January 1926
Career Lancashire, 1948–54; Worcestershire, 1955–8; Derbyshire, 1959–62
Tests 2
Debut v West Indies, Old Trafford, June 1950

Inns	NOs	HSc	Runs	Average	100s
4	2	4*	6	3.00	–

Runs	Wkts	Average	Best
228	9	25.33	5–63

DID YOU KNOW...?

England players who became vicars include Tom Killick, Vernon Royle and David Sheppard, and one of Doug Wright's names was Parson.

347. DOGGART George Hubert Graham
Born Earl's Court, London, 18 July 1925
Career Cambridge University, 1948–50; Sussex, 1948–61
Tests 2
Debut v West Indies, Old Trafford, June 1950

Inns	NOs	HSc	Runs	Average	100s
4	0	29	76	19.00	–

Runs	Wkts	Average	Best
–	–	–	–

348. PARKHOUSE William Gilbert Anthony
Born Swansea, Glamorgan, 12 October 1925
Died Carmarthen, Dyfed, 10 August 2000
Career Glamorgan, 1948–64
Tests 7
Debut v West Indies, Lord's, June 1950

Inns	NOs	HSc	Runs	Average	100s
13	0	78	373	28.69	–

Runs	Wkts	Average	Best
–	–	–	–

349. INSOLE Douglas John
Born Clapton, London, 18 April 1926
Career Cambridge University, 1947–9; Essex, 1947–63
Tests 9
Debut v West Indies, Trent Bridge, July 1950

Inns	NOs	HSc	Runs	Average	100s
17	2	110*	408	27.20	1

Runs	Wkts	Average	Best
–	–	–	–

350. SHACKLETON Derek
Born Todmorden, Yorkshire, 12 August 1924
Career Hampshire, 1948–69
Tests 7
Debut v West Indies, Trent Bridge, July 1950

Inns	NOs	HSc	Runs	Average	100s
13	7	42*	113	18.83	–

Runs	Wkts	Average	Best
768	18	42.66	4–72

351. HILTON Malcolm Jameson
Born Chadderton, Lancashire, 2 August 1928
Died Oldham, Lancashire, 8 July 1990
Career Lancashire, 1946–61
Tests 4
Debut v West Indies, The Oval, August 1950

Inns	NOs	HSc	Runs	Average	100s
6	1	15	37	7.40	–

Runs	Wkts	Average	Best
477	14	34.07	5–61

352. McINTYRE Arthur John William
Born Kennington, London, 14 May 1918
Career Surrey, 1938–63
Tests 3
Debut v West Indies, The Oval, August 1950

Inns	NOs	HSc	Runs	Average	100s
6	0	7	19	3.16	–

Runs	Wkts	Average	Best
–	–	–	–

353. SHEPPARD Lord David Stuart
Born Reigate, Surrey, 6 March 1929
Died Liverpool, 5 March 2005
Career Sussex, 1947–62; Cambridge University, 1950–2
Tests 22
Debut v West Indies, The Oval, August 1950

Inns	NOs	HSc	Runs	Average	100s
33	2	119	1172	37.80	3

Runs	Wkts	Average	Best
–	–	–	–

354. WARR John James
Born Ealing, Middlesex, 16 July 1927
Career Cambridge University, 1949–52; Middlesex, 1949–60
Tests 2
Debut v Australia, Sydney, January 1951

Inns	NOs	HSc	Runs	Average	100s
4	0	4	4	1.00	–

Runs	Wkts	Average	Best
281	1	281.00	1–76

355. TATTERSALL Roy
Born Bolton, Lancashire, 17 August 1922
Career Lancashire, 1948–60
Tests 16
Debut v Australia, Adelaide, February 1951

Inns	NOs	HSc	Runs	Average	100s
17	7	10*	50	5.00	–

Runs	Wkts	Average	Best
1513	58	26.08	7–52

356. STATHAM John Brian
Born Gorton, Manchester, 17 June 1930
Died Stockport, Cheshire, 10 June 2000
Career Lancashire, 1950–68
Tests 70
Debut v New Zealand, Christchurch, March 1951

Inns	NOs	HSc	Runs	Average	100s
87	28	38	675	11.44	–

Runs	Wkts	Average	Best
6261	252	24.84	7–39

357. WATSON Willie
Born Bolton-upon-Dearne, Yorkshire, 7 March 1920
Died Johannesburg, South Africa, 24 April 2004
Career Yorkshire, 1939–57; Leicestershire, 1958–64
Tests 23
Debut v South Africa, Trent Bridge, June 1951

Inns	NOs	HSc	Runs	Average	100s
37	3	116	879	25.85	2

Runs	Wkts	Average	Best
–	–	–	–

358. GRAVENEY Thomas William
Born Riding Mill, Northumberland, 16 June 1927
Career Gloucestershire, 1948–60; Worcestershire,
1961–70; Queensland, 1969–70 to 1971–2
Tests 79
Debut v South Africa, Old Trafford, July 1951

Inns	NOs	HSc	Runs	Average	100s
123	13	258	4882	44.38	11

Runs	Wkts	Average	Best
167	1	167.00	1–34

359. BRENNAN Donald Vincent
Born Bradford, Yorkshire, 10 February 1920
Died Ilkley, Yorkshire, 9 January 1985
Career Yorkshire, 1947–53
Tests 2
Debut v South Africa, Headingley, July 1951

Inns	NOs	HSc	Runs	Average	100s
2	0	16	16	8.00	–

Runs	Wkts	Average	Best
–	–	–	–

DID YOU KNOW...?

In his only two Tests, both in the 1950–1 Ashes series, England seamer John Warr had bowling figures of 0–142, 0–63 and 1–76 and batting scores of 4, 0, 0, 0.

360. LOWSON Frank Anderson
Born Bradford, Yorkshire, 1 July 1925
Died Pool-in-Wharfedale, Yorkshire, 8 September 1984
Career Yorkshire, 1949–58
Tests 7
Debut v South Africa, Headingley, July 1951

Inns	NOs	HSc	Runs	Average	100s
13	0	68	245	18.84	–

Runs	Wkts	Average	Best
–	–	–	–

361. MAY Peter Barker Howard
Born Reading, Berkshire, 31 December 1929
Died Liphook, Hampshire, 27 December 1994
Career Surrey, 1950–63; Cambridge University, 1950–2
Tests 66
Debut v South Africa, Headingley, July 1951

Inns	NOs	HSc	Runs	Average	100s
106	9	285*	4537	46.77	13

Runs	Wkts	Average	Best
–	–	–	–

362. CARR Donald Bryce
Born Wiesbaden, Germany, 28 December 1926
Career Derbyshire, 1946–63; Oxford University, 1949–51
Tests 2
Debut v India, Delhi, November 1951

Inns	NOs	HSc	Runs	Average	100s
4	0	76	135	33.75	–

Runs	Wkts	Average	Best
140	2	70.00	2–84

363. HOWARD Nigel David
Born Hyde, Cheshire, 18 May 1925
Died Douglas, Isle of Man, 31 May 1979
Career Lancashire, 1946–53
Tests 4
Debut v India, Delhi, November 1951

Inns	NOs	HSc	Runs	Average	100s
6	1	23	86	17.20	–

Runs	Wkts	Average	Best
–	–	–	–

364. KENYON Donald
Born Wordsley, Staffordshire, 15 May 1924
Died Worcester, 12 November 1996
Career Worcestershire, 1946–67
Tests 8
Debut v India, Delhi, November 1951

Inns	NOs	HSc	Runs	Average	100s
15	0	87	192	12.80	–

Runs	Wkts	Average	Best
–	–	–	–

365. RIDGWAY Frederick
Born Stockport, Cheshire, 10 August 1923
Career Kent, 1946–61
Tests 5
Debut v India, Delhi, November 1951

Inns	NOs	HSc	Runs	Average	100s
6	0	24	49	8.16	–

Runs	Wkts	Average	Best
379	7	54.14	4–83

366. SPOONER Richard Thompson
Born Stockton-on-Tees, County Durham, 30 December 1919
Died Torquay, Devon, 20 December 1997
Career Warwickshire, 1948–59
Tests 7
Debut v India, Delhi, November 1951

Inns	NOs	HSc	Runs	Average	100s
14	1	92	354	27.23	–

Runs	Wkts	Average	Best
–	–	–	–

367. LEADBEATER Edric
Born Huddersfield, Yorkshire, 15 August 1927
Career Yorkshire, 1949–56; Warwickshire, 1957–8
Tests 2
Debut v India, Bombay, December 1951

Inns	NOs	HSc	Runs	Average	100s
2	0	38	40	20.00	–

Runs	Wkts	Average	Best
218	2	109.00	1–38

368. POOLE Cyril John
Born Mansfield, Nottinghamshire, 13 March 1921
Died Balderton, Nottinghamshire, 11 February 1996
Career Nottinghamshire, 1948–62
Tests 3
Debut v India, Calcutta, Dec 1951–Jan 1952

Inns	NOs	HSc	Runs	Average	100s
5	1	69*	161	40.25	–

Runs	Wkts	Average	Best
9	0	–	–

369. TRUEMAN Frederick Sewards
Born Stainton, Yorkshire, 6 February 1931
Died Steeton, Yorkshire, 1 July 2006
Career Yorkshire, 1949–68
Tests 67
Debut v India, Headingley, June 1952

Inns	NOs	HSc	Runs	Average	100s
85	14	39*	981	13.81	–

Runs	Wkts	Average	Best
6625	307	21.57	8–31

370. LOCK Graham Anthony Richard
Born Limpsfield, Surrey, 5 July 1929
Died Perth, Western Australia, 30 March 1995
Career Surrey, 1946–63; Leicestershire, 1965–7; Western Australia, 1962–3 to 1970–1
Tests 49
Debut v India, Old Trafford, July 1952

Inns	NOs	HSc	Runs	Average	100s
63	9	89	742	13.74	–

Runs	Wkts	Average	Best
4451	174	25.58	7–35

371. MOSS Alan Edward
Born Tottenham, London, 14 November 1930
Career Middlesex, 1950–63
Tests 9
Debut v West Indies, Kingston, January 1954

Inns	NOs	HSc	Runs	Average	100s
7	1	26	61	10.16	–

Runs	Wkts	Average	Best
626	21	29.80	4–35

372. PALMER Charles Henry
Born Old Hill, Staffordshire, 15 May 1919
Died 31 March 2005
Career Worcestershire, 1938–49; Leicestershire, 1950–9; Europeans, 1945–6
Tests 1
Debut v West Indies, Bridgetown, February 1954

Inns	NOs	HSc	Runs	Average	100s
2	0	22	22	11.00	–

Runs	Wkts	Average	Best
15	0	–	–

373. APPLEYARD Robert
Born Bradford, Yorkshire, 27 June 1924
Career Yorkshire, 1950–8
Tests 9
Debut v Pakistan, Trent Bridge, July 1954

Inns	NOs	HSc	Runs	Average	100s
9	6	19*	51	17.00	–

Runs	Wkts	Average	Best
554	31	17.87	5–51

374. McCONNON James Edward
Born Burnopfield, County Durham, 21 June 1922
Died Altrincham, Cheshire, 26 January 2003
Career Glamorgan, 1950–61
Tests 2
Debut v Pakistan, Old Trafford, July 1954

Inns	NOs	HSc	Runs	Average	100s
3	1	11	18	9.00	–

Runs	Wkts	Average	Best
74	4	18.50	3–19

375. PARKS James Michael
Born Haywards Heath, Sussex, 21 October 1931
Career Sussex, 1949–72; Somerset, 1973–6

376. LOADER Peter James
Born Wallington, Surrey, 25 October 1929
Career Surrey, 1951–63; Western Australia, 1963–4
Tests 13
Debut v Pakistan, The Oval, August 1954

Inns	NOs	HSc	Runs	Average	100s
19	6	17	76	5.84	–

Runs	Wkts	Average	Best
878	39	22.51	6–36

377. TYSON Frank Holmes
Born Bolton, Lancashire, 6 June 1930
Career Northamptonshire, 1952–60
Tests 17
Debut v Pakistan, The Oval, August 1954

Inns	NOs	HSc	Runs	Average	100s
24	3	37*	230	10.95	–

Runs	Wkts	Average	Best
1411	76	18.56	7–27

378. ANDREW Keith Vincent
Born Oldham, Lancashire, 15 December 1929
Career Northamptonshire, 1953–66
Tests 2
Debut v Australia, Brisbane, Nov–Dec 1954

Inns	NOs	HSc	Runs	Average	100s
4	1	15	29	9.66	–

Runs	Wkts	Average	Best
–	–	–	–

379. COWDREY Michael Colin
Born Putumala, Ootacamund, India, 24 December 1932
Died Littlehampton, Sussex, 4 December 2000
Career Kent, 1950–76; Oxford University, 1952–4
Tests 114
Debut v Australia, Brisbane, Nov–Dec 1954

Inns	NOs	HSc	Runs	Average	100s
188	15	182	7624	44.06	22

Runs	Wkts	Average	Best
104	0	–	–

380. BARRINGTON Kenneth Frank
Born Reading, Berkshire, 24 November 1930
Died Needham's Point, Bridgetown, Barbados, 14 March 1981
Career Surrey, 1953–68
Tests 82
Debut v South Africa, Trent Bridge, June 1955

Inns	NOs	HSc	Runs	Average	100s
131	15	256	6806	58.67	20

Runs	Wkts	Average	Best
1300	29	44.82	3–4

DID YOU KNOW...?

Ken Barrington was the first England batsman to score centuries on all six major England Test grounds and against six other countries.

381. TITMUS Frederick John

Born St Pancras, London, 24 November 1932
Career Middlesex, 1949–82; Surrey, 1978; Orange Free
State, 1975–6
Tests 53
Debut v South Africa, Lord's, June 1955

Inns	NOs	HSc	Runs	Average	100s
76	11	84*	1449	22.29	–

Runs	Wkts	Average	Best
4931	153	32.22	7–79

382. RICHARDSON Peter Edward

Born Hereford, 4 July 1931
Career Worcestershire, 1949–58; Kent, 1959–65
Tests 34
Debut v Australia, Trent Bridge, June 1956

Inns	NOs	HSc	Runs	Average	100s
56	1	126	2061	37.47	5

Runs	Wkts	Average	Best
48	3	16.00	2–10

383. OAKMAN Alan Stanley Myles

Born Hastings, Sussex, 20 April 1930
Career Sussex, 1947–68
Tests 2
Debut v Australia, Headingley, July 1956

Inns	NOs	HSc	Runs	Average	100s
2	0	10	14	7.00	–

Runs	Wkts	Average	Best
21	0	–	–

384. SMITH Donald Victor

Born Broadwater, Sussex, 14 June 1923
Career Sussex, 1946–62
Tests 3
Debut v West Indies, Lord's, June 1957

Inns	NOs	HSc	Runs	Average	100s
4	1	16*	25	8.33	–

Runs	Wkts	Average	Best
97	1	97.00	1–12

385. RICHARDSON Derek Walter

Born Hereford, 3 November 1934
Career Worcestershire, 1952–67
Tests 1
Debut v West Indies, Trent Bridge, July 1957

Inns	NOs	HSc	Runs	Average	100s
1	0	33	33	33.00	–

Runs	Wkts	Average	Best
–	–	–	–

386. SMITH Michael John Knight

Born Westcotes, Leicester, 30 June 1933
Career Leicestershire, 1951–5; Oxford University, 1954–6;
Warwickshire, 1956–75
Tests 50
Debut v New Zealand, Edgbaston, June 1958

Inns	NOs	HSc	Runs	Average	100s
78	6	121	2278	31.63	3

Runs	Wkts	Average	Best
128	1	128.00	1–10

387. MILTON Clement Arthur

Born Bedminster, Bristol, 10 March 1928
Career Gloucestershire, 1948–74
Tests 6
Debut v New Zealand, Headingley, July 1958

Inns	NOs	HSc	Runs	Average	100s
9	1	104*	204	25.50	1

Runs	Wkts	Average	Best
12	0	–	–

388. DEXTER Edward Ralph

Born Milan, Italy, 15 May 1935
Career Cambridge University, 1956–8; Sussex, 1957–68
Tests 62
Debut v New Zealand, Old Trafford, July 1958

Inns	NOs	HSc	Runs	Average	100s
102	8	205	4502	47.89	9

Runs	Wkts	Average	Best
2306	66	34.93	4–10

389. ILLINGWORTH Raymond

Born Pudsey, Yorkshire, 8 June 1932
Career Yorkshire, 1951–83; Leicestershire, 1969–78
Tests 61
Debut v New Zealand, Old Trafford, July 1958

Inns	NOs	HSc	Runs	Average	100s
90	11	113	1836	23.24	2

Runs	Wkts	Average	Best
3807	122	31.20	6–29

390. SUBBA ROW Raman

Born Streatham, London, 29 January 1932
Career Cambridge University, 1951–3; Surrey, 1953–4;
Northamptonshire, 1955–61
Tests 13
Debut v New Zealand, Old Trafford, July 1958

Inns	NOs	HSc	Runs	Average	100s
22	1	137	984	46.85	3

Runs	Wkts	Average	Best
2	0	–	–

391. SWETMAN Roy

Born Westminster, London, 25 October 1933
Career Surrey, 1954–61; Nottinghamshire, 1966–7;
Gloucestershire, 1972–4
Tests 11
Debut v Australia, Sydney, January 1959

Inns	NOs	HSc	Runs	Average	100s
17	2	65	254	16.93	–

Runs	Wkts	Average	Best
–	–	–	–

392. MORTIMORE John Brian

Born Southmead, Bristol, 14 May 1933
Career Gloucestershire, 1950–75
Tests 9
Debut v Australia, Melbourne, February 1959

Inns	NOs	HSc	Runs	Average	100s
12	2	73*	243	24.30	–

Runs	Wkts	Average	Best
733	13	56.38	3–36

393. GREENHOUGH Thomas

Born Rochdale, Lancashire, 9 November 1931
Career Lancashire, 1951–66
Tests 4
Debut v India, Trent Bridge, June 1959

Inns	NOs	HSc	Runs	Average	100s
4	1	2	4	1.33	–

Runs	Wkts	Average	Best
357	16	22.31	5–35

394. HORTON Martin John
Born Worcester, 21 April 1934
Career Worcestershire, 1952–66; Northern Districts 1967–8 to 1970–1
Tests 2
Debut v India, Trent Bridge, June 1959

Inns	NOs	HSc	Runs	Average	100s
2	0	58	60	30.00	–

Runs	Wkts	Average	Best
59	2	29.50	2–24

395. TAYLOR Kenneth
Born Huddersfield, Yorkshire, 21 August 1935
Career Yorkshire, 1953–68; Auckland, 1963–4
Tests 3
Debut v India, Trent Bridge, June 1959

Inns	NOs	HSc	Runs	Average	100s
5	0	24	57	11.40	–

Runs	Wkts	Average	Best
6	0	–	–

396. PULLAR Geoffrey
Born Swinton, Lancashire, 1 August 1935
Career Lancashire, 1954–68; Gloucestershire 1969–70
Tests 28
Debut v India, Headingley, July 1959

Inns	NOs	HSc	Runs	Average	100s
49	4	175	1974	43.86	4

Runs	Wkts	Average	Best
37	1	37.00	1–1

397. RHODES Harold James
Born Hadfield, Derbyshire, 22 July 1936
Career Derbyshire, 1953–69
Tests 2
Debut v India, Headingley, July 1959

Inns	NOs	HSc	Runs	Average	100s
1	1	0*	0	–	–

Runs	Wkts	Average	Best
244	9	27.11	4–50

398. ALLEN David Arthur
Born Horfield, Bristol, 29 October 1935
Career Gloucestershire, 1953–72
Tests 39
Debut v West Indies, Bridgetown, January 1960

Inns	NOs	HSc	Runs	Average	100s
51	15	88	918	25.50	–

Runs	Wkts	Average	Best
3779	122	30.97	5–30

399. BARBER Robert William
Born Withington, Lancashire, 26 September 1935
Career Lancashire, 1954–62; Cambridge University, 1955–7; Warwickshire, 1963–9
Tests 28
Debut v South Africa, Edgbaston, June 1960

Inns	NOs	HSc	Runs	Average	100s
45	3	185	1495	35.59	1

Runs	Wkts	Average	Best
1806	42	43.00	4–132

400. WALKER Peter Michael
Born Clifton, Bristol, 17 February 1936
Career Glamorgan, 1956–72; Transvaal, 1956–7 to 1957–8; Western Province, 1962–3
Tests 3
Debut v South Africa, Edgbaston, 1960

Inns	NOs	HSc	Runs	Average	100s
4	0	52	128	32.00	–

Runs	Wkts	Average	Best
34	0	–	–

401. PADGETT Douglas Ernest Vernon
Born Bradford, Yorkshire, 20 July 1934
Career Yorkshire, 1951–71
Tests 2
Debut v South Africa, Old Trafford, July 1960

Inns	NOs	HSc	Runs	Average	100s
4	0	31	51	12.75	–

Runs	Wkts	Average	Best
8	0	–	–

402. MURRAY John Thomas
Born North Kensington, London, 1 April 1935
Career Middlesex, 1952–75
Tests 21
Debut v Australia, Edgbaston, June 1961

Inns	NOs	HSc	Runs	Average	100s
28	5	112	506	22.00	1

Runs	Wkts	Average	Best
–	–	–	–

403. FLAVELL John Alfred
Born Wall Heath, Staffordshire, 15 May 1929
Died Barmouth, Gwynedd, 25 February 2004
Career Worcestershire, 1949–67
Tests 4
Debut v Australia, Old Trafford, July–August 1961

Inns	NOs	HSc	Runs	Average	100s
6	2	14	31	7.75	–

Runs	Wkts	Average	Best
367	7	52.42	2–65

404. BROWN Alan
Born Rainworth, Nottinghamshire, 17 October 1935
Career Kent, 1957–70
Tests 2
Debut v Pakistan, Lahore, October 1961

Inns	NOs	HSc	Runs	Average	100s
1	1	3*	3	–	–

Runs	Wkts	Average	Best
150	3	50.00	3–27

405. RUSSELL William Eric
Born Dumbarton, Scotland, 3 July 1936
Career Middlesex, 1956–72
Tests 10
Debut v Pakistan, Lahore, October 1961

Inns	NOs	HSc	Runs	Average	100s
18	1	70	362	21.29	–

Runs	Wkts	Average	Best
44	0	–	–

406. WHITE David William
Born Sutton Coldfield, Warwickshire, 14 December 1935
Career Hampshire, 1957–71; Glamorgan, 1972
Tests 2
Debut v Pakistan, Lahore, October 1961

Inns	NOs	HSc	Runs	Average	100s
2	0	0	0	0.00	–

Runs	Wkts	Average	Best
119	4	29.75	3–65

407. SMITH David Robert
Born Fishponds, Bristol, 5 October 1934
Died Bristol, 17 December 2003
Career Gloucestershire, 1956–70
Tests 5
Debut v India, Bombay, November 1961

Inns	NOs	HSc	Runs	Average	100s
5	1	34	38	9.50	–

Runs	Wkts	Average	Best
359	6	59.83	2–60

408. KNIGHT Barry Rolfe
Born Chesterfield, Derbyshire, 18 February 1938
Career Essex, 1955–66; Leicestershire, 1967–9
Tests 29
Debut v India, Kanpur, December 1961

Inns	NOs	HSc	Runs	Average	100s
38	7	127	812	26.19	2

Runs	Wkts	Average	Best
2223	70	31.75	4–38

409. MILLMAN Geoffrey
Born Bedford, 2 October 1934
Died Bedford, 6 April 2005
Career Nottinghamshire, 1957–65
Tests 6
Debut v India, Calcutta, Dec 1961–Jan 1962

Inns	NOs	HSc	Runs	Average	100s
7	2	32*	60	12.00	–

Runs	Wkts	Average	Best
–	–	–	–

410. PARFITT Peter Howard
Born North Elmham, Norfolk, 8 December 1936
Career Middlesex, 1956–72
Tests 37
Debut v India, Calcutta, Dec 1961–Jan 1962

Inns	NOs	HSc	Runs	Average	100s
52	6	131*	1882	40.91	7

Runs	Wkts	Average	Best
574	12	47.83	2–5

411. COLDWELL Leonard John
Born Newton Abbot, Devon, 10 January 1933
Died Teignmouth, Devon, 6 August 1996
Career Worcestershire, 1955–69
Tests 7
Debut v Pakistan, Lord's, June 1962

Inns	NOs	HSc	Runs	Average	100s
7	5	6*	9	4.50	–

Runs	Wkts	Average	Best
610	22	27.72	6–85

412. STEWART Michael James
Born Herne Hill, London, 16 September 1932
Career Surrey, 1954–72
Tests 8
Debut v Pakistan, Lord's, June 1962

Inns	NOs	HSc	Runs	Average	100s
12	1	87	385	35.00	–

Runs	Wkts	Average	Best
–	–	–	–

413. LARTER John David Frederick
Born Inverness, Scotland, 24 April 1940
Career Northamptonshire, 1960–9
Tests 10
Debut v Pakistan, The Oval, August 1962

Inns	NOs	HSc	Runs	Average	100s
7	2	10	16	3.20	–

Runs	Wkts	Average	Best
941	37	25.43	5–57

414. SMITH Alan Christopher
Born Hall Green, Birmingham, 25 October 1936
Career Warwickshire, 1958–74; Oxford University, 1958–60
Tests 6
Debut v Australia, Brisbane, Nov–Dec 1962

Inns	NOs	HSc	Runs	Average	100s
7	3	69*	118	29.50	–

Runs	Wkts	Average	Best
–	–	–	–

415. EDRICH John Hugh
Born Blofield, Norfolk, 21 June 1937
Career Surrey, 1958–78
Tests 77
Debut v West Indies, Old Trafford, June 1963

Inns	NOs	HSc	Runs	Average	100s
127	9	310*	5138	43.54	12

Runs	Wkts	Average	Best
23	0	–	–

416. WILSON Donald
Born Settle, Yorkshire, 7 August 1937
Career Yorkshire, 1957–74
Tests 6
Debut v West Indies, Old Trafford, June 1963

Inns	NOs	HSc	Runs	Average	100s
7	1	42	75	12.50	–

Runs	Wkts	Average	Best
466	11	42.36	2–17

417. SHARPE Philip John
Born Shipley, Yorkshire, 27 December 1936
Career Yorkshire, 1958–74; Derbyshire, 1975–6
Tests 12
Debut v West Indies, Edgbaston, July 1963

Inns	NOs	HSc	Runs	Average	100s
21	4	111	786	46.23	1

Runs	Wkts	Average	Best
–	–	–	–

418. BOLUS John Brian
Born Leeds, Yorkshire, 31 January 1934
Career Yorkshire, 1956–62; Nottinghamshire, 1963–72; Derbyshire, 1973–5
Tests 7
Debut v West Indies, Headingley, July 1963

Inns	NOs	HSc	Runs	Average	100s
12	0	88	496	41.33	–

Runs	Wkts	Average	Best
16	0	–	–

419. BINKS James Graham
Born Hull, Yorkshire, 5 October 1935
Career Yorkshire, 1955–69
Tests 2
Debut v India, Bombay, January 1964

Inns	NOs	HSc	Runs	Average	100s
4	0	55	91	22.75	–

Runs	Wkts	Average	Best
–	–	–	–

420. JONES Ivor Jeffrey
Born Dafen, Carmarthenshire, 10 December 1941
Career Glamorgan, 1960–8
Tests 15
Debut v India, Bombay, January 1964

Inns	NOs	HSc	Runs	Average	100s
17	9	16	38	4.75	–

Runs	Wkts	Average	Best
1769	44	40.20	6–118

421. PRICE John Sidney Ernest
Born Harrow, Middlesex, 22 July 1937
Career Middlesex, 1961–75
Tests 15
Debut v India, Bombay, January 1964

Inns	NOs	HSc	Runs	Average	100s
15	6	32	66	7.33	–

Runs	Wkts	Average	Best
1401	40	35.02	5–73

422. BOYCOTT Geoffrey
Born Fitzwilliam, Yorkshire, 21 October 1940
Career Yorkshire, 1962–86; Northern Transvaal, 1971–2
Tests 108
Debut v Australia, Trent Bridge, June 1964

Inns	NOs	HSc	Runs	Average	100s
193	23	246*	8114	47.72	22

Runs	Wkts	Average	Best
382	7	54.57	3–47

 DID YOU KNOW...?

The only batsman to score 99 while carrying his bat was Geoff Boycott against Australia in 1979.

423. GIFFORD Norman
Born Ulverston, Lancashire, 30 March 1940
Career Worcestershire, 1960–82; Warwickshire, 1983–8
Tests 15
Debut v Australia, Lord's, June 1964

Inns	NOs	HSc	Runs	Average	100s
20	9	25*	179	16.27	–

Runs	Wkts	Average	Best
1026	33	31.09	5–55

424. CARTWRIGHT Thomas William
Born Coventry, Warwickshire, 22 July 1935
Career Warwickshire, 1952–69; Somerset, 1970–6; Glamorgan, 1977
Tests 5
Debut v Australia, Old Trafford, July 1964

Inns	NOs	HSc	Runs	Average	100s
7	2	9	26	5.20	–

Runs	Wkts	Average	Best
544	15	36.26	6–94

425. RUMSEY Frederick Edward
Born Stepney, London, 4 December 1935
Career Worcestershire, 1960–2; Somerset, 1963–8; Derbyshire, 1970
Tests 5
Debut v Australia, Old Trafford, July 1964

Inns	NOs	HSc	Runs	Average	100s
5	3	21*	30	15.00	–

Runs	Wkts	Average	Best
461	17	27.11	4–25

426. THOMSON Norman Ian
Born Walsall, Staffordshire, 23 January 1929
Career Sussex, 1952–72
Tests 5
Debut v South Africa, Durban, December 1964

Inns	NOs	HSc	Runs	Average	100s
4	1	39	69	23.00	–

Runs	Wkts	Average	Best
568	9	63.11	2–55

427. PALMER Kenneth Ernest
Born Winchester, Hampshire, 22 April 1937
Career Somerset, 1955–69
Tests 1
Debut v South Africa, Port Elizabeth, February 1965

Inns	NOs	HSc	Runs	Average	100s
1	0	10	10	10.00	–

Runs	Wkts	Average	Best
189	1	189.00	1–113

428. SNOW John Augustine
Born Peopleton, Worcestershire, 13 October 1941
Career Sussex, 1961–77
Tests 49
Debut v New Zealand, Lord's, June 1965

Inns	NOs	HSc	Runs	Average	100s
71	14	73	772	13.54	–

Runs	Wkts	Average	Best
5387	202	26.66	7–40

429. BROWN David John
Born Walsall, Staffordshire, 30 January 1942
Career Warwickshire, 1961–82
Tests 26
Debut v South Africa, Lord's, June 1965

Inns	NOs	HSc	Runs	Average	100s
34	5	44*	342	11.79	–

Runs	Wkts	Average	Best
2237	79	28.31	5–42

430. HIGGS Kenneth
Born Sandyford, Staffordshire, 14 January 1937
Career Lancashire, 1958–69; Leicestershire, 1972–86
Tests 15
Debut v South Africa, The Oval, August 1965

Inns	NOs	HSc	Runs	Average	100s
19	3	63	185	11.56	–

Runs	Wkts	Average	Best
1473	71	20.74	6–91

431. MILBURN Colin
Born Burnopfield, County Durham, 23 October 1941
Died Aycliffe Village, County Durham, 28 February 1990
Career Northamptonshire, 1960–74; Western Australia, 1966–7 to 1968–9
Tests 9
Debut v West Indies, Old Trafford, June 1966

Inns	NOs	HSc	Runs	Average	100s
16	2	139	654	46.71	2

Runs	Wkts	Average	Best
–	–	–	–

432. D'OLIVEIRA Basil Lewis
Born Signal Hill, Cape Town, South Africa, 4 October 1931
Career Worcestershire, 1964–80
Tests 44
Debut v West Indies, Lord's, June 1966

Inns	NOs	HSc	Runs	Average	100s
70	8	158	2484	40.06	5

Runs	Wkts	Average	Best
1859	47	39.55	3–46

433. UNDERWOOD Derek Leslie
Born Bromley, Kent, 8 June 1945
Career Kent, 1963–87
Tests 86
Debut v West Indies, Trent Bridge, June–July 1966

Inns	NOs	HSc	Runs	Average	100s
116	35	45*	937	11.56	–

Runs	Wkts	Average	Best
7674	297	25.83	8–51

434. AMISS Dennis Leslie
Born Harborne, Birmingham, 7 April 1943
Career Warwickshire, 1960–87
Tests 50
Debut v West Indies, The Oval, August 1966

Inns	NOs	HSc	Runs	Average	100s
88	10	262*	3612	46.30	11

Runs	Wkts	Average	Best
–	–	–	–

435. HOBBS Robin Nicholas Stuart
Born Chippenham, Wiltshire, 8 May 1942
Career Essex, 1961–75; Glamorgan, 1979–81
Tests 7
Debut v India, Headingley, June 1967

Inns	NOs	HSc	Runs	Average	100s
8	3	15*	34	6.80	–

Runs	Wkts	Average	Best
481	12	40.08	3–25

436. ARNOLD Geoffrey Graham
Born Earlsfield, Surrey, 3 September 1944
Career Surrey, 1963–77; Sussex, 1978–82; Orange Free State, 1976–7
Tests 34
Debut v Pakistan, Trent Bridge, August 1967

Inns	NOs	HSc	Runs	Average	100s
46	11	59	421	12.02	–

Runs	Wkts	Average	Best
3254	115	28.29	6–45

437. KNOTT Alan Philip Eric
Born Belvedere, Kent, 9 April 1946
Career Kent, 1964–85; Tasmania, 1969–70
Tests 95
Debut v Pakistan, Trent Bridge, August 1967

Inns	NOs	HSc	Runs	Average	100s
149	15	135	4389	32.75	5

Runs	Wkts	Average	Best
–	–	–	–

438. POCOCK Patrick Ian
Born Bangor, Caernarvonshire, 24 September 1946
Career Surrey, 1964–86; Northern Transvaal 1971–2
Tests 25

Debut v West Indies, Bridgetown, Feb–March 1968

Inns	NOs	HSc	Runs	Average	100s
37	4	33	206	6.24	–

Runs	Wkts	Average	Best
2976	67	44.41	6–79

 DID YOU KNOW...?

Keith Fletcher took seven hours and 3,289 balls to score a century at The Oval in 1974, the slowest Test century made in England.

439. FLETCHER Keith William Robert
Born Worcester, 20 May 1944
Career Essex, 1962–88
Tests 59
Debut v Australia, Headingley, July 1968

Inns	NOs	HSc	Runs	Average	100s
96	14	216	3272	39.90	7

Runs	Wkts	Average	Best
193	2	96.50	1–6

440. PRIDEAUX Roger Malcolm
Born Chelsea, London, 13 July 1939
Career Cambridge University, 1958–60; Kent, 1960–1; Northamptonshire, 1962–70; Sussex, 1971–3; Orange Free State, 1971–2 to 1974–5
Tests 3
Debut v Australia, Headingley, July 1968

Inns	NOs	HSc	Runs	Average	100s
6	1	64	102	20.40	–

Runs	Wkts	Average	Best
0	0	–	–

441. COTTAM Robert Michael Henry
Born Cleethorpes, Lincolnshire, 16 October 1944
Career Hampshire, 1963–71; Northamptonshire, 1972–6
Tests 4
Debut v Pakistan, Lahore, February 1969

Inns	NOs	HSc	Runs	Average	100s
5	1	13	27	6.75	–

Runs	Wkts	Average	Best
327	14	23.35	4–50

442. HAMPSHIRE John Harry
Born Thurnscoe, Yorkshire, 10 February 1941
Career Yorkshire, 1961–81; Tasmania, 1967–8 to 1978–9; Derbyshire, 1982–4
Tests 8
Debut v West Indies, Lord's, June–July 1969

Inns	NOs	HSc	Runs	Average	100s
16	1	107	403	26.86	1

Runs	Wkts	Average	Best
–	–	–	–

443. WARD Alan
Born Dronfield, Derbyshire, 10 August 1947
Career Derbyshire, 1966–76; Border, 1971–2; Leicestershire, 1977–8
Tests 5
Debut v New Zealand, Lord's, July 1969

Inns	NOs	HSc	Runs	Average	100s
6	1	21	40	8.00	–

Runs	Wkts	Average	Best
453	14	32.35	4–61

444. DENNESS Michael Henry
Born Bellshill, Lanarkshire, Scotland, 1 December 1940
Career Scotland, 1959–67; Kent, 1962–76; Essex, 1977–80
Tests 28
Debut v New Zealand, The Oval, August 1969

Inns	NOs	HSc	Runs	Average	100s
45	3	188	1667	39.69	4

Runs	Wkts	Average	Best
–	–	–	–

445. LUCKHURST Brian William
Born Sittingbourne, Kent, 5 February 1939
Died Canterbury, Kent, 1 March 2005
Career Kent, 1958–85
Tests 21
Debut v Australia, Brisbane, Nov–Dec 1970

Inns	NOs	HSc	Runs	Average	100s
41	5	131	1298	36.05	4

Runs	Wkts	Average	Best
32	1	32.00	1–9

446. SHUTTLEWORTH Kenneth
Born St Helens, Lancashire, 13 November 1944
Career Lancashire, 1964–75; Leicestershire, 1977–80
Tests 5
Debut v Australia, Brisbane, Nov–Dec 1970

Inns	NOs	HSc	Runs	Average	100s
6	0	21	46	7.66	–

Runs	Wkts	Average	Best
427	12	35.58	5–47

447. LEVER Peter
Born Todmorden, Yorkshire, 17 September 1940
Career Lancashire, 1960–76; Tasmania, 1971–2
Tests 17
Debut v Australia, Perth, December 1970

Inns	NOs	HSc	Runs	Average	100s
18	2	88*	350	21.87	–

Runs	Wkts	Average	Best
1509	41	36.80	6–38

448. WILLIS Robert George Dylan
Born Sunderland, County Durham, 30 May 1949
Career Surrey, 1969–71; Warwickshire, 1972–84; Northern Transvaal, 1972–3
Tests 90
Debut v Australia, Sydney, January 1971

Inns	NOs	HSc	Runs	Average	100s
128	55	28*	840	11.50	–

Runs	Wkts	Average	Best
8190	325	25.20	8–43

449. TAYLOR Robert William
Born Stoke-on-Trent, Staffordshire, 17 July 1941
Career Derbyshire, 1961–84
Tests 57
Debut v New Zealand, Christchurch, Feb–March 1971

Inns	NOs	HSc	Runs	Average	100s
83	12	97	1156	16.28	–

Runs	Wkts	Average	Best
6	0	–	–

450. HUTTON Richard Anthony
Born Pudsey, Yorkshire, 6 September 1942
Career Yorkshire, 1962–74; Cambridge University, 1962–4; Transvaal, 1975–6
Tests 5
Debut v Pakistan, Lord's, June 1971

Inns	NOs	HSc	Runs	Average	100s
8	2	81	219	36.50	–

Runs	Wkts	Average	Best
257	9	28.55	3–72

451. JAMESON John Alexander
Born Byculla, Bombay, India, 30 June 1941
Career Warwickshire, 1960–76
Tests 4
Debut v India, Old Trafford, August 1971

Inns	NOs	HSc	Runs	Average	100s
8	0	82	214	26.75	–

Runs	Wkts	Average	Best
17	1	17.00	1–17

452. GREIG Anthony William
Born Queenstown, South Africa, 6 October 1946
Career Border, 1965–6 to 1969–70; Sussex, 1966–78; Eastern Province, 1970–1 to 1971–2
Tests 58
Debut v Australia, Old Trafford, June 1972

Inns	NOs	HSc	Runs	Average	100s
93	4	148	3599	40.43	8

Runs	Wkts	Average	Best
4541	141	32.20	8–86

453. WOOD Barry
Born Ossett, Yorkshire, 26 December 1942
Career Yorkshire, 1964; Lancashire, 1966–79; Derbyshire, 1980–3; Eastern Province, 1971–2 to 1973–4
Tests 12
Debut v Australia, The Oval, August 1972

Inns	NOs	HSc	Runs	Average	100s
21	0	90	454	21.61	–

Runs	Wkts	Average	Best
50	0	–	–

454. LEWIS Anthony Robert
Born Swansea, Glamorgan, 6 July 1938
Career Glamorgan, 1955–74; Cambridge University, 1960–2
Tests 9
Debut v India, Delhi, December 1972

Inns	NOs	HSc	Runs	Average	100s
16	2	125	457	32.64	1

Runs	Wkts	Average	Best
–	–	–	–

455. OLD Christopher Middleton
Born Middlesbrough, Yorkshire, 22 December 1948
Career Yorkshire, 1966–82; Northern Transvaal, 1981–2 to 1982–3; Warwickshire, 1983–5
Tests 46
Debut v India, Calcutta, Dec 1972–Jan 1973

Inns	NOs	HSc	Runs	Average	100s
66	9	65	845	14.82	–

Runs	Wkts	Average	Best
4020	143	28.11	7–50

456. BIRKENSHAW Jack
Born Rothwell, Yorkshire, 13 November 1940
Career Yorkshire, 1958–60; Leicestershire, 1961–80; Worcestershire, 1981
Tests 5
Debut v India, Kanpur, January 1973

Inn	NOs	HSc	Runs	Average	100s
7	0	64	148	21.14	–

Runs	Wkts	Average	Best
469	13	36.07	5–57

457. ROOPE Graham Richard James
Born Fareham, Hampshire, 12 July 1946
Career Surrey, 1964–82; Griqualand West, 1973–4
Tests 21
Debut v India, Kanpur, January 1973

Inns	NOs	HSc	Runs	Average	100s
32	4	77	860	30.71	–

Runs	Wkts	Average	Best
76	0	–	–

458. HAYES Frank Charles
Born Preston, Lancashire, 6 December 1946
Career Lancashire, 1970–84
Tests 9
Debut v West Indies, The Oval, July 1973

Inns	NOs	HSc	Runs	Average	100s
17	1	106*	244	15.25	1

Runs	Wkts	Average	Best
–	–	–	–

459. HENDRICK Michael
Born Darley Dale, Derbyshire, 22 October 1948
Career Derbyshire, 1969–81; Nottinghamshire, 1982–4
Tests 30
Debut v India, Old Trafford, June 1974

Inns	NOs	HSc	Runs	Average	100s
35	15	15	128	6.40	–

Runs	Wkts	Average	Best
2248	87	25.83	4–28

460. LLOYD David
Born Accrington, Lancashire, 18 March 1947
Career Lancashire, 1965–83
Tests 9
Debut v India, Lord's, June 1974

Inns	NOs	HSc	Runs	Average	100s
15	2	214*	552	42.46	1

Runs	Wkts	Average	Best
17	0	–	–

461. GOOCH Graham Alan
Born Leytonstone, Essex, 23 July 1953
Career Essex, 1973–97
Tests 118
Debut v Australia, Edgbaston, July 1975

Inns	NOs	HSc	Runs	Average	100s
215	6	333	8900	42.58	20

Runs	Wkts	Average	Best
1069	23	46.47	3–39

DID YOU KNOW...?

Graham Gooch celebrated his forty-first birthday in 1994 by becoming the first batsman to score 2,000 runs on any Test ground (Lord's).

462. STEELE David Stanley
Born Bradeley, Staffordshire, 29 September 1941
Career Northamptonshire, 1963–84; Derbyshire, 1979–81
Tests 8
Debut v Australia, Lord's, July–August 1975

Inns	NOs	HSc	Runs	Average	100s
16	0	106	673	42.06	1

Runs	Wkts	Average	Best
39	2	19.50	1–1

463. WOOLMER Robert Andrew
Born Kanpur, India, 14 May 1948
Career Kent, 1968–84; Natal, 1973–4 to 1975–6; Western Province, 1980–1
Tests 19
Debut v Australia, Lord's, July–August 1975

Inns	NOs	HSc	Runs	Average	100s
34	2	149	1059	33.09	3

Runs	Wkts	Average	Best
299	4	74.75	1–8

464. EDMONDS Philippe Henri
Born Lusaka, Northern Rhodesia, 8 March 1951
Career Cambridge University, 1971–3; Middlesex, 1971–87; Eastern Province, 1975–6
Tests 51
Debut v Australia, Headingley, August 1975

Inns	NOs	HSc	Runs	Average	100s
65	15	64	875	17.50	–

Runs	Wkts	Average	Best
4273	125	34.18	7–66

465. BREARLEY John Michael
Born Harrow, Middlesex, 28 April 1942
Career Cambridge University, 1961–4; Middlesex, 1961–83
Tests 39
Debut v West Indies, Trent Bridge, June 1976

Inn	NOs	HSc	Runs	Average	100s
66	3	91	1442	22.88	–

Runs	Wkts	Average	Best
–	–	–	–

466. SELVEY Michael Walter William
Born Chiswick, Middlesex, 25 April 1948
Career Surrey, 1968–71; Cambridge University, 1971; Middlesex, 1972–82; Orange Free State, 1973–4; Glamorgan, 1983–4
Tests 3
Debut v West Indies, Old Trafford, July 1976

Inns	NOs	HSc	Runs	Average	100s
5	3	5*	15	7.50	–

Runs	Wkts	Average	Best
343	6	57.16	4–41

467. BALDERSTONE John Christopher
Born Huddersfield, Yorkshire, 16 November 1940
Died Carlisle, Cumbria, 6 March 2000
Career Yorkshire, 1961–9; Leicestershire, 1971–86
Tests 2
Debut v West Indies, Headingley, July 1976

Inns	NOs	HSc	Runs	Average	100s
4	0	35	39	9.75	–

Runs	Wkts	Average	Best
80	1	80.00	1–80

468. WILLEY Peter
Born Sedgefield, County Durham, 6 December 1949
Career Northamptonshire, 1966–83; Eastern Province, 1982–3 to 1984–5; Leicestershire, 1984–91
Tests 26
Debut v West Indies, Headingley, July 1976

Inns	NOs	HSc	Runs	Average	100s
50	6	102*	1184	26.90	2

Runs	Wkts	Average	Best
456	7	65.14	2–73

469. MILLER Geoffrey
Born Chesterfield, Derbyshire, 8 September 1952
Career Derbyshire, 1973–90; Natal, 1983–4; Essex, 1987–9
Tests 34
Debut v West Indies, The Oval, August 1976

Inns	NOs	HSc	Runs	Average	100s
51	4	98*	1213	25.80	–

Runs	Wkts	Average	Best
1859	60	30.98	5–44

470. BARLOW Graham Derek
Born Folkestone, Kent, 26 March 1950
Career Middlesex, 1969–86
Tests 3
Debut v India, Delhi, December 1976

Inns	NOs	HSc	Runs	Average	100s
5	1	7*	17	4.25	–

Runs	Wkts	Average	Best
–	–	–	–

471. LEVER John Kenneth
Born Stepney, London, 24 February 1949
Career Essex, 1967–89; Natal, 1982–3 to 1984–5
Tests 21
Debut v India, Delhi, December 1976

Inns	NOs	HSc	Runs	Average	100s
31	5	53	306	11.76	–

Runs	Wkts	Average	Best
1951	73	26.72	7–46

472. RANDALL Derek William
Born Retford, Nottinghamshire, 24 February 1951
Career Nottinghamshire, 1972–93
Tests 47
Debut v India, Calcutta, January 1977

Inns	NOs	HSc	Runs	Average	100s
79	5	174	2470	33.37	7

Runs	Wkts	Average	Best
3	0	–	–

473. TOLCHARD Roger William
Born Torquay, Devon, 15 June 1946
Career Leicestershire, 1965–83
Tests 4
Debut v India, Calcutta, January 1977

Inns	NOs	HSc	Runs	Average	100s
7	2	67	129	25.80	–

Runs	Wkts	Average	Best
–	–	–	–

474. BOTHAM Ian Terence
Born Heswall, Cheshire, 24 November 1955
Career Somerset, 1974–86; Worcestershire, 1987–91; Queensland, 1987–8; Durham, 1991–2
Tests 102
Debut v Australia, Trent Bridge, July–August 1977

Inns	NOs	HSc	Runs	Average	100s
161	6	208	5200	33.54	14

Runs	Wkts	Average	Best
10878	383	28.40	8–34

DID YOU KNOW...?

Ian Botham, who tried most things in his eventful career, walked the 880 miles from John O'Groats to Land's End in 1985 to raise money for the Leukaemia Research Fund. In 1988, he emulated Hannibal's feat of crossing the Alps on an elephant.

475. COPE Geoffrey Alan
Born Leeds, Yorkshire, 23 February 1947
Career Yorkshire, 1966–80
Tests 3
Debut v Pakistan, Lahore, December 1977

Inns	NOs	HSc	Runs	Average	100s
3	0	22	40	13.33	–

Runs	Wkts	Average	Best
277	8	34.62	3–102

476. ROSE Brian Charles
Born Dartford, Kent, 4 June 1950
Career Somerset, 1969–87
Tests 9
Debut v Pakistan, Lahore, December 1977

Inns	NOs	HSc	Runs	Average	100s
16	2	70	358	25.57	–

Runs	Wkts	Average	Best
–	–	–	–

477. GATTING Michael William
Born Kingsbury, Middlesex, 6 June 1957
Career Middlesex, 1975–98
Tests 79
Debut v Pakistan, Karachi, January 1978

Inns	NOs	HSc	Runs	Average	100s
138	14	207	4409	35.55	10

Runs	Wkts	Average	Best
317	4	79.25	1–14

478. RADLEY Clive Thornton
Born Hertford, 13 May 1944
Career Middlesex, 1964–87
Tests 8
Debut v New Zealand, Christchurch, February 1978

Inns	NOs	HSc	Runs	Average	100s
10	0	158	481	48.10	2

Runs	Wkts	Average	Best
–	–	–	–

479. GOWER David Ivon
Born   Tunbridge Wells, Kent, 1 April 1957
Career Leicestershire, 1975–89; Hampshire, 1990–3
Tests 117
Debut v Pakistan, Edgbaston, June 1978

Inns	NOs	HSc	Runs	Average	100s
204	18	215	8231	44.25	18

Runs	Wkts	Average	Best
20	1	20.00	1–1

480. EMBUREY John Ernest
Born   Peckham, London, 20 August 1952
Career Middlesex, 1973–95; Western Province, 1982–3 to
         1983–4; Northamptonshire, 1996–7
Tests 64
Debut v New Zealand, Lord's, August 1978

Inns	NOs	HSc	Runs	Average	100s
96	20	75	1713	22.53	–

Runs	Wkts	Average	Best
5646	147	38.40	7–78

481. BAIRSTOW David Leslie
Born   Bradford, Yorkshire, 1 September 1951
Died   Marton-cum-Grafton, Yorkshire, 5 January 1998
Career Yorkshire, 1970–90; Griqualand West, 1976–7 to
         1977–8
Tests 4
Debut v India, The Oval, Aug–Sept 1979

Inns	NOs	HSc	Runs	Average	100s
7	1	59	125	20.83	–

Runs	Wkts	Average	Best
–	–	–	–

482. BUTCHER Alan Raymond
Born   Croydon, Surrey, 7 January 1954
Career Surrey, 1972–86; Glamorgan, 1987–92
Tests 1
Debut v India, The Oval, Aug–Sept 1979

Inns	NOs	HSc	Runs	Average	100s
2	0	20	34	17.00	–

Runs	Wkts	Average	Best
9	0	–	–

483. DILLEY Graham Roy
Born   Dartford, Kent, 18 May 1959
Career Kent, 1977–86; Natal, 1985–6; Worcestershire,
         1987–92
Tests 41
Debut v Australia, Perth, December 1979

Inns	NOs	HSc	Runs	Average	100s
58	19	56	521	13.35	–

Runs	Wkts	Average	Best
4107	138	29.76	6–38

484. LARKINS Wayne
Born   Roxton, Bedfordshire, 22 November 1953
Career Northamptonshire, 1972–91; Eastern Province,
         1982–3 to 1983–4; Durham, 1992–5
Tests 13
Debut v Australia, Melbourne, February 1980

Inns	NOs	HSc	Runs	Average	100s
25	1	64	493	20.54	–

Runs	Wkts	Average	Best
–	–	–	–

485. STEVENSON Graham Barry
Born   Ackworth, Yorkshire, 16 December 1955
Career Yorkshire, 1973–86; Northamptonshire, 1987
Tests 2
Debut v India, Bombay, February 1980

Inns	NOs	HSc	Runs	Average	100s
2	1	27*	28	28.00	–

Runs	Wkts	Average	Best
183	5	36.60	3–111

486. TAVARE Christopher James
Born   Orpington, Kent, 27 October 1954
Career Kent, 1974–88; Oxford University, 1975–7;
         Somerset, 1989–93
Tests 31
Debut v West Indies, Trent Bridge, June 1980

Inns	NOs	HSc	Runs	Average	100s
56	2	149	1755	32.50	2

Runs	Wkts	Average	Best
11	0	–	–

 DID YOU KNOW...?

Against Australia in 1982, Chris Tavare set a record by not scoring a run off 89 consecutive balls.

487. ATHEY Charles William Jeffrey
Born   Middlesbrough, Yorkshire, 27 September 1957
Career Yorkshire, 1976–83; Gloucestershire, 1984–92;
         Sussex, 1993–7
Tests 23
Debut v Australia, Lord's, Aug–Sept 1980

Inns	NOs	HSc	Runs	Average	100s
41	1	123	919	22.97	1

Runs	Wkts	Average	Best
–	–	–	–

488. DOWNTON Paul Rupert
Born   Farnborough, Kent, 4 April 1957
Career Kent, 1977–9; Middlesex, 1980–91
Tests 30
Debut v West Indies, Port-of-Spain, February 1981

Inns	NOs	HSc	Runs	Average	Inns
48	8	74	785	19.62	–

Runs	Wkts	Average	Best
–	–	–	–

489. BUTCHER Roland Orlando
Born   East Point, St Philip, Barbados, 14 October 1953
Career Middlesex, 1974–90; Barbados, 1974–5; Tasmania,
         1982–3
Tests 3
Debut v West Indies, Bridgetown, March 1981

Inns	NOs	HSc	Runs	Average	100s
5	0	32	71	14.20	–

Runs	Wkts	Average	Best
–	–	–	–

490. JACKMAN Robin David
Born   Simla, India, 13 August 1945
Career Surrey, 1966–82; Western Province, 1971–2;
         Rhodesia, 1972–3 to 1979–80
Tests 4
Debut v West Indies, Bridgetown, March 1981

Inns	NOs	HSc	Runs	Average	100s
6	0	17	42	7.00	–

Runs	Wkts	Average	Best
445	14	31.78	4–110

491. ALLOTT Paul John Walter

Born Altrincham, Cheshire, 14 September 1956
Career Lancashire, 1978–91; Wellington, 1985–6 to 1986–7
Tests 13
Debut v Australia, Old Trafford, August 1981

Inns	NOs	HSc	Runs	Average	100s
18	3	52*	213	14.20	–

Runs	Wkts	Average	Best
1084	26	41.69	6–61

492. PARKER Paul William Giles

Born Bulawayo, Southern Rhodesia, 15 January 1956
Career Cambridge University, 1976–8; Sussex, 1976–91; Durham, 1992–3
Tests 1
Debut v Australia, The Oval, Aug–Sept 1981

Inns	NOs	HSc	Runs	Average	100s
2	0	13	13	6.50	–

Runs	Wkts	Average	Best
–	–	–	–

493. COOK Geoffrey

Born Middlesbrough, Yorkshire, 9 October 1951
Career Northamptonshire, 1971–90; Eastern Province, 1978–9 to 1980–1
Tests 7
Debut v Sri Lanka, Colombo, February 1982

Inns	NOs	HSc	Runs	Average	100s
13	0	66	203	15.61	–

Runs	Wkts	Average	Best
27	0	–	–

494. LAMB Allan Joseph

Born Langebaanweg, Cape Province, South Africa, 20 June 1954
Career Western Province, 1972–3 to 1981–2; Northamptonshire, 1978–95; Orange Free State, 1987–8
Tests 79
Debut v India, Lord's, June 1982

Inns	NOs	HSc	Runs	Average	100s
139	10	142	4656	36.09	14

Runs	Wkts	Average	Best
23	1	23.00	1–6

495. PRINGLE Derek Raymond

Born Nairobi, Kenya, 18 September 1958
Career Essex, 1978–93; Cambridge University, 1979–82
Tests 30
Debut v India, Lord's, June 1982

Inns	NOs	HSc	Runs	Average	100s
50	4	63	695	15.10	–

Runs	Wkts	Average	Best
2518	70	35.97	5–95

496. GREIG Ian Alexander

Born Queenstown, South Africa, 8 December 1955
Career Border, 1974–5 to 1979–80; Griqualand West, 1975–6; Cambridge University, 1977–9; Sussex, 1980–5; Surrey, 1987–91
Tests 2
Debut v Pakistan, Edgbaston, July–August 1982

Inns	NOs	HSc	Runs	Average	100s
4	0	14	26	6.50	–

Runs	Wkts	Average	Best
114	4	28.50	4–53

497. HEMMINGS Edward Ernest

Born Leamington Spa, Warwickshire, 20 February 1949
Career Warwickshire, 1966–78; Nottinghamshire, 1979–92; Sussex, 1993–5
Tests 16
Debut v Pakistan, Edgbaston, July–August 1982

Inns	NOs	HSc	Runs	Average	100s
21	4	95	383	22.52	–

Runs	Wkts	Average	Best
1825	43	42.44	6–58

498. FOWLER Graeme

Born Accrington, Lancashire, 20 April 1957
Career Lancashire, 1979–92; Durham, 1993–4
Tests 21
Debut v Pakistan, Headingley, August 1982

Inns	NOs	HSc	Runs	Average	100s
37	0	201	1307	35.32	3

Runs	Wkts	Average	Best
11	0	–	–

499. MARKS Victor James

Born Middle Chinnock, Somerset, 25 June 1955
Career Oxford University, 1975–8; Somerset, 1975–89; Western Australia, 1986–7
Tests 6
Debut v Pakistan, Headingley, August 1982

Inns	NOs	HSc	Runs	Average	100s
10	1	83	249	27.66	–

Runs	Wkts	Average	Best
484	11	44.00	3–78

500. COWANS Norman George

Born Enfield, St Mary, Jamaica, 17 April 1961
Career Middlesex, 1980–93; Hampshire, 1994
Tests 19
Debut v Australia, Perth, November 1982

Inns	NOs	HSc	Runs	Average	100s
29	7	36	175	7.95	–

Runs	Wkts	Average	Best
2003	51	39.27	6–77

501. COOK Nicholas Grant Billson

Born Leicester, 17 June 1956
Career Leicestershire, 1978–85; Northamptonshire, 1986–94
Tests 15
Debut v New Zealand, Lord's, August 1983

Inns	NOs	HSc	Runs	Average	100s
25	4	31	179	8.52	–

Runs	Wkts	Average	Best
1689	52	32.48	6–65

502. FOSTER Neil Alan

Born Colchester, Essex, 6 May 1962
Career Essex, 1980–93
Tests 29
Debut v New Zealand, Lord's, August 1983

Inns	NOs	HSc	Runs	Average	100s
45	7	39	446	11.73	–

Runs	Wkts	Average	Best
2891	88	32.85	8–107

503. SMITH Christopher Lyall
Born Durban, South Africa, 15 October 1958
Career Natal, 1977–8 to 1982–3; Glamorgan, 1979;
Hampshire, 1980–91
Tests 8
Debut v New Zealand, Lord's, August 1983

Inns	NOs	HSc	Runs	Average	100s
14	1	91	392	30.15	–

Runs	Wkts	Average	Best
39	3	13.00	2–31

504. PIGOTT Anthony Charles Shackleton
Born Fulham, London, 4 June 1958
Career Sussex, 1978–93; Wellington, 1982–3 to 1983–4;
Surrey, 1994–5
Tests 1
Debut v New Zealand, Christchurch, February 1984

Inns	NOs	HSc	Runs	Average	100s
2	1	8*	12	12.00	–

Runs	Wkts	Average	Best
75	2	37.50	2–75

505. LLOYD Timothy Andrew
Born Oswestry, Shropshire, 5 November 1956
Career Warwickshire, 1977–92; Orange Free State, 1978–9
to 1979–80
Tests 1
Debut v West Indies, Edgbaston, June 1984

Inns	NOs	HSc	Runs	Average	100s
1	1	10*	10	–	–

Runs	Wkts	Average	Best
–	–	–	–

506. BROAD Brian Christopher
Born Knowle, Bristol, 29 September 1957
Career Gloucestershire, 1979–83 and 1993–4;
Nottinghamshire, 1984–92; Orange Free State,
1985–6
Tests 25
Debut v West Indies, Lord's, June–July 1984

Inns	NOs	HSc	Runs	Average	100s
44	2	162	1661	39.54	6

Runs	Wkts	Average	Best
4	0	–	–

507. TERRY Vivian Paul
Born Osnabruck, Germany, 14 January 1959
Career Hampshire, 1978–96
Tests 2
Debut v West Indies, Headingley, July 1984

Inns	NOs	HSc	Runs	Average	100s
3	0	8	16	5.33	–

Runs	Wkts	Average	Best
–	–	–	–

508. AGNEW Jonathan Philip
Born Macclesfield, Cheshire, 4 April 1960
Career Leicestershire, 1978–90
Tests 3
Debut v West Indies, The Oval, August 1984

Inns	NOs	HSc	Runs	Average	100s
4	3	5	10	10.00	–

Runs	Wkts	Average	Best
373	4	93.25	2–51

509. ELLISON Richard Mark
Born Ashford, Kent, 21 September 1959
Career Kent, 1981–93; Tasmania, 1986–7
Tests 11
Debut v West Indies, The Oval, August 1984

Inns	NOs	HSc	Runs	Average	100s
16	1	41	202	13.46	–

Runs	Wkts	Average	Best
1048	35	29.94	6–77

510. COWDREY Christopher Stuart
Born Farnborough, Kent, 20 October 1957
Career Kent, 1977–91; Glamorgan, 1992
Tests 6
Debut v India, Bombay, Nov–Dec 1984

Inns	NOs	HSc	Runs	Average	100s
8	1	38	101	14.42	–

Runs	Wkts	Average	Best
309	4	77.25	2–65

511. ROBINSON Robert Timothy
Born Sutton-in-Ashfield, Nottinghamshire, 21 November
1958
Career Nottinghamshire, 1978–99
Tests 29
Debut v India, Bombay, Nov–Dec 1984

Inns	NOs	HSc	Runs	Average	100s
49	5	175	1601	36.38	4

Runs	Wkts	Average	Best
1	0	–	–

512. SIDEBOTTOM Arnold
Born Barnsley, Yorkshire, 1 April 1954
Career Yorkshire, 1973–91; Orange Free State, 1981–2 to
1983–4
Tests 1
Debut v Australia, Trent Bridge, August 1985

Inns	NOs	HSc	Runs	Average	100s
1	0	2	2	2.00	–

Runs	Wkts	Average	Best
65	1	65.00	1–65

513. TAYLOR Leslie Brian
Born Earl Shilton, Leicestershire, 25 October 1953
Career Leicestershire, 1977–90; Natal, 1981–2 to
1983–4
Tests 2
Debut v Australia, Edgbaston, August 1985

Inns	NOs	HSc	Runs	Average	100s
1	1	1*	1	–	–

Runs	Wkts	Average	Best
178	4	44.50	2–34

514. SMITH David Mark
Born Balham, London, 9 January 1956
Career Surrey, 1973–83 and 1987–8; Worcestershire,
1984–6; Sussex, 1989–94
Tests 2
Debut v West Indies, Kingston, February 1986

Inns	NOs	HSc	Runs	Average	100s
4	0	47	80	20.00	–

Runs	Wkts	Average	Best
–	–	–	–

515.   THOMAS John Gregory

Born   Trebanos, Glamorgan, 12 August 1960
Career   Glamorgan, 1979–88; Border, 1983–4 to 1986–7; Eastern Province, 1987–8; Northamptonshire, 1989–91
Tests   5
Debut   v West Indies, Kingston, February 1986

Inns	NOs	HSc	Runs	Average	100s
10	4	31*	83	13.83	–

Runs	Wkts	Average	Best
504	10	50.40	4–70

516.   SLACK Wilfred Norris

Born   Troumaca, St Vincent, Windward Islands, 12 December 1954
Died   Banjul, The Gambia, 15 January 1989
Career   Middlesex, 1977–88; Windward Islands, 1981–2 to 1982–3
Tests   3
Debut   v West Indies, Port-of-Spain, March 1986

Inns	NOs	HSc	Runs	Average	100s
6	0	52	81	13.50	–

Runs	Wkts	Average	Best
–	–	–	–

517.   FRENCH Bruce Nicholas

Born   Warsop, Nottinghamshire, 13 August 1959
Career   Nottinghamshire, 1976–95
Tests   16
Debut   v India, Headingley, June 1986

Inns	NOs	HSc	Runs	Average	100s
21	4	59	308	18.11	–

Runs	Wkts	Average	Best
–	–	–	–

518.   BENSON Mark Richard

Born   Shoreham, Sussex, 6 July 1958
Career   Kent, 1980–95
Tests   1
Debut   v India, Edgbaston, July 1986

Inns	NOs	HSc	Runs	Average	100s
2	0	30	51	25.50	–

Runs	Wkts	Average	Best
–	–	–	–

519.   RADFORD Neal Victor

Born   Luanshya, Northern Rhodesia, 7 June 1957
Career   Transvaal, 1978–9 to 1987–8; Lancashire, 1980–4; Worcestershire, 1985–95
Tests   3
Debut   v India, Edgbaston, July 1986

Inns	NOs	HSc	Runs	Average	100s
4	1	12*	21	7.00	–

Runs	Wkts	Average	Best
351	4	87.75	2–131

520.   MOXON Martyn Douglas

Born   Barnsley, Yorkshire, 4 May 1960
Career   Yorkshire, 1981–97; Griqualand West, 1982–3 to 1983–4
Tests   10
Debut   v New Zealand, Lord's, July 1986

Inns	NOs	HSc	Runs	Average	100s
17	1	99	455	28.43	–

Runs	Wkts	Average	Best
30	0	–	–

521.   SMALL Gladstone Cleophas

Born   St George, Barbados, 18 October 1961
Career   Warwickshire, 1980–97; South Australia, 1985–6
Tests   17
Debut   v New Zealand, Trent Bridge, August 1986

Inns	NOs	HSc	Runs	Average	100s
24	7	59	263	15.47	–

Runs	Wkts	Average	Best
1871	55	34.01	5–48

522.   DEFREITAS Phillip Anthony Jason

Born   Scotts Head, Dominica, 18 February 1966
Career   Leicestershire, 1985–8 and 2000–5; Lancashire, 1989–93; Boland, 1993–4 and 1995–6; Derbyshire, 1994–9
Tests   44
Debut   v Australia, Brisbane, November 1986

Inns	NOs	HSc	Runs	Average	100s
68	5	88	934	14.82	–

Runs	Wkts	Average	Best
4700	140	33.57	7–70

523.   RICHARDS Clifton James

Born   Penzance, Cornwall, 10 August 1958
Career   Surrey, 1976–88; Orange Free State, 1983–4
Tests   8
Debut   v Australia, Brisbane, November 1986

Inns	NOs	HSc	Runs	Average	100s
13	0	133	285	21.92	1

Runs	Wkts	Average	Best
–	–	–	–

524.   WHITAKER John James

Born   Skipton, Yorkshire, 5 May 1962
Career   Leicestershire, 1983–99
Tests   1
Debut   v Australia, Adelaide, December 1986

Inns	NOs	HSc	Runs	Average	100s
1	0	11	11	11.00	–

Runs	Wkts	Average	Best
–	–	–	–

525.   FAIRBROTHER Neil Harvey

Born   Warrington, Lancashire, 9 September 1963
Career   Lancashire, 1982–2002
Tests   10
Debut   v Pakistan, Old Trafford, June 1987

Inns	NOs	HSc	Runs	Average	100s
15	1	83	219	15.64	–

Runs	Wkts	Average	Best
9	0	–	–

526.   CAPEL David John

Born   Northampton, 6 February 1963
Career   Northamptonshire, 1981–98; Eastern Province, 1985–6 to 1986–7
Tests   15
Debut   v Pakistan, Headingley, July 1987

Inns	NOs	HSc	Runs	Average	100s
25	1	98	374	15.58	–

Runs	Wkts	Average	Best
1064	21	50.66	3–88

527. JARVIS Paul William
Born Redcar, Yorkshire, 29 June 1965
Career Yorkshire, 1981–93; Sussex, 1994–8; Somerset, 1999–2000
Tests 9
Debut v New Zealand, Christchurch, February 1988

Inns	NOs	HSc	Runs	Average	100s
15	2	29*	132	10.15	–

Runs	Wkts	Average	Best
965	21	45.95	4–107

528. CHILDS John Henry
Born Plymouth, Devon, 15 August 1951
Career Gloucestershire, 1975–84; Essex, 1985–96
Tests 2
Debut v West Indies, Old Trafford, June–July 1988

Inns	NOs	HSc	Runs	Average	100s
4	4	2*	2	–	–

Runs	Wkts	Average	Best
183	3	61.00	1–13

529. CURTIS Timothy Stephen
Born Chislehurst, Kent, 15 January 1960
Career Worcestershire, 1979–97; Cambridge University, 1983
Tests 5
Debut v West Indies, Headingley, July 1988

Inns	NOs	HSc	Runs	Average	100s
9	0	41	140	15.55	–

Runs	Wkts	Average	Best
7	0	–	–

530. SMITH Robin Arnold
Born Durban, South Africa, 13 September 1963
Career Natal, 1980–1 to 1984–5; Hampshire, 1982–2003
Tests 62
Debut v West Indies, Headingley, July 1988

Inns	NOs	HSc	Runs	Average	100s
112	15	175	4236	43.67	9

Runs	Wkts	Average	Best
6	0	–	–

531. BAILEY Robert John
Born Biddulph, Staffordshire, 28 October 1963
Career Northamptonshire, 1982–99; Derbyshire, 2000–1
Tests 4
Debut v West Indies, The Oval, August 1988

Inns	NOs	HSc	Runs	Average	100s
8	0	43	119	14.87	–

Runs	Wkts	Average	Best
–	–	–	–

532. MAYNARD Matthew Peter
Born Oldham, Lancashire, 21 March 1966
Career Glamorgan, 1985–2004
Tests 4
Debut v West Indies, The Oval, August 1988

Inns	NOs	HSc	Runs	Average	100s
8	0	35	87	10.87	–

Runs	Wkts	Average	Best
–	–	–	–

533. BARNETT Kim John
Born Stoke-on-Trent, Staffordshire, 17 July 1960
Career Derbyshire, 1979–98; Boland, 1982–3 to 1987–8; Gloucestershire, 1999–2002
Tests 4
Debut v Sri Lanka, Lord's, August 1988

Inns	NOs	HSc	Runs	Average	100s
7	0	80	207	29.57	–

Runs	Wkts	Average	Best
32	0	–	–

534. LAWRENCE David Valentine
Born Gloucester, 28 January 1964
Career Gloucestershire, 1981–91 and 1997
Tests 5
Debut v Sri Lanka, Lord's, August 1988

Inns	NOs	HSc	Runs	Average	100s
6	0	34	60	10.00	–

Runs	Wkts	Average	Best
676	18	37.55	5–106

535. NEWPORT Philip John
Born High Wycombe, Buckinghamshire, 11 October 1962
Career Worcestershire, 1982–99; Boland, 1987–8; Northern Transvaal, 1992–3
Tests 3
Debut v Sri Lanka, Lord's, August 1988

Inns	NOs	HSc	Runs	Average	100s
5	1	40*	110	27.50	–

Runs	Wkts	Average	Best
417	10	41.70	4–87

536. RUSSELL Robert Charles
Born Stroud, Gloucestershire, 15 August 1963
Career Gloucestershire, 1981–2004
Tests 54
Debut v Sri Lanka, Lord's, August 1988

Inns	NOs	HSc	Runs	Average	100s
86	16	128*	1897	27.10	2

Runs	Wkts	Average	Best
–	–	–	–

537. FRASER Angus Robert Charles
Born Billinge, Lancashire, 8 August 1965
Career Middlesex, 1984–2002
Tests 46
Debut v Australia, Edgbaston, July 1989

Inns	NOs	HSc	Runs	Average	100s
67	15	32	388	7.46	–

Runs	Wkts	Average	Best
4836	177	27.32	8–53

538. ATHERTON Michael Andrew
Born Manchester, 23 March 1968
Career Cambridge University, 1987–9; Lancashire, 1987–2001
Tests 115
Debut v Australia, Trent Bridge, August 1989

Inns	NOs	HSc	Runs	Average	100s
212	7	185*	7728	37.69	16

Runs	Wkts	Average	Best
302	2	151.00	1–20

 DID YOU KNOW...?

In the first Test of the 1997 Ashes series, Mike Atherton equalled a record by captaining England for the forty-first time and scored his 5,000th Test run.

539. MALCOLM Devon Eugene
Born Kingston, Jamaica, 22 February 1963
Career Derbyshire, 1984–97; Northamptonshire,
1998–2000; Leicestershire, 2001–3
Tests 40
Debut v Australia, Trent Bridge, August 1989

Inns	NOs	HSc	Runs	Average	100s
58	19	29	236	6.05	–

Runs	Wkts	Average	Best
4748	128	37.09	9–57

540. IGGLESDEN Alan Paul
Born Farnborough, Kent, 8 October 1964
Career Kent, 1986–98; Western Province, 1986–90;
Boland, 1991–2
Tests 3
Debut v Australia, The Oval, August 1989

Inns	NOs	HSc	Runs	Average	100s
5	3	3*	6	3.00	–

Runs	Wkts	Average	Best
329	6	54.83	2–91

541. STEPHENSON John Patrick
Born Stebbing, Essex, 14 March 1965
Career Essex, 1985–94 and 2002–4; Boland, 1988–9;
Hampshire, 1995–2001
Tests 1
Debut v Australia, The Oval, August 1989

Inns	NOs	HSc	Runs	Average	100s
2	0	25	36	18.00	–

Runs	Wkts	Average	Best
–	–	–	–

542. HUSSAIN Nasser
Born Madras, India, 28 March 1968
Career Essex, 1987–2004
Tests 96
Debut v West Indies, Kingston, February 1990

Inns	NOs	HSc	Runs	Average	100s
171	16	207	5764	37.18	14

Runs	Wkts	Average	Best
15	0	–	–

543. STEWART Alec James
Born Merton, Surrey, 8 April 1963
Career Surrey, 1981–2003
Tests 133
Debut v West Indies, Kingston, February 1990

Inn	NOs	HSc	Runs	Average	100s
235	21	190	8463	39.54	15

Runs	Wkts	Average	Best
13	0	–	–

544. LEWIS Christopher Clairmonte
Born Georgetown, Guyana, 14 February 1968
Career Leicestershire, 1987–91 and 1998–2000;
Nottinghamshire, 1992–5; Surrey, 1996–7
Tests 32
Debut v New Zealand, Edgbaston, July 1990

Inns	NOs	HSc	Runs	Average	100s
51	3	117	1105	23.02	1

Runs	Wkts	Average	Best
3490	93	37.52	6–111

545. MORRIS John Edward
Born Crewe, Cheshire, 1 April 1964
Career Derbyshire, 1982–93; Griqualand West, 1988–9
and 1993–4; Durham, 1994–9; Nottinghamshire,
2000–1
Tests 3
Debut v India, Lord's, July 1990

Inns	NOs	HSc	Runs	Average	100s
5	2	32	71	23.66	–

Runs	Wkts	Average	Best
–	–	–	–

546. WILLIAMS Neil Fitzgerald
Born Hope Well, St Vincent, West Indies, 2 July 1962
Died Kingstown, St Vincent, West Indies, 26 March
2006
Career Middlesex, 1982–94; Windward Islands, 1982–3
and 1989–90; Tasmania, 1983–4; Essex, 1995–8
Tests 1
Debut v India, The Oval, August 1990

Inns	NOs	HSc	Runs	Average	100s
1	0	38	38	38.00	–

Runs	Wkts	Average	Best
148	2	74.00	2–148

547. TUFNELL Philip Clive Roderick
Born Hadley Wood, Hertfordshire, 29 April 1966
Career Middlesex, 1986–2002
Tests 42
Debut v Australia, Melbourne, December 1990

Inns	NOs	HSc	Runs	Average	100s
59	29	22*	153	5.10	–

Runs	Wkts	Average	Best
4560	121	37.68	7–47

548. HICK Graeme Ashley
Born Harare, Zimbabwe, 23 May 1966
Career Worcestershire, 1984–to date; Northern Districts,
1987–9; Queensland, 1990–1; Auckland, 1997–8
Tests 65
Debut v West Indies, Headingley, June 1991

Inns	NOs	HSc	Runs	Average	100s
114	6	178	3383	31.32	6

Runs	Wkts	Average	Best
1306	23	56.78	4–126

549. RAMPRAKASH Mark Ravindra
Born Bushey, Hertfordshire, 5 September 1969
Career Middlesex, 1987–2000; Surrey, 2001–to date
Tests 52
Debut v West Indies, Headingley, June 1991

Inns	NOs	HSc	Runs	Average	100s
92	6	154	2350	27.32	2

Runs	Wkts	Average	Best
477	4	119.25	1–2

550. WATKIN Steven Llewellyn
Born Maesteg, Glamorgan, 15 September 1964
Career Glamorgan, 1986–2001
Tests 3
Debut v West Indies, Headingley, June 1991

Inns	NOs	HSc	Runs	Average	100s
5	0	13	25	5.00	–

Runs	Wkts	Average	Best
305	11	27.72	4–65

551. ILLINGWORTH Richard Keith
Born Bradford, Yorkshire, 23 August 1963
Career Worcestershire, 1982–2000; Natal, 1988–9;
Derbyshire, 2001
Tests 9
Debut v West Indies, Trent Bridge, July 1991

Inns	NOs	HSc	Runs	Average	100s
14	7	28	128	18.28	–

Runs	Wkts	Average	Best
615	19	32.36	4–96

552. MORRIS Hugh
Born Cardiff, 5 October 1963
Career Glamorgan, 1981–97
Tests 3
Debut v West Indies, Edgbaston, July 1991

Inns	NOs	HSc	Runs	Average	100s
6	0	44	115	19.16	–

Runs	Wkts	Average	Best
–	–	–	–

553. REEVE Dermot Alexander
Born Hong Kong, 2 April 1963
Career Hong Kong, 1982; Sussex, 1983–7; Warwickshire,
1988–96
Tests 3
Debut v New Zealand, Christchurch, January 1992

Inns	NOs	HSc	Runs	Average	100s
5	0	59	124	24.80	–

Runs	Wkts	Average	Best
60	2	30.00	1–4

554. SALISBURY Ian David Kenneth
Born Northampton, 21 January 1970
Career Sussex, 1989–96; Surrey, 1997–to date
Tests 15
Debut v Pakistan, Lord's, June 1992

Inns	NOs	HSc	Runs	Average	100s
25	3	50	368	16.72	–

Runs	Wkts	Average	Best
1539	20	76.95	4–163

555. MUNTON Timothy Alan
Born Melton Mowbray, Leicestershire, 30 July 1965
Career Warwickshire, 1985–99; Derbyshire, 2000–1
Tests 2
Debut v Pakistan, Old Trafford, July 1992

Inns	NOs	HSc	Runs	Average	100s
2	1	25*	25	25.00	–

Runs	Wkts	Average	Best
200	4	50.00	2–22

556. MALLENDER Neil Alan
Born Kirk Sandall, Yorkshire, 13 August 1961
Career Northamptonshire, 1980–6 and 1995–6; Otago,
1983–4 to 1992–3; Somerset, 1987–94
Tests 2
Debut v Pakistan, Headingley, July 1992

Inns	NOs	HSc	Runs	Average	100s
3	0	4	8	2.66	–

Runs	Wkts	Average	Best
215	10	21.50	5–50

557. TAYLOR Jonathan Paul
Born Ashby-de-la-Zouch, Leicestershire, 8 August 1964
Career Derbyshire, 1984–6; Northamptonshire, 1991–2001
Tests 2
Debut v India, Calcutta, Jan–Feb 1993

Inns	NOs	HSc	Runs	Average	100s
4	2	17*	34	17.00	–

Runs	Wkts	Average	Best
156	3	52.00	1–18

558. BLAKEY Richard John
Born Huddersfield, Yorkshire, 15 January 1967
Career Yorkshire, 1985–to date
Tests 2
Debut v India, Madras, February 1993

Inns	NOs	HSc	Runs	Average	100s
4	0	6	7	1.75	–

Runs	Wkts	Average	Best
–	–	–	–

559. CADDICK Andrew Richard
Born Christchurch, New Zealand, 21 November 1968
Career Somerset, 1991–to date
Tests 62
Debut v Australia, Old Trafford, June 1993

Inns	NOs	HSc	Runs	Average	100s
95	12	49*	861	10.37	1

Runs	Wkts	Average	Best
6999	234	29.91	7–46

560. SUCH Peter Mark
Born Helensburgh, Scotland, 12 June 1964
Career Nottinghamshire, 1982–6; Leicestershire, 1987–9;
Essex, 1990–2001
Tests 11
Debut v Australia, Old Trafford, June 1993

Inns	NOs	HSc	Runs	Average	100s
16	5	14*	67	6.09	–

Runs	Wkts	Average	Best
1242	37	33.56	6–67

561. ILOTT Mark Christopher
Born Watford, Hertfordshire, 27 August 1970
Career Essex, 1988–2002
Tests 5
Debut v Australia, Trent Bridge, July 1993

Inns	NOs	HSc	Runs	Average	100s
6	2	15	28	7.00	–

Runs	Wkts	Average	Best
542	12	45.16	3–48

562. LATHWELL Mark Nicholas
Born Bletchley, Buckinghamshire, 26 December 1971
Career Somerset, 1991–2001
Tests 2
Debut v Australia, Trent Bridge, July 1993

Inns	NOs	HSc	Runs	Average	100s
4	0	33	78	19.50	–

Runs	Wkts	Average	Best
–	–	–	–

563. McCAGUE Martin John
Born Larne, Northern Ireland, 24 May 1969
Career Western Australia, 1990–1 to 1991–2; Kent,
1991–2001
Tests 3
Debut v Australia, Trent Bridge, July 1993

Inns	NOs	HSc	Runs	Average	100s
5	0	11	21	4.20	–

Runs	Wkts	Average	Best
390	6	65.00	4–121

DID YOU KNOW...?

Pace bowler Martin McCague was a controversial choice for England's tour of Australia in 1994–5. Taunted as a 'traitor' (he learned his cricket in Australia), he conceded 96 runs in the only innings he bowled, was out for a duck, suffered a stress fracture and was never capped again.

564.   THORPE Graham Paul
Born   Farnham, Surrey, 1 August 1969
Career   Surrey, 1988–2005
Tests   100
Debut   v Australia, Trent Bridge, July 1993

Inns	NOs	HSc	Runs	Average	100s
179	28	200*	6744	44.66	16

Runs	Wkts	Average	Best
37	0	–	–

565.   BICKNELL Martin Paul
Born   Guildford, Surrey, 14 January 1969
Career   Surrey, 1986–to date
Tests   4
Debut   v Australia, Headingley, July 1993

Inns	NOs	HSc	Runs	Average	100s
7	0	15	45	6.42	–

Runs	Wkts	Average	Best
543	14	38.78	4–84

566.   RHODES Steven John
Born   Bradford, Yorkshire, 17 June 1964
Career   Yorkshire, 1981–4; Worcestershire, 1985–2004
Tests   11
Debut   v New Zealand, Trent Bridge, June 1994

Inns	NOs	HSc	Runs	Average	100s
17	5	65*	294	24.50	–

Runs	Wkts	Average	Best
–	–	–	–

567.   WHITE Craig
Born   Morley, Yorkshire, 16 December 1969
Career   Yorkshire, 1990–to date; Victoria, 1990–1
Tests   30
Debut   v New Zealand, Trent Bridge, June 1994

Inns	NOs	HSc	Runs	Average	100s
50	7	121	1052	24.46	1

Runs	Wkts	Average	Best
2220	59	37.62	5–32

568.   GOUGH Darren
Born   Barnsley, Yorkshire, 18 September 1970
Career   Yorkshire, 1989–2003; Essex, 2004–to date
Tests   58
Debut   v New Zealand, Old Trafford, June–July 1994

Inns	NOs	HSc	Runs	Average	100s
86	18	65	855	12.57	–

Runs	Wkts	Average	Best
6503	229	28.39	6–42

569.   CRAWLEY John Paul
Born   Maldon, Essex, 21 September 1971
Career   Lancashire, 1990–2001; Cambridge University, 1991–3; Hampshire, 2002–to date
Tests   37
Debut   v South Africa, Lord's, July 1994

Inns	NOs	HSc	Runs	Average	100s
61	9	156*	1800	34.61	4

Runs	Wkts	Average	Best
–	–	–	–

570.   BENJAMIN Joseph Emmanuel
Born   Christ Church, St Kitts, 2 February 1961
Career   Warwickshire, 1988–91; Surrey, 1992–99
Tests   1
Debut   v South Africa, The Oval, August 1994

Inns	NOs	HSc	Runs	Average	100s
1	0	0	0	0.00	–

Runs	Wkts	Average	Best
80	4	20.00	4–42

571.   MARTIN Peter James
Born   Accrington, Lancashire, 15 November 1968
Career   Lancashire, 1989–2004
Tests   8
Debut   v West Indies, Headingley, June 1995

Inns	NOs	HSc	Runs	Average	100s
13	0	29	115	8.84	–

Runs	Wkts	Average	Best
580	17	34.11	4–60

572.   CORK Dominic Gerald
Born   Newcastle-under-Lyme, Staffordshire, 7 August 1971
Career   Derbyshire, 1990–2003; Lancashire, 2004–to date
Tests   37
Debut   v West Indies, Lord's, June 1995

Inns	NOs	HSc	Runs	Average	100s
56	8	59	864	18.00	–

Runs	Wkts	Average	Best
3906	131	29.81	7–43

573.   GALLIAN Jason Edward Riche
Born   Manly, NSW, Australia, 25 June 1971
Career   Lancashire, 1990–7; Oxford University, 1992–3; Nottinghamshire, 1998–to date
Tests   3
Debut   v West Indies, Edgbaston, July 1995

Inns	NOs	HSc	Runs	Average	100s
6	0	28	74	12.33	–

Runs	Wkts	Average	Best
62	0	–	–

574.   KNIGHT Nicholas Verity
Born   Watford, Hertfordshire, 28 November 1969
Career   Essex, 1991–4; Warwickshire, 1995–to date
Tests   17
Debut   v West Indies, Old Trafford, July 1995

Inns	NOs	HSc	Runs	Average	100s
30	0	113	719	23.96	1

Runs	Wkts	Average	Best
–	–	–	–

575.   WATKINSON Michael
Born   Bolton, Lancashire, 1 August 1961
Career   Lancashire, 1982–2000
Tests   4
Debut   v West Indies, Old Trafford, July 1995

Inns	NOs	HSc	Runs	Average	100s
6	1	82*	167	33.40	–

Runs	Wkts	Average	Best
348	10	34.80	3–64

576. WELLS Alan Peter
Born Newhaven, Sussex, 2 October 1961
Career Sussex, 1981–96; Border, 1981–2; Kent, 1997–2000
Tests 1
Debut v West Indies, The Oval, August 1995

Inns	NOs	HSc	Runs	Average	100s
2	1	3*	3	3.00	–

Runs	Wkts	Average	Best
––	–	–	–

577. IRANI Ronald Charles
Born Leigh, Lancashire, 26 October 1971
Career Lancashire, 1990–3; Essex, 1994–to date
Tests 3
Debut v India, Edgbaston, June 1996

Inns	NOs	HSc	Run	Average	100s
5	0	41	86	17.20	–

Runs	Wkts	Average	Best
112	3	37.33	1–22

578. MULLALLY Alan David
Born Southend-on-Sea, Essex, 12 July 1969
Career Western Australia, 1987–8 to 1989–90; Hampshire, 1988 and 2000–4; Victoria, 1990–1; Leicestershire, 1990–9
Tests 19
Debut v India, Edgbaston, June 1996

Inns	NOs	HSc	Runs	Average	100s
27	4	24	127	5.52	–

Runs	Wkts	Average	Best
1812	58	31.24	5–105

579. PATEL Minal Mahesh
Born Bombay, India, 7 July 1970
Career Kent, 1989–to date
Tests 2
Debut v India, Edgbaston, June 1996

Inns	NOs	HSc	Runs	Average	100s
2	0	27	45	22.50	–

Runs	Wkts	Average	Best
180	1	180.00	1–101

580. EALHAM Mark Alan
Born Willesborough, Kent, 27 August 1969
Career Kent, 1989–2003; Nottinghamshire, 2004–to date
Tests 8
Debut v India, Trent Bridge, July 1996

Inns	NOs	HSc	Runs	Average	100
13	3	53*	210	21.00	–

Runs	Wkts	Average	Best
488	17	28.70	4–21

581. BROWN Simon John Emmerson
Born Cleadon Village, Sunderland, 29 June 1969
Career Northamptonshire, 1987–90; Durham, 1992–2002
Tests 1
Debut v Pakistan, Lord's, July 1996

Inns	NOs	HSc	Runs	Average	100s
2	1	10*	11	11.00	–

Runs	Wkts	Average	Best
138	2	69.00	1–60

582. CROFT Robert Damien Bale
Born Swansea, Glamorgan, 25 May 1970
Career Glamorgan, 1989–to date
Tests 21
Debut v Pakistan, The Oval, August 1996

Inns	NOs	HSc	Runs	Average	100s
34	8	37*	421	16.19	–

Runs	Wkts	Average	Best
1825	49	37.24	5–95

583. SILVERWOOD Christopher Eric Wilfred
Born Pontefract, Yorkshire, 5 March 1975
Career Yorkshire, 1993–2005; Middlesex, 2006–to date
Tests 6
Debut v Zimbabwe, Bulawayo, December 1996

Inns	NOs	HSc	Runs	Average	100s
7	3	10	29	7.25	–

Runs	Wkts	Average	Best
444	11	40.36	5–91

584. BUTCHER Mark Alan
Born Croydon, Surrey, 23 August 1972
Career Surrey, 1991–to date
Tests 71
Debut v Australia, Edgbaston, June 1997

Inns	NOs	HSc	Runs	Average	100s
131	7	173*	4288	34.58	8

Runs	Wkts	Average	Best
541	15	36.06	4–42

585. HEADLEY Dean Warren
Born Stourbridge, Worcestershire, 27 January 1970
Career Middlesex, 1991–2; Kent, 1993–9
Tests 15
Debut v Australia, Old Trafford, July 1997

Inns	NOs	HSc	Runs	Average	100s
26	4	31	186	8.45	–

Runs	Wkts	Average	Best
1671	60	27.85	6–60

586. SMITH Andrew Michael
Born Dewsbury, Yorkshire, 1 October 1967
Career Gloucestershire, 1991–2004
Tests 1
Debut v Australia, Headingley, July 1997

Inns	NOs	HSc	Runs	Average	100s
2	1	4*	4	4.00	–

Runs	Wkts	Average	Best
89	0	–	–

587. HOLLIOAKE Adam John
Born Melbourne, Australia, 5 September 1971
Career Surrey, 1993–2004
Tests 4
Debut v Australia, Trent Bridge, August 1997

Inns	NOs	HSc	Runs	Average	100s
6	0	45	65	10.83	–

Runs	Wkts	Average	Best
67	2	33.50	2–31

588. HOLLIOAKE Ben Caine
Born Melbourne, Australia, 11 November 1977
Died Perth, Australia, 23 March 2002
Career Surrey, 1996–2001
Tests 2
Debut v Australia, Trent Bridge, August 1997

Inns	NOs	HSc	Runs	Average	100s
4	0	28	44	11.00	–

Runs	Wkts	Average	Best
199	4	49.75	2–105

589. JAMES Stephen Peter
Born Lydney, Glamorgan, 7 September 1967
Career Glamorgan, 1985–2003
Tests 2
Debut v South Africa, Lord's, June 1998

Inns	NOs	HSc	Runs	Average	100s
4	0	36	71	17.75	–

Runs	Wkts	Average	Best
–	–	–	–

590. GILES Ashley Fraser
Born Chertsey, Surrey, 19 March 1973
Career Warwickshire, 1993–to date
Tests 52
Debut v South Africa, Old Trafford, July 1998

Inns	NOs	HSc	Runs	Average	100s
77	12	59	1347	20.72	–

Runs	Wkts	Average	Best
5544	140	39.60	5–57

591. FLINTOFF Andrew
Born Preston, Lancashire, 6 December 1977
Career Lancashire, 1995–to date
Tests 61
Debut v South Africa, Trent Bridge, July 1998

Inns	NOs	HSc	Runs	Average	100s
98	5	167	3077	33.08	5

Runs	Wkts	Average	Best
5720	179	31.95	5–58

592. TUDOR Alexander Jeremy
Born West Brompton, London, 23 October 1977
Career Surrey, 1995–2004; Essex, 2005–to date
Tests 10
Debut v Australia, Perth, November 1998

Inns	NOs	HSc	Runs	Average	100s
16	4	99*	229	19.08	–

Runs	Wkts	Average	Best
963	28	34.39	5–44

593. HEGG Warren Kevin
Born Whitefield, Manchester, 23 February 1968
Career Lancashire, 1986–2005
Tests 2
Debut v Australia, Melbourne, December 1998

Inns	NOs	HSc	Runs	Average	100s
4	0	15	30	7.50	–

Runs	Wkts	Average	Best
–	–	–	–

594. HABIB Aftab
Born Reading, Berkshire, 7 February 1972
Career Middlesex, 1992; Leicestershire, 1995–2001 and 2005–to date; Essex, 2002–4
Tests 2
Debut v New Zealand, Edgbaston, July 1999

Inns	NOs	HSc	Runs	Average	100s
3	0	19	26	8.66	–

Runs	Wkts	Average	Best
–	–	–	–

595. READ Christopher Mark Wells
Born Paignton, Devon, 10 August 1978
Career Nottinghamshire, 1998–to date
Tests 13
Debut v New Zealand, Edgbaston, July 1999

Inns	NOs	HSc	Runs	Average	100s
19	3	55	325	20.31	–

Runs	Wkts	Average	Best
–	–	–	–

596. GIDDINS Edward Simon Hunter
Born Eastbourne, Sussex, 20 July 1971
Career Sussex, 1991–6; Warwickshire, 1998–2000; Surrey, 2001–2; Hampshire, 2003
Tests 4
Debut v New Zealand, The Oval, August 1999

Inns	NOs	HSc	Runs	Average	100s
7	3	7	10	2.50	–

Runs	Wkts	Average	Best
240	12	20.00	5–15

597. MADDY Darren Lee
Born Leicester, 23 May 1974
Career Leicestershire, 1994–to date
Tests 3
Debut v New Zealand, The Oval, 1999

Inns	NOs	HSc	Runs	Average	100s
4	0	24	46	11.50	–

Runs	Wkts	Average	Best
40	0	–	–

598. ADAMS Christopher John
Born Whitwell, Nottinghamshire, 6 May 1970
Career Derbyshire, 1988–97; Sussex, 1998–to date
Tests 5
Debut v South Africa, Johannesburg, November 1999

Inns	NOs	HSc	Runs	Average	100s
8	0	31	104	13.00	–

Runs	Wkts	Average	Best
59	1	59.00	1–42

599. HAMILTON Gavin Mark
Born Broxburn, Scotland, 16 September 1974
Career Scotland, 1993–4; Yorkshire, 1994–2003; Durham, 2004
Tests 1
Debut v South Africa, Johannesburg, November 1999

Inns	NOs	HSc	Runs	Average	100s
2	0	0	0	0.00	–

Runs	Wkts	Average	Best
63	0	–	–

600. VAUGHAN Michael Paul
Born Eccles, Manchester, 29 October 1974
Career Yorkshire, 1993–to date
Tests 64
Debut v South Africa, Johannesburg, November 1999

Inns	NOs	HSc	Runs	Average	100s
115	8	197	4595	42.94	15

Runs	Wkts	Average	Best
537	6	89.50	2–71

601. SCHOFIELD Chris Paul
Born Rochdale, Lancashire, 6 October 1978
Career Lancashire, 1998–2004
Tests 2
Debut v Zimbabwe, Lord's, June–July 2000

Inns	NOs	HSc	Runs	Average	100s
3	0	57	67	22.33	–

Runs	Wkts	Average	Best
73	0	–	–

602. HOGGARD Matthew James
Born Leeds, Yorkshire, 31 December 1976
Career Yorkshire, 1996–to date; Orange Free State, 1998–9 to 1999–2000
Tests 58
Debut v West Indies, Lord's, June–July 2000

Inns	NOs	HSc	Runs	Average	100s
79	26	38	414	7.81	–

Runs	Wkts	Average	Best
6607	222	29.76	7–61

603. TRESCOTHICK Marcus Edward
Born Keynsham, Bristol, 25 December 1975
Career Somerset, 1993–to date
Tests 76
Debut v West Indies, Old Trafford, August 2000

Inns	NOs	HSc	Runs	Average	100s
143	10	219	5825	43.79	14

Runs	Wkts	Average	Best
155	1	155.00	1–34

604. SIDEBOTTOM Ryan Jay
Born Huddersfield, Yorkshire, 15 January 1978
Career Yorkshire, 1997–2003; Nottinghamshire, 2004–to date
Tests 1
Debut v Pakistan, Lord's, May 2001

Inns	NOs	HSc	Runs	Average	100s
1	0	4	4	4.00	–

Runs	Wkts	Average	Best
64	0	–	–

605. WARD Ian James
Born Plymouth, Devon, 30 September 1973
Career Surrey, 1992 and 1996–2003; Sussex, 2004–5
Tests 5
Debut v Pakistan, Lord's, 2001

Inns	NOs	HSc	Runs	Average	100s
9	1	39	129	16.12	–

Runs	Wkts	Average	Best
–	–	–	–

606. AFZAAL Usman
Born Rawalpindi, Pakistan, 9 June 1977
Career Nottinghamshire, 1995–2003; Northamptonshire, 2004–to date
Tests 3
Debut v Australia, Edgbaston, July 2001

Inns	NOs	HSc	Runs	Average	100s
6	1	54	83	16.60	–

Runs	Wkts	Average	Best
49	1	49.00	1–49

607. ORMOND James
Born Walsgrave, Coventry, 20 August 1977
Career Leicestershire, 1995–2001; Surrey, 2002–to date
Tests 2
Debut v Australia, The Oval, August 2001

Inns	NOs	HSc	Runs	Average	100s
4	1	18	38	12.66	–

Runs	Wkts	Average	Best
185	2	92.50	1 – 70

608. DAWSON Richard Kevin James
Born Doncaster, Yorkshire, 4 August 1980
Career Yorkshire, 2001–to date
Tests 7
Debut v India, Chandigarh, December 2001

Inns	NOs	HSc	Runs	Average	100s
13	3	19*	114	11.40	–

Runs	Wkts	Average	Best
677	11	61.54	4–134

609. FOSTER James Savin
Born Whipps Cross, Essex, 15 April 1980
Career Essex, 2000–to date
Tests 7
Debut v India, Chandigarh, December 2001

Inns	NOs	HSc	Runs	Average	100s
12	3	48	226	25.11	–

Runs	Wkts	Average	Best
–	–	–	–

610. JONES Simon Philip
Born Swansea, Glamorgan, 25 December 1978
Career Glamorgan, 1998–to date
Tests 18
Debut v India, Lord's, July 2002

Inns	NOs	HSc	Runs	Average	100s
18	5	44	205	15.76	–

Runs	Wkts	Average	Best
1666	59	28.23	6–53

611. HARMISON Stephen James
Born Ashington, Northumberland, 23 October 1978
Career Durham, 1996–to date
Tests 44
Debut v India, Trent Bridge, August 2002

Inns	NOs	HSc	Runs	Average	100s
58	16	42	504	12.00	–

Runs	Wkts	Average	Best
5056	175	28.89	7–12

612. KEY Robert William Trevor
Born Dulwich, London, 12 May 1979
Career Kent, 1998–to date
Tests 15
Debut v India, Trent Bridge, August 2002

Inns	NOs	HSc	Runs	Average	100s
26	1	221	775	31.00	1

Runs	Wkts	Average	Best
–	–	–	–

613. ANDERSON James Michael
Born Burnley, Lancashire, 30 July 1982
Career Lancashire, 2002–to date
Tests 13
Debut v Zimbabwe, Lord's, May 2003

Inns	NOs	HSc	Runs	Average	100s
18	12	21*	89	14.83	–

Runs	Wkts	Average	Best
1353	41	33.00	5–73

614. McGRATH Anthony
Born Bradford, Yorkshire, 6 October 1975
Career Yorkshire, 1995–to date
Tests 4
Debut v Zimbabwe, Lord's, May 2003

Inns	NOs	HSc	Runs	Average	100s
5	0	81	201	40.20	–

Runs	Wkts	Average	Best
56	4	14.00	3–16

615. JOHNSON Richard Leonard
Born Chertsey, Surrey, 29 December 1974
Career Middlesex, 1992–2000; Somerset, 2001–to date
Tests 3
Debut v Zimbabwe, Riverside Ground, June 2003

Inns	NOs	HSc	Runs	Average	100s
4	0	26	59	14.75	–

Runs	Wkts	Average	Best
275	16	17.18	6–33

616. KIRTLEY Robert James
Born Eastbourne, Sussex, 10 January 1975
Career Sussex, 1995–to date; Mashonaland, 1996–7
Tests 4
Debut v South Africa, Trent Bridge, August 2003

Inns	NOs	HSc	Runs	Average	100s
7	1	12	32	5.33	–

Runs	Wkts	Average	Best
561	19	29.52	6–34

617. SMITH Edward Thomas
Born Pembury, Kent, 19 July 1977
Career Cambridge University, 1996–8; Kent, 1996–2004; Middlesex, 2005–to date
Tests 3
Debut v South Africa, Trent Bridge, August 2003

Inns	NOs	HSc	Runs	Average	100s
5	0	64	87	17.40	–

Runs	Wkts	Average	Best
–	–	–	–

618. ALI Kabir
Born Moseley, Birmingham, 24 November 1980
Career Worcestershire, 1999–to date
Tests 1
Debut v South Africa, Headingley, August 2003

Inns	NOs	HSc	Runs	Average	100s
2	0	9	10	5.00	–

Runs	Wkts	Average	Best
136	5	27.20	3–80

619. BATTY Gareth Jon
Born Bradford, Yorkshire, 13 October 1977
Career Yorkshire, 1997; Surrey, 1999–2001; Worcestershire, 2002–to date
Tests 7
Debut v Bangladesh, Dhaka, October 2003

Inns	NOs	HSc	Runs	Average	100s
8	1	38	144	20.57	–

Runs	Wkts	Average	Best
733	11	66.63	3–55

620. CLARKE Rikki
Born Orsett, Essex, 29 September 1981
Career Surrey, 2002–to date
Tests 2
Debut v Bangladesh, Dhaka, October 2003

Inns	NOs	HSc	Runs	Average	100s
3	0	55	96	32.00	–

Runs	Wkts	Average	Best
60	4	15.00	2–7

621. SAGGERS Martin John
Born King's Lynn, Norfolk, 23 May 1972
Career Durham, 1996–8; Kent, 1999–to date
Tests 3
Debut v Bangladesh, Chittagong, Oct–Nov 2003

Inns	NOs	HSc	Runs	Average	100s
3	0	1	1	0.33	–

Runs	Wkts	Average	Best
247	7	35.28	2–29

622. COLLINGWOOD Paul David
Born Shotley Bridge, Tyneside, 26 May 1976
Career Durham, 1996–to date
Tests 15
Debut v Sri Lanka, Galle, December 2003

Inns	NOs	HSc	Runs	Average	100s
28	3	186*	1027	41.08	2

Runs	Wkts	Average	Best
245	1	245.00	1–33

623. JONES Geraint Owen
Born Kundiawa, Papua New Guinea, 14 July 1976
Career Kent, 2001–to date
Tests 31
Debut v West Indies, Antigua, April 2004

Inns	NOs	HSc	Runs	Average	100s
47	4	100	1109	25.79	1

Runs	Wkts	Average	Best
–	–	–	–

624. STRAUSS Andrew John
Born Johannesburg, South Africa, 2 March 197
Career Middlesex, 1998–to date
Tests 31
Debut v New Zealand, Lord's, July 2004

Inns	NOs	HSc	Runs	Average	100s
58	2	147	2597	46.37	10

Runs	Wkts	Average	Best
–	–	–	–

625. BELL Ian Ronald
Born Walsgrave-on-Sowe, Warwickshire, 11 April 1982
Career Warwickshire, 1999–to date
Tests 18
Debut v West Indies, The Oval, August 2004

Inns	NOs	HSc	Runs	Average	100s
32	5	162*	1287	47.66	5

Runs	Wkts	Average	Best
64	1	64.00	1–33

626. PIETERSEN Kevin Peter
Born Pietermaritzburg, South Africa, 27 June 1980
Career Natal, 1997–8 to 1999–2000; Nottinghamshire, 2001–4; Hampshire, 2005–to date
Tests 18
Debut v Australia, Lord's, July 2005

Inns	NOs	HSc	Runs	Average	100s
34	1	158	1597	48.39	5

Runs	Wkts	Average	Best
76	1	76.00	1–11

627. UDAL Shaun David
Born Farnborough, Hampshire, 18 March 1969
Career Hampshire, 1989–to date
Tests 4
Debut v Pakistan, Multan, November 2005

Inns	NOs	HSc	Runs	Average	100s
7	1	33*	109	18.16	–

Runs	Wkts	Average	Best
244	8	30.50	4–14

628. PLUNKETT Liam Edward
Born Middlesbrough, Yorkshire, 6 April 1985
Career Durham, 2003–to date
Tests 6
Debut v Pakistan, Lahore, Nov–Dec 2005

Inns	NOs	HSc	Runs	Average	100s
9	1	28	69	8.62	–

Runs	Wkts	Average	Best
601	16	37.56	3–17

629. BLACKWELL Ian David
Born Chesterfield, Derbyshire, 10 June 1978
Career Derbyshire, 1997–9; Somerset, 2000–to date
Tests 1
Debut v India, Nagpur, March 2006

Inns	NOs	HSc	Runs	Average	100s
1	0	4	4	4.00	–

Runs	Wkts	Average	Best
71	0	–	–

630. COOK Alastair Nathan
Born Gloucester, 25 December 1984
Career Essex, 2003–to date
Tests 9
Debut v India, Nagpur, March 2006

Inns	NOs	HSc	Runs	Average	100s
16	2	127	761	54.35	3

Runs	Wkts	Average	Best
–	–	–	–

631. PANESAR Mudhsuden Singh
Born Luton, Bedfordshire, 25 April 1982
Career Northamptonshire, 2001–to date
Tests 10
Debut v India, Nagpur, March 2006

Inns	NOs	HSc	Runs	Average	100s
13	8	26	51	10.20	–

Runs	Wkts	Average	Best
1037	32	32.40	5–72

632. SHAH Owais Alam
Born Karachi, Pakistan, 22 October 1978
Career Middlesex, 1996–to date
Tests 1
Debut v India, Mumbai, March 2006

Inns	NOs	HSc	Runs	Average	100s
2	0	88	126	63.00	–

Runs	Wkts	Average	Best
–	–	–	–

633. MAHMOOD Sajid Iqbal
Born Bolton, Lancashire, 21 December 1981
Career Lancashire, 2002–to date
Tests 5
Debut v Sri Lanka, Lord's, May 2006

Inns	NOs	HSc	Runs	Average	100s
5	1	34	63	15.75	–

Runs	Wkts	Average	Best
498	15	33.20	4–22

634. LEWIS Jonathan
Born Aylesbury, Buckinghamshire, 26 August 1975
Career Gloucestershire, 1995–to date
Tests 1
Debut v Sri Lanka, Trent Bridge, June 2006

Inns	NOs	HSc	Runs	Average	100s
2	0	20	27	13.50	–

Runs	Wkts	Average	Best
122	3	40.66	3–68

3 TOP 50 ENGLAND PLAYERS

DENNIS AMISS

A phlegmatic, determined opening batsman, Dennis Amiss was a patient accumulator of runs who had massive powers of concentration and an insatiable appetite for large scores. Though he made his Warwickshire debut in 1960, at the age of seventeen, it was not until 1965 that he established himself as a regular member of the county side, ending the season as Warwickshire's leading scorer with 1,433 runs. The following year, in August, he was picked for England for the fifth Test against the West Indies at The Oval – a memorable game in which Tom Graveney and John Murray hit hundreds, and Ken Higgs and John Snow put on 128 for the last wicket. Amiss scored 17 runs, but as England won by an innings, his performance was restricted to just one knock.

After a rocky beginning – 348 runs at an average of 18.31 in his first twelve Tests – Amiss amassed over 2,000 runs at an average of 71.33 with eight hundreds in the next twenty matches. From 1972 to 1974 he was England's outstanding run-getter, scoring 1,379 runs in a single year – just two runs short of Bobby Simpson's record Test aggregate in a calendar year. The total included his marathon match-saving, career-best innings of 262 not out made in February 1974 during the second Test at Sabina Park, Kingston. Had Bob Willis not survived for almost an hour during an unbroken last-wicket partnership, Amiss would have become only the fourth player to carry his bat through a completed innings for England, and his would have been the highest score in Tests. Another century followed in the fourth Test at Georgetown, Guyana, and then came scores of 188 against India in June and 193 against Pakistan in August during the home series.

Unfortunately, he was to follow this run of high scores with a series of depressing failures. In the 1974–5 Ashes series, he was completely overwhelmed by the formidable Australian pace attack and thereafter lost his wicket to Dennis Lillee on numerous occasions, suffering several blows to the head. But he did manage a remarkable double century against a rampant Michael Holding at The Oval in August 1976, and enjoyed a successful winter tour of India, where he made 179 in the first Test at Delhi, before joining the Packer bandwagon. Until this point, the image of Dennis Amiss had been one of a loyal and dedicated professional cricketer – he had received a record declared benefit from Warwickshire – but any bitterness was quickly forgotten.

He treated Warwickshire followers to another decade of fine batting, scoring 35,146 runs for the county – his confidence reinforced by protective headgear, which he was the first to market in Britain. Made an MBE for his services to cricket, Dennis Amiss has remained at Edgbaston as Warwickshire's much-respected chief executive.

MIKE ATHERTON

Michael Atherton captained England a record fifty-three times and played in sixty-three consecutive Tests between 1993 and 1998. He was troubled by a back injury for much of his international career, but his dogged determination and a successful training schedule gave him a longer Test career than might have been expected.

Captain of Cambridge, where he hit three centuries and a highest of 151 against Middlesex at Fenner's, he also led the Combined Universities on their enterprising giant-killing run in the 1989 Benson & Hedges Cup.

He made his Lancashire debut against Warwickshire in 1987, a summer in which he scored 1,183 first-class runs to become the first batsman since Sussex's Paul Parker in 1976 to make over 1,000 runs in a debut season.

In 1989, Atherton was awarded his county cap and selected to play for England in two Tests against Australia. He continued to score runs by the ton for Lancashire and he trod in some famous footprints at Trent Bridge in June 1990, when, at the age of twenty-two, he became the youngest Englishman to make a Test hundred since the twenty-one-year-old David Gower achieved the feat in India in 1978. That summer was also Atherton's first full season with Lancashire.

No one at Old Trafford did more to lead Lancashire's assault on the Britannic Championship, Benson & Hedges Cup and Refuge Assurance League – Atherton ended the campaign with 1,170 runs at an average of 78.00.

In 1993, Atherton followed Peter May, Ted Dexter, Mike Brearley and others to the tenancy of the captain's locker in the England dressing room. He was the springboard for an England innings, but was not always supported by his colleagues in terms of building decent totals. Atherton made his hundredth Test appearance against the West Indies at Old Trafford in the summer of 2000, which was a milestone that he reached at the same time as fellow batsman and wicketkeeper Alec Stewart. His mammoth innings of 185 not out against South Africa in the second Test at Johannesburg in December 1995 was his highest Test score.

Made an OBE in 1997, Michael Atherton returned from successful winter tours to Pakistan and Sri Lanka to play his last Ashes series in the summer of 2001 before announcing his decision to retire from first-class cricket.

TREVOR BAILEY

Trevor Bailey, who played his first game for Essex during the Second World War, was offered the position of assistant secretary with the county in 1948, which enabled him to devote all his time to playing first-class cricket after coming down from Cambridge.

In 1949, every possible distinction came to Bailey. He was selected by the MCC for its match against New Zealand and then played in four successive Test matches. During this four-match series, he took 6 wickets for 118 runs in his first Test, scored 93 runs in his second, in his third Test achieved bowling figures of 6–84 as well as 72 not out with the bat. He achieved the double, scoring 1,380 runs and capturing 130 wickets in 1949, and, in the match against Lancashire at Clacton, took all 10 wickets in the red rose county's first innings for 90 runs. Not surprisingly, he was chosen as one of *Wisden*'s Five Cricketers of the Year.

In 1950 he performed the hat-trick for his county side against Glamorgan at Newport, while in the return match at Brentwood, he took 7–0 in 29 balls. When injuries began to restrict his appearances for Essex, he managed to gain an FA Amateur Cup winners' medal while playing for Walthamstow Avenue against Leyton.

In 1953 he was appointed Essex's vice-captain, a position he was to hold until he took over as captain from Doug Insole nine years later. During the Test series against Australia, his innings of 71 in the fifth-wicket partnership of 163 with Willie Watson at Lord's saved the series for England, while in the winter tour to the West Indies, he turned in his best bowling figures in Test cricket, taking 7–34 at Kingston.

Though he had a reputation for some dour performances with the bat, he did hit a hundred before lunch in the 1955 encounter with Nottinghamshire at Southend. Two years later, in a Test match against the West Indies at Lord's, he took 7–44 in 21 overs – it was his fiftieth Test and his victims included Walcott, Weekes and Worrell. In 1959 Bailey scored 2,011 runs and took 100 wickets – the first time such a feat had been performed by an Essex player. In 1961, his first season as captain, he led by example, attaining the double for the seventh time. After he had repeated the achievement the following season, injuries began to restrict his appearances and in 1967 he decided to retire. Without doubt the finest all-round cricketer ever to play for Essex, Trevor Bailey went on to become an important member of the BBC's radio commentary team.

SYDNEY BARNES

Sydney Barnes was an intense man who bowled mainly fast spinners, and who, in so many games, wore the skin off his fingers so that the ball became smeared with his own blood. Barnes seemed almost always to be at loggerheads with officials and he missed at least five years during his peak – 1902–7 – because Test selectors found him so difficult to handle. But when he was bowling for England and he had it in his mind to get wickets, he was almost unplayable. Indeed, many believe he may have been the finest bowler of any era.

Barnes was a professional cricketer for forty-five years and in all classes of cricket he took 6,225 wickets at 8.31 each. Twelve times in his career he took all 10 wickets in an innings. In a match for Porthill in 1906 against Leek Highfield, he batted through the innings to score 76 and then took 10–12 with the ball.

In 1907, he took 112 wickets at 3.91 each, again took all 10 wickets against Leek Highfield and did the hat-trick twice in one innings against the powerful batting line-up of Silverdale. In twenty-seven Tests for England he took an amazing 189 wickets – 7 wickets per Test – at 16.43, and in just seven Tests against South Africa he took 83 wickets. In 1967, shortly before his death at the age of ninety-four, Barnes estimated, without a trace of modesty, that had he been playing in the modern era he could have taken 500 Test wickets.

At the age of twenty-eight he was playing in the Lancashire League, but after bowling to a much-impressed Archie MacLaren at the Old Trafford nets, he was signed by Lancashire. Though he played county cricket for two years, he fell foul of the England selectors and didn't return to Test cricket until the 1907–8 tour of Australia.

Sydney Barnes played his last Test series against South Africa in 1913–14 at the age of forty, when he took 49 wickets, including 17 wickets (8–56 and 9–103) at Johannesburg – a world record until Jim Laker topped him in 1956. Barnes took his 49 wickets in the first four Tests of the series, but missed the fifth at Port Elizabeth, blaming his withdrawal on the fact that South African officials, bitter that his bowling was ruining gate receipts, refused to pass the hat around to meet the expenses of his wife and son, who were with him on tour. At fifty-five, he headed the English first-class averages, and at fifty-six he bowled unchanged for three hours and took 8 wickets for 41 runs bowling for Minor Counties against South Africa. By the age of sixty-seven he was still taking wickets as a club professional, and at eighty he bowled an over of brisk pace and immaculate length in a benefit game featuring some of England's great names.

KEN BARRINGTON

Ken Barrington was one of the most prolific post-war batsmen in world cricket until a heart attack in 1968 ended his first-class career shortly before his thirty-ninth birthday. It was as a leg-spinner that Barrington was recommended to Surrey in 1947, but soon his promise as a batsman became obvious, and, after playing his first game for Surrey in 1953, he developed so quickly that two years later he played in his first Test.

Having the advantage of playing in a strong, confident side – during Surrey's seven-year reign as champions – Barrington began the 1959 season with a century in each innings against Warwickshire. Recalled to the England side, he went on to make twenty centuries, including at least two against each of England's opponents, and 6,806 runs, a number surpassed at the time of his retirement only by Wally Hammond, Colin Cowdrey, Don Bradman and Len Hutton.

His first two hundreds were made during the 1959–60 tour of the West Indies and for some years he made most runs on overseas wickets in India, Pakistan and Australia. He also developed a humorous presence on the field, skilled as he was in clowning and mime, which was something appreciated more by overseas crowds than English spectators.

Several times in Test matches he suddenly emerged from a period of inactivity to reach his hundred with a perfectly struck six. On one famous occasion in Melbourne, he made the fastest Test hundred of the year by an Englishman – in 122 balls – and played as boldly and as well as anyone could have asked. It was not until July 1964 that he made his first Test hundred in England, but, typically, when it did come it was extended to 256 in the marathon innings against Australia at Old Trafford. He was then dropped by the England selectors in 1965 after taking what was considered an excessive time to score 137 against New Zealand at Edgbaston in May, but this was a passing interlude in a career for Surrey and England which, though seldom spectacular, was immensely productive.

When he retired, Barrington became a popular manager or coach on England tours, and it was while he was assistant manager on the 1980–1 tour of the West Indies that, tragically, he suffered a second heart attack and died during the Test match at Bridgetown, Barbados.

IAN BOTHAM

Ian Botham is one of the greatest cricketers the world has ever seen. It is a measure of his stature that although he became the most prolific wicket-taker in history, he is likely to be remembered for his batting.

The Cheshire-born player was certainly not free from criticism during his career, being involved in court cases and frequently offending the cricketing authorities. There were times when he was accused of having a carefree attitude, others when he was called domineering. However, throughout the 1980s, Botham was the man who could turn Test matches on his own, the man whose entry to bat was enough to excite crowds to expectancy, the most charismatic cricketer of all.

In July 1977, the Somerset all-rounder received a Test call-up for the match against the Australians at Trent Bridge. He finished the first innings with figures of 5–74, his first wicket being Greg Chappell. In the winter, he scored his first Test century against New Zealand and by the end of 1978, during which he hit Pakistan with two centuries, he had produced his best Test analysis of 8–34 and was the hottest property in cricket. In 1979, Botham passed 1,000 runs and 100 Test wickets in his twenty-first Test, and in February 1980, in Bombay in India's Golden Jubilee Test, he scored 114 and took 13 wickets – the first player to score a century and take 10 or more wickets in a Test.

After two matches of the 1981 Ashes series, Botham resigned the England captaincy. The next Test was one of the most amazing in history and Botham's all-round performance was one of the greatest ever seen. With the ball he took 6–95 and with the bat he scored 50 runs and the match-winning 149 not out. The series continued with Botham in similar form – an outstanding 5–11 at Edgbaston and a superb 118 at Old Trafford. In the first Test of the winter tour of India he became the third player after Richie Benaud and Garry Sobers to score 2,000 Test runs and take 200 Test wickets.

Though a knee injury ended a run of 65 consecutive Tests for England, Botham would return for the 1984 series against the West Indies, and become the first player to complete the double of 3,000 Test runs and 300 Test wickets. In 1986, he achieved his greatest statistical feat in becoming the leading wicket-taker in Test cricket when he passed Dennis Lillee's total of 355.

Botham's figures for Somerset were usually less impressive than those achieved in Test-match cricket, and, after a well-publicized row following the club's sacking of his friends Joel Garner and Viv Richards, he joined Worcestershire, whom he helped to win the County Championship in 1988 and 1989. He moved to Durham in 1991, where he ended his first-class career.

It was inevitable that a man of Ian Botham's temperament and ability would attract headlines – he shoots, has flown with the Red Devils aerobatic team, crashed Saab cars and played professional football for Scunthorpe United. He has also walked from John O'Groats to Land's End for charity and made a trip over the Alps with elephants. Few cricketers have given more pleasure than Ian Botham.

GEOFF BOYCOTT

Geoff Boycott was one of the most controversial cricketers of modern times. No batsman compiled runs in a more single-minded and dedicated manner. At first sight, he was not obviously a batsman of the highest class, but his performances allowed no argument – 1,778 runs in his first full season and 2,110 runs in 1964.

In June 1967, he made 246 not out against India at Headingley, but spent nearly six hours over the first 100. The selectors had previously called for a positive approach to batting and this flagrant disregard for their requirements and the fact that it was not warranted by the state of the match meant that Boycott was dropped for the next Test. The 1970–1 season in Australia, however, was a personal triumph. His 657 Test runs at an average of 93.85 were instrumental in helping England to regain the Ashes.

In 1974, he voluntarily withdrew from Test cricket and did not return to the international scene until 1977. His comeback against Australia at Trent Bridge in the summer was dour and nerve-racking, but triumphant never-theless, for he made 107 and 80 not out. With his confidence high, he made an even more emotional century in the next Test in front of his home crowd at Headingley, his 191 runs also marking the milestone of his hundredth first-class century.

More ups and downs lay ahead. During the 1977–8 winter tour he succeeded to the English captaincy when Mike Brearley suffered a broken forearm, but after averaging 82.25 against Pakistan, in February 1978 at Wellington he had the galling experience of leading England in their first defeat by New Zealand. He also, not for the first time, found himself the centre of controversy over the way he captained and batted for Yorkshire. The responsibility on his shoulders had been great – his ability to play one long innings after another was desperately needed, particularly by a weak-batting Yorkshire side, whose captaincy he had taken over in 1971. It was no coincidence in his first year in charge he averaged over 100 runs.

During the 1981–2 tour of India, he passed Garry Sobers's record aggregate of runs in Test cricket. Soon after his return to England, he announced that he was to take part in a 'rebel' tour of South Africa. Like the other England Test players who went on the controversial tour, he was banned from Tests for three years. When the ban was lifted in 1985, Boycott found the competition for England places was fierce and he wasn't selected again. His Yorkshire career ended in 1986, although there were doubtless many more runs left in him.

Geoff Boycott was controversial to the end, but always insisted his figures spoke for him. His critics claimed the context was as important as the figures, but nobody can take away from him his career average of 56.83, his 8,114 Test runs (once the highest figure in the world), or his two averages of over 100 in a season, which still amount to a unique achievement.

JOHNNY BRIGGS

Johnny Briggs was one of the best left-arm spinners. He took 97 wickets against Australia and made six tours of that country, and would most surely have completed his century against them but for the illness that beset him.

Born in Nottinghamshire, he became a professional at Hornsea in East Yorkshire aged thirteen – following in his father's footsteps – and was taken on Lancashire's staff at sixteen. He made his first-class debut the following year – very young for those days – when he was virtually a specialist fielder. Then his batting developed and he went on to score a century for England against Australia in January 1885. His bowling tended to be mechanical, although he was short enough at 5 feet 5 inches to have flighted the ball. He focused on line and length, and his variation lay in the occasional ball turning into the right-hander.

By 1899, Briggs had taken 94 wickets against Australia. His county skipper, Archie MacLaren, exerted his influence on the selectors and Briggs was brought in for the Headingley Test of that summer. Naturally, he was very excited, the more so after taking three Australian wickets on the opening day. That evening he and some other England players went to a music hall in Leeds.

Briggs suffered a seizure and became deranged. The next day he was put on a train and sent to Cheadle Asylum, where he stayed for nine months.

He was allowed to leave in time to take part in the 1900 season and had recovered enough to take all 10 wickets in a Worcestershire innings. But he was soon to return to the asylum, where he would ultimately die in January 1902. Reports written after Briggs's death at the age of thirty-nine say that he had epilepsy like Colin Blythe, the left-armer who was beginning his career at the time Briggs was finishing his. One source states that the illness that afflicted Briggs derived from a bad attack of sunstroke in South Africa; another that it originated in a blow he received when bowling at The Oval and a ball was hit straight back at him. An X-ray also showed a bone pressing against the valve of his heart, which suggests that the spasms may have resulted from the blood not being able to circulate freely.

DENIS COMPTON

Denis Compton was a popular and colourful sporting hero in 1940s Britain. A natural at both cricket and football, he thrilled the crowds with his unorthodox and, at times, cheeky play.

Few English batsmen have risen to the top at an earlier age than Compton. At just eighteen, in 1936 he played his first match for Middlesex against Sussex, batting at number 11 in the Whitsun match at Lord's. Within a month he had made the first of his 123 first-class centuries, and by the end of the season there were many who thought he should have gone to Australia with Gubby Allen's MCC side. He played in his first Test against New Zealand in the summer of 1937 and in all subsequent home Tests up to the outbreak of war, making 102 in his first innings against Australia at Trent Bridge in June 1938.

In 1947, Compton embarked on his golden year and his memorable record-breaking partnerships with Bill Edrich. When he had made a hundred, he often considered that enough, unless the requirements of the side made it important for him to go on. In this particular year, with Middlesex challenging successfully for the County Championship, he went on often! His 1947 record of 3,816 runs and 18 centuries in a season is unlikely ever to be beaten.

The following year, he played what many regard as his greatest innings – an unbeaten 145 against Australia at Old Trafford, overcoming Ray Lindwall at his most hostile and returning to the crease after being knocked out and retiring hurt when on 4 not out. He went to South Africa in 1948–9 and made his famous 300 in three hours at Benoni, easily the fastest triple century ever made.

Despite an operation to remove a fragment of bone from his right knee, he was still able to play an astonishing innings of 278 in a little under a run a minute against Pakistan at Trent Bridge in July 1954, but in November 1955 he had to have his kneecap removed. Again he returned with a hundred for his county side – against Somerset – and when fit enough to play in the last Test against Australia in August 1956, he made a brilliant 94.

Compton captained Middlesex jointly with Bill Edrich in 1951 and 1952, an unusual arrangement which recognized the talents of two superb players, but he had perhaps too much of the cavalier spirit to be a truly outstanding captain. After the 1957 season he retired, making 143 and 48 in his last match for Middlesex.

As a footballer, Denis Compton played as a dashing left-winger for Arsenal from 1936 to 1950. He won a League Championship medal in 1948, and, in his second-last match, an FA Cup winners' medal. These were his only football honours because the war took his best years, and, although he was a wartime international for England, he did not make the official list.

COLIN COWDREY

Few players in the world have spent longer at the top in post-war cricket than Colin Cowdrey, whose Test career began in Australia in 1954–5. When he retired, his 114 Test appearances had established a new record and his 7,624 Test runs were the highest number scored by an Englishman.

Cowdrey first played for Kent in 1950. The following year, he made an impressive 106 for the Gentlemen against a strong Players side at Scarborough. Two half-centuries for the Gentlemen against the Australians at Lord's in 1953 confirmed his swift advance towards the England team.

In 1954, when he was captain of Oxford University, he was twelfth man in the last Test against Pakistan at The Oval and a somewhat unexpected selection for the MCC tour of Australia and New Zealand. Sadly, the tour began on a tragic note when, on Cowdrey's arrival in Perth, he learned of the sudden death of his father, who had been a tremendous inspiration to his cricket. However, it was his partnership with Peter May at Sydney in December that turned the second Test and the series in England's favour. Then, in the next Test at Melbourne, it was his remarkable innings of 102 – out of his side's total of only 191 – that started England on the way to success in the third Test.

In the 1950s, the England innings would thrive or fall with Cowdrey and May. Indeed, it was their historic stand of 411 at Edgbaston in the summer of 1957 that had a decisive effect on the series with the West Indies. Cowdrey followed 154 at Edgbaston with 152 in the next Test at Lord's.

In Australia, during the 1962–3 tour, Cowdrey made his highest first-class score, 307 against South Australia in Adelaide. Later in 1963, in the Lord's Test against the West Indies, his arm was broken by a short ball from Wes Hall. At the end of a dramatic match, he had to come in for the last two balls to earn England a draw – which he did, fortunately, as the non-striker.

During the 1967–8 tour of the West Indies, Cowdrey batted magnificently, scoring 534 runs in the series, including 71 at Port-of-Spain, to give England the only win of the Test series (the other four matches all resulting in draws). The following summer at Edgbaston saw him play in his hundredth Test, and to celebrate this achievement he hit yet another century against opponents Australia.

The 1974–5 England team touring Australia had been ravaged by injuries, and so, at the age of forty-two, Cowdrey was needed to join the rest of the team in their battle against Dennis Lillee and Jeff Thomson. He responded with skill and character, and managed to score his last century against the Australians – his innings of 151 not out steering Kent to victory by four wickets.

In 1986, Colin Cowdrey's appointment as MCC President for the county's bicentenary the following year was well received by all connected with Kent cricket. Knighted in 1992 and raised to the peerage five years later, Lord Cowdrey of Tonbridge was a true sportsman – charming, gentle and friendly.

TED DEXTER

Known throughout the world as 'Lord Ted', Ted Dexter was one of the most dashing batsmen and most gifted all-round cricketers to play for England in modern times. He captained the Cambridge University team in 1958 and two years later took over the captaincy of Sussex.

Having played his first Test against the New Zealand tourists in 1958, Dexter was sent out to Australia during the 1958–9 tour when Willie Watson and Ramon Subba Row were injured. He played in two Tests there, and, on the New Zealand section of the tour, made his maiden Test century, scoring 141 in the Christchurch Test, which England won by an innings and 99 runs. A year later he was selected for the tour of the West Indies, and, though it was a much criticized choice, he played the fast bowling with great zest and topped the Test batting averages. He was batting at number three when he made his second century of the series at Georgetown in March, ensuring that England could not lose the match.

In the first Test of the 1961 series against Australia at Edgbaston, he earned England a draw with a second innings of 180, and in the decisive fourth Test at Old Trafford he played a spectacular innings of 76 at a run a minute, putting England in the position of needing only 106 runs from their last 9 wickets. However, after Dexter's dismissal, they collapsed, and the game and ultmaitely the series were lost.

Dexter became captain of England when he took the MCC side to India and Pakistan in 1961–2, and subsequently led England in Australia in 1962–3. Few who witnessed it will ever forget his innings of 93 in the second Test at Melbourne, when he set England on the road to victory, having scored 70 and 99 in the first Test.

Though Dexter scored a number of centuries, he is best remembered by many for his innings of 70 in 81 minutes in the Lord's Test of June 1963 against the West Indian fast bowlers, Wes Hall and Charlie Griffith, then in their menacing prime.

He remained captain until he stood for Parliament in October 1964 and had to delay his acceptance of the invitation to tour South Africa. When he eventually went, it was as vice-captain to Mike Smith. He did not captain England again and slipped out of regular first-class cricket. However, when Sussex's batting became depleted by injury in 1968, Dexter returned to action and made an immediate impact, scoring 203 against Kent at Hastings in his first innings. He was then selected for the last two Tests against the Australians, the excitement his return caused further illustrating the great loss English cricket suffered when 'Lord Ted' retired. He took up numerous business interests until, in 1989, he became the first paid Chairman of Selectors for England.

BASIL D'OLIVEIRA

Basil D'Oliveira became more significant than he could possibly have imagined when he walked out on to the field to play for England at Lord's in 1966. He gave new and hitherto unimagined hope to millions of black South Africans.

As early as 1956, D'Oliveira had begun to write from his Cape Town home to England in the hope of finding coaching instruction so that he could help to teach the game to others in his community. He performed with such dazzling success in minor cricket, on very poor grounds and matting wickets, that word of his talent reached England via John Arlott and Glamorgan's Peter Walker. As a result he was invited to join Middleton in the Central Lancashire League. He needed £200 for the air fare and the sum was partially raised by raffles, fêtes and matches held in the area around his tenement home.

It was a wise investment for 'Dolly', as he became known, for by the end of the 1960 season he was ahead of Garry Sobers at the top of the league batting averages. He played with great success with Middleton for four years before Tom Graveney persuaded him he could make the grade in county cricket. He then spent 1964 qualifying for Worcestershire, making a century against the Australians, and in 1965, at the age of thirty-three, he was the only batsman in the County Championship to score more than 1,500 runs.

D'Oliveira found it difficult to believe that he had been picked to play for England against the West Indies at Lord's in June 1966. It is said that he was so proud of his England cap that he wore it in bed! He was more or less a regular in the England side for six years, making the highest score of his career – 158 runs – in the final Test against Australia at The Oval in 1968, as he, John Edrich (with 164 runs) and Derek Underwood (with figures of 7–50) effectively won the Test. Later that year, he was the innocent cause of an international incident when, picked to replace Tom Cartwright for the MCC tour of South Africa after he had been controversially omitted in the first place, he was refused entry and the tour was cancelled.

Long after losing his place in the England side, D'Oliveira continued to display his class for Worcestershire. He was capable of anything when the mood was right – once almost winning a Benson & Hedges Cup final at Lord's single-handedly, despite a severe leg injury, and once keeping Yorkshire in the field for more than a day while compiling 227 at Hull in

1974 – purely because a Yorkshire bowler had annoyed him with a reference to his colour.

On retiring, he became Worcestershire's coach – a man of rare fighting qualities, he overcame many hurdles in his unprecedented career, doing honour to the game of cricket.

BILL EDRICH

Bill Edrich made his debut as a young cricketer for Norfolk in the Minor Counties Championship of 1934. Thirty-five years later, in 1969, he was back playing for them. During the intervening decades, Edrich had gained fame as one half of a partnership that had devastated bowling for both Middlesex and England immediately after the Second World War – Compton was the other half.

Edrich was also a good footballer and played a number of games for Tottenham Hotspur, but it was as a professional cricketer that he established himself at an early age. Though lacking the genius or range of Compton, Edrich had other qualities – courage, fearlessness, resolution in adversity – that imprinted themselves on the imagination of the cricketing public. In only his second full season for Middlesex, he joined the select band of batsmen who have made 1,000 runs before the end of May, and played in four Tests against Don Bradman's Australians in summer 1938. But he met with little success during both that series and the subsequent tour of South Africa in the winter of 1938–9, the exception being the notorious 'timeless' Test in Durban in March 1939, in which he made a magnificent 219 in the second innings.

After the war, however, the selectors' faith was handsomely justified. His partnerships with Denis Compton in 1947 for Middlesex in their Championship-winning year and for England against South Africa became legendary. Among the most remarkable were an unbroken stand of 287 in just over two and a half hours against Surrey at The Oval, another partnership of 227 in a little over two hours at Leicester, and 370 against South Africa at Lord's in June. At Grace Road they opened the second innings with 66 runs needed in 25 minutes, which they made with seven minutes to spare. In that season, Bill Edrich made 3,539 runs, an aggregate exceeded in cricket history only by Denis Compton in the same year.

Sturdily built, he was short of inches and yet he seemed to relish facing a fast bowler. A brave hooker and a quick cutter, he was particularly adept at the pulled drive. It was not a classic or attractive method, but, allied with his pugnacious temperament, it was good to watch and effective. In his heyday, Bill Edrich had been a fast bowler who, from just a few yards' run and with a slinging action, worked up surprising pace and took some useful wickets. In later years, he acquired a happy touch as joint captain of Middlesex with Compton for two seasons and as captain from 1953 to 1957. Married five times, he was certainly a man who lived life to the full and played his cricket the same way.

JOHN EDRICH

Tenacious, courageous and totally phlegmatic, John Edrich served England loyally over thirteen years and 77 Tests. A cousin of former England and Middlesex batsman Bill Edrich, he left Norfolk some twenty years after his famed relation and joined Surrey.

In 1959, his first full season, he had made 1,799 runs, including a century in each innings of his second Championship match against Yorkshire, during which he was struck on the left hand by a lively ball from Fred Trueman. The injury healed slowly and his hand was again badly damaged by Frank Tyson in the last match of the season. An orthopaedic surgeon finally solved the problem by grafting a piece of leg bone into the hand, giving rise to the joke that Edrich was the only batsman who could be struck on the hand and given out lbw!

After establishing himself as a Test batsman with an innings of 120 against Australia at Lord's in June 1964, Edrich enjoyed some astonishing success the following summer when he made an unbeaten 310 against New Zealand at Headingley. In 1969, when England lost the bulk of its experienced batting – Ken Barrington, Colin Cowdrey and Tom Graveney – there was still John Edrich. He illustrated his pre-eminence by finishing the season far ahead of the field on top of the first-class batting averages, having made 2,238 runs at an average of 69.93.

Following a fine tour of Australia in 1970–1, however, he lost some consistency and his Test place. His future seemed to lie in a new role as captain of Surrey, but England could not manage without his resolution and he returned in 1974–5 for a winter tour in which the Australian pace attack broke hearts as well as fingers. During the fourth Test at Sydney, Edrich had two ribs cracked by a short ball from Dennis Lillee. Giving not an inch of ground, the thirty-eight-year-old then had an outstanding home series on slower pitches against the same tormentors. In August he piled up 175 in the second Test at Lord's – his seventh century against the Australians – and in the fourth Test at The Oval he was bowled by Lillee four runs short of yet another century.

A year later, he was called up again and batted resolutely against the fierce West Indies pace attack. In the relative tranquillity of county cricket, Edrich, who scored 29,305 first-class runs for Surrey at an average of 46.07, became the eighteenth batsman to score a hundred centuries when he made 101 not out against Derbyshire at The Oval. Later the same month he scored two centuries in the match against Kent. In 1977, he was made an MBE and he retired a year later.

GODFREY EVANS

Godfrey Evans was a brilliant, extrovert wicketkeeper, one of the greatest ever seen. He relished the big occasions and managed to combine acrobatic showmanship with glovework of the highest class.

With a reputation already established as a batsman, Evans joined the Kent staff in 1937. During his trials, he was pressed into service as a keeper and startled onlookers referred to him as 'another Ames'. Studying both Les Ames and Kent's other Test wicketkeeper, 'Hopper' Levett, allowed Evans to continue his education behind the stumps. But the war put paid to his immediate ambition and in 1946 he returned to Canterbury with much to prove.

While Ames decided to concentrate on his batting and Levett returned to the Second XI, Evans seized his opportunity with both hands. In August 1946, he was called up to play in the third Test against India at The Oval. That autumn he set sail to Australia and New Zealand with the MCC party under Wally Hammond, and, having been omitted from the first disastrous Test at Brisbane (which England lost by an innings and 332 runs), kept his place for a record twenty-seven consecutive matches thereafter.

Evans was dropped in 1949 and 1951, but otherwise represented as near automatic a Test selection as any England player until his retirement in 1959. In 1950, against the combined wiles of Ramadhin and Valentine, he scored 104 at Old Trafford. Two years later, he had his most successful season with the bat, scoring a second Test hundred at Lord's (98 of which came before lunch) and making 1,241 runs for his county.

Godfrey Evans had all the qualities of a born wicketkeeper: a superb pair of hands, agility, balance, anticipation, and, perhaps most of all, vitality. He was a shrewd tactician, spotting weaknesses in a batsman and passing on the tips to the bowlers. He was so enthusiastic that he would keep up a non-stop chatter of encouragement to his teammates, both in the changing-room and on the field of play. At his best, Evans was capable of making catches and taking stumpings, something which no other player would have even a considered chance of doing. He was superb standing back, good near the stumps and possibly the fastest mover anywhere.

Evans's subsequent career led him from pub tenancy to public relations. Perhaps his best-known position was as cricket adviser to Ladbrokes, for whom he set the infamous 500–1 odds on the 1981 Test at Headingley.

ANDREW FLINTOFF

In the summer of 2005, Andrew Flintoff established himself as England's greatest all-round cricketer since the days of Ian Botham.

In his early county and international career, Flintoff was considered a raw but unfulfilled talent. Though the Lancastrian made his Test debut for England in 1998 against South Africa, his struggle to make the grade at county level continued. He found his form only intermittently, though when he did he was often explosive. In 2000, he hit an unbeaten 135 against Surrey in the semi-finals of the NatWest Trophy, which David Gower described as 'the most awesome innings we are ever going to see on a cricket field'.

It was around this time that the England management team said they were unhappy with his fitness and weight, and, after losing his England place, he remodelled his bowling action and gained a place on the 2001–2 tour of India. Despite possibly his worst international batting form, Flintoff later saw the tour as a turning point in his career. In the final crucial one-day match, he was entrusted with bowling the final over with India needing 11 to win. He ran out Anil Kumble and then bowled Srinath with successive balls to win the match, before ripping off his shirt in celebration.

In March 2002, he scored his maiden Test century against New Zealand at Christchurch, and the following year he scored a century and three fifties in the five-Test series against South Africa. He continued to excel on the tour of the West Indies in 2004, taking 5–58 in the Barbados Test at Bridgetown and scoring a century in Antigua. Shortly afterwards he was named as a *Wisden* Cricketer of the Year.

Injury prevented him from bowling in the 2004 NatWest one-day series against New Zealand and the West Indies, but he played as a specialist batsman, scoring two centuries in the series and hitting seven sixes in one innings. He matched this haul in the second Test against West Indies at Edgbaston in July 2004, hitting a first-class best of 167 runs. Over the course of England's record-breaking summer, he hit a half-century in all seven victorious Tests against the Kiwis and West Indies. At the end of the season he was named as the inaugural winner of the ICC One-day Player of the Year award and the Professional Cricketers' Association Player of the Year.

Following the Test series in South Africa, Flintoff flew home for surgery on his left ankle, leading to worries that he might not regain fitness for the Ashes series, but fortunately these fears were never realized. In the second Test at Edgbaston he was made Man of the Match after he broke Ian Botham's 1981 record of six sixes in an Ashes Test match. England went on to win by 2 runs and Michael Vaughan subsequently dubbed the match 'Fred's Test' in honour of 'Freddie' Flintoff's achievements. For his performance throughout the Ashes series, he was named Man of the Series by Australian coach John Buchanan. His outstanding achievement also won him the inaugural Compton-Miller medal.

In October 2005, Flintoff shared the Sir Garfield Sobers Trophy for the ICC Player of the Year award with South Africa's Jacques Kallis. Two months later, he was named BBC Sports Personality of the Year, and in the New Year's Honours List for 2006 he was made an MBE for his role in England's successful Ashes side. In Vaughan's enforced absence, Flintoff captained England and was viewed as a great success in the drawn series with India – his contributions with bat and ball ensured that he was made Player of the Series. In April 2006, he was named *Wisden* Leading Cricketer in the World.

GRAHAM GOOCH

When Graham Gooch was appointed captain of England against the West Indies at The Oval in the summer of 1988 he became England's fourth captain of the series. By that time he had become his country's leading batsman, although his start in Test cricket had been somewhat inauspicious.

In July 1975, after hitting the first of his 94 centuries for Essex, Gooch was called into the Test side a little prematurely, making his debut against the pace of Dennis Lillee and Thomson at Edgbaston. Despite making 0 and 0, he was retained for the second Test at Lord's, but then disappeared from Test cricket until 1978, when he returned against Pakistan as Geoff Boycott's opening partner.

When Essex won the County Championship in 1979, Gooch gave the team an attacking look right from the start. In the Benson & Hedges final against Surrey, he played a magnificent innings of 120 in the first of a run of successes in the Lord's finals.

After being run out on 99 in the third Test at Melbourne in February 1980, his first ton came against the West Indies at Lord's the following June, when he scored a magnificent 123 out of the first 165 runs. In winter 1980–1 he toured the Caribbean and was England's most successful batsman by far, scoring 116 at Bridgetown and 153 at Kingston to average 57.50 in the series. However, after captaining a rebel tour to South Africa, he was banned from Test cricket for three years.

Playing for Essex in 1982, Gooch hit the Sussex attack for 198 not out in a Benson & Hedges Cup zonal match – the highest score made in a one-day competition in England. Two years later he was the first man in 1984 to reach 2,000 runs, scoring 2,559, the highest by an Essex player in a season.

Gooch returned to the England side in 1985 to face the Australians, and in the final Test at The Oval hit 196 as England won the Ashes. He became captain of Essex in 1986, but, despite leading the county to their third Championship title in four years, he relinquished the post after a couple of seasons – though he was later reappointed.

After accepting the role of England captain, he became a national hero when he led the team to victory over the West Indies at Kingston in March 1990, and he came close to doing the same at Port-of-Spain, where he was forced to retire from the match with a broken finger.

The year 1990 belonged to Graham Gooch. He hit 154 as England beat New Zealand at Edgbaston in July, and followed this later that same month with innings of 333 and 123 in the victory over India at Lord's. His triple century was the highest innings ever played by an England captain.

Capable of the destruction of any attack, Gooch lifted the spirits of English cricket by his own supreme example, coming as it did after a few years of unhappiness and controversy. When he retired from first-class cricket in 1997, he was both England's and Essex's leading run-getter of all time.

DARREN GOUGH

The first product of Yorkshire's cricket school, Darren Gough made a startling entry into the County Championship in the summer of 1989 when aged just seventeen. The wicket of former England captain Mike Gatting was one of five the teenager claimed in the match. However, after this remarkable start, a back injury ruined the rest of his season and he didn't return until August.

The next three seasons rarely hinted that he would become a consistently accurate quick bowler, but in 1993 his off-cutter developed and he began to bowl the yorker with devastating effect. That season he produced his best figures in the County Championship, with 7–42 against Somerset at Taunton. Awarded his county cap, he was selected to go to Holland with an England XI. After playing in a one-day international against New Zealand in 1994, Gough made his Test debut in the summer against the Kiwis at Old Trafford, reviving England's innings with a lusty 65.

In 1995, Gough took 4 wickets in 5 balls, including a hat-trick in the match against Kent, and followed this with new best figures of 7–28 against Lancashire in a non-Championship fixture at Headingley.

The following year, he not only had his best season with the ball, taking 66 wickets at 22.69 runs apiece, but also scored his maiden first-class century with a knock of 121 against Warwickshire. At Test level, Gough's best figures with the ball came in front of his home crowd at Headingley, in August 1998, when he took 6–42 against South Africa, helping England to a surprise 2–1 series win.

On the 1998–9 tour of Australia, Gough performed the hat-trick for the first time for England in the final Test at Sydney. He played in two World Cups, but was sidelined for the entire series against New Zealand in 1999 because of a career-threatening injury.

Passionately committed, even in the bleakest of situations, he was named Man of the Series against the West Indies in 2000, thanks to a haul of 25 wickets that included Brian Lara's scalp on five occasions. With the bat he was Dominic Cork's foil during England's dramatic two-wicket win at Lord's in July. During the curse of the 2001 Ashes series, he became only the eighth English bowler to reach 200 Test victims.

Currently playing his county cricket with Essex at the time of writing, the winner of BBC's Strictly Come Dancing still harbours hopes of a recall to both the Test side and, most definitely, England's 2007 World Cup squad.

DAVID GOWER

David Gower has been described as the most accomplished England batsman of his generation and his languid, graceful style has been likened to that of Frank Woolley, another great left-hander born in Kent.

After drifting into a first-class cricket career because he was bored with his law studies, Gower joined Leicestershire and made his debut in 1975, the season the county went on to win the Championship for the first time in their ninety-six-year history. Gower made his Test debut against Pakistan at Edgbaston in June 1978, when he hit his first ball for four and went on to make 58. Later that season, he made his first Test century against New Zealand at

The Oval. In December 1978 he made his first century against Australia at Perth, and when India visited England in summer 1979 he hit an unbeaten 200 in the first Test at Edgbaston.

There followed a lean period that culminated in his being dropped for the first Test against the West Indies in 1980. He was still not fulfilling his potential when he toured Australia in 1982–3, but in the World Series Cup, a bonanza of one-day matches that followed the Test series, he made three centuries against New Zealand. Having made over 1,000 runs in five Tests and ten WSC matches, he was named Benson & Hedges International Cricketer of the Year.

Later appointed England captain, he probably regretted his first period in charge as the West Indies beat England 5–0 during the summer of 1984 – the worst defeat ever inflicted on England. However, in 1984–5 he led with tact and shrewdness through a most difficult tour of India which saw the assassinations of Prime Minister Mrs Gandhi and Percy North, the British Deputy High Commissioner. England lost the first Test in Bombay, but won the series 2–1, not least because of Gower's calm and control.

In 1985, Gower and his team regained the Ashes from an Australian side weakened by the defections of a rebel tour of South Africa. In the third Test at Trent Bridge, he made his first century as England captain and in the fifth at Edgbaston, he hit his highest ever Test score of 215. He scored 732 runs in the series, at an average of 81.33.

The following year, after a poor tour to the West Indies, when his captaincy was criticized as being too lenient, he was replaced by Mike Gatting. He was later reinstated for the 1989 series against Australia, but after a heavy 4–0 defeat, he was not only deprived of the captaincy, but was not even selected for the trip to the West Indies. He won back his place in 1990, however, and in August made an unbeaten century against India at The Oval. He joined Gooch's team to go to Australia, and made two centuries during the winter 1990–1 series, but was later guilty of a breach of discipline with an ill-judged flying escapade.

On leaving Leicestershire, he joined Hampshire, but he never seemed to have a great appetite for the county game, preferring instead the drama and gravitas of Test-match cricket.

W. G. GRACE

W. G. Grace was surely the greatest player the game has ever known or will know. After steadily building a local reputation, he took a step forward in 1863 when he played against professional bowling of the highest calibre when the All England XI came down to play twenty-two men of Bristol on Durdham Down.

In 1866, he was only eighteen years of age when he played his first major innings, making 224 for All England against Surrey, despite leaving the match early in order to run a hurdle race at Crystal Palace, which he won! Even in those early years, he seemed to be breaking conventions.

In 1868 he played what he always thought was his best innings when he scored an all-run 134 at Lord's on a terrible wicket out of the Gentlemen's 201 against the Players. He scored two hundreds for the South in a match against the North of the Thames at Canterbury, the first time such a feat had been achieved since William Lambert at Lord's in 1817.

Soon to become internationally famous, Grace toured Canada and the United States in 1872, where he was hailed as 'the Champion Batsman of Cricketdom and a monarch in his might'.

In 1874, Grace scored 1,000 runs and took 100 wickets in eleven consecutive matches – a phenomenal feat. Two years later, he scored 2,622 runs and, in the month of August, he scored highly in three successive innings: 344 for the MCC against Kent at Canterbury, 177 against Nottinghamshire at Clifton, and then his highest score for Gloucestershire, 318 not out against Yorkshire at Cheltenham.

In 1880 he hit 152 at The Oval in the first match in this country between England and Australia. He was thirty-two years old when he played in his first Test and had already scored some 20,000 first-class runs, the record for a debutant. There were suggestions that, because he was putting on weight and was very heavy for so young a man, he may have passed his best. Nevertheless, over the next nineteen years he scored 1,098 Test runs at an average of 32.29, though he had to battle against his increasing size for the rest of his life as a cricketer.

In what may be termed the second part of his career, a climax was reached in 1895. In May, he scored 1,016 runs at an average of 112.88, including 288 against Somerset, to become the first man ever to score a hundred first-class hundreds.

In 1899, W. G. Grace split with Gloucestershire. The Cricket Committee had heard he had been offered employment with the London County Club, which was just being formed at Crystal Palace. The County Committee wrote to W. G., asking which matches he intended to play for Gloucestershire. He was furious because he had played in all Gloucestershire's first-class matches in the season so far, and so he replied to the committee by sending his resignation and inviting *them* to choose teams for all future games.

In a first-class career which stretched from 1865 to 1908, W. G. Grace scored, according to *Wisden*, 54,896 runs and took 2,876 wickets. His record should include all other games, in which he collected about 45,000 more runs and 4,500 wickets. If these were added up, they would reach totals never imagined before: some 100,000 runs and over 7,000 wickets.

TOM GRAVENEY

Tom Graveney had a natural talent for the game of cricket and this, plus a recommendation from his elder brother Ken, who was already on the Gloucestershire staff, brought him to Bristol. He was soon established as the most promising young batsman in the country.

In 1951, Graveney scored 2,291 runs, his best performance coming in the match against Northamptonshire at Bristol, when he hit 103 and 105 not out. In 1951–2, he was England's number three on the tour to India, Pakistan and Sri Lanka, his aggregate total of 1,393 runs including six centuries. The following season, he scored 2,066 runs and was selected as one of *Wisden's* Cricketers of the Year.

In 1953–4, he represented the MCC in their fixture against British Guyana at Georgetown. Graveney scored 231 as he and Willie Watson added 402 for the fourth wicket – still a record for any English touring team. The following summer, he hit 222 against Derbyshire at Chesterfield, his highest score for Gloucestershire. In 1956, he topped the county batting averages, scoring 2,397 runs. In the match against Essex, he produced a remarkable performance, scoring more than half his team's total in both innings of the match – 100 out of 153 followed by 67 out of 107. Also that season, against Glamorgan at Newport, Graveney scored a magnificent 200 out of his side's total of 298, his runs scored on a turning wicket against the spin of Jim McConnon and Don Shepherd.

Though he had made his Test debut in July 1951, it was 1957 before Graveney won a regular place in the side. He hammered the West Indian bowlers all round Trent Bridge in July, scoring a glorious 258 in the process. He followed this up the next month with 164 at The Oval in the fifth Test, while on the county circuit he hit hundreds in each innings of the match against Warwickshire.

He played for Gloucestershire for twelve years and was their captain for the last two, leading them to the runners-up spot in the County Championship in 1959. By the time 1960 came round, the Gloucestershire committee couldn't make up its mind whether or not it wanted an amateur or professional captain, with the result that Graveney was relieved of the captaincy. Having scored 19,705 runs, he left to play for Worcestershire in 1961. At New Road, he improved as a player, helping his new county win the Championship in 1964 and 1965, scoring 2,385 runs and 1,768 runs respectively.

Graveney played all his strokes with elegance, perfect timing and style, and is the only cricketer to score more than 10,000 runs for two different counties. In the 1968 New Year's Honours List he was made an OBE for his services to cricket. In the early part of his career, some selectors and Test captains wondered whether Graveney had the right temperament to succeed at the highest level. The former MCC President's seventy-nine Test appearances, 4,882 runs, eleven centuries and average of 44.38 prove that they need not have worried.

TONY GREIG

Tony Greig made his county debut for Sussex against Lancashire in May 1967 at the age of twenty. Standing at an impressive 6 feet 8 inches, the slim, blond Greig saved Sussex with 156 runs in his first match and it was clear a new star had risen. He scored 1,299 runs and took 67 wickets in his first season.

In 1970, Greig played for the England XI against the Rest of the World, before making his Test debut against Australia two years later. In the first Test at Old Trafford in June 1972, he was top scorer in both innings with 57 and 62, and he also took a total of 5 wickets in the England victory. The following winter he toured India, where he was a popular figure, and in the fifth Test in Bombay he made his first Test century, 148, and shared in a record fifth-wicket stand for England of 254 with Keith Fletcher.

In 1973–4, he had an extremely successful tour of the West Indies, where his competitiveness got him into trouble in the first Test at Port-of-Spain. On the last ball of the second day, Julien played the ball back down the pitch and Greig, seeing Kallicharran out of his ground, threw down the wicket. Kallicharran, who was only making his way back to the pavilion, was given out. It took an off-the-field agreement between captain, umpires and officials to reinstate the West Indian batsman and possibly prevent uproar the following day. Apart from contributing two centuries, Greig played a major part in England's making a draw of the series when, in the final Test, he changed his bowling style from medium swing and seam to off-breaks. He took 8–86 and 5–70, the best figures produced by an England bowler against the West Indies at that time.

In 1975, Greig was appointed England captain and the following year, when the West Indies visited England, he made a combative but ill-considered remark about making them grovel: in the event the West Indian fast bowlers were merciless in inflicting a 3–0 defeat.

His style of leadership was beginning to weld a more successful England side, however, and the tour of India in 1976–7 was a triumph – India lost the first three Tests to a touring side for the first time ever. Then his role in World Series Cricket became known. The immediate result was the loss of the captaincy to Mike Brearley. He was never forgiven by the establishment and within a couple of years, his first-class career had ended.

He became managing director of an insurance company set up by Kerry Packer and a cricket presenter on Channel 9 television. During the Packer affair, he was articulate, polite and reasonable in his assertions that all was for the best as far as the welfare of cricketers was concerned, a claim that bears examination now the dust has settled.

Tony Greig deserves to be remembered not as a player who vaguely besmirched the name of cricket, as some traditionalists would like to have it, but as one of England's best captains and all-rounders.

WALLY HAMMOND

In 1924, while playing for Gloucestershire against Middlesex on a terrible wicket at Bristol, Wally Hammond amazed everyone. Gloucestershire had been dismissed for only 31 runs and Middlesex themselves could muster only 74. In Gloucestershire's second innings, Hammond scored a majestic, unbeaten 174 in only four hours, enabling his side to go on to win the match.

Hammond's class was obvious, but many judges thought him too head-strong, playing too many shots. This theory was certainly dispelled in the match against Lancashire at Old Trafford in August 1925, when Hammond scored 250 not out against the pace of Ted McDonald and the off-spin of Cecil Parkin and Dick Tyldesley.

During the winter of 1925–6, Hammond was bitten by a mosquito and contracted an illness for which the Caribbean doctors had no answer. He was shipped back to England and spent most of the 1926 season in hospital. Despite this, he returned to English cricket a great batsman – a remarkable achievement considering a year earlier he had been close to death.

In May 1927, he scored 1,000 runs in only twenty-two days and ended the season with 2,522 runs in the Championship at an average of 72.05. The following year he scored 2,474 runs at 82.46, and, in the match against Surrey, held 10 catches, a feat that will stay in the record books for ever. In all first-class matches that summer, Hammond made 78 catches, which was yet another record for a fieldsman other than a wicketkeeper. This was also the season that he performed his best bowling, taking 9–23 against Worcestershire.

In 1928–9 he toured Australia in Percy Chapman's side. He outshone every-one, amassing 905 runs, which remains the largest number of runs scored in a Test series by an English batsman. At Sydney, he scored 251, at Melbourne, 200, and at Adelaide, 119 and 17. His batting average for the Test series was a mere 113.12! Both aggregate and average remain a record in Australia.

In 1935 he became the quickest compiler of a hundred hundreds, having scored his first century in 1928. He was at his best three years later, both in the County Championship and at Test level. For Gloucestershire, he scored seven hundreds in eight consecutive innings, his highest being 271 against Lancashire at Bristol. For England, at Lord's, he scored a masterly 240 after Australian paceman Ernie McCormick had blasted out Charlie Barnett, Len Hutton and Bill Edrich for just 31 runs. He went on to play in eighty-five Test matches, scoring 7,249 runs at an average of 58.45. For Gloucestershire, he scored 33,664 runs at 57.05 and produced a highest score of 317, made against Nottinghamshire at Gloucester in 1936.

After remarrying, he left England for Durban, but his life in South Africa seemed dogged by bad luck. He invested all his savings in the motor trade, but within a few years his capital had vanished. In 1959 he was involved in a horrific crash and suffered a fractured skull. He never really recovered from that and, in 1965, aged sixty-two, he died after suffering a heart attack. A genius of his time, Wally Hammond was worshipped by the crowds and revered by his colleagues.

JACK HOBBS

Renowned as a very modest and self-effacing man, Jack Hobbs was popularly referred to as 'The Master', while Percy Fender, who saw much of his play and was a shrewd judge of cricket, called him 'the greatest batsman the world has ever known'.

His cricket career was one of immense success. He scored more runs than anyone else (61,237); more centuries (197); and more seasonal totals of 2,000 or more on seventeen occasions. However, he was by no means a creature of statistics, which had little meaning for him. The eldest of six children from a poor background, he had virtually no coaching, yet he grew up to be an almost flawless batsman.

Tom Hayward saw him playing in his native Cambridge and recommended him to Surrey, and, after satisfying the county at his trial and after a period of residence, he was given his first-team debut. In the match against the Gentleman of England, captained by W. G. Grace, he scored 88, while in his second against Essex, he made 155 and was immediately awarded his county cap.

His Surrey career was to last for thirty historic years until 1934 and he ceased to play for England only four years before his retirement. During his career, he had four opening partners with whom he was especially successful – Tom Hayward and Andy Sandham for Surrey, and Wilfred Rhodes and Herbert Sutcliffe for England. His 352 with Hayward against Warwickshire at The Oval in 1909 was their highest partnership together. The best-remembered stand between Hobbs and Rhodes was their 323 at Melbourne against Australia in February 1912, which is still the highest ever made for the first wicket for England against Australia. After the First World War, Sandham succeeded Hayward, and together they shared in sixty-three stands of over 100. But it is his partnership with Yorkshire's Herbert Sutcliffe that is best remembered. Their batting alliance was remarkable for their understanding of each other's running and their joint mastery of difficult pitches, such as that at The Oval in August 1926, when England won back the Ashes last held before the war.

In the 1920s, Hobbs stood supreme on all pitches and against all types of bowling, and when he was taken ill with appendicitis during the 1921 series against Australia, it was akin to a national disaster. He went to Australia on five MCC tours and to South Africa twice before the First World War.

Just as he had overlapped the Grace era in his youth, so he overlapped the Bradman era in 1930 when he played in his last Test series at the age of forty-seven. He started well against the Australians, scoring 78 and 74 in the first Test at Trent Bridge, which England won by 93 runs, but he did not pass 50 again. The last of his sixty-one Tests was at The Oval in August, in which England made 405 in the first innings, Hobbs contributing 47, but the home side were beaten eventually by an innings.

In 1934, his last first-class season, Hobbs was asked by George Duckworth of Lancashire to play in his benefit match at Old Trafford. He went out and scored 116 and 51 not out. With Sandham once again, he put on 184. Lancashire were champions that year and Hobbs's century was the only one scored against them in the Championship.

After retirement as a player, he took up cricket journalism. In 1953, he became the first cricketer to receive a knighthood in recognition of his services to sport.

LEN HUTTON

Len Hutton won recognition as one of the greatest batsmen in cricket history through many prodigious feats, one of the earliest being his 364 in the fifth Test of the 1938 Ashes series. It was the longest innings and the highest Test total up to that time and, at 903–7, it remains the highest innings played in an Ashes series to date.

In his first Test, played in June 1937 against New Zealand, Hutton made 0 and 1, but in his second, he made the first of nineteen Test hundreds. He began the 1938 series against Australia with another century and an opening stand of 219 with Charlie Barnett. He finished it with his record-breaking 364, made in thirteen hours and seventeen minutes. In the last season before the war, he made 196 against the West Indies at Lord's, and in the last pre-war Test in August 1939, he attained 73 and 165 not out at The Oval.

Many of Hutton's most important innings, before the advent of May and Cowdrey, were played sustaining an uncertain England batting side. One at Lord's in June 1948 he batted so unimpressively that he was dropped for the next Test – a strange decision in retrospect, for he played Ray Lindwall and Miller at their fastest supremely well. This was especially marked in 1950–1, when he averaged 88.83 during the Ashes series.

In South Africa, in 1948–9, he batted with Cyril Washbrook all through a day's play in Johannesburg and they scored 359 for the first wicket. In 1951, he made his hundredth hundred at The Oval for Yorkshire against Surrey, and the next year captained England against India.

At Lord's, in 1953, he made 145 against Australia and that winter became the first professional to take an MCC side overseas. In the West Indies, England lost the first two Tests, but won the third and fifth, in which the captain made 169 and 205 respectively. Though he missed much of the first series against Pakistan in 1954, his mind was on the 1954–5 tour of Australia, where he led England shrewdly and effectively to one of their most decisive victories against the Aussies. His form in the tour matches was as impeccable as ever – he made over 1,000 runs in Australia – but after the two Tests against New Zealand that followed, he left international cricket and then announced his retirement from the game after injuries had restricted his appearances for Yorkshire in 1955.

England never lost a Test series under his command – a tribute to his leadership. Knighted for his services to cricket, he continued to be involved in the game following his retirement, both in the press box and as a Test selector, his deep appreciation of cricket finding a new and most successful outlet.

RAY ILLINGWORTH

Having made his Yorkshire debut in 1951, Ray Illingworth soon established himself as an important member of the county side and two years later scored his maiden century, 146 not out against Essex at Hull. As a bowler, though, he had to bide his time behind Bob Appleyard and Johnny Wardle, and it wasn't until the appointment of Ronnie Burnet as captain that Illingworth came into his own.

In 1957, he produced his best bowling figures for the county, taking 9–42 against Worcestershire at New Road, and two years later he made his highest score for Yorkshire, hitting 162 against the Indian tourists. He was a member of the team that ended Surrey's domination and gained Yorkshire seven championships.

Then, in 1969, following a dispute over his contract, he moved to Leicestershire as captain, enjoying a remarkable renaissance that included the captaincy of his country and doubling the length of his international career.

Within months of his move, Colin Cowdrey became injured and Illingworth was given the England captaincy. Even after his predecessor regained his fitness, Illingworth remained first choice and provided perfect justification for the selectors' decision when his side regained the Ashes in 1970–1 and retained them in 1972. He captained England thirty-one times and was succeeded by Mike Denness after England were beaten in 1973 by West Indies – he had chosen to miss the 1972–3 series in India and Pakistan.

Illingworth epitomized the philosophy of the professional. A remarkably shrewd leader, he earned the unyielding respect of his team, although at times his single-mindedness forfeited goodwill. At Sydney in 1970–1, he led his side from the field in protest against some crowd loutishness. He was a creator of runs rather than a trailblazer and he would have been even more productive had he batted higher in the order. By the end of his career he had scored 24,134 runs and taken 2,072 wickets, testimony to his all-round talents.

But even more than this, his successful practical brand of captaincy set him apart. With Leicestershire, he produced results that must have made every Yorkshireman wince. Despite the orthodoxy of his own game, he made an enormous impact on the development of cricket, particularly the tactics of one-day competition. He led Leicestershire to wins in the Benson & Hedges Cup in 1972 and 1975, and they were beaten finalists in 1974. That year they also became champions of the John Player League. But Illingworth's greatest triumph in county cricket came in 1975, when he led Leicestershire to their first County Championship.

In 1979, he retired from first-class cricket and returned to Yorkshire as manager. Three years later, in the midst of the troubles that beset the county club, he took over as captain and the following year led Yorkshire to the Sunday League Championship. On leaving Yorkshire for the last time in 1983, he became a radio and TV commentator before taking up the post of England team manager.

DOUGLAS JARDINE

Few captains have excited as much passion and controversy as Douglas Jardine; none has been more successful. He was born in India, where his father, who had scored a century in the Varsity match of 1892, had a most successful career in the legal profession. Jardine returned to Britain at the age of nine and went to Winchester before heading off to Oxford University. He began to play for Surrey while still at university and he won his first Test cap in 1928, playing against the West Indies both at Lord's and Old Trafford, where he was run out for 83.

He toured Australia with the English team in 1928–9, and, playing in all five Test matches, scored 341 runs at the commendable average of 42.63. The skills he displayed throughout the year led to his being named a *Wisden* Cricketer of the Year for 1928. Cool and aloof, batting in the brightly coloured Harlequin cap, Jardine was barracked by the Australians, who saw him as symbolic of the Imperial order, the British establishment. It is recorded that during one tour match, Australian player Hunter Hendry expressed his sympathies to Jardine for the jeers he was getting from the crowd, to which Jardine replied, 'All Australians are uneducated and an unruly mob.'

He became England captain in 1931, leading the side in three Tests against New Zealand. The following season, he was England's captain in India's inaugural Test match at Lord's in June and was top scorer, with innings of 79 and 85 not out.

Jardine was also appointed captain of the English touring team to Australia in 1932–3 and used the Bodyline tactics – fast bowling to a leg-side field – ruthlessly and effectively against his opposition. He also appreciated the benefit of psychologically boosting his own players: on the boat trip out to Australia, he encouraged his team to foster a hatred for the Australian players and to refer to Don Bradman exclusively as 'the little bastard'. In Australia, Harold Larwood and Bill Voce repeatedly hit the Australian batsmen with fast balls, causing outrage amongst Australian fans. The England captain insisted his tactic was not designed to cause injury and that he was leading his team in a sportsmanlike and gentlemanly manner, arguing it was up to the Australian batsmen to play their way out of trouble.

Jardine and his team returned to England as heroes, having convincingly won back the Ashes 4–1. He was invited by the MCC to captain England again for the Tests against India, but decided that he had no wish to lead England again, resigning before the 1934 Ashes tour.

Douglas Jardine was only thirty-three when he retired from cricket and was arguably the best number five batsman in the world at the time. It is doubtful if England has ever had a better captain and he was one of the few amateurs of his period who won places in the side on the merit of their batting.

ALAN KNOTT

At The Oval in 1976, Alan Knott broke the world record for the number of Test victims – a statistic that proved the class of the latest in a long line of great wicketkeepers from Kent. A man who always inspired his teammates with his exuberance and enthusiasm, he also won Test matches with his batting skills.

Voted England's Best Young Cricketer in 1965, he arrived on the Test scene two years later, before replacing Jim Parks on the 1967–8 tour of the West Indies. England won the fourth Test on a generous Sobers declaration, but only after Knott, with an unbeaten 69, had helped Cowdrey to rectify their first innings. Even more vital was his 73 not out, which saved the match and the rubber in the fifth Test.

Now an established wicketkeeper, Knott's work behind the stumps became an inspiration for every bowler. Neat and lithe, he developed even further agility with continual exercise. His liking for early-morning calisthenics earned him a room to himself on more than one tour. On the field, his wheeling and stretching between deliveries and battered 'lived-in' pads became trademarks. His uninhibited stroke-play also brought him five Test centuries. Despite the barrage of short balls in Australia in 1974–5, his 106 not out at Adelaide in January 1975 made him only the second wicketkeeper to reach three figures for England against Australia – his Kent predecessor Les Ames was the other.

It was not until the spring of 1977 that his triumphant record-breaking career was threatened. One of the English Packer signatories, he was chosen for the summer Tests against Australia and continued to justify his inclusion with 12 catches, some of them brilliant. An important 135 in the third Test at Trent Bridge, his finest innings, served to inspire Geoff Boycott, who was deeply bogged down in his comeback match. Knott's strokes were as cheeky and inventive as ever, and brought him a five and 18 fours. His final score beat Les Ames's record for a wicketkeeper in Ashes Tests, and the stand of 215 with Boycott equalled the England sixth-wicket record against Australia, set in 1939 by Len Hutton and Joe Hardstaff.

In 1977–8 he missed the England tour of Pakistan and New Zealand, and played instead for Kerry Packer in Australia, thus ending a run of sixty-five consecutive Tests for his country, a record later equalled by Ian Botham.

Returning to England, tired after years of continuous cricket, Knott decided not to play for Kent in the following season. He returned to the county side after the establishment made peace with Packer, and regained his Test place in 1980. The following year, he became the first wicketkeeper to record 100 victims against Australia. But he had expressed an unwillingness to tour regularly, which made his Test place insecure, and when he joined the South African 'rebels' in 1981–2, he effectively lost it for good. His total of 269 Test victims places him fourth in the list of the world's wicketkeepers, but the figure could well have been higher.

JIM LAKER

Yorkshire-born Jim Laker will always be remembered for one of the most extraordinary feats in cricket history – his 19 wickets for 90 runs against Australia at Old Trafford in 1956. No one else in the history of the first-class game has ever taken more than 17 wickets in a match. Yet Laker, with his off-spin, took 19 against Australia, while another highly skilled spin bowler, Tony Lock, took only one at the other end.

Within two years of his first-class debut for Surrey, he was playing for England. In his first full season, in 1947, he finished seventh in the first-class bowling averages with 79 wickets, and that winter went to the West Indies with Gubby Allen's MCC team, playing in his first Test in Barbados and taking 7–103 in the first innings.

The Australians of 1948 played him with a confidence their successors seldom emulated. After they had made 404–3 in the last innings at Headingley, Laker, who had several chances dropped off his bowling, but was still learning the off-spinner's trade, was one of those left out of the side in subsequent Tests. For a while, his career marked time, but he burst into the record books in the Test trial at Bradford in 1950, when, on a drying pitch, he took 8 'Rest' wickets for 2 runs, completely ruining the match as a trial. However, the selectors were still not convinced that he was a valuable bowler on good pitches and he was not a regular choice for England, though his 10–119 against South Africa at The Oval in 1951 had much to do with the team's victory there.

In 1952, Surrey's seven-year run of Championship successes began with Laker playing an important part, and, a year later, he and Lock bowled out Australia at The Oval. The Ashes were finally recovered after nineteen years.

Laker's greatest triumphs were to come in 1956, when he took 46 wickets in the series against Australia, at an average of 9.60. In addition to his overall bag of 19 wickets at Old Trafford, he became the first player to take 10 wickets in an innings more than once; he had accomplished the feat earlier in the season with 10–88 for Surrey also against the Australians. Sadly, his later years with Surrey were marred by disagreements, and after his retirement in 1959, he wrote a controversial book which caused the MCC to withdraw his honorary membership and to lose his pavilion privileges at Surrey. Happily, though, these were restored within a few years and the incident forgotten. Laker returned to first-class cricket for a time in the early 1960s, playing a number of matches for Essex. When he finally left the first-class scene, he maintained his association with the game, becoming a successful television commentator and writer. He died after a short illness in 1986.

HAROLD LARWOOD

Many people well placed to judge believe that Harold Larwood was the fastest and best fast bowler in cricket history. It was, therefore, all the sadder that his career should have declined among the bitterness of the Bodyline controversy, in which he was one of the two central figures.

Leaving school at fourteen to become a labourer in the local mine, he also began to play for the village cricket team. By eighteen he was invited to trial for Nottinghamshire, where he was offered a professional contract and starred with bat and ball. Larwood was, by this stage, a fearsome bowler. His run-up, which was relatively short, yet beautifully balanced and accelerating gradually, at once attracted attention, and his marvellously supple, easy, textbook action left no doubt of his quality. Though he made his Test debut in June 1926, he didn't secure a regular place in the side for another two years, when in the first Test at Brisbane, he took 6–32. Stories of Larwood's speed have entered cricket mythology. In a match against Tasmania on this 1928–9 tour, he is said to have sent a bail 60 metres.

Before the 1932–3 tour, he had taken only 45 Test wickets, but under the captaincy of Arthur Carr, Larwood had been a great force for Nottinghamshire, playing a big part in their Championship win of 1929. Eight times in all he took 100 wickets in a season – from only ten full seasons. In Australia, on that unhappy tour, he bowled superbly to his orders. Though it was the short ball, fast and accurate, that undermined the batsmen, he could put in a devastating yorker at will. In the first Test, Larwood took 5 wickets in each innings and thereafter he was the spearhead of England's attack, taking 33 wickets in all. And in the final Test, at Sydney, which was to be the last of his career, he went in as nightwatchman and made 98 runs in two and a quarter hours.

His departure from Test cricket was not entirely due to the aftermath of Bodyline and the reluctance of selectors to open old wounds, but also to an injury to his left foot. It had been under great pressure, not only from the ordinary demands of fast bowling, but also from those extra times he thumped the ball short of a length.

He played on for Nottinghamshire until 1938, but latterly was merely a fast-medium bowler operating off a short run. Inevitably his name at that time had associations in Australia, but after the Second World War, he, his wife and five daughters emigrated there. His part in the 1932–3 series had been forgiven and forgotten, and he became a much-respected Australian citizen.

GEORGE LOHMANN

Regarded as one of the greatest bowlers of all time, George Lohmann posted the finest Test average of any long-standing bowler, taking 112 Test wickets at 10.75 each in eighteen appearances for England.

He was one of the great Surrey trio of quick bowlers, along with Bill Lockwood and Tom Richardson. Essentially a medium-pacer with a surprise fast ball, he picked up wickets more through deception than speed. He made his Test debut against the touring Australians in the summer of 1886, and in the third Test at The Oval he took 12 wickets (7–36 and 5–68), and England won by an innings.

Being the leading first-class wicket-taker, Lohmann was chosen to tour Australia in 1886–7 with Alfred Shaw's team. In the second Test in Sydney, he took a record 8–35 to help England to a 71-run victory.

In the abnormally dry English summer of 1887, he showed himself to be far ahead of any bowler – taking 154 wickets when the next best was 114. He also made the highest score of his career, 115 against Sussex at Hove.

The following year, a summer as wet as the previous one had been dry, Lohmann took full advantage of the dreadful pitches on which most matches were played, taking 209 wickets at only 10.90 each. His 62 runs in the second Test of the 1888 series against Australia at The Oval, came as England made 317 and he was again a hero, with 11 wickets at 13 runs each.

In 1889, Lohmann took over 200 wickets again and took 9 wickets in an innings for the first time against Sussex. The following year, he took a career-best 220 wickets and in 1891 he was the leading English wicket-taker for the seventh successive year. On the following year's tour of Australia, he bowled wonderfully well, taking 8–58 on a dry wicket in Sydney.

After the 1892 season had ended, a dreadful shock came when it was announced that Lohmann had contracted tuberculosis. In an effort to improve his health, he left for South Africa and did not play for Surrey in 1893 or 1894. By 1895, his health had recovered sufficiently for him to play once again for Surrey, and the following winter he toured South Africa. He was so unplayable that he took 35 wickets in three matches on the matting. Partnering Sammy Woods, Lohmann took a haul in South Africa that included 7–38 and 8–7 at Port Elizabeth and 9–28 at Johannesburg. This was England's best Test bowling until Jim Laker took all 10 in an innings in 1956.

After his all-conquering feats in South Africa, Lohmann decided to stay there, hoping the climate would help his breathing problems. He managed the South African tourists to England in 1901, but by then, at the age of only thirty-six, he was dying of tuberculosis.

ARCHIE MACLAREN

Archie MacLaren was an outstanding batsman for many years and is remembered chiefly for two achievements. For Lancashire against Somerset at Taunton in 1895, he scored 424 in seven hours fifty minutes, with a six and 62 fours. It was then the highest score made in a first-class match, beating W. G. Grace's 344 of 1876. Then, twenty-six years later, at the age of forty-nine, he selected and captained the first team to defeat Warwick Armstrong's Australian side of 1921, who were touring in England. MacLaren, who by then had retired from active cricket, declared that he could pick a team to beat the triumphant Australians, calling his team 'An England XI'. They won the game by 28 runs, after being bowled out for 43 in the first innings.

He made an early mark when he won his colours for Harrow at the age of fifteen, and scored 55 and 67 against Eton. In 1890, also against Eton, the eighteen-year-old made 76 out of a total of 133, batting with a maturity that surprised many informed observers. In the same year, he was invited to play for his native county Lancashire, and, in his first innings for them, scored 108. In 1894, at the age of twenty-two, he was made captain of the county and held that post for all but two seasons until 1907.

When W. G. Grace retired from the England captaincy in 1899, Archie MacLaren, who had not yet played a first-class match that season, was invited to succeed him. In his first match in office, against Australia at Lord's in June, England followed on, but on a most difficult pitch MacLaren made 88 not out, the highest score of the match for his side. When he took out the team of 1901–2, his 116 at Sydney made him the first man to score four centuries in Test cricket and the last England captain to make a hundred in Australia for fifty-seven years, until Peter May in 1958–9.

He was always less happy playing in England, where the damper weather adversely affected his lumbago, than in Australia, where he toured three times. On those visits, he scored 2,769 runs at an average of over 50 and was regarded there as probably the finest batsman in the world.

For Lancashire, whom he led to the County Championship title in 1904, when they went through the summer unbeaten, he scored 15,735 runs at an average of 33.34, a great achievement when one considers that the wickets in those days were of variable quality and, more often than not, were quite unplayable.

Following his retirement from the first-class game, Archie MacLaren, at the age of fifty-one, played for the MCC against New Zealand at Wellington in 1923 and scored 200 not out. He was also county coach, but after a number of disagreements with the Lancashire Committee he ended his long association with the county.

PETER MAY

For a period in the 1950s, Peter May was regarded as the best batsman in the world. His Test career spanned less than ten years, yet in that time he captained England a then record forty-one times.

A year after a playing his first match for Surrey in 1950, May made his Test debut against South Africa at Headingley, and it was a sign of the concentration and phlegmatic temperament he was to show so often later on that he made 138. Soon, he was acknowledged as the batsman who would take over the mantles of Len Hutton and Denis Compton.

He was vice-captain to Hutton on the triumphant tour of Australia in 1954–5 and it was his 104 at Sydney in the second Test that turned the series towards England after they had lost the first Test and been 74 runs behind in the first innings of the second. On his return to England, May found himself appointed captain because Hutton was ill. He led England thirty-five times in succession, beginning with the magnificent series of 1955 against South Africa. He scored brilliant hundreds at Lord's and Old Trafford, averaging 97.00 in the series.

The following year, in a low-scoring series against Australia, he averaged 90.00 and shared in a memorable fourth-wicket partnership of 187 with Cyril Washbrook at Headingley, after England had lost 3 wickets for 17 runs.

May was then at his peak and his failure in the 1956–7 Test series in South Africa has never been satisfactorily explained. He played as well as ever in other matches on the tour, but fell to brilliant catches and the like in the Tests. But back at home in June 1957, he soon showed this was merely a fleeting failure, for when England began their second innings in the first Test at Edgbaston 288 runs behind West Indies, May batted for nearly ten hours, making 285 not out and sharing in a fourth-wicket stand of 411 with Colin Cowdrey.

Early in 1958, May played two of his best innings for Surrey – 174 against Lancashire at Old Trafford and 165 against the New Zealanders at The Oval. But that winter, he led an ageing side in Australia, and, though he still batted well himself, the team were beaten by Richie Benaud's more aggressive Australians.

In 1959, he suffered a painful illness midway through the season. He was struck down again during the tour of the West Indies that winter and missed the 1960 season, but returned to play against Australia in 1961 before retiring.

Tall, elegant and powerful, Peter May had an orthodox method. He played very straight and had all the strokes, except perhaps the hook. He combined, as few others have, the grace, strength and classic mould of the old-fashioned amateur with the professional competitiveness now needed in the highest class. His services to cricket did not end with his wonderful record on the field. After retiring, he served on MCC and TCCB committees, and was also a Test selector and Chairman of Selectors from 1982 to 1989.

BOBBY PEEL

The Yorkshire and England left-arm spinner ranks as one of the finest bowlers of the 1890s. His record in Test matches, though somewhat flattered by the primitiveness of the pitches, is still remarkable.

Peel emerged in first-class cricket for Yorkshire in 1882 and quickly established himself as a skilful left-arm spin bowler with extraordinary accuracy of pitch and the ability to bowl a fast ball that obtained many wickets. His ability was regarded so highly by 1884 that, even though he was relatively inexperienced, Alfred Shaw took him to Australia in 1884–5. He found that up-country batting techniques were as crude as the pitches and he took 321 wickets against teams like the XXII of Ballarat at 4 runs each. He appeared in all three Tests, taking 21 wickets, but, after losing form, didn't play Test cricket again until 1887–8.

He played superbly at the Sydney Cricket Ground in February 1888, taking 9 wickets for 58 runs, and was England's match-winner. In the extremely wet summer of 1888, Peel took 100 wickets for the first time and, on a series of sticky wickets, took 24 wickets for fewer than 8 runs each in the three Tests against Australia including 11–68 in the deciding match at Old Trafford. He accomplished a number of bowling feats that year, the most remarkable of which saw him take 8–12 and 6–21 against Nottinghamshire.

Over the following years, Peel took over 100 wickets every year, except in 1891, when he took only 99! However, owing to competition from bowlers such as Johnny Briggs, Bobby Peel did not make consistent appearances in the England Test side. He headed the first-class bowling averages in 1893 and took a career-best 180 wickets in 1895 – his 15–50 against Somerset and 10–59 against Gloucestershire were both match-winning performances.

His excellent bowling on hard and true Australian pitches in the tour of 1894–5 seemed to cement his place as the best slow bowler in the world, though perhaps he is best remembered on this tour for being the first player in Test cricket history to have been dismissed four times in succession without scoring.

The summer of 1896 saw Peel develop so much as a batsman that he hit three centuries during one of England's driest Mays on record. That summer, he played in just one Test against Australia; he took 6–23 in the second innings, helped to restrict them to just 44 runs, and recorded his hundredth Test wicket against them, the first Englishman to reach that landmark.

The end of his career, when it came, was as singular as the man. He got drunk, too drunk to stand, but insisted on presenting himself to the Yorkshire captain Lord Hawke on the field at the start of play, before, so legend has it, relieving himself against the sightscreen. Not surprisingly, he was dismissed by the county for unbecoming conduct.

DEREK RANDALL

Derek Randall gave immense pleasure to spectators and television audiences around the world and emerged as one of the real characters in the game. For one so dedicated to cricket he came relatively late to the game, making his Nottinghamshire debut in 1972 at the age of twenty-one. Within three years, he had emerged as one of the best batsmen on the county circuit and on a Trent Bridge wicket possessing sufficient pace and bounce to allow Bob Willis to have match figures of 9–106, he hit an unbeaten 153, an innings that included a final fifty scored in a breathtaking twenty-three minutes.

Having made his one-day international debut for England against the West Indies at Lord's in 1976, when he scored 88 after coming in with his side on 31–4, he went on to win the English Man of the Series award. After he had made his Test debut against India at Calcutta in January 1977, the Centenary Test two months later was his first against Australia, where England were set an impossible 463 to win. His splendid innings of 174 took the team to within 45 runs of a much stronger and more confident side. It earned him his Test place in 1977, when England won the Ashes. His innings of 79 at Old Trafford ended unluckily leg-before, but Randall was certainly close to his form of the Centenary Test. At Headingley, he caught Marsh to give England the rubber and instantly celebrated by turning a rather exuberant cartwheel.

After a run of ordinary scores on the Pakistan–New Zealand tour of 1977–8, Randall was chosen for the 1978–9 tour of Australia. Every state game brought him a fifty or a century, and his form continued at Brisbane, in the first Test, where he contributed innings of 75 and 74 in England's first win of the Ashes series. Yet there were many who thought Randall should never have been picked for the tour in the first place. His best innings was a ten-hour 150 in the fourth Test at Sydney, as England won by 93 runs.

In 1979, he became the only player to score a double century (209) and a century (146) in the same match as Nottinghamshire beat Middlesex. Over the next couple of years, Randall played little Test cricket, but Nottinghamshire's Championship win in 1981 was a great consolation.

Just when it seemed his Test career was over, he was recalled for the first Test of 1982 against India in June and celebrated with a glorious innings of 126. Touring Australia in 1982–3 he topped the Test averages with 365 runs at 45.63, including a top score of 115 in the first Test at Perth.

Randall was an extrovert, effervescent, enthusiastic player. He communicated a tremendous sense of fun and enjoyment, yet beneath his clowning was a very shrewd cricket brain, a marvellous eye and a gift for improvisation, which made him such an exciting player to watch.

WILFRED RHODES

Wilfred Rhodes took more first-class wickets than anyone else has, or ever will, unless one-day games are ranked as first-class. He alone has amassed a total of over 4,000 wickets. He alone has taken a hundred wickets in a season twenty-three times.

Having made his debut for Yorkshire in 1898, following Peel's enforced and hasty retirement, Rhodes dismissed 261 batsmen in 1900 and 251 more the following year. But he was not able to play Test cricket in those two prime years of his, for the Yorkshire committee would not allow him and George Hirst to tour Australia in the intervening winter. It was not until 1903–4, when he was already in relative decline, that he visited Australia and bowled more successfully than any English slow bowler has ever done there.

At Melbourne, he had the assistance of an old-fashioned sticky, but still had eight chances missed off him as he took 15 wickets for 124 – they were his best figures in Test cricket to that point. In his early years, Rhodes actually spun the ball off a wart, which may have been a contributory factor in his decision to cease being a specialist bowler. In any event, he started to open the batting for his county and later went on to open the batting for England as well, with Jack Hobbs.

The third part of Rhodes's career, after the First World War, was equally amazing. He dropped down the order to number five for Yorkshire and so revived his bowling that he was the best slow left-armer again in the immediate post-war period, heading the national averages from 1919 to 1923 inclusive, as he had not done since 1901.

Then, in 1926, he returned to the top of the national averages and, aged forty-eight, did the double for the sixteenth, final and record-setting time. He was recalled by England's selectors for final Test against Australia at The Oval – his 45 overs bringing him 6 wickets for 79 runs, a match victory and, most importantly, the Ashes.

After the sudden death of Roy Kilner, Yorkshire suddenly found themselves short of bowlers. Rhodes had no chance to pick his moments now and he passed the age of fifty in October 1927. He still had three more seasons in the game and one MCC tour to the West Indies, when he represented England again, at the age of fifty-two, easily the oldest player in Test cricket.

He played in a total of fifty-eight Test matches, taking 127 wickets. His stand of 323 with Jack Hobbs at Melbourne in 1911 is still the highest stand for England for the first wicket in an Ashes series Test, and his stand of 130 with Tip Foster at Sydney in 1903 is still the highest for England's last wicket in any Test match, proof of his ability to bat as an opener and a tail-ender.

By the end of the Second World War, Wilfred Rhodes had lost his sight, but he continued to attend cricket matches regularly, claiming to be able to follow everything from the sounds. Appropriately, he died during a Test match against New Zealand, which was being played at his favourite ground of Headingley.

ARTHUR SHREWSBURY

Arthur Shrewsbury was a slight, retiring, quiet man who was widely regarded as competing with W. G. Grace for the accolade of being the best batsman of the 1880s. Grace himself, when asked whom he would most like in his side, replied simply, 'Give me Arthur.' He showed great promise from an early age and was selected for the Colts of England against MCC when he was barely seventeen, for Nottinghamshire – then quite the strongest county – at nineteen, and for the Players against the Gentlemen at twenty.

Ill health held him back, however; he was always frail, until, at the age of twenty-five, the long sea voyages and the sun of his first visit to Australia in 1881–2 steadied him physically and he settled down to twenty years of utter consistency. He had an extremely high average for his period – 36.66 (59 centuries) in all first-class cricket; 35.47 in his twenty-three Tests, with three centuries. He joined James Lillywhite and Alfred Shaw in organizing four trips to Australia. He made his Test debut on the first, 1881–2, and he captained the side in 1884–5 and 1886–7. In the fifth Test of the 1884–5 series in Melbourne, he hit 105 not out, becoming the first England captain to score a century in a Test match.

Shrewsbury was a purist batsman: patient, poised and regarded as the master on bad wickets. One of the stories told about him at Trent Bridge is that as he walked out of the pavilion to bat after lunch, in the days before a tea interval was allowed, he used to say to the pavilion attendant, 'Bring me out a cup of tea at half past four, Kirk,' and he would usually be there waiting for it!

He is credited with playing two of the great innings of Test cricket, both against Australia: 164 out of a total of 353 – on a Lord's pitch that one of his opponents considered 'impossible' – in July 1886; and seven years later, again at Lord's, he made 106 out of 334 (in the course of which he became the first batsman to reach 1,000 runs in Tests) against Turner, 'The Terror', on a hideous 'sticky'.

In 1902, his last season, at the age of forty-six, Shrewsbury scored two centuries in a match for the first time and was top of the first-class batting averages with 1,250 runs at 50.00. But the following year, believing that his career was at an end after a bout of depression that convinced him he was suffering from an incurable disease, he shot himself.

Famous, popular and modest, Arthur Shrewsbury was much mourned and is still remembered with great respect in Nottinghamshire.

JOHN SNOW

Fast bowler John Snow joined Sussex as a batsman but he bowled so quickly and with such movement that anyone who saw him firing away knew he would become a great pace bowler.

His progress through first-class cricket was not rapid and he didn't become a regular in the Sussex side until 1964. However, the next season he took over 100 wickets and made his Test debut against New Zealand at Lord's in Fred Trueman's last match.

Against the West Indies in 1966, Snow took a modest 12 wickets, but made his most significant contribution in the fifth Test at The Oval, where he scored an unbeaten 59 in a last-wicket partnership of 128 with Ken Higgs.

After a mediocre series against India the following summer, he cemented his reputation on England's winter tour of the Caribbean. He played in four Tests, and took 27 wickets at 18.66, including 7–49 on his Caribbean debut at Kingston in February, and 5–86 in the next Test at Bridgetown. In the fifth Test, at Georgetown, he dismissed Garry Sobers with his first ball, just as he had done at The Oval in 1966, to finish with 10 wickets in the match, including 6–60.

Snow's best series for England came in the controversial Ashes tour of Australia in 1970–1. In six Tests, he took 31 wickets at 22.83, finishing off the fourth at Sydney with his best Test figures of 7–40. In the seventh Test, again at Sydney, England needed a draw to win the Ashes. Umpire Lou Rowan cautioned Snow for intimidatory bowling and the pair clashed. When Snow went off to field at long leg, in front of the notorious Paddington Hill, a drunken spectator reached over the fence to grapple with him and the fast bowler was showered with beer cans. Illingworth duly led his team from the field in protest, and the umpires warned the Englishmen that the game would be forfeited, along with the Ashes. In the second innings, Australia needed only 223 to win, but even with Snow in hospital after breaking the index finger of his bowling hand, England won by 62 runs.

The England pace bowler was again embroiled in controversy during the summer of 1968. In the first Test at Lord's, he scored 73, his highest knock at international level. It was in this match that he knocked Sunil Gavaskar off his feet as the Indian was trying for a quick single. Snow was ordered to apologize and was left out of the team for the Old Trafford Test as a punishment.

Sadly, he never toured again with England and he gained a reputation for being moody and obstinate. However, he was England's answer to Dennis Lillee and Massie during the 1972 campaign against Australia, taking 24 wickets at 23.12 runs apiece and helping his side to draw the series 2–2 to retain the Ashes he had won for them some eighteen months earlier. He might well have been the first to challenge Fred Trueman's record of 307 Test wickets but for injury and the intervention of Kerry Packer.

Snow, who took 883 wickets for Sussex, is also likely to remain the only international fast bowler to have two volumes of verse published.

BRIAN STATHAM

During a nineteen-year career, Brian Statham was a highly popular player, both on and off the field; everyone admired the level-headed manner in which he dealt with adversity as well as adulation. Most fast bowlers possess a volatile nature that sometimes gets them into trouble, but there was never the slightest suggestion of Statham giving offence. In this way he contrasted markedly with his England partner Fred Trueman: the Yorkshireman was all fire and brimstone, the Lancastrian more phlegmatic.

He made his county debut on his twentieth birthday and in his first season had several successes, notably against Somerset at Bath, where in one spell he took 5 wickets for 5 runs. Before the summer was over, he had been awarded his county cap and then the following winter he was called upon to reinforce the injury-hit MCC team in Australia. He did not play in any Tests, but in March 1951 he made his England debut against New Zealand at Christchurch.

Following his Test debut, Brian Statham was usually an automatic choice for England, featuring in the strong sides that won and retained the Ashes in the 1950s. His partnerships with Frank Tyson and Fred Trueman often found him playing a supporting role, but neither would deny the large part he played in their own successes. However, with just a little bit more luck he could have been the more successful partner.

After 1963, it seemed that Statham's Test career was over, but he came back for one match against South Africa at The Oval in August 1965, and with 5–40 and 2–105 he completed 250 Test wickets. Among them were his 7–39 against South Africa at Lord's in June 1955 and 7–87 against Australia at Melbourne in January 1959.

Outside Test cricket, he topped 100 wickets in thirteen seasons, ten in succession from 1957 to 1966, and his triumphs included three hat-tricks: against Sussex at Old Trafford in 1956, for MCC against Transvaal at Johannesburg in 1956–7 and against Leicestershire, again at Old Trafford, in 1958. At Coventry in 1957 he took 15 wickets (8–34 and 7–55) in the match with Warwickshire and another 15 (7–71 and 8–37) against Leicestershire in 1964. His benefit in 1961 showed the esteem in which he was held for it brought him over £13,000.

In 1965, he took over the captaincy of Lancashire and was made a CBE in the New Year's Honours list of 1966. However, the next season, he relinquished the county leadership and retired in 1968.

Few bowlers have attained such accuracy at such a biting pace, but Statham had his own dictum and his own motivation: 'If they miss, I hit,' he would explain with a wry smile.

ALEC STEWART

The rise of model professional Alec Stewart to the position of England captain surprised many. It wasn't that the pedigree was absent – his father, Mickey, a former Test player and Surrey captain, also managed England – but even though Stewart was a good batsman and wicketkeeper, he was considered low down in the pecking order for the England captaincy.

Success didn't come easy to him. Though he always appeared to be a well-organized, busy, bat-twirling player, capable of making entertaining runs, in the early days he seemed to lack the commitment needed to register big scores. In fact, if Stewart hadn't developed his wicketkeeping, he might not have received his chance in international cricket as early as he did.

Having made his Surrey debut a couple of years earlier, Stewart established himself in the county side in 1983, scoring his maiden first-class century, 118, against Oxford University. He continued to score runs freely and in 1986 topped the county batting averages with 1,665 runs at 46.54. He topped the batting averages again the following summer, and, after a successful 1989 season, when his 1,633 runs included his first double hundred – 206 not out against Essex – he was selected to tour the West Indies, making his Test debut in a 9-wicket win at Sabina Park, Kingston. Also in 1989, Stewart held 11 catches for Surrey in the match against Leicestershire, thus equalling the world first-class record.

Dropped from the England side after a disastrous 1990–1 tour of Australia, he was rather surprisingly recalled to the side to keep wicket in the final Test against the West Indies in August 1991. It was an opportunity he could not afford to miss and he took it. Two weeks later, he scored his first Test century: 113 not out against Sri Lanka at Lord's. His highest Test score of 190 was made against Pakistan at Edgbaston in 1992 and he ended the series as England's leading run-getter, with 397 runs at 56.71.

He was captain of England on fourteen occasions, and the highlight of his spell in charge was the home series triumph over South Africa in the summer of 1998. He went on to skipper England during the World Cup of 1999, when the home side were very disappointing.

He was the leading run-maker in Test cricket during the 1990s, scoring 6,407 runs at an average of more than 40 – narrowly pipping Mark Waugh to the honour when he made 95 against South Africa at Durban in December 1999. In the summer of 2000 he overtook Graham Gooch as England's most-capped one-day player, with 170 appearances. Also that summer he equalled Adam Gilchrist's one-day record for wicketkeeping dismissals – six against Zimbabwe at Old Trafford.

As England's most-capped Test player with 133 appearances to his name, Alec Stewart deserves the highest praise and respect for his massive contribution to English cricket.

HERBERT SUTCLIFFE

Herbert Sutcliffe was arguably the greatest opening batsman in cricket history and undoubtedly one of the greatest players of any type the game has known. He was a batsman of immense concentration, unflinching courage, imperturbable temperament and consistent success.

During the First World War he was commissioned into the Green Howards, but on his return he went straight into the Yorkshire team for the first post-war season of 1919. He scored 1,839 runs, so impressive a start that after a single season he was chosen as one of *Wisden*'s Five Cricketers of the Year.

He then embarked on a distinguished career, making his Test debut at Edgbaston against South Africa in June 1924. He scored 64 in his first innings, 122 in his second in the following Test at Lord's, and averaged 75.75 for five innings. That winter, Sutcliffe established himself as England's leading batsman, with an amazing aggregate of 734 runs in five Tests against Australia.

During 1925 and 1926 his skill was a primary factor in Yorkshire having the longest unbeaten run in county cricket – an amazing seventy matches without loss until early 1927, and, after three defeats, a further fifty-eight games without loss until 1929. In 1930, a summer of hot, thundery weather that produced some exceptionally bad pitches, Sutcliffe averaged 64.22 in all matches and 87.61 in four Tests – he missed the second due to injury and this probably cost England the Ashes.

In 1931 he scored four centuries in consecutive innings and averaged an unbelievable 97.00 in one of the worst summers on record. The following year, for Yorkshire against Essex at Leyton, he and Percy Holmes put on 555 for the first wicket, a record until 1976 when Waheed Mirza and Mansoor Akhtar made 561 for Karachi Whites against Quetta.

Herbert Sutcliffe was the only player to top 1,000 runs in each of the twenty-one inter-war seasons. In twelve of those seasons, he scored more than 2,000 and 3,000 in another three. Altogether he made 149 centuries, seventeen of them of 200 or more, and over his entire career he averaged 51.95, while as a measure of his capacity for rising to the great occasion, in all Test cricket his average was 60.73.

He was also an interesting character. When he emerged from the wartime officers' mess, he set out to convert his native accent to standard southern English, unlike his Yorkshire contemporaries. This gave rise to some suspicion in the dressing room, until in 1927 he was offered the Yorkshire captaincy as a professional. Refusing it, he said that he would be happy to play under any other captain.

Herbert Sutcliffe was, as his subsequent career in business demonstrated, a man with a cool, clear mind and purpose. Always immaculately turned out, he was infallibly courteous – to everyone, which is true courtesy.

MAURICE TATE

Affectionately known as 'Chubby', Maurice Tate was twenty-seven before he became a pace bowler and twenty-nine before he represented England. Despite this late start and the legacy of being 'Poor' Fred Tate's son, he became one of the masters of Test cricket. A big man with the face of a cherub and a hearty sense of humour, Tate was a born swing bowler. Yet it was as a hard-hitting batsman and slow-medium off-break bowler like his father that Maurice Tate first made a living out of cricket.

Despite two decades of service for his county, Sussex, Fred Tate will for ever be remembered for dropping a vital catch and losing his wicket, the last of the England innings, when his side needed only four runs to win in an Ashes match at Old Trafford in July 1902. With tears in his eyes, poor Fred had announced in the dressing room that back home he had a little lad who would make up for his failures.

At Eastbourne, in 1922, Maurice Tate became fed up with his inability to get through the defence of Philip Mead, the Hampshire opener. Letting the ball go as fast as he could, he pitched it on Mead's off stump, from where it cut back and knocked the leg stump clean out of the ground. Sussex captain Arthur Gilligan encouraged Tate to perfect his new style of bowling and in the next season, Tate took 219 wickets, followed by 205 in 1924 and 228 in 1925. In each season he also scored more than 1,000 runs.

In June 1924, he made a Test debut that made Poor Fred and the rest of England cry with joy. Snaring the wicket of Fred Susskind with his first delivery for England, Tate finished his first Test innings with 4–12, helping Gilligan to rout South Africa for 30 in 75 balls after England had made 438 at Edgbaston.

Tate overtook Gilligan as England's premier strike bowler before long and finished his first Test series with 27 wickets at 15.70, taking his best Test figures of 6–42 at Headingley.

He was quick to perfect his outswinger and leg-cutter, but, although he took nearly 3,000 first-class wickets in twenty-five years, he was often plagued by the sight of the ball just missing the outside edge of the bat.

Against the mighty 1930 Australian team without Don Bradman at Hove, he had the visitors at 69–6, dismissing Bill Ponsford, McCabe, Jackson, Fairfax, Richardson and a'Beckett while conceding just 18 runs.

Tate finished his first-class career in 1937, having taken 2,783 wickets and hit 21,698 runs. For many years, he opened the bowling and the batting for Sussex, hitting twenty-three first-class hundreds and even going in first for England at one stage. In his prime it was said that Tate was the world's best bowler on a batsman's wicket. His career highlights include 9–71 for Sussex against Middlesex in 1926; match figures of 14–58 for Sussex against Glamorgan in 1925; 100 not out for England against South Africa in 1929; and 203 for Sussex against Northamptonshire in 1921.

GRAHAM THORPE

One of the world's best left-handed batsman, Graham Thorpe was earmarked as a first-class cricketer as soon as he joined the Oval playing staff in 1988, although he forced his way into the first team primarily as a bowler who could bat.

In 1989, at the age of nineteen, he hit a brave century against a Hampshire side that included Malcolm Marshall and ended his first season with 1,132 runs at 45.28. His reward for an immensely promising full debut season was a place on the England 'A' tour of Zimbabwe, an expedition which convinced most judges that a full England cap was only another good season away.

Though he continued to score runs freely for the next few seasons, including 1,895 at 45.58 in 1992, it was the summer of 1993 before he finally made the senior side. Making his England debut against Australia at Trent Bridge in July, Thorpe scored an unbeaten 114 in his country's second innings in a drawn game. This was a fairy-tale start to his international career, but Thorpe had to wait until his fifteenth Test appearance for his second century, 123 against Australia at Perth in February 1995.

The following summer, Thorpe failed to register a century in the series against the West Indies, but he was still England's leading run-getter with 506.

In June 1997, he made 138 against Australia at Edgbaston, when coupled with Hussain's 207 in a fourth-wicket partnership of 288, and helped England to win by 9 wickets. He also ended the series as England's top batsman with 453 runs at 50.13.

After missing the 1999–2000 tour to South Africa for family reasons, he was soon restored to the England side and was a major success on the 2000–1 winter tours of Pakistan and Sri Lanka. He scored his seventh Test century, 118, against Pakistan in Lahore in November 2000, when he shared in a 166-run partnership with Yorkshire's Craig White. Just as important was his unbeaten 64 in fading light in the final Test in Karachi, where England secured their first Test series win in Pakistan for thirty-nine years.

More solid batting from Thorpe helped England secure their fourth successive series win against Sri Lanka, scoring 269 runs at 67.25 against the magic of Muttiah Muralitharan. He batted for six and a half hours in the crucial third Test at Colombo, remaining undefeated with match-winning knocks of 113 and 32.

During the course of the tour to New Zealand in March–April 2002, he hit his highest ever Test score of 200 not out in the first Test at Christchurch.

Thorpe, who went on to score 6,744 runs in 100 Tests, had an unusual mixture of brilliance and resilience and all the qualities that the England fans love to see – grit, flair and guts.

FRED TRUEMAN

Characters in cricket are not appreciated until they have retired or at least reached a seniority that gives their peculiar individuality a lovable quality. Thus it was some time before Fred Trueman, 'Fiery Fred' to many, was fully appreciated in all quarters.

The son of a miner, Trueman worked briefly in the pits before making his first appearance for Yorkshire at the age of eighteen. His immense promise was obvious and in June 1952 he made his Test debut against India at Headingley. In four Test matches, on lively pitches, he took 29 wickets at 13.31 apiece, including 8–31 at Old Trafford.

The next summer he played only once against Australia, and though he went to the West Indies with Len Hutton's team in winter 1954, his brash forthright manner frequently got him into trouble. Though he took 134 wickets in 1954, the selectors did not call on him for the trip to Australia and the Ashes were won without him.

Trueman was not fit in 1956 and was again left out of a touring side, this time bound for South Africa. However, he had gained considerable experience by this time, and from 1957 to 1963 he was at his peak. In his later years a touch of prudence made his batting more productive overall and he made three first-class hundreds between 1963 and 1965.

In January–March 1960, against the West Indies, Trueman took 21 Test wickets and kept clear of the controversy that had surrounded him on the previous tour. He enjoyed his best home season later that year, taking 175 wickets, and it was not until 1967 that he took fewer than 100 wickets in a season. He also took 25 wickets against the touring South Africans. The following year, he took 20 more against Australia, including match figures of 11–86 at Headingley, where he made the most of a poor wicket and enabled England to win by 8 wickets.

At Lord's, in June 1962, he took 6–31 when Pakistan were bowled out for 100 on the first day, and in the series he added 22 wickets to the growing list.

Against Frank Worrell's triumphant West Indians of 1963, he took 11 wickets in the famous second Test at Lord's, followed by 12 at the next match at Edgbaston. His 7–44 in the last innings brought England their only win of the series, and was a model of how conditions that allowed the ball to move in the air and off the seam could be exploited. In that series, his tally of wickets was 34.

In the Ashes series the following year, Trueman was still the major wicket-taker, but he was dropped for the fourth Test and there were suggestions that his Test career might be over. However, he was recalled for the final Test at The Oval, where he dismissed Redpath and McKenzie with successive balls before shortly afterwards making Neil Hawke his 300th victim.

His farewell season might almost have been stage-managed. Yorkshire won their third successive Championship in 1968, and with Trueman at the helm inflicted the first defeat on the visiting Australians.

Trueman was Yorkshire to the core, which made a brief return in one-day matches for Derbyshire somewhat incongruous. He later joined BBC Radio's *Test Match Special* team, where his comments sometimes earned less respect than his bowling had!

DEREK UNDERWOOD

Quiet and undemonstrative, with a shuffling gait, Derek Underwood enjoyed a career probably unique among English bowlers, although at first sight, he didn't look the type of cricketer to break records and upset traditions.

After a remarkable first season for Kent in 1963, when he became the youngest bowler ever to take 100 wickets, he took 9–28 the next year against Sussex at Hastings and 9–37 against Essex at Westcliff in 1966. He made his Test debut in 1966 against the West Indies at Trent Bridge, and though he didn't take a wicket, he bowled 43 overs for 86 runs in the second innings and batted with obstinacy to share a last-wicket stand of 65 with Basil D'Oliveira.

Underwood's greatest triumph was to follow in August 1968, in the final Test against Australia at The Oval. On the last day there was a thunderstorm and after it finally became possible to resume play, only seventy-five minutes remained. If the wicket were to become difficult as it dried, then Underwood clearly had the potential to become the match-winner. Forty minutes passed before it did, at which point one man fell to D'Oliveira. Underwood took the last wickets in 27 balls to win the match with six minutes to spare, level the series and finish with figures of 7–50.

In the three-match summer series against New Zealand in 1969 he was in devastating form, taking 24 wickets at 9.16 runs apiece. He also played an important part in the recovery of the Ashes in 1970–1, taking 16 wickets and containing the batsmen while the pace bowlers recovered.

At times the selectors overlooked him, and in 1972 he was omitted from the team until the fourth Test at Headingley in July, where he returned match figures of 10–82. The match caused much controversy as a freak storm and subsequent strong sunshine led to a fungus removing the grass from the wicket, thus allowing spin from the start.

In the winter of 1974–5, he bowled steadily in Australia before coming into his own in the fifth Test, at Adelaide, when he had a damp patch to bowl into on the opening day and finished with figures of 7–113.

Against the all-conquering West Indians of 1976, he took the most wickets for England in the series – 17 – and a few months later, on the successful tour of India, his 29 wickets at 17.55 topped anything even the Indian spinners could achieve.

'Deadly' Derek was one of the English players who signed for World Series Cricket in 1977, wanting security for his wife and daughter. Afterwards he seemed unsure of an automatic Test place, despite taking his haul of wickets to 297. He decided to accept an invitation to join the 'rebel' tour of South Africa and was banned from Tests for three years. He was still bowling well enough to merit consideration in 1985, when the ban was lifted, but the selectors ignored him.

Though he took 2,465 first-class wickets, perhaps his greatest pleasure came playing for his county side Kent, in 1984, when he scored his maiden century, 111, against Sussex at Hastings.

MICHAEL VAUGHAN

Captain of the England cricket team when they won the Ashes in 2005, Michael Vaughan used to watch Yorkshire playing at Sheffield in his childhood. On one occasion, during the tea interval, he was playing on the outfield with his friends when the then Yorkshire head coach Doug Padgett spotted his natural talent from the balcony of the pavilion. Padgett put down his cup of tea and went to get the boy's details. But unfortunately, he was born in Manchester and at the time Yorkshire had a strict policy of picking only county-born players. Later, when the rule was relaxed, Padgett got him to come to the academy and immediately signed him.

Vaughan captained the England Under-19 team and played his first Test for England in Johannesburg in November 1999. With England in the perilous state of 4 wickets down for just 2 runs, he soon demonstrated his maturity and flair as a batsman, particularly his trademark cover-drive.

In May 2001, he scored his first Test century, against Pakistan, and seven months later he became the second Englishman after Graham Gooch to be given out for handling the ball during a Test. The following year, he scored 900 runs in seven Tests against Sri Lanka and India, including his highest innings score to date, 197, against India at Trent Bridge. Two Tests later, also against India, he scored 195.

During the 2002–3 Ashes series, Vaughan proved that he could perform against the best team in the world. In the second Test, at Adelaide, he made a superb 177 and 41; in the fourth Test, at Melbourne, he made an aggressive 145; in the fifth and final Test, at Sydney, Vaughan made a spectacular match-winning 183, before falling to a dubious leg-before decision. He became the first visiting batsman for thirty-two years to score over 600 runs in a series against Australia. In total he scored 1,458 Test runs in 2002, the third highest for a calendar year in Test history. During this magnificent run of form, Vaughan also rose to the position of number-one batsman in the world, the first Englishman to achieve this feat since Graham Gooch.

In July 2004, against the West Indies, he became the eighth player to score a century in each innings of a Test match, scoring 103 and 101 not out at Lord's in the first Test.

During the 2005 Ashes series, Vaughan, who had been appointed England captain in July 2003, made 166 in the third Test at Old Trafford, eventually leading his side to victory in the Ashes for the first time since Mike Gatting's team in the 1986–7 series in Australia. For Vaughan it was the culmination of a five-year journey, for after whitewashing first New Zealand (3–0), then West Indies (4–0) in 2004, and recording a memorable 2–1 series win in South Africa in 2004–5, he then achieved the ultimate prize with a 2–1 triumph in arguably the greatest Ashes series of all time.

HEDLEY VERITY

Slow left-arm spinner Hedley Verity's apprenticeship was mostly spent as a professional in the Yorkshire and Lancashire Leagues. In fact he didn't play first-class cricket until the age of twenty-five, largely because of the imposing presence of Wilfred Rhodes in the Yorkshire side.

In 1931, his first full season playing for Yorkshire, he was selected for England, ahead of White or Parker, and took 10–36 in a county game against Warwickshire at Headingley. The following season he took all 10 wickets in an innings for a second time and for just 10 runs – the cheapest 'all ten' in history. Yorkshire's opponents were Nottinghamshire, who had led the home side on first innings. Indeed, the Notts batting went so deep that at number eleven was Sam Staples, a player who had done the double.

For Yorkshire, Verity was forever taking 7–20 or 7–40, enviable figures for today's spinners. In 1933, he took 17 wickets in one day, one of only three occasions in the history of cricket when this has been achieved.

For England, facing the Australians at Lord's in June 1934, he enjoyed a triumphant spell when, first, he caught and bowled Don Bradman on a dry pitch, then trapped the Australians on a wet if not a sticky one, so that in a single day he took 14 wickets for 80 runs off 44.3 overs. In his second innings, Bradman was caught off a cross-batted swipe at Verity, born of frustration. This performance helped England to their only Ashes victory at the ground in the twentieth century. In fact Verity dismissed Don Bradman on eight occasions in Tests, more than any other bowler, and once opened the batting in a Test, against Australia at the Adelaide Oval on the 1936–7 Ashes tour.

Thorough and methodical in his private life as well as his cricket, Hedley Verity prepared for war by studying military tactics. Despite his professional status, he was commissioned as a captain in the Green Howards, and it was as he was leading his men into action in Italy that he was fatally wounded at the age of thirty-eight.

It is certain that Verity had much more life and more cricket in him. On the very last day of county cricket before the competition was suspended, Verity was part of the Yorkshire team playing against Sussex at Hove. He set up a fine win by skittling the opposition for just 33 in their second innings, returning the exceptional analysis of 6–1–9–7.

CYRIL WASHBROOK

Although the Second World War arrived just as Cyril Washbrook was being discussed as a possible Test opener, he survived the hostilities with his batting form intact to become the Lancashire half of a renowned Roses opening partnership with Len Hutton.

A few weeks after his arrival at Old Trafford in 1933, Washbrook played for the Lancashire Second XI against Yorkshire and scored 202 not out – the first time the names of Washbrook and Hutton appeared together on the same scorecard. He was then promoted to the first team and in his second game he scored 152 against Surrey. Four years later he won his first Test cap against New Zealand at The Oval, when teammate Eddie Paynter had to withdraw through injury.

After the war, he was chosen to tour Australia and New Zealand in the winter of 1946–7. Hutton and Washbrook opened the England innings in all five Ashes Tests, the series marking the beginning of their association as England's first-wicket pair. In the third Test, at Melbourne, he achieved a personal triumph, scoring 62 in England's first innings, followed by 112, his first Test century, in the second. At Adelaide, the match was drawn, but Hutton and Washbrook gave their finest performance as openers with two century partnerships.

Over the next season, runs flowed freely from Washbrook's bat and his qualities as an opener with Hutton for England and Winston Place for Lancashire were acknowledged and admired wherever cricket was played. He took part in four of the five Tests against Australia in 1948, missing the match at The Oval only through injury. He averaged 50.85 and scored more than any other England batsman, except Compton. In the third Test at Old Trafford, he was 85 not out in England's second innings and looked well set for a century when a declaration was made in an abortive attempt to win the match. In the next match, at Headingley, he scored 143 in the first innings and 65 in the second, and shared with Hutton a century stand in each innings, a performance which established a new world record, for the feat had never been accomplished twice by the same batsmen.

Washbrook toured South Africa in 1948–9 and averaged 60.22. He and Hutton set up a new record for an opening partnership in the second Test at Johannesburg, their stand of 359 being made in exhausting conditions, 6,000 feet above sea level.

After an unsuccessful tour of Australia in 1950–1, he was not selected again until 1956, when he was forty-two years old. Persuaded to play in the Headingley Test, he joined Peter May at the crease when England were on 17–3. Between them and Jim Laker's superb bowling display they decided the rubber, Washbrook having scored 98 vintage runs before succumbing inevitably to a forcing shot.

Lancashire's first professional captain, he served two spells as a Test selector and was President of his beloved red rose county.

BOB WILLIS

Following an erratic start in county and Test cricket, Bob Willis, a gangling, rather open-chested fast bowler, developed into England's leading wicket-taker, and appeared in more Test matches than any other fast bowler.

After two years playing for Surrey, Willis joined Warwickshire in 1972, and in his first season he helped his new county to their first County Championship in twenty-one years, taking 8–44 including a hat-trick against Derbyshire at Edgbaston.

During his earlier spell with Surrey, he had flown out to Australia as a replacement for the injured Alan Ward in the Ashes series that England would ultimately win. He played in four Tests, took 12 wickets at 27.41, and thus began a long and rewarding association with the England Test team.

Willis was England's most aggressive bowler against the West Indies at home in 1973, on tour in 1973, and also in 1974, when he was England's fastest bowler. After the 1974–5 Ashes series, however, Willis flew home for knee operations and many thought he would go the same way as the injury-prone Alan Ward. Thankfully, he returned as quick as ever and on the normally dead wickets of India, took 20 wickets at 16.75 apiece.

By 1977 Bob Willis was in peak form. He produced his best first-class figures when he achieved 8–32 for Warwickshire against Gloucestershire at Bristol, and against the touring Australians took 27 wickets at 19.77 runs apiece, including 7–78 at Lord's.

Despite more knee surgery and an early return home flight from the Caribbean in 1980–1, Willis reserved his greatest performance when facing Kim Hughes's Australians in a match in which Ian Botham's unbeaten 149 allowed the home team a slender lead of 129 in the third Test at Headingley in July 1981. The Australians were cruising at 56–1 and Willis was looking like a spent force. He found he couldn't bowl as he wanted to when charging uphill

TOP 50 ENGLAND PLAYERS 241

and into the wind, and so he pleaded with Mike Brearley for a shot at the Kirkstall Lane end. On a pitch that was becoming more and more unreliable, Willis got his way and some much-needed wickets. Aiming at the cracks in the pitch, just short of a length, he sent them down in one of the truly inspired spells of Test bowling. Willis finished with 8–43 – Australia surrendered their last 9 wickets for 55 and lost one of the most thrilling Test matches by 18 runs.

He was a surprising choice as England captain in 1982 and it was a role the Warwickshire paceman never seemed comfortable with, prior to handing over the captaincy to David Gower.

It is Bob Willis's all-out pace and determination and, of course, that memorable day in 1981, for which he will be best remembered.

FRANK WOOLLEY

Frank Woolley was one of the finest all-rounders the game has seen. In a career lasting more than thirty years, he scored more first-class runs than anyone but Jack Hobbs, and took over 2,000 wickets at an average of under 20. He is also the only non-wicketkeeper to have held more than 1,000 catches.

Woolley made his Test debut in August 1909, playing for England against Australia at The Oval. It was in this same season that, along with Arthur Fielder, he set the Kent record for the tenth wicket, when they put on 235 against Worcestershire at Stourbridge.

In 1910, he achieved the double for the first time, scoring 1,050 runs and taking 132 wickets. The following season, in a match against Somerset at Tunbridge Wells, he scored a century in each innings. During the close-season tour of Australia, he scored an unbeaten 303 against Tasmania at Hobart.

Woolley took a keen interest in new bats. He always had four heavy bats made for him, each weighing around 2 lb 6 oz, calculating that this number would cover his season's needs. It was ironic that a man of Woolley's brilliant batting ability should be turned down by the Army during the First World War because of poor eyesight.

In 1919, when cricket playing was resumed, Woolley performed the hat-trick for the only time in his career against Surrey at Blackheath. In the 1921 season, during which he completed the double for the fifth time, he is best remembered for his performance in the second Test at Lord's against Australia. He held England together against Gregory and McDonald, scoring 95 out of 187 and 93 out of 283, playing his strokes with plenty of time to spare against the powerful Australians.

In 1923, he hit the highest score of his career in this country, racking up 270 runs against Middlesex at Canterbury. Five years later, after producing another couple of double hundreds, he scored his highest number of runs in a season, with 2,894 at an average of 59.06. In 1929, Woolley, who had been surprisingly overlooked for the 1929–30 tour of Australia, hit four consecutive centuries in the County Championship.

Two years later, he made 2,011 runs, his top score being 224 against the New Zealand tourists at Canterbury. It was while making those runs that he and Les Ames put on 277 for the fifth wicket to set up a Kent record. He also completed a hundred before lunch on two occasions, the first against Surrey at Blackheath in 1930 and then three years later when Derbyshire visited Canterbury.

After his retirement from the game he was elected a life member of the MCC and Kent and also the county committee. He remained quite active into his late eighties, and, in January 1971, he flew to Australia to watch the last two Tests. Nine months later, in Canada, he married for the second time, his first wife having died some ten years earlier.

One of the most elegant of left-handed all-rounders, Frank Woolley died in Nova Scotia in October 1978, aged ninety-one.

4 ENGLAND'S TEST GROUNDS

THE OVAL

The memorable oval shape of the ground in Kennington, south London, dates back to around 1790 when an oval road was first laid around what was originally a cabbage garden and later a market garden. After the failure of a number of proposed building projects, the area was first opened as a cricket ground in 1845 – the original turf coming from Tooting Common – and used by the Montpelier Club following its expulsion from its own ground in nearby Walworth.

The first match to be played on the ground is recorded as having taken place on 13 May 1845 between Mr Fould's XI and Mr Houghton's XI. The first Surrey game was played on 21 and 22 August 1845 between the Gentlemen of Surrey and the Players of Surrey. Following the formal inauguration of the county club, the first Surrey CCC match was staged with neighbours Kent in 1846, while the first County Championship match occurred in 1873 against Sussex.

Significantly, in September 1880, The Oval was to host the first Test match on English soil between England and Australia, the two oldest nations in Test cricket. W. G. Grace scored 152 for England and Billy Murdoch replied for Australia with 153 not out, yet it was the hosts who won by five wickets. The game was made famous with England fielding three brothers in their team – W. G., E. M. and G. F. Grace. As well as hosting cricket tournaments, the ground was also used for football matches, and was the venue for the FA Cup Final in 1872, and again between 1874 and 1892.

The Oval is also the venue where the legend of the Ashes was born in August 1882. England, chasing only 85 to win, slumped from 51–2 to 78 all out. The next morning, *The Sporting Times* published its famous mock obituary regarding the death of English cricket, and the resulting Ashes matches have been fiercely contested ever since.

The Oval has, of course, witnessed many famous matches. In August 1902, England's dramatic one-wicket win over Australia was inspired by Gilbert Jessop's sensational hundred. In August 1934, Australia scored 701 as Don Bradman (244) and Bill Ponsford (266) put on 451 for the second wicket. Four years later, England scored 903–7 declared as they beat Australia by an innings and 579 runs, with Len Hutton making 364. Also notable was the occasion in summer 1948, when, on his last appearance in Test cricket, Don Bradman was bowled for a duck by Eric Hollies of Warwickshire, which meant that he finished his Test career with a batting average of 99.94, agonizingly short of the century mark. In terms of outstanding bowling performances, one of the best at The Oval in recent years was Devon Malcolm's 9–57 against South Africa in 1994.

ENGLAND'S RECORDS AND SCORES AT THE OVAL

TEST MATCHES

Highest innings total for England
903–7 declared v Australia, 1938

Highest innings total against England
708 by Pakistan, 1987

Lowest innings total for England
52 v Australia, 1948

Lowest innings total against England
44 by Australia, 1896

Highest individual innings for England
364 by Len Hutton v Australia, 1938

Highest individual innings against England
291 by Viv Richards for West Indies, 1976

Best bowling performance in an innings for England
9–57 by Devon Malcolm v South Africa, 1994

Best bowling performance in an innings against England
9–65 by Muttiah Muralitharan for Sri Lanka, 1998

Best bowling performance in a match for England
13–57 by Sydney Barnes v South Africa, 1912

Best bowling performance in a match against England
16–220 by Muttiah Muralitharan for Sri Lanka, 1998

LIMITED-OVERS INTERNATIONALS

Highest innings total
347–4 by New Zealand v USA, 2004

Lowest innings total
103 by England v South Africa, 1999

Highest individual innings
145* by Nathan Astle for New Zealand v USA, 2004

Best bowling performance
5–26 by Ronnie Irani for England v India, 2002

OLD TRAFFORD

Old Trafford in Manchester has been the home of Lancashire cricket since 1857 when the ground was newly opened. The first match ever staged at Old Trafford was between Manchester CC and Liverpool CC, and, in 1860, the inaugural first-class match saw England facing Another England XI. Lancashire CCC was formed four years later, and the first county match on home soil was against Middlesex in 1865.

Old Trafford's first day of Test cricket in July 1884 was washed out, and consequently produced a draw between England and Australia. In the Ashes Test of 1888, Yorkshire's Bobby Peel finished with match figures of 11–68 as Australia, bowled out for 81 in their first innings, were forced to follow on in the wake of England's 172. After a disastrous start – at one point they had 7 runs on the board for the loss of 6 wickets – their fortunes improved slightly when Turner and Lyons added 48. Despite the attempt at a fightback, Australia ended up losing by an innings and 21 runs shortly before lunch on the second day, making this the shortest Test match of all time.

In the 1902 Ashes game, which was known as 'Tate's match', the visitors enjoyed a narrow victory when England's Fred Tate, who needed just four runs to win the game, was bowled by Saunders. Fifty-four years later in another classic Ashes encounter came 'Laker's match', which featured an outstanding example of spin bowling, all from the Stretford End, in which England bowler Jim Laker took 9–37 in the first innings followed by 10 wickets in the second, ending up with match figures of 19–90. In 1964, Bobby Simpson scored 311 for Australia out of their total of 656–8 declared, while Ken Barrington (256) and Ted Dexter (174) replied for England in a game in which both sides passed the 600-run mark. During the 1981 Ashes series, the Australian bowlers faced an inspired Ian Botham, while in 1995, in dramatic fashion, Dominic Cork achieved a hat-trick against the West Indies.

Old Trafford is well known for attracting large crowds. The record attendance is 78,617 for the 1926 Roses match – 46,000 passed through the gates on the first day. Though the ground capacity is now classed as 19,000, a crowd of 22,000 crammed into Old Trafford in 1999 for the Pakistan v India World Cup game. Despite losing out as a venue for the 2009 Ashes series, Old Trafford regularly sells out for all forms of international cricket.

ENGLAND'S RECORDS AND SCORES AT OLD TRAFFORD

TEST MATCHES

Highest innings total for England
627–9 declared v Australia, 1934

Highest innings total against England
656–8 declared by Australia, 1964

Lowest innings total for England
71 v West Indies, 1976

Lowest innings total against England
58 by India, 1952

Highest individual innings for England
256 by Ken Barrington v Australia, 1964

Highest individual innings against England
311 by Bobby Simpson for Australia, 1964

Best bowling performance in an innings for England
10–53 by Jim Laker v Australia, 1956

Best bowling performance in an innings against England
8–31 by Frank Laver for Australia, 1909

Best bowling performance in a match for England
19–90 by Jim Laker v Australia, 1956

Best bowling performance in a match against England
11–157 by Lance Gibbs for West Indies, 1963

LIMITED-OVERS INTERNATIONALS

Highest innings total
318–7 by Sri Lanka v England, 2006

Lowest innings total
45 by Canada v England, 1979

Highest individual innings
189* by Viv Richards for West Indies v England, 1984

Best bowling performance
5–14 by Glenn McGrath for Australia v West Indies, 1999

LORD'S

Still widely regarded as the home of cricket, Lord's, in St John's Wood, north-west London, derives its name not from any association with the aristocracy (as is sometimes thought), but from its founder, Thomas Lord.

It was opened in 1814, and soon become a major venue as cricket developed into the world's leading sport in the nineteenth century. It was not until July 1884 that England met Australia in the first Test match at Lord's – The Oval having led the way as a host for Test cricket. Nowadays, the Lord's Test match is regarded as the highlight of the season.

Before the arrival of the Test match, the most important fixture was between the Gentlemen and Players, which was still popular when it was discontinued in 1963 after the abolition of amateur status. Apart from the occasional interruption, teams from Eton and Harrow have met regularly at Lord's since 1822. More famous matches and innings have been played at Lord's than on any other ground in the world, and many of its historic moments are recorded in the museum that stands just behind the pavilion. For example, Lord's was the scene of 'Cobden's match' in 1870, when F. C. Cobden took three wickets with the last three balls of the game to win the University match for Cambridge by two runs.

One of the most bizarre incidents on the ground occurred during the 1926 England–Australia Test. Early on the Monday morning, it was found that water had saturated a part of the square during the night, someone having connected a hose with the water supply. It had penetrated to the pitch, but only in the middle and no harm was done. The incident was never satisfactorily explained, but these days the ground is guarded throughout the night.

During the twentieth century, England managed to beat Australia only once at Lord's – their sole victory coming in June 1934 under the captaincy of Bob Wyatt. Prior to 1934, the previous England victory at Lord's was way back in 1896. When the two sides met at the round in June 1961, England had gone eighteen Tests without defeat, but the Lord's hoodoo was to strike again: only one England batsman reached a half-century, as Australia won by five wickets. Not even winning the toss for a twelfth consecutive match could help the home side. When Ray Illingworth's side retained the Ashes in 1972, they suffered a mauling at Lord's, where the hero was debutant Bob Massie, who bagged 16–137. Twenty-five years later, Glenn McGrath ripped through the England batting, taking 8–38 and leaving the shell-shocked hosts all out for 77.

In July 2005, in the first Test of the Ashes series, Lord's was also the location for the Australians' sole win of the tournament, once again thanks in part to some damaging bowling in both innings by McGrath.

ENGLAND'S RECORDS AND SCORES AT LORD'S

TEST MATCHES

Highest innings total for England
653–4 declared v India, 1990

Highest innings total against England
729–6 declared by Australia, 1930

Lowest innings total for England
53 v Australia, 1888

Lowest innings total against England
42 by India, 1974

Highest individual innings for England
333 by Graham Gooch v India, 1990

Highest individual innings against England
259 by Graeme Smith for South Africa, 2003

Best bowling performance in an innings for England
8–34 by Ian Botham v Pakistan, 1978

Best bowling performance in an innings against England
8–38 by Glenn McGrath for Australia, 1997

Best bowling performance in a match for England
15–104 by Hedley Verity v Australia, 1934

Best bowling performance in a match v England
16–137 by Bob Massie for Australia, 1972

LIMITED-OVERS INTERNATIONALS

Highest innings total
334–4 by England v India, 1975

Lowest innings total
107 by South Africa v England, 2003

Highest individual innings
138* by Viv Richards for West Indies v England, 1979

Best bowling performance
5–30 by Daniel Vettori for New Zealand v West Indies, 2004

TRENT BRIDGE

Trent Bridge in Nottingham became a cricket ground thanks to the enterprise of William Clarke. After he moved from the Bell Inn (which is still located in Nottingham's main square) to the Trent Bridge Inn, he laid out a cricket ground on the land at the back of his new home, which he opened for use in 1841. In 1919, Nottinghamshire County Cricket Club purchased both the inn, which they later sold, and the ground, which has been in their sole ownership ever since.

The first Test match at Trent Bridge was played in 1899 against Australia. It was W. G. Grace's last appearance for England, and, when the match ended on 3 June, he was forty-five days short of his fifty-first birthday. By a strange coincidence, the only other Englishman to play Test cricket at an advanced age, Wilfred Rhodes – who was fifty-two years and six months when he played his last game in April 1930 – made his debut in this game.

The great Australian side of 1948 opened the Test series with an eight-wicket win at Trent Bridge. Early on the first day, England were reduced to

74–8, which seemed to set the tone for the entire five-match series. Australia topped 500 in the first innings as Don Bradman scored his twenty-eighth Test century on his final tour of England. In August 1965, the Pollock brothers, Graeme and Peter, led South Africa to a famous victory. Twenty-four years later, Australians Mark Taylor and Geoff Marsh hit the England attack all over the ground when they batted throughout the first day and made a total of 301 without loss. In 1993, Graham Thorpe became the first Englishman – since Frank Hayes in 1973 – to score a hundred on his Test debut. The Surrey left-hander hit 114 in his second innings and helped England end a run of seven straight Test defeats. In the same match, which ended in a draw, England skipper Graham Gooch passed the milestone of 8,000 Test runs.

ENGLAND'S RECORDS AND SCORES AT TRENT BRIDGE

TEST MATCHES

Highest innings for England
658–8 declared v Australia, 1938

Highest innings total against England
602–6 declared by Australia, 1989

Lowest innings total for England
112 v Australia, 1921

Lowest innings total against England
88 by South Africa, 1960

Highest individual innings for England
278 by Denis Compton v Pakistan, 1954

Highest individual innings against England
261 by Frank Worrell for West Indies, 1950

Best bowling performance in an innings for England
8–107 by Bernard Bosanquet v Australia, 1905

Best bowling performance in an innings against England
8–70 by Muttiah Muralitharan for Sri Lanka, 2006

Best bowling performance in a match for England
14–99 by Alec Bedser v Australia, 1953

Best bowling performance in a match against England
11–129 by Bill O'Reilly for Australia, 1934

LIMITED-OVERS INTERNATIONALS

Highest innings total
391–4 v Bangladesh, 2005

Lowest innings total
138 by Sri Lanka v Pakistan, 1975

Highest individual innings
152 by Andrew Strauss for England v Bangladesh, 2005

Best bowling performance
6–31 by Paul Collingwood for England v Bangladesh, 2005

HEADINGLEY

Cricket and rugby football have been played at Headingley in Leeds since 1890, when the first important match was staged between the North and the touring Australians. The following year, Headingley staged Yorkshire's inaugural first-class match against Kent, and in June 1899, the ground hosted its first Test match, against Australia.

Spectators at Headingley have, over the years, witnessed a number of outstanding spectacles, including a couple of triple Test centuries by Don Bradman. In July 1930, in the first innings, Bradman scored 309 of his eventual 334 total in just one day, which is the only time a batsman has scored 300 in one day of a Test match. Four years later the Leeds crowd witnessed a similar feat when the legendary batsman scored 304 runs.

England opener John Edrich also made a triple Test hundred at the ground – an unbeaten 310 – against New Zealand in July 1965, and, quite appropriately, Yorkshire's Geoff Boycott brought up his hundredth hundred at Headingley against Australia in 1977. Four years later, Headingley would play host to a match that many people regard as the greatest comeback in the history of Test cricket, when England turned round a likely defeat to beat Australia by 18 runs. The home side had been forced to follow on 227 runs behind Australia's first-innings declaration of 401–9, and were struggling at 135–7 in their second innings. However, a dazzling display with the bat from Ian Botham (149*) and a superb piece of bowling from Bob Willis (8–43) turned the tables on the Australians, and set the pace for the rest of the 1981 Ashes series.

Much of the development at Headingley was undertaken by Sir Edwin Airey, a building contractor, who, in 1932, undertook improvements designed to establish Headingley as a major cricket venue. Unlike the majority of Test grounds, Headingley has no pavilion, so the players use a modern dressing-room square of the wicket.

ENGLAND'S RECORDS AND SCORES AT HEADINGLEY

TEST MATCHES

Highest innings total for England
550–4 declared v India, 1967

Highest innings total against England
653–4 declared by Australia, 2002

Lowest innings total for England
76 by South Africa, 1907

Lowest innings total against England
61 by West Indies, 2000

Highest individual innings for England
310* by John Edrich v New Zealand, 1965

Highest individual innings against England
334 by Don Bradman for Australia, 1930

Best bowling performance in an innings for England
8–43 by Bob Willis v Australia, 1981

Best bowling performance in an innings against England
7–37 by Jason Gillespie for Australia, 1997

Best bowling performance in a match for England
15–99 by Colin Blythe v South Africa, 1907

Best bowling performance in a match against England
11–85 by Charles Macartney for Australia, 1909

LIMITED-OVERS INTERNATIONALS

Highest innings total
324–2 by Sri Lanka v England, 2006

Lowest innings total
93 by England v Australia, 1975

Highest individual innings
152 by Sanath Jayasuriya for Sri Lanka v England, 2006

Best bowling performance
7–36 by Waqar Younis for Pakistan v England, 2001

EDGBASTON

Established in 1882, Edgbaston was the youngest of England's six regular Test grounds until the inauguration of the Riverside ground in Chester-le-Street in May 2003. The ground was originally a 'meadow of rough grazing land' and belonged to Lord Calthorpe until he allowed the club to lease it for cricket purposes.

The first ever match to be played on the new ground was between an England XI and the Australians in 1886, while the first county match hosted at

Edgbaston saw Warwickshire entertain Kent in 1894. Eight years later, the Birmingham ground was finally recognized as a suitable venue for Test matches, and in May 1902, England met Australia in the first Test of the series. Australia were bowled out for a mere 36 runs; Wilfred Rhodes was the chief wicket-taker with figures of 7–17 from 11 overs. Test matches continued to be played until 1929, although there was a considerable gap until 1946, but since the end of the Second World War it has remained a regular venue.

Throughout its history, Edgbaston has provided the setting for a number of exciting Ashes matches. In summer 1981, Ian Botham proved himself to be the scourge of the Aussies when they needed just 146 to win the fourth Test and take a 2–1 lead in the series. The tourists reached 105–4, needing just 41 for victory on the fourth afternoon. But Botham had other ideas, and took 5–11 in 14 overs as England scraped home by 29 runs. Over the last decade or so, Edgbaston, the scene of Brian Lara's 1994 world record 501 not out, has developed a reputation for low scoring, so when Australia were bowled out for 118 inside three hours on the first morning of the first Test in June 1997, it appeared that another runs-deprived contest was on the cards. But England made 478–9 declared, thanks largely to a match-winning stand of 288 between Hussain (207) and Thorpe (138).

ENGLAND'S RECORDS AND SCORES AT EDGBASTON

TEST MATCHES

Highest innings total for England
633–5 declared v India, 1979

Highest innings total against England
608–7 declared by Pakistan, 1971

Lowest innings total for England
89 v West Indies, 1995

Lowest innings total against England
30 by South Africa, 1924

Highest individual innings for England
285* by Peter May v West Indies, 1957

Highest individual innings against England
277 by Graeme Smith for South Africa, 2003

Best bowling performance in an innings for England
7–17 by Wilfrid Rhodes v Australia, 1902

Best bowling performance in an innings against England
7–49 by Sonny Ramadhin for West Indies, 1957

Best bowling performance in a match for England
12–119 by Fred Trueman v West Indies, 1963

Best bowling performance in a match against England
10–115 by Muttiah Muralitharan for Sri Lanka, 2006

LIMITED-OVERS INTERNATIONALS

Highest innings total
320–8 by England v Australia, 1980

Lowest innings total
70 by Australia v England, 1977

Highest individual innings
171* by Glenn Turner for New Zealand v East Africa, 1975

Best bowling performance
5–11 by Shahid Afridi for Pakistan v Kenya, 2004

BRAMALL LANE

Bramall Lane in Sheffield was home to Yorkshire county cricket in the early days and its spectators could always be relied upon for enthusiastic support during the course of a game, and would even acknowledge good play by the opposition when it was warranted. Unfortunately, the venue was never an ideal location for cricket, as it was first and foremost a football ground, the home of Sheffield United. Indeed, Bramall Lane staged international soccer matches, as well as the 1912 FA Cup Final replay between Barnsley and West Bromwich Albion.

It came as a complete surprise, therefore, when Bramall Lane was chosen to stage the third Test in the 1902 Ashes series against Australia – the bad light (from the smoke produced by the numerous local factories) being blamed for England's 143-run defeat. Owing to poor attendances throughout the three-day Test, the fixture was not repeated, although the ground did host one of the Victory Tests in 1945. Although the county club moved its headquarters to Leeds in 1903, Bramall Lane remained a regular venue for County Championship matches until 1973, when, due to economic pressures, Yorkshire played their final Championship game there. In the winter, Sheffield United filled in the open side of the Bramall Lane ground with a new stand, which brought to an end the future of cricket at the football club.

ENGLAND'S RECORDS AND SCORES AT BRAMALL LANE

TEST MATCHES

Highest innings total for England
195 v Australia, 1902

Highest innings total against England
289 by Australia, 1902

Lowest innings total for England
145 v Australia, 1902

Lowest innings total against England
194 by Australia, 1902

Highest individual innings for England
63 by Archie MacLaren v Australia, 1902

Highest individual innings against England
119 by Clem Hill for Australia, 1902

Best bowling performance in an innings for England
6–49 by Sydney Barnes v Australia, 1902

Best bowling performance in an innings against England
6–52 by Monty Noble for Australia, 1902

Best bowling performance in a match for England
7–99 by Sydney Barnes v Australia, 1902

Best bowling performance in a match against England
11–103 by Monty Noble for Australia, 1902

RIVERSIDE GROUND

The Riverside ground was first used by Chester-le-Street CC in the 1890s, but it wasn't until more than a hundred years later, in 1992, that the ground became properly developed to the standard worthy of hosting cricket internationals.

The original ground had a somewhat limited capacity, although a crowd of 5,000 squeezed in to watch the 1972 Gillette Cup tie against Surrey. But all the hard work needed to build up the status of the ground paid off in May 1999, when the home of Durham CCC was awarded a couple of matches in that summer's World Cup.

In June 2000, England played a NatWest Series one-day game that was watched by 15,000, and three years later, the Chester-le-Street venue became the first new Test ground in England to be established since 1902, when it was chosen to host an England v Zimbabwe three-day Test.

ENGLAND'S RECORDS AND SCORES AT THE RIVERSIDE GROUND

TEST MATCHES

Highest innings total for England
447–3 declared v Bangladesh, 2005

Highest innings total against England
316 by Bangladesh, 2005

Lowest innings total by England
416 v Zimbabwe, 2003

Lowest innings total against England
94 by Zimbabwe, 2003

Highest individual innings for England
162* by Ian Bell v Bangladesh, 2005

Highest individual innings against England
82* by Aftab Ahmed for Bangladesh, 2005

Best bowling performance in an innings for England
6–33 by Richard Johnson v Zimbabwe, 2003

Best bowling performance in an innings against England
4–64 by Heath Streak for Zimbabwe, 2003

Best bowling performance in a match for England
8–97 by Matthew Hoggard v Bangladesh, 2005

Best bowling performance in a match against England
4–64 by Heath Streak for Zimbabwe, 2003

LIMITED-OVERS INTERNATIONALS

Highest innings total
290–4 by Zimbabwe v West Indies, 2000

Lowest innings total
101 by England v New Zealand, 2004

Highest individual innings
126* by Mahela Jayawardene for Sri Lanka v England, 2006

Best bowling performance
5–42 by James Franklin for New Zealand v England, 2004

5 ENGLAND'S TEST RECORDS

HIGHEST INNINGS TOTALS BY ENGLAND

903–7 dec.	England v Australia	The Oval	1938
849	England v West Indies	Kingston	1929–30
658–8 dec.	England v Australia	Trent Bridge	1938
654–5	England v South Africa	Durban	1938–9
653–4 dec.	England v India	Lord's	1990
652–7 dec.	England v India	Chennai	1984–5
636	England v Australia	Sydney	1928–9
633–5 dec.	England v India	Edgbaston	1979
629	England v India	Lord's	1974
627–9 dec.	England v Australia	Old Trafford	1934
619–6 dec.	England v West Indies	Trent Bridge	1957
617	England v India	Trent Bridge	2002
611	England v Australia	Old Trafford	1964
608	England v South Africa	Johannesburg	1948–9
604–9 dec.	England v South Africa	The Oval	2003
595–5 dec.	England v Australia	Edgbaston	1985
594	England v India	The Oval	1982
593–6 dec.	England v New Zealand	Auckland	1974–5
593	England v West Indies	St John's	1993–4
592–8 dec.	England v Australia	Perth	1986–7
589	England v Australia	Melbourne	1911–12
583–4 dec.	England v West Indies	Edgbaston	1957
580–9 dec.	England v New Zealand	Christchurch	1991–2
577	England v Australia	Sydney	1903–4
576	England v Australia	The Oval	1899
571–8 dec.	England v India	Old Trafford	1936
570–7 dec.	England v South Africa	Durban	2004–5
568	England v West Indies	Port-of-Spain	1967–8
568	England v West Indies	Lord's	2004
567–8 dec.	England v New Zealand	Trent Bridge	1994
566–9 dec.	England v West Indies	Edgbaston	2004
564	England v India	Trent Bridge	1996
562–7 dec.	England v New Zealand	Auckland	1962–3
560–8 dec.	England v New Zealand	Christchurch	1932–3
559–9 dec.	England v South Africa	Cape Town	1938–9

559–8 dec.	England v India	Kanpur	1963–4
558–6 dec.	England v Pakistan	Trent Bridge	1954
558	England v Australia	Melbourne	1965–6
554–8 dec.	England v South Africa	Lord's	1947
551	England v Australia	Sydney	1897–8
551	England v South Africa	Trent Bridge	1947
551–6	England v Sri Lanka	Lord's	2006
550	England v New Zealand	Christchurch	1950–1
550–4 dec.	England v India	Headingley	1967

LOWEST INNINGS TOTALS BY ENGLAND

45	England v Australia	Sydney	1886–7
46	England v West Indies	Port-of-Spain	1993–4
52	England v Australia	The Oval	1948
53	England v Australia	Lord's	1888
61	England v Australia	Melbourne	1901–2
61	England v Australia	Melbourne	1903–4
62	England v Australia	Lord's	1888
64	England v New Zealand	Wellington	1977–8
65	England v Australia	Sydney	1894–5
71	England v West Indies	Old Trafford	1976
72	England v Australia	Sydney	1894–5
75	England v Australia	Melbourne	1894–5
76	England v South Africa	Headingley	1907
77	England v Australia	The Oval	1882
77	England v Australia	Sydney	1884–5
77	England v Australia	Lord's	1997
79	England v Australia	Brisbane	2002–3
82	England v New Zealand	Christchurch	1983–4
84	England v Australia	The Oval	1896
87	England v Australia	Headingley	1909
87	England v Australia	Melbourne	1958–9
89	England v West Indies	Edgbaston	1995
92	England v South Africa	Cape Town	1898–9
92	England v Australia	Melbourne	1994–5
93	England v New Zealand	Christchurch	1983–4
93	England v West Indies	Old Trafford	1988
95	England v Australia	Old Trafford	1884
95	England v Australia	Melbourne	1976–7
99	England v Australia	Sydney	1901–2
99	England v South Africa	Lord's	1994

BATTING RECORDS

OVER 4,000 RUNS IN A TEST CAREER

G. A. Gooch	8,900	J. B. Hobbs	5,410
A. J. Stewart	8,463	I. T. Botham	5,200
D. I. Gower	8,231	J. H. Edrich	5,138
G. Boycott	8,114	T. W. Graveney	4,882
M. A. Atherton	7,728	A. J. Lamb	4,656
M. C. Cowdrey	7,624	M. P. Vaughan	4,595
W. R. Hammond	7,249	H. Sutcliffe	4,555
L. Hutton	6,971	P. B. H. May	4,537
K. F. Barrington	6,806	E. R. Dexter	4,502
G. P. Thorpe	6,744	M. W. Gatting	4,409
M. E. Trescothick	5,825	A. P. E. Knott	4,389
D. C. S. Compton	5,807	M. A. Butcher	4,288
N. Hussain	5,764	R. A. Smith	4,236

HIGHEST INDIVIDUAL INNINGS

364	L. Hutton v Australia at The Oval, 1938
336*	W. R. Hammond v New Zealand at Auckland, 1932–3
333	G. A. Gooch v India at Lord's, 1990
325	A. Sandham v West Indies at Kingston, 1929–30
310*	J. H. Edrich v New Zealand at Headingley, 1965
287	R. E. Foster v Australia at Sydney, 1903–4
285*	P. B. H. May v West Indies at Edgbaston, 1957
278	D. C. S. Compton v Pakistan at Trent Bridge, 1954
262*	D. L. Amiss v West Indies at Kingston, 1973–4
258	T. W. Graveney v West Indies at Trent Bridge, 1957
256	K. F. Barrington v Australia at Old Trafford, 1964
251	W. R. Hammond v Australia at Sydney, 1928–9
246*	G. Boycott v India at Headingley, 1967
243	E. Paynter v South Africa at Durban, 1938–9
240	W. R. Hammond v Australia at Lord's, 1938
231*	W. R. Hammond v Australia at Sydney, 1936–7
227	W. R. Hammond v New Zealand at Christchurch, 1932–3
221	R. W. T. Key v West Indies at Lord's, 2004
219	W. J. Edrich v South Africa at Durban, 1938–9
219	M. E. Trescothick v South Africa at The Oval, 2003
217	W. R. Hammond v India at The Oval, 1936
216*	E. Paynter v Australia at Trent Bridge, 1938
216	K. W. R. Fletcher v New Zealand at Auckland, 1974–5
215	D. I. Gower v Australia at Edgbaston, 1985

214*	D. Lloyd v India at Edgbaston, 1974
211	J. B. Hobbs v South Africa at Lord's, 1924
210	G. A. Gooch v New Zealand at Trent Bridge, 1994
208	D. C. S. Compton v South Africa at Lord's, 1947
208	I. T. Botham v India at The Oval, 1982
207	M. W. Gatting v India at Madras, 1984–5
207	N. Hussain v Australia at Edgbaston, 1997
206	L. Hutton v New Zealand at The Oval, 1949
205*	E. H. Hendren v West Indies at Port-of-Spain, 1929–30
205*	J. Hardstaff Jnr v India at Lord's, 1946
205	L. Hutton v West Indies at Kingston, 1953–4
205	E. R. Dexter v Pakistan at Karachi, 1961–2
203	D. L. Amiss v West Indies at The Oval, 1976
202*	L. Hutton v West Indies at The Oval, 1950
201	G. Fowler v India at Madras, 1984–5
200*	D. I. Gower v India at Edgbaston, 1979
200*	G. P. Thorpe v New Zealand at Christchurch, 2001–2
200	W. R. Hammond v Australia at Melbourne, 1928–9

MOST CENTURIES

G. Boycott	22	A. J. Stewart	15
M. C. Cowdrey	22	M. P. Vaughan	15
W. R. Hammond	22	I. T. Botham	14
K. F. Barrington	20	N. Hussain	14
G. A. Gooch	20	A. J. Lamb	14
L. Hutton	19	M. E. Trescothick	14
D. I. Gower	18	P. B. H. May	13
D. C. S. Compton	17	J. H. Edrich	12
M. A. Atherton	16	D. L. Amiss	11
H. Sutcliffe	16	T. W. Graveney	11
G. P. Thorpe	16	M. W. Gatting	10
J. B. Hobbs	15	A. J. Strauss	10

HIGHEST PARTNERSHIP FOR EACH WICKET

1st	359	L. Hutton & C. Washbrook v South Africa at Johannesburg, 1948–9
2nd	382	M. Leyland & L. Hutton v Australia at The Oval, 1938
3rd	370	W. J. Edrich & D. C. S. Compton v South Africa at Lord's, 1947
4th	411	M. C. Cowdrey & P. B. H. May v West Indies at Edgbaston, 1957
5th	254	K. W. R. Fletcher & A. W. Greig v India at Mumbai, 1972–3
6th	281	A. Flintoff & G. P. Thorpe v New Zealand at Christchurch, 2001–2

7th 197 M. J. K. Smith & J. M. Parks v West Indies at Port-of-Spain, 1959–60
8th 246 L. E. G. Ames & G. O. B. Allen v New Zealand at Lord's, 1931
9th 163* M. C. Cowdrey & A. C. Smith v New Zealand at Wellington, 1962–3
10th 130 R. E. Foster & W. Rhodes v Australia at Sydney, 1903–4

BOWLING RECORDS

MOST WICKETS

I. T. Botham	383	S. P. Harmison	175
R. G. D. Willis	325	G. A. R. Lock	174
F. S. Trueman	307	M. W. Tate	155
D. L. Underwood	297	F. J. Titmus	153
J. B. Statham	252	J. E. Emburey	147
A. V. Bedser	236	H. Verity	144
A. R. Caddick	234	C. M. Old	143
D. Gough	229	A. W. Greig	141
M. J. Hoggard	222	P. A. J. DeFreitas	140
J. A. Snow	202	A. F. Giles	140
J. C. Laker	193	G. R. Dilley	138
S. F. Barnes	189	T. E. Bailey	132
A. Flintoff	179	D. G. Cork	131
A. R. C. Fraser	177	D. E. Malcolm	128

HAT-TRICKS

W. Bates	England v Australia at Melbourne, 1882–3
J. Briggs	England v Australia at Sydney, 1891–2
G. A. Lohmann	England v South Africa at Port Elizabeth, 1895–6
J. T. Hearne	England v Australia at Headingley, 1899
M. J. C. Allom	England v New Zealand at Christchurch, 1929–30
T. W. J. Goddard	England v South Africa at Johannesburg, 1938–9
P. Loader	England v West Indies at Headingley, 1957
D. G. Cork	England v West Indies at Old Trafford, 1995
D. Gough	England v Australia at Sydney, 1998–9
M. J. Hoggard	England v West Indies at Bridgetown, 2003–4

WICKETKEEPING RECORDS

OVER 100 DISMISSALS IN TESTS

		Tests	Caught	Stumped
269	A. P. E. Knott	95	250	19
241*	A. J. Stewart	82	227	14

219	T. G. Evans	91	173	46
174	R. W. Taylor	57	167	7
165	R. C. Russell	54	153	12
124	G. O. Jones	31	119	5
112*	J. M. Parks	43	101	11

* Excluding catches taken in the field.

TEN DISMISSALS IN A TEST

11	R. C. Russell	England v South Africa at Johannesburg, 1995–6
10	R. W. Taylor	England v India at Bombay, 1979–80

FIELDING RECORDS

MOST CATCHES

I. T. Botham	120		N. Hussain	67
M.C. Cowdrey	120		F. E. Woolley	64
W. R. Hammond	110		F. S. Trueman	64
G. P. Thorpe	105		M. A. Butcher	61
G. A. Gooch	103		W. Rhodes	60
M. E. Trescothick	95		G. A. R. Lock	59
G. A. Hick	90		M. W. Gatting	59
A. W. Greig	87		K. F. Barrington	58
M. A. Atherton	83		L. Hutton	57
T. W. Graveney	80		K. W. R. Fletcher	54
A. J. Lamb	75		M. J. K. Smith	53
D. I. Gower	74		J. M. Brearley	52

MOST TEST MATCH APPEARANCES

A. J. Stewart	133		D. L. Underwood	86
G. A. Gooch	118		W. R. Hammond	85
D. I. Gower	117		K. F. Barrington	82
M. A. Atherton	115		L. Hutton	79
M. C. Cowdrey	114		T. W. Graveney	79
G. Boycott	108		A. J. Lamb	79
I. T. Botham	102		M. W. Gatting	79
G. P. Thorpe	100		D. C. S. Compton	78
N. Hussain	96		J. H. Edrich	77
A. P. E. Knott	95		M. E. Trescothick	76
T. G. Evans	91		M. A. Butcher	71
R. G. D. Willis	90		J. B. Statham	70

ENGLAND TEST CAPTAINCY RECORD

	Tenure	Matches	Won	Lost	Drawn
James Lillywhite	1876–7	2	1	1	0
Lord Harris	1878–84	4	2	1	1
A. Shaw	1881–2	4	0	2	2
A. N. Hornby	1882–4	2	0	1	1
Hon. Ivo Bligh	1882–3	4	2	2	0
A. Shrewsbury	1884–7	7	5	2	0
A. G. Steel	1886–8	4	3	1	0
W. W. Read	1887–92	2	2	0	0
W. G. Grace	1888–99	13	8	3	2
C. A. Smith	1888–9	1	1	0	0
M. P. Bowden	1888–9	1	1	0	0
A. E. Stoddart	1893–8	8	3	4	1
Sir T. C. O'Brien	1895–6	1	1	0	0
Lord Hawke	1895–9	4	4	0	0
A. C. MacLaren	1897–1909	22	4	11	7
P. F. Warner	1903–6	10	4	6	0
Hon. F. S. Jackson	1905	5	2	0	3
R. E. Foster	1907	3	1	0	2
F. L. Fane	1907–10	5	2	3	0
A. O. Jones	1907–8	2	0	2	0
H. D. G. Leveson-Gower	1909–10	3	1	2	0
J. W. H. T. Douglas	1911–24	18	8	8	2
C. B. Fry	1912	6	4	0	2
Hon. L. H. Tennyson	1921	3	0	1	2
F. T. Mann	1922–3	5	2	1	2
A. E. R. Gilligan	1924–5	9	4	4	1
A. W. Carr	1926–9	6	1	0	5
A. P. F. Chapman	1926–31	17	9	2	6
R. T. Stanyforth	1927–8	4	2	1	1
G. T. S. Stevens	1927–8	1	0	1	0
J. C. White	1928–9	4	1	1	2
Hon. F. S. G. Calthorpe	1929–30	4	1	1	2
A. H. H. Gilligan	1929–30	4	1	0	3
R. E. S. Wyatt	1930–5	16	3	5	8
D. R. Jardine	1931–4	15	9	1	5
C. F. Walters	1934	1	0	1	0
G. O. B. Allen	1936–48	11	4	5	2
R. W. V. Robins	1937	3	1	0	2
W. R. Hammond	1938–47	20	4	3	13
N. W. D. Yardley	1946–50	14	4	7	3
K. Cranston	1947–8	1	0	0	1

	Tenure	Matches	Won	Lost	Drawn
F. G. Mann	1948–9	7	2	0	5
F. R. Brown	1949–51	15	5	6	4
N. D. Howard	1951–2	4	1	0	3
D. B. Carr	1951–2	1	0	1	0
L. Hutton	1952–5	23	11	4	8
D. S. Sheppard	1954	2	1	0	1
P. B. H. May	1955–61	41	20	10	11
M. C. Cowdrey	1959–69	27	8	4	15
E. R. Dexter	1961–4	30	9	7	14
M. J. K. Smith	1963–6	25	5	3	17
D. B. Close	1966–7	7	6	0	1
T. W. Graveney	1968	1	0	0	1
R. Illingworth	1969–73	31	12	5	14
A. R. Lewis	1972–3	8	1	2	5
M. H. Denness	1973–5	19	6	5	8
J. H. Edrich	1974–5	1	0	1	0
A. W. Greig	1975–7	14	3	5	6
J. M. Brearley	1977–81	31	18	4	9
G. Boycott	1977–8	4	1	1	2
I. T. Botham	1980–1	12	0	4	8
K. W. R. Fletcher	1981–2	7	1	1	5
R. G. D. Willis	1982–4	18	7	5	6
D. I. Gower	1982–9	32	5	18	9
M. W. Gatting	1986–8	23	2	5	16
J. E. Emburey	1988	2	0	2	0
C. S. Cowdrey	1988	1	0	1	0
G. A. Gooch	1988–93	34	10	12	12
A. J. Lamb	1989–91	3	0	3	0
A. J. Stewart	1992–2001	15	4	8	3
M. A. Atherton	1993–2001	54	13	21	20
N. Hussain	1999–2003	45	17	15	13
M. A. Butcher	1999	1	0	0	1
M. P. Vaughan	2003–6	33	19	6	8
M. E. Trescothick	2004–5	2	1	1	0
A. Flintoff	2005–6	6	2	2	2
A. Strauss	2006	4	3	0	1

6 ENGLAND'S ONE-DAY INTERNATIONAL RECORDS

HIGHEST TEAM TOTALS FOR ENGLAND

391–4 (50 overs)   England v Bangladesh at Trent Bridge, 2005
363–7 (55 overs)   England v Pakistan at Trent Bridge, 1992
334–4 (60 overs)   England v India at Lord's, 1975
333–9 (60 overs)   England v Sri Lanka at Taunton, 1983
327–4 (50 overs)   England v Pakistan at Lahore, 2005–6
325–5 (50 overs)   England v India at Lord's, 2002
322–6 (60 overs)   England v New Zealand at The Oval, 1983
321–7 (50 overs)   England v Sri Lanka at Headingley, 2006
320–8 (55 overs)   England v Australia at Edgbaston, 1980
307–5 (50 overs)   England v India at The Oval, 2004
306–5 (55 overs)   England v West Indies at The Oval, 1995
306–5 (47.2 overs)   England v Pakistan at Karachi, 2000–1
304–8 (50 overs)   England v South Africa at East London, 2004–5
302–5 (55 overs)   England v Pakistan at The Oval, 1992
302–3 (50 overs)   England v Sri Lanka at Adelaide, 1998–9
301–7 (50 overs)   England v Ireland at Belfast, 2006

LOWEST TEAM TOTALS FOR ENGLAND

86   (32.4 overs)   England v Australia at Old Trafford, 2001
88   (46.1 overs)   England v Sri Lanka at Dambulla, 2003–4
89   (37.2 overs)   England v New Zealand at Wellington, 2001–2
93   (36.2 overs)   England v Australia at Headingley, 1975
94   (31.7 overs)   England v Australia at Melbourne, 1978–9
101   (32.5 overs)   England v New Zealand at Chester-le-Street, 2004
103   (41 overs)   England v South Africa at The Oval, 1999
107   (34.2 overs)   England v Zimbabwe at Cape Town, 1999–2000
110   (31.5 overs)   England v Australia at Melbourne, 1998–9
111   (38 overs)   England v South Africa at Johannesburg, 1999–2000
114   (39 overs)   England v West Indies at Bridgetown, 1985–6
115   (43.4 overs)   England v South Africa at East London, 1995–6
117   (41 overs)   England v Australia at Sydney, 2002–3
118   (30 overs)   England v Zimbabwe at Harare, 1996–7

HIGHEST INDIVIDUAL SCORES

167*   R. A. Smith   v Australia at Edgbaston (Texaco Trophy), 1993

158   D. I. Gower   v New Zealand at Brisbane (World Series Cup), 1982–3

152   A. J. Strauss   v Bangladesh at Trent Bridge (NatWest Series), 2005

142*   C. W. J. Athey   v New Zealand at Old Trafford (Texaco Trophy), 1986

142   G. A. Gooch   v Pakistan at Karachi (2nd ODI), 1987–8

137   D. L. Amiss   v India at Lord's (World Cup), 1975

137   M. E. Trescothick   v Pakistan at Lord's (NatWest Series), 2001

136   G. A. Gooch   v Australia at Lord's (Texaco Trophy), 1989

131   K. W. R. Fletcher   v New Zealand at Trent Bridge (World Cup), 1975

130   D. I. Gower   v Sri Lanka at Taunton (World Cup), 1983

130   M. E. Trescothick   v West Indies at Gros Islet (5th ODI), 2003–4

129*   G. A. Gooch   v West Indies at Port-of-Spain (2nd ODI), 1985–6

129   R. A. Smith   v India at Gwalior (5th ODI), 1992–3

128   R. A. Smith   v New Zealand at Headingley (Texaco Trophy), 1990

127   M. A. Atherton   v West Indies at Lord's (Texaco Trophy), 1995

126*   G. A. Hick   v Sri Lanka at Adelaide (Carlton & United Series), 1998–9

125*   N. V. Knight   v Pakistan at Trent Bridge (Texaco Trophy), 1996

124   W. Larkins   v Australia at Hyderabad (Nehru Cup), 1989–90

123   A. Flintoff   v West Indies at Lord's (NatWest Series), 2004

122   D. I. Gower   v New Zealand at Melbourne (World Series Cup), 1982–3

122   N. V. Knight   v West Indies at Barbados (1st ODI), 1997–8

121   M. E. Trescothick   v India at Calcutta (1st ODI), 2001–2

121   M. E. Trescothick   v Sri Lanka at Headingley (NatWest Series), 2006

119   M. E. Trescothick   v Zimbabwe at Colombo (ICC Champions), 2002–3

118   A. J. Lamb   v Pakistan at Trent Bridge (Prudential Trophy), 1982

118   A. D. Brown   v India at Old Trafford (Texaco Trophy), 1996

117*   C. T. Radley   v New Zealand at Old Trafford (Prudential Trophy), 1978

117*   G. A. Gooch   v Australia at Lord's (Texaco Trophy), 1985

116*   D. Lloyd   v Pakistan at Trent Bridge (Prudential Trophy), 1974

116   A. J. Stewart   v India at Sharjah (Champions Trophy), 1997–8

116   K. P. Pietersen   v South Africa at Centurion (7th ODI), 2004–5

115*   M.W. Gatting   v India at Pune (1st ODI), 1984–5

115   G. A. Gooch   v Australia at Edgbaston (Texaco Trophy), 1985

115   G. A. Gooch   v India at Bombay (World Cup), 1987–8

115   N. Hussain   v India at Lord's (NatWest Series), 2002

114*   D. I. Gower   v Pakistan at The Oval (Prudential Trophy), 1978

114*   M. E. Trescothick   v South Africa at The Oval (NatWest Series), 2003

113*   M. A. Atherton   v Australia at The Oval (Texaco Trophy), 1997

113   N. H. Fairbrother   v West Indies at Lord's (Texaco Trophy), 1991

113   N. V. Knight   v Pakistan at Edgbaston (Texaco Trophy), 1996

113   M. E. Trescothick   v Ireland at Belfast (Only ODI), 2006

112*   G. A. Gooch   v New Zealand at The Oval (Texaco Trophy), 1990

112* P. D. Collingwood v Bangladesh at Trent Bridge (NatWest Series), 2005
111* N. V. Knight   v Australia at Sydney (VB Series), 2002–3
111 C. W. J. Athey   v Australia at Brisbane (World Series Cup), 1986–7
109 D. I. Gower   v New Zealand at Adelaide (World Series Cup), 1982–3
109 G. A. Hick   v Australia at Adelaide (Carlton & United Series), 1998–9
109 M. E. Trescothick v India at Lord's (NatWest Series), 2002

MOST RUNS

A. J. Stewart	4,677	I. T. Botham	2,113
M. E. Trescothick	4,335	M. W. Gatting	2,095
G. A. Gooch	4,290	N. H. Fairbrother	2,092
A. J. Lamb	4,010	A. J. Strauss	1,847
G. A. Hick	3,846	M. A. Atherton	1,791
N. V. Knight	3,637	M. P. Vaughan	1,730
D. I. Gower	3,170	K. P. Pietersen	1,364
A. Flintoff	2,573	B. C. Broad	1,361
R. A. Smith	2,419	V. S. Solanki	1,014
G. P. Thorpe	2,380	G. Boycott	1,082
N. Hussain	2,332	D. W. Randall	1,067
P. D. Collingwood	2,251		

MOST CENTURIES

M. E. Trescothick	12	P. D. Collingwood	2
G. A. Gooch	8	V. S. Solanki	2
D. I. Gower	7	A. J. Strauss	2
G. A. Hick	5	G. Boycott	1
N. V. Knight	5	B. C. Broad	1
D. L. Amiss	4	A. D. Brown	1
A. J. Lamb	4	N. H. Fairbrother	1
R. A. Smith	4	K. W. R. Fletcher	1
A. J. Stewart	4	M. W. Gatting	1
A. Flintoff	3	N. Hussain	1
K. P. Pietersen	3	W. Larkins	1
M. A. Atherton	2	D. Lloyd	1
C. W. J. Athey	2	C. T. Radley	1

HIGHEST PARTNERSHIP FOR EACH WICKET

1st   200   V. S. Solanki & M. E. Trescothick v South Africa at The Oval, 2003
2nd 202   D. I. Gower & G. A. Gooch v Australia at Lord's, 1985
3rd   213   N. H. Fairbrother & G. A. Hick v West Indies at Lord's, 1991

4th   226   A. Flintoff & A. J. Strauss v West Indies at Lord's, 2004
5th   174   A. Flintoff & P. D. Collingwood v India at The Oval, 2004
6th   150   G. O. Jones & M. P. Vaughan v Zimbabwe at Bulawayo, 2004–5
7th   110   C. White & P. D. Collingwood v Sri Lanka at Perth, 2002–3
8th   67   B. C. Hollioake & D. Gough v Pakistan at Headingley, 2001
9th   100   L. E. Plunkett & V. S. Solanki v Pakistan at Lahore, 2005–6
10th   50*   D. Gough & S. J. Harmison v Australia at Chester-le-Street, 2005

HUNDRED ON DEBUT

D. L. Amiss   103   England v Australia at Old Trafford, 1972

CARRYING BAT THROUGH INNINGS (Side all out)

N. V. Knight   125*   England v Pakistan at Trent Bridge, 1996
A. J. Stewart   100*   England v West Indies at Trent Bridge, 2000

BOWLING RECORDS

MOST WICKETS

D. Gough	234	M. A. Ealham	67
I. T. Botham	145	C. C. Lewis	66
P. A. J. DeFreitas	115	C. White	65
A. Flintoff	109	S. J. Harmison	64
R. G. D. Willis	80	A. D. Mullally	63
J. E. Emburey	76	N. A. Foster	59
J. M. Anderson	75	G. C. Small	58
A. R. Caddick	69	A. F. Giles	55

HAT-TRICKS

J. M. Anderson   England v Pakistan at The Oval, 2003
S. J. Harmison   England v India at Trent Bridge, 2004

WICKETKEEPING RECORDS

OVER 100 DISMISSALS IN A CAREER

		ODIs	Caught	Stumped
163	A. J. Stewart	170	148	15

This total excludes catches taken in the field and matches when not wicketkeeper.

SIX DISMISSALS IN AN INNINGS

6 (all caught)   A. J. Stewart   England v Zimbabwe at Old Trafford, 2000

FIELDING RECORDS

MOST CATCHES

G. A. Hick	64	G. P. Thorpe	42
P. D. Collingwood	48	N. Hussain	40
M. E. Trescothick	47	I. T. Botham	36
G. A. Gooch	45	N. H. Fairbrother	33
N. V. Knight	44	A. Flintoff	32
D. I. Gower	44	A. J. Lamb	31

ALL-ROUND RECORDS

50 RUNS AND 5 WICKETS IN A MATCH

G. A. Hick	80 and 5–33	v Zimbabwe at Harare, 1999–2000
R. C. Irani	53 and 5–26	v India at The Oval, 2002
P. D. Collingwood	112* and 6–31	v Bangladesh at Trent Bridge, 2005

1,000 RUNS AND 100 WICKETS

I. T. Botham	2,113 runs and 145 wickets
A. Flintoff	2,573 runs and 109 wickets

MOST ONE-DAY INTERNATIONAL APPEARANCES

A. J. Stewart	170	M. P. Vaughan	74
D. Gough	158	R. A. Smith	71
G. A. Gooch	125	M. A. Ealham	64
M. E. Trescothick	123	R. G. D. Willis	64
A. J. Lamb	122	A. F. Giles	62
G. A. Hick	120	J. E. Emburey	61
I. T. Botham	116	A. J. Strauss	61
D. I. Gower	114	M. A. Atherton	54
P. A. J. DeFreitas	103	A. R. Caddick	54
P. D. Collingwood	100	C. C. Lewis	53
N. V. Knight	100	G. C. Small	53
A. Flintoff	99	V. S. Solanki	51
M. W. Gatting	92	C. White	51
N. Hussain	88	R. D. B. Croft	50
G. P. Thorpe	82	A. D. Mullally	50
N. H. Fairbrother	75	J. M. Anderson	50

7 ENGLAND'S WORLD CUP CAMPAIGNS

1975 WORLD CUP

Sixty-three years after the first attempt to organize a 'World Championship' of cricket, when a tournament hampered by bad weather was organized between England, Australia and South Africa in 1912, the ill-fated experiment was not attempted again until 1975, when, following the success of the domestic one-day competition, the six Test-playing nations (England, Australia, New Zealand, West Indies, India and Pakistan) were joined by East Africa and Sri Lanka in the first World Cup.

ENGLAND v INDIA at Lord's, 7 June 1975

England 334–4 (Amiss 137, Fletcher 68, Old 51*)
India 132–3
England won by 202 runs

England's score of 334–4 from 60 overs was the highest ever made in a major limited-overs match in England and was fashioned from the earliest overs with Dennis Amiss and John Jameson finding gaps in the field with powerful strokes. Amiss reached a superlative century in the 37th over, missing a century before lunch by just two runs, and after an uncertain start Keith Fletcher also found top gear. Chris Old and captain Mike Denness hammered the dispirited Indian side for 89 off the final 10 overs. Even at the halfway stage, the match seemed over and all that remained was entertainment. But the shirt-sleeved crowd was to be denied even that as Sunil Gavaskar batted through India's 60 overs for 36 not out. Gundappa Viswanath tried bravely to raise a decent total, but the funereal performance left India with practically little chance of qualifying for the semi-finals on scoring rate. Their performance defied explanation, as England's bowlers were never put to the test.

ENGLAND v NEW ZEALAND at Trent Bridge, 11 June 1975

England 266–6 (Fletcher 131)
New Zealand 186 (Morrison 55, Greig 4–45)
England won by 80 runs

England, put in to bat, lost both openers at 27 and 28 respectively, but Keith Fletcher and Frank Hayes took control against the New Zealand bowlers, whose length was not immaculate, as well as some brilliant fielding. Hayes went in the 32nd over, but Mike Denness supported Fletcher and, for much of their 16 overs together, led in a stand of 66. Chris Old then played a vital role by striking vigorously in a partnership of 53 in the final 5 overs when every fieldsman was on the boundary. Fletcher was run out for 131 off the last ball of the innings. In reply, John Lever removed New Zealand's best batsman Glenn Turner, this after being called for a wide when the ball bounced over the batsman's head. It soon became heavy going for the Kiwis, who managed only 53 runs in the first 20 overs. With half the innings gone, 184 runs were still needed and, with Derek Underwood and Old bowling extremely tightly, any real hopes New Zealand might have had soon disappeared.

ENGLAND v EAST AFRICA at Edgbaston, 14 June 1975

England 290–5 (Amiss 88, Wood 77, Hayes 52)
East Africa 94 (Snow 4–11, Lever 3–32)
England won by 196 runs

England's match with East Africa was one of the more one-sided of their World Cup campaign. The home side cruised along at almost 5 runs an over, with Dennis Amiss and Barry Wood posting 158 for the first wicket and Frank Hayes stroking 52 runs in 43 minutes with two hefty sixes. East Africa's first 4 wickets fell to John Snow at a personal cost of 5 runs, and only Ramesh Sethi, whose 30 was stretched over 32 overs, resisted for long. The innings extended into the 53rd over, at which point the poorest-equipped of the eight competing teams bowed out of the Cup having handled the abrasive experience bravely.

ENGLAND v AUSTRALIA at Headingley, 18 June 1975

England 93 (Gilmour 6–14, Walker 3–22)
Australia 94–6 (Old 3–29)
Australia won by 4 wickets

On a day when the toss became an all-important one to win, it is a pity that this semi-final should have been relegated to a previously used pitch. Despite England's great fightback, the game was as good as over by the time 20 overs had been bowled. Gary Gilmour, given preference over Jeff Thomson with the new ball, reduced England to 36–6 with the astonishing personal analysis of 6–10. It was an inspirational piece of swing bowling and with the exception of Tony Greig, superbly taken by Rod Marsh behind the wicket, all the early England batsmen were trapped playing back to the swinging ball. Even after Geoff Arnold had taken Alan Turner's wicket, it seemed that Australia were coasting to an easy win, but John Snow then dismissed both Chappell brothers in successive overs during the course of a fine spell of hostile pace bowling. Dramatically, the game was thrown wide open by Chris Old, who dismissed Rick McCosker, Ross Edwards and Marsh, and with Australia on 39–6, 16 wickets had crashed for a paltry 132 runs. Any hopes of a sensational England victory were thwarted by Doug Walters and, of course, Gilmour.

1979 WORLD CUP

Between this and the previous World Cup, the Packer 'circus' had torn cricket asunder, and despite a 'peace' agreement signed shortly before, England and Australia chose not to field their Packer players, whereas the other teams were at full strength.

ENGLAND v AUSTRALIA at Lord's, 9 June 1979

Australia 159–9 (Hilditch 47)
England 160–4 (Gooch 53, Brearley 44)
England won by 6 wickets

The Australians went into this 60-over match hopelessly short of cricket practice but, although batting first, they made a good start, with Rick Darling making a useful 25 and Andrew Hilditch missing out on a half-century by just 3 runs. However, the middle order and tail end had a nightmare game. Not since the 1975 final against the West Indies, when five Australians including both the Chappells ran themselves out, has a side so handicapped itself by its disastrous running between the wickets. Rodney Hogg made early inroads into the England batting, and at 5–2 the home side was on the ropes. Fortunately, Graham Gooch looked in complete control from the start, and, aided by skipper Mike Brearley, he led England to victory by 6 wickets.

ENGLAND v CANADA at Old Trafford, 14 June 1979

Canada 45 (Dennis 21, Old, 4–8, Willis 4–11)
England 46–2
England won by 8 wickets

Even though Canada had put up a resolute performance in their opening match against Pakistan, they were soundly beaten in this game in Manchester. The Canadian batsman had no answer to the pace of Bob Willis and Chris Old, and were bowled out for just 45 runs in 40.3 overs. England went on to win by 8 wickets, and in doing so, were guaranteed a place in the semi-finals as Pakistan had beaten Australia.

ENGLAND v PAKISTAN at Headingley, 16 June 1979

England 165–9 (Gooch 33, Gower 27)
Pakistan 151 (Asif Iqbal 51, Hendrick 4–15)
England won by 14 runs

Even with Pakistan's Sarfraz Nawaz unfit, England struggled after being put into bat against the bowling of Imran Khan and Sikander Bakht, and then lost 3 key wickets to Majid Khan, whose 12 overs cost only 27 runs. In reply, however, Mike Hendrick had a field day, beating the bat time after time, but also finding the edge when it mattered to take 4–15. Asif Iqbal, though, played an excellent innings and took Pakistan from 31–5 to the brink of victory. Geoff Boycott had already bowled well in the win over Australia and again he did an invaluable job. With less than 4 overs remaining, after an absorbingly tight match, Sikander was well caught by Hendrick off Boycott at deep mid-off, and England recorded a 14-run victory.

ENGLAND v NEW ZEALAND at Old Trafford, 20 June 1979

England 221–8 (Gooch 71, Brearley 53, Randall 42*)
New Zealand 212–9 (Wright 69)
England won by 9 runs

In the 1979 semi-final, the home side took the decision to play an extra batsman and rely on Geoff Boycott and Graham Gooch to bowl 12 overs between them. New Zealand's Richard Hadlee bowled well at the start, but England's two most consistent batsman in this tournament, Gooch and Mike Brearley, both hit half-centuries before Derek Randall coming in at number seven hit an invaluable 42 not out. The Nottinghamshire batsman's outstanding fielding – he ran out two New Zealand players – along with Brearley's astuteness in the field, enabled England to scrape home by 9 runs to win a coveted place in the final.

ENGLAND v WEST INDIES at Lord's, 23 June 1979

West Indies 286–9 (Richards 138*, King 86)
England 194 (Brearley 64, Boycott 57, Garner 5–38)
West Indies won by 92 runs

West Indies, the best side in the competition, would end up deserved victors of the second World Cup tournament. With Bob Willis unfit, England again opted to go into the match with four front-line bowlers, leaving Graham Gooch and Geoff Boycott to share responsibility for 12 overs. Despite having had success with the ball in previous rounds, Boycott found the West Indies batsmen more than he could manage. The match-winning partnership came from Collis King and Viv Richards. Coming together at 99–4 with very little batting left, they added 139 runs in 21 overs, despite the fact that England's fielding was the best ever produced by a home side at Lord's. Derek Randall ran out Gordon Greenidge, and Mike Brearley took a superb running catch of a high ball to dismiss Andy Roberts, while Phil Edmonds made one diving save after another. England's target of 286, though demanding, was by no means out of range. At tea after 25 overs, England were 79 without loss, but even with a number of good hitters of a ball in the side – Graham Gooch, David Gower, Ian Botham, Derek Randall and Wayne Larkins – none of them, when the time came, had a chance to shine, though Gooch and Randall made a frantic 48 together. In the 48th and 50th overs, Joel Garner took 5 of England's last 7 wickets, making it a proud day for West Indian cricket.

1983 WORLD CUP

This year saw the elevation of Sri Lanka to Test status and so only one qualification place was available via the ICC Trophy, which went to Zimbabwe. The 1983 World Cup also saw a change of format: the two groups of four stayed the same as the two previous tournaments, but this time the teams faced each other twice each, thus doubling the number of matches played at group stage.

ENGLAND v NEW ZEALAND at The Oval, 9 June 1983

England 322–6 (Lamb 102, Tavare 45, Gatting 43)
New Zealand 216 (Crowe 97, Willis 2–9)
England won by 106 runs

England's first opponents of the tournament never threatened to reproduce the form that had flattened England the previous winter. Man of the Match Allan Lamb was England's chief destroyer with a superb century, ably assisted by Chris Tavare, Mike Gatting and Ian Botham. New Zealand bowler Martin Snedden returned unenviable figures of 2–105 in his 12 overs, the highest number of runs conceded by a bowler in the World Cup. The Kiwis struggled from the start of their reply against the tight bowling of Bob Willis and Graham Dilley, and their only glimmer of hope came from Martin Crowe, the younger of the Crowe brothers, who was unluckily run out three runs short of his century.

ENGLAND v SRI LANKA at Taunton, 11 June 1983

England 333–9 (Gower 130, Lamb 53)
Sri Lanka 286 (de Alwis 58*, Mendis 56, Marks 5–39, Dilley 4–45)
England won by 47 runs

The West Country crowd, some of whom queued from 2.15 a.m. until the gates opened at 8.15 a.m., were treated to a superb performance by David Gower. He hit five sixes, one of which completed his century, while Allan Lamb shared the action with two more. The only disappointment for the Taunton spectators was the early run-out of local hero Ian Botham, after failing to make a single run. An impressive England total (one short of their highest World Cup score) did not frighten the Sri Lankans, who batted with determination and skill right down the order. Somerset's pride was restored with Vic Marks's effective off-spinners claiming 5–39, but Gower was naturally named Man of the Match, his superb innings having set up the England victory.

ENGLAND v PAKISTAN at Lord's, 13 June 1983

Pakistan 193–8 (Zaheer Abbas 83*, Willis 2–24)
England 199–2 (Fowler 78*, Lamb 48*, Gower 48)
England won by 8 wickets

The match that most people had expected would be the most crucial in Group A never quite took off. Pakistan's batting was unconvincing and their running between the wickets was often fraught with danger. Only Gloucestershire's Zaheer Abbas calmed the proceedings with an unbeaten 83 not out, but why he batted at number five instead of number three was a mystery. Bob Willis was again the pick of the England bowlers, taking the first two wickets in a fiery spell at the start of the Pakistan innings. In reply, Graeme Fowler had a steady start, but gained confidence throughout the match and remained unbeaten on 78, while Allan Lamb and David Gower again provided the entertainment.

ENGLAND v NEW ZEALAND at Edgbaston, 15 June 1983

England 234 (Gower 92*, Fowler 69, Hadlee 3–32)
New Zealand 238–8 (Coney 66*, Howarth 60, Willis 4–42)
New Zealand won by 2 wickets

Memories of the previous winter's tour came flooding back as England let a winning position slip to a penultimate-ball defeat. Graeme Fowler again batted well at the head of the England innings, but it was David Gower who once more looked the best of the English batsmen. New Zealand's Jeremy Coney won the Man-of-the-Match award by virtue of a delightfully controlled innings after New Zealand had found themselves 4 wickets down for only 75 runs. Bob Willis bowled his heart out to take 4–42, but he was not backed up by the home side's other quick bowlers, and England had to endure their first loss of the tournament.

ENGLAND v PAKISTAN at Old Trafford, 18 June 1983

Pakistan 232–8 (Javed Miandad 67, Ijaz Faqih 42*)
England 233–3 (Fowler 69, Tavare 58)
England won by 7 wickets

Fresh from a dressing down from the Chairman of Selectors after their defeat by New Zealand, England played an efficient game of cricket to dispose of Pakistan for the second time in the group matches. Javed Miandad and Ijaz Faqih provided the backbone of the Pakistani score, the highlight of which was the devastating run-out of Miandad by Ian Botham fielding at backward cover. There is no doubt that Miandad could have turned the game, but, as it was, England, with an opening partnership of 115 between Man of the Match Graeme Fowler and Chris Tavare, never looked in danger as Lamb accelerated to an unbeaten 38 runs to take the team to victory and guarantee them a place in the semi-final.

ENGLAND v SRI LANKA at Headingley, 20 June 1983

Sri Lanka 136 (Botham 2–12, Marks 2–18, Willis 1–9)
England 137–1 (Fowler 81*)
England won by 9 wickets

An easy 9-wicket victory provided England with a gentle warm-up for their semi-final match against India. Norman Cowans made his first World Cup appearance, replacing the injured Graham Dilley. Bob Willis conceded just one run per over as well as removing the dangerous Brendon Kuruppu, while Ian Botham at last bowled enthusiastically and Vic Marks once again had a tidy game. In reply to Sri Lanka's modest total, Graeme Fowler and David Gower ensured that the match was over by tea. For his tremendous economy of bowling (9–4–9–1), Bob Willis was named Man of the Match.

ENGLAND v INDIA at Old Trafford, 22 June 1983

England 213 (Fowler 33, Tavare 32, Kapil Dev 3–35)
India 217–4 (Yashpal Sharma 61, Patil 51*, Amarnath 46)
India won by 6 wickets

The turning point of this Old Trafford semi-final came as early as the 17th over, when Chris Tavare pushed a defensive bat at Roger Binny – a rare enough occurrence in itself with England galloping along at 4 an over – and edged it to Syed Kirmani. Incredibly, it marked the last moment of England's apparent dominance in the game. With the ball keeping low, Allan Lamb and Mike Gatting were badly inconvenienced, unable to attack off the back foot with any safety. Even so, at 107–2, a score of 250 was still possible, but wickets began to tumble quickly and at 160–6 it was left to Graham Dilley and Paul Allott to take the score into the 200s.

For the first time in seven World Cup matches, Willis and Dilley bowled to only one close fielder, compared with the usual two slips and a gulley from their group matches. The five main bowlers did a good enough containing job, but a third-wicket partnership of 96 between Mohinder Amarnath and Yashpal Sharma, aided by a fine half-century by Sandeep Patil, saw India home by 6 wickets with 5 overs remaining. India then went on to beat West Indies by 43 runs in the final.

1987 WORLD CUP

In 1987, the Cricket World Cup was hosted outside England for the first time, India and Pakistan the chosen hosts. The format of the tournament remained much the same, the only difference being the reduction of overs from 60 to the now standard 50 per side.

ENGLAND v WEST INDIES at Gujranwala, 9 October 1987

West Indies 243–7 (Richardson 53, Logie 49, Dujon 46, Foster 3–53)
England 246–8 (Lamb 67*, Gooch 47, Hooper 3–42)
England won by 2 wickets

England launched their 1987 World Cup campaign with an extraordinary and fortunate victory as Allan Lamb produced an incredible variety of boundary strokes in the final overs to transform a match that seemed to have slipped irretrievably away from his team. After Mike Gatting had won the toss and put the West Indies in to bat, Phil DeFreitas and Neil Foster had quickly taken the initiative. However, Richie Richardson played some brilliant shots as England's fielding was exposed in the intense heat. Neil Foster, though expensive, removed Richardson, Viv Richards and Gus Logie when they were going well, and helped to slow the West Indian innings down.

In reply, Graham Gooch anchored the England innings after the early losses of Chris Broad and Tim Robinson, but it was Lamb, with 89 needed from the last 10 overs, who was ably supported lower down the order by John Emburey and DeFreitas, who helped to see England safely home.

ENGLAND v PAKISTAN at Rawalpindi, 13 October 1987

Pakistan 239–7 (Salim Malik 65, Ijaz Ahmed 59, DeFreitas 3–42)
England 221 (Gatting 43, Abdul Qadir 4–31)
Pakistan won by 18 runs

A match that had been postponed until its reserve day because of a saturated outfield produced a win for Pakistan, despite Imran Khan suffering from a stomach ailment that had prevented him from bowling. Mike Gatting again preferred to field first, and though Phil DeFreitas and Neil Foster initially bowled a tight line, Salim Malik rode his luck to make 65 in an innings marked by hard hit pulls and drives, while Ijaz Ahmed, a brilliant natural player, made a handsome 59 off as many balls. England made too steady a start in their innings, and though Gatting batted well, Javed Miandad had cleverly held one over of Abdul Qadir in reserve. The bowler had already played brilliantly to dismiss Graham Gooch and Tim Robinson, but with England 186–4 in the 43rd over, Qadir returned to remove Allan Lamb and Paul Downton in his final over. Wasim Akram and Salim Jaffer bowled well in their second spells and England lost their last 6 wickets for only 15 runs.

ENGLAND v SRI LANKA at Peshawar, 17 October 1987

England 296–4 (Gooch 84, Lamb 76, Gatting 58)
Sri Lanka 158–8 (Ranatunga 40, Emburey 2–26)
England won by 108 runs (rain rule)

England gained their second win of the tournament by virtue of an impressive scoring rate during a rain-affected match. Mike Gatting won the toss and decided to bat. England's batsmen then paced their effort to perfection – Graham Gooch top-scored with 84 from 100 balls as he and Chris Broad laid the foundation for a large score with an opening stand of 89. Then each successive partnership raised the tempo. Gatting with 58 from 63 balls, Man of the Match Allan Lamb scoring 76 from 58 balls, and John Emburey with 30 not out from 19 balls were in such command that 101 runs were plundered from the last 10 overs. Phil DeFreitas and Gladstone Small bowled accurate opening spells to lift Sri Lanka's required run-rate to more than 6 an over. Then spinners Emburey and Eddie Hemmings were able to exert a stranglehold over the Sri Lankan batsmen by bowling their 20 overs for 57 runs, and taking 2 wickets each.

ENGLAND v PAKISTAN at Karachi, 20 October 1987

England 244–9 (Athey 86, Gatting 60, Imran Khan 4–37)
Pakistan 247–3 (Ramiz Raja 113, Salim Malik 88)
Pakistan won by 7 wickets

Pakistan strode confidently into the semi-finals on home ground with a 7-wicket win. Imran Khan and Wasim Akram bowled some hostile overs early on and both England openers Graham Gooch and Tim Robinson went cheaply. However, Bill Athey and Mike Gatting then developed a partnership that began modestly, and blossomed into a stand of 135 before both batsmen were dismissed with the score on 187–4. The scene was set for an all too traditional England collapse, but with Neil Foster hitting an unbeaten 20, the last 7 wickets managed to add 57 runs. In Pakistan's innings, Ramiz Raja and Mansoor Akhtar gave the home side an admirable start before Salim Malik joined Raja following Akhtar's run-out. Both batsmen were dropped a number of times, but the match was already won bar the shouting when the second-wicket pair were at last given out on 243–3.

ENGLAND v WEST INDIES at Jaipur, 26 October 1987

England 269–5 (Gooch 92, Lamb 40, Patterson 3–56)
West Indies 235 (Richardson 93, Richards 51, DeFreitas 3–28)
England won by 34 runs

England's sixth win in seven matches against the West Indies more or less assured them of a semi-final place. Graham Gooch was given the Man-of-the-Match award for a well-paced innings. In turn, Bill Athey, Mike Gatting, Allan Lamb and Phil DeFreitas gave Gooch valuable assistance before John Emburey and DeFreitas milked runs from the last few overs. At 147–2, Richie Richardson and Viv Richards had got West Indies into such a strong position that they only needed to place the ball in the gaps to win. Richards had hit Emburey for one enormous six, which must have carried nearly 150 yards, and twice swept Eddie Hemmings over the square-leg boundary, but was ultimately outwitted by Hemmings, who saw him move and tossed the ball up to the off-stump. Three good catches by wicketkeeper Paul Downton combined with steady bowling to complete England's victory.

ENGLAND v SRI LANKA at Pune, 30 October 1987

Sri Lanka 218–7 (Dias 80, Hemmings 3–57)
England 219–2 (Gooch 61, Robinson 55, Gatting 46*, Athey 40*)
England won by 8 wickets

England made sure of securing a place in the semi-final when Sri Lanka failed to take advantage of batting first against a disciplined England bowling attack. Roy Dias showed the complete range of strokes of which he was capable in a fine innings of 80, including the shot of the tournament when he hit Gladstone Small for six over mid-wicket. In reply, Graham Gooch, despite dislocating a finger when missing a sharp slip catch in the first over, and Tim Robinson, who was in his element, added 123 for the first wicket with marvellous assurance, and Bill Athey and Mike Gatting finished the job with 8 overs and 4 balls to spare.

ENGLAND v INDIA at Bombay, 5 November 1987

England 254–6 (Gooch 115, Gatting 56, Maninder Singh 3–54)
India 219 (Azharuddin 64, Hemmings 4–52)
England won by 35 runs

England reached their second World Cup Final thanks mainly to Graham Gooch's majestic innings of 115 off 136 balls on a wicket everyone knew would take spin. Once Tim Robinson and Bill Athey had perished in vain attempts to find their timing, Mike Gatting took his cue from Gooch and the two added 117 in 19 overs. Although Maninder Singh claimed both their wickets, his 10 overs had nevertheless cost 5 runs each on a pitch prepared to his liking. The faithful Allan Lamb made the most of the final over and when Phil DeFreitas uprooted Sunil Gavaskar's off-stump in the third over, England were on top. Captain Gatting had an unexpected problem when Eddie Hemmings's first 3 overs went for 26 runs, but the canny old pro came back to remove Mohammad Azharuddin, Kapil Dev and Ravi Shastri in a devastating spell that saw him take 4–21 in 34 balls.

ENGLAND v AUSTRALIA at Calcutta, 8 November 1987

Australia 253–5 (Boon 75, Veletta 45*)
England 246–8 (Athey 58, Lamb 45, Gatting 41)
Australia won by 7 runs

The fourth World Cup Final proved to be a fantastic occasion. Australia's victory was the nineteenth out of twenty-seven matches in the tournament to have been won by the side batting first. Having won the toss, Australia capitalized by rattling to 52 in the first 10 overs as both Gladstone Small and Phil DeFreitas bowled too short, often down the leg side. England were rescued by Neil Foster, who produced a near-perfect first spell in which he bowled Geoff Marsh with a delivery that held its off-stump line, and conceded just 16 runs in 8 overs, thus preventing Dean Jones from getting into his stride. Eddie Hemmings and John Emburey, and to a lesser extent Graham Gooch (who had been pressed into service because of Small's problems), kept Australia to a total of 253 despite an inventive innings of 45 not out by Mike Veletta.

When England went out to face Australia's bowling line-up, Tim Robinson was out leg-before, playing back to Craig McDermott's third ball, but Gooch and Bill Athey played without great difficulty until Simon O'Donnell came on for a fine spell of medium-paced bowling. Athey was run out for 58, which, with England on 170–4, put pressure on incoming batsman Mike Gatting, who played some fine shots before getting a top edge as he tried to reverse-sweep Allan Border's first ball. With Allan Lamb quickly into his stride, and dangerous hitters like Emburey and DeFreitas to come, all was not yet lost for England. They needed 8 an over off the last 10, and though DeFreitas brought the crowd to its feet by hitting McDermott for four, six, four off successive balls in the 48th over, Steve Waugh bowled straight and to a full length, and Australia became the holders of the World Cup just less than a year after losing the Ashes at home.

1992 WORLD CUP

The 1992 World Cup marked a turning point in the history of the competition. The first to be held in the southern hemisphere, hosted jointly by New Zealand and Australia, the tournament was greatly expanded. South Africa had rejoined the Test ranks, Zimbabwe had been given Test status, and thus the contest consisted of the same eight teams that had taken part in the 1987 tournament plus South Africa. Day/night cricket also made its debut, along with the use of the white ball and the wearing of coloured clothing.

ENGLAND v INDIA at Perth, 22 February 1992

England 236–9 (Smith 91, Gooch 51)
India 227 (Shastri 57, Reeve 3–38)
England won by 9 runs

England began their campaign with a victory over India that was rather more comfortable than the scorecard might suggest. Gooch scored a half-century, but ended his innings with a runner, having suffered severe cramp. Robin Smith pulled and cut savagely until he was brilliantly caught by Mohammad Azharuddin in the gully for 91, the first of 6 England wickets that fell for 27 runs, during a period in which only Neil Fairbrother shone briefly. After a promising start, India lost Kris Srikkanth and Azharuddin in quick succession before Ravi Shastri, who had held up one end, was dropped and run out off the same ball by Phil DeFreitas. There then followed a comedy of errors in which Subroto Banerjee was involved in three run-outs in a gallant attempt to steal victory in the last over.

ENGLAND v WEST INDIES at Melbourne, 27 February 1992

West Indies 157 (Arthurton 54, Lewis 3–30, DeFreitas 3–34)
England 160–4 (Gooch 65, Hick 54)
England won by 6 wickets

England's bowlers exploited to the full a seaming pitch and the mischievous white balls to dismiss West Indies for a meagre 157 and lay the foundations for a convincing victory. Chris Lewis found the edge to dismiss both Brian Lara and Richie Richardson in the opening overs, though Keith Arthurton, whose brave 54 contained two sixes, was easily the best of the West Indian batsmen. Graham Gooch was in fine form and straight-drove both Curtly Ambrose and Malcolm Marshall to the boundary in a fine innings of 65. When he was stumped, giving Carl Hooper the charge, Graeme Hick assumed control and took England to 156 before offering Roger Harper a return catch that the giant screen suggested bounced first.

ENGLAND v PAKISTAN at Adelaide, 1 March 1992

Pakistan 74 (Pringle 3–8, Botham 2–12)
England 24–1
No Result

Having bowled out Pakistan for 74 on a drying pitch that gave the seamers no end of assistance, England were confounded by wretched weather. Seven of the eleven batsmen dismissed in this match were caught in the cordon between wicketkeeper and gully, which was a clear indication of the state of the pitch. Derek Pringle took a miserly 3–8 in 8.2 overs, while Ian Botham bowled his 10 overs for 12 runs. Dermot Reeve bowled a highly amusing over in which Aaqib Javed played and missed at every ball. England's reply was twice interrupted before a deluge brought the contest to a premature close.

ENGLAND v AUSTRALIA at Sydney, 5 March 1992

Australia 171 (Moody 51, Botham 4–31)
England 173–2 (Gooch 58, Botham 53)
England won by 8 wickets

Ian Botham gave one of his most devastating performances as England strolled to their easiest win so far in the tournament. He took 4 wickets in 7 balls and then shared in an opening partnership of 107 with Graham Gooch, dominating the bowling from the outset. Tom Moody and Dean Jones had laid steady foundations, and Steve Waugh and Allan Border were looking to launch their assault when Botham produced his remarkable 7-ball spell. In no mood to linger when England started their reply, Botham began his aggressive demolition of the Australian bowling. He fell eventually to a diving leg-side catch by Ian Healy, and by the time Gooch was bowled by Waugh for a more tempered half-century, the game was all but won.

ENGLAND v SRI LANKA at Ballarat, 9 March 1992

England 280–6 (Fairbrother 63, Stewart 59, Botham 47, Hick 41)
Sri Lanka 174 (Lewis 4–30, Reeve 2–14)
England won by 106 runs

With 10 overs remaining, the England innings erupted with Lancashire's Neil Fairbrother and Surrey's Alec Stewart adding 80 at about a run a ball. When Fairbrother was caught at deep mid-wicket for 63, Chris Lewis responded in style, plundering 20 runs from the 6 balls he faced – the final 5 overs yielding 73 runs. When Sri Lanka came in to bat they made a good start thanks mostly to the England attack, which for once strayed from its usual line and length. However, under the pressure of having to sustain a run-rate of nearly 6 an over, the Sri Lankans eventually succumbed, with Chris Lewis the pick of the England bowlers. England's massive victory was marred only by Graham Gooch's forced departure from the field due to a hamstring injury.

ENGLAND v SOUTH AFRICA at Melbourne, 12 March 1992

South Africa 236–4 (Wessels 85, Hudson 79)
England 226–7 (Stewart 77, Fairbrother 75*, Snell 3–42)
England won by 3 wickets (rain rule)

Alec Stewart, Neil Fairbrother and Chris Lewis overcame the treacherous rain rule to ensure England's place in the semi-final with victory off the penultimate ball of a thrilling match. Blighted by injury to three of their bowlers, and with Small's 2 overs yielding 14 runs, England struggled to contain Kepler Wessels and Andrew Hudson, who shared an opening stand of 151. With wickets in hand, however, South Africa failed to make full use of their last 15 overs. In reply, England raced to 62 without loss, only to be thwarted by rain and a recalculation of their target. Requiring a further 164 in 29 overs, Ian Botham, Robin Smith and Graeme Hick were all out within the space of 7 balls, victims of their own impatience. Stewart and Fairbrother batted purposefully in their match-winning partnership of 66 in 13 overs, and it was Lewis with 33 runs from 22 balls who took England to the brink of victory.

ENGLAND v NEW ZEALAND at Wellington, 15 March 1992

England 200–8 (Hick 56, Stewart 41)
New Zealand 201–3 (Jones 78, Crowe 73*)
New Zealand won by 7 wickets

England were let down in the second half of their innings after Alec Stewart and Graeme Hick had made a comfortable start. Following their dismissal, Robin Smith, Allan Lamb, Derek Pringle and Phil DeFreitas all holed out in the deep with Dermot Reeve valiantly holding up one end. In reply, Mark Greatbatch set off at a blistering pace, lofting the ball over the fielders confined to the 30-yard ring and took New Zealand past 50 in the 10th over before pulling a Botham ball straight to DeFreitas at square-leg. Andrew Jones and Martin Crowe then put on 108 in 23 overs, a stand that ended only when

Hick threw down the stumps to run out Jones, but Crowe secured victory with 9.1 overs to spare.

ENGLAND v ZIMBABWE at Albury, 18 March 1992

Zimbabwe 134 (Botham 3–23, Illingworth 3–33)
England 125 (Brandes 4–21)
Zimbabwe won by 9 runs

Having been bowled out for 134, Zimbabwe could not have held much hope of avoiding another trouncing. But on an uneven seaming pitch on which only Dave Houghton and Iain Butchart had been able to cope, Eddo Brandes took Graham Gooch's wicket with the first ball of the innings. Ian Botham was then adjudged to have edged a ball, though he clearly thought otherwise, and when Graeme Hick became Brandes's fourth victim England were 43–5. Neil Fairbrother and Alec Stewart added 52 in 24 overs in a dour but valuable partnership, but after their departure England, with one wicket left, were left with 1 over to make 10 runs for victory. Gladstone Small chipped the first ball to mid-wicket and the unthinkable had happened.

ENGLAND v SOUTH AFRICA at Sydney, 22 March 1992

England 252–6 (Hick 83)
South Africa 232–6 (Hudson 46, Rhodes 43)
England won by 19 runs (rain rule)

With South Africa requiring 22 runs from 13 balls to defeat England in this semi-final, a heavy downpour interrupted play for ten minutes. When the match resumed after numerous consultations, the target was revised to 21 runs from one ball! A disgusted Brian McMillan patted a single and set off for the pavilion in understandably high dudgeon, while the crowd hooted their derision at this farcical ruling. Kepler Wessels later accepted that he had taken a calculated risk when he opted to field first since the prospect of rain was obvious. At the start of the England innings, the ball moved around, but then Allan Donald and Richard Snell became so wayward that after 15 overs England were 84–2. The batting side was then able to consolidate throughout the middle overs without taking undue risks and they finished with a total of 252 from 45 overs. The main contributor was Graeme Hick, who made 83 from 90 balls. He was well supported by Dermot Reeve, who took 17 off Allan Donald's last over. When South Africa came in to bat Andrew Hudson gave his side the start they needed and he was followed by a mixture of big hitting and adventurous running by Jonty Rhodes and Adrian Kuiper. South Africa were always slightly behind the run rate and though the chances are that England would just about have scraped home, the truth is that we will never know for sure.

ENGLAND v PAKISTAN at Melbourne, 25 March 1992

Pakistan 249–6 (Imran Khan 72, Javed Miandad 58, Inzamam-ul-Haq 42,
   Pringle 3–22)
England 227 (Fairbrother 62, Mushtaq Ahmed 3–41)
Pakistan won by 22 runs

In this fifth World Cup Final, Pakistan won the toss and opted to bat under a mercifully cloudless sky. Yet within 10 overs, Imran Khan and Javed Miandad, veterans of five World Cups, were at the wicket after Derek Pringle had removed both Aamer Sohail and Ramiz Raja. After 34 overs, Pakistan had stuttered to 113–2, but in the next 16 they plundered 136 vital runs. Once the two experienced players had gone after adding 139 together, Inzamam-ul-Haq and Wasim Akram ran amok. They clubbed the England bowling to all parts of the ground as Pakistan reached a total of 249–6.

England's response began disastrously. Ian Botham was caught behind off Akram. He was furious to miss out on such an occasion and his temper was not improved when Sohail gave him some hints regarding the swiftest route back to the pavilion. Imran introduced Mushtaq Ahmed into the attack and he accounted for both Graeme Hick and Graham Gooch as England slumped to 69–4. Allan Lamb and Neil Fairbrother then added 72 before Akram was recalled into the attack, and he dismissed Lamb followed by Chris Lewis in successive balls. England were left needing 108 from 15 overs with just Fairbrother and the tail left. The game ended in a similar way to the 1987 Final, with Phil DeFreitas flailing away valiantly but to no avail. For England, this was a huge disappointment but no disgrace. Gooch, having experienced his third defeat in a World Cup Final, refused to make any excuses and praised the Pakistani performance as well as the commitment of his own team during the tournament.

1996 WORLD CUP

The 1996 tournament was expanded to allow participation from non-Test-playing teams. The preliminary rounds were in two groups of six, with eight teams advancing to the quarter-finals. The tournament returned to Asia, with games spread over three countries, India, Pakistan and Sri Lanka. The pre-tournament lead-up was overshadowed by security concerns, particularly on the part of the Australian side. Sri Lanka was undergoing internal political turmoil with threats of disruption by the Tamil rebel groups, and after a massive bomb blast in Colombo in late January, the Australian team decided that they would forfeit their preliminary-round matches in Sri Lanka rather than travel there. A week later the West Indies board followed suit.

ENGLAND v NEW ZEALAND at Ahmedabad, 14 February 1996

New Zealand 239–6 (Astle 101)
England 228–9 (Hick 85, Nash 3–26)
New Zealand won by 11 runs

The sixth World Cup got off to a flying start as underdogs New Zealand beat England in the first match of the tournament. After winning the toss and putting New Zealand in, Mike Atherton saw his side drop four straightforward catches. The first was the one that mattered most when Graham Thorpe at slip put down Nathan Astle. After this escape, Astle went at the England bowlers with relish, reaching his 50 off 65 balls, and by the 20th over, New Zealand were 90–1. Astle then settled into the anchor role as Chris Cairns thumped 36 from 30 balls. The England bowlers stuck at it and were rewarded with the wickets of Astle and Cairns either side of the 200 mark. Hick, who had been unable to complete his bowling because of a hamstring problem, emerged with a runner when England came out to bat, and he and Alec Stewart set about the New Zealand bowling. Not even the loss of Stewart and then Thorpe could stop Hick until he was run out after Neil Fairbrother and Atherton (who was Hick's runner) hesitated long enough for Roger Twose to throw down the stumps. England then hit out and perished.

ENGLAND v UNITED ARAB EMIRATES at Peshawar, 18 February 1996

United Arab Emirates 136 (Smith 3–29)
England 140–2 (Thorpe 44*)
England won by 8 wickets

In a one-sided encounter, England polished off the opposition professionally, hardly needing to break into a gallop. The crowd, small but vocal, was almost more absorbing than the game. One spectator had brought his cockerel, which sat placidly on his lap, and a contortionist hopped up and down on the terraces, his feet wrapped about his chin. The Emirates chose to bat first and made 136 off 48.3 overs with Mazhar Hussain topscoring with 33. For England Neil Smith took 3 UAE wickets off 8 balls and finished with 3–29. Then he was used as Alec Stewart's opening partner and hit four boundaries in his 27 off 31 balls before twice vomiting and being forced to leave the pitch unwell. All England's batsmen reached double figures with Graham Thorpe and Neil Fairbrother at the crease when the winning runs were made.

ENGLAND v HOLLAND at Peshawar, 22 February 1996

England 279–4 (Hick 104*, Thorpe 89)
Holland 230–6 (van Noortwijk 64, Zuiderent 54, de Leede 41)
England won by 49 runs

When faced with an opposition of Dutch part-timers, England did a professional job of overcoming their competitors. Graeme Hick's second one-day international hundred came on a flat, low pitch that suited him well. Yet in his 143-run partnership with Graham Thorpe, he was uncharacteristically outscored, collecting only 53. Thorpe's timing was excellent and many of his runs came from finely angled dabs behind the stumps. His 89 took 82 deliveries before he tried to whip Roland Lefebvre through the on-side. Hick, more static, gave two half-chances in his unbeaten 104, which took 133 balls and included two sixes and six boundaries. As far as the England bowling attack was concerned, Dominic Cork made the early breakthrough, trapping the dangerous veteran Noel Clarke, leg before wicket, before losing his line and later his rhythm, bowling both wides and no-balls. Phil DeFreitas was the pick of the England bowlers, despite a fifth-wicket partnership of 114 in 25 overs between van Noortwijk and Zuiderent, an eighteen-year-old schoolboy. Both made half-centuries, but Holland fell short – the small margin of defeat being almost a moral victory.

ENGLAND v SOUTH AFRICA at Rawalpindi, 25 February 1996

South Africa 230 (Martin 3–33)
England 152 (Thorpe 46, Pollock 2–16)
South Africa won by 78 runs

After Gary Kirsten and his opening partner Steve Palframan had put on 56 in the first 13 overs of South Africa's innings, Peter Martin dismissed Palframan and a good underarm throw by Alec Stewart accounted for Kirsten. South Africa's middle-order batsmen tried to take control, but succumbed to tight bowling and fielding. Warwickshire's Neil Smith remained at the top of the England batting order to plunder some early-over runs, but the ploy failed despite the absence of Allan Donald with an upset stomach. Following the early dismissal of Graeme Hick, Graham Thorpe hit the first boundary in 19 overs before falling to Pat Symcox. The fast bowlers showed some spirit with Phil DeFreitas in his hundredth international, hitting Symcox over mid-wicket for the game's only six. He put on 42, England's highest stand, with Dominic Cork, but by then it was a lost cause with more than 10 runs an over needed three-quarters of the way through the innings.

ENGLAND v PAKISTAN at Karachi, 3 March 1996

England 249–9 (R. Smith 75, Atherton 66, Thorpe 52*)
Pakistan 250–3 (Saeed Anwar 71, Ijaz Ahmed 70, Inzamam-ul-Haq 53*,
   Aamer Sohail 42)
Pakistan won by 7 wickets

At 134–0, halfway through their allotted overs, England had been well positioned to make a score close on 300, but they fell away against the might of

Aamer Sohail and Salim Malik. As soon as Robin Smith, who had batted with a runner for the last 20 runs of his partnership due to suffering from cramp, was given out to Malik, 9 wickets fell for 102 runs. When Pakistan batted, Sohail flashed the ball through the off-side and his cultured left-handed partner Saeed Anwar introduced himself to England with a fine 71, after hitting eight hundreds against other nations. Richard Illingworth and Dermot Reeve managed to slow the over rate sufficiently to keep everyone guessing as to the result, but two expensive overs by Graeme Hick broke that spell. Between the dismissals of Anwar and Ijaz Ahmed, Pakistan added 75. There was soon no doubt as to who would be the victors of this hard-fought match.

ENGLAND v SRI LANKA at Faisalabad, 9 March 1996

England 235–8 (DeFreitas 67)
Sri Lanka 236–5 (Jayasuriya 82, Gurusinha 45)
Sri Lanka won by 5 wickets

England were defeated in the quarter-finals not only by Sri Lanka, but also by an impressive plan of attack beyond their imagination. England had scored 31 runs before they lost their first wicket, and then a couple of poor decisions went against them. Thus it was left to England's middle and lower order to produce the goods. Phil DeFreitas posted his maiden 50 in 101 one-day internationals and went on to reach 67 off 64 balls with two sixes. Apart from DeFreitas, though, nobody else gained any momentum until Darren Gough scored a run a ball and Dermot Reeve almost managed the same. England hit 18 fours in their total of 235–8, but Sri Lanka's opening batsman Jayasuriya hit 13 fours and three sixes from only 44 balls. He also struck four consecutive fours off spinner Richard Illingworth, who opened the bowling as a novelty. The first 6 overs from the Pavilion end – shared by Illingworth, Gough and DeFreitas – cost a total of 76 runs. The Sri Lankan 100 came up after just 11.3 overs. If Jayasuriya hadn't been stumped down the leg-side he would have made the fastest century in all one-day internationals. He was well supported by Gurusinha and Aravinda de Silva, but the Sri Lankans could afford to take their foot off the throttle, using up 14 overs in knocking off the last 42 runs for victory without any further mishaps.

1999 WORLD CUP

In 1999, the Cricket World Cup came back to England. Once again there were twelve participating teams placed in two groups. The nine Test-playing nations were joined by Bangladesh, Kenya and Scotland. The top three in each group qualified for the Super Six stage, which was played on a league basis, and the top four then made it to the knockout semi-finals.

ENGLAND v SRI LANKA at Lord's, 14 May 1999

Sri Lanka 204 (Kaluwitharana 57, Mullally 4–37)
England 207–2 (Stewart 88, Hick 73*)
England won by 8 wickets

During the early stages of their innings, the Sri Lankan batsmen played and missed at both Darren Gough and Ian Austin, but managed to survive. It took Alan Mullally to make the first breakthrough, and 3 more wickets soon followed. Sri Lanka showed their mettle in recovering, with Romesh Kaluwitharana hitting a fine half-century before Nasser Hussain took a sensational catch to end his steady partnership with Arjuna Ranatunga. When England batted, Alec Stewart wasn't so much back in form as playing from memory and he scored a fine 88. Graeme Hick, never under pressure, found the gaps immediately and saw off Muttiah Muralitharan, who was Sri Lanka's most dangerous bowler even though the pitch offered him nothing.

ENGLAND v KENYA at Canterbury, 18 May 1999

Kenya 203 (Tikolo 71, Shah 46, Gough 4–34)
England 204–1 (Hussain 88*, Hick 61*)
England won by 9 wickets

England went one better than the result achieved in their opening match by losing only 1 wicket, that of Alec Stewart, as they eased to a rain-delayed victory over Kenya. After losing an early wicket, Ravi Shah and Steve Tikolo put on 100 for the second wicket before Darren Gough was recalled into the attack. The Yorkshire paceman ripped the heart out of the middle order with only Thomas Odoyo getting to grips with his bowling. In fact, Odoyo struck Alan Mullally for a splendid six over square leg as he went on to make 34. Odoyo was also the only Kenyan to take a wicket, knocking back Stewart's off-stump after he and Nasser Hussain had put on 45 for England's first wicket. Then the rain fell again, but at 5.56 p.m. Kenyan skipper Asif Karim agreed to return to the field even though it was still drizzling and England had faced only 20 overs. A no-result was then a possibility, but Hussain and Graeme Hick saw England home.

ENGLAND v SOUTH AFRICA at The Oval, 22 May 1999

South Africa 225–7 (Gibbs 60, Klusener 48*, Kirsten 45)
England 103 (Donald 4–17)
South Africa won by 122 runs

On a cloudy morning at The Oval, Gary Kirsten and Herschelle Gibbs came good, taking a particular fancy to Angus Fraser and Robert Croft, the latter bowling out of the match and the tournament after his 2 overs (including a massive six from Gibbs) had cost 13. It was therefore left to Alan Mullally and Mark Ealham to frustrate the batsmen and change the course of the innings after Graeme Hick had hung on to Gibbs's lofted sweep. Kirsten soon followed and when Mullally castled Jacques Kallis, South Africa had lost 3 wickets for just 1 run. Darren Gough also finally had some luck – Jonty Rhodes and Shaun Pollock in successive balls – and though Lance Klusener and Mark Boucher muscled 51 off the last 7 overs, 226 runs was a gettable target. However, South Africa bowled and fielded like champions-in-waiting and both Nasser Hussain and Alec Stewart were back in the pavilion with just 6 runs on the board. Allan Donald then ripped through England's batting with leg-cutters of variable pace. First Graham Thorpe, who had hit him for a four the previous delivery, then Andrew Flintoff, Mark Ealham and Neil Fairbrother followed. Meanwhile, Steve Elworthy had removed Hick in the battle of the Zimbabweans, and England found themselves well and truly beaten.

ENGLAND v ZIMBABWE at Trent Bridge, 25 May 1999

Zimbabwe 167–8 (Mullally 2–16)
England 168–3 (Thorpe 62, Hussain 57*)
England won by 7 wickets

After England had won the toss and bowled as usual, the pitch seamed obligingly and the Zimbabweans never really got into their stride. Although Grant Flower made 35 and Andrew Flintoff helped with five wides, Zimbabwe had no answer to the bowling of Angus Fraser and Alan Mullally. England's fielding was also top-class with Graham Thorpe taking a superb catch at slip, Fraser galloping into the deep from his position at mid-on to cling on to a skyer and Nasser Hussain superbly running out Andy Flower. Alec Stewart failed again with the bat, as did Graeme Hick against his ex-compatriots, but Hussain and in particular Thorpe batted supremely well before the Surrey left-hander was out to a hand-wringing reflex catch by Alistair Campbell. Flintoff should have been the next man in, but instead Neil Fairbrother emerged from the pavilion, and in 5 overs he and Hussain made the 9 runs needed for victory.

ENGLAND v INDIA at Edgbaston, 29 & 30 May 1999

India 232–8 (Dravid 53, Ganguly 40)
England 169 (Ganguly 3–27)
India won by 63 runs

What had started out as a workout in the sun for England turned as dark as the thunderclouds that later rolled over Edgbaston as news filtered through of Zimbabwe's stunning performance against South Africa at Chelmsford. Suddenly England, who had looked a safe bet to qualify for the Super Six, had to beat India. England's bowlers restricted the Indian batsmen well on a slowish pitch that made driving difficult. Rahul Dravid produced a patient half-century and he was well supported by Sourav Ganguly before Darren Gough returned to the attack to pick up a couple of wickets. A target of 233 seemed eminently attainable for England, but as the cloud cover over Birmingham increased, Debasis Mohanty took 2 wickets with successive legal deliveries, separated by a wide. The umpires conferred about the weather, but decided to stay on and almost immediately a furious Nasser Hussain was bowled by Ganguly. Then the downpour began and with England 73–3 from 20.3 overs, the game became the first match of the tournament to spill over into a second day. Graham Thorpe was adjudged leg-before to Javagal Srinath from a ball that seemed to be going down leg-side, and Neil Fairbrother, who nudged his way to 29, found he had too much to do alongside the three all-rounders in the England side. Soon it was all over for England – the match, and the rest of the tournament.

2003 WORLD CUP

The 2003 Cricket World Cup was hosted by South Africa for the first time, the format being the same as four years earlier. The tournament was dogged by controversy with the political situation in Zimbabwe resulting in England refusing to play the Zimbabweans on 13 February and having points deducted.

ENGLAND v HOLLAND at East London, 16 February 2003

Holland 142–9 (de Leede 58*, Anderson 4–25)
England 144–4 (Knight 51, Vaughan 51, van Bunge 3–16)
England won by 6 wickets

England's tortured build-up to the World Cup finally got under way against Holland, and a professional performance allowed Nasser Hussain's team to side-step a potential banana skin, although there was disappointment that the Dutch survived the full 50 overs. James Anderson was the pick of the England bowlers, taking 4–25, and Holland were in a mess at 31–5 until being led to respectability by the experienced Tim de Leede, who made an unbeaten 58. England lost Marcus Trescothick early, before Nick Knight and Michael Vaughan both hit half-centuries in a match-winning stand of 89. Leg-spinner Daan van Bunge took quick wickets to interrupt the procession, but Ian Blackwell brought matters to a conclusion with five fours from the 11 balls he faced.

ENGLAND v NAMIBIA at Port Elizabeth, 19 February 2003

England 272 (Stewart 60, Trescothick 58, van Vuuren 5–43)
Namibia 217–9 (A. J. Burger 85, Keulder 46, Irani 3–30)
England won by 55 runs

The match against Namibia saw another victory for England, but it was not an impressive performance as their batsmen gave away wickets with a series of sloppy shots. In fact, at one stage of the Namibian innings, England were in with a chance of losing the match through a combination of rain and the Duckworth/Lewis method. With Nasser Hussain nursing a neck injury, Alec Stewart skippered the side and only he and Marcus Trescothick managed half-centuries. Rudi van Vuuren, who played in the last Rugby World Cup for Namibia, took 5–43 in England's total of 272. Jan-Berrie Burger won the Man-of-the-Match award for a spirited run-a-ball 85, and he and Danie Keulder put on 97 together. Eventually England's bowlers got their act together, with the result that the Namibian challenge faltered and the game slowly petered out.

ENGLAND v PAKISTAN at Cape Town, 22 February 2003

England 246–8 (Collingwood 66*, Vaughan 52)
Pakistan 134 (Shoaib Akhtar 43, Anderson 4–29, White 3–33)
England won by 112 runs

During the course of the England innings, Shoaib Akhtar finally produced the delivery he had been waiting to unleash on the world with the last ball of his second over. The Rawalpindi Express clocked 100.2 mph on the speed gun as an unruffled Nick Knight turned the ball to square leg. It was Wasim Akram and Waqar Younis who unsettled the England top order, but that England eventually posted a respectable total was down to two of their side's least experienced one-day batsmen, Michael Vaughan and Paul Collingwood, although the Yorkshire batsman was caught first ball off a Wasim no-ball. Akhtar's party was gate-crashed by twenty-year-old James Anderson, who officially announced himself a force on the international stage, destroying Pakistan's top order. Bowling his 10 overs straight through, he took 4–29, and at the end of his spell, Pakistan found themselves reduced to 67–6. It was only Shoaib Akhtar's efforts with the bat that saved his side from further embarrassment.

ENGLAND v INDIA at Durban, 26 February 2003

India 250–9 (Dravid 62, Tendulkar 50, Yuvraj Singh 42)
England 168 (Flintoff 64, Nehra 6–23)
India won by 82 runs

India's victory owed much to the spirited knocks made by Sachin Tendulkar, Rahul Dravid and Yuvraj Singh. Tendulkar and Virender Sehwag took Andy Caddick and James Anderson's opening spells apart, punishing anything off line or length. Despite the last 4 balls of India's innings all producing wickets, Yuvraj Singh had hit 42 off 38 balls to ensure India's attack had plenty of ammunition with which to bowl. Man of the Match Ashish Nehra, who wrecked England's innings with a mesmerizing spell of left-arm pace bowling, took 6–23 – his analysis being the third best in World Cup history. Only Andrew Flintoff, who had taken 2–15 off his own 10 overs, with an innings of 64, played him with any confidence. At 107–8 England were reeling, but Flintoff, aided by Caddick, pushed England up to a score of some respectability. However, this defeat left England with a stiff task ahead if they were to reach the Super Six stage.

ENGLAND v AUSTRALIA at Port Elizabeth, 2 March 2003

England 204–8 (Stewart 46, Flintoff 45, Bichel 7–20)
Australia 208–8 (Bevan 74*, Caddick 4–35)
Australia won by 2 wickets

The game began so well for England after they had won the toss and had chosen to bat first. Marcus Trescothick and Nick Knight rattled up 66 from the first 9 overs against the bowling of Glenn McGrath and Brett Lee. But the introduction of Andy Bichel seemed to dash all those early hopes and England lost 5 wickets for 21 runs. Only a stand of 90 in 25 overs between Alec Stewart and Andrew Flintoff prevented a rout. Bichel, though, was unstoppable as he took 7–20, the second-best figures by an Australian in one-day international cricket. In reply, Andy Caddick then removed Australia's top four batsmen in a devastating spell with just 48 runs on the board. Ashley Giles later removed Andrew Symonds and Brad Hogg, and at 135–8 the reigning champions were reeling. But they would lose no further wickets as Michael Bevan produced a painstaking unbeaten 74 and Bichel racked up 34 not out to see the Australians to victory.

ENGLAND'S OVERALL PERFORMANCES IN WORLD CUP CRICKET

Matches	Won	Lost	Tied	No Result	Win %
50	31	18	0	1	63.00%

	Played	Won	Lost	No Result
v Australia	5	2	3	0
v Canada	1	1	0	0
v East Africa	1	1	0	0
v Holland	2	2	0	0
v India	6	3	3	0
v Kenya	1	1	0	0
v Namibia	1	1	0	0
v New Zealand	6	3	3	0
v Pakistan	9	4	4	1
v South Africa	4	2	2	0
v Sri Lanka	7	6	1	0
v UAE	1	1	0	0
v West Indies	4	3	1	0
v Zimbabwe	2	1	1	0

8 SUMMARY OF ENGLAND'S RECORDS AND RESULTS

ENGLAND v AUSTRALIA – TEST SERIES RECORDS

HIGHEST INNINGS TOTAL

England	in England	903–7 dec. at The Oval, 1938
	in Australia	636 at Sydney, 1928–9
Australia	in England	729–6 dec. at Lord's, 1930
	in Australia	659–8 dec. at Sydney, 1946–7

LOWEST INNINGS TOTAL

England	in England	52 at The Oval, 1948
	in Australia	45 at Sydney, 1886–7
Australia	in England	36 at Edgbaston, 1902
	in Australia	42 at Sydney, 1887–8

HIGHEST MATCH AGGREGATE

1,753 runs for 40 wickets at Adelaide, 1920–1

LOWEST MATCH AGGREGATE

291 runs for 40 wickets at Lord's, 1888

HIGHEST INDIVIDUAL INNINGS

England	in England	364	L. Hutton at The Oval, 1938
	in Australia	287	R. E. Foster at Sydney, 1903–4
Australia	in England	334	D. G. Bradman at Headingley, 1930
	in Australia	307	R. M. Cowper at Melbourne, 1965–6

HIGHEST AGGREGATE OF RUNS IN A SERIES

England	in England	732	D. I. Gower (6 Tests), 1985
	in Australia	905	W. R. Hammond, 1928–9
Australia	in England	974	D. G. Bradman, 1930
	in Australia	810	D. G. Bradman, 1936–7

RECORD WICKET PARTNERSHIPS

ENGLAND

1st	323	J. B. Hobbs & W. Rhodes at Melbourne, 1911–12
2nd	382	L. Hutton & M. Leyland at The Oval, 1938
3rd	262	W. R. Hammond & D. R. Jardine at Adelaide, 1928–9
4th	288	N. Hussain & G. Thorpe at Edgbaston, 1997
5th	206	E. Paynter & D. C. S. Compton at Trent Bridge, 1938
6th	215	L. Hutton & J. Hardstaff Jnr at The Oval, 1938
	215	G. Boycott & A. P. E. Knott at Trent Bridge, 1977
7th	143	F. E. Woolley & J. Vine at Sydney, 1911–12
8th	124	E. H. Hendren & H. Larwood at Brisbane, 1928–9
9th	151	W. H. Scotton & W. W. Read at The Oval, 1884
10th	130	R. E. Foster & W. Rhodes at Sydney, 1903–4

AUSTRALIA

1st	329	G. R. Marsh & M. A. Taylor at Trent Bridge, 1989
2nd	451	W. H. Ponsford & D. G. Bradman at The Oval, 1934
3rd	276	D. G. Bradman & A. L. Hassett at Brisbane, 1946–7
4th	388	W. H. Ponsford & D. G. Bradman at Headingley, 1934
5th	405	S. G. Barnes & D. G. Bradman at Sydney, 1946–7
6th	346	J. W. Fingleton & D. G. Bradman at Melbourne, 1936–7
7th	165	C. Hill & H. Trumble at Melbourne, 1897–8
8th	243	M. J. Hartigan & C. Hill at Adelaide, 1907–8
9th	154	S. E. Gregory & J. M. Blackham at Sydney, 1894–5
10th	127	J. M. Taylor & A. A. Mailey at Sydney, 1924–5

BEST INNINGS BOWLING ANALYSIS

England	in England	10–53	J. C. Laker at Old Trafford, 1956
	in Australia	8–35	G. A. Lohmann at Sydney, 1886–7
Australia	in England	8–31	F. Laver at Old Trafford, 1909
	in Australia	9–121	A. A. Mailey at Melbourne, 1920–1

BEST MATCH BOWLING ANALYSIS

England	in England	19–90	J. C. Laker at Old Trafford, 1956
	in Australia	15–124	W. Rhodes at Melbourne, 1903–4
Australia	in England	16–137	R. A. L. Massie at Lord's, 1972
	in Australia	13–77	M. A. Noble at Melbourne, 1901–2

HIGHEST AGGREGATE OF WICKETS IN A SERIES

England	in England	46	J. C. Laker	1956
	in Australia	38	M. W. Tate	1924–5
Australia	in England	42	T. M. Alderman (6 Tests)	1981
	in Australia	41	R. M. Hogg (6 Tests)	1978–9

RESULTS SUMMARY

Year	Hosts	Tests	England wins	Australian wins	Draws	Series winner
1876–7	Australia	2	1	1	0	Draw
1878–9	Australia	1	0	1	0	Australia
1880	England	1	1	0	0	England
1881–2	Australia	4	0	2	2	Australia
1882	England	1	0	1	0	Australia
1882–3	Australia	3	2	1	0	England
1882–3	Australia	1	0	1	0	Australia
1884	England	3	1	0	2	England
1884–5	Australia	5	3	2	0	England
1886	England	3	3	0	0	England
1886–7	Australia	2	2	0	0	England
1887–8	Australia	1	1	0	0	England
1888	England	3	2	1	0	England
1890	England	2	2	0	0	England
1891–2	Australia	3	1	2	0	Australia
1893	England	3	1	0	2	England
1894–5	Australia	5	3	2	0	England
1896	England	3	2	1	0	England
1897–8	Australia	5	1	4	0	Australia
1899	England	5	0	1	4	Australia
1901–2	Australia	5	1	4	0	Australia
1902	England	5	1	2	2	Australia
1903–4	Australia	5	3	2	0	England
1905	England	5	2	0	3	England
1907–8	Australia	5	1	4	0	Australia
1909	England	5	1	2	2	Australia
1911–12	Australia	5	4	1	0	England
1912	England	3	1	0	2	England
1920–1	Australia	5	0	5	0	Australia
1921	England	5	0	3	2	Australia
1924–5	Australia	5	1	4	0	Australia
1926	England	5	1	0	4	England
1928–9	Australia	5	4	1	0	England
1930	England	5	1	2	2	Australia
1932–3	Australia	5	4	1	0	England
1934	England	5	1	2	2	Australia
1936–7	Australia	5	2	3	0	Australia
1938	England	4	1	1	2	Draw
1946–7	Australia	5	0	3	2	Australia
1948	England	5	0	4	1	Australia
1950–1	Australia	5	1	4	0	Australia
1953	England	5	1	0	4	England
1954–5	Australia	5	3	1	1	England
1956	England	5	2	1	2	England

Year	Hosts	Tests	England wins	Australian wins	Draws	Series winner
1958–9	Australia	5	0	4	1	Australia
1961	England	5	1	2	2	Australia
1962–3	Australia	5	1	1	3	Draw
1964	England	5	0	1	4	Australia
1965–6	Australia	5	1	1	3	Draw
1968	England	5	1	1	3	Draw
1970–1	Australia	6	2	0	4	England
1972	England	5	2	2	1	Draw
1974–5	Australia	6	1	4	1	Australia
1975	England	4	0	1	3	Australia
1976–7	Australia	1	0	1	0	Australia
1977	England	5	3	0	2	England
1978–9	Australia	6	5	1	0	England
1979–80	Australia	3	0	3	0	Australia
1980	England	1	0	0	1	Draw
1981	England	6	3	1	2	England
1982–3	Australia	5	1	2	2	Australia
1985	England	6	3	1	2	England
1986–7	Australia	5	2	1	2	England
1987–8	Australia	1	0	0	1	Draw
1989	England	6	0	4	2	Australia
1990–1	Australia	5	0	3	2	Australia
1993	England	6	1	4	1	Australia
1994–5	Australia	5	1	3	1	Australia
1997	England	6	2	3	1	Australia
1998–9	Australia	5	1	3	1	Australia
2001	England	5	1	4	0	Australia
2002–3	Australia	5	1	4	0	Australia
2005	England	5	2	1	2	England

Matches played in England:

England	43 wins
Australia	46 wins
	62 draws

Matches played in Australia:

England	54 wins
Australia	80 wins
	26 draws

Total:

England	97 wins
Australia	126 wins
	88 draws

ENGLAND v SOUTH AFRICA – TEST SERIES RECORDS

HIGHEST INNINGS TOTAL

England	in England	604–9 dec. at The Oval, 2003
	in South Africa	654–5 at Durban, 1938–9
South Africa	in England	682–6 dec. at Lord's, 2003
	in South Africa	572–7 at Durban, 1999–2000

LOWEST INNINGS TOTAL

England	in England	76 at Headingley, 1907
	in South Africa	92 at Cape Town, 1898–9
South Africa	in England	30 at Edgbaston, 1924
	in South Africa	30 at Port Elizabeth, 1895–6

HIGHEST MATCH AGGREGATE

1,981 runs for 35 wickets at Durban, 1938–9

LOWEST MATCH AGGREGATE

378 runs for 30 wickets at The Oval, 1912

HIGHEST INDIVIDUAL INNINGS

England	in England	219	M. E. Trescothick at The Oval, 2003
	in South Africa	243	E. Paynter at Durban, 1938–9
South Africa	in England	277	G. C. Smith at Edgbaston, 2003
	in South Africa	275	G. Kirsten at Durban, 1999–2000

HIGHEST AGGREGATE OF RUNS IN A SERIES

England	in England	753	D. C. S. Compton, 1947
	in South Africa	656	A. J. Strauss, 2004–5
South Africa	in England	714	G. C. Smith, 2003
	in South Africa	625	J. H. Kallis, 2004–5

RECORD WICKET PARTNERSHIPS

ENGLAND

1st	359	L. Hutton & C. Washbrook at Johannesburg, 1948–9
2nd	280	P. A. Gibb & W. J. Edrich at Durban, 1938–9
3rd	370	W. J. Edrich & D. C. S. Compton at Lord's, 1947
4th	197	W. R. Hammond & L. E. G. Ames at Cape Town, 1938–9
5th	237	D. C. S. Compton & N. W. D. Yardley at Trent Bridge, 1947
6th	206*	K. F. Barrington & J. M. Parks at Durban, 1964–5

7th   115   J. W. H. T. Douglas & M. C. Bird at Durban, 1913–14
8th   154   C. W. Wright & H. R. Bromley-Davenport at Johannesburg, 1895–6
9th   99   A. Flintoff & S. J. Harmison at The Oval, 2003
10th   92   C. A. G. Russell & A. E. R. Gilligan at Durban, 1922–3

SOUTH AFRICA

1st   338   G. C. Smith & H. H. Gibbs at Edgbaston, 2003
2nd   267   G. C. Smith & G. Kirsten at Lord's, 2003
3rd   319   A. Melville & A. D. Nourse at Trent Bridge, 1947
4th   214   H. W. Taylor & H. G. Deane at The Oval, 1929
5th   192   G. Kirsten & M. V. Boucher at Durban, 1999–2000
6th   171   J. H. B. Waite & P. L. Winslow at Old Trafford, 1955
7th   123   H. G. Deane & E. P. Nupen at Durban, 1927–8
8th   150   G. Kirsten & M. Zondeki at Headingley, 2003
9th   137   E. L. Dalton & A. B. C. Langton at The Oval, 1935
10th   103   H. G. Owen-Smith & A. J. Bell at Headingley, 1929

BEST INNINGS BOWLING ANALYSIS

England   in England   9–57   D. E. Malcolm at The Oval, 1994
               in South Africa 9–28   G. A. Lohmann at Johannesburg, 1895–6
South Africa   in England   7–65   S. J. Pegler at Lord's, 1912
               in South Africa 9–113   H. J. Tayfield at Johannesburg, 1956–7

BEST MATCH BOWLING ANALYSIS

England   in England   15–99   C. Blythe at Headingley, 1907
               in South Africa 17–159   S. F. Barnes at Johannesburg, 1913–14
South Africa   in England   10–87   P. M. Pollock at Trent Bridge, 1965
               in South Africa 13–192   H. J. Tayfield at Johannesburg, 1956–7

HIGHEST AGGREGATE OF WICKETS IN A SERIES

England   in England   34   S. F. Barnes, 1912
               in South Africa 49   S. F. Barnes, 1913–14
South Africa   in England   33   A. A. Donald, 1998
               in South Africa 37   H. J. Tayfield, 1956–7

RESULTS SUMMARY

Year	Hosts	Tests	England wins	South African wins	Draws	Series winner
1888–9	South Africa	2	2	0	0	England
1891–2	South Africa	1	1	0	0	England
1895–6	South Africa	3	3	0	0	England

Year	Hosts	Tests	England wins	South African wins	Draws	Series winner
1898–9	South Africa	2	2	0	0	England
1905–6	South Africa	5	1	4	0	South Africa
1907	England	3	1	0	2	England
1909–10	South Africa	5	2	3	0	South Africa
1912	England	3	3	0	0	England
1913–14	South Africa	5	4	0	1	England
1922–3	South Africa	5	2	1	2	England
1924	England	5	3	0	2	England
1927–8	South Africa	5	2	2	1	Draw
1929	England	5	2	0	3	England
1930–1	South Africa	5	0	1	4	South Africa
1935	England	5	0	1	4	South Africa
1938–9	South Africa	5	1	0	4	England
1947	England	5	3	0	2	England
1948–9	South Africa	5	2	0	3	England
1951	England	5	3	1	1	England
1955	England	5	3	2	0	England
1956–7	South Africa	5	2	2	1	Draw
1960	England	5	3	0	2	England
1964–5	South Africa	5	1	0	4	England
1965	England	3	0	1	2	South Africa
1994	England	3	1	1	1	Draw
1995–6	South Africa	5	0	1	4	South Africa
1998	England	5	2	1	2	England
1999–2000	South Africa	5	1	2	2	South Africa
2003	England	5	2	2	1	Draw
2004–5	South Africa	5	2	1	2	England

Matches played in England:

England	26 wins
South Africa	9 wins
	22 draws

Matches played in South Africa:

England	28 wins
South Africa	17 wins
	28 draws

Total:

England	54 wins
South Africa	26 wins
	50 draws

ENGLAND v WEST INDIES – TEST SERIES RECORDS

HIGHEST INNINGS TOTALS

England	in England	619–6 dec. at Trent Bridge, 1957
	in the West Indies	849 at Kingston, 1929–30
West Indies	in England	692–8 dec. at The Oval, 1995
	in the West Indies	751–5 dec. at St John's, 2003–4

LOWEST INNINGS TOTAL

England	in England	71 at Old Trafford, 1976
	in the West Indies	46 at Port-of-Spain, 1993–4
West Indies	in England	54 at Lord's, 2000
	in the West Indies	47 at Kingston, 2003–4

HIGHEST MATCH AGGREGATE

1,815 runs for 34 wickets at Kingston, 1929–30

LOWEST MATCH AGGREGATE

309 runs for 29 wickets at Bridgetown, 1934–5

HIGHEST INDIVIDUAL INNINGS

England	in England	285*	P. B. H. May at Edgbaston, 1957
	in the West Indies	325	A. Sandham at Kingston, 1929–30
West Indies	in England	291	I. V. A. Richards at The Oval, 1976
	in the West Indies	400*	B. C. Lara at St John's, 2003–4

HIGHEST AGGREGATE OF RUNS IN A SERIES

England	in England	506	G. P. Thorpe (6 Tests), 1995
	in the West Indies	693	E. H. Hendren, 1929–30
West Indies	in England	829	I. V. A. Richards, 1976
	in the West Indies	798	B. C. Lara, 1993–4

RECORD WICKET PARTNERSHIPS

ENGLAND

1st	212	C. Washbrook & R. T. Simpson at Trent Bridge, 1950
2nd	291	A. J. Strauss & R. W. T. Key at Lord's, 2004
3rd	303	M. A. Atherton & R. A. Smith at St John's, 1993–4
4th	411	P. B. H. May & M. C. Cowdrey at Edgbaston, 1957
5th	150	A. J. Stewart & G. P. Thorpe at Bridgetown, 1993–4
6th	205	M. R. Ramprakash & G. P. Thorpe at Bridgetown, 1997–8

7th   197   M. J. K. Smith & J. M. Parks at Port-of-Spain, 1959–60
8th   217   T. W. Graveney & J. T. Murray at The Oval, 1966
9th   109   G. A. R. Lock & P. I. Pocock at Georgetown, 1967–8
10th 128   K. Higgs & J. A. Snow at The Oval, 1966

WEST INDIES

1st   298   C. G. Greenidge & D. L. Haynes at St John's, 1989–90
2nd 287* C. G. Greenidge & H. A. Gomes at Lord's, 1984
3rd 338   E. D. Weekes & F. M. M. Worrell at Port-of-Spain, 1953–4
4th 399   G. S. Sobers & F. M. M. Worrell at Bridgetown, 1959–60
5th 265   S. M. Nurse & G. S. Sobers at Headingley, 1966
6th 282   B. C. Lara & R. D. Jacobs at St John's, 2003–4
7th 155* G. S. Sobers & B. D. Julien at Lord's, 1973
8th 99   C. A. McWatt & J. K. Holt at Georgetown, 1953–4
9th 150   E. A. E. Baptiste & M. A. Holding at Edgbaston, 1984
10th 70   I. R. Bishop & D. Ramnarine at Georgetown, 1997–8

BEST INNINGS BOWLING ANALYSIS

England	in England	8–103	I. T. Botham at Lord's, 1984
	in the West Indies	8–53	A. R. C. Fraser at Port-of-Spain, 1997–8
West Indies	in England	8–92	M. A. Holding at The Oval, 1976
	in the West Indies	8–45	C. E. L. Ambrose at Bridgetown, 1989–90

BEST MATCH BOWLING ANALYSIS

England	in England	12–119	F. S. Trueman at Edgbaston, 1963
	in the West Indies	13–156	A. W. Greig at Port-of-Spain, 1973–4
West Indies	in England	14–149	M. A. Holding at The Oval, 1976
	in the West Indies	11–84	C. E. L. Ambrose at Port-of-Spain, 1993–4

HIGHEST AGGREGATE OF WICKETS IN A SERIES

England	in England	34	F. S. Trueman, 1963
	in West Indies	27	J. A. Snow, 1967–8
West Indies	in England	35	M. D. Marshall, 1988
	In West Indies	30	C. E. L. Ambrose, 1997–8

RESULTS SUMMARY

Year	Hosts	Tests	England wins	West Indian wins	Draws	Series winner
1928	England	3	3	0	0	England
1929–30	West Indies	4	1	1	2	Draw
1933	England	3	2	0	1	England
1934–5	West Indies	4	1	2	1	West Indies

Year	Hosts	Tests	England wins	West Indian wins	Draws	Series winner
1939	England	3	1	0	2	England
1947–8	West Indies	4	0	2	2	West Indies
1950	England	4	1	3	0	West Indies
1953–4	West Indies	5	2	2	1	Draw
1957	England	5	3	0	2	England
1959–60	West Indies	5	1	0	4	England
1963	England	5	1	3	1	West Indies
1966	England	5	1	3	1	West Indies
1967–8	West Indies	5	1	0	4	England
1969	England	3	2	0	1	England
1973	England	3	0	2	1	West Indies
1973–4	West Indies	5	1	1	3	Draw
1976	England	5	0	3	2	West Indies
1980	England	5	0	1	4	West Indies
1980–1	West Indies	4	0	2	2	West Indies
1984	England	5	0	5	0	West Indies
1985–6	West Indies	5	0	5	0	West Indies
1988	England	5	0	4	1	West Indies
1989–90	West Indies	4	1	2	1	West Indies
1991	England	5	2	2	1	Draw
1993–4	West Indies	5	1	3	1	West Indies
1995	England	6	2	2	2	Draw
1997–8	West Indies	6	1	3	2	West Indies
2000	England	5	3	1	1	England
2003–4	West Indies	4	3	0	1	England
2004	England	4	4	0	0	England

Matches played in England:

England	25 wins
West Indies	29 wins
	20 draws

Matches played in the West Indies:

England	13 wins
West Indies	23 wins
	24 draws

Total:

England	38 wins
West Indies	52 wins
	44 draws

ENGLAND v NEW ZEALAND – TEST SERIES RECORDS

HIGHEST INNINGS TOTALS

England	in England	567–8 dec. at Trent Bridge, 1994	
	in New Zealand	593–6 dec. at Auckland, 1974–5	
New Zealand	in England	551–9 dec. at Lord's, 1973	
	in New Zealand	537 at Wellington, 1983–4	

LOWEST INNINGS TOTALS

England	in England	126 at Edgbaston, 1999	
	in New Zealand	64 at Wellington, 1977–8	
New Zealand	in England	47 at Lord's, 1958	
	in New Zealand	26 at Auckland, 1954–5	

HIGHEST MATCH AGGREGATE

1,294 runs for 36 wickets at Christchurch, 2001–2

LOWEST MATCH AGGREGATE

390 runs for 30 wickets at Lord's, 1958

HIGHEST INDIVIDUAL INNINGS

England	in England	310*	J. H. Edrich at Headingley, 1965
	in New Zealand	336*	W. R. Hammond at Auckland, 1932–3
New Zealand	in England	206	M. P. Donnelly at Lord's, 1949
	in New Zealand	222	N. J. Astle at Christchurch, 2001–2

HIGHEST AGGREGATE OF RUNS IN A SERIES

England	in England	469	L. Hutton, 1949
	in New Zealand	563	W. R. Hammond, 1932–3
New Zealand	in England	462	M. P. Donnelly, 1949
	In New Zealand	341	C. S. Dempster, 1929–30

RECORD WICKET PARTNERSHIPS

ENGLAND

1st	223	G. Fowler & C. J. Tavare at The Oval, 1983
2nd	369	J. H. Edrich & K. F. Barrington at Headingley, 1965
3rd	245	J. Hardstaff Jnr & W. R. Hammond at Lord's, 1937
4th	266	M. H. Denness & K. W. R. Fletcher at Auckland, 1974–5
5th	242	W. R. Hammond & L. E. G. Ames at Christchurch, 1932–3
6th	281	G. P. Thorpe & A. Flintoff at Christchurch, 2001–2

7th   149   A. P. E. Knott & P. Lever at Auckland, 1970–1
8th   246   L. E. G. Ames & G. O. B. Allen at Lord's, 1931
9th   163* M. C. Cowdrey & A. C. Smith at Wellington, 1962–3
10th 59   A. P. E. Knott & N. Gifford at Trent Bridge, 1973

NEW ZEALAND

1st   276   C. S. Dempster & J. E. Mills at Wellington, 1929–30
2nd   241   J. G. Wright & A. H. Jones at Wellington, 1991–2
3rd   210   B. A. Edgar & M. D. Crowe at Lord's, 1986
4th   155   M. D. Crowe & M. J. Greatbatch at Wellington, 1987–8
5th   180   M. D. Crowe & S. A. Thomson at Lord's, 1994
6th   141   M. D. Crowe & A. C. Parore at Old Trafford, 1994
7th   117   D. N. Patel & C. L. Cairns at Christchurch, 1991–2
8th   104   D. A. R. Moloney & A. W. Roberts at Lord's, 1937
9th   118   J. V. Coney & B. L. Cairns at Wellington, 1983–4
10th 118   N. J. Astle & C. L. Cairns at Christchurch, 2001–2

BEST INNINGS BOWLING ANALYSIS

England   in England   7–32 D. L. Underwood at Lord's, 1969
               in New Zealand   7–47 P. C. R. Tufnell at Christchurch, 1991–2
New Zealand   in England   7–74 B. L. Cairns at Headingley, 1983
               in New Zealand   7–143 B. L. Cairns at Wellington, 1983–4

BEST MATCH BOWLING ANALYSIS

England   in England   12–101 D. L. Underwood at The Oval, 1969
               in New Zealand   12–97   D. L. Underwood at Christchurch, 1970–1
New Zealand   in England   11–169 D. J. Nash at Lord's, 1994
               in New Zealand   10–100 R. J. Hadlee at Wellington, 1977–8

HIGHEST AGGREGATE OF WICKETS IN A SERIES

England   in England   34   G. A. R. Lock, 1958
               in New Zealand   19   D. Gough, 1996–7
                                19   A. R. Caddick, 2001–2
New Zealand   in England   21   R. J. Hadlee, 1983
               in New Zealand   15   R. O. Collinge, 1977–8
                                15   R. J. Hadlee, 1977–8

RESULTS SUMMARY

Year	Hosts	Tests	England wins	N. Zealand wins	Draws	Series winner
1929–30	New Zealand	4	1	0	3	England
1931	England	3	1	0	2	England
1932–3	New Zealand	2	0	0	2	Draw

Year	Hosts	Tests	England wins	N. Zealand wins	Draws	Series winner
1937	England	3	1	0	2	England
1946–7	New Zealand	1	0	0	1	Draw
1949	England	4	0	0	4	Draw
1950–1	New Zealand	2	1	0	1	England
1954–5	New Zealand	2	2	0	0	England
1958	England	5	4	0	1	England
1958–9	New Zealand	2	1	0	1	England
1962–3	New Zealand	3	3	0	0	England
1965	England	3	3	0	0	England
1965–6	New Zealand	3	0	0	3	Draw
1969	England	3	2	0	1	England
1970–1	New Zealand	2	1	0	1	England
1973	England	3	2	0	1	England
1974–5	New Zealand	2	1	0	1	England
1977–8	New Zealand	3	1	1	1	Draw
1978	England	3	3	0	0	England
1983	England	4	3	1	0	England
1983–4	New Zealand	3	0	1	2	New Zealand
1986	England	3	0	1	2	New Zealand
1987–8	New Zealand	3	0	0	3	Draw
1990	England	3	1	0	2	England
1991–2	New Zealand	3	2	0	1	England
1994	England	3	1	0	2	England
1996–7	New Zealand	3	2	0	1	England
1999	England	4	1	2	1	New Zealand
2001–2	New Zealand	3	1	1	1	Draw
2004	England	3	3	0	0	England

Matches played in England:

England   25 wins
New Zealand   4 wins
             18 draws

Matches played in New Zealand:

England   16 wins
New Zealand   3 wins
             22 draws

Total:

England   41 wins
New Zealand   7 wins
             40 draws

ENGLAND v INDIA – TEST SERIES RECORDS

HIGHEST INNINGS TOTAL

England	in England	653–4 dec. at Lord's, 1990
	in India	652–7 dec. at Madras, 1984–5
India	in England	628–8 dec. at Headingley, 2002
	in India	591 at Bombay, 1992–3

LOWEST INNINGS TOTAL

England	in England	101 at The Oval, 1971
	in India	102 at Bombay, 1981–2
India	in England	42 at Lord's, 1974
	in India	83 at Madras, 1976–7

HIGHEST MATCH AGGREGATE

1,614 runs for 30 wickets at Old Trafford, 1990

LOWEST MATCH AGGREGATE

482 runs for 31 wickets at Lord's, 1936

HIGHEST INDIVIDUAL INNINGS

England	in England	333	G. A. Gooch at Lord's, 1990
	in India	207	M. W. Gatting at Madras, 1984–5
India	in England	221	S. M. Gavaskar at The Oval, 1979
	in India	224	V. G. Kambli at Bombay, 1992–3

HIGHEST AGGREGATE OF RUNS IN A SERIES

England	in England	752	G. A. Gooch (3 Tests), 1990
	In India	594	K. F. Barrington, 1961–2
India	in England	602	R. Dravid (4 Tests), 2002
	in India	586	V. L. Manjrekar, 1961–2

RECORD WICKET PARTNERSHIPS

ENGLAND

1st	225	G. A Gooch & M. A. Atherton at Old Trafford, 1990
2nd	241	G. Fowler & M. W. Gatting at Madras, 1984–5
3rd	308	G. A. Gooch & A. J. Lamb at Lord's, 1990
4th	266	W. R. Hammond & T. S. Worthington at The Oval, 1936
5th	254	K. W. R. Fletcher & A. W. Greig at Bombay, 1972–3
6th	171	I. T. Botham & R. W. Taylor at Bombay, 1979–80

7th   125   D. W. Randall & P. H. Edmonds at Lord's, 1982
8th   168   R. Illingworth & P. Lever at Old Trafford, 1971
9th   103   C. White & M. J. Hoggard at Trent Bridge, 2002
10th   70   P. J. W. Allott & R. G. D. Willis at Lord's, 1982

INDIA

1st   213   S. M. Gavaskar & C. P. S. Chauhan at The Oval, 1979
2nd   192   F. M. Engineer & A. L. Wadekar at Bombay, 1972–3
3rd   316   G. R. Viswanath & Yashpal Sharma at Madras, 1981–2
4th   249   S. R. Tendulkar & S. C. Ganguly at Headingley, 2002
5th   214   M. Azharuddin & R. J. Shastri at Calcutta, 1984–5
6th   130   S. M. H. Kirmani & Kapil Dev at The Oval, 1982
7th   235   R. J. Shastri & S. M. H. Kirmani at Bombay, 1984–5
8th   128   R. J. Shastri & S. M. H. Kirmani at Delhi, 1981–2
      128   A. Kumble & M. Kaif at Nagpur, 2005–6
9th   104   R. J. Shastri & Madan Lal at Delhi, 1981–2
10th   63   A. B. Agarkar & A. Nehra at Lord's, 2002

BEST INNINGS BOWLING ANALYSIS

England   in England   8–31   F. S. Trueman at Old Trafford, 1952
          in India   7–46   J. K. Lever at Delhi, 1976–7
India   in England   6–35   L. Amar Singh at Lord's, 1936
          in India   8–55   M. H. Mankad at Madras, 1951–2

BEST MATCH BOWLING ANALYSIS

England   in England   11–93   A. V. Bedser at Old Trafford, 1946
          in India   13–106   I. T. Botham at Bombay, 1979–80
India   in England   10–188   C. Sharma at Edgbaston, 1986
          in India   12–108   M. H. Mankad at Madras, 1951–2

HIGHEST AGGREGATE OF WICKETS IN A SERIES

England   in England   29   F. S. Trueman, 1952
          in India   29   D. L. Underwood, 1976–7
India   in England   17   S. P. Gupte, 1959
          in India   35   B. S. Chandrasekhar, 1972–3

RESULTS SUMMARY

Year	Hosts	Tests	England wins	Indian wins	Draws	Series winner
1932	England	1	1	0	0	England
1933–4	India	3	2	0	1	England
1936	England	3	2	0	1	England

Year	Hosts	Tests	England wins	Indian wins	Draws	Series winner
1946	England	3	1	0	2	England
1951–2	India	5	1	1	3	Draw
1952	England	4	3	0	1	England
1959	England	5	5	0	0	England
1961–2	India	5	0	2	3	India
1963–4	India	5	0	0	5	Draw
1967	England	3	3	0	0	England
1971	England	3	0	1	2	India
1972–3	India	5	1	2	2	India
1974	England	3	3	0	0	England
1976–7	India	5	3	1	1	England
1979	England	4	1	0	3	England
1979–80	India	1	1	0	0	England
1981–2	India	6	0	1	5	India
1982	England	3	1	0	2	England
1984–5	India	5	2	1	2	England
1986	England	3	0	2	1	India
1990	England	3	1	0	2	England
1992–3	India	3	0	3	0	Draw
1996	England	3	1	0	2	England
2001–2	India	3	0	1	2	India
2002	England	4	1	1	2	Draw
2005–6	India	3	1	1	1	Draw

Matches played in England:

England	23 wins
India	4 wins
	18 draws

Matches played in India:

England	11 wins
India	13 wins
	25 draws

Total:

England	34 wins
India	17 wins
	43 draws

ENGLAND v PAKISTAN – TEST SERIES RECORDS

HIGHEST INNINGS TOTALS

England	in England	558–6 dec. at Trent Bridge, 1954
	in Pakistan	546–8 dec. at Faisalabad, 1983–4
Pakistan	in England	708 at The Oval, 1987
	in Pakistan	636–8 dec. at Lahore, 2005–6

LOWEST INNINGS TOTALS

England	in England	130 at The Oval, 1954
	in Pakistan	130 at Lahore, 1987–8
Pakistan	in England	87 at Lord's, 1954
	in Pakistan	158 at Karachi, 2000–1

HIGHEST MATCH AGGREGATE

1,344 runs for 40 wickets at Old Trafford, 2001

LOWEST MATCH AGGREGATE

509 runs for 28 wickets at Trent Bridge, 1967

HIGHEST INDIVIDUAL INNINGS

England	in England	278	D. C. S. Compton at Trent Bridge, 1954
	in Pakistan	205	E. R. Dexter at Karachi, 1961–2
Pakistan	in England	274	Zaheer Abbas at Edgbaston, 1971
	in Pakistan	223	Mohammad Yousuf at Lahore, 2005–6

HIGHEST AGGREGATE OF RUNS IN A SERIES

England	in England	453	D. C. S. Compton, 1954
	in Pakistan	449	D. I. Gower, 1983–4
Pakistan	in England	488	Salim Malik, 1992
	in Pakistan	431	Inzamam-ul-Haq, 2005–6

RECORD WICKET PARTNERSHIPS

ENGLAND

1st	198	G. Pullar & R. W. Barber at Dacca, 1961–2
2nd	248	M. C. Cowdrey & E. R. Dexter at The Oval, 1962
3rd	267	M. P. Vaughan & G. P. Thorpe at Old Trafford, 2001
4th	233	A. N. Cook & P. D. Collingwood at Lord's, 2006
5th	192	D. C. S. Compton & T. E. Bailey at Trent Bridge, 1954
6th	166	G. P. Thorpe & C. White at Lahore, 2000–1

7th 167 D. I. Gower & V. J. Marks at Faisalabad, 1983–4
8th 99 P. H. Parfitt & D. A. Allen at Headingley, 1962
9th 76 T. W. Graveney & F. S. Trueman at Lord's, 1962
10th 79 R. W. Taylor & R. G. D. Willis at Edgbaston, 1982

PAKISTAN

1st 173 Mohsin Khan & Shoaib Mohammad at Lahore, 1983–4
2nd 291 Zaheer Abbas & Mushtaq Mohammad at Edgbaston, 1971
3rd 363 Mohammad Yousuf & Younis Khan at Headingley, 2006
4th 322 Javed Miandad & Salim Malik at Edgbaston, 1992
5th 197 Javed Burki & Nasim-ul-Ghani at Lord's, 1962
6th 269 Mohammad Yousuf & Kamran Akmal at Lahore, 2005–6
7th 112 Asif Mujtaba & Moin Khan at Headingley, 1996
8th 130 Hanif Mohammad & Asif Iqbal at Lord's, 1967
9th 190 Asif Iqbal & Intikhab Alam at The Oval, 1967
10th 62 Sarfraz Nawaz & Asif Masood at Headingley, 1974

BEST INNINGS BOWLING ANALYSIS

England	in England	8–34	I. T. Botham at Lord's, 1978
	in Pakistan	7–66	P. H. Edmonds at Karachi, 1977–8
Pakistan	in England	7–40	Imran Khan at Headingley, 1987
	in Pakistan	9–56	Abdul Qadir at Lahore, 1987–8

BEST MATCH BOWLING ANALYSIS

England	in England	13–71	D. L. Underwood at Lord's, 1974
	in Pakistan	11–83	N. G. B. Cook at Karachi, 1983–4
Pakistan	in England	12–99	Fazal Mahmood at The Oval, 1954
	in Pakistan	13–101	Abdul Qadir at Lahore, 1987–8

HIGHEST AGGREGATE OF WICKETS IN A SERIES

England	in England	22	F. S. Trueman, 1962
	in Pakistan	17	A. F. Giles, 2000–1
Pakistan	in England	22	Waqar Younis, 1992
	in Pakistan	30	Abdul Qadir, 1987–8

RESULTS SUMMARY

Year	Hosts	Tests	England wins	Pakistan wins	Draws	Series winner
1954	England	4	1	1	2	Draw
1961–2	Pakistan	3	1	0	2	England
1962	England	5	4	0	1	England

Year	Hosts	Tests	England wins	Pakistan wins	Draws	Series winner
1967	England	3	2	0	1	England
1968–9	Pakistan	3	0	0	3	Draw
1971	England	3	1	0	2	England
1972–3	Pakistan	3	0	0	3	Draw
1974	England	3	0	0	3	Draw
1977–8	Pakistan	3	0	0	3	Draw
1978	England	3	2	0	1	England
1982	England	3	2	1	0	England
1983–4	Pakistan	3	0	1	2	Pakistan
1987	England	5	0	1	4	Pakistan
1987–8	Pakistan	3	0	1	2	Pakistan
1992	England	5	1	2	2	Pakistan
1996	England	3	0	2	1	Pakistan
2000–1	Pakistan	3	1	0	2	England
2001	England	2	1	1	0	Draw
2005–6	Pakistan	3	0	2	1	Pakistan
2006	England	4	3	0	1	England

Matches played in England:

England	17 wins
Pakistan	8 wins
	18 drawn

Matches played in Pakistan:

England	2 wins
Pakistan	4 wins
	18 drawn

Total:

England	19 wins
Pakistan	12 wins
	36 drawn

ENGLAND v SRI LANKA – TEST SERIES RECORDS

HIGHEST INNINGS TOTALS

England	in England	551–6 dec. at Lord's, 2006
	in Sri Lanka	387 at Kandy, 2000–1
Sri Lanka	in England	591 at The Oval, 1998
	in Sri Lanka	628–8 dec. at Colombo, 2003–4

LOWEST INNINGS TOTALS

England	in England	181 at The Oval, 1998
	in Sri Lanka	148 at Colombo, 2003–4
Sri Lanka	in England	141 at Edgbaston, 2006
	in Sri Lanka	81 at Colombo, 2000–1

HIGHEST MATCH AGGREGATE

1,401 runs for 24 wickets at Lord's, 2002

LOWEST MATCH AGGREGATE

645 runs for 36 wickets at Colombo, 2000–1

HIGHEST INDIVIDUAL INNINGS

England	in England	174	G. A. Gooch at Lord's, 1991
	in Sri Lanka	128	R. A. Smith at Colombo, 1992–3
Sri Lanka	in England	213	S. T. Jayasuriya at The Oval, 1998
	in Sri Lanka	201*	M. S. Atapattu at Galle, 2000–1

HIGHEST AGGREGATE OF RUNS IN A SERIES

England	in England	354	M. E. Trescothick, 2002
	in Sri Lanka	269	G. P. Thorpe, 2000–1
Sri Lanka	in England	277	M. S. Atapattu, 2002
	in Sri Lanka	334	D. P. M. de S. Jayawardene, 2003–4

RECORD WICKET PARTNERSHIPS

ENGLAND

1st	168	M. E. Trescothick & M. P. Vaughan at Lord's, 2002
2nd	202	M. E. Trescothick & M. A. Butcher at Edgbaston, 2002
3rd	167	N. Hussain & G. P. Thorpe at Kandy, 2000–1
4th	128	G. A. Hick & M. R. Ramprakash at The Oval, 1998
5th	173	K. P. Pietersen & P. D. Collingwood at Lord's, 2006
6th	87	A. J. Lamb & R. M. Ellison at Lord's, 1984
	87	A. J. Stewart & C. White at Kandy, 2000–1
	87	A. Flintoff & G. J. Batty at Colombo, 2003–4
7th	63	A. J. Stewart & R. C. Russell at Lord's, 1991
8th	102	A. J. Stewart & A. F. Giles at Old Trafford, 2002
9th	53	M. R. Ramprakash & D. Gough at The Oval, 1998
10th	91	G. P. Thorpe & M. J. Hoggard at Edgbaston, 2002

SRI LANKA

1st	99	R. S. Mahanama & U. C. Hathurusinghe at Colombo, 1992–3
2nd	109	W. U. Tharanga & K. C. Sangakkara at Lord's, 2006
3rd	262	T. T. Samaraweera & D. P. M. de S. Jayawardena at Colombo, 2003–4
4th	153	D. P. M. de S. Jayawardene & T. M. Dilshan at Kandy, 2003–4
5th	150	S. Wettimuny & L. R. D. Mendis at Lord's, 1984
6th	138	S. A. R. Silva & L. R. D. Mendis at Lord's, 1984
7th	93	K. C. Sangakkara & H. D. P. K. Dharmasena at Kandy, 2000–1
8th	53	H. P. D. K. Dharmasena & W. P. U. C. J. Vaas at Kandy, 2000–1
9th	105	K. M. D. N. Kulasekara & W. P. U. J. C. Vaas at Lord's, 2006
10th	64	J. R. Ratnayake & G. F. Labrooy at Lord's, 1988

BEST INNINGS BOWLING ANALYSIS

England	in England	7–70	P. A. J. DeFreitas at Lord's, 1991
	in Sri Lanka	6–33	J. E. Emburey at Colombo, 1981–2
Sri Lanka	in England	9–65	M. Muralitharan at The Oval, 1998
	in Sri Lanka	7–46	M. Muralitharan at Galle, 2003–4

BEST MATCH BOWLING ANALYSIS

England	in England	8–115	P. A. J. DeFreitas at Lord's, 1991
	in Sri Lanka	8–95	D. L. Underwood at Colombo, 1981–2
Sri Lanka	in England	16–220	M. Muralitharan at The Oval, 1998
	in Sri Lanka	11-93	M. Muralitharan at Galle, 2003–4

HIGHEST WICKET AGGREGATE IN A SERIES

England	in England	14	M. J. Hoggard, 2002
	in Sri Lanka	18	A. F. Giles, 2003–4
Sri Lanka	in England	16	M. Muralitharan, 1998
	in Sri Lanka	26	M. Muralitharan, 2003–4

RESULTS SUMMARY

Year	Hosts	Tests	England wins	Sri Lankan wins	Draws	Series winner
1981–2	Sri Lanka	1	1	0	0	England
1984	England	1	0	0	1	Draw
1988	England	1	1	0	0	England
1991	England	1	1	0	0	England
1992–3	Sri Lanka	1	0	1	0	Sri Lanka
1998	England	1	0	1	0	Sri Lanka
2000–1	Sri Lanka	3	2	1	0	England
2002	England	3	2	0	1	England
2003–4	Sri Lanka	3	0	1	2	Sri Lanka
2006	England	3	1	1	1	Drawn

Matches played in England:

England	5 wins
Sri Lanka	2 win
	3 draws

Matches played in Sri Lanka:

England	3 wins
Sri Lanka	3 wins
	2 draws

Total:

England	8 wins
Sri Lanka	5 wins
	5 drawn

ENGLAND v ZIMBABWE – TEST SERIES RECORDS

HIGHEST INNINGS TOTALS

England	in England	472 at Lord's, 2003
	in Zimbabwe	406 at Bulawayo, 1996–7
Zimbabwe	in England	285–4 dec. at Trent Bridge, 2000
	in Zimbabwe	376 at Bulawayo, 1996–7

LOWEST INNINGS TOTALS

England	in England	147 at Trent Bridge, 2000
	in Zimbabwe	156 at Harare, 1996–7
Zimbabwe	in England	83 at Lord's, 2000
	in Zimbabwe	215 at Harare, 1996–7

HIGHEST MATCH AGGREGATE

1,220 runs for 36 wickets at Bulawayo, 1996–7

LOWEST MATCH AGGREGATE

621 runs for 30 wickets at Lord's, 2000

HIGHEST INDIVIDUAL INNINGS

England	in England	137	M. A. Butcher at Lord's, 2003
	in Zimbabwe	113	N. Hussain at Bulawayo, 1996–7
Zimbabwe	in England	148*	M. W. Goodwin at Trent Bridge, 2000
	in Zimbabwe	112	A. Flower at Bulawayo, 1996–7

HIGHEST AGGREGATE OF RUNS IN A SERIES

England	in England	225	M. A. Atherton, 2000
	in Zimbabwe	241	A. J. Stewart, 1996–7
Zimbabwe	in England	178	M. W. Goodwin, 2000
	in Zimbabwe	135	A. D. R. Campbell, 1996–7

RECORD WICKET PARTNERSHIPS

ENGLAND

1st	121	M. A. Atherton & M. R. Ramprakash at Trent Bridge, 2000
2nd	137	N. V. Knight & A. J. Stewart at Bulawayo, 1996–7
3rd	68	A. J. Stewart & N. Hussain at Bulawayo, 1996–7
4th	149	G. A. Hick & A. J. Stewart at Lord's, 2000
5th	148	N. Hussain & J. P. Crawley at Bulawayo, 1996–7
6th	149	A. J. Stewart & A. McGrath at Chester-le-Street, 2003
7th	66	A. McGrath & A. F. Giles at Lord's, 2003
8th	32	C. P. Schofield & A. R. Caddick at Trent Bridge, 2000
	32	A. F. Giles & R. L. Johnson at Lord's, 2003
9th	57	A. F. Giles & M. J. Hoggard at Lord's, 2003
10th	28	J. P. Crawley & P. C. R. Tufnell at Bulawayo, 1996–7

ZIMBABWE

1st	20	D. D. Ebrahim & M. A. Vermeulen at Lord's, 2003
2nd	127	G. W. Flower & A. D. R. Campbell at Bulawayo, 1996–7
3rd	129	M. W. Goodwin & N. C. Johnson at Trent Bridge, 2000
4th	122	M. W. Goodwin & A. Flower at Trent Bridge, 2000
5th	29	A. Flower & A. C. Waller at Bulawayo, 1996–7
6th	54	S. M. Ervine & T. J. Friend at Chester-le-Street, 2003
7th	79	A. Flower & P. A. Strang at Bulawayo, 1996–7
8th	41	A. Flower & H. H. Streak at Bulawayo, 1996–7
9th	51	T. J. Friend and R. W. Price at Lord's, 2003
10th	31	B. C. Strang & M. Mbangwa at Lord's, 2000

BEST INNINGS BOWLING ANALYSIS

England	in England	6–33	R. L. Johnson at Chester-le-Street, 2003
	in Zimbabwe	4–40	D. Gough at Harare, 1996–7
Zimbabwe	in England	6–87	H. H. Streak at Lord's, 2000
	in Zimbabwe	5–123	P. A. Strang at Bulawayo, 1996–7

BEST MATCH BOWLING ANALYSIS

England	in England	7–42	E. S. H. Giddins at Lord's, 2000
	in Zimbabwe	6–137	P. C. R. Tufnell at Bulawayo, 1996–7
Zimbabwe	in England	6–87	H. H. Streak at Lord's, 2000
	in Zimbabwe	7–186	P. A. Strang at Bulawayo, 1996–7

HIGHEST AGGREGATE OF WICKETS IN A SERIES

England	in England	11	J. M. Anderson, 2003
	in Zimbabwe	8	R. D. B. Croft, 1996–7
Zimbabwe	in England	9	H. H. Streak, 2000
	in Zimbabwe	10	P. A. Strang, 1996–7

RESULTS SUMMARY

Year	Hosts	Tests	England wins	Zimbabwe wins	Draws	Series winner
1996–7	Zimbabwe	2	0	0	2	Draw
2000	England	2	1	0	1	England
2003	England	2	2	0	0	England

Matches played in England:

England	3 wins
Zimbabwe	0 wins
	1 draw

Matches played in Zimbabwe:

England	0 wins
Zimbabwe	0 wins
	2 draws

Total:

England	3 wins
Zimbabwe	0 wins
	3 draws

ENGLAND v BANGLADESH – TEST SERIES RECORDS

HIGHEST INNINGS TOTALS

England	in England	528–3 dec. at Lord's, 2005
	in Bangladesh	326 at Chittagong, 2003–4
Bangladesh	in England	316 at Chester-le-Street, 2005
	in Bangladesh	255 at Dhaka, 2003–4

LOWEST INNINGS TOTALS

England	in England	447–3 dec. at Chester-le-Street, 2005
	in Bangladesh	295 at Dhaka, 2003–4

Bangladesh   in England   104 at Chester-le-Street, 2005
                in Bangladesh   138 at Chittagong, 2003–4

HIGHEST MATCH AGGREGATE

917 runs for 33 wickets at Dhaka, 2003–4

LOWEST MATCH AGGREGATE

795 runs for 23 wickets at Lord's, 2005

HIGHEST INDIVIDUAL INNINGS

England	in England	194	M. E. Trescothick at Lord's, 2005
	in Bangladesh	113	M. E. Trescothick at Dhaka, 2003–4
Bangladesh	in England	82*	Aftab Ahmed at Chester-le-Street, 2005
	in Bangladesh	59	Hannan Sarkar at Dhaka, 2003–4

HIGHEST AGGREGATE OF RUNS IN A SERIES

England	in England	345	M. E. Trescothick, 2005
	in Bangladesh	208	M. P. Vaughan, 2003–4
Bangladesh	in England	155	Javed Omar, 2005
	in Bangladesh	114	Mushfiqur Rahman, 2003–4

RECORD WICKET PARTNERSHIPS

ENGLAND

1st	148	M. E. Trescothick & A. J. Strauss at Lord's, 2005
2nd	255	M. E. Trescothick & M. P. Vaughan at Lord's, 2005
3rd	155	M. E. Trescothick & I. R. Bell at Chester-le-Street, 2005
4th	187*	I. R. Bell & G. P. Thorpe at Chester-le-Street, 2005
5th	116	N. Hussain & R. Clarke at Chittagong, 2003–4
6th	63	N. Hussain & C. M. W. Read at Chittagong, 2003–4
7th	41	G. P. Thorpe & G. J. Batty at Dhaka, 2003–4
8th	8	A. F. Giles & R. L. Johnson at Chittagong, 2003–4
9th	5	A. F. Giles & M. J. Saggers at Chittagong, 2003–4
10th	28	A. F. Giles & M. J. Hoggard at Chittagong, 2003–4

BANGLADESH

1st	50	Javed Omar & Nafis Iqbal at Chester-le-Street, 2005
2nd	108	Hannan Sarkar & Habibul Bashar at Dhaka, 2003–4
3rd	31	Javed Omar & Aftab Ahmed at Lord's, 2005
4th	24	Javed Omar & Habibul Bashar at Chester-le-Street, 2005
5th	70	Habibul Bashar & Khaled Mashud at Chester-le-Street, 2005
6th	60	Mushfiqur Rahman & Khaled Mashud at Dhaka, 2003–4
7th	29	Mushfiqur Rahman & Khaled Mashud at Dhaka, 2003–4

8th   34   Khaled Mashud & Mohammad Rafique at Dhaka, 2003–4
9th   60   Aftab Ahmed & Tapash Baisya at Chester-le-Street, 2005
10th 13   Mohammad Rafique & Enamul Haque Jnr at Chittagong, 2003–4

BEST INNINGS BOWLING ANALYSIS

England	in England	5–38	S. J. Harmison at Chester-le-Street, 2005
	in Bangladesh	5–35	S. J. Harmison at Dhaka, 2003–4
Bangladesh	in England	2–91	M. Mortaza at Chester-le-Street, 2005
	in Bangladesh	4–60	M. Mortaza at Chittagong, 2003–4

BEST MATCH BOWLING ANALYSIS

England	in England	8–97	M. J. Hoggard at Chester-le-Street, 2005
	in Bangladesh	9–79	S. J. Harmison at Dhaka, 2003–4
Bangladesh	in England	2–91	M. Mortaza at Chester-le-Street, 2005
	in Bangladesh	5–141	M. Rafique at Dhaka, 2003–4

HIGHEST AGGREGATE OF WICKETS IN A SERIES

England	in England	14	M. J. Hoggard, 2005
	in Bangladesh	9	S. J. Harmison, 2003–4
		9	R. L. Johnson, 2003–4
Bangladesh	in England	4	M. Mortaza, 2005
	in Bangladesh	10	M. Rafique, 2003–4

RESULTS SUMMARY

Year	Hosts	Tests	England wins	Bangladesh wins	Draws	Series winner
2003–4	Bangladesh	2	2	0	0	England
2005	England	2	2	0	0	England

Matches played in England:

England	2 wins
Bangladesh	0 wins
	0 draws

Matches played in Bangladesh:

England	2 wins
Bangladesh	0 wins
	0 draws

Total:

England	4 wins
Bangladesh	0 wins
	0 draws

LIMITED-OVERS INTERNATIONALS RESULTS

	Played	Won	Lost	Tied	No Result
Australia	85	34	47	2	2
South Africa	34	11	21	1	1
West Indies	70	29	37	0	4
New Zealand	54	25	25	1	3
India	57	26	29	0	2
Pakistan	63	35	26	0	2
Sri Lanka	37	19	18	0	0
Zimbabwe	30	21	8	0	1
Bangladesh	7	7	0	0	0
Associates	8	8	0	0	0
Total	445	215	211	4	15